Advance Praise for

WALLED

"In this brave and powerful book, Sylvain Cypel tells the painful truth of how Israelis and Palestinians have become locked inside their own nationalist nightmares, in which many on each side see only their own suffering, feel only their own pain, and cannot imagine themselves except through a violent political, physical, and emotional denial and exclusion of the other. He shows peace can only come from Israel's unconditional withdrawal from the occupied Palestinian territories, and a commitment by both peoples to accept the existence, identity, and experience of the other, and accepting that all people have an equal right to freedom and justice."

—**Zia Mian, Princeton University**

"This is a wonderfully clarifying, persuasive, and informed account of the tragic ordeal that daily haunts Israelis and Palestinians. If only everyone could read and ponder *Walled*, peace for these two peoples might yet be attainable. It is a necessary book for anyone who cares and wants to understand what can be done."

—**Richard Falk, author of** *The Declining World Order*; **Visiting Distinguished Professor, Global Studies, UCSB**

"Sylvain Cypel has given us a masterful tableau of Israeli Jewish 'group-think' as it pertains to the Jewish 'self' and the Palestinian 'other.' Turning on their head notions of victim and victimizer, right and wrong, truth and deception, Cypel allows the historical record to speak for itself. By describing different historic events and their interpretations and by quoting statements from political and military leaders, intellectuals, and simple people, the author paints a deeply disturbing picture. He suggests that being locked in by a 'system' of denial, Israeli Jewish society is prevented from moving forward."

—**Miriam R. Lowi, author of** *Water and Power*; **Professor, Department of Political Science, The College of New Jersey**

WALLED

Israeli Society
at an
Impasse

Sylvain Cypel

Other Press • New York

Text designer: Kaoru Tamura
This book was set in Electra LH Regular by Alpha Graphics of Pittsfield, NH.

10 9 8 7 6 5 4 3 2 1

Library of Congress Cataloging-in-Publication Data

Cypel, Sylvain.
   [Emmurés. English]
   Walled : Israeli society at an impasse / by Sylvain Cypel.
     p. cm.
   Translated from the French.
   Includes bibliography and index.
   ISBN-13: 978-1-59051-210-4
   ISBN-10: 1-59051-210-3
   1. Arab-Israeli conflict. 2. Palestinian Arabs–Government policy–Israel.
3. Israel–Politics and government. I. Title.
   DS119.7.C9313 2007
   956.9405'4–dc22

                      2006027133

To my children, who are Jewish in a different way from me,
I who am Jewish in a different way from my father,
who was Jewish very differently from his father. But a thread,
not at all invisible, binds all these generations.

All human beings are born free and equal in dignity and in law. They are endowed with reason and conscience and must act toward one another in a spirit of brotherhood.

—Universal Declaration of the Rights of Man

It's he, the other, always the other, who puts us in a situation where we use force. Excuse me: where we are obliged to use force. For ultimately he's the one who started it. All we did was react. Maybe another time, when they've gained understanding—forcibly, by force, since all they understand is force—we'll be able to talk with them. If there's ever anyone to talk with. . . . That's what we say. It's exactly what they say, too.

—Yaakov Raz, Introduction to Motti Golani's *Milkhamot Lo Kor'ot MeAtzman—Al Zikaron, Koakh OuBekhirah* (Wars Never Come by Themselves: On Memory, Force, and Choice)

Contents

PART *One*
Memories, Self-Images, Images of the Other

1. TANTURA:
THE REPRESSED FLOODS BACK IN

2. THE "PURITY OF ARMS":
HOW TO ESCAPE FROM AN "OCEAN OF LIES"

3. "A VILLA IN THE JUNGLE":
THE ISRAELIS' PERCEPTION OF THEIR ENVIRONMENT

4. "THESE SEMITES–THEY ARE ANTI-SEMITES":
WE ARE WHAT WE WERE BORN TO BE

5. "SOMETHING LIKE A CAGE":
THE DILEMMAS OF THE ISRAELI HISTORIAN

6. TOM SEGEV VS. GIDEON LEVY:
THE "IMMUNIZATION" OF ISRAELI STUDENTS

7. AN "ARTIFICIAL STATE":
INTERNAL PALESTINIAN OBSTACLES TO
UNDERSTANDING THE ISRAELIS

PART *Two*
Israelis, Palestinians: The Temptation to Do the Worst

8. MUTE ORACLES:
THE TRANSFORMATION OF ISRAEL AFTER THE SIX DAYS' WAR

9. "WE MISSED AN EXTRAORDINARY OPPORTUNITY":
THE GREAT WASTE OF THE PEACE TALKS

10. "SERIAL LIARS":
CREATING A USEFUL IMAGE OF THE ENEMY

11. "SHARON IS SHARON IS SHARON":
THE CREEPING "PIED-NOIRIZATION" OF ISRAEL

12. "TERRORISM: TELL ARAFAT TO
STOP THIS NONSENSE":
THE FAILURE OF THE PALESTINIAN AUTHORITY

13. THE BRUTALIZATION OF ISRAELI SOCIETY
AND THE RADICALIZATION OF NATIONALISM

14. "AN INSANE LOGIC, A FORM OF SUICIDE":
THE ISRAELIS CONFRONT THEIR MORAL FAILURE

15. "THE HIDDEN PLOT OF OUR LIVES":
COMPETING FOR VICTIMHOOD

16. FORWARD:
ISRAELI SOCIETY AFTER THE EVACUATION OF GAZA

ACKNOWLEDGMENTS

I want first of all to thank *Le Monde*, which allowed me to work on my favorite subject under conditions unique in the French press. The name of this newspaper alone opens doors often closed to others.

Then I want to thank Princeton University, which provided me with unequaled working conditions for three months. Nowhere but at Princeton can one find a library gathering in one place materials of such quantity and quality on the Middle East. I am particularly grateful to Professor Abdallah Hammoudi, director of the Institute for the Transregional Study of the Middle East, for his availability and valuable advice, and to his assistant, the invariably gracious Gregory Bell, without whose aid I would have lost precious time. The personal welcome of Professor Hammoudi and his wife, Professor Myriam Löwi, was of great help to me at this rather lonely time.

I thank all the participants in or observers of the conflict who were willing to grant me interviews as I was working on this book, and all my friends, Israelis and Palestinians, who will sometimes recognize their ideas whether I agree with them or not.

Olivier, Menahem, Liliane, Ezra, and Ariel, each in his or her own way, helped me make progress in writing or clarifying various parts of the book.

I must also express my gratitude to Hugues Jallon, my editor at La Découverte, who helped me check my natural tendency to get distracted.

Finally, I can never thank my family enough for having endured my absences and moods with love and good humor.

WALLED

INTRODUCTION

With Yasser Arafat gone and George W. Bush in his second term, Israel appears triumphant. From the military point of view it has largely overcome the insurrection of the Palestinians, the second intifada. Moreover, on the day Arafat was buried, its American ally announced the creation of a future Palestinian state, possibly as early as 2009—that is, after the end of its mandate and sixteen years after the famous "mutual recognition" at the time of the Oslo Accords in 1993. All this on condition that its new leaders would by then have established a democracy in their as yet nonexistent state, and that they undertake to support the "struggle against terrorism." Failing that, the Palestinians will have to keep on waiting.

Four and a half years after the onset of the new intifada in September 2000 and thousands of deaths later (four-fifths of them Palestinians, the other fifth Israelis, the great majority of them civilians),[1] Palestinian society is bled dry, fragmented, and on the verge of chaos. Yet Israeli society, tense as ever, is also in disarray. The two interlocutors are walled by their certainties: for most Israelis, the need to overcome terrorism, and, for most Palestinians, the need to maintain resistance. Many on both sides understand that these modes of confrontation ultimately lead to impasse.

While the Palestinians are defending themselves, in the current state of affairs, it's impossible to imagine that fighting will succeed in making the Israeli army retreat from their territories. No matter: As long as the Israelis don't feel safe, they, the Palestinians, will not have been defeated. They will show that they are there, an unmovable obstacle. As for the Israelis, they know or sense that the victory their generals keep on saying is on the horizon, the eradication of terrorism, is largely illusory; no wall of protection or security barrier will prevent terrorists inclined to risk death from trying to get beyond these obstacles nine times without success only to succeed on the tenth try. And even if terrorism is wiped out it's clear that the question of real national independence for the Palestinians will remain. As long as there is no solution, sooner or later the rebellion will begin again.

At the same time, nearly all Israelis reject the idea of a general abandonment of the occupied territories, at least not without claiming victory first. Such a retreat would be seen as a terrible political defeat, setting up a frightening perception of Israel in the eyes of the world—and most of all the Arab world—the image of a loser. So they cobble together absurd plans, finding docile interlocutors among the Palestinians, or withdrawing from a given area of occupied territory in order to preserve the essential part of it. A bit of land here, a bit of land there, with the IDF (Israeli Defense Force), the army, involved in it all. Do anything, just don't let go of the occupied territories.

How, after a peace process in which Israel and the Palestinian Liberation Organization (PLO) offered one another mutual recognition and engaged in negotiations from 1993 to 2000, have Israelis and Palestinians gotten to this point? Why have all Israeli governments since 2001—those of Ehud Barak, Ariel Sharon, and Ehud Olmert—systematically turned their backs on any form of political negotiation with the president of the PLO, whoever he may be, thereby strengthening the position of the Islamists of Hamas to the point where the latter won a completely democratic election? Why has this approach, based on the primacy of security interests, not to mention the actual political stakes, proved an utter failure time and time again? And why have the Palestinians themselves largely come to support the Islamist party under the conviction that, where Israel is concerned, only what is called "armed action" pays off in the long run?

This book sets out to examine such questions. This English-language version was completed at the beginning of 2006, just after the Palestinian and Israeli legislative elections. The second intifada, which broke out in late September 2000, had for the first time given birth to the victory, by a wide margin, of an Islamist party, Hamas. For the Israelis, it had brought Sharon's successors to power at the head of a new party, Kadima, which advocates the ongoing repression of the Palestinian people but, also for the first time on the right side of the Israeli political map, has broken away from the ideology of a Greater Israel.

THE VICTIM POSITION

September 29, 2000: the second intifada is triggered. Why just then? The day before, Ariel Sharon had visited the Esplanade of the Mosques. When he was the foreign minister of the former right-wing government, neither he nor any other member of the cabinet had ever gone there. The symbolism was too strong and the consequences of ignoring it predictable. Overlooking the Temple Mount of the Jews, the Al-Aqsa Mosque, located on the Plaza, is the third holiest place for Muslims; for many Palestinians it represents their hope of one day seeing East Jerusalem become the capital of their future state.

In 1996, when Prime Minister Benyamin Netanyahu disregarded the warnings of security officials and authorized the reopening of a tunnel in the excavations of the ruins located under Al-Aqsa, the Palestinians were incensed. The Army responded with bullets. The heads of the Internal Security Service, Shabak (better known by its former name, Shin Bet), had intervened to avoid a breakdown of negotiations between Israel and the Palestinian Authority. "The soldiers open fire, like [they were] shooting ducks. . . . [T]his has to be stopped right away, because we're attacking the honor of the Palestinian Authority. They're not just going to stand there," Israel Hasson, the number two man in Shin Bet, told the Israeli officers (Enderlin 2002, pp. 55–56). The Palestinian police, too, had begun to shoot. Hasson and his counterparts negotiated a return to calm. The death toll: sixty-seven Palestinians, thirteen Israeli soldiers. Everyone could see how quickly the lighting of even the smallest fuse at Al-Aqsa could explode the powder keg.

In 1999 the Labor leader Ehud Barak came to power. In July 2000 he entered into negotiations for a "global and definitive peace" with the PLO at the Camp David summit meetings, with the Americans serving as intermediaries. The meetings failed. In front of President Bill Clinton, Barak and Yasser Arafat undertook to renounce violence. After July, the talks continued more loosely. On September 26, for the first time, the Israeli prime minister received Arafat at his home for dinner. On the preceding day he had authorized Ariel Sharon to "visit" the Esplanade of the Mosques, escorted by police. Perhaps in the political situation he was in after the failure at Camp David he could not have done otherwise. Perhaps he wanted to show Arafat how risky it was to refuse his offers. As head of the opposition, Sharon knew what he was doing: he was demonstrating that, if he were in power, any restoration of Palestinian sovereignty over East Jerusalem, and hence over the Temple Mount, would be definitively ruled out, and that Israel was "at home throughout Jerusalem," Al-Aqsa included. Nothing happened on this September 28, or almost nothing. Several dozen young people were dispersed.

The following day, the 29th, a Friday and hence the Muslim day of prayer, the young Palestinians flared up. The Israeli police sent in two thousand men. After prayers dozens of young people began to throw stones at the faithful and the tourists at the Wailing Wall on the lower level. The crowd of worshipers in Al-Aqsa Square did not scatter, and the Israeli police resorted to truncheons and tear gas. Soon, when the policemen themselves were hit by stones, they opened fire. Seven people were killed and around two hundred wounded, some of them right under the portico of the mosque, including not only young people but also older ones unconnected with the stone throwers. The news spread on the airwaves. Immediately that afternoon, and especially the next day, huge demonstrations filled the streets. Israeli police and soldiers, sometimes hit by stones and sometimes without waiting to be attacked, once again fired on the crowd. New victims fell, most of them young.

As in 1996, armed Palestinians began to fire back. But this time the Israeli services negotiated nothing with their counterparts. Barak demanded that Arafat immediately and unilaterally put an end to the violence, or the IDF would continue shooting. The demonstrations grew larger. On the fifth day Israel sent its first missile into a residential area, aiming at a building associated with Fatah, Arafat's organization. During the first intifada (1987–1993) the Israeli army had never had recourse to tanks or aircraft.

When I interviewed leaders and ordinary individuals as a special envoy of *Le Monde* in Israel and Palestine at the beginning of the intifada, I was struck by the consistency with which they all barricaded themselves in the victim position. On the Palestinian side, which in the early phase experienced 90 percent of the casualties, all I heard about was the "savagery" of the Israelis. Excessive force had certainly been used, but one question, to which there was no reply, aroused uneasiness: Why had the young Palestinians initially shown their anger by throwing stones at a crowd of Israeli worshipers who had no part in Sharon's "provocation"? What did this say about their general relationship to the Israelis—not just to Israel as an occupying state, but to all Israelis? "If you endorse this as harmless," I said to a lay instructor at Bir Zeit University, "tomorrow you won't denounce Hamas's attacks on civilians in Israel." He raised his shoulders in rage: "If the Israelis continue to shoot down our kids like that, they're going to get attacked soon." Neither he nor I imagined the level of suicidal terrorism that the intifada would produce.

On the Israeli side, the refusal to consider disturbing facts seemed even more flagrant to me. Political leaders on the right and the left, intellectuals, ordinary people, all repeated the same argument: the Palestinians had used Sharon's appearance on the esplanade to initiate acts of violence; the rest was just propaganda. They ignored the killings of the following day or thought they had no significance. When I observed that the Israeli police had fired on an unarmed crowd, the response rang out uniformly: "*Lo meshaneh*" (That makes no difference). Shooting at the crowd was a non-event, a quibble on the part of the Palestinians. Nothing fundamental had happened that day. Israel had been attacked and had to defend itself.

I pointed out in vain that Al-Aqsa was not just any place, that killing and wounding civilians at the entrance to a venerated site of Islam was not an indifferent act, that in shooting anywhere else the Israeli soldiers would not have evoked such an emotional response. The reply was always the same: "There or anywhere, what does it matter? The Palestinians were just waiting for an opportunity." This was the final point, enabling the Israelis to consolidate their victim position, place the others in the position of the aggressor, and ask themselves no questions.

Questions like these, for example: "If the Palestinians were just waiting for a favorable opportunity to rise up violently while falsely posing as victims, why give them one?" or: "Would the police have fired on an unarmed crowd if the crowd had consisted of Jews?" Shulamit Aloni had formulated these questions in an interview with me on October 21, 2000, shortly after the onset of the intifada. A former Israeli Minister of Education from the Labor Party, Aloni said she was appalled by what had happened at Al-Aqsa. She was almost alone in asking such questions in Israel.

Since my meeting with her I have been haunted by a nightmare. If by chance there were a real accord between the two parties, if there were plans for an Israeli military withdrawal putting an end to the occupation of the Palestinians, there would always be some diehard willing to do anything to prevent it. Another Baruch Goldstein, in despair at seeing his dream for a Greater Israel vanish, would commit a new massacre, be it at Al-Aqsa or at the Cave of the Patriarchs in Hebron.[2] Or a young Palestinian would manage to blow himself up at the Wailing Wall. You didn't want to understand the importance of Al-Aqsa? Well, an eye for an eye.

These are horror fantasies. Nourished by the spirit of vendetta that holds sway in each camp, they arise after each "targeted liquidation" of a political leader or opposing terrorist by the Israelis, after each Palestinian attack. I then recall the way the current conflict was triggered and my meeting with Shulamit Aloni. The old lady, former leader of the secular Zionist camp, has been less alone since then. Many of the Israeli pacifists who spontaneously adhered to the consensus in October 2000 admit today that Israel did indeed initiate the current cycle of violent acts. And most have dropped the idea that once prevailed among almost all Israelis, namely that the Camp David fiasco in July 2000 was due solely to Arafat's refusal to compromise.

Most Israelis, however, are still convinced that after Camp David the Palestinians responded with violence to offers that in fact were as generous as could be. They remain so even after the Geneva Pact, drawn up by former Israeli minister Yossi Beilin and former Palestinian minister Yasser Abed Rabbo in October 2004 as a model of a possible accord, "granted" the Palestinians, point by point, basically everything that the Israelis had refused them three years earlier, reducing their so-called generosity of that time to more just proportions. But few people in Israel are as yet disposed to hear this truth. As for the Palestinians, who have reverted so abundantly to the failed recipes of terrorism, their repression and enclosure are increasing, and their young people are escalating the level of their political demands.

THE ROLE OF DENIAL

A major theme of this book is the fundamental role played by denial in Israeli–Palestinian relations. The term is to be understood in its accepted meaning: refusal to acknowledge the truth of a fact or assertion. In the Israeli–Palestinian context, denial is accompanied by the creation of a diabolical image of the other, denying his actual reality, and hence also by the creation of a self-image denying or distorting one's own history and actions—all of this so as to confirm one's own position as righteous and a victim in all circumstances.

With twelve chapters on the Israelis, two on the Palestinians, and two final chapters on both, this book will seem unbalanced. It is, first and foremost, a book on Israeli society. Having lived in Israel for twelve years and closely followed its development professionally, I know this society much better than the other. I know Hebrew, not Arabic. And yet, because denial is at the center of the relationship between Israelis and Palestinians, because the history and behavior of the one side can't be understood without an awareness of the influence of the other, and also because the denial enclosing each side is in turn sustained by its being the object of denial on the part of the other, it was impossible to focus on Israeli society without mentioning the Palestinians. The two peoples are mingled, physically and mentally. And never has this conflictual intertwining been so strong as it is today.

Beyond the vicissitudes of politics, the construction of the wall of separation Israel is building inside the West Bank has never been interrupted. But the people being walled are not only the ones we can see and imagine. By enclosing the Palestinians behind a wall, with watchtowers and barbed wire, the Israelis are walling themselves into a dramatic impasse. "Any structure built on unawareness of the suffering of others is bound to come crashing down. Watch out: You are dancing on a roof that rests on tottering pillars," Avraham Burg, former president of the Jewish Agency, the highest authority of the Zionist movement, said to his compatriots. Describing an evolution toward "an unrecognizable and hateful Jewish state," he described a country tragically digging itself into a moral crisis.[3] "We don't hear anything anymore," he said shortly thereafter, painting a picture of an Israeli society immured in "unawareness" of the other.[4]

Though it refers to historians, this book is not a history of Israel or the Israeli–Palestinian conflict. Nor, though it refers to the works of sociologists, is it a work of sociology. Nor, finally, is it an eyewitness account, though it presents a number of personal recollections and symptomatic anecdotes, experienced firsthand or reported. Yet it's a bit of all that: a journalist's observations in the service of a study of mentalities. For it bears on the way the dominant mentalities in Israel have been forged, the mindsets in which the society represents itself and represents the Palestinians, and on the major lines of force within it that lead each to rejection of the other. It confirms the unawareness Burg described, as well as the mindsets that lead to opening. For the greater the denial of the humanity of the other, the greater the development of an antidote to this unawareness.

Why and how have the Israelis come to wall in the Palestinians as they continue, mentally for the most part, to wall themselves in a political impasse legitimizing the daily oppression of an entire people? And how does the denial mounted by the Palestinians to the constitution by the Israelis of a national society strongly sustain the Palestinians' own behavior? These questions form the framework of this study.

The book is divided into two parts in which past and present shed light on one another. The first part is more specifically concerned with the past and the ongoing relevance of the events that marked it—in particular the creation of Israel and the concomitant expulsion of the Palestinians from their land in 1947–1950—and with the implications on both sides of the concealment of these events. This part of the book aims to show how, when we refuse to face up to the past, we also deny the reality of the present.

The second part deals with the changes that have come about since the other founding event of modern Israel identity, the Six Days' War in 1967. Here I address the way in which certain initial tropisms of the Jewish national movement, Zionism, have reemerged with greatly increased power, and with the way in which certain other tendencies have been gradually marginalized. The aim here is to show how the immurement in the denial of reality is structuring the current relationship to the Palestinians and moving the entire society in a new direction. By now the historical center that shaped Israeli society has disappeared, to the point where someone like Ariel Sharon, who was always the staunch enemy of the Palestinian national movement, came to be regarded as a centrist on the political map. A large majority of Israelis think they are protecting themselves from any introspective assessment by becoming fixed in what the writer David Grossman calls the cult of force.[5] A minority fear that this process will lead the country toward disaster.

Although there is certainly denial on both sides of the conflict, it is much more constitutive among the Israelis. To begin with, it does not occur in similar contexts. Politically and physically, the Palestinians are the dominated. Their land has been occupied for thirty-nine years in the territories, or they have been second-class citizens in Israel itself for fifty-nine years, and this is not to mention those who are refugees in Arab countries. The Israelis are the dominators: they determine the entire political, legal, and social setting of the daily life they impose on the Palestinians. The denial of that reality, moreover, can be seen most clearly on the Israeli side, where there is a systematic effort to present the conflict in terms of two adversaries in a situation of parity.

For the Palestinians, the refusal to accept the constitution of an Israeli nation-state, a refusal that, for many of them, existed from the beginning or has been revived, is tied to their initial despoliation. In other words, for the Palestinians the denial of the other is anchored in their own *reality*. For the Israelis the refusal to recognize the reality of a Palestinian people and the national character of their resistance is the result of *another denial of reality*, an even more constitutive one: they deny that they expelled the Palestinians and that they dominate them today by unworthy means. It is surely because denial is more obvious on the Israeli side that, for those who observe the terrible routine of the occupation, the tendency to stand at a distance from it is also more important there.

For, in the movement toward the recognition of the other, the road is paradoxically harder for the Israelis. In terms of self-image, the price to be paid is higher. It is they, and not the Palestinians, who had to make the greater mental and political effort to sign the Oslo Accords. Nor did these accords come as a great surprise in Palestinian political circles. For years Arafat had been making speeches preparing Palestinian public opinion for the turning point of the recognition of Israel. There was nothing similar on the Israeli side. There, Oslo struck like a thunderbolt. No prime minister had prepared public opinion for such a radical turn of events. On the very eve of its recognition, the PLO was still considered by the Israelis to be a terrorist organization that would never be recognized. And we all remember that dramatic scene of the signing of the accords in front of the White House: Arafat overdoing it as usual, and opposite him a tense Itzhak Rabin, and Rabin's moment of pulling back before being pushed by Bill Clinton toward the man whom, up to that time, he had never called anything but the "terrorist-in-chief."

From the onset of the intifada, the role played by denying the most obvious facts—hiding or minimizing them, and often simply by being ignorant of them—all part of the way each side looks at itself and creates a false identity for the other, has seemed to me to be a central element in the fundamental attitudes of both peoples. We have only to leaf through the textbooks distributed to schoolchildren for fifty years to see how each side, in its own way, passes along a narrative corresponding to a self-representation that serves its national interests: on the Palestinian side an absolute victim, powerless and without responsibility for its own destiny in the face of colonial machination; on the Israeli side a people pure of hand and thirsting for peace, confronting an adversary that has no national identity but is an eternal aggressor.

Though the general forms of this denial are occasionally similar, its nature and manifestations are neither identical or equal. For the side historically vanquished, the Palestinians, it is often rougher, sometimes subtly or even overtly anti-Semitic. For the historical victors, the Israelis, the denial is more categorical, more sophisticated, but equally imbued with racism.

To be sure, in what will soon be sixty years of existence, especially in the phase following the mutual recognition between Israel and the PLO, steps have been taken in the direction of a collective modification in the way each side views itself and the other. With regard to the actual events occurring during the war of independence of the Jewish state in 1948, more and more Israeli historians have been corroborating what Palestinian historical studies have been claiming for a long time. In the nonreligious school system in Israel the most extravagant claims have been deleted from textbooks. Among the Palestinians there have been efforts to take into account the magnitude of the Shoah in thinking about the birth of Israel. Since the 1980s the term *Israeli* has regularly replaced *Jew* in official Palestinian political discourse.

Yet in situations of high tension, when the conflict floods the entire field of thought and feeling, or rather when feeling banishes rational thought, structural denials and the need to confirm one's own victim image quickly come to the fore. And the stronger the denial of the other and of one's own role in the situation imposed on one, the greater the tendency to exploit on one's own behalf the denial manifested by the adversary. And the greater, too, the tendency to violence toward him, and the subsequent entangled, mutually exclusive feelings of vulnerability, omnipotence, and impunity.

What can the Palestinians do in the face of the firepower of the Israeli tanks and air force? What can they do, cordoned off as they are, when the army razes their homes and orchards in order to "improve visibility"? Most of them eventually conclude that the Israelis, and, to their minds, Jews in general, are inherently barbaric.

What can the Israelis do in the face of determined terrorists when each foiled attack, each destroyed house, doubles the number of candidates for martyrdom, when each new civilian victim quadruples that number? Eradicate the infrastructure of terrorism, Israeli leaders and generals proclaim. Fine, replies Uri Avnery, the old politician of Gush Shalom (Peace Bloc). But then, he says, you have to admit that the infrastructure of terrorism is the occupation itself. The occupation is the terrain on which terrorism prospers, borne along by desire for liberation. A large majority of Israelis are still unable to understand this, even if they are becoming more aware of it in a confused way. For most of them terrorism, especially since it appears overwhelmingly suicidal, can only be a phenomenon disconnected from reality and rooted in the insanity of the Palestinians' hatred for Israel and the Jews, or in Islam itself, or in both.

The concealment of the reality constituted by the occupation of a people so as to preserve a chosen self-image explains the shifting back and forth between present and past described in this book. Today's events can be understood only if we take into account the processes underlying the identity formation of these two peoples. Certainly the memory of the past, evoked by the protagonists, has surged up powerfully at the present time. Since he came to power, hasn't Ariel Sharon announced his ambition to carry on the 1948 war because, as he says, "it isn't over"[6]? Haven't many Palestinians denounced what they see as the treachery of anyone who tries to work out a solution that does not include a general return of the 1948 and 1967 refugees to their homes?

The concealment or distortion of present-day facts, large or small, the denial of the suffering inflicted by the occupation on those who have endured it for thirty-nine years, like the denial of the reality of the Israelis' fundamental fears and the means necessary to circumvent these fears, can be understood only through an analysis of the long process that forged them, immuring both adversaries. Historically, the most brutal manifestation of this denial has been the simple nonrecognition of the other party. Politically, at the outset the PLO did not recognize either the state of Israel or Israeli society as a national entity. Originally, it advocated the departure of Jews born abroad; later, until 1988, its watchword became that of a secular and democratic Palestine, accepting the presence of Jews only as a religious community and denying them any national character. Then came Oslo: the Israelis existed as such. After Oslo failed, "the Jews" have once again replaced "the Israelis" for most Palestinians.

In a mirror image of this shift, Golda Meir, Israeli prime minister in the 1970s, summed up the entire historical relationship of the Zionist movement to the native-born Palestinians in her famous statement that the Palestinians did not exist as such but were simply Arabs (see Elder and Zertal 2006). She said this in order to ward off fate at the very time when, having been engulfed by history, the Palestinians were reemerging as a people. Here again what was denied was the existence of the other side's specific national identity. The first intifada followed. After Oslo, the Palestinians were said to exist. After Oslo failed, "the Arabs" have once again replaced "the Palestinians" for most Israelis.

For a long time, and to a great extent even today, this nonrecognition has been accompanied by a denial of the most elementary facts. Thus the Zionist movement said it bought the land of Israel in due form—which, for 87 percent of the land, was a lie. The Palestinians, they claimed, fled voluntarily in 1948, and so Israel played no role in the refugee problem, which it was up to the Arab countries to solve. As for the PLO, minimized up to 1993 as a mere "terrorist organization," its character as a national movement was denied.

The first intifada (1987–1993), the so-called "stone-throwing revolt" of Palestinian youth on the West Bank and in Gaza, ended in the Oslo Accords. Why did that peace process shatter? Why, in 2000, did the Jewish population of Israel adhere almost unanimously to the notion of "Israel's generosity" at Camp David in the face of "Arafat's unwillingness to make peace"? Why did the failure of the process negotiated there immediately reactivate deep existential fears on both sides, with each people convinced that the other was aiming to make it disappear? Why did the Israelis at first almost unanimously endorse the unprecedentedly brutal repression of the new Palestinian uprising and then of an entire population? Why, after several weeks, did the Palestinians opt for terrorism against civilians in Israel? Why were Palestinian leaders unable to present their own people, the Israelis, and the international community with a plan clearly stating their political objectives? Why did the Israeli left, traditionally pacifist, initially swing in favor of national unity? Why did the Israelis bring to power Ariel Sharon, the most discredited politician in their country, a man whose career was marked by a series of crimes? Why, on the other hand, did many Palestinians gradually shift toward the political views of the Islamists? How did the idea of a new expulsion of the Palestinians from their country regain such legitimacy in Israel? And how have the young people of the second intifada once again rallied behind the idea of a final abolition of the Jewish state?

The answers to these questions have to do with the way each side, using the logic in which it has immured itself, has fostered the other side's radicalism. Yet after years of hopes for peace, the sudden reemergence of closed systems based on the delegitimization of the opponent, along with the formidable power of their logic, can't be explained solely on the basis of prior events. Deeper movements are at work.

During my stay in Israel I quickly observed the way that, magnified or concealed, the past fills the present. Two dates would immediately come to the lips of those I spoke to, Israelis and Palestinians, young and old, politicians, intellectuals, soldiers, and people from all walks of life: 1948 and 1967. The first of these years is that of the partition of the historic Palestine under the British mandate, the second marks the conquest of that territorial integrity by Israel. What was obvious to me time and again was not so much that mutually exclusive narratives were put forth, each of them aiming to justify its position—"We accepted the partitioning of the country, but the Palestinians refused it" on the one side, "The Israelis drove us out and have since refused to acknowledge their wrongdoings and leave us our freedom" on the other—but instead how a remembered *relationship* corresponds to the account of the events.

This is a relationship in which the rewriting of history through partial, and partisan, truths, and the concealment of facts, plays a central role. In contrast, some of the people I spoke with (although there were very few in the initial phase of the conflict) rejected this rewriting. Unable to make their voices heard among the majority, they felt a kind of despair and pessimism regarding the destiny promised to their own people. Here too there was a clear difference between Israelis and Palestinians.

Many in this small minority of Israelis chose the "exile in silence" that the Algerian Frenchman Albert Camus had adopted in 1956–1958. As Michael Ben Yair, former legal adviser to the Rabin government, told me, "I wrote publicly that we had established an apartheid in the territories, that nothing is worse than the daily humiliation we make the Palestinians undergo, that our society is rotting from within from its wish to dominate another people by force. Now I keep quiet. There's no point in saying what people don't want to hear."[7]

On the Palestinian side the silence took another form. After four weeks of intifada, the physician and former Communist leader Mustafa Barghouti told me this:

> In firing on us so intensely the Israeli army is pushing us to armed reaction. This would be a major error. But Arafat will go in the direction of guerrilla warfare. What's preventing him from issuing a call to the people: next Friday a general strike, everyone out on the streets, not one weapon, not one stone in hand, everyone in Jerusalem? What would the Israelis do, fire on peaceful crowds? But Arafat won't do it. He's incapable of thinking in terms of popular mobiliza-

tion. All he knows is armed struggle or secret diplomacy. And if the Palestinians were to demonstrate today, there would be thousands of "Down with the Occupation" banners but also some "Down with Arafat" ones. That's why he'll go in the direction of armed struggle.[8]

Would Dr. Barghouti say this in public? No, he explained to me: resistance to the oppressor must prevail over disagreements.

At bottom, the reality of the Israeli–Palestinian conflict is relatively simple to observe. On one side, for thirty-nine years a state, Israel, recognized by the entire international community, has occupied a territory outside its 1967 borders. The consequences of this occupation, beginning with the colonization and annexation of East Jerusalem, have been regularly deemed illegal in international law. On the other side is a national movement, the PLO, which officially claims the establishment of a state in these same territories. As long as the occupation continues, no one can see how, by some miracle, a viable solution could come about. The end of the occupation might not bring the end of the conflict or of the spirit of conflict. But, without it, no future of coexistence is possible.

The problem is that the overwhelming majority of Israelis do not feel like foreigners in these occupied territories, which, as they have been taught since kindergarten, form part of Eretz Yisrael, "their" biblical land. The Palestinians, for their part, do not consider Israel a foreign place; most of their parents or grandparents were forced to leave it, and their family memory is marked by that exile.

But another element is even more basic to the predominant mentalities, and that is the vividness of the ideological models in place when the two national movements were coming into existence and taking shape. Israel is the culmination of a national Jewish movement, Zionism, which emerged in Eastern Europe at the beginning of the last century. Beyond its colonial aspects (understood in the strict sense: the emigration of a population coming from elsewhere and the conquest of the land) as they were espoused at the time, Zionism, like other national movements— Polish, Ukrainian, Serbian, Croatian—that arose in the same area, was characterized from the outset by a profound ethnicism. It is steeped in the cult of "roots," of the relationship to the land, the privileging of cultural specificity, the equation of nation and religion, and national emancipation via separation from others, if necessary by their exclusion.

Despite the ravages of ethnicism in the twentieth century, and despite the evolution of modern societies in which hybridity is increasingly becoming the norm (a phenomenon that creates multiple new problems and is uniformly rejected by nationalist, populist, and extreme right-wing movements), Israeli society in its entirety has remained deeply imbued with an ethnocentrism that has become more intense during the occupation of the Palestinian territories. Covering a story in a small, disadvantaged town, Kiryat Malakhi, in 2003, I was struck by the sight of a map of "Eretz Yisrael," the Land of Israel on the wall of a kindergarten room. It depicted no borders of the Jewish state, no Arab city of the occupied territories, but everything related to the "roots" of the Jewish people in those territories was there: the Cave of the Patriarchs in Hebron, the walls of Jericho, the Temple in Jerusalem, and the so-called Tomb of Joseph in Sishem (Nablus). This kindergarten was part of the public school system, not part of the network of religious schools. Before 1967 this map would have been unthinkable. In thirty years the relationship to the "Land of Israel" has gradually replaced the relationship to the state in Israeli minds.

Faced with a government acting as heir to the Zionist tradition, Palestinian nationalism as represented by the PLO is a classic Arab anticolonialist movement along the lines of those created between 1930 and 1950. For Yasser Arafat's Fatah, its kingpin, the Algerian NLF (National Liberation Front) has been a special model. According to the Algerian historian Mohammed Harbi (2004), the ideology of the NLF was characterized by "an ethnocultural nationalism taking identity as a natural given and the people as an organic community" (p. 39).[9] An outgrowth of the Palestinian exile, the PLO is steeped in this ethnocultural concept. Despite the disastrous failure of independence movements in the Arab world, all of which have lapsed into nepotism and negligence, despite the door largely left open to Islamism by the failure of these regimes, and despite the terrible damage later wrought on its own people by the blind violence implemented by the NLF in order to get rid of the French occupier, the PLO remained stuck in its models. In the so-called freed territories stingily allotted to it by Israel after Oslo, it established a pathetic "power" modeled on the failed ethnocultural nationalist regimes of the Arab world, similarly leaving the door wide open to Islamism. Before marrying a Christian Palestinian woman, Arafat asked her to convert to Islam.

From this point of view, beyond the domination of one side by the other that remains the heart of the problem, what we also see in Israel and Palestine is the confrontation between two national movements, the first of which is a hundred years late on the level of political mentality, the second fifty years. In different ways, but equally deeply, both are marked by a fundamental ethnicism. Each of the two sides, though acutely aware of the inevitable presence of the other, basically wishes it would disappear. In the brief period of rapprochement after Oslo, this wish was partially consigned to oblivion, both side knowing how unrealistic it is. With the second intifada, it has now reemerged, stronger than ever, reshaping the mentalities of the two societies.

In 2002, on a soundproofing wall along the Tel Aviv–Haifa highway, an advocate of a new general expulsion of the Palestinians wrote in large letters: "No more Arabs, no more attacks." Mocking the absurdity of the wish for the disappearance of the other, an Israeli pacifist added: "No more Jews, no more victims" of attacks.

ISRAEL REAL, ISRAEL DISEMBODIED:
The Journalist, Honesty, and Emotions

A study like this can only be written with the acknowledgment that its own reflections, too, are subject to deep emotions. I investigated Camp David and covered the recent intifada, from both sides, during its first thirty months. I did so as honestly as possible. Honesty in the gathering of facts and the need to determine their degree of significance seem to me to be cardinal virtues of the journalist's profession, in contrast to objectivity, a subjective term prized by those who in fact judge it by the yardstick of their own convictions.

Yet I never covered the Israeli–Palestinian conflict with the same eye, the same ear, as in other situations, and this for two reasons. First, raised in a family that counted as its most important concerns the Shoah[10] and

Zionism, I lived in Israel for twelve years during the 1960s and 1970s. I studied there and served in the army. I worked, got married, and raised children there. I was politically active on the extreme left. I have family there and many friends, including some of my dearest ones. I also know many Palestinians, some of whom I also count as friends. For twenty-five years I have visited Israel frequently for professional or private purposes. In short, when I'm there I feel more at home there than anywhere else, and the conflict unfolding there is closer to me than any other.

The second reason is that no other conflict in the world arouses such passionate interest, sometimes sincere, sometimes sickening, and not only among those who, as Jews, Arabs, or Muslims, feel personally concerned. Though many other wars are by far more devastating, especially for civilians, as in Chechnya or various places in Africa, none has had such an emotional charge in terms of identification with one or the other side, and none has led to such hidden blindness, deafness, anathemas, tensions, and inner unrest. Nor has any led to such distortions, exaggerations, half-truths, and concealment of facts despite the exceptional extent of academic research and media coverage.

There is no journalist discussing the Israeli–Palestinian conflict in France who has not found the amount of mail from readers on this subject to be disproportionate in comparison with mail on other burning issues of the day. These letters are rarely calm discussions; as a rule, when they are not filled with insults and threats, they denounce what they see as the disinformation perpetrated by the newspaper or the journalist. The same is true of the partisan spirit in which Le Monde is regularly accused of being Zionist by one side, anti-Semitic by the other.

Given my background, it would have been surprising if, despite my efforts at honesty and professional discipline, I were not myself affected by the passion this conflict generates. But affected does not mean infected. A journalist's duty is not to an illusory "balanced treatment" but to the honest collection of facts and their accurate placement in local and historical contexts in the face of denials and concealments on the part of those for whom emotion prevails over any other consideration, and for whom the representation of events in the media will always count more than their reality. This duty is what gradually gave rise to this book.

I have always been struck by the fact that, admired or condemned, Israel and its society have often been spoken of in the outside world in a disembodied, monolithic way. Stereotyped imagery is not unique to Israelis, but in their case it reaches proportions rarely found elsewhere. For facile imagery, whether positive ("the only democracy in the Middle East") or negative ("the colonizers"), masks more complex realities. The 1990s had begun to open up a field of observation more attentive to the diversity and contradictions of this society. Outside Israel the resumption of armed conflict in 2000, with the focus of all attention solely on the political and military aspects, has led to an even more powerful recrudescence of the stereotypes promoted by distance.

Since that time some people have been unable to speak of the Israelis except in terms of global denunciation. Others, mobilized in Israel's defense, can no longer hear the slightest criticism. For both foes and admirers, an imaginary country, one in which the way one portrays it to oneself replaces the realities, has taken over the domain of reflection. Some of my Israeli friends, too, obsessed with what they see as the other side's monstrousness, have become resistant to any criticism. But in general it is by far easier to discuss Israel, its politics, its lapses, and its crimes with many Israelis without fear of ostracism than it is with many dyed-in-the-wool intellectuals, French or American, who are ready to decry in the strongest terms any thought considered dissident. These intellectuals are referring to an imaginary Israel that most Israelis themselves know does not exist. All one has to do is read the Hebrew daily press—which is no paragon of honesty but remains a source of an important diversity of information—to see how ridiculous it is to view this country with monolithic adulation.

The corollary of the fixation of Israel in a negative imaginary form is the propensity to "Sharonize" all Israelis collectively as monsters. The inverse corollary is the positive notion of the fundamental purity of all Israelis, including Sharon, his supporters, and his successors. The admirers of Israel abroad conceal or minimize a number of disturbing phenomena: the emergence of a racism spreading so deeply that it is not even perceived as such, the powerful rise of mystical religiosity and superstitions, the legitimization of the idea that the Arabs should be thrown out

once and for all, the daily implementation of means of repression contrary to law and morality, the upsurge in internal social violence, and the
like. Yet these phenomena are taken for granted by many Israelis and reviled by others, who, Israelis themselves, are not scary anti-Semites. Politicians, officers, professors, artists, journalists, young people: these are the
voices that will be heard in this book.

I happen to be a Jew, and not one of those who have only recently discovered their Jewishness. In insulting letters I receive, or on the Internet
sites specializing in hunting down "disinformation," where I am sometimes
a target, it is generally another formula that is used to characterize me: I am
subject to "self-hatred." This view comes from people who, mired in denial, tend for example to mobilize all their energy to "demonstrate" that
the child Mohammed Al-Doura was not killed by the Israeli army on the
third day of the intifada but are otherwise indifferent or inclined to justify
the deaths of hundreds of other Palestinian children who have been killed
since then. Those who condemn this alleged self-hatred are usually the same
people who find nothing to reproach in the most reprehensible acts committed by their own side. Understood in this sense, and not in its Sartrean
meaning, "self-hatred" as used today in communitarian Jewish circles is
ultimately just the banal equivalent of the epithets "bad Frenchman" or "un-
American" uttered by other people in other circumstances.

Behind this accusation we see the aggressive refusal to take the least
critical look at oneself. People who are able to take a critical distance from
themselves have always seemed to me to be more worthwhile and less
dangerous than those who are convinced they have no faults or who present
themselves that way. And if being moved by the deprivation of freedom
and dignity imposed by Israel on the Palestinian people for so long means
being "a Palestinian-loving Jew," in the disgusted reproach of a letter I
received, I am quite willing to plead guilty,[11] even though, since we are
in the realm of the emotions, the fate of the Jews is of more personal concern to me. "The main question," Admiral Ami Ayalon, former head of
Shin Bet (Israel's internal intelligence service), told me, "is what are we making of ourselves, what do we want to make of ourselves?"[12] As the historian
Nazmi El-Jubeh, a former official of the Palestinian Popular Liberation
Front, replied in an echo, this question "also applies to the Palestinians."[13]

One

Memories, Self-Images,
Images of the Other

ONE

TANTURA
The Repressed Floods Back In

What do the Israelis know about their own history? About the Palestinians' history? What are they trying to ignore, evade, minimize, or mask? A recent incident, one that seemed insignificant and went relatively unnoticed, offers a striking example of how people position themselves with regard to these questions and how Israeli society has regressed in its ability to examine itself since the outbreak of the intifada.

MAY 23, 1948: *Was There a Massacre?*

No two ways about it: This man is an old-style kibbutznik, almost a caricature, a vestige of a past that has all but disappeared from the Israeli landscape. Face furrowed by sun and sweat, impressive mustache, sandals, loose-fitting shorts of worn denim, a checked shirt open at the chest. A paunchy 60-something, this former *mapamnik*, a member of the left-wing Zionist party Mapam (better known for its youth movement, Hashomer Hatzair) and an activist in Meretz, the present-day Israeli left-wing Labor movement, is named Theodore Katz. Whether he was named after the most famous Theodore in Israel, Theodore Herzl, the founder of Zionism, isn't known, but no one here calls him anything but Teddy.

For six years Teddy has been living a nightmare. His name appeared periodically in the press in 2001–2002, often in a bad light though

sometimes in his defense, for he was the involuntary hero of an affair—
the so-called Tantura Affair—that he helped set in motion before it turned
on him and devoured him.

On May 23, 1948, a week after the birth of Israel, was or wasn't there a
massacre of civilians in that small Palestinian town, committed by soldiers
of a regiment of Palmakh, the elite troops of Haganah, the principal Jewish army detachment of that time, led by the Labor majority of the *yishuv*,
as the Jewish community was called before it became Israel? Katz and his
supporters are convinced there was; their opponents denounce the claim
as a fabrication and Katz as a forger. Ever since the affair got underway
and, he says, obsesses him and spoils his nights,[1] he never goes anywhere
without a heavy briefcase. In the briefcase are five hundred bound pages
of testimony.

It all began in 1985. Like many kibbutzniks of his generation, Teddy
was a latecomer to higher education. He majored in Jewish and Middle-
Eastern history, got excellent grades, and received a bachelor's degree. He
then started on a master's degree in Middle-Eastern history, but his studies were interrupted by a personal drama: in late 1989 his 20-year-old
daughter was killed in an auto accident. "I was devastated," he says. He
did not feel able to resume his studies until 1997, at which time he proposed Haifa as his thesis topic: What had happened there in 1948? Quite
a lot is already known about Haifa, he was told; why not write on the surrounding area? That sounded fine.

Teddy is not a brilliant historian, let alone someone adept at handling
concepts. What he enjoys is microhistory, the monograph, and at his level
of study that was also what was called for. His aim was like that of Benny
Morris, the precursor of the New Historians in Israel, who said he wanted
"to describe what happened, not more, not less" (see Vidal and Algazy 1998,
p. 187). This apparently simple ambition, foregoing interpretation, is nevertheless the most difficult part of the historian's work. Method and organization are not the strong points of Katz as an investigator, but the man has an
undeniable talent: he is persistent, and in this way he gradually found witnesses and got them to talk about events occurring fifty years earlier.

After the initial spadework he decided to concentrate on five villages
that had disappeared: Tantura, nowadays divided between the kibbutz

Nakhsholim and the moshav (semi-collective farm) Dor; Ja'ba, which
became the moshav Geva Carmel; Izzim, which became Keren Maaral;
Ail Ghazal, now divided between Ofer and Ein Ayala; and Um El-Zeinat,
whose land was annexed to the Jewish town of Eliakim.

He began by seeking eyewitness reports from Palestinians, most of
whom had become refugees. "Immediately," he says, "I noted that when
I mentioned the name Tantura, a village of 1,500 souls at the time, the
only remnant of which is a hovel by the sea 20 kilometers from Haifa,
people blanched. Some fell silent. Others asked me what I knew. I didn't
know anything. Then some old Palestinians began to say, 'Tantura, a
big massacre.'"

The reports gradually accumulated, sometimes contradictory when it
came to timing or precise locations but agreeing on the basic point: many
civilians were killed by Israeli soldiers on May 23, 1948, after all combat
had ceased. Teddy Katz then spoke with surviving soldiers of the Thirty-
Third Battalion of the Alexandroni Brigade of Palmakh, which had conquered the town during the war of Israeli independence. He questioned
135 people in all, Jews and Arabs, 65 of them on Tantura alone, including
20 former soldiers of Palmakh.

All the Arab witnesses confirmed that there had been a slaughter; many
mentioned a father, brother, husband, or neighbor who was "taken away
and never came back" before they themselves were driven out. And they
remembered hearing gunshots long after the battle in which the village
was taken. Two men—Abu Mashayekh, living in Tulkarm, and Okab
Yahia, living near Bremen, in Germany—said they had witnessed the
killing. Among the Israelis, according to Katz, seven confirmed that "serious things happened." Three of these people—Mikha Vitkon, who died
in June 2003; Tuvia Lishanski, an officer of Shai, the Palmakh intelligence service at the time, now also deceased; and Motel Sokoler, who
personally buried the bodies—were unequivocal about the reality of a
slaughter. General Shlomo Ambar, at the time a low-ranking officer of
the battalion, is quoted by Katz as follows: "When I saw what the soldiers had done, I couldn't bear it; I went away." He added no further
details. The other Israelis who were questioned do not recall any criminal acts.

After two years of investigation Katz was no longer in doubt. He wrote his thesis, which in essence says this: the attack on Tantura by three companies of the Thirty-Third Alexandroni Battalion of Palmakh began around 3 a.m. The defenders were at a disadvantage, and the first Israeli forces took the main entrance at 5 a.m. By 8 the last Palestinian fighters had surrendered. According to Katz, the killings began at that time, in two different ways.

In one set of deaths, civilians were separated, with women, children, and old people on one side, men between 14 and 50, approximately, on the other. The latter were taken to the beach near the cemetery. Many were killed there after being asked to hollow out the sand in which their own bodies would later be thrown. After cross-checking, Katz estimated that between eighty and ninety people were murdered in this way. The witness Mikha Vitkon said soldiers told him that Nakhman Carmi, who according to Vitkon was "a bit crazy," and who would later become assistant secretary general in the Israeli Ministry of Defense, "took out his parabellum pistol and shot them in the head one after the other." According to the testimony, the killing stopped at the intervention either of an officer or of Israeli civilians of the neighboring village of Zikhron Yaakov who had taken part in the sorting process and called out, "Stop that" to the soldiers. Several Palestinian witnesses mentioned the name Yakov Epstein, also known as Yakov El-Mukhtar, who was said to have intervened to stop the massacre.

Other murders took place during house-to-house searches by Palmakh officers who had lists of names of people to arrest. According to the witnesses, a corporal, Nahum Kaplinski, came up to men in the street, his Browning rifle in hand, and asked each one where his weapon was. "He immediately killed those who said they didn't have one," Katz reports. "As for the ones who replied, 'It's at home,' he went with them to their house, took their weapon, and they didn't come back out." A group of soldiers "fired on everything that was moving" in the streets. Abu Mashayekh said that he saw an Israeli he knew, Rehavia Altschuler from the town of Benyamina, intervene, asking one of the killers, Shimshon Mashwitz, to stop the bloody madness.

Abu Mashayekh: Shimshon reloaded two or three times.

Teddy Katz: What time was it?

Mashayekh: Two or three in the afternoon.

Katz: How far away were you?

Mashayekh: More than 20 meters.

Katz: About 30 meters?

Mashayekh: Yes.

"How many deaths in all, two hundred?" Katz asked Lishanski. "Maybe," the latter replied. "I didn't stay till the end. After that, I don't know. But there were a lot." Sokoler, who was sent to bury the bodies, said he "stopped counting" after burying two hundred and thirty. He included in this list the eighty-five people from the beach. But there are inconsistencies in his account. At one moment he mentioned fifty Palestinians killed in combat, "around a hundred" in the streets; further on he estimates that "in the battles a dozen [Palestinians] were killed, no more." "When did you leave the scene?" Katz asked. "A day and a half later. They were buried with their clothes," Sokoler replied.

Katz put the accounts in the context of a slaughter occurring after the last Palestinian fighters had surrendered. He gave the most important accounts in an appendix. The university examiners gave his thesis the high grade of 97 (out of 100). End of Act 1.

THE KATZ AFFAIR

On January 21, 2000, the daily newspaper *Maariv* published a long article entitled "Massacre at Tantura." It set forth Katz's argument and questioned the commander of the Palmakh force that had beseiged the village, Bentzion Fridan, who, when interviewed by Katz, had strongly denied that any criminal act had been committed by his men. He categorically rejected the charge that civilians had been killed; no Palestinian died at Tantura except in combat, he asserted. "It was war. . . . The enemy doesn't carry a sign saying he has no intention of shooting at you. When you see him,

you shoot. . . . We advanced street by street, and that's why many people
were killed," he added.

On April 6, 2000, Fridan and several veterans of the Thirty-Third Battalion of the Alexandroni Brigade sued on the grounds of defamation, demanding 1.1 million shekels from Katz, the equivalent at the time of around
250,000 euros (300,000 dollars nowadays). The reasoning behind the lawsuit was that the battles had not stopped early in the day but continued
until the evening, explaining the number of Palestinian victims.

Judge Drora Pilpel set the hearing for the end of December. The date
is not irrelevant. In April 2000 the mood in Israel was one of negotiation
with the Palestinians. Nine months later it had totally changed: the Camp
David summit had failed, and the intifada had begun. In December the
atmosphere favored national unity, and it was not good to be an outsider.

In contrast to his opponents, members of a military unit that is legendary in Israel, Katz was not a well-known personality, nor did he have connections. He was defended by his cousin, the attorney Amatzia Atlas, and
three members of Adallah, a Nazareth law association for human rights,
together with a leading light of the bar, Avigdor Feldman, a defender of
grand humanitarian causes and also a powerful intellectual and poet. The
Alexandroni veterans chose the law firm headed by Giora Erdinast, who
happened to be married to the daughter of one of the plaintiffs. Both sides,
then, were to some extent among family.

One of his defenders told Katz, "We won't even need our Palestinian
witnesses to carry the day; the soldiers' accounts will be enough." But at the
beginning of the hearings Erdinast, representing the plaintiffs, surprised the
other side. Excellent lawyer that he was, he was not interested in the actual
content of the accounts. He asked Katz to provide him with all the tapes of
the witnesses and had them analyzed in detail. In six cases he determined
that sentences appearing in the appendix of the master's thesis were not on
the tapes. Questioned by the judge, Katz replied that the witnesses had
continued talking while he was changing the cassettes, and so he had also
taken notes. Where were the originals of the notes? "I moved. Everything
was in boxes. I found some of the notes, others not," Katz answered.

Erdinast, citing a Palestinian witness, Abu Nayef, who said he had been
"saved by someone from Zikhron Yaakov," asked Katz: "Saved from what,

from death?" "I replied, 'I guess so,'" Katz said later. "I had sixty-three hours of tape recordings on Tantura. I no longer remembered every detail." The plaintiffs' lawyer brandished the written account: the witness had said he was saved from "being arrested," not from death. And so, Erdinast claimed, Katz was falsifying the accounts. When another Palestinian witness, Abu Fimi, said he had left at 11 a.m, Erdinast said in astonishment that Katz claimed the slaughter went on all afternoon, and so his witness could not have seen it. This was "false testimony," he asserted devastatingly. The line of attack was set: Katz had falsified or distorted the accounts. His entire argument was null and void; he was a forger.

With the exception of his cousin, his lawyers were not anxious; the bravado of the other side did not impress them. (Later an internal commission of the University of Haifa would demonstrate that the soldiers' lawyer, too, had twisted certain accounts for the purposes of his case.) Katz's lawyers were impatiently awaiting the appearance of the witnesses; the weaknesses of their client's work would then be canceled out by the quantity and unanimity of the accounts, and the contradictions in the veterans' statements would be revealed.

But Teddy was feeling ill. "One week after the plaintiffs lodged their complaint," he said, "I had a stroke. On the second day of the trial I had a terrible sense of faintness." His cousin, the lawyer Amatzia Atlas, then advised him to meet with the plaintiffs, but without his other lawyers. The meeting took place that very evening, December 19, and lasted several hours.

On a number of occasions before the beginning of the trial, his adversaries had already suggested an "arrangement": Katz would recant, and they would drop the suit. Teddy had always refused. But the pressure mounted the closer the trial date came. "My wife received telephone calls from people saying, 'Where's your guy? Out again, fucking Arab corpses?' She couldn't take it anymore." Now, in the absence of his other counsels, Katz attended the meeting with his cousin, other family members, the lawyer for the plaintiffs, and four of the plaintiffs themselves. Everyone asked him to recant. His cousin told him that the outcome of a trial is never certain, that he was running the risk of spending his life paying out that goddamn million shekels. The veterans, according to Katz, kept on talking to his wife: "'Why are you going through all this trouble? Let him sign, and that'll be the end of it.'"

His wife wanted to be done with the whole matter. Then, too, the mood in Israel was one of national unity. It didn't matter too much what had really happened at Tantura; maybe there had been some shameful acts. But now that terrorism was once again being mounted against Israel, was this a time to wash dirty linen in public?

It went on and on and on. One of the people questioning Katz noted that he was being sued for defamation on account of a word, "massacre," that was not even used in his master's thesis. It was the newspaper *Maariv* that had written "massacre"; Katz had spoken only of "large-scale killing of civilians." He had not said "massacre" precisely because that word suggests premeditation, whereas he was convinced that what had occurred was a spontaneous, bloody outburst of insanity on the part of a few individuals. This being the case, his questioners said, there would be no shame involved in admitting that there hadn't been a massacre. In the end Teddy Katz signed a document in which he admitted to "knowingly and systematically falsifying testimony. . . . No massacre was committed by the soldiers of the Alexandroni Brigade." And he agreed to have his retraction published in the newspapers.

That was it. It was after midnight. He felt like vomiting. His cousin and lawyer, Atlas, went back with him in a taxi.

Katz claims he told Atlas that he had made a terrible mistake and wanted to revoke his signature, to which Atlas replied, "Sleep; you're not feeling well." The next day Katz demanded that Atlas immediately repudiate the agreement made with the opposite side, whereupon the lawyer resigned without advising the plaintiffs of his client's change of mind. At the hearing Giora Erdinast, the veterans' lawyer, triumphantly brandished the retraction signed by Katz, informing the judge that his clients no longer wished to pursue their lawsuit.

Katz's other attorneys were stunned: this had all gone on behind their backs. As for Katz himself, he begged the president of the tribunal to disregard the document. "Under family pressure," he said, he had had "a moment of weakness."[2] He no longer stood by his retraction, and this was his definitive position. He urgently wanted this trial, he continued, because his thesis had only revealed the truth: many Palestinian civilians were executed at Tantura on May 23, 1948, apart from any combat situation.

Taken aback, the judge called a recess. At noon she announced her decision: she validated the retraction and the subsequent withdrawal of the lawsuit. Teddy was devastated, as were his lawyers, who felt betrayed by their client. Avigdor Feldman appealed to the Supreme Court for a reversal of the decision and a continuation of the trial. The highest judicial authority in Israel affirmed Judge Pilpel's decision. When his thesis was rejected by the University of Haifa, Katz revised it, adding an appendix with supplementary testimony, and presented it again. Although a new thesis jury rejected it, the university decided in spite of everything to give the "forger" his master's degree, a highly unusual occurrence.

Since that time Teddy Katz has been obsessively gathering additional evidence on Tantura. But he wanders around like an man undone, repeating to anyone willing to listen that he's "a jerk" who "screwed up" everything. Attorney Feldman summed up the Katz Affair with a terrible statement: "The whole thing began and ended among Jews. The Arabs, the victims, were totally excluded from a story that was originally theirs: none of them was able to testify."[3]

And indeed, what can be said about all those old Palestinians, most of whom came to Tel Aviv from various refugee camps and places in the occupied territories to tell what they had gone through that day, fifty-two years ago: what they saw and heard, and what became of them and their relatives when the gunfire ceased? They had been 15, 20, 25 years old. They had lost a father, a son, sometimes a brother. Mostafa Abu-Masri, 13 at the time, lost "a dozen family members" before being driven out (Pappe 2004, p. 66). Afterward their village was razed to the ground. "They were waiting patiently in a room for their turn to tell their story," Feldman reported, "and they were told 'Go home; no one here is interested in your story.'"

WHAT THE KATZ AFFAIR REVEALS ABOUT ITS PROTAGONISTS

First of all, the Katz Affair is enlightening because of its banality. Its main protagonist is banal, a student historian whose methodology is sometimes faulty and often confused. I would have to agree that spending a few hours with him is a rather inconclusive experience, since the man seems so lost and chaotic today. This does not in any way change the contents of the testimony he gathered on tape. Also banal, if one may venture to say so, are the facts in question. Not in themselves, of course, nor for any of the victims, but in the context of what really matters about the War of 1948: the collective expulsion, and not the murder, of the Palestinians. The affair is also banal and enlightening for what it says about Israeli society, the attitudes and behaviors predominant there today.

THE MAN

Why did he "screw everything up," signing a retraction and then correcting himself? Why did he agree to a meeting with his adversaries without telling his primary attorneys? Feldman does "not at all believe the version about the momentary weakness of mind, nor the failing health." "No," he says, "Katz botched it all because he was ambivalent. He's not a very good historian, but he's a good Zionist."

To be sure, Katz is not a historian on the order of Ilan Pappe or someone like Michel Warshawski, who has broken with the ideology of the Jewish state. Warshawski (2000), a longtime defender of the Palestinian cause, describes himself as a "militant anticolonialist" who does not even claim to be a "post-Zionist." On the contrary, Teddy Katz is what the Israelis call "a good guy." "I'm a Zionist," he explains. "Not like Sharon, obviously. But Zionism is the Jewish emancipation movement, a national homeland in Zion, the construction of a Jewish state. Not the expulsion of the inhabitants, and certainly not ethnic cleansing. Zionism means respecting Jews and hence respecting all peoples; it means affirming everyone's right to life, land, and water. If I evict people and starve them, I'm a bad Zionist and a bad Jew."[4]

Ilan Pappe and Michel Warshawski are hardened — if one can ever really be so — against the attacks against them in Israel. But Katz always felt part of the Israeli consensus, even if, as an activist in Meretz, he was not at its epicenter. All he wanted to do was study an event that had been concealed, and the result was that he was accused of being a forger. He was not prepared for that.

A rather good speaker, he had in 1999 represented his party in a great many meetings held to help secure the victory of Barak, the man of the left, over Netanyahu, the leader of the right. In 2001 Meretz asked him to stay in the background. It was hard to come to terms with the presence, on the speaker's platform, of someone held by public opinion to be a forger.

THE COURT AND THE UNIVERSITY

Why did Judge Pilpel validate Katz's signature on a document despite the fact that he went back on his decision in her presence? According to the University of Tel Aviv astrophysicist Elya Leibowitz (son of the famous philosopher Yeshaayahu Leibowitz), who took a close interest in this matter, no political bias was involved; all that happened was that the judge "intelligently accepted the opportunity Katz offered her with his temporary retraction, so that the trial wouldn't take place. She believed that determining historical truth is not the role of a court. Justice is there to say whether a given person did or did not commit a given crime, not to resolve the way events unfolded."[5]

Avigdor Feldman, the star attorney, confirms this: "Another judge could have reprimanded Katz for his about-faces, fined him for contempt of court, and continued the trial. But Judge Pilpel actually didn't want this trial. Moreover, before it began, she had let it be understood that if the University of Haifa joined the defense of its student, she would dismiss the case."[6]

But the University of Haifa dropped its student and along with him its own thesis jury, refusing to stand by a thesis it had previously deemed very good. The timing was not insignificant. The intifada had begun, and with it increasing repression of the Palestinian population and the first Palestinian terrorist attacks. In Israel the omnipresent feeling was one of existential struggle. Who supported the legendary veterans of the Alexandroni Brigade, in which Ariel Sharon had been an officer? The cream of the establishment. Who supported Katz? Ilan Pappe; the spokespeople for the Palestinians of Israel, who knew that the accounts of a massacre at Tantura had been related both by Palestinian historians and in humble dwellings; and a few Jewish intellectuals who either did not doubt the reality of the massacre or believed that a historical work could not be the object of a lawsuit. All of them also generally rejected the consensus according to which the Palestinians were solely responsible for the failure of the Camp David negotiations and the outbreak of the intifada. In a situation of high political tension, the University of Haifa chose the side to which it naturally belonged.

Six months later, the internal commission appointed by its rector, the philosopher Aharon Ben Zeev, rendered its verdict, which the journalist-writer Tom Segev called "embarrassing."[7] As far as Katz was concerned, Segev said, gathering oral testimony of course "calls for professional skills," thus giving credence to the idea that in this regard Katz had fallen short. Yet the verdict was much more embarrassing for the veterans. For, Segev continued, "the report does not say that Katz made this whole story up. On the contrary, it holds that some of the veterans really did recall a massacre." According to Segev the report expressed the view that former General Shlomo Ambar, who had admitted to Katz that he had left because he could not bear what the soldiers were doing, "in fact confirmed that there was indeed a massacre, though he subsequently denied this."

THE KATZ AFFAIR, THE ATTITUDE OF THE PLAINTIFFS, AND PUBLIC OPINION

From the outset the behavior of the veterans was astounding. Why did some of them confide in Katz and later deny their statements, accusing him of falsification? Apparently because the researcher had been able to win their trust. They spoke to him in confidence because he was an Israeli, "one of us." Hence their rage at seeing their confessions made public and their later denials. "Normally," said Avigdor Feldman, "claiming that they had been defamed they would have absolutely wanted the trial to proceed to a conclusion, with a decision by the judge in their favor. But instead they did all they could to prevent the hearing of witnesses, their aim being to interrupt the trial. Then they activated their effective communications network, which hammered home the message that there had been no massacre at Tantura."[8]

And in fact, after the aborted trial, the veterans kept on proclaiming that the court had found in their favor, that Katz had recanted, and that they had been found blameless. And they found a lot of support in the media;

the well-known editorialist Dan Margalit, for example, conveyed their views.[9] But the veterans' surprising attitude did not stop there. According to the historian Ilan Pappe, "Ever since the end of the trial I've declared time and again that there really was a massacre at Tantura. In contrast to Katz, I'm willing to use the term 'massacre' because I don't see how it differs from 'large-scale killing of civilians.' And I say to the veterans, 'So accuse me of defamation! I'm waiting.'"[10] Up to now they have not done so. Why?

Pappe (2000), whose own book of historical investigations is much more serious than Katz's, suggests an explanation. Look, he says, bringing out his documents: this is what we find in the archives of the army. On June 1, 1948, nine days after the alleged massacre, the very day Menahem Begin accepted the integration of his ultranationalist militia, Etzel, in the Alexandroni and Givati Brigades of Tsahal, the newly created IDF, the man who would be its first chief of staff, General Yaakov Dori, wrote to the commander of the Alexandroni Brigade. He said he had had "information to the effect that at Tantura our soldiers committed many acts of sabotage *after* the conquest, entirely unnecessarily. Please let us know whether these facts are accurate, so that they will no longer recur in the future." The word "after" was underlined by General Dori in his message. As for the "acts of sabotage," the Hebrew expression used, *maassei khabalah*, can have several meanings in addition to "acts of sabotage," including "terrorist acts." The Hebrew word for "terrorist" is *mekhabel*, which has the same root as *khabalah* (sabotage, destruction).

In short, what this document describes are acts committed after the battle and wholly unnecessarily, and the chief of staff is demanding that they not recur. We can see why the veterans were reluctant to sue Ilan Pappe for defamation, especially since Pappe has available other archived official documents. Thus, on June 9, 1948, the commander of a base near Tantura wrote to Dori: "I've been to see the common grave and all is in order."[11]

AN OLD TECHNIQUE: *Challenging the Opponent's Legitimacy*

Regardless of the methodological faults of Katz's work, in view of the testimony of some thirty Palestinian survivors and the initial confessions of seven former Palmakh soldiers, all of which are in agreement; in view of Chief of Staff Dori's message and the reply he gave; in view of the veterans' refusal to go after Ilan Pappe; and in view of the report of the university's internal commission of inquiry, we may hold with a relatively small margin of error that an elite Israeli battalion did indeed commit a massacre, or a "large-scale killing," of civilians on May 23, 1948, in the village of Tantura. Moreover, this is the unanimous opinion of all those who have examined the dossier with no preconceived bias.

It was not the opinion of all those for whom the defense of Israel, in the political circumstances of the intifada, was more important than the search for truth. Thus the left-wing Israeli intellectual Ilan Greilsammer, a political scientist at Bar Ilan University, denounced in the name of ethics the fact that, to pay the expenses of his trial, Katz got a subsidy of $8,000 from Faisal Husseini, who at the time was the head of Orient House, the unofficial representative of the PLO in Jerusalem (later closed by Ariel Sharon). A scandal! "The Tantura affair was a godsend for Palestinian propaganda," wrote Greilsammer (2002). "There are ethical boundaries that should never be overstepped, and I think the 'Tantura researcher' overstepped them here, and by far. . . . If we learned that a researcher from the Institute of Political Science in Paris, sued on account of his revelations of crimes committed by French police units during the war in Algeria, paid for his defense with the aid of the Algerian government, wouldn't this cause, shall we say, a certain uneasiness?"

We may note in passing that Greilsammer's analogy, colonialist crimes in Algeria, itself causes "a certain uneasiness" in its firm conviction about what really happened at Tantura. The analogy shows that Greilsammer himself basically has no doubts regarding the crime. But this fact does not interest him. What counts is to delegitimize Katz in the eyes of public opinion, presenting him as a traitor and the delight of enemy propaganda. If this is taken for granted, who can then regard the facts themselves as important?

The renowned historian and former Israeli ambassador to Paris Eli Barnavi (2002) is even more direct. Speaking of "an alleged massacre," he writes that Teddy Katz's thesis was "conducted under conditions unpleasantly reminiscent of the negationist theses defended at the University of Lyons-III: slapdash work; clear ideological bias; obvious incompetence of the thesis directors and members of the jury; and, finally, a lawsuit by the survivors of the brigade, following which the student was forced by the court to admit that he had to a great extent manipulated the evidence he gathered." Everything is here: deny the killing and send the Palestinian witnesses back to their nonexistence, slander in the very name of denouncing slander, cast aspersions on the integrity of the researcher and the academic jury, manipulate the facts by lying about both the magnitude of the errors ascribed to Katz and the actual conditions of his retraction, and ignore the report of the university's internal commission of inquiry (which, moreover, found that Katz's methodological errors were in no way owing to any malevolent intention). To top it all off, there is the striking lapse on the part of a historian highly skilled in his use of the French language: mention of the "lawsuit by the *survivors of the brigade*" (emphasis added!).

Reading between the lines here, we see the logic of denial and its outcome: the delegitimization of the opponent and the inversion of meaning that changes the aggressors into victims. If the word *survivor* applies to anyone in the Tantura case, is it to the soldiers who, as everyone agrees, sustained some losses during an initial battle in which they overcame the village and then engaged in killing, or observed the killing passively, or intervened to stop it? Or does it apply to those who, precisely, *sur*-vived, lived on, and were unable to testify at the trial: the Palestinian townspeople? The lapse truly seems like an involuntary product of the deeply anchored tendency of so many Israelis, even when some among them commit crimes, to see themselves as the primary victims, the survivors.

Here, in the attitudes of two Israeli historians, we are at the heart of the mechanisms of denial. This is all the more unfortunate because Greilsammer had published a study of the New Historians, scholars who had worked diligently for twenty years to reestablish the historical truths concealed since 1948. As for Barnavi, he was one of the first in Israel to work toward revamping history textbooks so as to remove the most entrenched propagandistic ravings, especially with regard to the War of 1948. But the crisis triggered by the failure of the Camp David negotiations and the onset of the Palestinian intifada tilted the vast majority of Jewish Israelis toward the conviction that they were once again in an existential battle, a conviction that, as we shall see, is not purely irrational. At least initially, situations of warlike confrontation always create powerful pressures to strengthen national consensus and conceal facts both present and past, and as a result to reject everyone who does not conform.

Not so long ago Katz, Barnavi, and Greilsammer were on the same side — broadly speaking, that of Shalom Akhshav (Peace Now), Israeli pacifists by common consent. But the intifada revealed differences. Like many of their kind, Barnavi and Greilsammer opted for consensual retraction. If they denied the truth of past facts and sought to delegitimize the man who revealed them, this was also because, with the explosion of the new conflict, they had to deny present facts. Like former minister Shlomo Ben Ami, they found themselves in the camp of Arafat's accusers. In contrast, from the beginning Professor Menahem Klein (Ben Ami's adviser) was critical of the plausibility of the "generous" Israeli offers at Camp David. As for Teddy Katz, because he had revealed killings committed fifty-two years earlier he unwittingly found himself among those banished from the consensus, defamed, and miserable.

Katz found it very hard to cope with his ostracism: "For God's sake, we are not responsible for the War of 1948. The Arabs started it. [He is almost shouting.] So what do we have to be afraid of, fifty-six years later? The reassuring version of the conquerors won't allow us to continue to live in this part of the world if we persist in denial and in inventing false official truths."[12] And indeed, why, despite the accumulation of evidence, does Tantura still have to be denied? Why was this so essential, so constitutive of Israeli experience in 2001–2002? Why can't the authorities, or a man like Barnavi, say, even if only as an incomplete truth, "There was a war on. In wars, crimes are committed. It is very likely that a war crime was committed by Israelis at Tantura. This is highly regrettable." Why does Tantura have to remain an "alleged massacre"? Why make Teddy Katz into a forger? What, as he asks, is there to be afraid of?

AN INADMISSIBLE REALITY FROM THE PAST?

"Israelis and Arabs committed war crimes both before and after 1948. The issue is not Tantura. It is that the majority of Israelis must now internalize their share of responsibility in the creation of the Palestinian tragedy, and that to the extent they have not done so peace has no chance." So wrote Tom Segev.[13] In itself the killing at Tantura is not representative of the profound nature of the War of 1948. To be sure, and we shall return to this, there were more massacres of Palestinian civilians than the popular official version of history has let on since the 1950s. That version systematically limits itself to the single case of Deir Yassin on April 9, 1948, and perceives that massacre as insignificant because it was committed by militants of Etzel and Lehi, two ultranationalist paramilitary organizations supposedly uncontrolled by the *yishuv* leadership. But consider similar historical situations. Just as the means of Israeli repression in the occupied territories today are not comparable to what happened at Setif (Algeria), Vukovar (Croatia), or Grozny (Chechnya), so the massacres are not the most striking aspect of the War of 1948. What identifies this war and the indelible impression it left on the peoples of the region is the interconnection of the crushing Israeli victory and the likewise massive expulsion of the Palestinian population. It is also the fact that this interconnection was long denied in Israel and still remains largely concealed.

For, to return to Tantura, a question naturally arises. Both Katz and the historian Ilan Pappe, for example, are convinced that, in contrast to orders given in other massacres, there was no order to commit slaughter in this town. They are also convinced that the killing was not premeditated, and that the murderers represented only a small group of the soldiers in the battalion. According to Pappe, what occurred was a "fit of madness" in a few soldiers who went wild and drew others into their bloody insanity before they were stopped.[14] In Katz's view the motive for the killing was undoubtedly vengeance. When the last Palestinian fighters raised the white flag and the Israelis approached, a Palestinian shot at them, fatally wounding a member of Palmakh. This treachery ignited the rage of his companions. Some days earlier the scouts of the Alexandroni Brigade had fallen in an ambush; it was said that they were found with their sex organs in their mouths and that some soldiers took reprisal against the inhabitants of the first Arab town they besieged.

In this view the Tantura killings were different in terms of motive from most of the others committed by troops of the *yishuv* at the time. For major atrocities were generally perpetrated with the admitted aim of terrorizing the population and driving them into flight, not for ad hoc vengeance. Thus Benny Morris (1999) speaks of the psychological warfare launched by General Yigal Allon in the northern part of Galilee on May 12, 1948, as his men drew near each Arab town and tossed in tracts with this message in Arabic: "If you don't flee immediately, you will all be slaughtered, your daughters will be raped" (p. 213).

More generally, in the 1990s, while newspaper articles on the works of the New Historians were not overwhelming in their impact, the testimony and accounts they related of the 1948 massacres were substantial enough to be read by many Israelis. Among the first of these reports was a long article by Gai Erlich appearing in *Ha'Ir*, the weekly city magazine published in Jerusalem by *Haaretz* on May 6, 1992. Basing his report on the evidence compiled and the archives consulted by the Israeli military historian Aryeh Itzhaki, director of the IDF archives in the 1960s, Erlich speaks of the "conspiracy of silence" surrounding the massacres committed by elite Israeli troops against the Palestinian population before and after the creation of the state of Israel and concludes that "a dozen massacres were committed in the course of the War of Independence (more than fifty victims each time), and around a hundred of other small acts of killing (of individuals or small groups of people)." He quotes Itzhaki as follows: "The time has come; a generation has gone by and it is now possible to face up to the ocean of lies in which we were brought up. In almost every town conquered during the War of Independence acts were committed that are defined as war crimes, such as blind killings, massacres, and even rapes. The only question is to know how to confront this evidence."

What is at issue here is not knowing whether the vision set forth by an entirely mainstream historian, at the time teaching in the Department of Israeli Studies of the religious Bar Ilan University, corresponds to reality (which, as we shall see, is the case). All that matters at this point is to note two phenomena.

First, the works of the New Historians, the New Sociologists, and various Israeli journalists and writers, as well as the relatively numerous articles in mass publications, did not at the time lead to a thoroughgoing revision of the dominant historiography, which up to then had been uniform.

Second, while a verdict like Itzhaki's, much more terrifying in its scope and systematic approach than Katz's and corroborated in the 1990s by other articles and evidence, did to be sure give rise to debate, it did not entail the same delegitimization that Katz came up against. This is why Daniel Dor, a linguist and media specialist from the University of Tel Aviv, is convinced that under other circumstances, that is, were it not for the fact that the Katz Affair and the trial had not come at a time of such great tension during the intifada, Katz's thesis would have sparked the usual outraged reactions but would not have caused either such a denial of the facts he reveals or such brutal delegitimization of its author. The problem, Dor said,

> is not what Katz says, but that he's saying it today. The function of the denial is to evade the contents of facts and focus on the stakes they bring into play. Many things could have been expressed in Israel in the past, especially the recent past. But with the onset of the intifada those facts and ideas became inaudible for most Israelis. People no longer wanted to hear or know. For us, what's at stake in this intifada is the recognition of our own responsibilities in the failure of the peace process with the Palestinians. In this sense it brings us back to our initial responsibilities in the formation of the very identity of the other nation. The political circumstances of confrontation have taken us Israelis back to the founding mechanisms of our identity, those of the "virginity" of Israel in the face of aggressive Arab refusal.[15]

Nevertheless, Dor thinks of himself as optimistic: "The Israelis and the Palestinians," he said in the same interview, "are two very romantic peoples. I am convinced that if, tomorrow, there were to be a general retreat from the occupied territories, a viable Palestinian state were to be founded, and a true peace established, and if a Truth and Reconciliation Commission were set up, a lot of people would spontaneously begin to tell the truth. Because these truths would become audible again."

Perhaps. Let us at least agree with him on the commonplace idea that the ability to overcome denial, to break away from it, to confront the evidence, as the former chief archivist of the IDF says, depends to a great extent on the political situation and the feeling of safety of those who have to deal with it. In the last years of the first intifada (1987–1993), and especially after the Oslo accord of mutual recognition between the PLO and the state of Israel in August 1993, a great deal could be said and written in Israel about the past, and about the nature of the occupation undergone by the Palestinians, without seeming taboo. After the failure of Camp David in July 2000 and the renewal of confrontation with the Palestinians, the wheel abruptly turned in the opposite direction. It was impossible to justify a repression — one that soon became very violent — of the civilian Palestinian population and to deny committing war crimes in the present, and at the same time to deal with war crimes committed in the past.

The Katz–Tantura Affair is symptomatic of the magnitude of the Israelis' denial of facts, of history, of the identity of the other, and hence of their own identity. Beyond the way it unfolded in its immediate context, how can we explain this? The most glaringly obvious explanation of all is the boundless fear that an emergence from denial would entail. What makes a very large majority of Israelis anxious today is the spiral of consequences: If the official version of what happened at Tantura is false, are other official versions also false? And if they are, how far does the concealment reach? Why does it exist?

These questions go beyond Tantura. What is at stake in the Israelis' refusal to take responsibility for the creation of the Palestinian refugee problem is first of all their self-image as perpetual victims of aggression. Then there is what follows from this self-image: if Israel is the victim, and is *only* a victim, its moral superiority over its aggressor goes without saying. Thus the challenging of this moral superiority is intolerable; it leads either to a reinforcement of denial (and the accompanying violent fury against anything and anyone that impedes it) or to a profound crisis of identity.

Six generations of Israelis have been born since the beginning of the Zionist movement, three of them since the birth of the state of Israel. A modern language has been created there and a complex new Jewish society constituted, one that is both united and fragmented yet still strong. But the revelation of the slightest flaw, the revelation of the least stain, whether in the past or, as we shall soon see, in the present, seems to evoke such fear that it challenges not only the existence but the very legitimacy of this society in the eyes of a large majority of its own members.

THE EXPURGATED MEMORY OF THE 1948 GENERATION

For the vast majority of Israelis, 90 percent of whom did not experience them and have been presented with a fictive version of them, the events of 1948 are known, vaguely apprehended, or, most often, wholly unknown. Yet these events haunt their collective memory. And their boundless concealment of the memory goes a long way toward explaining their present attitudes.

In 1948 Tikva Honig-Parnass, a 76-year-old retired teacher and third-generation Israeli whose grandfather, Eliahu Honig, was the first director of the Ottoman postal service in Jerusalem, belonged to the Harel regiment of Palmakh, the elite Labor brigades. In the 1970s she became a fierce opponent of the occupation of the territories and made the acquaintance of many Palestinians. One day in 1995 she was walking in the mountains surrounding Jerusalem with a Palestinian friend, the archeologist Mahmoud Hawari, who began to talk about the town his family had come from, a town that had once existed there. The name of the village, Saris, near the Israeli settlement of Shoresh, meant absolutely nothing to Honig-Parnass. Yet she had fought in this zone and well remembered the places and towns that no longer exist today: Irtouf, Beit Jamal, and others. She clearly recalled Abu Gosh, the town of Palestinian Christians near the headquarters of her brigade and still in existence, and saw once again the residences of British officials and the water station a bit further down the road. But not the village of Saris.

"For several long minutes," she relates,

> I stubbornly insisted that Mahmoud was mistaken: there had been nothing in this place. It was impossible, I kept on repeating, that I wouldn't remember. "If you fought here you can't not have seen it," he told me. Suddenly I felt an enormous internal tension.

Everything came back to me. Not only had his village existed after all, but I saw myself again, taking an evening stroll in the empty streets after the evacuation of its inhabitants. And I recalled the pleasure I felt at the time. Not only had I erased the stones from my memory, but I had forgotten the people who lived here. We had been mentally prepared for the expulsion, and for the mental erasure of what we were doing.[16]

Tikva Honig-Parnass (1998) movingly described how her mother, before she died, had given her the letters that Tikva had sent her as an 18-year-old soldier in wartime. And she described how one of these letters, written in a newly conquered town on paper that still bore, in Arabic and English, the letterhead of the landlord who had since "departed"—Ahmed N. Sharabati, manager of the Irtouf gas station B.P. 712, Jerusalem, Palestine—had been a motivating force in helping her become aware of how the tragedy of the Palestinian refugees had come about. Since that time she has spoken of how she gradually deconstructed her memory to uncover facts, not only events in which she had taken part but the general facts of the expulsion that had been hidden, erased from collective memory and its transmission.

In its radicality, the case of Tikva Honig-Parnass exemplifies how the entire generation called *Dor Tashakh*, the generation that fought in 1948 and created the state of Israel, sought to cover over the traces of the past, banishing the most fundamental facts to the abyss of repression. Only a few Israelis have undertaken the work of memory, revealing its flaws and, sometimes, its gaps, an effort that has inevitably led to a deconstruction of the country's founding myths. Yet the work of Palestinian historians like Rashid Khalidi (Khalidi and colleagues 1992), Nur Masalha (1995), and Elias Sanbar (1984) and of the Israeli New Historians enables us to form a clear picture of what really happened in 1948 and what official Israeli historiography has long been anxious to rewrite from the ground up, literally inverting the meaning and implications of events, a rewriting that still plays a major role in the Israelis' image of themselves.

The basic result of this war, the expulsion of the Palestinian population from the territories forming the Jewish state at its beginnings, is often called "Israel's original sin."[17] Though this term is immediately understandable, given its religious connotation I don't find it the most appropriate. It suggests a reprehensible and incriminating act, one that people try to silence out of a sense of guilt. I prefer "stain," a stain that is unseen not because it has been washed out but because it has been covered up. A dark stain. For, even if it means approving the evidence in principle and accepting its consequences to the point of being willing to see it multiply, as the pioneer of the New History, Benny Morris, has done since then,[18] no serious historian nowadays can deny that evidence: for the Palestinians, 1948 was what we would now, after the recent war in the Balkans, call a vast ethnic cleansing.[19]

The intensity of the extraordinary feeling of freedom, of resurrection, that brought about the establishment of Israel, a feeling that was obviously due to the time at which it occurred (immediately following the Shoah), seized not only Zionists but also a large number of Jews—as well as non-Jews—filling them with pride. How can that be reconciled with any historical account that might induce a conflicting feeling of guilt or, at the very least, of responsibility for the fate that befell the other nation? From this point of view, the most activist right-wing party of the *yishuv*, the so-called revisionist Zionists,[20] in the minority politically up to 1977, was always able to manage this contradiction more comfortably by assuming much less guilt for the reality of the expulsion of the Palestinians and, if need be, justifying it. The increasing influence of the far-right view of history on Israeli society, to the point where it became the majority view, is primarily due to the ongoing occupation. The longer a nation is occupied, the longer the occupiers themselves get used to the rule of force. This influence also explains the resurgence of the idea of the legitimacy of the transfer of the Palestinians, which had disappeared from people's minds and discussions from 1950 to 2000—along with the essential Palestinian question, the issue of the expulsion.

As Gideon Levy, the famous columnist from *Haaretz*, says, "1948 was Israel's finest hour, the culmination of a mad dream: the formation of an independent Jewish state." At the same time, he observes, "it was our darkest hour, in which we committed war crimes on a large scale. And did so in all good conscience."[21]

This conjunction, this radical incompatibility between heroism and crime, was amply marked out for two generations, in which the acomplishment of the ambitions of the *yishuv* was covered with glory while its motivations and its consequences for the native inhabitants were hidden or ignored. This was what was most urgently at stake for the nascent state. As Amnon Raz-Krakotzkin, Professor of Judaism at Beersheva University, puts it, the members of the 1948 generation, from its leaders on down, would try not only to "hide, and hide from themselves," the rift in the identity of the newly formed nation, but also to systematically seal it off each time it appeared by forging a historical narrative corresponding to the noble, heroic figure of the perennial victim who succeeds in overcoming a persistently hostile fate and a depraved enemy.[22]

Even when fissured and altered as the reality of the historical facts was reestablished, this victim figure is still widespread in the awareness of the Israelis, and explains many of their reactions to events and the way they spontaneously interpret these events to themselves. This is the figure that the *hasbara*, the Israeli communications media, promotes in all situations. It reemerged with more power than ever at the beginning of the intifada, accounting for the almost universal feeling among Israeli Jews that they had been cheated in the peace process by a sly adversary who had concealed his intentions and wanted nothing but war. For the Israelis' automatic self-image as victims is inseparable from the image, necessarily wholly aggressive, that they have formed of the other side. It is this same self-image that an Israeli "moral camp" is making a point of challenging today.

TWO

THE "PURITY OF ARMS"
How to Escape from an "Ocean of Lies"

AN OFFICIAL VERSION: *The Israelis as "Just, Absolute, and Sole Victims"*

In 2000 Benny Morris published *Tikkun Taout*, his first work to appear in Hebrew. The title has a double meaning. The literal translation is "correcting a mistake," which suggests the restoration of historical facts; the second meaning is based on the biblical and literary connotation of *tikkun*, namely "reparation": improving mankind, accomplishing and pursuing the work of God.

Gideon Levy's review of the book for the literary supplement of *Haaretz* was entitled "Maybe there was no other way, but why all the years of lying?" The Hebrew title sums up Levy's view of the matter, and his article is the most accomplished of all the writings, published in Israel since the early 1990s, that reveal the fear sparked by the discovery of the hidden face of the past.

Levy had been a longtime member of a group of young Israeli intellectuals called the Peres Boys, who fervently backed the idea of a historic reconciliation with the Palestinians and supported the Oslo Accords. Then he began to distance himself, criticizing more and more directly the political positions of the various Israeli governments, especially the pursuit of the settlement policy, and going on to take a supremely isolated position in which, after the failure of Camp David and the onset of the intifada, he was bitterly opposed to the official versions of these events. "Ah," he says at the beginning of his article on *Tikkun Taout*, "how good we were (and what bad deeds we committed), how just we were (and what unhappiness we brought about), how beautiful we were (and what ugliness our hands created). And, ah, how innocent we were! And what lies we spread. Lies and half-truths that we told to ourselves and to the world." Here Levy joins the former chief archivist of the IDF, Aryeh Itzhaki, who, as we have seen, thought it was time for Israelis to leave "the ocean of lies" in which they had been brought up.

One of the revelations of Morris's book involves the discussions at the Twentieth Zionist Congress, held in Zurich in August of 1937. These discussions were largely devoted to the theme of the transfer out of Palestine of the Arab population. There was a near consensus on this principle. As important a Labor leader as Menahem Ussishkin, a strong believer in the expulsion, justified the transfer by saying that a Jewish state could not be formed with half of its population being Arabs; such a state, he said, would not last a half hour.[1] And in fact the participants at the congress spent much more time discussing how the Arabs would be driven out and what the political impact would be than they did on the basic subject of the meeting, which was taken for granted.

This discussion took place in the context of the work of the Peel Commission, which had been sent from London to explore ways of ending the hostilities between Jews and Arabs and was the first group to contemplate the option of a transfer of populations to separate the two sides. Berl Katzenelson, another preeminent Zionist and labor leader, hoped to bring about this transfer after an accord with London and the Arab states, on condition, Morris reports him as saying, that the transfer be extensive in scope. Morris also reports that David Ben Gurion, president of the board of directors of the Jewish Agency, the fulcrum of the Zionist movement, was quick to agree: the transfer would make widespread settlement possible, especially since the Arabs still owned a lot of uninhabited land. It was important, Ben Gurion said, that the plan come from the Peel Commission, not from the congress.

But what Morris shows above all in *Tikkun Taout* is this: not only did the Jewish Agency create a very discreet Transfer Committee and hold a full discussion of plans to expel the Palestinian population ten years before the expulsion took place, but its directors decided to keep these discussions secret, to withdraw them from the official archives, and, for the future, to deny the slightest suggestion that the implementation of an expulsion was methodical and preconceived. Yet on January 30, 1941, Chaim Weitzmann, who would become the first president of the Jewish state, mentioned "the transfer of a half million Arabs" from Palestine in the presence of the Soviet ambassador to London.[2] And Ben Gurion was under no illusions: "It is hard to imagine a transfer without recourse to force," he wrote in an internal memorandum in October of the same year.[3] "They lied, oh, how they lied," lamented the furious Gideon Levy, stating that these lies were then institutionally codified and inserted in a mythological vision—that Israel never expelled or wanted to expel anyone—lasting to this day for the vast majority of Israelis.

Why, Levy asks, did the Israeli leadership undertake a systematic rewriting of events once the expulsion was carried out between 1947 and 1949? For example, in the early 1950s the *mistanenim*, the infiltrators caught seeking to enter Israel, were presented as bloodthirsty terrorists, although a large majority them were just *fellahin*, peasants, who had been driven out and were trying to reach their old homesteads from the other side of the border so as to recover some possessions or at least find out what had become of them. In his tireless quest for answers and his conviction that answers are essential today if the conflict is to end ("If you want to understand the Palestinian uprising, read Morris," he writes), he provides a framework of explanation: "The Arabs were always the bad guys, and we were the just, absolute, and sole victims. That's what we've been told."[4]

This leitmotiv still forms the basis for the attitude of the average Israeli, acting as the most forceful catalyst for the man in the street, politicians, and the intelligentsia alike. It took root in the events of 1948 and their immediate aftermath, underpinning the formation of the *yishuv* in the next fifty years. Levy describes how, when he returned from covering a story in a town in the occupied territories in the summer of 2003, he told a relative that the inhabitants had been living there for five days with no water whatsoever, the supply having been cut off. "Why," she asked, "didn't they pay their bill?" For her, if the water is cut off it means a late payment; why would it be otherwise for the Palestinians? "That's how we are," says Levy despondently. "It's almost a Pavlovian reflex to think that the other side's distress has got to be their own fault and that we're never to blame."

PRIMARY ELEMENTS OF THE INITIAL ISRAELI DENIAL

Ask an Israeli what happened on November 29, 1947 and 95 percent of the time the instant reply will be: "The United Nations voted for the creation of the state of Israel." This is correct, but it is precisely the kind of half-truth that led to the centering of subsequent discourse on the alleged Arab rejection of the partition of Palestine that had been accepted by Israel. It effectively places the fault, the original sin, entirely on the enemy's side.

The reality was that Resolution 181 of the U.N. General Assembly recommended a plan for dividing Palestine into *two* independent states, one Arab and the other Jewish, intended to be linked by an economic union. This resolution has never, to my knowledge, appeared in its entirety in Hebrew. The *yishuv* retained only the part of it that corresponded to its own expectations, casting out of their minds the disturbing principles underlying it. In fact, as if foreseeing the risks entailed by the implementation of the plan, the resolution stipulated, among other things, that no expropriation of land owned by an Arab in the Jewish state, or by a Jew in the Arab state, would be permitted except for public benefit. We know what became of that part of the resolution: Israel granted itself the lands of the "absent" inhabitants, an area amounting to about 60 percent of its own territory (without counting the Negev, almost none of which was listed in the land registry, though a number of Bedouins were also displaced from it).

While it might be asked why these details matter, the main point is that the Jews accepted the partition while the Arabs rejected it. From the historical perspective things are not so simple. For the acceptance of the partition by the *yishuv* was accompanied by a number of premises, never spelled out but fundamental, and as far as they were concerned perceived as existential. The first of these amounted to rejecting any constitution of the second state that the partition was supposed to establish. In the view of the leaders of the *yishuv*, if the Jewish state was to be born it was imperative that the concomitant Palestinian Arab state *not* be born.

Hence the negotiations with the Hashemite monarchy of Transjordan, undertaken even before the U.N. vote, aimed at blocking the creation of a Palestinian state. At the end of 1947, as the historian Avi Schlaim (1988) notes, there were two plans for partition, not one. The first came from New York. It bore the official seal of the international community and called for the creation of two independent states. The other was secretly conceived at Naharayim by agreement between the Zionists and Hashemites. It envisaged the creation of a single state and the annexation of the rest of Palestine by Jordan.[5]

The second hidden Israeli premise underlying the rejection of disturbing aspects of the U.N. partition was the entirely warranted conviction that the creation of the Jewish state would mean a war with the surrounding nations, a war that, if Israel were to win it, would lead to an extension of its borders. A political realist, Ben Gurion accepted the borders of the partition only as an untenable makeshift arrangement that the facts on the ground would soon repeal. "We are inclined to accept the creation of a Jewish state on a significant portion of Palestine, even as we confirm our right to all of Palestine," he declared to U.N. representatives two months before the vote on the resolution (cited in Flapan 1987, p. 58). And, to persuade his many Labor allies who were grumbling at the abandonment of the original plan to conquer what today would be called Greater Israel, that is, all of mandatory Palestine,[6] he added: "As soon as we gain power, once our state is established, we'll annul [the partition] and will spread out over all the territory of Israel" (see Navon 2001). Here he was merely repeating an idea he had put forth ten years earlier: "[A] Jewish state in a part [of Palestine] is not an end, but a beginning. Our possession is important not only for itself. . . . [We thereby] increase our power, and every increase in power facilitates getting hold of the country in its entirety. Establishing a [small] state . . . will serve as a very potent lever," as he wrote in 1937 to his son Amos (cited in Morris 1999, p. 138).

The third premise had to do with the acute awareness, deeply rooted in the overwhelming majority of *yishuv* leaders from both labor and revisionist camps, that the Jewish state would be only nominally Jewish if the partition took place according to the recommendations of the U.N. Left-wing Zionists from Mapam were the only ones to mount a bit of resistance, supporting the idea of a binational state of Israel. For, if the U.N. resolution had been implemented as it was written, this state would in fact have been binational from the outset. According to the plan for partition, it would include 45 percent of the native inhabitants, a Palestinian population that, given the difference in the rate of demographic growth relative to the Jews, and regardless of the pace of Jewish immigration, would inevitably become a majority in short order.

There are many statements by *yishuv* leaders showing that there could be no such possibility as far as they were concerned. For them, what was fundamentally at stake was a radical alteration of the ethnic distribution in the coming Jewish state. And what alteration could be more radical than the implementation of the longed-for transfer? Ernest Bevan, the British Labor leader who headed the Mandate, explained well before the U.N. resolution was adopted that no diplomatic solution to the partitioning of Palestine would be viable without a transfer of populations, and that if this transfer were not spelled out in the resolution it would necessarily follow come what may. As soon as the United Nations voted, some Zionists were acutely aware of this; Hannah Arendt, for example, warned against the consequences, predicting that the Palestinians would inevitably be driven out and their rights violated (Raz-Krakotzkin 2001a).

In fact, given the vote by the U.N., an Arab victory in 1948 would have certainly meant the end not only of the state of Israel but also of the physical presence of a native Jewish community in Palestine. On the other hand, in the minds of the *yishuv* leaders an Israeli victory could not come about except by the massive expulsion of the Palestinians, this being the only way to anchor a Jewish state as a fact, to ensure that the demographic balance would not quickly shift in the direction of an Arab majority in that state.

Taken together, these three unspoken principles constructed the primary fable of official Israeli historiography, one drummed in for two generations up to the 1990s: the Arabs left voluntarily. Of all the legends that were created, that of the voluntary flight of the Palestinians has suffered most from the work of the New Historians in Israel. Apart from those for whom blindness or cynicism is second nature, nothing is left of it.

The data are simple. The partition allocated 14,000 square kilometers to the future Jewish state, which at the time included 558,000 Jews and 455,000 Arabs, and 11,500 square kilometers to the Arab state of Palestine, including 804,000 Palestinians and only 10,000 Jews. One hundred six thousand Arabs and 100,000 Jews were living between Bethlehem and Jerusalem, an area that was intended to be an international zone, but that would never see the light of day. To the Palestinians living in the Jewish state would be added 470,000 inhabitants of the territories Israel would conquer during the war. Of these 875,000 Palestinians who found themselves in what constituted Israel at the end of the war, only 150,000 were left after the new expulsions following the cease-fire with the Arab states. The others, that is, 82 percent, were driven out, half of them by military force, the rest under the combined influence of threat, terror, and a deep feeling of abandonment and powerlessness.

The key period of massive expulsions, April–July 1948, also gave rise to the legend that Arab leaders called on their people to leave. Benny Morris (1999) has determined not only that there is no evidence for this, but also that Israeli archives reveal precisely the opposite: "In no case did a [Palestinian] population abandon its homes before an attack" (p. 255). For a long time the official Israeli version claimed that such appeals for departure were made by the Mufti and other Arab leaders so that their armies could clear Palestine and throw the Jews into the sea. Morris shows that the story is a fabrication on the part of Israeli leaders, who were perfectly aware that the opposite was the case. Debating with one of his most scathing critics, the Israeli historian Shabtai Teveth, whose aim is to lend credence to the official version at least for the period preceding the establishment of the Hebrew state, Morris (1990) stated that the intelligence services of Haganah and the western diplomatic missions in the Middle East at that time heard, noted, and cited orders and appeals to the Palestinians from King Abdallah, the commander of the Arab Liberation Army Fawzi Kawoukji, and Radio Damascus, asking them to remain in their homes or, if they had already gone into exile, to return to Palestine.

Homes and entire towns were erased from the map, sometimes very soon after their conquest, sometimes not until 1952. In all, some four hundred Palestinian towns and villages, out of a total of five hundred, disappeared.[7] According to Simha Flapan (1987), most of these had been burned, dynamited, and mined immediately after the expulsion of their inhabitants. With the exception of the towns of Ramleh and Lydda, in the large cities like Haifa, Safed, Tiberias, Jaffa, and part of Jerusalem, the expulsion was implemented *before* the onset of the Israeli–Arab war, and the apartments of the "absentees" were allocated even before it ended. In Jaffa Israelis quarreled over possession of certain "abandoned" villas. In Jerusalem the most beautiful Ottoman houses in a residential quarter were allocated to deserving Palmakh officers.

The reality is that the expulsion was desired, coordinated, and accompanied by systematic atrocities against, and killing of, civilians, with town properties razed on order (at first in a very unequal fashion from one area to another), and that nearly half of this expulsion was carried out even before the Arab states attacked Israel. The facts that Palestinian historians, working from testimony, had made plain long ago have by now been so abundantly confirmed by both military and political directives (although on the Israeli side some archives remain inaccessible) that the attempt to deny them seems pathetic. We need only point to the words used in the reports of local commanders as they appear in the archives of the IDF: a certain village had been "cleansed" (in Hebrew *tuhar*, which can also be translated as "purified"); in a certain area the "cleansing operation" (*mivtzah nikayion*) had been a success. The terms were immediately understood for what they meant: the population had been driven out.

As we have seen, the idea of the transfer of the local Arab population had been put forward for a long time by a number of *yishuv* leaders[8] and seriously discussed for some ten years before it was decided to partition Palestine. But a wish, even if its fulfilment is ardently hoped for, is not the same as a premeditation of the act at the moment it is committed. No formal general plan for expulsion, or at least no project drawn up in this sense, has been discovered by historians. However, there are many indications—including, of course, the famous "Plan D," adopted by the chief of staff of Haganah on March 28, 1948, when the expulsions were already in progress—that provided what Morris (1987) calls a strategic and ideological anchor for the phase of massive military offensives and transfers. Simha Flapan notes that this plan provided for the "destruction of villages and enemy armies, and, in the case of opposition while searches were being carried out, for the expulsion of populations to points beyond the borders of the state" (cited in Vidal and Algazy 1998, pp. 67–68).

The historian Ilan Pappe (2002) recalls how intent he had been on learning whether there had been a general plan for driving out the Palestinians in 1948, until he realized that he was on the wrong track. His investigations led him to conclude that an essential element in the implementation of a project that had taken a long time to come to fruition did not depend on a preexisting master plan. What was needed was an *atmosphere*, indoctrinated people, an ideological community, and leaders at every link in the chain of command who would know what to do when the moment arrived, even if they had received no explicit orders along these lines. And indeed, when the first expulsions were undertaken no local officer received an order to stop them. Everyone understood from then on what direction was to be followed, without any need for an explicit formulation.

Isn't the denial of the evidence for the intention to expel, like the conviction shared by the overwhelming majority of the Jews of the *yishuv* that this was the precondition for the ongoing existence of the state of Israel, ultimately proof in itself? From then on all the leaders of Israel would hammer home not only that the Palestinians had fled voluntarily but that their state "had not driven out a single Arab."[9]

What is the deeper meaning of such an instantaneous annulment of a historical fact, since recognized as both obvious and fundamental, that provided the Jewish identity of the state with its physical materiality? Let us return to the questions that torment Gideon Levy (2000). "Maybe," Levy writes, "we had to act as we did. Maybe there was no other possibility. But why lie all these years? Why not say, 'One right came up against another, one victim came up against another, and the result was inevitable. We had to drive them out. It was them or us.' That would be much more persuasive than the lie."

Why wasn't that said? Why did the Israelis wall themselves into a denial of the facts and their responsibility for them? Doubtless because this more balanced version, too, would not have been free of contradictions. According to Levy, when we begin to consider matters from the perspective of shared responsibility it soon appears that a number of acts committed by the Israelis had nothing inevitable about them. In addition, firmly setting a lie in place is a better way to create a prestigious self-image than admitting the truth. Acknowledgment of an expulsion that was at least strongly desired, and that had been implemented at the same time as the establishment of the state, would clash with the fundamental assumptions of the *yishuv*. Accepting a balance, a sort of equality of victimhood in relation to the Palestinians ("one victim came up against another"), would have amounted to knocking down one of the cornerstones of the general view of the majority of the *yishuv*—its deeply rooted self-image as sole victim, the eternal injured party entirely without aggression. And at a time when, even though only a tiny number of Shoah survivors formed part of the shock troops implementing the expulsion in the War of 1948, the very recent extermination of the Jews of Europe helped to give the *yishuv* the status of putative political heirs to the victims of the crime of crimes.

Simha Flapan, an ideologue of the left-wing Zionist party Mapam, sums up this attitude as follows:

> For most of the Jews of Palestine, the Palestinian Arabs were always marginal, living outside of Jewish society, even if they constituted the majority. Their presence was felt only when they took up arms against what they considered a Zionist encroachment on their rights and their property. And what [the Palestinians] considered a defense was perceived by the Zionists as the intrusion of violence into the peace-making efforts of the Jewish settlers. . . . The uprightness that enabled the Jews to defy accepted ethical norms was intensified by the fact that they projected onto the Arabs the anger and wish for vengeance they felt with regard to the Nazis. This process was facilitated by propaganda, which constantly depicted the Arabs as the disciples of Hitler. [cited in Vidal and Algazy 1998, p. 150]

Thus to say, "It was them or us; there was no other possibility" would have meant admitting that, however involuntarily, ethnic cleansing was intrinsic to the nature of the *yishuv*. The concept "them or us" was in fact basic for the ultranationalist right wing on the Israeli side, which was much less inclined than the Labor leaders to cite universal values.[10] It meant falling into line with the positions of someone like Vladimir Jabotinsky, the historical head of revisionist Zionism, who had long stated that the conflict with the surrounding Arabs was insoluble, that the Jewish settlement was an assault on the indigenous population, and that there was no point in imagining that it wouldn't react; only the installation of a "wall of steel," only an iron hand would show the Arabs how useless it was to hope for an end to Zionism. "Them or us, us against them" entailed endorsing a view of the conflict based on ethnicity, a view in which, right or wrong, might meant right.[11]

The vision of the primacy of force was quickly instilled in Israeli society, structuring its entire notion of safety even though it was taken up incompletely and ambivalently. After the occupation of 1967 it helped create a disturbed, schizophrenic self-image in which, in the name of legitimate self-defense, the justification for the worst misdeeds was mixed with the perpetuation of their denial. But in the aftermath of 1948 this vision still clashed with the image that the leadership of the *yishuv* was seeking to promote, that of a conflict between one camp bearing the values of civilization, peace, progress, emancipation, and freedom against the retrograde and aggressive camp of "the Arabs" in general. As a consequence this leadership chose to establish as official history the denial of facts and responsibilities.

THE MISSING PAST IN LITERATURE

When the war in Kosovo broke out in 1999 an Israeli editorialist exclaimed, in substance, "How lucky we were that there was no CNN in 1948, or the whole world would have been able to see in Palestine the images we're seeing today." He was referring to the televised images of the columns of Kosovars fleeing to nearby Albania or Macedonia. *Dor Tashakh*, the generation of 1948 and its fighters above all, could not have failed to see the columns of Palestinians on the roads, in cars, on carts, on the backs of mules, and most of all on foot, usually by the dozens and hundreds, and, after the evacuations of the large cities, by the tens of thousands: 60,000 fled Haifa in three days after the bombings, 70,000 were evacuated at gunpoint from Lydda and Ramleh, some in trucks prepared in advance by the Israelis, some on donkeys.

Fifty years after the fact, the former 1948 soldier Tikva Honig-Parnass (1998) tried to understand what had motivated her to participate actively in the expulsion, in all good conscience and with the feeling that she was on the side of justice. In letters she sent to her mother at the time she found "the complete concealment of the 'enemy' as human" characteristic of her and her companions in arms at the time. She speaks of the "transparency" of the indigenous population in the eyes of her generation, a population with which she had had no contact up to then and before whom she "passed without seeing them." And she mentions "the supposed absence of affect, neither joy nor hatred, toward the Palestinian Arabs." This attitude, she says, "corresponded to the view of the Arabs as an 'environmental objective' that had to be dealt with rationally." It also corresponded to the upbringing of this generation, reared in the cult of the "new Jew" definitively exempt from the sad assumptions that had allegedly affected the Jews of the *galut* (diaspora), making them "weak" and "sick," with "sentimentality" being the worst of their foibles.

Honig-Parnass cites one of the letters she wrote to her mother:

> Among our scouts are two Americans who came here only a month and a half ago. Terrific guys. But yesterday, when they saw all these Arabs, these women and children returning to their village starving, they took pity on them. In the evening they began to shout. They said that if the Jewish state isn't able to take charge of the economy of the territories it conquers, then there's no need for it to wage this war. They also said that Arabs shouldn't be killed when there was absolutely no need to do so. [p. 26]

In short, she concluded in her letter, "these idealistic Zionists, with their philanthropic attitude to life and the world are sometimes very irritating." In retrospect she notes how typical this passage was for the generation of

1948: "In contrast to the distance and indifference I showed to the fate of these hungry women and children, I expressed lively feelings of scorn and anger toward the men who had dared to show human feelings toward them" (p. 26).

Fifty-five years later, in the second intifada, the same "distance and indifference" regarding the fate of the Palestinians and the methods used against them emerged powerfully within Israeli society, accompanied by similar mockery of the Israeli "softies" indignant at the repression and dehumanization in the daily life of the Palestinians, and by overt scorn for any compassionate attitudes, which were seen as the symptom of a perverse weakness and a reprehensible self-hatred.

To avoid the potential spread of a "very irritating" compassionate attitude, which might lead to a political challenge, it was decided to conceal the facts of collective memory. As we shall see in more detail, in Israeli textbooks up to the mid-1990s the civilian aspects of the War of Independence were dealt with in a few lines: "fled voluntarily . . ." End of discussion. From the political point of view there was no "Palestinian question."

Literature, being independent of political directives, offers a striking example of this concealment of the essential facts of the past. In 1950 the Israeli writer S. Yzhar (Yzhar Smilanski) published a short story called "Khirbet Khizeh" (The Ruin of Khizeh), describing the siege of a town by Israeli forces, the atrocities, the expulsion. The work was quite famous in Israel but led to no rethinking of the writing of history. Twenty-seven years later, using a screenplay by Daniela Carmi, the Israeli film director Ram Levy turned it into a television film that sparked various debates. The main argument was whether it should be shown on public television. The compromise was that it would be shown, but not in prime time. The soufflé fell fast.

After "Khirbet Khizeh" it would be thirty-five years before a new literary work spoke of the hidden events of the past. This was the three-part novel of Netiva Ben Yehuda called *Meb'ad Laavotot* (The Path of Links), likewise based on personal memories, published in 1985. The author focuses on the massacre at Ein Zeitun and the atrocities and acts of humiliation committed against Palestinian civilians. In the years

WALLED

following, the recollection of the events of 1948 has gradually become part of Israeli intellectual and artistic life, but only to an extent that remains marginal.

"THE PALESTINIANS DON'T EXIST," NOR DO THE REFUGEES

The two primary historical reconstructions, the one that ignores the "disturbing aspects" of the United Nations plan for partition, and the one that transforms the victims of ethnic cleansing into people responsible for their own fate,[12] created two axioms that would last for almost forty years in Israel's governmental actions as well as in the popular mind.

In the first view, as repeated in several versions by Golda Meir, diplomat and prime minister from 1969 to 1974, "It's not as if there were a Palestinian People" (London *Times*, July 15, 1969); she saw them only as Arabs. The second view also denies the essence of the Palestinians' identity, that they are, above all, a people of refugees.

For a long time there were no more "refugees" just as there were no "Palestinians," since the individuals in question had, it was claimed, chosen to leave. There were only people who had made the wrong choice at the wrong moment. Let the leaders of the Arab countries where they now live take care of them; the refugees are not a problem that concerns Israel.

With the reemergence of an organized national Palestinian movement, the occupation of Gaza and the West Bank from 1967 on, and especially the first intifada in 1987, cracks gradually appeared in the first of these reconstructions. Acceptance of the existence of the Palestinians by the Israelis and the Palestinian acknowledgment of the reality of Israel led to the Oslo Accords. From then on, few people in Israel, even among the fiercest opponents of Oslo, have contested the existence of the Palestinians. On the contrary, to return to Jabotinsky and his wall of steel, the most consistent enemies of the Palestinians, including an ultranationalist like Rabbi Benny Elon, head of the "transfer party," now justify their refusal of territorial compromise precisely because of the irreducible national character of the opponent.[13]

From this point of view the Palestinians have won: the years of their oblivion in official Israeli historiography and the notion that they do not exist as a distinct entity have largely faded from the awareness of Israelis. But certainly not all Israelis; for someone like Education Minister Limor Livnat, the Palestinians still do not exist as such but are an integral part of the Arab nation. "In fact Arafat, born in Cairo," she wrote, "is an Egyptian."

On the other hand, the taboo against discussion of responsibility for the creation of the refugee problem continues to be extraordinarily powerful. What does the head of the Israeli government, Ariel Sharon, together with Shimon Peres, the last active representative of the "generation of 1948," have to say fifty-three years later? Speaking of the talks with the Palestinian Authority at Taba in December 2000 and January 2001, he took offense: "The issue was Israel's acknowledging its responsibility in the refugee problem, whereas the Israelis have nothing for which to reproach themselves on this subject."[14] His predecessor, Labor leader Ehud Barak, likewise declared that Israel could not accept historical responsibility for the creation of the problem.[15]

The difference between these two views is considerable. The first one acts to maintain the radical denial of Ben Gurion, a position that had been chipped away at for twenty years and now needed restoration (Livnat, Sharon's education minister, made this her job from the time she took office in March 2001): Israel had done nothing for which it had to reproach itself. The second view is much more sophisticated and from a political point of view, much more difficult to hold. As Barak puts it, whatever the Israelis may have done, they "cannot" acknowledge it. He does not say why, but we may guess the reason, since the admission of any historical responsibility in the fate of the Palestinian people would give rise in Israel to fear about the preservation of its own image.

At that time Sharon represented the Israelis who believe there is ultimately no solution to the conflict other than finishing the task undertaken in 1948. Repeated polls from 2000 to 2004 indicated that there are many such people who dream of *going all the way*, as Morris puts it; if there is nothing to feel guilty about in the transfer of 1948, why would it be illegitimate to want to repeat it? Barak expressed the perspective of those who think it best to forget that old story with all its complications, but who also know that it is useless to pretend that the Palestinian problem does not exist. Such people would welcome a separation, on condition that the Israelis are assured continuing domination over their adversary/partner. As we shall see later on, this factor was the key to the failure of the Camp David negotiations.

DAVID AND GOLIATH

Various other mythologized historical reconstructions emerging from the War of 1948 have remained very much present to this day, all of them connected with a national identity formed on the basis of being a victim wholly without aggression in act or intent.

On this model, the primary reconstruction is that of David confronting Goliath. It comes straight from the vision of the War of 1948 as it was presented to the population: a small state invaded by five states, 600,000 Jews against 30 million Arabs. Beyond the fact that this vision ignores a fundamental point, namely that Israel enjoyed the political support of both the White House and the Kremlin—at that time a unique and crucial advantage—it is silent on the brute reality of the respective military forces. We now know that, even in the short period following the attack of the Arab countries, two or three weeks during which it experienced real military difficulties, the *yishuv* had a military superiority that would increase to the point where it became crushing. It maintained this superiority from the outset, both at the time of the civil war with the Palestinians and the "Arab bands" that came to their aid before and after the U.N. resolution, and at the time of the attack of the Arab states until the cease-fire accords.

This superiority in quantity and quality, both of "human materiel,"[16] as the generals call it, and of weapons, tanks, artillery, and aviation, has been established by historians. On May 15, 1948, the attacking Arab forces deployed 28,000 soldiers. Opposite them, Morris (1999) writes, Haganah had between 30,000 and 35,000 men, and Irgun and Lehi, the two armed revisionist groups, together had 3,000. By mid-July the Israeli Defense Forces had nearly 65,000 men, the Arab armies nearly 40,000 men on Palestinian territory.

Moreover, the Jewish forces, better armed and much better provisioned than the enemy, were able to get around the embargo decreed by the U.N. and achieve exclusive mastery in the air. But we must put ourselves in the context of that time to understand that the heads of the *yishuv* themselves were in part surprised by the scope of their military superiority, which had not seemed evident to them when the civil war turned ugly in December 1947. (A clear victor did not emerge from the war until March 1948, when the tide turned in favor of the *yishuv*.) That is, Israel's superiority was not in evidence on May 15, 1948, when the phase of conventional warfare began: "Haganah commanders judged the chances of victory at fifty-fifty" (Morris 2003, p. 239).[17]

"Fifty-fifty" chances are enough to cause fear for the worst, but that is not David against Goliath. All we can say is that in order to preserve this stereotype, no Israeli history textbook has ever presented the brute facts just mentioned. The result is that the outcome of a war of 600,000 against 30 million, in which Israel crushed its opponents and increased its territory by 46 percent, can only be understood as a miracle, one reinforcing the most chauvinistic and mystical presuppositions at work in the country (cf. the 1958 textbook quoted in Podeh 2003, p. 103).

To this day the image of David against Goliath is still deeply anchored in Israeli minds. It originates in the same assertion: that Israel remains a tiny state surrounded by a sea of hostility. The grounds for this assertion go a long way toward explaining Israeli fears, although, as we shall see, it is not sufficient in itself. After all, when transposed to the political and military domain this image of the little boy defending himself against an enormous and powerful opponent seems even more unreal today, at the dawn of the twenty-first century and in the current unipolar world, than it was fifty-seven years ago.

In some ways it brings to mind the attitude of yesterday's communists, who justified each aggression on the part of the U.S.S.R. against a rebellious population in one of its satellites by appealing to the fact that, appearances to the contrary, Moscow was the small power that had to defend itself against the imperialist monster. For example, in his first big press conference the former commander in chief, General Moshe Yaalon, after likening the Palestinian threat to "a cancer" he was treating by "chemotherapy" and envisioning "all sorts of other solutions," including "the need to amputate organs," said the following: "Two societies are in competition for one piece of land, and to a certain extent for their existence. I don't think there is an existential threat for Palestinian society. There is one for us. In other words, there is an asymmetry here, but in reverse. Everyone thinks we are Goliath and they [the Palestinians] are David, but I maintain that it is the opposite."[18]

We must not believe that the Goliath threatening the existence of Israel is not the Arab world or the Islamic world but "Palestinian society." We must not believe what we see, the general explains. For we might automatically see an asymmetry between Israel, with its internationally recognized territory established on 78 percent of mandatory Palestine, enjoying the unwavering military and diplomatic support of Washington, with an army that is by far the most powerful in the region; with its F-16s, Apaches, tanks, missiles, and atomic bomb; with its educated elite and its developed economy. And all this over against an exhausted society maintained under occupation and denied all right of self-determination, restricted to a minimal piece of land, a society cordoned off at the will of the occupier and now also walled in, whose military means have been reduced to machine guns, mortars, and makeshift explosives, and whose citizens are subject to the good will of Israeli soldiers in carrying out the smallest of their daily activities.

This view, the general tells us, is mistaken. On the contrary, it is Palestinian society that is the Goliath, while Israel remains little David, armed only with his slingshot, facing a mighty giant. The denial of reality, the reversal claimed by General Yaalon, would be ridiculous if its consequences were not so tragic—for the Palestinians, first of all, but without question for the Israelis as well.

MORAL SUPERIORITY OVER THE ENEMY

A final important mythology sums up all the ones we have been discussing. It is mythology in the strongest sense—that is, a mental construct of major symbolic power, both constitutive and, if need be, mystifying. This is the notion of the purity of arms, in Hebrew *tohar haneshek*. In Israel, the expression is a true archetype, endlessly repeated in all situations by its politicians, military leaders, educators, and poets. It reappears all the more forcefully, of course, in every situation of conflict.

Purity of arms? We can understand that soldiers are the objects of veneration, especially in young nations and in the period following their creation at the end of armed conflict. Yet we may wonder by what blindness a human community, whatever it may be, comes to ascribe purity to the instruments of death its soldiers employ. And we may ask a further question, since, in the political and social domain, we know how the aspiration to "purity" in general, given the experience of the past century, can give rise to terrible acts of violence. Purity as a political dogma often leads to purification: political, ethnic, or other kinds of cleansing.

The concept of the purity of arms carries with it the assumption of an ethical superiority over the opponent, and the corresponding moral inferiority of the latter. It appears before 1948 in the Palmakh, the shock troops of Haganah, according to Uri Ben Eliezer, a sociologist at the University of Haifa specializing in the Israeli army: "It came from the revolutionary socialist tradition of the *yishuv* leadership and simultaneously evokes notions of morality, a high level of awareness, and ideological motivation. The War of Independence would then establish this expression as a badge of identity of the intrinsic and superior moral stature of the Israeli army."[19]

The underlying idea is clear: because the intention of the national Jewish movement—bringing about emancipation and salvation—is pure, the political or military means by which it is implemented must be pure, either by definition or as a result. This shift—from the end to the means, from the intention to the act—was practiced in its highest form during the triumph of Stalinism, when the revolution and the dictatorship of the proletariat were intended to launch the emancipation of humanity as a whole; with this purest of ambitions, the gulag could only be a lie. The transfer of the Palestinians would be all the easier because the Israeli army always was and still is the object of enormous pride: the venerated symbol of the transformation of the Jew into a new, strong being, and a true social melting pot for a population that is largely the result of immigration.

Although the IDF, like any army, is governed by hierarchy and discipline, it offers an atmosphere of camaraderie and simple relationships, along with a degree of independence and assumption of responsibility in its ranks that can be explained only by the strong support of its members, career officers and conscripts alike, for its aims. Uri Ben Eliezer believes that, over time, the IDF has largely abandoned its traditional role as a focal point for "a nation-state in arms,"[20] yet it remains true to this role to a great extent, if not, as in 1948, for the purposes of an expulsion then, since 1967, for the purposes of the occupation and the protection of the settlers. This is so despite the fact that, precisely in the name of patriotism, many young Israelis object to equating the purity of their nation's intentions with the alleged purity of the means it employs to oppress another nation.

The weapons of the early period were not in fact pure. To return one last time to Tantura: even if the massacre was inspired by vengeful rage, it was not an isolated instance. And there were other such events in 1948. Tom Segev is right in saying that both parties committed war crimes back then, but such crimes were much more numerous and systematic on the Israeli side. It is not that the Arabs were more ethical in waging war, but they were, quite simply, in retreat most of the time.

A massacre, says Arieh Itzhaki, the former head of the IDF's archives, implies deliberate killing of between 50 and 250 victims in a single episode, whether these are civilians, including old people, women, and children (often by blowing up houses with the occupants locked inside), or civilians and Palestinian soldiers who had been taken prisoner and were killed with a bullet to the back of the head before being thrown into a common ditch. This happened at Ein Zeitun, Eilabun, Jish, Safsaf, Lydda, Sasa, Dawayima, Majdal-Kroum, Balad El-Sheikh, and Salha. And, of course, at Deir Yassin. Some cases are not as well confirmed. For example, Benny Morris (1999) writes that before the attack on Tiberias, atrocities were committed at Khirbet Nasser ad-Din. Itzhaki lists a dozen such collective murders and a hundred instances of the pillaging, brutality, and killing of small groups of noncombatants, events that, each time, terrorized the inhabitants of the town and the surrounding areas and played an important role in their "flight." The Palestinians calculate a larger number of massacres.

The question here is why Israeli historical accounts mention only one such incident: the massacre at Deir Yassin, a town bordering Jerusalem, on April 9, 1948, of between 110 and 254 civilians. The simplest answer is that this event was carried out in an especially repugnant way and became known very quickly, so that it could not be denied. The Haganah official Tsvi Ankori stated as follows in 1982: "I went into six or seven homes and saw genitals that had been cut off and women's bellies crushed" (cited in Gresh and Vidal 2003, p. 148). There were also accounts of rape and torture before the victims were killed. Inhabitants of Deir Yassin were exhibited in chains in the markets of Jerusalem before being killed. This butchery was immediately condemned by the Labor leaders of the *yishuv*, and Ben Gurion sent his apologies to King Abdallah. Four days later Arab soldiers took their revenge on an armed convoy of Jewish civilians and soldiers, killing seventy people, and on the Jewish settlers of Gush Etzion.

But there is a more fundamental reason why this massacre is the only one mentioned in Israeli historiography. It was perpetrated by the forces of Etzel (or Irgun) and Lehi (the Stern Group, ultranationalist dissident militias of the *yishuv*). When Ben Gurion washed his hands of all responsibility for the massacre, ascribing it to uncontrolled elements, the leaders of these two organizations were left choking with indignation. In this phase of the war, all their operations were coordinated with Haganah (the Laborite armed forces), and Deir Yassin was no exception, they said. Since that time various witnesses, including former Palmakh officers, have confirmed the version given by the attacking forces. But why did the ultranationalists quickly give up the defense of their cause? Apparently because everyone preferred to believe that Deir Yassin was a single exception to the rule.

This was clearly the view of the Labor leaders of the *yishuv*. Nearly all the other massacres were the work of its troops, which had ten times the manpower of the ultranationalist militias. But the crimes of Palmakh had to be denied and concealed in the name of purity of arms, immaculate intentions. With Deir Yassin as the sole exception, the purity of the rule was proven—preserving the fundamental innocence of the acts founding Israel's collective identity. Irgun and its successors, Herut and then Likud, were content to leave matters there. Arguing with the Labor Party about Deir Yassin would have meant opening a Pandora's box,

since the ultranationalists would inevitably have had to bring up similar massacres committed by their partner and competitor, Palmakh,
damaging the collectivity and its image not only in its own eyes but in
the eyes of the world.

Thus in his memoirs Menahem Begin (1972), head of Irgun, could speak
of the propaganda lies about Jewish atrocities at Deir Yassin. Once the
law of the majority was accepted, implying the renunciation, at least for
the time being, of the idea of Greater Israel, and once their troops joined
those of Tsahal (the new IDF), the former terrorist leaders Begin and Itzhak
Shamir, now patriots and statesmen, adopted the Labor concept of purity
of arms as the supreme symbol of Israel and its army.

The power of this symbolic notion, together with the central importance
of its primary vehicle, the IDF, made public opinion resistant to all further revelations of major atrocities in the past as well as to later, detailed
accounts of inexcusable behavior up to the time of the two intifadas. This
was the case with crimes committed during the so-called reprisal operations in the early 1950s. The most famous of these was the attack on Kibya
on October 15, 1953, in which Battalion 101 under Ariel Sharon, using a
method often employed in 1948, booby-trapped the houses of the village
before entering it and, firing freely, killing sixty people, most of whom were
women and children. Then there was the slaughter of hundreds of Egyptian prisoners after the Sinai campaign in 1956, committed in cold blood
by troops under the man who was Sharon's second in command for years,
the future chief of staff Rafael Eytan. As part of this campaign some 500
unarmed Palestinian civilians were also massacred in the Gaza Strip during and after its conquest. On this occasion Colonel Uri Ben Ari was relieved of his duties. He later rejoined the IDF and ended his career as a
brigadier general (see Morris 1999).

It was after the Suez campaign, basically as a result of the massacre
committed by Israeli troops in the Israeli Arab village of Kafr Kassem on
October 29, 1956, that the IDF formally inscribed the notion of purity of
arms in its code of conduct, along with the right to refuse to carry out
"manifestly illegal orders" invoked nowadays by Israeli soldiers who refuse
to take part in the repression of the Palestinians. The concept of purity of
arms also led to the ignoring of the new expulsion in 1967, later totally

banished from collective memory, of some 250,000 additional Palestinians and the Arab population of the Golan, and it enabled public opinion to remain indifferent during the bombing of Beirut in 1982. Ultimately, the concept of the purity of the Israeli army served as a constant, astonishing self-justification in the two intifadas.

With the passing of time, as Israel became more deeply involved in the repression of the other nation, and as the means of repression became more intense, popular belief in the legend of purity of arms began to crumble. The result was two mutually exclusive trends. For a minority, the rejection of such methods and the denunciation of the inpurity of the Israeli military, and for a majority the justification of the most frightful acts with no concern for morality. But even in its battered state, the legend still serves as a shield against questioning, continuing on as a reflexive self-defense mechanism that, as Gideon Levy would say, is almost Pavlovian.

In *Testimonies*, a documentary film by the Israeli director Ido Sela (1993) about the first intifada (1987–1993), the commanding officer of a reserve battalion, Matti Ben Tsur, a clinical psychologist by profession, relates a dreadful experience. In the course of a perfectly ordinary event, a nighttime search carried out in a refugee camp in Tulkarm, his group of soldiers knocked on a door for a long time. Sounds could be heard from within, but no one opened. In accordance with instructions, he tossed a tear-gas grenade inside. A family was there, paralyzed with fear. After a few minutes a man rushed out carrying a two-year-old girl. Before the Palestinian ambulance could get there, an Israeli medical aide found that she was dead of suffocation by the gas.

Ben Tsur recalls how he shouted at the Palestinian father, a man of 40, "reproaching him for not having opened the door" and striking him violently. "I saw myself," he says, "spending the rest of my days with the image of that little girl." He also recalls how he then had to describe this trauma to his family and friends, as if to receive their forgiveness. At this point the filmmaker asks him, "Didn't you think to ask forgiveness from the Palestinian family?" The Israeli psychologist remains silent for a long minute before replying, "I never thought of that possibility. I was angry at that family. Your question is not relevant. They're the ones who should have asked me for forgiveness. They're the ones who put me in that situation; they didn't open the door, didn't take the child up onto the roof [after the grenade was thrown]."

Testimony of this kind reveals the clear conscience typical of the average Israeli. According to the soldier, the Palestinian family are the ones who should apologize. They were unarmed and terrified in their apartment, but the Israeli soldier's grenade was pure. He too was afraid, with no way of knowing in advance what he would find in that house. But his *intention* was not to kill. He would have preferred not to throw that grenade; *they* are the cause of his nightmares. The reaction exemplifies the conditioning brought about by denial. The soldier does not blame the situation that brought about the event, namely the military occupation and domination. He does not ask himself what he, personally, is doing there, in the middle of the night, knocking on the doors of terrorized civilians in a refugee camp. No, he blames the victim. If those Palestinians had only opened the damned door, there wouldn't have been a dead child and he would not be having nightmares.

Today, however, the doctrine of purity of arms has also become the reference cited by many Israelis who refuse to participate in the dehumanization of the occupied population. In January 2004, Lieutenant Colonel Eitan Ronen sent his military insignia back to the chief of staff with the following message: "Human life has lost all value, and the values with which we were raised, such as the purity of arms, have become a bad joke."[21] This at the same time that purity of arms remains the knockdown argument of all those who favor the methods employed by the IDF in its so-called fight against terrorism, where it is the argument used to decisively void any accusation of the amorality of its use of force.

Twenty-seven Israeli war pilots, including the legendary Yftah Spector, signed a statement indicating their refusal to carry out future bombings of the occupied territories, especially the inhabited areas. To swat a fly, one of the men explained, you don't use an ax, and if you do so knowingly it's because you're not concerned about the consequences.[22] The commander of the Air Force, General Dan Halutz, today's chief of staff, replied immediately, evoking the IDF's purity of arms and accusing the pilots themselves of being immoral, traitors in wartime.

Yet there was an important shade of difference. For a long time the so-called purity had found expression in the straightforward denial of the facts called into question. Now, however, when the "refusenik" pilots denounced a systematic and deliberate policy, the general admitted "errors." But he immediately added that the Israeli army was the most moral of all the armed forces of the world. Translated into modern-day language, what the dogma of the purity of arms means to the citizens of Israel is that, even if weapons in their hands should happen to be dirty at some point, they are still cleaner than weapons in any other hands. Thus General Halutz had declared, a year earlier, that after his pilots released a one-ton bomb that killed the Hamas leader Salah Shehadeh and seventeen other people — including ten children — living in the same building, he himself, sitting in his cockpit, felt nothing but a slight gust of air.

TZADKANUT: *Systematic Self-Justification*

The effect of all these historiographical mythologies and rewritings has been to set in stone an attitude that in modern Hebrew is called *tzadkanut*, meaning "good conscience" or "systematic self-justification," the spontaneous tendency to see oneself as "good, just, beautiful, and innocent," as Gideon Levy puts it.

This need to conceal or deny disturbing truths for the sake of a stable identity is in no way confined to Israelis. As Woody Allen quipped, the Austrians "are a nation convinced that Hitler was German and Beethoven Austrian." Like Gideon Levy, the novelist Thomas Bernhard could no longer endure the spontaneous, reassuring self-justification at work in his own society. The remarkable Holocaust Museum in Washington, D.C., offers an excellent way to establish forever the universal meaning of the Shoah, but, despite long discussions, there is still no museum dedicated to slavery. A museum to commemorate the greatest crime against humanity committed by others, on foreign soil, yes. A museum to commemorate another great collective crime of the modern era, committed by Americans on American soil, against people whose great-grandchildren are Americans, no. It's probably still too soon.

Coming to terms with a flawed past implies a political *aggiornamento* that enables a society to turn its back, at least partially, on nationalism and, obviously, on ethnocentrism, without fearing disintegration, the aim being to construct itself in a different way. If the Federal Republic of Germany was able to draw up a balance sheet for its past, this was because, apart from a few nostalgia buffs and perverse historians, there was nothing good to hold onto from the Hitler era. The collective turn to democracy and to the European arena that was gradually forming also explains why this assessment was much more important in West Germany than in the German Democratic Republic. Stalinist ideology, with its fortress mentality, made sure that the events of the Hitler era were readily adapted to political ends; actually analyzing them was of much less interest.

Likewise, if the extent of the crimes of the colonial past of the great European powers can be better evaluated today, and responsibility taken, this is above all because colonialism is no longer perceived as an ideal of civilization. In Poland, on the other hand, historically the victim of the imperialist ambitions of Germany, whether Prussian or Hitlerian, and of Russia, czarist or Soviet, nationalism and the church created and still maintain the perception that they are forces of resistance and emancipation and thus find it much harder to confront the deep anti-Semitism of the country's recent past. So too the nationalism promoted by Kemal Atatürk, still quite strong in Turkey as a movement claiming to be a force for freedom, which stubbornly persists in denying the genocide of the Armenians.

The denial of facts and the inversion of responsibilities, like the conviction of moral superiority over one's enemies that allows their delegitimization, are the mainstays of the intellectual functioning and political attitudes of a great many Israelis, and since the founding of the country have been desired and fostered by the entire machinery of the state apparatus. That is what is summed up in the concept of *tzadkanut*. To paraphrase Sartre, in an ideal world the executioner would never forget his terrible crime and the victim would manage to forget enough of his suffering so that he could put himself back together. In reality, generally speaking, what occurs is the opposite: the executioner often forgets very quickly and has no trouble repressing what he has done, and the victim retains a lifelong memory of his misfortune and the pain it brought. Even while gradually being abandoned by an increasingly important minority, at the deepest level for an overwhelming majority of Israelis, two demands are at work, becoming stronger as the conflict becomes entrenched. The first is that the whole world must never forget the abomination inflicted on the Jews. The second, equally strong, is that the wrongs committed by Israel against the Palestinians must be completely forgotten.

Here there will be comments, scandalized or, paradoxically, relieved, aimed at discrediting the author of these lines once and for all: So this is what we've come to, comparing Israel to the Nazis! I shall try to show that, on the contrary, all comparisons of this type, however frequent (and including wild statements to this effect in Israel itself) seem to me to be false and unworthy. What matters here is not to compare acts, or their degree of abomination, or their political or symbolic implications, or, clearly, to deny the specific nature of the Shoah, but to determine the workings of an extremely widespread attitude. What is at issue is the imperative need, perfectly legitimate, to remember the suffering, existing alongside the need, equally intense but illegitimate, to forget the suffering inflicted on the other. A person with this twofold tendency would be described as having a paradoxical split in his behavior. How, then, can we define a society steeped in this duality?

THREE

"A VILLA IN THE JUNGLE"
The Israelis' Perception of Their Environment

THE KEYWORD *BITAKHON*: *Security*

It was 1973. Visiting my aunt, my son, 4 years old at the time, asked her point blank, "Sara, do you know Nasser?"

"Of course, honey," she replied. "Who hasn't heard of Nasser?" The Egyptian *rais* had died three years earlier.

"Oh good! You know Nasser, my daddy's friend?"

My aunt looked at the child, half appalled and half incredulous. A bomb rolling under her feet wouldn't have been more startling. Seeing her distress, the boy then came out with these astonishing words: "You know, Auntie, Nasser isn't like the other Arabs. He wears nice clothes and he speaks Hebrew."

Nasser was an Israeli Arab, a student at Hebrew University. He was very different from the Arabs my son saw every day in Jerusalem: construction workers who came from the occupied territories to work at the building sites surrounding our district. The child had long believed that "Arab" and "construction worker" (hence "badly dressed") were synonymous. My aunt, who happened to be a very kind woman by nature, was not reassured, however. She could not get her mind around the fact that I, a student, could associate with an Arab, though he was a student as well. The only Arab she knew in her town, Holon, was the gardener who came to trim the shrubbery in the senior center her husband directed. At most she would exchange an occasional "hello" with him. Ever since she left the kibbutz where she had lived after her arrival from her native Ukraine in 1938, she had gotten to know no other Arabs and had no intention of doing so. What would she have in common with them? Besides, let everyone stay where they belong. The less you have to do with them, the better.

At the time this was the least hostile attitude among the people. In contrast to her husband, a leftist Labor Party member, for whom the Palestinians in general, and those from the occupied territories in particular, had to be treated with an iron hand "because that's all they understand," my aunt felt that it would be better to have peace without the territories than the territories without peace. She had a vague premonition of what the occupation would mean in the end, but the ultimate basis for her attitude was that she didn't want to live with Arabs in a state in which they would be the majority. In Israel the Arab is a source of fear, automatically perceived by most people as disturbing, deceitful, suspect—at best, "too different." What is more, he doesn't like us either. So if he attacks you, you have to defend yourself. As for the rest, better ignore him.

I didn't tell my aunt that this Nasser was more infatuated with my son than with my wife and me, and that we trusted him enough to let him occasionally take the child to the movies in the Arab part of East Jerusalem, to see one of the kung fu films both of them loved. She would never have understood that.

Whether the Arab is being talked about or relegated to silence, whether the times are tense or relatively calm, the fact of the relationship itself is invariably in the forefront of the preoccupations, thoughts, and daily agenda of the Israelis. It always forms a large portion of the news, written or broadcast. Even when it is not being discussed it is never far away, always somehow in the air, although the two societies, Jewish and Arab, live in separate compartments. Unless they make a special effort, the vast majority of Jewish Israelis seldom have occasion to be in contact with Arabs, even Israeli Arabs. Subject to the draft until the age of 49, most men are liable to find themselves in contact with Arabs during their annual period of service in the reserves. But then, the contact is one of pure domination.

Before it becomes nuanced, socialized, and politicized, for most people this relationship starts out monolithic: "us" on one side, "the Arabs" on

the other. It is by far the most powerfully uniting element in Jewish Israeli society, confronted as that society is with the wide variety of its dis-
similar and often antagonistic "tribes": various religious groups and more
or less traditional laypeople; Ashkenazim and Sephardim; older generations bearing the glory of the *tkuma* (rebirth) and building of the state;
new generations of sabras (native Israelis) and new immigrants (90 percent of whom came from the former Soviet republics in the 1990s); the
westernized, educated inhabitants of the coastal areas; the underprivileged
inhabitants of "development towns"; and so on.

The way this society portrays its Arab opposite numbers both in intel-
lectualized forms and in popular manifestations is, on the whole, based
on a very deep sense of superiority in terms of civilization and culture
(Western), politics (democratic), and intellect, onto which is grafted willful ignorance and indifference along with fantasy projections onto the
Arab, all these giving rise to denial of his possible suffering and, more
generally, of his real identity—in extreme cases of his simple humanity.
Not just ordinary people but also a large number of intellectuals will readily
tell you that the Arabs have "a different sense from ours" of life and death,
that an Arab mother has many children and "doesn't suffer the same way
we do" if one of them dies.

One of the best-known anecdotes in Israel is the one about the scorpion and the frog. "Get me across the stream," the scorpion asks the frog.
"But you'll sting me when we're halfway across," says the frog anxiously.
"You have nothing to be afraid of," replies the scorpion. "I don't know
how to swim. If I sting you, I'll die in the water with you." So they set off
across the stream, and in the middle the scorpion stings the frog. "But
why?" the latter cries in agony. "Because that's the way I am," replies the
poisonous creature.

This story is considered very funny. That's the way the Arab is: wholly
irrational. He'll kill you even if he dies doing so. Those people don't operate the way "we" do, don't have the same feelings. This is said as though
it were obvious.

Such a relationship has political consequences: a necessary and imperi-
ous domination, with the priority being security. The concept of *bitakhon*,
"security," has always, and in almost all circumstances, held first place in

the determination of Israeli politics and social attitudes toward the Arabs. It stems from past experience, from the time of the formation of the *yishuv*, and is based on deterrence, deterrence being perceived as essential in assuring the permanence of a society that prefers to distance itself from its environment (but whose members rushed to visit the pyramids as soon as the peace treaty with Egypt was signed). Finally, the provision of security is seen as necessary for the survival of the nation, in order to preserve a balance of power tilted strongly in Israel's favor.

In 2002 I met former general Avraham "Abrasha" Tamir, who upon retiring from active service was appointed director of the Israeli National Security Council. For fifteen years he had been an adviser to four different prime ministers. I left the meeting torn between a feeling of alarm and a barely suppressed fit of hysterical laughter. The man had not concealed his criticism of the political views of Ariel Sharon, whom he considered "an imbecile," security matters included. He began by stating in no uncertain terms that Israel's security doctrine had been fixed for all time by David Ben Gurion and since then had never been questioned in a coherent way by anyone. The backbone of this doctrine was that the country's definitive borders would be those of the armistices of 1949 with the Arab nations, which had been the borders of Israel up to 1967. Ultimately, he said in a tone that brooked no contradiction, Israel would live in peace within those borders and no others. But before this inevitable outcome, there was still such a long way to go.

General Tamir then launched into a description, lasting four hours, of the security conditions necessary for the advent of that blessed day. The list was endless. To the extent that these conditions were not fulfilled, Israel would never be able to withdraw from the occupied territories, at least not completely. Security first! This is how matters had stood since 1967, and, given the extraordinarily complex and imperative nature of this list of conditions, this is how they would stand for a very long time to come.

At the end of this meeting an association of ideas led me to recall a booklet, bought in one of the great Coptic churches of Cairo, that had evoked the same reaction of hilarity in the face of the absurd. It was a commentary by Pope Shenuda III of the Coptic Orthodox Church on the commandment, "Thou shalt not kill." This, according to His Holiness, is the fundamental precept of the Bible. Now, he says, we know that there are countless situations in which killing is permitted. And he lists them: when a woman betrays her husband, when a girl dishonors her family, and so forth. Here too the list went on endlessly. And the good pope concluded that, apart from these many situations in which it is permitted to take someone's life, killing is absolutely forbidden. Like Shenuda III, brave General Tamir began by stating the law and then went on to enumerate the countless reasons for not applying it.

Ultimately, the Israeli "imperative strategic conditions" are and have always been merely a powerful ideological construct based on an Orientalist view of the Arab world—we shall be returning to the notion of Orientalism—that likewise presupposes an imperative need to maintain a favorable balance of forces and affects political relationships with the other side. Hence the automatically aggressive behavior, often, though not always, said to be preventive but always presented and perceived as defensive. The wall of separation, said to be necessary for security, a structure that shuts the Palestinians behind a high concrete barrier, a deep impassable ditch, or barbed wire, is its latest manifestation.

This concept brought Israel its greatest military successes, those of 1948, 1956, 1967, 1973, and 1982. It has often ended by collapsing one day like a house of cards as a result of a basic failure to understand, or a belated understanding of, the adversary and the policies he opposes. Unfortunately, this never leads to any deep questioning of why the vision has failed.

To take one example: from 1967 to 1973 General Moshe Dayan explained time and again that he would rather have Sharm el-Sheikh without peace with Egypt than peace without Sharm el-Sheikh. He had many reasons, the main one being the strategic depth of the Sinai in the face of the most powerful of Arab armies. Surprised by the attack by Egypt and Syria in October 1973, Israel won the Yom Kippur War militarily but lost it politically. The relationship with Washington established in 1972 by Anwar el-Sadat after his break with the Soviets had changed the nature of his conflict with Israel in the eyes of U.S. Secretary of State Henry Kissinger. Four years later, at Camp David, Menahem Begin agreed to give the Sinai back, down to the last inch.

In the end, the total withdrawal from the Sinai and peace offered more security than Sharm el-Sheikh and its alleged strategic importance. A witness to the scene told me how Dayan, a typical sabra (a kind of pear, sweet inside, prickly outside, nickname of native Israelis), explained the matter to the settlers near El Arish. The army will withdraw from the Sinai, he told them, but the treaty will allow you to remain there if you wish. You will be Israeli citizens in a foreign country. "Will we have the right to raise the flag in the town square and sing Hatikva [the Israeli national anthem]?" one settler asked. "No," Dayan replied, and then said: "You'll be able to do that, but in your bathrooms."

Yet subsequent Israeli governments did not challenge any of the fundamental assumptions of their security strategy—on the contrary. Since 1969 this doctrine had been based on the establishment of two so-called defensive barriers. The first was the Bar Lev Line, named after a former chief of staff, a kind of reinforced Maginot Line in front of the Suez Canal that made the Sinai a huge buffer zone between Egypt and Israel. The second was the famous Allon Plan for the construction of two large bands of settlements on the West Bank along with the military presence necessary for their defense: one along the June 1967 border (the "Green Line"), the other in the Jordan valley opposite Jordan and its majority Palestinian population, which made it possible to keep the West Bank under Israeli control. The Bar Lev Line had crumbled under a deluge of Egyptian bombs and water cannons; it was crossed by the Egyptians in a few hours' time in 1973 as Sadat overturned the political order. No matter: since security still dominated political thinking, the Allon Plan was felt to be all the more imperative. A decision was made to speed up the settlement of the Palestinian territories. It took fifteen more years of this before the first Palestinian intifada broke out.

By a sort of absurd determinism, from Ben Gurion to Barak to the second Camp David summit, the automatic tendency of the Israeli elites to favor the option of domination for what were said to be security motives won out almost every time over the understanding of what was really at stake, and hence over the search for political compromise. Thus the outcome of the Israeli withdrawal from Lebanon in 2000 was evidence of how "security" outweighed the most glaringly obvious evidence. For eighteen years Israel had occupied South Lebanon, leaving only under attack by Hezbollah. As the toll of the dead and injured in the military mounted, the people of Israel were being worn down for a political gain they no longer saw as worthwhile.

When, shortly thereafter, the second intifada broke out, what was the primary lesson learned by Israeli leaders and the overwhelming majority of the population from the bloody Lebanese adventure? That the withdrawal from Lebanon had been a major error, because it had given the Palestinians ideas.

The argument was not unfounded. After the failure at Camp David many Palestinians concluded from the example of Lebanon that Israel would never put an end to a military occupation except under force. But very few Israelis came to the opposite conclusion, though it was obvious from the facts: after Tsahal's withdrawal from South Lebanon, and despite Ariel Sharon's repeated attempts to heat up this area again, and also despite the outbreak of the intifada, the border between Israel and Lebanon had remained exceptionally calm. The end of the occupation did not trigger increased violence but the opposite.

As we shall see, the priority Israel gives to security over political solutions is what ultimately explains the failure of the peace process begun at Oslo. In 1988 Defense Minister Itzhak Rabin reacted to the outbreak of the first intifada by declaring the need to "break the bones"[1] of Palestinian stone throwers, advice that some Israeli soldiers and police took literally. Only later did he come to understand what the heads of Shin Bet, on the ground, ascertained relatively fast, namely that the insurrection did not have much in common with the so-called Arab revolt of 1936–1939, which was the analogy Rabin had in mind, and that "breaking" young Palestinians would not alter the remobilization that was under way in Palestinian society to end the occupation. Yet soon after the signing of the Oslo Accords the preoccupation with security once again got the upper hand, leading the peace process to an impasse.

Finally, the need, perceived as essential, to maintain a dominant balance of power over the Arab and Palestinian environment explains why in Israel, as compared to other modern democracies, an unusually large number of generals have moved successfully into politics at the highest level—along with the number of noncommissioned officers who have attained the highest governmental positions in Israel's history. In the 1970s Amnon Kapeliouk, an Israeli reporter from *Le Monde*, used to attach the label "general" to the ministers who had been just that. The list, extremely long, gave readers the impression of a military junta. "What can I do?" he replied. "In France we always say 'General de Gaulle' although he had been out of the army for a longer time than those generals."

Yes, but in France there was only one such general. In Israel there were dozens: Generals Allon, Dayan, Yadin, Bar Lev, Rabin, Gur, and so on. And they were not only ministers but special advisers, cabinet heads, ambassadors, and mayors. This situation has continued: a right-wing general, Ariel Sharon, succeeded the left-wing General Ehud Barak as prime minister in 2001. And, to replace General "Fuad" Ben Eliezer, a hawk, at the top of the list of candidates in the 2002 legislative elections, Labor activists chose a dove, General Amram Mitzna. In Israeli public opinion a general will usually start out with more credit, including political credit, than a civilian. This automatic trust arises from the notion that a military man will necessarily know better than a politician how to deal with the Arabs: he has "played ball" with them close up.

For *bitakhon*, the urgent need for security, also has a major influence in shaping the most widespread popular attitudes among the Jews of Israel, attitudes often expressed in very brutal, racist ways, sometimes with more sophistication. As long as he watches his step, the Arab is ignored. At best, if he keeps a low profile, you can even be "generous" with him. But you can't stop mistrusting him for a minute, and if he raises his head you put him right back in his place.

Ariel Sharon provided a caricature of his own view of the Palestinian. One month after coming to power, with the intifada well underway, he described his strategy as follows: "The first stage is to restore security. . . . At the beginning you take steps to improve [the living conditions] of the Palestinians who are not implicated in terrorism, those who want to take home a piece of bread and raise their children, and at the same time we fight the terrorists according to a coherent and long-term plan." He added that this strategy would require "keeping our eyes wide open and remaining vigilant. Very vigilant: giving them [the Palestinians] the bare minimum."[2] Between suspicious paternalism and bludgeoning, Sharon knows only two kinds of Palestinians: those who are concerned only with their daily bread, to whom he is willing to give a bare minimum, and the others, whose demands are much greater and hence illegitimate, whom he groups under the generic heading of terrorists.

His Labor predecessor Ehud Barak, who conducted the Camp David negotiations, where he was willing to "grant" the Palestinians much more than the minimum but much less than the generosity later claimed for him, represents another aspect of his society's fundamental and predominant view. On many occasions Barak has used the following metaphor to characterize the situation of Israel within the Arab world: the Jewish state is "a villa in the jungle."[3] The image speaks volumes about the way Barak sees himself and the Arab world: Israel is an island of modernity, prosperity, and propriety in a natural, savage environment that has to be tamed to prevent it from encroaching.

Taming, dominating the surroundings so as not to be swallowed up by this jungle: this is the idea summed up in the key term *bitakhon*. Everything that is at stake for the society and the state of Israel is contained in the common understanding of a single word. In one poll after another a majority of Israelis always come out in favor of such domination. Yet the heads of security see it as the main threat looming over Israel's future. Three years after the beginnings of the repression of the second intifada, four former heads of Shin Bet uttered a cry of warning. Israel, they proclaimed, is heading toward disaster if it does not understand the nature of the Palestinian uprising. The solution, they said in effect, was not to strike harder and harder in the hope of putting an end to terrorism but to move toward a political solution involving the inevitable withdrawal from the Palestinian territories and the dismantling of the settlements.[4] The methods used against the Palestinian population, they added, are not only ineffective; they are also shameful.

One week later, a poll showed how Israelis reacted to this suggestion. Fifty-one percent of the respondents believed that the four former heads of the secret services were wrong to speak out in public. Thirty-six percent considered Israel's policy toward the Palestinians "appropriate," 25 percent "too soft," and 35 percent "too hard." The title of the article reporting the poll was "Sixty-one percent of Israelis want to continue or step up" the repression.[5]

INSTITUTIONAL PARADOXES
OF ISRAELI SOCIETY

Israeli society is often paradoxical, its complexity hard to understand. It is very dynamic and for the most part Westernized, with intellectual, professional, and political elites, including certain religious milieus, deeply influenced by the United States. The two societies, Israeli and American, have in common that they were founded by people in mass flight from disaster, oppression, or great poverty, people imbued with a sense of mission who conquered a territory by erasing the native inhabitants. After all, one of the first companions of Theodor Herzl, the founder of Zionism, was Israel Zangwill, who developed the concept of the melting pot.

What is the name of the very trendy café at the University of Tel Aviv? Café To Go, in English, its name answering the question asked by servers at the counters of American coffee shops: "For here or to go?" Every student knows what this expression implies, since at one point or another in their studies 80 percent of Israeli doctoral candidates spend some time in Western universities, generally American ones. For three decades American culture has had a huge impact—both on lifestyles (through sports, for example) and on ways of thinking. Consider political, economic, and intellectual freedom: nearly everything can be expressed in Israel, from challenges to the Jewish state to the most racist public statements. But the weight of this freedom is inversely proportional to the way democratic freedoms are registered in actual facts.

There are other manifestations of growing Americanization. In the late 1990s, when the "Internet bubble" was at its fullest, the second highest number of startups listed on Nasdaq for foreign countries were in Israel, behind Canada but ahead of Germany, Great Britain, the Scandinavian countries, Japan, Australia, and France. In 2002, at noon on the day after the Super Bowl, a sports commentator on the main Israeli television news program indicated that 400,000 people in a country of 6 million, a country in which American football is not played, had watched this game in the middle of the night. "No question about it," the sportscaster exclaimed, "we're the fifty-first state of the union!"

And in *Elvis in Jerusalem* the historian and journalist Tom Segev (2002) develops the (controversial) idea that the Americanization of life in his country, which he considers positive, is the most striking, and, in his view, all but inevitable symptom of its achievement of normality, normality being identified with democratization—the de facto acceptance of its non-Jewish component—and the abandonment of Zionist ideology, necessarily through modernization. "There is life after Zionism," he concludes (p. 161).

Others, however, view the Americanization of Israeli society and its elites as a dangerous development, especially because it presents the risk of powerfully reinforcing communitarian influences and social divisions that are already very present. The most "American" politician who ever governed Israel was Benyamin Netanyahu, who, with the aid of a large political marketing firm in Washington, brought together under his name a coalition of groups (the religious, Sephardim, ultranationalist chauvinists, Russian immigrants), each in itself a minority, between 1966 and 1999. But no one in Israel contests the reality of this rampant Americanization. To win aganst his rival, Ehud Barak, too, then had to make use of the services of an American political marketing firm.

At the same time, Israeli society is also Levantine in many ways, beginning, for example, with its basic foods, typical of the Mashreq: hummus, fava beans, shashlik, and the like. Though the Sephardim, the great majority of whom come from Muslim countries, have been marginalized in Israel up to now, they represent no less than 45 percent of Israeli Jews, and their influence is significant in many aspects of social and cultural life, for example in some recent popular music and in literature. Israeli society is also largely secular, but in a way that is closer to the American model than that of Western Europe; this is a secularism in which faith and tradition still carry crucial values, but where the idea of prohibition, if only in the form of discussing the banning of the Muslim headscarf or some other religions sign in school, would seem inconguous, common as these signs are everywhere.

For this society is also theocratic in some ways: in its family law, obviously, where rabbis rule supreme, but also in its civil law, where a person's religion (Jewish, Muslim, Christian) has long been noted on personal identity papers alongside citizenship (Israeli) and nationality (Jewish, Arab, Druse, Cherkassian, etc.). What is more, the proportion of the religious in the population has been strongly on the rise in the last thirty years, the quest for spirituality being apparent in the increasing number of people returning to observance and to the major growth of sects from Scientology to varieties of Zen.

With its citizens originating from all over the world in successive waves of immigration from very different backgrounds and cultures, this society is also deeply communitarian. Membership in a community, or fidelity to one, as in the United States, remains a striking feature, marked in different ways, depending on their origins, by deep and more global tensions between Western and Oriental Jews. In the long run, however, for example through intermarriage between Jews of different communities, the melting pot is a more tangible reality in Israel than in other societies largely composed of recent immigrants, such as the United States or Australia. Israeli society is simultaneously very united and strongly imbued with what the writer David Grossman calls "individualism and each man for himself."[6] Social relations are warm and direct, scarcely policed, but also characterized by a glaringly obvious brutality. When this crude individualism joins the triumphant pioneering spirit, the result is both a great dynamism and an arrogant stubbornness about what one considers one's rights that accords little importance to other people. This has not kept Israel from also producing many writers of great sensitivity, alongside "national poets" of a more warlike type.

Finally, this society is Jewish in the very identity of the state it created, inscribed as such in its fundamental laws. But it is not only Jewish, since 20 percent of its citizens are Palestinian. It is democratic in many ways, first of all on the electoral level, even though for a long time any expression of Arab or Palestinian nationalism was in point of fact prohibited. At the same time it is institutionally discriminatory and nondemocratic in other ways—mainly with regard to this minority of Palestinian citizens of Israel, as Judge Orr's commission of inquiry noted once again in September 2003.[7] I shall not mention in detail the many forms of political and socioeconomic discrimination aimed at the Arab citizens of Israel since the founding of the state: everything is done to marginalize them in education, land use, city planning, housing, access to civil service, and the like. Here are only two examples that have wide symbolic bearing.

First, the Kaadan Affair. In 1995 a 44-year-old nurse, Adel Kaadan, and his wife Iman, Israeli citizens from the Arab town of Bakka el-Gharbieh, applied to buy a plot of land in Katzir, a nearby Jewish area, so they could move there with their children. They had replied to a small advertisement calling on those who wished to buy land to take advantage of local facilities. The Kaadans met with a refusal on the part of the owners, the Israeli Land Authority and the Jewish National Fund (or KKL), a subsidiary of the Jewish Agency, the supreme organ of the worldwide Zionist movement, which owns most of the land in Israel, including the land from which Palestinians were driven out between 1947 and 1950. The Fund told the couple that the plots of land in Katzir were closed to non-Jews. The Kaadans petitioned the Supreme Court, which, on March 8, 2000, found in their favor. Its president, Aharon Barak, wrote in his decision that "not only do the values of the state of Israel as a Jewish state not require discrimination on the basis of religion or nationality, but, on the contrary, these very principles forbid it."[8] Yet he did not go so far as to demand that the Jewish National Fund implement the ruling immediately. As far as I know, the Kaadans have still not been able to move to Katzir.

Another famous affair involved the townspeople of Ikkrit and Birim. Like so many others, they had been driven out in 1948. Their case is exceptional in that as Christians they were on good terms with nearby Jews, who intervened in their favor, so that they were later authorized to return. In the meantime, obviously, their land had been distributed among the local Jews, including those from the leftist kibbutz Birim. It was in their particular case that Israeli law invented the category of "absent-present." Noting their absence, the state of Israel or its agencies appropriated the property of the 700,000 expelled Palestinians (the 1950 law pertaining to absentees). But what was to be done about the land belonging to these rare refugees authorized to return? From now on, the legislature decided, they would be "absent-present," present citizens of the state of Israel but treated as absent.

The inhabitants of Ikkrit and Birim have still not regained their land or homes. Installed opposite their former property in "temporary" tents they have long refused to leave, refugees in their own country, they have won all the lawsuits they brought. But the state and its organs, appealing the decision, have kept on refusing to return their property. The Supreme Court was still discussing the matter fifty-eight years after the fact.

These affairs are symptomatic of the two main problems facing Israel. The first has to do with identity. When the state was created, the *yishuv* decided . . . not to decide on what its institutional nature would be. For various reasons, not the least of which were that the religious were against defining Israel as a republic (they are awaiting the restoration of the kingdom of David with the coming of the messiah), and that Ben Gurion prefered to see them in the government so as to be able to control them better than if they were outside it, the founder of Israel chose not to decide. Thus, in the absence of a constitution, Israeli constitutional law consists of various "fundamental laws"; of these, two of the first five stipulate that it is a "Jewish and democratic state." This definition is ambiguous, to say the least. Democracy is a form of political government, not the definition of the institutional character of a state. We know of dictatorial republics and democratic monarchies. As a basis of the republic, the equality of citizens is supposed to go without saying in Israel. But it is not clearly established by law, which allows for numerous exceptions guaranteed by law or the regulations of state organs.

As for "Jew," the term is problematic in itself. First because in fifty-eight years the Knesset, the Israeli parliament, has still not ruled on what it refers to. Since 1948 the question, "Who is a Jew?" has come up time and again there. It touches on the prerogatives of the rabbinate, on the Jews of the diaspora who are, or are not, to be granted the right of return, and on many other institutional aspects. In what sense, then, is Israel Jewish? Without a definition, the meaning of the term remains subject to interpretation. The meaning most commonly accepted in Israel is more ethnic and national than religious. Thus Israel is the state of the "nationality," in the old Marxist sense of the term, that by far constitutes its large majority: the Jews. And everyone naturally understands this.

As the historian Shlomo Sand of the University of Tel Aviv sums up the matter, "In liberal Israeli democracy 80 percent of the population knows that the state does not belong to 100 percent."[9] The Jews know perfectly well that the state is theirs, not that of the 20 percent of Palestinian Israeli citizens, who are merely tolerated. As objects of discrimination, the latter, too, are acutely aware of the imbalance. As Shulamit Aloni, who was a minister in the Labor Party and then in Meretz, quipped in 2002, "Israel is a 'democratic' state for the Jews, a 'Jewish' state for the Arabs" who live there.[10]

How many times during the 1970s did I hear in the courtyard of the Hebrew University in Jerusalem discussions during which Jewish students would say to their Arab counterparts, "This is our country, not yours." Those with the best intentions would end by saying, "All you have to do is accept that and be quiet." The more aggressive would end with "Go away." It was no surprise that, in a time of extreme tension, signs saying *Aravim, lekhu mipo* ("Arabs get out") would appear in right-wing demonstrations I attended. This signs were aimed not only at the Palestinians of the occupied territories who, it was hoped, would be "transfered" elsewhere, but in a vague way to all Arabs, Israeli citizens included.

The anthropologist Jeff Halper, one of the leaders of Gush Shalom (Peace Bloc), is much more outspoken. "Israel," he says, "is more an ethnocracy than a democracy: it is a democracy reserved for the ethnic group that wields power"[11] and happens to be in the overwhelming majority, if only with reference to the borders internationally recognized in 1967 within which Israeli democracy applies. (Beyond these, in the occupied territories, institutional occupation and segregation have been the case for thirty-nine years.) An ethnocracy? The term may be considered outrageous. Yet what is the major symbolic import of the Kaadan Affair? What, in fact, are the practical consequences of the constitutionally national-ethnic nature of the state of Israel?

The first of these consequences is the feeling of appropriation, identification, and security that it inspires in those who benefit from it. The problem is that the state is not the only Jewish entity. The Land of Israel, too, is intrinsically Jewish. This is not specifically laid down in the funda-mental laws, but the Israeli Land Authority stipulates that the land can-not be sold or leased to a non-Jew. What would we say about another democratic state that gave the right to vote and social security coverage to all its citizens but legally barred a subset of them—Blacks, Arabs, Jews, Asians, tall people, hunchbacks—from owning land? Yet this has always been the case in Israel on the basis of purely national-ethnic criteria.

The clause prohibiting the sale of land to non-Jewish citizens has still not been stricken from the regulations of the government department in charge of state-owned land. So it is not surprising to see the recent increase in openly segregationist proposals in Israel. Thus Rabbi Druckman, from the National-Religious Party, proposed in July 2002 that the prohibition against selling land to non-Jews be explicitly stated in law, knowing that in practice it was aimed only at Arab citizens. And a majority of the Knesset's commission on laws voted for a proposal to withdraw citizenship from any Israeli Arab marrying a Palestinian from the occupied territories.

Nor is it surprising that discussions of "demographic risks" are officially conducted in an overtly segregationist tone in Israel. Many democratic countries discuss ways to limit the entry or the presence of certain catego-ries of immigrants on their soil. But suppose that in France, the United States, or elsewhere the government moved to establish a policy to reduce the birthrate of a specific category of *citizens*: Blacks, Arabs, Jews, or Asians. As we shall see, this is what is being done in Israel.

The Ikkrit–Birim Affair is even more symbolic of the basic problems confronting Israeli democracy. It seems a priori incomprehensible that the state refuses to allow some of its own citizens, who, at its initiative, were authorized to return to their land after being driven out, to recover that land. In reality, the stakes are crucial. For over fifty years these towns-people have had available a decision of an Israeli court authorizing their return. And in point of fact, whatever it may say, Israel has indeed recog-nized United Nations Resolution 194 of December 11, 1948, implying the right of return for Palestinian refugees, since its recognition figures in the preamble of the resolution admitting Israel to membership in the U.N. The fear, explains Avigdor Feldman, the attorney for the "absent-present" townspeople, is that today a restitution, even a partial one, of the property belonging to the people who were expelled, even if the latter returned legally and enjoy citizenship, "would constitute a precedent, a *de jure* acknowledgment of the Palestinians' right of return." At issue is the question of 1948. "Our society," Feldman says, "is still very childish, fearful. This makes us unable to face up to the darkest aspects of our history."[12] Childishness and fear, resulting from denial of the past and the actual role of Israel in the creation of the refugee problem, also render Israel unable to guarantee its own citizens equality before the law.

NATIONAL UNITY AND
CENTRIFUGAL TENDENCIES

Democratic and segregationist, secular and partially theocratic, Jewish and not only Jewish—all these contradictory components of Israeli society appear with greater or lesser intensity depending on the time period in question. For all of them are, first and foremost, tightly encompassed in the general body of sociopolitical attitudes governing the relation to the other: the Palestinian so close by and the Arab in general. This body of attitudes basically revolves around the imperative need to dominate the other, owing to the fear aroused by the thought of what would happen if this domination were to end. The more tense and conflictual this relation to the other, even degenerating into warfare, the more it has dominated the Israelis' relation to themselves—and, as a consequence, the more the internal conflicts tend to be damped down so as to give precedence to a single sacred unity. In contrast, the more relatively peaceful the relation with the environment, the more Israel's internal centrifugal tendencies tend to come to the fore.

It is not by accident that movements stemming from feelings of discrimination on the part of the Jewish population of Oriental origin have emerged each time there has been relative calm vis-à-vis the Arabs. Thus the social explosions of Sephardic Jews at Wadi Salib (Haifa) and Beersheba in 1959, protesting the discrimination against them, especially in hiring, arose in a period of a relative reduction in tension at the borders following the triumph of the Israeli operation at Suez in 1956 and the evacuation of the

Sinai and Gaza in 1957. Similarly, a radical movement of Sephardic youth, the Black Panthers, was formed at the beginning of the 1970s after the crushing of the Arab armies in June 1967, when the Israelis, drunk with a feeling of power and security, thought they had eradicated all external military threats for a long time to come. Finally, the dazzling electoral success of the Sephardic religious party Shas occurred during the Oslo period, when Israel began to believe in the possibility of peace with the Palestinians. Once the second intifada broke out, this party lost half of its electoral strength: many voters who had chosen it more for its Sephardic orientation than for its religiosity now favored Sharon, with his emphasis on the iron hand, over their earlier intrinsic identitarian claims.

Nor is it by chance that the New Historians, whose work had preceded the 1993 signing of the Oslo Accords by several years, were published in Hebrew and brought about real public discussion only in the mid-1990s. Those years, moreover, were not exclusively marked by retrospective consideration of what some saw as the stigma of 1948 and its antecedents. They were for the most part years of introspection, as Israeli researchers focused on questions like the relationship of the Zionist movement to Jewish history in general and to the Shoah, or its relationship to the immigration of Oriental Jews. This was also a time of openness, of growing interest in the Arab world and the Palestinians. "With peace possibly in view," says the scholar Shlomo Sand,

> Oslo gave rise to the possibility of an academic and intellectual body of work that wasn't devoted to constructing a self-congratulatory national awareness, as had been the case up to that time, but considered a normalized civil society and its history from a critical point of view, the criticism no longer being perceived as a challenge to the legitimacy and permanence of the nation. Hence the emergence at that time of the expression *post-Zionism*. Israeli society proved willing to question its founding mythologies and its constitutive assumptions because fear was on the wane.[13]

In contrast, after the failure of the negotiations at Camp David, with a political campaign immediately launched to convince the public (who

wanted nothing but to be convinced) that this failure could only be the
exclusive fault of the Palestinians, and with the premonition of a resurgence of conflict, almost overnight the diversity of Israeli civil society
narrowed down, giving way to former self-justifying certitudes. Critical
voices were marginalized and became inaudible for a long time.

This pattern of questioning the founding mythologies and dominant
imperatives established under the banner of security, followed by the
gradual abandonment of the challenges, was also evident on the institutional level. Toward the end of the 1990s a partial rewriting of textbooks
was undertaken, revamping the conventional account of the nation's past.
At the same time the Supreme Court adopted a series of historic decisions,
like the one in the Kaadan Affair that nullified the prohibition against
selling land to non-Jews, or the one in which military censors were obliged
to allow the publication of the news that hostages (Sheikh Obeid and other
Lebanese Shiite leaders) were being held by Israel, having been captured
with the avowed aim of exchanging them for Israelis imprisoned in Lebanon or Iran. Or the decision of September 6, 1999, in which, for the first
time, torture in Israel was declared illegal after having been authorized
for decades.[14]

THE COLONIAL QUESTION

A further question remains: Is Israel a colonialist state? Answer: yes and
no. For both the Israelis and the Palestinians, an unequivocal reply to this
question — that Israel is not at all colonialist or is so totally or solely — is a
central element in the denial of the opposite side.

In Israel, with the exception of some recent historiographical works,
the idea of likening Zionisn and the Jewish state to colonialism, either
today or in the past, is vigorously rejected. And it is precisely this refusal
to take into account the historical colonial aspects of the country and its
society, and the consequences for the Palestinians, that prevents so many
Israelis from seeing the other nation as their equal and achieving a reconciliation. Conversely, the idea that Israel and its society are colonialist and
nothing but colonialist has led the Palestinians from failure to failure. For

this idea is naturally associated with another, one not overtly expressed except by certain noted Islamists and yet very alive in the minds of all Palestinians, which implies that if Israel is merely a colonial formation it is ultimately bound to disappear.

Albert Memmi's classic text *The Colonizer and the Colonized* (1957) was reprinted in France in 2002.[15] I had read this book as a teenager, at the urging of a group leader in the Zionist youth movement I belonged to. Reading it again forty years later gave me a glimpse of what the group leader's motive had been at the time. At the end of the book Memmi compares, with some justice, the situation of the diasporic Jew to that of the Black person in America. He describes both as a kind of internal colonized group denied any possibility of assimilation; their liberation, Memmi writes, will come about through gaining their own autonomy and proclaiming their status of Jew or Black. All the training I received in my Zionist youth movement days was aimed at explaining that the assimilation or even the acceptance of the Jew in the diaspora was a hopeless illusion,[16] against the nature of things.

According to this view, which forms the basis of Zionism, the assimilation of the Jew or his acceptance by society as a proclaimed Jew are impossible, because the milieu stubbornly refuses to grant him this even when appearances would seem otherwise. Given the intrinsic permanence and recurrent resurgence of anti-Semitism, all attempts to improve the condition of the Jew are therefore doomed to ultimate failure. But, it was said in this youth movement, assimilation is also impossible because, for many reasons, the Jew is inherently unassimilable, with the most fundamental of those reasons being that a people without a state is, as it were, sick, abnormal, and incurable as long as that situation lasts.

The logical conclusion is that Israel is the only path to the emancipation of the Jews. The establishment of their state will return them to normality and, it was added, would finally give them independent means of security. Jews living outside Israel were perpetuating their own abnormality. In contrast, Israel had put an end to an abominable situation, that of the congenital weakness of the Jews in exile, creating a new Jew, strong and independent. As for achieving normality, the joke had it that this would come about when the Jews stopped being only doctors, physicists, and violinists and had their own thieves and criminals. In short, this would be the day when, in a normal state, there would be as many crooks as there were emulators of Sigmund Freud, Albert Einstein, or Yehudi Menuhin.

Rereading this book today, after having lived for twelve years in Israel and returning there many times, arouses a combination of incredulity and wonder. Colonizer and colonized: what one finds here is a description, sometimes amazingly accurate, of the sociopsychological and political relationships linking . . . the Israeli and the Palestinian. From those points of view, as Sartre writes in his introduction to Memmi's book, "all is said" (p. 22).

And at the same time all is not said. It quickly becomes apparent that the economic logic underlying the colonizer–colonized relations portrayed by Memmi is largely inapplicable to the Israeli–Palestinian situation. In other words, colonial economic exploitation, which is the basis of the attitudes Memmi is studying, is essentially weak or nonexistent in Israel. This is so, to a large extent, even in the Israeli settlement venture within the occupied territories, where, apart from certain cases of agricultural exploitation in Gaza and the Jordan valley, the Jewish settlers are not economically dependent on the sweat of the indigenous population. What is happening there essentially involves moving people in and occupying land.[17]

We should not forget here that most of the dwellings in which Israelis live in the occupied territories, including East Jerusalem, as well as nearly all of the splendid highways reserved for the settlers alone, have been built for the past thirty-nine years by Palestinian labor.[18] Nor should we conceal the fact that the establishment of Israel came about via a classic colonial mechanism: appropriating the land of the natives. What is more, the colonization of the country, right down to the systematic use of the term, was amply assumed to be just that by the leaders of the yishuv up to the 1950s—that is, as long as colonialism was perceived in the great Western democracies to be a civilizing force. We shall not recall here the countless writings, from Herzl, the founder of Zionism, and Ben Gurion, the father of the Jewish state, to ideologues of the extreme left, like Ber Borochov, and the extreme right, like Zeev Jabotinsky, that have all historically claimed the idea of colonization.

However, the Israeli economy as a whole is not based on indigenous labor and is only slightly dependent on it. On the contrary, from the outset, with the exception of certain historical situations and certain activities like construction or, in part, agriculture, its entire ambition has been precisely *not* to have to depend on the sweat of the native. It was to form a nation apart from him and, if need be, in opposition to him, but not with him, not through his economic exploitation. From this perspective there is a radical difference from the colonial situation as described by Memmi. However, another very important difference is also involved: Memmi mercilessly points to what he calls "the mediocrity" (p. 70) of the colonial elites. But the quality of Israeli elites—intellectual, scientific, technological, and artistic—is the opposite of the mediocrity of those colonizing societies that are fundamentally dependent on their own mother countries. And the quality of these elites can be explained only by the inherently autonomous nature, constitutive of a nation-state, of Israeli society.

On the other hand, the attitudes described by Memmi are similar, sometimes surprisingly so, to those met almost every day in Israel if one is aware of them. And they lead to segregationist behavior, popular as well as institutional, that is typically colonial in nature as Memmi portrays it. Entire pages could be cited, so striking are the similarities. Pages, for example, in which he explains how the notion of "privilege" (p. 33) is at the heart of the relationhip of the colonist ("a pioneer" [p. 29]) to the colonized, and leads to "paternalism that likes to think of itself as generous, once racism and inequality are admitted." For the most overt paternalism, Memmi says, "protests as soon as the colonized population makes demands" (p. 94). Here, in one concise sentence, is the essence of the Camp David negotiations.

Or we might cite the pages in which Memmi depicts the mentality of the "little" white man, the dupe and victim of the relationship of the "big" colonizer to the colonized, the colonizer whose interests he nevertheless defends with a fervor the more necessary it becomes, both practically and symbolically, to maintain his privileged status relative to those situated below him: the natives. This is a state of affairs that applies very exactly to the great majority of Jews in the so-called development towns and the suburbs of the large cities of Israel.

Memmi also speaks of "the tone that marks the way the master always addresses the slave" (p. 39), a tone that often goes hand in hand with "an unbearable moralism" (p. 46) characteristic of those on the side of the colonizers who, humanely, are upset by the most scandalous aspects of the relationship to the native and find themselves faced with the spitefulness and sarcasm of their compatriots. Notice for example the pitying or aggressive scorn that most Israelis reserve for the "beautiful souls" who object to the way the Palestinians are treated.

Memmi describes the colonizer's reaction to the terrorism activated by liberation movements, actions that are perceived as nothing but sheer abjection disconnected from all social reality. The colonizer, Memmi writes, "is hardly swayed by the argument that the cruelty of the oppression explains the blindness of the reaction" (p. 54). On the contrary, he uses the most upsetting and reactionary characteristics of the colonized as an excuse to refuse them their freedom or to impose conditions under which he could agree to make some gesture toward them. These are in fact conditions by which "the colonizer who accepts himself for what he is seeks to legitimize" his domination (p. 67). "He justifies everything, stubbornly pretending not to have seen any of the misery that is staring him in the face" (p. 68).

Here is where Memmi's account shows the most striking similarities to the Israeli–Palestinian situation. "Having benefited from a usurpation," he writes, "the colonizer now has to inscribe it in laws and a moral code. If he is to take full advantage of his victory, he must cleanse himself of the conditions under which it was won. Hence his zeal, astonishing in a victor, with regard to trivial details. He tries to falsify history by having texts rewritten and [by] dulling memories" (pp. 73–74). Thus, in 1995, the Israeli government asked Itzhak Rabin to withdraw from the English translation of his memoirs the pages relating his active role in the expulsion of the inhabitants of Lydda and Ramleh in 1948, and especially Ben Gurion's answer to his question about what was to be done with these people. Drive them out, the father of the state of Israel had replied. Rabin complied with the ministers' request, and this passage was withdrawn.

The colonizer must "strive time and again to absolve himself," Memmi says, "taking every opportunity to parade his own virtues in public and pleading his cause with bitter stubbornness so as to seem heroic and grand. At the same time . . . the colonizer depicts the colonized in the most negative terms, taking action, if need be, to devalue and annihilate him" (p. 75). His aim is to create "a stark contrast between the two images: his own image of glory and the contemptible image of the colonized. This self-justification," Memmi concludes, "is actually tantamount to an ideal reconstruction of the two protagonists of the colonial drama" (pp. 75–76).

Everything said by people like Ehud Barak or Shlomo Ben Ami immediately after the failure of Camp David, especially with regard to Yasser Arafat, is summed up in Memmi's description.

Written at a time when the colonial liberation movement was far from being a widespread success in the world, Memmi's less persuasive points seemed to contribute to excusing colonialism's most reactionary features, explaining them only by reference to the colonial relationship and casting them in a potentially positive light. Since that time the dreadful toll exacted by nationalist groups that, once in power, have so often sunk into nepotism, corruption, and racism obliges us to reconsider the excuses thought up by Memmi and so many other advocates of decolonization for these anticolonialist movements. Ultimately it obliges us to put a complete stop to making excuses for them.

The most striking example is Memmi's account of the colonizer's racism as contrasted with that of the colonized: the former, like the modern European racist, feels more hate and scorn than fear; the colonized feels admiration alongside fear. While these definitions also often apply to the racist aspects of the Israeli–Palestinian relationship, it is no longer possible to support the conclusions Memmi draws from them. When the racism of the colonized is perceived not as aggressive but as defensive, it leads Memmi to argue that, even though such xenophobia and racism obviously contain negative elements, they can be the prelude to a positive movement: the regaining of control by the colonized. Since then we have learned that racism and xenophobia never lead to anything but racism and xenophobia.

Yet on the whole Memmi's account remains extraordinarily astute when it comes to the popular attitudes prevailing in Israel toward the Arabs. He mentions, for example, the stereotype of "incredible laziness" (p. 99); here the Arab is perceived as a backward child, "perverse, someone with bad instincts, a thief" (p. 102), and he speaks of how deeply familiar the colonized are with destitution and of their "well-known ingratitude and insatiability" (p. 102) in the face of the kindnesses offered to them. Memmi is also accurate in his description of the terms used to stigmatize the colonized. "They are never differentiated," he writes, "but are swallowed up in an anonymous collectivity: 'they're this,' 'they're all the same'" (p. 104), one never knows with them, "one can't count on them," (p. 105) and the like, right down to the time-honored expression, now an absolute platitude in Israel, as it was in French North Africa a century ago: "Arab work" (p. 131), uttered scornfully to characterize any activity, not specifically Arab, of mediocre quality.

According to Memmi, the characteristics colonizers ascribe to the colonized are mutually exclusive. But who in Israel, checking off the contradictions, many bordering on the absurd, between these collective stereotypes ascribed in their totality to "the Arabs"—they are crafty but also idiots, they are hospitable but treacherous, they laugh at death but are cowards— has not met with the reply, "You obviously don't know them." These words are always proclaimed in a definitive tone, as if self-evident, and are quickly followed by another cliché, similarly conclusive: "All they understand is force."

Historically, on the ninth day of the intifada, when the generals, including Prime Minister Barak, were convinced that striking harder and harder was all that was needed to get Arafat to put a final stop to the violence, meanwhile failing to take into account the conditions under which this violence had arisen, Gideon Levy wrote: "We have always held that force is the only thing the Arabs understand. On the contrary, the truth turns out to be that force is our own official language."[19] Not only had Israel always automatically sought to resolve problems by force in the early days, he added, but Israel itself yields only to force. It would never have given back the Sinai if Sadat hadn't made war in 1973, he reminded his readers, nor would it ever have recognized the PLO without the first intifada or left South Lebanon without the ongoing guerrilla warfare of Hezbollah. Today we might add that a right-wing government would never have evacuated the settlers from Gaza without the second Palestinian insurrection. This is how the process of disavowal works: one ascribes one's own tendencies to the other side so as to be better able to deny them in oneself.

In his introduction to the book by Motti Golani (2002), head of the Geography Department at the University of Haifa, Yaakov Raz, professor of Asian studies at the University of Tel Aviv, expressed the same idea in a different way:

> It's he, the other, always the other, who puts us in a situation in which we use force. Excuse me, where we *are obliged* to use force. For ultimately he's clearly the one who started it. All we did was react. Maybe another time, when they've understood—forced into it, by force, because force is all they understand—we'll be able to talk with them. If there's anyone to talk with. That's what we say. That's exactly what 'they' say, too. Not only can't we see the other and talk to him, but it's absolutely forbidden to do so. He's not allowed to have a name, the other, or a past, a history, plans, descendants, dreams, suffering, loves, and misfortunes. Because if we understood his history, if we saw his loves and his fears, if we knew his plans and his dreams, maybe, God forbid, we would discover how much he's like us—almost the spitting image. And then we would no longer be able to hit him so hard.

"You don't know them; all they understand is force." When you hear those "obvious facts" in Israel, you can be sure that the person saying them belongs to one of the following categories: those, few in number, who as soldiers, settlers, foremen on construction sites, or distinguished Orientalists, have a direct or intellectually formed relationship of domination with the Arabs, or those, the vast majority, who on the contrary never ("God forbid!") have the slightest contact with an Arab. The less acquaintance people have with specific Arabs, the less contact with them as separate individuals, the more they claim to know them as a whole. And because this self-centered logic is also self-contained, they add that it is precisely because they know them so well . . . that they have no close contact with any of them.

How and why does a society that contains historical colonialist elements but also contains other elements that are sharply antagonistic to classic colonialist exploitation come to develop attitudes that recall, almost word for word, those of the European colonists of the Maghreb described by Memmi? The novelist-philosopher himself leads us to the beginnings of an answer. In a later preface, written in 1966, he explains that he thought he had portrayed the relations of the colonizer and the colonized; he realized that they generalized to the categories of the oppressor and the oppressed. Or, as we would say today, of the dominators and the dominated.

THE "ANIMAL NATURE" OF THE ARAB

As we have seen, Ehud Barak compared Israel to a villa in the jungle. Many Israeli leaders are in the habit of using animal analogies. "The Arabs are proliferating in Jerusalem like ants," proclaimed the former Sephardic Grand Rabbi Ovadia Yossef in 2001 during a sermon on Tisha B'Av (the holiday commemorating the destruction of the First Temple). This same rabbi had caused a scandal when, the following summer, he compared the Palestinians to snakes.[20] Barak did not arouse such outraged commentaries, even though he had chosen to describe the Palestinian leaders as crocodiles, adding, "The more you feed them, the hungrier they are,"[21] words that speak volumes about the mind of a man, still prime minister at the time, who was supposed to continue to negotiate with them.

This is an important detail, because when Barak uttered these words the outbreak of the intifada was one month away, and it reveals how prepared he was intellectually to understand why it broke out. Before him, former chief of staff Raphael Eytan had compared the Arabs to cockroaches, and still earlier, Menahem Begin saw them as two-footed animals (khayot du-ragliot). Similar statements by dozens of other top-ranking Israeli officials could be cited.

In short, the Arabs are seen as animals in the surrounding jungle one looks out on from one's villa. These are images, of course, but they are not perceived as fundamentally illegitimate. Stemming from deep emotions, they are generally used in times of high tension or great frustration, as in the case of Barak after the failure of his strategy at Camp David. They did not prevent Begin from signing a peace treaty with Egypt or the head of the Sephardi Jews from coming out several times in favor of a possible

Israeli retreat from the occupied territories. But they are symptomatic of a profound resentment that surfaces powerfully whenever there is conflict. And some go further, making them into openly racist theories. Thus Rabbi Itzhak Ginsburg, author of a book glorifying Baruch Goldstein, the man who committed mass murder against Muslim worshipers in the Cave of the Patriarchs in Hebron in 1994, a book entitled *Barukh Hagever* (Baruch the Male), was quoted in *Maariv* as saying that "the Arabs are closer to the animal than to the human."[22]

The problem is not that a fanatical rabbi expresses unbridled racist ideas in a major daily newspaper with a freedom of tone that would make a born-again American preacher like Jerry Falwell pale with envy (Falwell had to apologize for saying only that Mohammed was the first terrorist in history). The problem is that *Maariv* allotted an unprecedented four pages to the Ginsburg interview, with his photo covering page one of its supplement under a headline reading, in large red letters, "The Arab Has Little Intelligence; His Nature Is Animal-Like"—a sentence appearing in the interview—without seeing the need to distance itself at any time from what was said or to warn the reader about its import. On the contrary, the rabbi, who had headed the talmudic school at Joseph's Tomb in the center of the Palestinian town of Nablus, was presented as a great Torah scholar, a man worthy of respect who was professing an opinion as valid as any other.

The problem is that this interview did not cause any scandal in Israel, either among the authorities or the readership of the newspaper. Why? Because Rabbi Ginsburg was simply expressing, in extreme terms, a very diffuse attitude in Israeli society, one combining scorn for and great alienation from the Arab. This attitude began to be discredited in the 1990s, only to reemerge strongly with the intifada, creating a rift in Israel itself between those who were horrified by it in the name of simple morality and those for whom the popular saying, "A good Arab is a dead Arab" is merely common sense. The same goes for another phrase, heard a thousand times in Israel, uttered in a tone of hope or regret: "How much easier everything would be if there were no Arabs!" Here too we find a disturbing similarity to Memmi's comment that the quip to the effect that "all would be perfect were it not for the natives" (p. 86) is more serious than it appears to be.[23]

The underpinnings of this feeling of "common sense" are very deep and very old. They explain why the books of the Israeli New Historians and the newspaper articles on the facts of the past that have appeared since the late 1980s have not led to a thoroughgoing revision of historiography or an intensive discussion about the future of relations with the Palestinians and the Arabs in general. They explain why articles published since the onset of the intifada by Amira Hass, Gideon Levy, Akiva Eldar, Professor Zeev Sternhell, the former legal adviser to the Rabin government Michael Ben Yair, and many others refuting the official version of the failure of the Oslo process and discussing the criminal forms of the repression mounted against the Palestinians, along with the highly detailed reports by Israeli non-governmental organizations on human rights, have for the most part come up against a wall of indifference if not outright hostility.

TEACHING CONTEMPT

In a poll of Israeli high-school students taken in the spring of 1997, three and a half years before the onset of the intifada, 40 percent of the respondents stated that they hated the Arabs and 60 percent expressed a strong impulse to vengeance.[24]

In 1999 Professor Daniel Bar-Tal of the University of Tel Aviv conducted a study of 124 Hebrew history, geography, and civics textbooks published between 1950 and 1990 and used in college preparatory courses. His conclusion was that these books had long promoted a stereotyped image, paternalistic and demonizing at the same time, of the Arab as fatalistic and primitive, possessing a tribal sense of hospitality but cruel, immoral, thieving, and bloodthirsty (cf. Raviv and colleagues 1999). In contrast, the Jewish *yishuv* of Palestine, described as constantly under attack by natives who were threatening without provocation, was described as pioneering and industrious, a community that revived a land neglected for two millennia by Arabs who were, at best, unproductive, content to live on a piece of pita and a few olives. With time, the stereotypes of the Arab tended to become less crude. But however polished and sophisticated, the essential view of cultural superiority was scarcely changed.

In 1985 Adir Cohen, one of Israel's greatest educators, an integral part of the country's pioneer culture and a prolific author (works on Martin Buber; the pedagogue Makarenko; Janusz Korczak, the teacher in the Warsaw Ghetto who left for the extermination camps with the children in his institution; and many other topics), published a book whose title in English would be *The Ugly Face in the Mirror—The Arab–Israeli Conflict in Hebrew Children's Books*. Cohen had made a semantic study of some 1,700 children's books published since 1967 and studied a group of pupils between the ages of 10 and 12 in a Jewish school in Haifa. The astonishing results alarmed the researcher, leaving him very uneasy about their implications.

Five hundred and twenty of the works studied presented a degraded and deeply negative view of the Arab: 66 percent portrayed him as violent, 52 percent as wicked, 37 percent as a pathological liar, and 28 percent as sly. Out of eighty-six books for young children, Cohen found twenty-one cases in which Arabs were described as lethal, thirteen in which they were called murderers. Terms like *animal, snake, bloodthirsty, warlike*, and *dirty* were recurrent. As for the replies of the young pupils to the five questions Cohen asked them, they merely reproduced these racist stereotypes. Seventy-five percent saw the Arab as a murderer, a kidnapper, and a terrorist. Eighty percent spontaneously described him as dirty. Ninety percent believed that he had no right to the Land of Israel. Cohen concluded that the demonization of the Arab as a disturbing and vile figure was part and parcel of a system of shared convictions perceived as legitimate in history books and children's books alike.

In the 1970s, when my son was in second grade, his teacher explained in class that "the Palestinians are Philistines," the very people who, according to the Bible, were the enemies of the Hebrews, capturing Samson by a ruse and condemning him to death before the giant tore down the pillars of their temples. Besides, she told them, aren't the Hebrew word for Philistines, *Plishtim*, and the Arabic word for Palestine, *Filastin*, the same? What an incredible reversal, when we recall that throughout the centuries what has been called the teaching of contempt in the catechism began with the idea that the Jews, as such, were the very people who, two thousand years earlier, had killed Jesus.

The collective endorsement of the teaching of contempt, in school or in novels and other books for children, interwoven with a veritable cult of force and the self-justifying claim of victimhood that accompanies every manifestation of aggression—especially when instigated by Israel—goes a long way toward explaining the attitudes of so many Israelis and their indifferent, disdainful, or demonizing views. Since the late 1980s, as is the case with history textbooks (of which there will be more to say), the new novels and stories for children have been partially expurgated to remove the most overt racism. But what could a book like *Samir and Jonathan*, an admirable novel for teenagers by Daniela Carmi (2002), written precisely with the aim of undermining all the racist stereotypes, achieve in the face of a "servile culture" that was still so strongly in evidence?

It should be noted that a good third of students in Israel attend religious schools, where, over time, the demonization of the other has often become terrifying, with the Arab frequently identified as the reincarnation of Amalek the Amalekite, the sworn enemy, even worse than the Philistine, of the Hebrew people.

In 1976 Salah, an Israeli Palestinian friend studying law in Tel Aviv, invited our 7-year-old son to spend Easter vacation week in his village in the Galilee. He had a brother there of the same age. When we came to get our child, Salah's father asked him, "Will you tell the other kids in school that you spend a week in an Arab village?" Our son burst out laughing: "Impossible," he said. "They wouldn't believe me. Or else I might scare them a lot." "So what will you tell them?" the old Palestinian pressed on. "I'll tell them I was on a kibbutz"—a kibbutz where we in fact used to go on occasion, visiting other friends. Jewish ones.

Everyone in his own house, nursing a heritage of fear and ignorance.

FOUR

"THESE SEMITES—
THEY ARE ANTI-SEMITES"
We Are What We Were Born to Be

SOURCES OF ISRAELI ORIENTALISM

"The question of Orientalism, the school of thought that 'absenti-
fies' colonized peoples by freezing them in an image corresponding to the need to dominate them, is at the heart of the Israeli-Palestinian
conflict," says the Princeton anthropologist Abdallah Hammoudi.[1] For
we cannot understand Israel without referring to Orientalism, given that
its classic form has always dominated the academic and intellectual relationship to the Arab environment there.

A form of social science applied to the peoples of the East beginning in
the second half of the nineteenth century, Orientalism should not be reduced to a single perspective, still less to the caricatural or racist views
that have sprung up here and there since the attacks of September 11, 2001,
reviving the forgotten accents of the grand years of so-called colonial science, the most aggressive—and unscientific—expression of which is provided, for example, by Oriana Fallaci (2002).

A review of the various Orientalist approaches is not possible here. Instead, I propose to confine this discussion to their most recent and most
accomplished expression, found in the work of Bernard Lewis (at least
the Bernard Lewis of the last twenty years). As Hammoudi has observed,
this approach is based on the idea that the Arab–Muslim world is marked

by cultural constants that are inherent in it and constitutive of it. We need look no further to explain the state of its current sociopolitical glaciation. According to this view, these constants take the form of a congenital backwardness that has led the society to miss out on the march of progress, that is, industrial and democratic development, and essentially explain the huge demonstrations that have appeared there since the Iranian revolution of 1979 in favor of rejecting the West, especially the United States. They also explain the political and economic degeneration that has befallen the entire area since the end of the colonial era. The key to this backwardness is believed to lie in Islam itself. After a brief phase of civilization, first Arab and then Ottoman, producing a culture superior to what was going on around it that was responsible for its expansion into Central and Southern Europe, Islam, rooted in its constitutive incapacity to separate the individual from the collective, proved to be an insurmountable cultural obstacle to the achievement of modernity by these countries.

An analyst of this degeneration and a ceaseless, lifelong critic of the regimes embodying it in the Arab countries, Edward Said (1979) centers his refutation of present-day Western Orientalism on the idea that this static, nearly ahistorical vision reduces the Arab–Muslim world to a virtual category that is unable to grasp its dynamic heterogeneity (for Said, the global, static terms "the Arabs," "Islam," "the Jews," "Christianity," "the Americans," and the like are in general unreal fabrications). The origins of this view, whose influence he tried to uncover in Western literature in particular, are already apparent in the great Orientalists of the nineteenth century, from Renan to Massignon.

For Said, modern Orientalism is nothing but the manifestation of a form of neocolonialism and the fruit of ignorance. At the heart of this ignorance there is a method, which consists in tacking onto the object of research one's own ideological presuppositions along with certain major Western concepts, starting with the nation-state, which is seen as the keystone of progress. In contrast, any lack of familiarity with this notion and what it implies in local cultures is identified with the inability to climb aboard the train to modernity. The undeclared or unconscious aim of this method is to fabricate an Oriental reality that corresponds to one's own need to dominate. The Arab–Muslim world, says Said, cannot be understood apart

from a changing and complex perspective that takes into account its interaction with the different kinds of imperialism, colonial or not, that have
subjected it politically and economically for two centuries.

Various forms of Orientalism have flourished in the Jewish community of Palestine from its beginnings up to the present day. They first appeared in explicitly colonial ways as put forth candidly or crudely by the
leaders of the *yishuv*. For the reaction of the first pioneers to the indigenous human beings they found was divided between disgust and paternalism. Morris (1999) cites Eliezer Ben Yehuda, who modernized the
Hebrew language, as saying that he was overcome by "a depressing feeling of horror" upon his first contact, in 1881, with what he called "our
cousin Ishmael" (p. 44). As for the future father of the nation, David Ben
Gurion, Morris relates his comment that the inhabitants of Palestine
"made a very good impression" on him when he arrived there; "one might
say they are like big children" (p. 44). Ben Gurion was 20 at the time.

The most sophisticated and knowing expression of the Israeli Orientalist
attitude today, an academic version of the popular sentiment that oscil-
lates between arrogance and outright hostility, is found in a moderate form,
for example, in the renowned scholar of Islam Emmanuel Sivan, in an
aggressive and often crude form in another Israeli scholar, the Near-East
specialist Shimon Shamir, and with variations in the famous political
commentator Ehud Yaari, and Daniel Pipes, a similarly learned figure in
neoconservative American Judaism, adviser to the White House and editor of *The Middle East Quarterly*.

In Israel today, with some well-known exceptions like Haim Gerber,
professor of Muslim history at the Hebrew University, the Orientalist view
of the Arab–Muslim world continues to prevail in the university departments of Near-Eastern, Arabic, and Islamic studies — departments, moreover, that have traditionally furnished a major part of the intelligence
services. Together, in one way or another, these views lead to a justification for dominating the Palestinian space and, beyond it, the Near-Eastern
region, through stigmatization of the political and social backwardness of
the Arab–Muslim world and what is regarded as its unprovoked natural
aggressiveness against the values of Western civilization. Hence the emphasis
on the threat this world poses for Israel, whose democratic character,

though entirely reserved for Jewish citizens alone, is the very emblem of its superiority as a civilization.

The Orientalist viewpoint prevailing in the intellectual and mental representation of the Arab, however, has a foundation perceptibly different from the classic Western forms of Orientalism. Like them, it is a result of the initial process of colonization, which entailed the discovery of the indigenous population and the way its treatment was then rationalized. But it is much more the result of a second vector, the ideological particularities inherent in Jewish nationalism, that is, Zionism, that emerged at the end of the nineteenth century and ended in the formation of a new nation-state. Beyond their personal interpretations, three contemporary historians, Zeev Sternhell, Benny Morris, and Georges Bensoussan, among others, have set forth abundantly and honestly all the historical factors necessary for the understanding of the origins and development of the Israeli Orientalist perspective. All three base their work almost exclusively on internal sources. But, each in his own way, they are part of a movement to liberate the writing of Israeli history, with its tradition of reverence and hagiography.

Sternhell (1996), a historian of political ideas, studies the implications of the predominance of what he calls fundamental identitarian values on Israeli socialism, which was the chief driving force behind the establishment of the *yishuv* and then of the state of Israel. This constructivist form of socialism, he writes, "was never anything but a local variant of European national socialism, born of the encounter of anti-Marxist and antireformist socialist currents on the one hand and ethnic, cultural, and religious nationalism on the other. Compared with the other branches of socialism, European national socialism, he adds, owes its uniqueness to its adherence to the principle of the primacy of the nation," which, he considers, "governed all the others, beginning with the universalist principles of socialism" (pp. 18–19).[2]

Sternhell also shows the national model on which the *yishuv* was based: a nation that was not perceived as a crucible for the integration of various populations and the ultimate embodiment of universal values as conveyed, with important differences, by the French and American Revolutions, and producing the entire range of West-European universalist thought, liberal or revolutionary—the "thought of Locke, Kant, Toqueville, John Stuart Mill, and Marx" (p. 23). Instead, this was to be a nation "of the Herderian, not to say tribal, type" (p. 26), constituted in and through the exclusion of others, as developed among the peoples of the czarist and Austro-Hungarian empires in which the Jews of Central and Eastern Europe lived: "a nationalism based on ethnicity, culture, and history" in which identity was formed "around religion, language, and folklore, perceived as manifestations of specific biological or racial characteristics" (p. 29), as was the case, Sternhell notes, with Polish, Romanian, Slovak, Serbian, and Ukrainian forms of nationalism. These forms, within populations that were often mixed, with numerous national minorities, all envisioned the construction of a state on land that was more or less homogeneous ethnically, emptied of "other" groups. With the probable exception of Czech nationalism, this is true of nearly all the states that have emerged in Eastern Europe and the Balkans in the past hundred and fifty years, but also, in another context, of the Bareso-Maurassian French counterrevolutionary nationalism at the turn of the twentieth century. Like other ethnic nationalist movements, this was based on the land, religion, culture, roots, language, and folklore of the ethnic group.

In the case of the nationalism that would establish Israel, we may add the value placed on territorial origins, especially important because these were physically immaterial for the first Zionists, born thousands of miles away, and for this reason all the more invested with mythic status. This valuation was based on the central role of the Bible in the preservation of Judaism. The idea was present from the beginnings of the national Jewish movement in a fundamental way, through the choice of the Holy Land, seen as the only area able to motivate colonization and ultimately to bring about national regeneration.

Yet the relation to the Bible was marginal at first, since belief and faith were alien to the founding fathers of Israel. However, given time and the need, once Israel was created, to anchor it in a national history centered around a "two-thousand-year-old aspiration" to be reborn as a state, and above all with the conquest of new territory in 1967 and the emerging power of a new Jewish mysticism, the Bible came to play an increasingly crucial role in Israeli nationalism. The risk of capsizing negotiations, as happened at Camp David, in order to retain sovereignty over the Temple Mount, would have seemed exorbitant to the Ben Gurion of the years 1910–1950. "But who needs a Jewish Vatican?" Moshe Dayan, Ben Gurion's most legitimate political son, could still exclaim in 1969. In contrast, thirty years later the need for sovereignty over the Esplanade of the Mosques / Temple Mount seemed obvious and imperative to almost the entire Israeli political class, with the notable exception of Yossi Beilin.

The "ethnoreligious criteria" at the heart of Israeli identity, Tony Judt (2003) has recently written, seemed like "an oddity among modern nations," nations in which, given the necessities of globalization, hybrid populations are becoming the norm, and in which partitioning to maintain the original purity of the ethnic, religious, or cultural community, a frequent propensity that feeds the fear aroused by globalization, seems reactionary in the etymological sense of the term: the expression of a wish to stem a development that is inevitable but is seen as frightening.

THE INFLUENCE OF ETHNICISM ON THE JEWISH NATIONAL MOVEMENT

At time passed, the primacy of ethnoreligious criteria as the basis of Jewish nationalism as it emerged at the end of the nineteenth century was maintained and strengthened in Israel. They led first and foremost, obviously, to the marginalization of the Arabs living there, a policy intended by its institutions and largely accepted by the Jewish population, all the more so in the occupied territories after 1967, where the Palestinians were deprived of all rights until 1993.

But these criteria were also at work within Jewish society, especially in the antagonism between Ashkenazim and Sephardim. The latter, long called *schwartzen* (blacks) in the popular parlance of the former, were also subject to diffuse racism and an aggressive form of social discrimination and, because they came from Muslim countries, were seen by many Ashkenazim as inferior. Marked by the profound ethnicism of their own national movements, the first generations of pioneers could only regard with contempt these Oriental Jews from Yemen, Morocco, Iraq, and elsewhere, whose

Levantine culture, rites, and superstitions seemed to be symptomatic of a cultural inferiority. The Israeli national poet Nakhman Bialik (1873–1934) is said to have asked, "Do you know why I don't like the Arabs? Because they're too much like the Oriental Jews."

As the recent history of the nation had been opened to study, so these ethnicist criteria began to be the targets of criticism, in the 1990s, from sociologists like Uri Ram (1993) and Baruch Kimmerling (2001). But, deep down, beyond their conflict with the Ashkenazim, the Sephardim have remained within modern Israeli nationalism, adding to the fundamental ethnicist relationship—the one to the Arabs—their own tendencies, historically forged and strongly rooted in the Muslim world. This ethnicism resurged even more forcefully with the onset of the intifada, in its hard forms with the legitimized spread of the ultranationalist mystique of land and blood and the social validation of the idea of a new expulsion of the Palestinians, as well as in its more open forms, more inclined to compromise, with the fear of the long-term consequences of an excessive intermingling with the Palestinians. Applied by Ariel Sharon in the annexationist sense in which he understood it, the idea of erecting a wall of separation between Israelis and Palestinians first came from the left wing. From this point of view present-day Israeli nationalism remains deeply imbued with the ethnic-religious logic of its roots.

In this logic the bond of belonging by birth and origin triumphs over any other loyalty, any other ethical or political value. The basic assumption involves "us" on the one side, "them" on the other, under all circumstances, and, essentially, "them against us." The virtues of solidarity, of the affective bond, are raised to the status of unconditionality.

This is the logic found in the *volkisch* nationalist movements of Central Europe and the Balkans, as in the old clan-based or tribal thinking of the Mediterranean rim. It is also amply present among the Arabs, in their relations both among themselves and toward the minority groups living in their midst. It is a logic in which belonging to the original group is irreducible: one is what one was born into by virtue of one's family; district; temple, synagogue, or mosque; one's clan; region; and, on the broadest level, one's ethnicity of origin. From the smallest circle outward, each level of belonging maintains, with the larger one surrounding it, a relationship that at once demands self-preservation, and hence hostility toward the larger circle, and solidarity with the next larger circle in the face of the still larger ones.

Within each circle, the chief driving force, above any rationality or universal standard, is the feeling of shared emotion, collective solidarity. In the case of Israel, a very familiar popular expression, taken up by many a politician (beginning with Ben Gurion himself, who liked to refer to it), has it that "It doesn't matter what the *goyim* think; what matters is what the Jews are doing." The *goyim* are the gentiles, the non-Jews, and the others—all the others—and their opinion are of little account because one knows that they will naturally be hostile by nature. All that counts is what "we" do, for only "we" can guarantee our own interests. The popular expression might not be of too much consequence, might be merely an outcome, upsetting but unavoidable for the time being, of a tragic historical experience, all the more so because this experience is recent. But transposed to the political level, it takes the following form: twice in the 1990s the head of the Likud, Benyamin Netanyahu, centered his political campaign around the publicity slogan, "Netanyahu is good for the Jews." He is the one for whom all that matters is his people's welfare and only theirs. Conversely, he is the one who will not be concerned with the welfare of the other.

In the logic of those who are steeped in what Jacques Derrida called the herd compulsion, those, as Georges Brassens sang, "who were born somewhere," the quest for truth, justice, fairness, and the simple objective observation of facts are always subordinate to the preservation of group interests, interests always deemed superior because they guarantee the group's cohesion and flow from its changeless purity. The collective is never responsible for any misdeed; its identity is automatically never anything but immaculate.

This is a cocoon logic, offering all kinds of advantages, beginning with the signal one of knowing a priori that one will benefit from the support of the collective in all situations, whatever one's own acts. For the guarantee of the collective's solidarity is an individual shield for each of its members. Hence the automatic call for closing ranks in adversity, no matter the grievance of which one is the object.

When a group of Palestinians from Sabra and Shatila began judicial proceedings against Ariel Sharon for the 1982 massacre committed in these refugee camps in Lebanon by Christian Phalangists, who were coordinating their activities with the IDF, what was the reply of the man who was Israel's defense minister at the time? It was not just himself as an individual, Sharon said, but the Jewish people who were being indicted. Here we have the same logic as the one by which so many Serbs come to the defense of Slobodan Milosevic—to avoid recognizing that it is not just Milosevic but the Serbs as a collective entity who are being put in the dock. And it is the logic that made leaders of the Black community in the United States line up behind O. J. Simpson in a reflex of solidarity when he was accused of murder. What matters most is to preserve "our own."

In this way of thinking whoever breaks the bond of loyalty is challenging the purity of the collective and is automatically seen as a traitor. Returning as a reporter in November 2000, at the very beginning of the intifada, I got an odd telephone from Jerusalem call one evening. The man began by asking whether I was the son of Jacques Cypel (my father had been a French Zionist leader between 1950 and 1980). After verifying that this was indeed the case, he informed me that he had known him well. He then vehemently accused me of having written a "scandalous" article saying that the settlers in the Palestinian territories were "tired," which, he stated sharply, was "absolutely false."

The article in question was intended to show that the term *settlers*, used of the Israelis living in the occupied territories, covered a variety of different situations, that, as it were, there were settlers and settlers. Some, I had written, were strongly motivated by ideology, while others had moved to the occupied territories for more prosaic reasons such as the economic opportunities they had been offered. Nowhere in the article did the word *tired* appear, but I had given three examples of exasperated settlers. In a letter to *Haaretz* a farmer from the Jordan valley reproached the army for not defending him and his village against the depredations committed in his fields by Palestinians, adding that he would leave the area if this situation persisted. On a television news program a woman had explained that the government had moved her to Gilo, a Jewish quarter of East Jerusalem fired on by Palestinian snipers, and that for the safety of her children she was demanding to be relocated to a less exposed area. And the mayor of a town in the occupied territories had resigned from Yesha, the organization representing the Israeli settlements, criticizing its support for Greater Israel and settlements like the one in the center of Hebron, when a peace accord would in any case call for the abandonment of many settlements.

These three people, revealing attitudes on the part of Jewish inhabitants of the occupied territories rarely set forth in the media, which generally focus on the ultranationalist settlers, had been expressed publicly. Every Israeli could have seen or heard them. So what, then, was "false" in this article, I asked. A long silence followed my question. Then the man asked me, without transition, "Where were you born, sir?" I told him. "Ah," he said, "that's where I knew your father." There followed another long silence, and, having no intention of pursuing a conversation on family matters, I ended it.

What was the meaning of this apparently incoherent phone call? When I thought it over, the implicit message seemed clear. It was of little importance that the facts reported had been confirmed, nor that they had been made public in Israel. But they should not be mentioned in a French newspaper, a foreign newspaper, by someone who was himself Jewish, and the son of a well-known Zionist to boot, since they could be prejudicial to Israel. Among ourselves certain things could be said. But before foreigners it was scandalous to expose publicly the least fissure in the collective, the least flaw in solidarity.

Ethnicism is a projection onto sociopolitical terrain of the primary emotional disposition: one does not betray one's children, one's parents, those whom one loves; one naturally protects them under all circumstances. Transposed from the individual to the collective level, ethnic, clan-based, or partisan, this primal solidarity, the impossibility of breaking the affective bond and the prohibition against so doing, has terrifying effects. "My mother can't be a murderer," cried the communist lawyer André Blumel in the 1949 Kravchenko trial held in Paris, in a direct appeal to emotion aimed at denying legitimacy to any denunciation of the crimes of Stalinism. Transposed from the national level to that of the working class, the party spirit that blinded so many communist militants and intellectuals operated in the same way as ethnicist logic. The U.S.S.R. (Blumel's "mother"), the Party, could only receive unfailing solidarity and, as a result, could only be pure of any stain, just as, for the so-called "organic" Jewish intellectuals, any description of Israel or of Ariel Sharon regarding their policies toward the Palestinians, and the accompanying war crimes, could only be anti-Semitic, or, when they came from Israelis or Jews, the result of self-hatred. "Them against us" is the mode of mental functioning that explains why so many Israelis know deep down or perceive privately that crimes against the Palestinians are committed in their name yet refuse to admit this, at least publicly, in front of the "others," since this would mean betraying the fundamental affiliation and running the risk of expulsion from the cocoon that ensures their loved ones' solidarity.

In the face of crime, the ethnicist, communitarian logic of denial, like the "party spirit" of yesteryear's Stalinists, always has two phases. The first consists of ignoring and denying disturbing realities and delegitimizing whoever tries to bring them to light. There were neither camps nor terror in the U.S.S.R., and whoever claimed the contrary could only be a fascist or a fascist's "objective ally" (as the Communists used to define anyone criticizing the policy of the U.S.S.R.). The reasoning here is the same: Israel commits no war crimes, and whoever mentions them can only be anti-Semitic or someone who plays the game of anti-Semites. In the second phase, when the evidence is glaringly obvious, one proceeds to the minimization and justification of the facts in question. There was no revolution without repression of the enemies of the people, but, whatever forms this repression took, Stalin and the revolution remained the beacon of the future. Terrorism can't be combated without collateral damage, but the IDF, its leaders keep repeating, remains the most moral army in the world.

This is because the "other," a phobic figure, transparent but obsessional and invasive, is always the one who determines what you do. He never appears except as a threat to the collectivity and its cohesion, responsible for all the misfortunes that befall it, and his presence becomes a barricade against any evaluation, any introspective consideration of your own part in these same misfortunes. How to recognize an adherent of ethnic, communitarian, clannish thinking? The mechanism is always the same:

mention to him any misdeeds whatsoever of his camp, and, in an almost Pavlovian reflex, he will speak of the misdeeds, the defects, the crimes, and the monstrousness of the opposite camp.

This same logic also leads huge sections of the Arab–Muslim world to demonize Israel and America so as better to avoid any assessment of their own failures and conceal them. Thus a certain popular press in Egypt holds Israel, and sometimes the Jews in general, responsible for the shameful evils affecting that country: AIDS, drugs, prostitution, and the like. What brings shame to oneself, every stain, must be concealed and its revelation denounced as a lie. And when this fails, when the blemish (or what is perceived as such) is too visible by far, it can never be anything but the fault of the other, that figure of evil.

This attitude is very deeply entrenched in Israel. Like a groundswell, it strongly reemerged with the intifada, there too taking forms that were sometimes grotesque and sometimes much more elaborate. Thus among members of Shas (the orthodox Sephardic party) a rumor stemming from its most obscurantist rabbis was spread about at that time, to the effect that the mother of Shimon Peres was an Arab. A "friend of Arafat's" can't re-ally be Jewish. I personally heard this crazy, demonizing idea put forth by young activists of the religious party who believed it in all sincerity. And, in their circles, it was much more widespread than one might imagine.

This rumor that was entertained about Peres not being a Jew was of course extreme. Just as is the obsession of a small group in Israel that, through a cockamamie reconstruction of the facts, seeks to persuade the entire world that the death of the child Mohammed Al-Doura in Gaza, on the third day of the current intifada, was caused not by the Israeli army but by the Palestinians themselves. Worse, that this murder was just a macabre scenario staged by the Palestinians, the child actually having been neither wounded nor killed.

These attitudes, grotesque as they are, are symptomatic of a much more general tendency found on the most official level: the inversion of facts and meaning, the denial of what one knows to be reality. Was the intifada sparked by Israeli killing on the Esplanade of the Mosques? No matter: it was the Palestinians who began the violence. The aggression, the fault, the evil can in no case come from within our own side. And, whatever the facts may be, legitimacy is always ours, since the other, even in a situation of extreme weakness, is an immeasurable threat. So what remains is to bury oneself in denial, to theorize a way to shrug off the facts. Thus the thing to do is not to try to determine as precisely as possible what the facts are but instead to argue that the facts in themselves are meaningless and to discuss only the way they are represented. Was or wasn't there a massacre at Jenin during the Israeli Operation Defensive Shield in the spring of 2002? If so, then Israel is surely a monster. But, since there was no such massacre, then Israel is pure as the driven snow. Who cares what really happened?

VERY OLD ARGUMENTS STILL IN THE NEWS

In the course of an investigation into Camp David that I was carrying out in the fall of 2000, I had a meeting with Gidi Grinstein. An assistant to Gilead Sher, Ehud Barak's chief adviser, this young lawyer had taken part in July's tripartite summit. A deep admirer of Barak, whom he compared to Winston Churchill during our meeting, Grinstein proved to be useful and precise. He did not try to evade questions until we came to the discussions, or rather nondiscussions, held by the Camp David committee on the refugees. Why had the Israeli negotiators Dan Meridor and Eliakim Rubinstein stubbornly persisted in rejecting any acknowledgment of Israel's primary responsibility in the creation of the refugee problem? "Listen," Grinstein replied, cutting me short. "That all happened at a time when transfers of populations were permitted."[3]

This was rather too quick a summarization on the part of the young Israeli lawyer. There were indeed various transfers of populations in Europe during the years from 1920 to 1950, but not all of them were as readily permitted as he wanted to have it believed, nor are they all comparable. Who would see as equally legitimate the transfers, diplomatically agreed on, between the Greek and Turkish populations, whatever the suffering that they gave rise to, and Stalin's forced deportations of the Chechens? But Grinstein's reaction was symptomatic. First because it implied an acknowledgment of the reality of the expulsion. And then by what it said about

Grinstein himself and his state of mind, by its insertion into a historical context that, whatever its effects lasting up to the present day, still remained permissible in his view.

In Eastern Europe in the nineteenth century, of all the intermingled peoples and communities from the Baltic countries to the Balkans, the Jewish population, especially in the czarist residence zone to which it was confined (from Kovno to Odessa and from Lodz to eastern Kiev, where the first supporters of Zionism would be recruited), was by far the one most bullied institutionally and most systematically victimized by ethnicist condemnation. The great waves of pogroms in the years 1881–1884 and 1903–1906 and the Beilis trial in 1913[4] would be the culmination of these racist acts of violence at the turn of the twentieth century, the source, along with extreme poverty, of a continuous Jewish immigration toward the West before the Nazis and their local henchmen physically exterminated this population.

In this crucible, from which there would spring many political, nationalist, and socialist movements seeking escape from the yoke of St. Petersburg and Vienna, the issue of the emancipation of the Jew would emerge as a concomitant of the critique of the situation of the Jew. This was a critique of his submission and of his withdrawal into himself, a withdrawal that was imposed by official power and a hostile, often violently anti-Semitic environment but also one that was demanded by notable Jews, religious and secular, and by many of their followers, since they saw it as the guarantee of Jewish continuity. Thus intermarriage between Jews and non-Jews was seen as an abomination not only by the anti-Semites but by a very large number of Jews as well, by no means only religious ones, who were deeply convinced that each union with a non-Jew could only mean either a loss for Jewry or a later failure of the marriage, secular hostility being constitutive of the *goy*, the gentile. Underlying this conviction is the same inclination on the part of members of other long-oppressed minorities: the legacy of a memory of unhappiness. It can be seen in the character Spike Lee presents in his film *Jungle Fever* (1991), a black preacher who greets his son's new girlfriend, a white woman, with an icy silence and then asks her what she knows about slavery.

This attitude of the religious and communitarian Jewish institutions, which put up with the confinement imposed on them, instrumentalizing it as the basis of their own permanence, would be harshly criticized by all the emancipatory Jewish movements as indicative of a hateful ghetto mentality. More generally, the aspiration to win freedom from racist oppression and the oppressive restraints of self-enclosure had a great deal to do with the fact that, in the nineteenth and twentieth centuries, the Jews played such an exceptionally large role in all the intellectual movements of rupture; socialism, revolution, and psychoanalysis were the most notable forms, but the aspiration to rupture also appeared in the sciences, the arts, and literature.

Emerging in Germany at the end of the eighteenth century, the secular movement called *Haskala* (Enlightenment), in its hope to integrate the Jews into their societies and to attain universal values (thus its name), prefigured both future tendencies toward assimilation and those aiming at the affirmation of cultural identity. In some ways it even prefigured the rise of Zionist nationalism. Later on the major trend, by far, in socialism was to favor the whole idea of assimilation and hence of the disappearance of the Jew as such once anti-Semitism was eradicated (an ambiguous attitude, to be sure, since the triumphant Leninism in the U.S.S.R. identified a Jewish "nationality").

Whereas the Bund, the Jewish socialist party present throughout Yiddishland, advocated the recognition of this nationality's rights through its cultural autonomy, Zionism advocated its liberation through constitution as a nation-state in Palestine. The Bund was shaped by a deep empathy for the "little people" of the shtetl (the Jewish town in the residence zone) and the Jewish workers' districts in the growing industrial cities, but socialism and Zionism turned their backs on it with a pronounced hostility, though each in a different way. Socialism rejected the ethnic or cultural solidarity of the ghetto, deeming it contrary to internationalism, Zionism what it saw as the ghetto's diasporic mentality, the result of weakness and dependence. The hostility of the Zionist movement appeared, for example, in a declared aversion to Yiddish (a confused aversion, however, because it was combined with nostalgia), Yiddish being in their view the language of the weak and the conquered although it was the mother tongue of most Zionist leaders.[5]

Yet all three movements—socialism, Bundism, and Zionism—grew up in direct opposition to the traditional Jewish institutions and were fought by them. But their shared criticism of what they saw as the ghetto mentality, considered retrograde by all three, like their criticism of the cowardice of highly placed Jews, differed on one crucial point.

While for the socialists and Bundists, who saw themselves as internationalists, the ghetto mentality was first and foremost a sign of imprisonment, an obstacle to emancipation and the accession of the Jew to a position of equality, for the nationalists, including socialists of this tendency, it signified what they saw as the congenital weakness of the Jew. Reviled by the various socialist movements claiming universal values, the profound ethnicism of the ghetto mentality, which was the result both of the general strength of this perception in all the surrounding populations and of the special situation of the Jews, who were in fact located on the very bottom rung of the ladder of ethnical relationships, became an integral part of the dominant attitudes of Jewish nationalism. The Shoah would later confirm the nationalists in their conviction that the Jews clearly could expect nothing from others and, if they were to survive, could trust only themselves; it followed that the solidarity of the Jewish nation was under all circumstances the supreme value.

When it emerged, says Zeev Sternhell (1996), the Jewish national movement was no different from the other ethnicity-based national movements appearing at the same time in Central and Eastern Europe. "It wasn't worse, more violent, or more intolerant. Nor was it better, except in one respect: it hadn't developed its feelings of ethnic superiority with regard to the Arabs" (p. 30). Yet Georges Bensoussan (2002) and Benny Morris have offered abundant evidence to the contrary. And indeed, why would the Jewish national movement have been spared feelings of superiority to their environment, so near and yet so different, and the contempt toward it that affected the other *volkisch* national movements of Central Europe that arose at the same time?

For ethnicist nationalism, the other does not exist, or exists only in his relationship to one's own national redemption. Thus, very generally speaking, he is seen as an obstacle, especially if he also puts forth concurrent national or identitarian claims. Hence the natural tendency of this kind of nationalism to consider only the defects of the other, be they real or mentally projected onto him, and the threat he represents, instead of seeking to understand him and take his realities into account so as to open pathways to a common future. Hence also the tendency to demonize him endlessly, and the corollary, namely the need to dominate him precisely because he never exists except in a threatening form. As a result, this domination simply fuels the threat and proves it by the absurdity of its reality.

This way of thinking explains why so many national movements arising among people who were themselves oppressed and subjected in the czarist and Austro-Hungarian empires could be deeply poisoned by anti-Semitism or hatred for the Gypsies, at the same time as they themselves aspired to freedom. For it is under the sway of the same mental mechanisms that Louis Farakhan's Nation of Islam in the United States can emerge today as the heir to the Blacks' past of suffering and slavery and develop an anti-white racism—as well as an anti-Semitic racism and sometimes even an anti-Arab racism, surely an extreme point for Muslims. In itself, when accompanied by the closed logic of ethnicism, the aspiration to escape the state of domination or submission is no protection against anything, and especially not against racism, especially when one is or has been the victim of it oneself. How many nationalist movements of subjected peoples, once independence is achieved, have begun by denying their minorities access to the rights that they themselves were previously denied?

The recent works of Bensoussan and Morris outdo each other in demonstrating how a strong ethnicist inclination was evident from the time of the yishuv and how certain debates agitating Israel today with regard to the Palestinians, especially the tendency to justify all forms of domination and the pressure for rejection it arouses within the country, have been present there, almost word for word, for over a century.

Benny Morris (1999) describes how, on a visit to Ottoman Palestine, the theoretician of cultural Zionism Asher Ginsburg, who took the name Ahad Haam, was alarmed to find that the first Jewish pioneers were developing "a tendency to despotism as happens always when a slave turns

into master"; apparently, Morris says, "the settlers appear to have commonly referred to their [Arab] laborers as 'mules,' an analogy drawn from
the Talmudic comparison between asses and Canaanite slaves" (pp. 47–
48). Since the time of the first two *aliyot* (waves of immigration) there have
been two elements constitutive of the way the indigenous population is
perceived by the majority of the *yishuv*: on the one hand there is the usual
attitude of the colonist toward the native,[6] composed of ignorance (paternalistic or aggressive) and domination; on the other hand the tendency to
see in the native's resistance to being despoiled a local manifestation of
the congenital anti-Semitism of the *goy*, the non-Jew, whose potential anti-
Semitism is feared on the basis of experience.

Bensoussan (2002) relates how, when the writer Yosef Haim Brenner
moved to Palestine in 1909, he was "gripped by the tragic vision of what
he called the cowardice of the Jew in the diaspora" (p. 424) who simply
transposed to the new situation the interethnic relationships he was familiar with from his native Ukraine: "For Brenner, Jewish-Arab relations
in Palestine were merely a Near-Eastern version of the old conflict that
set Jews and Christians against one another in Europe. . . . The Arab had
taken the place of the muzhik or cossack. One form of barbarity replaced
the other, but the solitary vulnerability of the Jews remained the same. As
did their anguish" (p. 424). The Arab "mule" became the local counterpart of the Russian or Ukrainian anti-Semitic muzhiks, the Polish peasants or workmen feared for their excesses in the form of pogroms during
their annual pilgrimages to the Black Virgin of Czestochowa. No matter
that in the *moshavot*, the first Jewish settlements in Ottoman Palestine,
the master–slave relation mentioned by Ahad Haam was reversed, for the
fellah or small local tenant farmer was the victim of the progressive expansion of the new colony. This expansion, wrote Eliezer Ben Yehuda in
1882, had to be carried out "covertly, bit by bit, . . . quietly, . . . like silent
spies" with the aim of *increasing our numbers here until we are [in the]
majority.* He went on to say, "We shall easily take away the country if we
only do it through stratagems . . ."(cited in Morris 1999, p. 49, emphasis
in original).

From the beginnings of the *yishuv* this relation to the Arabs, combining paternalism and colonialist contempt, indifference and ethnicist

demonization, was the object of internal criticism, albeit always on the part of a minority. The constant focus of this criticism was the long-term risk of a relation to the other that served only to exacerbate the conflict. The majority replied that any manifestation of weakness would encourage a naturally hostile environment to further aggression.

From time to time two minority tendencies would emerge. One was critical but internal. Often with alarm, it feared that by favoring the use of force, a constant source of humiliation for the Arabs, and by denying the identity of the Palestinians, the Jewish community of Palestine and later the state of Israel would be heading toward a disastrous outcome for themselves. The other tendency, for ethical or political reasons or both, would at one time or another end up breaking away from the *yishuv* and taking the perspective of its opponent, the despoiled native.

The first of these two tendencies, rallying under the banner of what would now be called pacifism, is still a minority view within the Jewish community but, in moments of high tension, will for the most part unite with it before distancing itself once again in the face of the inappropriate or excessive use of force against the Arabs. It nevertheless remains more representative numerically than the second group, which in various ways turned its back on Zionism, taking up with communism or certain religious groups; or, after the establishment of Israel, advocating the formation of a "Hebrew people" as distinct from the Jewish people, as in the Canaanite movement of the 1950s; or finally, more prosaically, by returning to the diaspora.

Thus in 1909 the man who would become the most famous mayor of Tel Aviv, Meir Dizengoff, denounced the slogan "conquest of work" put forth by the two Zionist-socialist parties at that time, Hapoel Hatzair and Poalei Tsion, which were demanding the expulsion of Arab workers from the economy of the *yishuv*, reserving it for Jewish workers alone. "How," he exclaimed, "can Jews, who demand emancipation in Russia, rob the rights of, and act selfishly toward, other workers upon coming to Eretz Yisrael?" (cited in Morris 1999, p. 51).[7] Yet the ideal of Jewish labor can be understood only in the context of the declared ambition to create an autonomous society, one with its economic structures, social strata, political institutions, and schools separated and even disconnected from the

Arab surroundings. During the same period the first armed militia, Hashomer, was formed within the *yishuv*, its aim being to impose Jewish labor by force. Some settlers were quick to denounce its "brutality... [and] inhumanity" (p. 68) toward the natives. These are the words of Shmuel Tolkovsky from the *moshava* (settlement) of Rehovot, who, in 1913, castigated the violent and humiliating behavior of the Hashomer guards: "We Jews who ourselves suffered from persecutions and ill-treatment for thousands of years, . . . from us a minimally humane approach could have been expected. Not to beat unarmed and innocent people with a whip, out of mere caprice" (cited in Morris 1999, p. 53).

Forty years before the Shoah, then, Jewish suffering was being invoked to support diametrically opposed motives, by some, like Brenner, to justify the demonization of the Arabs and the need to repress them, and by others, like Tolkovsky, to refuse to endorse their mistreatment. To this day the Jews of Israel make reference to historical suffering from these same two perspectives—for most of them in order to highlight the savagery of the Arabs or Palestinians, for some to condemn the inhumanity of their own political or military leaders.

Thus the dehumanization of the Palestinian was already present in identical terms almost one hundred years before the behavior of Israeli law-and-order forces in the second intifada were decried in recent statements by Avraham Burg, former president of the Knesset and the Jewish Agency ("hateful," "humiliating"); the writer Batya Gur ("intolerable"); Amos Shoken, owner of *Haaretz*, considered the newspaper of record, who in October 2003 came out in favor of the refusenik Israeli pilots ("depressing"); and Avraham Shalom, former head of the internal security services, formerly known as a hard-liner ("shameful"). The present-day moral camp in Israel also reveals the same enraged incomprehension of how members of a historically persecuted group can, as the settler Tolkovsky said ninety years ago, act without a minimum of humanity.

The issue, then as now, is the ethnicist lens through which the other is perceived, one that validates his domination by an iron hand and leads to his humiliation. In Israel today, as earlier in the *yishuv*, the methodical violence inflicted on the other, presented as merely defensive in consequence of the refusal to take account of his real identity and his humanity, is what prompts the strong condemnation of the politics of force and self-justification that denies equal rights, and even equality, to the Palestinians.

Brit Shalom (Covenant for Peace) was formed in the late 1920s in rejection of the ethnicist view. Here the philosopher Martin Buber joined the great Kabbala scholar Gershom Sholem, and Yehuda Magnes, the founder of the Hebrew University, was a close ally. The group advocated the establishment of a binational state for the Jews and Arabs of Palestine in order to avoid an endless war. Amnon Raz-Krakotzkin (2001a) quotes Magnes as saying that the Jews' civilizing mission was to enter the promised land not in the manner of Joshua but bringing peace and doing nothing contrary to universal morality. As we shall see, Ariel Sharon's favorite biblical text is precisely the story of Joshua's conquest of Canaan. Already in those early years, as Raz-Krakotzkin reports, Sholem was distressed to see Zionism carried off by a national and theological vision of redemption. He feared that it would end up like the Sabbatean movement under the false messiah Sabbatai Tsvi, which had a considerable success in the last third of the seventeenth century among the disinherited Jewish masses of Asia Minor and Central and Eastern Europe before it finally collapsed.

This threat of the ultimate catastrophic consequences of the politics of force and humiliation was what led various members of Mapam, the Zionist left, to denounce the behavior of the IDF in 1948. Benny Morris (1990) quotes Mapam's ideological leader, Meir Yaari, as deploring the fact that, after the large-scale expulsions and numerous acts of violence in the fall of 1948, Israeli soldiers were turning the Arabs into slaves and firing on unarmed women and children. On November 14, 1948, Aharon Zisling, minister of agriculture in the first Israeli government and likewise a member of Mapam, wrote to Ben Gurion about the atrocities committed by these soldiers. Brokenhearted and in anguish — "I can't sleep at night," he writes — he compares the behavior of the Jews to that of the Nazis (see Segev 1991, p. 26).[8] Aharon Cohen, head of the party's Arab department, noting that before the creation of the state a deliberate expulsion of Palestinian civilians had been underway for months, wrote in a memorandum that, although others might rejoice, he was ashamed and frightened; by winning the war and losing the peace, he said, Israel, once created, would live by the sword (Morris 1990, p. 46).

The belief that by living by the sword and committing irreparable criminal acts against the local population Israel was losing its soul and running a great risk was what inspired Hannah Arendt, a paradoxical Zionist, between the 1940s and the 1950s. Her conviction was accompanied by the key idea that in abandoning his role of universal pariah and hence the universalist par excellence, the Jew was abandoning himself when he assumed the position of the dominator. Raz-Krakotzkin (2001a) shows how, in the 1940s, halfway between liberal Zionism and the autonomist national ideology of the historian Shimon Dubnov, Arendt began to fear that when the Jews became a nation they would adopt the same values that had led to their exclusion throughout history, the values espoused in ethnicist thinking. She quickly became a fierce critic of Ben Gurion's policies toward the Arabs.

Nevertheless, in the mid-1960s, the appearance of her book *Eichmann in Jerusalem*, which described the trial of the man who had organized the transportation of Jews to the extermination camps, made her the target of extremely violent hostility on the part of Israeli and international Jewish institutions. She wrote: "I know, or believe, that if a catastrophe were to sweep away the Jewish state for whatever reasons, and even if those reasons lay in its own madness, this might perhaps be the final catastrophe for the entire Jewish people, and it little matters what each of us might think at that moment" of the policies carried out by Israel.[9]

Setting out from an iconoclastic religious point of view in the mystico-nationalist storm that took hold of Israel after the conquest of the Palestinian territories in 1967, the scholar and philosopher Yeshaayahu Leibowitz immediately came to equally radical conclusions, reviving the "catastrophist" vision of the future should Israel forcefully impose an occupation on millions of Arabs. As soon as the ultranationalists of Gush Emunim (Bloc of the Faithful) made their appearance, Leibowitz denounced them as the equivalent of the Hitler Jugend and saw in the mystique of the Land of Israel and the sanctification of the Wailing Wall and the Cave of the Patriarchs in Hebron, which Gush Emunim promoted, a new form of idolatry contrary to the religious foundations of Judaism. Until his death in 1993 he tirelessly called for a withdrawal from the territories in order to save Israel.

Thus from within the Zionist consensus[10] and from the early days of the *yishuv*, there were those who thought the continuation of the politics of the iron hand and the denial of the rights of the Palestinians would lead to disaster and the possible disappearance of the state of Israel. This view holds true today among people like Avraham Burg, who speaks of a rottenness within Israel; Michael Ben Yair, former legal adviser to the Rabin government, who says that "amorality has become the norm in Israel";[11] and Ami Ayalon, former head of Shin Bet.

The Palestinian historian Elias Sanbar recalls how, when he was invited to speak at an American university during the first intifada (1987–1993), he met a famous Israeli professor of international relations, General Yehoshafat Harkabi, who had been head of military intelligence in the 1950s, and got on well with him. One afternoon during the Gulf War Harkabi invited him to have a cup of tea. He was feeling depressed. Speaking of the latest news about the IDF's repression of the young Palestinian stone-throwers, he suddenly said to Sanbar, "You know, I know how this will all end. We Israelis are a crazy, suicidal people. We're going to squash you, annihilate you. And then the Arab world will annihilate us. And nothing will be left either of you or of us."[12]

It is this idea, the idea of the final catastrophe resulting from the crushing of the other, that in times of high tension has regularly emerged at the margin among people who, for political or moral reasons, challenge the dominant and dominating Israeli view of the Arabs. It is what, today, motivates the hundreds of refuseniks who ever since the outbreak of the intifada have refused to serve in the occupied territories so as not to "oppress, expel, starve, and humiliate an entire people."[13]

DISCOUNTING THE OTHER

In contrast to these marginal views, which are mocked with condescension ("beautiful souls," "utopians" who fail to take into account the monstrousness of the Arab, though to be sure these utopians can prove themselves useful to those who scorn them, since they demonstrate the humanism of the Israeli undertaking) or, more often, reviled with hostility ("traitors," "deserters in wartime," said General Dan Halutz in 2003), the ethnicist view has deeply influenced not only shared attitudes in Israel but also their intellectual representations.

As early as the 1905 Zionist Congress in Basel the delegate Yitzhak Epstein declared, "We have forgotten one small matter: There is in our beloved land an entire nation, which has occupied it for hundreds of years and has never thought to leave it. . . . We are making a great psychological error. . . . While we feel a deep love for the land of our forefathers, we forget that the nation who lives in it today has a sensitive heart and a loving soul" (cited in Morris 1999, p. 57).[14] This initial forgetfulness is the basis for the fabrication of the image of the other and the conviction that he acts the way he does, submissively or aggressively, because of his nature, a nature that is an inherent cultural constant independent of the relationship to the Jewish immigrant (or the occupying colonial power) and later to the Israeli citizen.

The alternative of either natural submissiveness or irrational but likewise natural aggression was mentioned earlier in connection with the words of Ariel Sharon, who divides the Palestinians into two basic categories: those who are concerned with feeding their families and craven, barbarous terrorists. It appeared in the earliest days of the *yishuv*. The famous educator Yossef Vitkin, arriving from Belarus in 1897, saw the native laborer as "almost always a submissive servant, who may be exploited . . . and accepts lovingly the expressions of his master's power and dominion" (cited in Morris 1999, p. 43). In contrast, the activist settler Moshe Smilansky wrote as follows: "We must not forget that we are dealing here with a semi-savage people, which has extremely primitive concepts. And this is his nature: If he senses in you power—he will submit and will hide his hatred for you. And if he senses weakness—he will dominate you." Moreover, Smilansky continued, the Arabs have developed "base values . . . to lie, to cheat, to harbor grave [unfounded] suspicions and . . . a hidden hatred for the Jews. These Semites—they are anti-Semites" (cited in Morris 1999, pp. 43–44). Thus those who sought to conquer this land clandestinely and by cunning, as Ben Yehuda recommended, are the very same people who ascribe a lying and deceitful nature to the other as soon as he refuses to accept domination. (Morris goes on to offer many citations demonstrating how the leaders of the small *yishuv* "tried for decades to camouflage their real aspirations" [p. 63] to seize land, dreaming of being able to expel the local population so as to establish their state there.)

We find exactly the same attitudes seventy years later, in the period following the occupation of the West Bank and Gaza. Given the feebleness of the Palestinians' reaction, feebleness that was due to their recent, resounding defeat in 1967 and to the fact that the reorganization of their national movement after the "Catastrophe" of 1948 was still in limbo, a huge majority of Israelis persuaded themselves that the "liberal" nature of their occupation would be easily accepted by those who experienced it. "They're used to being under occupation; they've always been. By us or the Hashemites, whom they don't like either; for them nothing has changed." "With us, at least, they'll be better off than under the Jordanians. They've got everything to gain." Such sentiments could be heard all over Israel in the years after 1967, expressed not only by ultranationalists on the right but also by members of the Labor Party seeking to convince themselves that the occupation would not give rise to any calamities.

What remained was to find the means to validate this self-persuasion in actual fact, that is, to eradicate any ideas the Palestinians might have about national solidarity. The army and the special services got to work, hunting down nationalists, communists, and syndicalists, tens of thousands of whom passed through Israeli prisons in the next twenty years. In the mid-1970s, less than a decade after the beginning of the occupation, the Israeli writer Amos Keinan noted that there was not a single Palestinian family in the occupied territories in which someone had not been arrested at least once and jailed for at least one day. In contrast, when the first intifada broke out in 1987 the sudden physical resistance to occupation led immediately to the reemergence of the conviction that the violent nature of the Palestinian was the key to his attitude, so that one had to begin by "breaking his bones." The same reaction appeared after the failure of the Camp David negotiations, when Ehud Barak found it disconcertingly easy to get the overwhelming majority of Israelis to agree on the "duplicity" of Yasser Arafat and the Palestinians, who had "chosen violence" when Israel had "offered them everything."

Keeping silent about the reality of the other, believing that dominating him is natural, and demonizing him as soon as he puts forth any violent identitarian claims are the pillars of Orientalism Israeli style. We may recall the well-known words of Golda Meir, the longtime head of diplomacy, when she became prime minister (1970–1974): "There is nothing that can be called a Palestinian people" (Man 1993). Departments of history, Near-Eastern studies, and Islamic studies in Israeli universities elaborated this view for many years, denying the Palestinians any inherent national character, so that each of their uprisings could be regarded as an aggression against the *yishuv*, and later Israel, devoid of any identitarian element beyond the tribal and barbaric.

As early as 1886 the settler Haim Hissin, who had arrived with the Biluim, the first wave of Zionist immigration, judged that the Arabs were "in [the] process of degeneration" because they "lacked any patriotic feeling" (cited in Morris 1999, p. 43), patriotism evidently being the major distinctive sign of regeneration. The conviction or self-persuasion that there was no such thing as a Palestinian national awareness was probably the chief ingredient of the Orientalism prevailing in Israeli universities for decades. It was joined by a tendency to demonize the Muslims' relation to Jews (the mirror image of the well-known tendency of many Arab intellectuals to idealize this relation in the nostalgic celebration of the Golden Age of Islam, concealing or minimizing the status of *dhimmi* accorded to Jews, that is, believers who were protected as long as they remained submissive, and the tendency of Islamists to favor the passages of the Koran that demonize Jews).

As a counterpart of the perception of the Arab as someone who naturally accepts subjugation, a silence surrounding the real identity and national aspirations of the Palestinian accompanies the entire history of the *yishuv* and the vision of its leaders. Ella Shohat (1991), an Israeli anthropologist at Columbia University, has shown how documentary films made in the years from 1920 to 1940 either completely pass over the Arab presence in Palestine, making no reference to it as if it were physically nonexistent, or almost systematically reduce the Arab to a single type, that of the uncouth fellah content with a pita and a few olives, and almost never depicting him as a city dweller.

Similarly, the historian Georges Bensoussan (2002) tackles the "relative silence surrounding a question that, nevertheless, preys on everyone's mind, a question everyone is familiar with" (p. 424), the Arab question. According to Bensoussan, "far from being connected with contempt of the colonial kind, . . . constructing the Jewish nation by strengthening one's own culture presupposes ignoring the culture of the natives" (pp. 424, 427).

This inclination is very deeply rooted indeed, although, contrary to Bensoussan's assertion that it is not incompatible with colonialist contempt, it is in fact its complement. It is the direct result of the ethnicist nature of Jewish nationalism. You are solely concerned with yourself and your own aims, and these are seen as valid regardless of the consequences for others, who are viewed purely in terms of their reaction, be it submission or revolt. You construct yourself without taking into account these natives, though they are there before your eyes in great numbers, not seeing them for as long as you can get by without seeing them.

This willful ignorance, as Bensoussan calls it, has a price. "The silence on the 'Arab question,'" he writes, "broken only by a few literary allusions, shows just how violent the internal turmoil was. . . . Thus Zionism in the Land of Israel seems to be afflicted with schizophrenia, the 'Arab question' being silenced there because it contradicts the self-image. The problem is hidden, which makes it possible for life to go on in conformity with the image one has of oneself, that of a humanist respectful of human rights" (p. 428). This self-centered "schizophrenia" has a corollary: the fabrication of a diametrically opposite image of the Arab that in fact corresponds to one's own needs. If the Jewish national movement is humanistic and legitimate (and, for a very long time, had to be relegitimated vis-à-vis not only the Mandatory power but also the hesitations of the Jewish diaspora), the Palestinian national movement must be entirely ignored or at least minimized. And when it becomes too obvious, it must be delegitimized as nonhumanist, and sometimes even as nonhuman.

This nationalism is alleged to not exist because, for people like Golda Meir, the Palestinians do not exist as a people: "One of our central myths has held that there is no Palestinian national identity. We [Israelis] have instinctively defined every Arab uprising in this country, from 1920 to the intifada, as a gang outburst," writes the political scientist Zeev Sternhell.[15] Since manifestations of nationalism on the part of the indigenous population are without basis in reality, they can only be perverse, depraved, barbaric, an illegitimate invention. Have the Palestinians become a refugee nation since 1948? Not really, goes the reply, since they were not driven out but left voluntarily. As for the permanence of the refugee camps, it is solely due to the unhealthy wish of the Arab states to use the refugees against Israel for political ends by refusing to integrate them into their own populations. There can be no doubt that, if they were to do so, these Palestinians would instantly lose all vestiges of national identity or any budding aspirations to it. As for the PLO, it was denied any role as a nationalist movement until 1993. And once the Oslo parentheses were closed seven years later, there was a rapid return to the earlier Orientalism seeking other ways to discredit, if not to negate, the Palestinian Authority through the figure of its principal leader.

Multiple loyalties to clan, religion, region, nation, and the Arabs as a group, loyalties that are sometimes complementary, sometimes in conflict, constitute the identity of the peoples of the Mashrek, Palestinians and others, the relative weight of each of these components varying with historical circumstances and the modalities of the colonial past. Faced with this situation, Israeli Orientalism has made an effort to favor certain elements—global ones like Arabness and Islam, or reductive ones like tribe, clan, the particular family or religious group—to the detriment of elements tending to mark out a distinct nation. Israeli historiography is characterized by two wishes: on the one hand the wish to privilege everything that, across time, has bound the Jews together as one and the same entity, a single nation, systematically marginalizing all centrifugal and heterogeneous elements in Jewish history, and on the other the wish to highlight, just as systematically, all the divisive factors in the Arab world, especially among the Palestinians, emphasizing whatever tends to show that the idea of a nation is alien to them.

Up until the 1990s, and still quite often today, Orientalist grammar has referred to the Palestinians remaining in Israel after 1948 by the neutral term "minorities" (*miutim*). This word is perceived in two ways. The first is generalizing: for the ordinary Israeli, it is automatically understood to designate those who, while living in the country, are not Jews, and every-one is well aware that these are the Israeli Arabs. In ministries and mu-nicipalities the person in charge of Arab issues is called the "minorities official." In the army, "minority units" consist of non-Jewish soldiers: Bedouins, Druses, and Cherkassians; the others, that is, around 90 per-cent of Israeli Arabs, are not called up.

The second meaning, in contrast, is reductive and politically significant. It entails the idea that this population is multiple and divided ("minorities," in the plural), that it does not form a single group or have a common iden-tity and common interests, that what characterizes it is its irreducible het-erogeneity. "Minority individuals" are identified by their ethnic or religious origin: they are first and foremost Muslims, Christians, Druses, Bedouins, Cherkassians, and the like—everything but Palestinians.

The Israeli sociologist Baruch Kimmerling has devoted a great deal of effort to studying what this attitude means: not naming reality for what it is. Designating the Palestinian population remaining in Israel with the plural word "minorities" makes it possible to confer individual rights on its members but there can be no collective right, since it has no acknowl-edged collective existence. At the same time, though in a hidden man-ner, this population is the object of collective prohibitions. We have seen this, for example, in the de facto prohibition against acquiring land. By forging this notion of "minorities" in the plural, Israeli Orientalism ratio-nalizes an inability to perceive the Arab environment in its complexity, and it does so all the more easily because this rationalization corresponds to a need. Moreover, in the Arab Orient, the thoroughly artificial parti-tioning imposed in 1919 by the United Kingdom and France was added to the interaction among the multiple components of identity. The result is that one is simultaneously a member of a given family, a Muslim or Christian, a Palestinian, and an Arab, or a member of a given tribe and, at the same time, for example, an Iraqi, Arab, Shiite, and so forth.

These identities are not only various but also variable. Depending on the situation, one of the general identity components will predominate over the others. This complexity does not encourage the spontaneous establishment of differentiated nation-states, seen by Orientalism as the only perfect form of government, even if it is not irreducibly hostile to it.

But Israeli Orientalism operates with simple categories: if the Palestinian nation is not constituted in the ways it is familiar with, it does not exist. And so much the better, since the opposite case would have been upsetting. As a result, instead of seeking to understand the complexity of the Palestinian people, Orientalism will try hard to use this complexity as an excuse to deny the existence of a national identity. It will emphasize everything that reduces Arab societies, first and foremost the Palestinians, to a congenital and irremediable cultural archaism. To caricature this view only slightly: since the Arab and Palestinian elites reflect the peasant, tribal backwardness of their societies of origin, their politically retrograde character is an irreducible part of them.

FIVE

"SOMETHING LIKE A CAGE"
The Dilemmas of the Israeli Historian

ISRAELI ORIENTALISM APPLIED TO HISTORY

In a recent study, Haim Gerber (2003), professor of Muslim history at the University of Jerusalem, shows the extent to which the dominant cultural view became so powerful in Israel, and why it continues to be. According to Gerber, even a New Historian like Benny Morris, when he observes the Palestinians, stresses what, according to Gerber, he sees as "the natural characteristics of a primitive society" and "feels no need to demonstrate" them (p. 25). Thus Israeli Orientalism fails to consider not only the beginnings of Palestinian nationalism under the Ottoman Empire but also the repressive nature of the British policy that succeeded the Sublime Porte and, in order to ward off this nationalism, consistently favored the most feudal tendencies among the natives. What has been forgotten today is that the Grand Mufti of Jerusalem, before lapsing into collaboration with the Nazis, was a creature of the British, in the literal sense of the term: they created his job so that he could be their privileged representative, using his influence to hold back the aspirations of the Palestinian middle class.

Gerber also notes how, in the mid-1940s, the Orientalist Yaakov Shimoni, "unable to conceive of the possibility that the indigenous population could have feelings of genuine nationalism, . . . sees every opposition to Zionism as 'extremism' or a result of 'incitement.' Left to themselves, the Arab masses would have embraced Zionism and recognized its total beneficence to them" (p. 24; cf. Shimoni 1947). In the same period the Israeli Marxist Orientalist Yossef Vaschitz, ignoring the dispossession of the natives, also "had at his disposal a ready-made intellectual tool to explain away Palestinian self-perception: the landowners were afraid of the rise in the standard of living, businessmen were afraid of competition, and the masses were incited [to riot] by their leaders" (Gerber 2003, p. 25; cf. Vischitz 1947). Thus, Gerber concludes, what was seen as the violence of the Arab masses against the Jewish immigrants or British colonial power could only have been the result of manipulation, since the Arabs themselves lacked any national solidarity.

Given this view of the indigenous population, Israeli Orientalists universally marginalize the emergence of regional Arab forms of nationalism under the Ottoman Empire, just as they ignore any social change that might lead to a form of national identity emerging from within; the concept of the nation, in their view, could only have been imported from outside Muslim societies, to which it is said to be culturally alien. In the case of the Palestinians, the Orientalists are even more inclined to minimize its manifestations. So what if one of the two first local press organs, founded in 1911, was entitled *Filastin* (*Palestine*)? What was then emphasized was the idea that, if there was a Palestinian nationalism at the time, it was merely an appendage to an emergent pan-Syrian nationalism. Palestinian nationalism could not exist in its own right, or even coexist with other political forms of identitarian claim.

As an aspect of Orientalism, ethnicist thinking consists in retaining as evidence only what corresponds to its own presuppositions. Accordingly, it was the retrograde attitudes of the Palestinian elites, and only of that group, that, even for Morris, determined the Palestinian rejection of partition in 1947, not the social and political implications of this division. It was the "fatal weakness of Palestinian Arab society" with its "primitive and inefficient" agrarian economy, a society "largely apolitical and uninvolved in national affairs," that explains its inability to resist the emergence of the Israeli nation-state (Gerber 2003, p. 24, citing Morris 1987). The combined effect on this society of British colonial domination and the establishment of the *yishuv* is simply erased from memory, Gerber observes, in favor of the Palestinians' supposed national immaturity. In Morris's view, "Commitment and readiness to pay the price for national self-fulfillment presumed a clear concept of the nation, . . . which the Palestine's Arabs . . . by and large completely lacked. Most [of them] had no sense of separate national or cultural identity to distinguish them from, say, the Arabs of Syria, Lebanon, or Egypt" (Gerber 2003, p. 24, citing Morris 1987). We shall see further on how, in a sort of mirror effect, most Palestinian historians and sociologists tend to retain as explanations of what they call the "catastrophe" of 1948 only the elements connected with colonial policy, ignoring those having to do with the actual lateness of their national movement and the political carelessness of their elites.

With this view fixed in its mind, Orientalism Israeli style is especially inclined to efface the profound significance of the Palestinians' Great Revolt of 1936–1939 and its consequences for their inability to mount a resistance to their expulsion in 1948. This armed revolt, the most important to emerge in the part of the Arab world under British domination, stemmed from the fact that London, in contrast to the Ottoman Empire, ever since it took control of the territory in 1917, had constantly crushed anything in the social, economic, intellectual, and, especially, political domains that could contribute to the formation of an independent national society.

The revolt was drowned in blood. The colonial army did everything it could to break it, cordoning off the population whenever possible, even taking the extreme measure of bombing entire villages. In this they had the support of militias from the yishuv.[1] This was the time of the definitive creation of the myth that Zeev Sternhell (1997) describes, the myth that there is no Palestinian national identity, each Arab uprising being merely gang activity. And this was the time of the systematic adoption, in all circumstances, of the terms armed bands and, later, terrorists to characterize any armed or simply violent Palestinian demonstration, necessarily lacking any rational motivation and hence any national political meaning.[2]

Palestinian society emerged weakened from its insurrection, its backbone broken, as Gerber (2003) writes, dislocated and politically crushed by the British. Benny Morris evades the reality of this repression. "Possibly the most unsettling of his claims," Gerber continues, "is that the Mandate provided a *nursery* of state building that the Palestinians failed to take advantage of but which the Zionists exploited to the full" (p. 36, emphasis in original). This is in fact Morris's central thesis: the Jews of the *yishuv*, united and with a highly developed national awareness, were able to profit from the opportunities offered by the occupiers; the Arabs of Palestine, socially backward and lacking national awareness, were unable to do so and paid the price.

"The truth," Gerber replies, "is that this nursery of state building did exist," but solely for the *yishuv*. "The overall impression one gets [from studying this period]," he continues, is that the *yishuv* "was not really considered [by the Mandatory power] a society under occupation, a state within a state" (p. 36), in contrast to the indigenous Palestinians. The *yishuv*, Gerber writes, developed its own state organs alongside those of the British, its own militia and educational system, under the iron rule of London, all these being denied to the Palestinians or offered to them under unacceptable conditions. Thus between 1920 and 1930 the Palestinians twice refused the suggestion that they form a common parliament with the Jews. Why? Because, although they were three or four times more numerous, London offered them parliamentary representation only equal to that of the Jewish community.

In studying the differences, both well known and hidden, in the way the two populations were treated by the Mandatory power, it is interesting, Gerber observes, "to compare the way Britain suppressed [their] two revolts," that of the Palestinians in 1936 and that of the Jews ten years later.

> The suppression of the Arab revolt was brutal and cruel, . . . [including] indiscriminate killing of villagers, . . . the stripping of women to make sure that they were not men in disguise, and tying village leaders on trains as human shields. . . . Such acts against Jews would have been inconceivable. [In comparison,] the suppression of the Jewish revolt was almost a Boy Scout affair. The worst moment of this suppression was the so-called Black Saturday of June 1946, in which the British army searched for hidden weapons and arrested some second-rank Zionist leaders, who were held for a number of

months and never brought to trial. Compare to this [the] large number of executions of the leaders of the Arab revolt and the forced exile
of countless others. . . . In 1948 most of the potential leadership of
the Palestinians was either dead, in prison, or in exile, hardly a "nursery of state-building," and hardly equal treatment to that shown to
the Zionist movement. Morris does not give weight to this massive
repression as a major factor in the collapse of Palestinian society.
[p. 37]

Thus the Orientalist view, even when most inclined to bring brute historical facts to light in an honest manner, as is the case with Benny Morris, evades the role played by colonialism: the Jews of the *yishuv*, a nation
in the making, knew how to take advantage of the opportunities offered
by the British; if the Palestinians did not have this ability, this was solely
because they lacked the foundations of nationhood. Here too the mirror effect of the denial of reality is fully operative. By retaining only the
colonialist features of the *yishuv* and emphasizing only its privileged relations with the Mandatory power, Palestinian historians and political scientists refused for a long time to admit the establishment and existence of
a new Israeli nation with its own qualities.

In conforming to an ideological need, the Orientalist view has practical political consequences. Thus after 1948 Israeli authorities claimed for
themselves the juridical arsenal of the Mandatory "laws of exception"
(administrative internment without a charge or verdict, banishment without trial, etc.), laws that had sometimes been used against them in the
past, in order to apply them to the Palestinians, and, just as after 1967,
they adopted a political attitude very similar to that of the British toward
the Palestinians inside the newly occupied territories. The Palestinians'
nationalism was denied any legitimacy on account of their supposed nonexistence as a people; for a long time the Israelis spoke of "the Arabs of
the territories," the local counterparts of the citizen "minorities" of the
state, just as Israeli politicians never simply named the PLO, instead regularly calling it "the terrorist organization known as the PLO." Similarly,
for twenty-five years the Israeli authorities tried hard to track down people
of importance in the occupied territories, heads of large families or

religious dignitaries, and set them up as partners so as to create an obstacle to any form of national unity in the dominated society. To counter Palestinian nationalism and reduce it to its alleged nonexistence, Ariel Sharon, commander of the southern front in the early 1970s, surreptitiously financed the Muslim Brotherhood and the building of mosques in the Gaza Strip.

The first intifada, in 1987, put an end to the fantasy that denied any national sentiment to the Palestinians and favored their most retrograde structures. But Sharon, a great expert when it came to this view, revived it as an integral part of his strategy as soon as he came to power in March 2001. General Meir Dagan, Sharon's chief security adviser, whom he later placed at the helm of Mossad, stated in December of that year that Sharon's plan in the face of the second intifada, a plan developed before his election, was to isolate the Palestinians into separate pockets so that he could then negotiate with local representatives, thereby discrediting the Palestinian national leadership.[3]

This logic, coming straight from the ideological Orientalism that had been flourishing for decades and its practical consequences, is this: since the Palestinians do not exist as a people, and since their archaic cultural constants render them incapable of attaining national modernity as envisioned by the Western mind, all that remains to be done is bend one's efforts to proving the truth of these assertions.

The view of a *yishuv* and, later, an Israel eternally progressive and modern, legitimizing the domination, and, if need be, the repression, of the other, goes hand in hand with the view of an Arab society lagging decisively behind that of Israel, a society that must be deemed even more backward than it actually is so that it can be maintained in a state of weakness. Hence the denial of the reality of the other is inseparable from the ulterior mechanism of justification that validates it. All one has to do is compare the resources allotted to the settlers in the territories since 1967 with those granted to the indigenous population in terms of infrastructure for roads, aquifers, schools, and sanitary facilities, enormous in the first case (more than double the average sums disbursed to collectivities within Israel itself) and all but zero in the second case. Then listen to learned Orientalists explaining in all seriousness what the man in the street is sure of because he has heard it repeated so often, namely that the Arabs are clearly unable to make milk and honey flow.

"THERE IS NO PARTNER"

The logic of reversal invariably presents coercive measures as defensive ones, protections against the opponent's aggression, measures that are generally preventive (or preemptive, to use a word that became fashionable after September 11 as part of the Americans' "new strategic doctrine"). As such they require no evidence for this aggression.

The same logic, again, transposed to the political domain of relations with the Arab world, leads to a key phrase summing up the entire history of Israeli diplomacy: "There's no one to discuss things with." After 1967 Golda Meir was in the habit of saying, "I'm waiting for someone to knock on my door, but no one comes." This was true even at the very time when Israel rejected the Rogers Plan, proposed by Richard Nixon's secretary of state, for withdrawal from the occupied territories, or when its own services were holding secret talks with the Hashemites before objecting to their suggestions for a peace accord involving a complete Israeli withdrawal from the territories.

"There is no partner": this was the argument Ehud Barak automatically deployed after Camp David to deny the reality of the proposals he had been offered. The Palestinians made no counterproposals at the summit, his services claimed at first. Then, as the truth about the negotiations slowly made its way into Israel despite the attempts of the communications machine to counter it, a new rhetoric was devised, aimed at discrediting these counterproposals: they were merely a decoy meant to hide the Palestinians' true ambition, which was always the same, namely to annihilate Israel. Israel buttressed this claim by citing the Palestinians' demand that the right of return of their refugees be recognized in principle, as established in international law. It completely discounted the proposals set forth by the Palestinian negotiators to minimize the practical application of this right, using as an excuse the Palestinians' alleged wish, concealed and overt, to destroy the Jewish state from within.

The mechanism of denial is usually easy to decode. First, the facts do not exist. Second, if their existence is confirmed, they are interpreted in such a way as to discredit them, and policies are formulated with the aim of restoring their desired nonexistence. Consider, for example, the PLO. In the first phase, it was stated that the PLO does not represent the Palestinians but is merely a terrorist organization that cannot possibly be recognized. In the second phase, once it became clear that the PLO cannot be ignored, if coming to an agreement with it proves impossible under desirable conditions, this proves its illegitimacy. The Palestinians at Camp David were insincere, concealing their double game. At best they were incapable of making adequate decisions, an incapacity that can be explained only by their duplicity or their irrationality, precisely because the proposals they were offered were as favorable as can be imagined.

This initial reaction of denial, strongly undermined in Israel during the first years after the Oslo Accords, surfaced with renewed vigor right after the failure at Camp David. It appears in a recent book published in the United States by Yaacov Lozowick (2003), who is in charge of the archives at Yad Vashem, the Shoah museum in Israel. What would be best for Israel, Lozowick writes, is a true peace without the settlements, if only such a proposal were made. On March 28, 2002, fifteen months before his book appeared, after a meeting of its twenty-two heads of state and government in Beirut (the PLO was represented, though Arafat was unable to attend), the Arab League offered Israel full recognition and the establishment of normal relations in exchange for a retreat to the internationally recognized borders, those of June 6, 1967; acceptance of a Palestinian state in the territories with East Jerusalem as its capital; and what it termed a just solution to the refugee problem. Lozowick deliberately ignores this proposal, as though it had never existed.

Nor was there any official reaction to it in Israel itself at the time, as though it were virtual, without substance or interest. The media hardly mentioned it. Lozowick does not even try to argue that this proposal was, say, insincere, that the peace offered was not a true one or that, by calling for a just solution to the refugee problem, it was deceptively concealing the Arabs' eternal will to destruction, which line of argument, with variable components, is the usual second stage of the outburst of denial in the face of the facts. On the contrary, the matter is much simpler: no one is offering us peace in exchange for quitting the settlements. This is set forth as obvious, something everyone accepts. Pushed to its extreme, Israeli denial borders on autism.

Three months after September 11, 2001, the attacks were seen as "a kind of 'Hanukkah miracle' for Israel, coming just as Israel was under increasing international pressure because of the ongoing conflict with the Palestinians" (Benn 2001). Speeches given by Ephraim Halevy, head of Mossad at the time, and General Uzi Dayan, president of the Israeli National Security Council, suggested that the attacks "placed Israel firmly on the right side of the strategic map with the U.S., and put the Arab world at a disadvantage" (p. 1). The "miracle" brought by Al Qaeda's attacks was the confirmation of the entire traditional Orientalist vision in Israel, that of an Arab–Muslim region as the source of all threats.

From this time on, and up until the American war in Iraq, these same infinitely comforting phrases were repeated over and over again like a litany by a great many politicians and so-called experts in Israel. They boiled down to a few simple ideas: before September 11, people didn't believe us; they didn't want to listen to us; now they'll understand us better. For we Israelis know what the deep, immutable reality of the entire Arab and Muslim world is, beginning with the Palestinians. Our image of them was well founded, for they are invariably threatening and terrorist by nature. The proof was right there on September 11: the Arab world is the heart of darkness. And the only country in which polls showed most respondents in favor of the entry of the United States into war in Iraq, by a percentage higher than in America itself, was Israel.

BENNY MORRIS, AN ISRAELI HISTORIAN TORN BETWEEN ETHNICISM AND HISTORICAL TRUTH

When ethnicist thinking prevails, at least in the initial phases of conflictual situations when direct confrontation obliterates all landmarks, its crude version is always what sets the tone. For this is where the values and mechanisms of this way of thinking are most consistently expressed. Them against us. They're the aggressors, we're the victims. And the more the facts contradict this self-perception, the more it leads to their denial and inversion. Goliath isn't Goliath, he's David. The Israeli police opened fire on an unarmed crowd on the Esplanade of the Mosques. No matter; it was the Palestinians who began the violence.

After the failure of the Camp David negotiations, this consistent ethnicist view was once again brutally imposed on Israeli society, carrying along a large number of former advocates of the Oslo process. Very few Israeli intellectuals were able to resist the ill wind that blew on everyone at that time. Given the difficulty in crushing the intifada and the methods used to that end by the government and the army, some of these people gradually came to distance themselves to some extent from the position of their own camp.[4]

Among these intellectuals, the evolution in the views of Benny Morris illustrates the consequences of mixing ethnicism with the particular kind of Orientalism long found in Israeli universities. Setting out from the same premises as Teddy Katz, and emerging from the same crucible, Morris gradually came to diametrically opposite conclusions from those of the apprentice historian of the Tantura Affair.

Like Katz, Morris came from Hashomer Hatzair, the Zionist youth movement furthest on the left. And like him, but twenty years earlier and with a much broader scope, he looked into the realities of the war of 1948. Ostracized in academia, he published his first book, *The Birth of the Palestinian Refugee Problem*, in the United States in 1987. As a positivist historian, he rejects the use of oral testimony, relying solely on written texts. Thus he worked with Hebrew and English archives (he does not know Arabic) and helped to bring many of them to light.

His groundbreaking conclusion was, in essence, that "half of the Palestinian refugees fled at the time; the other half were indeed forcibly driven out" by Israel.[5] Morris is careful not to characterize facts; he simply relates them. Thus, for example, although he emphasizes that there is no written evidence for the specific orders of expulsion issued by leaders of the *yishuv*, he gives a full account of orders given locally. For many years, in one book and article after another, he gradually challenged the entire Israeli narrative, mythological and fallacious, concerning the War of Independence.

Morris claims that he belongs to the Zionist left. Yet no one, or almost no one, listened to him back then. Reviled by many of his colleagues who skillfully purveyed the official account of a heroic and pure past, and marginalized in his own university, Morris, against his will, became the object of an attempted recuperation by post-Zionists, with whom he does not identify. He claimed to be simply a historian, one who makes a watertight separation between ideology on the one hand and, on the other, historical investigation, honest and devoid of ideological constraints.

Then came the failure at Camp David and the new intifada. With dizzying speed, like Amos Oz and the vast majority of supporters of the Peace Now movement, to which he belonged, Morris began to denounce the turpitude of the Palestinian Authority, which was said to have refused Israel's generosity and triggered violence. But whereas Oz and many members of Peace Now slowly returned to a critique of Israel's policy toward the Palestinians, Morris followed his path all the way to the end. Or rather, he followed the two parallel paths, historical and ideological, on which he had set out.

We are now going to trace this remarkable change. The first researcher in Israel to undertake the revelation of historical facts that were the most painful for the collective memory—and the most systematically concealed— Morris came out and called these events what they were, an ethnic cleansing, something he had always refused to do. Yet, under the influence of the ethnicism and profound Orientalism condemned by Haim Gerber, he also undertook to justify them and even to advocate their repetition.

In the course of an interview with Morris in the spring of 2002, I commented that the exact percentages of refugees who had been driven out by force in 1948 and those who fled out of panic were ultimately of little importance, that in wartime civilians are in any case civilians and always naturally flee before the advance of the enemy army, and that the key issue was that Israel opposed their return in the immediate postwar period. Morris lost his temper; he seemed to be shaken to the core. "You're absolutely right!" he replied with vehemence. "The crucial point has to do with the meetings of the Israeli government in the summer of 1948, when it was decided that the Palestinians would not be authorized to return to their homes after the battles. But I agree with those decisions, because I'm a Zionist."

Up to that time Morris's Zionist convictions had not interfered with his work. He would never have argued a cause, either denying or justifying a given fact. All that interested him, he used to say, were the facts and the establishment of the truth. Now, pursuing his remarks, he told me that today the Palestinians, "by their acts, warrant whatever might happen to them. If there's a regional war, and the Palestinians, including the Arabs of Israel, prevent the army from making war, the IDF will have to expel them. They'll have only themselves to blame."[6]

Five months later, in *The Guardian*, Morris (2002b) took a further step. After recalling that "the idea of the transfer [of populations] is as old as modern Zionism and has accompanied its evolution and praxis during the past century," and showing, with the support of citations, how Theodor Herzl, the founder of Zionism; David Ben Gurion, who headed Israel's first government; and Haim Weitzmann, its first president, spoke out in favor of the wholesale expulsion of the Arabs of Palestine, he concluded as follows: "One wonders what Ben Gurion—who probably could have engineered a comprehensive rather than a partial transfer in 1948, but refrained—would have made of all this were he now somehow resurrected. Perhaps he would now regret his restraint. Perhaps, had he gone the whole hog, today's Middle East would be a healthier, less violent place, with a Jewish state between the Jordan and the Mediterranean and a Palestinian Arab state in Transjordan."

Thus the man who was the first in his country to reveal the expulsion of the Palestinians, tirelessly combating the stubborn official denial of the facts, had come to regret that the father of the Jewish state hadn't gone all the way in 1948.

Morris was going to show what going all the way involved. In the winter of 2004, when his most recent book, *Righteous Victims*, came out in Hebrew, he gave a long interview to Ari Shavit of *Haaretz*. This is an incredible interview from a man crippled by contradictions and inner suffering, deeply pessimistic, nearly schizophrenic, whose naming of what the War of 1948 had been, along with the prominence of the Orientalist view of "the Arab," makes any nuanced judgment impossible and seems to justify in advance the worst crimes.

This interview is the first time Benny Morris calls the expulsion of the Palestinians in 1948 an "ethnic cleansing."[7] He explains that he came to this conclusion because he had access to "many documents that were not available" when he wrote his first book in 1987. In 1948, Morris now says, "there were far more Israeli acts of massacre than I had previously thought. To my surprise, there were also many cases of rape." He tells of his discovery of explicit orders given to units of Haganah, the Labor militia that would provide most of the future cadres of the IDF, "to uproot the villagers, expel them and destroy the villages themselves." In passing, he confirms Teddy Katz's thesis on Tantura: "War crimes were committed." In connection with the massacres in many villages during Operation Hiram in the Galilee in October 1948, he adds: "There was an unusually high concentration of executions of people against a wall or next to a well in an orderly fashion. That can't be chance. It's a pattern."

Morris shows, as a historian, how on several occasions the orders for expulsion followed the visit of the prime minister to the headquarters of the units that undertook them: "From April 1948 Ben Gurion is a transferist. . . . There is no explicit order of his in writing, but . . . the entire leadership understands that this is the idea. The officer corps understands what is required of them. Under Ben Gurion, a consensus of transfer is created."

Morris goes on to justify this deliberate policy of expulsion in ideological terms: "There is no justification for acts of rape. There is no justification for acts of massacres. Those are war crimes," he says.

> But in certain conditions, expulsion is not a war crime. I don't think that the expulsions of 1948 were war crimes. You can't make an omelet without breaking eggs. You have to dirty your hands. . . . A society that aims to kill you forces you to destroy it. When the choice is between destroying or being destroyed, it's better to destroy. . . . There are circumstances in history that justify ethnic cleansing. I know that this term is completely negative in the discourse of the 21st century, but when the choice is between ethnic cleansing and genocide—the annihilation of your people—I prefer ethnic cleansing. . . . That is what Zionism faced. It was necessary to cleanse the

hinterland and cleanse the border areas and cleanse the main roads. It was necessary to cleanse the villages from which our convoys and our settlements were fired on. . . . I know it doesn't sound nice, but that's the term they used at the time. I adopted it from all the 1948 documents in which I am immersed.

On the one hand, on the basis of his archival research Morris the historian was the first to expose the attempts at transfer made by the leaders of the *yishuv*. He likewise contributed to the restoration of the historical truth concerning the real risks run by the *yishuv* and the state of Israel in 1948. On the other hand, Morris the ideologue and Orientalist now develops the arguments, beginning with the risk of genocide in 1948, that he himself had helped to demystify. "I feel sympathy for the Palestinian people, which truly underwent a hard tragedy," he goes on to say. "But if the desire to establish a Jewish state here is legitimate, there was no other choice" than, to use his term, uproot the Palestinians. When the journalist asks, "And morally speaking you have no problem with that deed?" Morris replies, "That is correct. Even the great American democracy could not have been created without the annihilation of the Indians"—a claim that raises as much doubt about its historical validity as astonishment at the calmness with which it was made.

From here on in, the inversion of meaning becomes the rule, based on this leitmotiv repeated millions of times by Israelis of every stripe and every background, a kind of collective "close sesame" that shuts all doors, beginning with that of doubt: "No other choice." In Hebrew this is expressed in two words that sound like an identitarian slogan: *ein breira*. Then all the usual artillery of self-justification can be rolled out, beginning with relativizing the acts of one's own camp so as to narrow the scope of their consequences. "You have to put things in proportion," Morris argues in the Shavit interview. Once expulsion isn't a war crime, there remain the massacres, but they are of little importance, as if these massacres hadn't been intended precisely to hasten the mad flight of civilians: "These are small war crimes. . . . In comparison to the massacres that were perpetrated in Bosnia, that's peanuts," he says.

What is implied here is that, if there is no other choice, this is because the other is a monster, a barbarian, as were no doubt the Indians who had to be annihilated in order for the American democracy to exist. Morris then sets forth the most crude Orientalist ideas, ideas their proponents usually surround with an ethereal veil:

> There is a deep problem in Islam. It's a world whose values are different. A world in which human life doesn't have the same value as it does in the West, in which freedom, democracy, openness and creativity are alien. . . . Revenge plays a central role in the Arab tribal culture. Therefore, the people we are fighting and the society that sends them [to kill us] have no moral inhibitions. If [that society] obtains chemical or biological or atomic weapons, it will use them. If it is able, it will also commit genocide.

The rest of the interview shows that, when it comes to the absence of moral inhibitions, Morris is the very example of how one's own inclinations are attributed to the other.

> *Journalist*: A large part of the responsibility for the hatred of the Palestinians rests with us. After all, you yourself showed us that the Palestinians experienced a historical catastrophe.
>
> *Reply*: True. But when one has to deal with a serial killer it's not so important to discover why he became a serial killer. What's important is to imprison the murderer or to execute him. . . . The barbarians . . . want to take our lives. . . . At the moment [Palestinian] society is in the state of being a serial killer. It is a very sick society. It should be treated the way we treat individuals who are serial killers. . . . We have to try to heal the Palestinians. Maybe over the years the establishment of a Palestinian state will help in the healing process. But in the meantime, until the medicine is found, they have to be contained so that they will not succeed in murdering us.
>
> *Journalist*: To fence them in? To place them under closure?
>
> *Reply*: Something like a cage has to be built for them. I know that sounds terrible. It is really cruel. But there is no choice. There is a wild animal there that has to be locked up in one way or another.

At that point anything goes, including, Morris says, the clash of civilizations described by Samuel Huntington, a theory Morris supports in a much less nuanced way than the American scholar. "The Arab world as it is today is barbarian," he tells the interviewer. There follows a whiff of the talk of a Le Pen or a Jerry Falwell about the Muslim invasion of the West, in the face of which it must protect itself: The West today, Morris says outright, "resembles the Roman Empire of the fourth, fifth, and sixth centuries: The barbarians are attacking it and they may also destroy it." And, he continues,

> The phenomenon of the mass Muslim penetration into the West and their settlement there is creating a dangerous internal threat. . . . [The Romans] let the barbarians in and they toppled the empire from within. . . . The war between the civilizations is the main characteristic of the 21st century. . . . It's not only a matter of bin Laden. This is a struggle against a whole world that espouses different values. And we [Israelis] are on the front line. Exactly like the Crusaders, we are the vulnerable branch of Europe in this place.

What is most extraordinary about this Janus-faced Morris, historian and Orientalist at the same time, is that although the one face had earlier analyzed the blindness of the other, this analysis did not prevent him from lapsing into the second view at a later time. Just one of many examples that could be cited is the account in his most recent book, *Righteous Victims* (1999), about the reactions to the onset of the great Palestinian revolt in 1936:

> The outbreak of the revolt shocked the Yishuv, [who] had grown accustomed to relative quiet. The Zionist leaders' public attitude was summed up by Chaim Weitzmann: "On one side, the forces of destruction, the forces of the desert, have risen, and on the other stand firm the forces of civilization and building. It's the old war of the desert against civilization, but we will not be stopped." Rhetoric aside, however, the Jews realized that they were sitting on a volcano, that the Yishuv's growth could not but spark native resistance. "There is

no choice" (*ein breira*) surfaced like a fatalistic battle cry; the Yishuv would have to live by the sword . . .

[A]gain, the Jews made a conscious effort to minimize the importance of what was afoot; again, anti-Zionist outbreaks were designated "pogroms," a term that belittled the phenomenon, demonized the Arabs, and, in a peculiar way, comforted the Jews—it obviated the need to admit that what they faced was a rival national movement, rather than Arabic-speaking Cossacks and street ruffians. Commentators who ventured the term "revolt" took care to place it in quotation marks, signifying deprecation or doubt. And when they did acknowledge the existence of an Arab nationalist movement, they tried to delegitimize it by branding it immoral and terroristic. [pp. 135–136]

One is left speechless at the way Morris the historian is describing in advance his own current ideological approach, since the accuracy of his historical observation is the exact reverse of the conclusions he reaches today. The expression *ein breira*, "no choice," he had said in his earlier works, was indicative at the time of both a failure to understand the other and an attempt at self-persuasion. Morris now takes it up as his own view. Whereas before he had written that Weitzmann's vision, in 1936, of a conflict between civilization and the barbaric desert revealed blindness to Palestinian national reality, he later adopted this very notion.

Let us listen to him in the Shavit interview once again: "I don't see the suicide bombings as isolated acts. They express the deep will of the Palestinian people. That is what the majority of Palestinians want. They want what happened to the bus to happen to all of us."

This is where the logic of ethnicism ultimately leads: the opposing camp as a whole is dehumanized. What we are dealing with here, in short, is a kind of terrorist nation, criminal and monstrous, entirely swept up in what Morris calls a "cultural dementia." Israel, as an enlightened and generous democracy, might try to cure this madness, according to Morris, but the problem is so ingrained that he has no illusions about the chances for success. "Ideologically," he says in the interview, "I support the two-state solution. . . . But in practice, in this generation, a settlement of that kind will not hold water." Pending an unlikely future cure by Israeli medicine, what remains is to put the Palestinians "in a cage" and, if they continue to behave as a terrorist nation, to contemplate their definitive transfer outside the borders, beyond Jordan.

For, after reproaching Ben Gurion for hesitating, for leaving incomplete the job of expelling all the Palestinians from all of Palestine in 1948, Morris goes on to say that, if asked whether he is in favor of expelling the Arabs "from the West Bank, Gaza and perhaps even from Galilee, and the Triangle" (the two latter cases referring to Palestinians of Israeli nationality, whom Morris calls "a fifth column" and "a time bomb"), he would reply that this would be neither ethical nor realistic under present conditions. "But," he says, "I am ready to tell you that in other circumstances, apocalyptic ones, which are liable to be realized in five or ten years, I can see expulsions." If the existence of Israel is threatened, these would be justified. Things have come full circle. Yes, Morris says, Israel did indeed engage in ethnic cleansing fifty-seven years ago, and yes, it must be prepared for another one. *Ein breira*: there is no choice.

Benny Morris's intellectual approach seems inconsistent: the more progress he makes in uncovering the misfortune inflicted on the other nation and the denial of this misfortune — and it took him twenty years to finally arrive at the same conclusions as his Palestinian counterparts regarding a deliberate ethnic cleansing undertaken between 1947 and 1950 — the more he subscribes to the most aggressive arguments, justifying in advance the possible perpetration of new crimes. This evolution is the outcome of an internal conflict between his honesty as a historiographer and his adhesion to the values of ethnicism. Hence his conclusions: If the Palestinians' "healing" does not depend primarily on their ceasing to be an occupied people (which is not possible in this generation), a nation of refugees whose distress is denied, and second-class citizens in Israel, if their intrinsic barbarity is at the root of their entire society, a society in which individuals are identified only in terms of their belonging to their collectivity, then acknowledging the misfortune imposed on them or their right to self-determination will change nothing.

In the 1980s Morris and the Israeli historian and journalist Tom Segev published, one after the other, the first two books discussing Israel's responsibility in the expulsion of the Palestinians in 1948. Segev told me that his own "line in the sand would be a new expulsion. If Israel implemented that, I could no longer identify with this country."[8] Morris has now reached the point of justifying in advance the crossing of this line in the sand. Segev shares the ideas of the Peace Bloc, which sees the occupation as the infrastructure of terrorism, and those of Avraham Burg, for whom the Palestinian human bombs "shed blood in our restaurants to take away our appetite" because "in their homes their children and parents are suffering from hunger and humiliation."[9] Morris, on the other hand, agrees with Avigdor Lieberman, the far-right leader and author of a plan for the "cantonization" of the Palestinians, their imprisonment in controlled Bantustans. Meanwhile, he awaits his chance to support someone like Benny Elon, the rabbi and former minister who preaches the Palestinians' transfer.

Twenty years ago both Segev and Morris set out from identical premises. Their diametrically opposite evolutions follow the course of Israeli society, which, with the intifada, lost its traditional political center as three-quarters of Israeli Jews rallied under the banner of security at any cost, whence the success of Ariel Sharon, their most consistent representative. The other 25 percent became more and more vocal in their challenge to the impasse brought about by this approach and the repression inflicted on another nation. For the intensity of the questions now being leveled at this society, an intensity that explains the sudden resurgence of the repressed past, leaves little room for middle-of-the-road solutions.

According to *Haaretz*, the interview with Benny Morris led to a deluge of replies. Here are excerpts from two of them.[10]

"The initial impulse is to try to refute Prof. Morris, especially over the eradication, not to say the annihilation, of the hope for conciliation and true peace, today or in the foreseeable future, between the Israeli people and the Palestinian people—on top of which the impression is that he does this with the greatest joy," writes Benny Mizrahi, a reader from Ramat Gan, a large suburb of Tel Aviv, who is apparently a former supporter of peace with the Palestinians. "Afterward," he continues, the doubt begins to creep in. Maybe he is not exaggerating at all in his apocalyptic forecasts? Maybe he's simply right, and things will never be better here and peace is a pipedream? For me, at least, the interview, I am not ashamed to say, marks my personal watershed. It legitimizes earnest soul-searching that I have been engaged in for the past three years and more, relating to the fundamentals of my political beliefs and positions. These beliefs are now undergoing a serious shock, not to say a sharp change. Thanks to Prof. Morris, or rather because of him, I am finally succeeding in articulating my conclusions to myself.

Adam Keller of Holon, another large suburb of Tel Aviv, has the exact opposite reaction:

> The historian Benny Morris uncovered documents that reveal the reality of what happened in 1948 in all its ugliness and monstrousness. However, Benny Morris the person is unwilling and incapable of coping with the moral implications of what he discovered and revealed. Indeed, the State of Israel as it is today could not have arisen if Ben Gurion had not carried out large-scale ethnic cleansing. . . . By the way, I . . . doubt that the "American democracy" of our day is such a wonderful creation that it confers moral justification on the annihilation of the Indians, as Morris claims.
>
> That doesn't mean we have to dismantle Israel or the United States. Even a child born of rape has the right to go on living once he has come into the world. It does mean that the State of Israel should recognize the terrible injustice its establishment inflicted on the Palestinian people and compensate them, and certainly that it should refrain from inflicting further injustices, as we are doing day in and day out, and as Morris recommends that we go on doing more intensively.

These two letters reveal the dividing line separating Israel society into two camps that are growing further and further apart. Now that it can no longer go on denying the actuality, for both Israel and the Palestinians, of the founding events, the first camp tends to accept them "with no pangs of conscience."[11] Since this acceptance, like the denial that preceded it, is based on the fundamental ethnicist assumption of the other side's intrinsic barbarity, any conciliation, not to mention reconciliation, must be seen as unrealistic. The only choice is to finish the job, to strike harder and harder until these savages capitulate. If the caging of the Palestinians turns out to be insufficient to cure their "dementia," if these madmen persist in wanting to remove the bars of their cage in order to breathe freely, what will have to be done? Expel them once again, and this time all of them? And if a new expulsion should manage only to exacerbate their "dementia" and that of the entire Arab and Muslim world, then what? Exterminate them?

On the other side of the fault line, the break with ethnicism also leads to a wish to be done with the problem, starting with the ignorance of the past. As the Israeli Adam Keller says, today's Israelis are responsible, not for acts committed by their grandparents, but for acts committed now. And what matters in the present is to stop denying both past acts and the injustices of the present. Specifically, Keller says, understanding and accepting the acts of the past leads to putting an end to the military occupation of the West Bank and Gaza and to the laws of segregation within Israel.

SIX

TOM SEGEV VS. GIDEON LEVY
The "Immunization" of Israeli Students

WHAT A YOUNG PERSON IN ISRAEL CAN KNOW

"The people we call 'New Historians' are the investigators who are setting out to reestablish the true facts of our history," Tom Segev told me on May 2, 2002. "The term *new* is inappropriate," added the eminent *Haaretz* columnist, himself a historian:

> We should say "first historians," because in the past official Israeli historiography had reflected not the search for truth but the need to construct a satisfactory "national version." The need was twofold: to close ranks in the face of a hostile Arab environment and to build a consensual image that validated and justified the new state in which the emancipation of the Jews had culminated. It left no room for acknowledging the slightest misdeed. The New Historians were the first to conduct their research outside these ideological constraints, to write true history.
>
> But there is another reason why the term *New Historians* is inappropriate. Despite the official version of history, anyone who wanted to know that the reality of the past did not correspond to the authorized version could have done so before these historians published their works. Their great contribution is to have demonstrated, with the opening of certain archives, that the Israeli historical narrative

was inauthentic. Basically, however, they brought nothing new to the realm of knowledge. Anyone who wished to could have learned perfectly well that the Arabs had not left the country voluntarily, as was said when I was a child.

In response, Gideon Levy, another famous columnist for *Haaretz*, was up in arms. In an interview on July 10, 2003, he protested as follows:

We could know what? And how, if I may ask? How could I personally have learned anything beside what I was taught? I went to the best schools in Tel Aviv. When I went off to college all I knew was that the U.N. "voted for the creation of the state of Israel"; that the Arabs opposed this and made war on us; that, alone against six states with superior weapons, a tiny and heroic Israel won out after nearly disappearing. And that was that. The Palestinians? They didn't exist; all we heard about was "Arabs" in general. Afterwards they left at the behest of "Arab leaders," who, we were told, promised them they could return to their homes once the Jews were thrown into the sea. Nothing was ever said about the Arab reality of Palestine. Its inhabitants were totally concealed by the historical narrative. We didn't know how many of them there were. They appeared not as people who lived and worked, who had apartments, shops, and fields, but only in the form of "Arab bands," hostile to the Jews, against whom our parents had to fight. They "left voluntarily." Fine, good riddance, but we had no part in it and it wasn't our affair. It was the problem of the Arab countries who refused to take care of them because they themselves were very wicked. How in God's name could I have known, at age 20, that this whole view was either an outright lie or contained omissions? By what means could I have understood that this was a fairy tale? That our responsibilities were systematically shoved under the rug?

The conflicting arguments of Segev and Levy are in fact both well founded. In 1984, three years before Benny Morris's first book appeared, Segev had himself published 1949: *The First Israelis*, in which, without access to archives, he deconstructed large sections of official Israeli history. And a great many Israelis always knew, more or less consciously, that there were black holes in their history from which the gaze was to be averted. As we have seen, with very few exceptions the "Palmakh generation" kept silent about, or hid from its memory, the expulsion of the Palestinians, retaining only the victim position and the epic sweep of events. Yet, at this same time, there were signs of another version of the facts, one that removed the cloak of silence and invisibility covering the Palestinians in official historiography and restored their place in a tangible reality. Such signs were continuously put forth, in scattered bits and pieces, even by the highest government authorities, as well as in the press and in works of literature.

As early as 1961 Akiva Orr and Moshe Machover, two activists who broke with the Israeli Communist Party, published *Peace, Peace, When There Is No Peace* under the collective name of A. Israeli, the title taken from a biblical passage.[1] Relying almost exclusively on a careful reading of the Israeli press and official statements and communiqués at the time of the events in question and several years thereafter, and noting the sequence of changes in the versions presented, the authors succeeded in revealing or reevaluating numerous established facts hidden from collective memory, highlighting what was obvious. They found that gradually, after an initial phase in which the version presented was invariably self-justifying, there was an almost systematic emergence of bits of information that radically contradicted the first account of matters relating to the period 1948–1958, including the so-called flight of the Palestinians, though the logic of that account had nevertheless been imposed on people's awareness.

Thus, thirty-six years before detailed studies by Israeli authors like Simha Flapan (1987), Avi Schlaim (2000), Charles Enderlin (1997), and, more recently, Moti Golani (2002) showed the vacuity of the claim that Israel has never stopped desiring peace in the face of Arab hostility, Orr and Machover, simply on the basis of consulting official articles and statements, demonstrated how Israel had regularly closed the door to various possibilities for diplomatic progress with the Arab world.

Throughout the period from 1950 to 1970, long before the opening of archives enabling the New Historians to dismantle the main distortions of the approved historiography, it was therefore possible to pick up signal flares, few but powerful, illuminating the hidden aspects of the past. Thus, for example, addressing students at the Haifa Technion in the spring of 1969, Moshe Dayan told them straight out: "Villages were built in place of Arab villages. You don't even know the names of these Arab villages, and I don't blame you, because the geography books disappeared. And not only do these books no longer exist, but the Arab villages don't either. Nahalal rose on the site of Mahloul, Kibbutz Gvat on the site of Jibta, Kibbutz Sarid on the site of Huneifis, and Kfar Yehoshua on the site of Tel Al Shuman. There isn't a single place built in this country where, before, there wasn't an Arab population."[2] This idea had been only very rarely expressed up to that point; quite the contrary, the whole image constructed around Palestine had been that of an empty country.

Yet anyone living in Israel could have readily noticed that what is unspoken is seldom totally unknown. In 1968, in the kibbutz where I lived, my friend Michael, who was also French and had recently arrived, came back one evening in a state of shock. For some time he had been wondering what a fragment of tower was doing in the middle of the field where he worked. He had thought it might be a dried-up well, but the ruin seemed to be too high to have been the rim of a well. That day he had asked a kibbutznik who was working alongside him. "That's not a tower, it's a minaret," the latter replied abruptly. What was this minaret doing in a field? "It's all that's left of the mosque." But why the hell a mosque in the middle of a field? "You dumb or something? There wasn't just a mosque here, there was a whole village." All Michael could see in front of him were long furrows and irrigation hoses. What happened to the village? "It was razed, like all the other Arab villages around here. Boy, you sure are clueless!" Yes, Michael was clueless.

This anecdote says less about a young man who had idealistically come from France to live on a kibbutz than it says about his interlocutor. The latter was a sabra, a native Israeli, in his early thirties, a tireless worker who had been 12 or 13 in 1948. Too young to have taken part in the War of

Independence, but, like his entire generation, he had seen, heard, and understood. Not the event in its entirety, of course, but enough to know that an action had been undertaken to eradicate for all time every physical reminder of the existence of the Palestinians who had lived there. Or at least almost every such reminder, since for some unknown reason this fragment of a minaret had remained standing, an incongruous trace of a vanished town and the people who had lived in it, one of many vestiges that Israelis pass by without seeing them or wondering what they represent. How many Israelis, like this young sabra, didn't need the opening of the archives or the New Historians to know what had taken place?

But what was the nature of this knowledge then, and what is it now? It was and remains fully inserted in a complex system combining elements of concealment, repression (as in the case of Tikva Hoenig-Parnass mentioned above), and retroactive justification of the facts when outright denial is no longer feasible. Ever since the creation of Israel this system has been fostered by the state apparatus, which, through many channels—army, ministries, education, diplomacy, the media—has overseen the concealment or disguising of facts.

Yet this system is not the same as the machinery for announcing official truths in totalitarian states. Because the state and society of Jewish Israel are largely democratic, the system has lasted only because it adheres as closely as possible to the expectations of those at whom it is aimed, to their eagerness to see themselves as victims of aggression in all circumstances. Israeli writing, profuse as it is, has long concealed the basic facts of 1948 from younger generations. Hence Gideon Levy's argument is also perfectly well founded. In 1948 he hadn't been born. How could the Israelis, then and now, especially the young people, come by an honest acquaintance with the recent past of their own country?

As Amnon Raz-Krakotzkin, Professor of Jewish Studies at Beer Sheva, observes,[3] school textbooks are the most conclusive evidence for the authorized version of itself that a national community, especially one recently constituted, seeks to present of the underpinnings of its collective identity. I will not dwell on general history here, as it is taught in Israeli colleges and high schools. Carefully selected in accordance with ideological imperatives and devoting primary attention to the history of the Jews, it is neither better nor worse than in other modern nations of recent origin, and even older ones. Until very recently "the Gauls" were considered the ancestors of the French, and until the 1960s colonialism was still presented in a very favorable light in France. The Napoleonic period is still largely mythologized. And didn't forty years have to pass before the image of a unilaterally resisting French nation, imposed by De Gaulle and the Communists in 1945, began to crumble?

In Israel the educational credo emphasizes the internal history of the Jewish people, usually unconnected to the general history of the countries of the diaspora, in which, during two thousand years of exile, the Jews never stopped hoping for the reconstruction of an independent state. Two thousand years of a Jewish community always identical to itself, a time essentially consisting of an uninterrupted series of persecutions culminating with, on the one hand, the emergence of Zionism to put an end to them, and, on the other hand, the Shoah, which the Jews were unable to withstand precisely because they lacked such a state.[4]

As for the history of the country itself, the Land of Israel, Raz-Krakotzkin notes ironically that it passes "directly from the destruction of the Second Temple to the arrival of the first Zionist pioneers." What happened between the first and nineteenth centuries? Who lived there? In general, an Israeli pupil can know nothing about this other than that "Jews lived there through this entire time," a phrase endlessly repeated in textbooks and aimed at reinforcing the idea that exile never put an end to hope, nor, more important still, to the physical relation to the Land of Israel. For a young Israeli, for nearly two millennia this country had no existence beside the one inscribed in the imagination of the Jews of exile (*galut*), an imagined history that is widely taught, often through reconstructions intended to endorse the idea of the expectation, enduring through the ages, of redemption in a national form. It is not surprising that no textbook of Israeli history has ever published a map of the populations of Mandatory Palestine.

Yaakov Hazan, the noted Marxist-Zionist leader, is said to have advocated what was called the conquest of the Galilee in the 1930s by referring to the area as a place where there was nothing but stones, scorpions, and Bedouins. Perhaps not a land without people, as the Zionist slogan had it, but at least arid, abandoned by its occupants, Bedouins, in short by nomads. In reality there were some one hundred fifty villages in the Galilee, and several cities. In the daily life of the average Israeli, the people living there, people who were still living there fifty-eight years ago, are just as invisible in the history books as are their descendants, who still live there.

The Israeli government charged the historian Bentzion Dinour, who was named minister of education in 1951, with the task of codifying the teaching of history. Historians, Dinour said, do not describe the whole of history but just what they consider important, inevitably reflecting their subjective beliefs and the perspective of their time. The writing of history, this view makes clear, must serve the political interests of the present. Dinour originated the 1953 law requiring that the teaching of history in Israel must "instill patriotism and the desire to serve and preserve the nation."[5]

For over fifty years textbooks would transmit this same heroic vision, biased, invalid, and incomplete, of events preceding and following the establishment of the state, along with the image of an "Arab" with no real existence, let alone a national one, in the Land of Israel save in the form of a perpetual aggressor and his voluntary flight. This mythological representation[6] corresponded both to the consensus of the *yishuv* regarding its native interlocutor and to the directives issued by Ben Gurion.[7]

The Israeli scholar Eli Podeh (2003) has recently published a remarkable study of the sociohistorical narrative elaborated since the creation of the state, ranging over all domains: the general view of Islam and the Ottoman Empire, the relationship of the first Zionist settlers to the Arab environment, the presentation of the wars of 1948, 1956, and 1967, and the treatment of the issue of the Arab minority in Israel. He adduces many examples of the way in which cognitive dissonance with regard to the other is at work in Israeli educational circles, and the conditions under which some individuals and groups are described in a manner radically different from accounts of the reference group, becoming targets of the projection of negative traits, including those that the people expressing the projections fear in themselves.[8] This is the relation to the other handed down from one generation to the next as part of its values and beliefs, a process in which, as Podeh shows, textbooks and the accompanying reference works and maps are important vehicles.

Podeh shows the abiding influence of the vision of a congenitally retrograde Palestinian (and, more generally, an Arabo-Muslim) world in works
appearing between 1900 and 1990, parallel to the systematic glorification of
the *yishuv*, and later of Israel, as bearers of civilizing values. In this regard
the illustrations are often even more striking than the texts; the maps show
a deliberate wish to erase the traces of the Palestinian past, especially the
very recent past, while the pictures try to impose the Orientalist vision of a
uniquely backward Arab environment.

The most worrisome aspects concern the treatment of Islam, and not
just in books written for the network of religious schools. Thus a widely
available high-school text by Avivi and Perski, published in 1957, stresses
the fact that the Jews taught the Arabs monotheism, after which the latter, with their vivid imagination and impressionable nature, invented their
own monotheism on the basis of Jewish stories and legends with which
they were fascinated. In another book, the Jewish tribes of seventh-century
Arabia are described as upright, respectable, and brave, the Arab tribes
following Mohammed as wily and treacherous. "Mohammed invented
nothing," explained Yaakov Levi (1948, p. 39). Islam, Podeh shows, is
presented as an amorphous farrago put together from the great cultures
of the Jews, Persians, Greeks, and Romans, the Jewish contribution to
Islam being deemed especially important.

Such a view merely draws on arguments developed from the time of
the late nineteenth century under the influence of the colonial conquest
in Western Orientalist circles, especially in France, though the textbooks
in question do so in a way that places a higher value on Judaism. These
arguments tend to portray Muslim religion and culture as hybrid, limited
in scope, and inferior to the Judeo-Christian tradition. Nearly fifty years
before Bin Laden and the somewhat Islamophobic theories legitimized
nowadays by intellectuals in Washington and Paris, Islam was already
being described in these books as the religion of the sword, and its adherents, Podeh shows, as thieves and pillagers.

In short, what we have here is a culture of contempt quite similar, in
its racist logic, to what is being taught today about Jews and Christians
in so many madrasas throughout the Islamic world. Later on, textbooks
used in the public educational system of Israel were often shorn of the

most controversial passages concerning Islam. In contrast, instruction provided in Israeli religious networks, whether Ashkenazi or Sephardi, orthodox or affiliated with the National Religious Party, has salvaged them, strongly emphasizing the worst errors. The result is that generations of Israelis have been educated in a degrading vision of the Arab and Islam.

In September 1968 I left the kibbutz to study in Jerusalem. My dormitory was located in the working-class district of Katamonim, opposite a huge, empty stretch of land. Upon arriving, I saw a group of children in front of the portico of the building. Laughing and shouting, they were having a good time throwing pebbles at a small column of Palestinians crossing the wasteland, obviously workmen returning home after a day of labor. This was more a perverse game than a true act of aggression, since the pebbles did not reach the workmen, who were about 40 meters away. The children were about 12 or 13, no older. There were only four or five of them, as opposed to over twenty Palestinians, all adults. Yet faced with the amused shouts of the urchins—*rukh, rukh* ("run, run")—their sole reaction was to bend their backs and hurry their pace.

This was at the very beginning of the occupation. No wonder that, thirty-three years later, in the days following the death by Israeli gunfire of thirteen Israeli Palestinian protesters on October 1, 2000, several actual raids were carried out against the people of various Arab locales in Israel, with no intervention by the police.[9]

Eli Podeh shows that, in accordance with the Orientalist perception, the teaching of history based on the denial and concealment of facts was consciously seen in Israel as a national mission right from the beginning. Thus Michael Ziv, head of the high-school division of the Ministry of Education in the 1950s and author of many textbooks, wrote that schools must guide students to clearly adopt the precise attitude accepted by society, with the presentation of history geared to inculcating that society's values. His successor in the years 1958–1972, Naftali Tson, was even clearer on this score. Teachers, he indicated, must select facts demonstrating values of sacrifice and heroism on Israel's part.

From this perspective, Podeh notes, the Israeli educational system was similar to those in other developing countries that gained independence in the same period. Nor, one might add, was it different from the French system imposed on the peoples of the colonies. In Israel, however, above and beyond the overvaluation of what Israeli academicians like to call the national ethos, the rewriting of facts, in its much shorter time span, was much more important, as was the programmatic demonization of the other, in this case the Arab.

This tendency would be reinforced from time to time over the years and simultaneously counteracted by a slow erosion of the grand mythologies. The Labor politician Aharon Yadlin, vice minister of education in 1964, then minister in 1974, developed the theory of immunizing pupils against any challenge to the official version of Israeli–Arab relations. After the war of June 1967 the vaccination consisted in never presenting the Arabs' viewpoint except in the context of their wishing to destroy Israel, and in modifying the terms used in textbooks—for example speaking of "liberated," not "occupied," territories—and setting the historical right of the Jewish people over and against any dire inclination toward what he called a guilty conscience on the part of the student.

Podeh shows how, beginning in the 1970s, the passage of time slowly, though marginally, began to erode the historical accounts in Israeli textbooks. He also shows how the contradictions in the setting forth of facts first began to emerge in these years, including the presentation of the refugee question. Thus a 1978 work maintains that the Palestinians fled but also mentions that they were sometimes evacuated. Another, from 1988, notes that they were encouraged to flee. Then there came the first intifada, the Oslo Accords, and the writings of the New Historians—in this case not so much their books, since most were first published abroad in English, not in Hebrew—as their articles and interviews in a press that provided them with an important echo. Polemics began to appear, describing the reality of the nation's past and the mythologized narratives forged to accompany its first steps.

The result was the publication, between 1996 and 1999, of the first textbooks attempting to present a revised version, freed of its most crude mythologies, of the country's modern history. Of special importance were the two-volume history by Eli Barnavi and Eyal Naveh, and Eliezer Dumke's textbook, also in two volumes.[10] Neither of these works perpetuated the intentionally propagandistic inventions of the past, and they also differed from their predecessors insofar as they were less imbued with patriotic ideology and lacked the demeaning portrayals of Israel's Arab environment. And, particularly in the case of Barnavi and Naveh, for the first time the attempt was made to engage students in thinking about possibly revising images of the past while respecting the basic historical credo imposed since the 1950s. This applied especially to the military realities of the victory of 1948, where the fable of "little David" was abandoned.

This new vision of the past influenced the administrative structures of the state. For example, Podeh calls attention to a teachers' guide published in 1999, calling on instructors to show that, in contrast to the commonly accepted image of a vastly outnumbered Jewish community, the Jews of 1948 had a significant advantage over the Arabs, which explains their victory.

Without ever mentioning the data revealed by the New Historians, Barnavi and Naveh, in particular, presented the two official versions of the creation of the Palestinian problem: the Israeli version as it had always been taught and the contrasting version in which there was an expulsion based on a plan established in advance by the leaders of the Zionist movement. Though they admitted that in certain places the Palestinians did indeed face a local politics of forced expulsion, they strewed their textbook with terms that had been used for fifty years (the Arabs fled, left, abandoned their homes) and ultimately refused to come out in favor of either view, condemning them both as erroneous and concluding that the exile of the Palestinians was simply the result of the war. And the war in question had broken out only because the Arab camp, including the Palestinians, had rejected the partition of the country. Thus, as Amnon Raz-Krakotzkin observed in an interview on July 4, 2003, even though this new presentation, freed of the most undeniably propagandistic elements, was more respectful of certain facts, "in entirely disconnecting the creation of the refugee question from the very establishment of the state of Israel and the implications of that establishment, we are still dealing with the key idea of self-justification: the victim is ultimately responsible for his own misfortune."

THE VICISSITUDES OF AUTHORIZED
HISTORIOGRAPHY: *A Study of a Recent Textbook*

What are young Israelis being taught today? I learned in a large Tel Aviv bookstore that in 2003 the best-selling work was a book whose English title would be *The Age of Dread and Hope, 1870–1970* (Avieli-Tabibian et al. 2001). The chapter on the struggle for national independence (pp. 291–314), from which the following quotations are taken, discusses the period between the United Nations resolution on the partitioning of Palestine on November 29, 1947, to the cease-fire agreements with the Arabs in the summer of 1949. Less drastic than Barnavi and Naveh on the Palestinian question, this textbook is symptomatic both of a return to the official version and of the impossibility of going all the way back to that version.

Thus the book is more precise than its predecessors on the exact nature of the plan for partition, though without recalling the demographic constitution of the Jewish state envisioned by the plan. But there is still no return to the sources. The day after the U.N. vote, "the War of Independence began with gunshots aimed at travelers on a Jewish bus. . . . Six travelers were killed" (p. 298). This is the sentence introducing the section entitled "The Arabs Begin the War." In contrast, Morris (1999) writes that it is unclear "whether the ambushes were triggered by the U.N. resolution or by a desire to avenge an earlier LHI [Lehi] raid, which had left five Arabs dead" (p. 190). Where Morris emphasizes a civil war between two communities for control of the region, a war that, even before the adoption of the plan for partition, began with attacks, reprisals, and terrorist acts on both sides—"From the first," he writes, "the IZL [Irgun], the LHI [Lehi], and to a lesser degree the Haganah used terror attacks against civilian and militia centers" (p. 197)—the book for high-school seniors written by Ketziah Avieli-Tabibian and her colleagues sees only an Arab initiative against a *yishuv* attacked without warning.

This first phase of the war, she writes, "began at the instigation of the Arabs on November 30, 1947, and was characterized by acts of terror" (p. 299). A list of the most important Arab military and terrorist attacks is provided. Reading this book, a student would never get precise information about any attack or terrorist act perpetrated by the forces of the *yishuv* during this period. Thus the notion of the Arab refusal of the partition, with no other explanation of how the *yishuv* actually accepted the U.N. resolution, remains the key element of this narrative. And the idea of exclusively Arab aggression is reinforced by the fact that the only victims mentioned are Jews.

There follows an account of the strategy employed by the leaders of the *yishuv*, a strategy presented as solely defensive, in a "civil war" from which Palestinian civilians are singularly absent. The description is limited to "Arab attacks" on Jewish civilians and confrontations with "Arab bands," a generic term that, as in the old historiography, refers to the Palestinian militias of Abdelkader Al-Husseini and the Arab Army of Liberation of Fawzi Al-Kawoukji, as well as to the small groups of defenders of Palestinian villages, armed with rusty old guns, confronting the offensives of various armed Jewish militants. Since no numerical data are presented regarding the relative military strength of the two communities in this initial phase of the war, just as nothing is said of the Israeli conquests and the first forced displacements of the Palestinian population, the student reading this book must find it absolutely miraculous that, despite their all-out aggression, "the Arabs never managed, in this phase, to seize the smallest Jewish locality" (p. 300), in contrast to the multiple victories of the *yishuv* militia.

Whereas all serious investigators conclude that, as of December 15, 1947, that is, two weeks after the U.N. vote, Israel undertook what Morris (1999) calls a "switch to the offensive" (p. 197), Avieli-Tabibian maintains that, up to April 1948, one month before the creation of the state, "the initiative in the military struggle was in the hands of the Arabs" (p. 301). The initiative changed sides, she explains, with Operation Nakhshon, begun by the Haganah on April 15 in accordance with Plan Dalet, endorsed by the leadership of the *yishuv*.

We have seen what this plan really called for: the organized cleansing of the Palestinian populace both from the territory devolving to Israel in the partition and from the areas situated in the future Palestine and conquered by Israel before and after its creation. Avieli-Tabibian merely indicates the motive behind Plan Dalet: "To defend Jewish areas a territorial continuity between them had to be created," and the aims of the plan:

"the control of the [nascent] Hebrew state and the defense of its borders," with no clear definition of the territory or borders in question, whether those of the U.N. partition or those of the conquest. "The towns of Tiberias, Haifa, Jaffa, Safed, Bet Shean and Saint John of Acre were conquered. A lot of their Arab inhabitants fled," the author writes (p. 302), with no further explanation of how this flight was carried out.

"At the height of Operation Nakhshon there occurred a difficult event that left its imprint on the relations of the two peoples," she adds (p. 301). This is obviously the massacre at Deir Yassin. As in the old historiography, this textbook mentions no other massacre of civilians during this period, maintaining the fiction of Deir Yassin as an exception (see Chapter 2 of this book). The facts are acknowledged: "The inhabitants were killed; the number is not clear, between 100 and 254 people, and the attack created a difficult trauma for the Arabs and reinforced their flight" (p. 301). The word *massacre* does not appear, however—no doubt, according to Gideon Levy, because "in politically correct Israeli terminology, this word is reserved solely for Jewish victims."[11]

Many other examples of the systematically biased presentation of events could be cited. Thus, where other investigators who have studied the question are concerned to analyze the ambiguities in the policy of the British in the period preceding their departure and the creation of Israel—45 percent of Palestinians were expelled *before* the offensive of the Arab states, hence under the eyes of British troops—Avieli-Tabibian mentions London's attitude only when it is favorable to the Arab camp, in contradiction to historical evidence. The war with the Arab countries, which attacked Israel from the time of its creation, is related in the same vein, with the same striking absence of key elements, the same partial presentation of facts. Thus the account of the meeting between Golda Meir and King Abdallah of Transjordan on May 11, 1948, four days before the creation of the new country, is limited to the fact that it convinced the *yishuv* leadership of the imminent invasion of the Arab states. Nothing is said of the prior negotiations between the Hashemite monarchy and the *yishuv* leaders, negotiations known for a very long time by Palestinian authors and analyzed in detail by the Israeli historians Avi Schlaim (1988) and Simha Flapan (1987). These negotiations led to the collusion that barred the creation of an Arab Palestinian state, with Abdallah respecting his undertaking not to touch the territory initially granted to Israel during the battles.

The first phase of the war, properly speaking, in which Israel experienced real military difficulties—the Egyptians advanced to within 40 kilometers of Tel Aviv before being driven back, and Israel in turn invaded the Sinai—and its leaders envisioned the annihilation of the state, is overvalued, just as at the time the *yishuv* leadership overestimated the strength of the Arab forces. But the actual strength of those forces, which put them at a disadvantage relative to Israel, is totally ignored. On the contrary: "The [international] embargo hit the state of Israel hard," Avieli-Tabibian explains to the students (p. 308). According to Morris (1999), however, this embargo did a major disservice to the Arab cause with only a minimal effect on the *yishuv*.

The "Ten-Day Period," July 9–18, 1948, following the first truce imposed by the United Nations Security Council, was marked by conquests and massive expulsions from Palestinian villages and towns, especially Lydda (today called Lod) and Ramleh. The account of this period in Avieli-Tabibian's textbook is especially interesting. "The IDF conquered the cities of Lod and Ramleh, and their Arab inhabitants were expelled. Up to that time the Lod–Ramleh zone was an organizational area for the force commanded by Hassan Salameh, one of the Mufti's supporters" (p. 310). What 18-year-old student could understand why the author uses the term *expelled* here for the first time in black and white, a term banished from textbooks for so long? And why are Lod and Ramleh the only cases mentioned, whereas this was a general measure? Because today too much material has come to light, in Israel itself, about what really happened in these two cities that were cleansed of their inhabitants in a highly organized fashion (and after major atrocities; 250 people were slaughtered by the Palmakh in Lod), in an operation under the iron rule of General Ygal Allon and led by a certain Itzhak Rabin. This was the incident Rabin later described in his memoirs (written in Hebrew), before he complied with the government request to delete the passage from the English version.

The essential point remains that, in Israel, the ethnic cleansing carried out between 1947 and 1949 can still be erased or silenced, but certain pieces of evidence cannot be denied. At least with regard to Lod and Ramleh, it can no longer be claimed that their inhabitants fled. How to circumvent this contradiction? The admission of the facts will be supplemented by a brief phrase of contextualization supposedly enabling students to justify the expulsion or at least minimize its extent: it was at Lod and Ramleh, they are told, that the forces supporting the Mufti were concentrated. This is a way of identifying the population of these cities with Israel's worst enemy in the popular imagination. What does the textbook implicitly tell students? To be sure, the people of these cities, women, children, and old folks, were expelled by military force according to a preestablished plan, but they were allies of our worst enemies. You can't make an omelet without breaking eggs.

This tendency to "contextualize," with the aim of minimizing the negative aspects of Israeli behavior in the war, appears throughout the chapter in question. Mentioning the "assassination" by three members of the Lehi of Count Folke Bernadotte, the U.N. special envoy in the region, on September 17, 1948, the book immediately explains that Bernadotte "had raised the question of the return of the Arab refugees to their areas" and "had acted to prevent the arrival in Israel of draft-eligible young people"; "these projects had raised a hue and cry in Israeli public opinion and resulted in his assassination" (p. 311). Here too the crime is explicable, and, given the unworthy behavior and plans ascribed to him, the victim is to blame for his tragic fate.

With the mention of Lod and Ramleh the Palestinian population vanishes from the textbook's account, which is nothing but battles with heavy losses and military successes for the Israelis, reappearing only at the very end. The final paragraph deserves to be widely quoted:

> The result of the war was that around half of the Arabs living in the Mandatory Land of Israel, nearly 600,000 people, became refugees. For the most part their uprooting was a direct consequence of the war and not the fruit of a preestablished plan on the part of the Jews or the Arabs. The departure of the Arabs from the Land of Israel began shortly after November 29, 1947, the date of the U.N. partition. At first it was rich urban families who left. This weakened the

determination of those who stayed behind. With the increase in
military activities and the victories of the Haganah, later of the IDF,
the departure of the Arabs from cities and towns, motivated by fear
of the warring armies, gained momentum. There was no plan by the
leaders of the state and the army to expel the Arabs from the Jewish
state. In places where relations between Jews and Arabs were good,
explicit orders were given not to expel the inhabitants. This was done
in Abu Gosh and in Faradis, near Zikhron Yaakov, as well as in Acre
and Haifa. The expulsion of the inhabitants of Ramleh and Lod, however, was endorsed at the political level. Their leadership contributed to the panicked stampede of the Arabs. It had no clear policy
and gave no clear directive on how to behave. On account of the
military defeat and the refugee problem the Arabs call the war of 1948,
which we call the War of Independence, the *Naqba*, which means
"catastrophe." [pp. 313–314]

    This assessment calls for a semantic study, since each phrase and choice
of wording is full of contradictions, paradoxes, and ellipses as a result of
an attempt to settle, without referring to them, multiple debates between
the old history and the New Historians, and between Israeli and Palestinian arguments. Yet this is the assessment that is being presented today to
the future high-school graduates of Israel.

    What can a young reader make of it? If there was no wish or plan for
expulsion, why were explicit orders for non-expulsion issued in some
places? The upside-down presentation of reality is especially flagrant in
the cited case of Faradis. This village was located near the Israeli town of
Zikhron Yaakov, at the time inhabited by private Jewish farmers who
employed many peasants from Faradis. As happened elsewhere, they intervened with the authorities to spare the villagers so as not to lose all their
employees at once. Thus the example of Faradis illustrates exactly the
opposite of what is claimed: the non-expulsion of its inhabitants was not
due to a deliberate wish not to expel them, as the textbook says, but, on
the contrary, to a specific intervention aimed at sparing those Palestinians from the common fate. Moreover, with the exception of Faradis and
another village, Jisser el-Zarka, all the others in the surrounding area (in-

cluding Tantura) were cleansed and then razed. And what about Haifa, emptied of three-quarters of its Arab population after intensive bombing, given here as an example of non-expulsion? Why no reference to Majdal, today Ashkelon, whose population was entirely expelled to Gaza well *after* the cease-fire accords with Egypt?

Finally, and especially, in the sole case in which the term *expulsion* is used, the case of Lydda and Ramleh, we are told that "endorsement at the political level" was needed for it to proceed. How could it possibly have been otherwise? Why specify this? Did expulsions take place elsewhere without this endorsement and with no plan in place? How can an Israeli high-school senior, already imbued with years of patriotic and self-justifying teaching, understand that the expulsion of the Palestinian population in 1948 was accepted as implicit and that this is why it did not require any written plan and its implementation no special political endorsement. And in fact that in the case of Lydda and Ramleh the scope of the expulsion, over 70,000 people at one stroke, was so important that military leaders demanded an explicit (oral) agreement from David Ben Gurion before proceeding?

The insistence on speaking only of "the Mandatory Land of Israel" and never of "Palestine," which is what it was called at the time of the British Mandate, and only of "the Arabs living in Israel," never "the Palestinians," is a legacy of traditional Orientalist historiography, a way of continuing the 1948 denial of the other, a national entity in the same land. But why speak of the "nearly half" of the native population that became refugees and not the proportion that makes sense, that of the refugees from the territory that became Israel, namely the more than 80 percent of the Palestinians who would have been living there had the expulsion not taken place? These were the only "Arab refugees" in the war. As for the figure of 600,000, it comes from a British report written in 1949. Since that time reliable estimates for the period 1947–1950 have been placed at between 700,000 and 750,000. The textbook prefers to remain with the lowest estimate. Yet this is progress, since for many years the figure in Israeli textbooks was given as around 350,000 to 400,000.

These few lines, with their inconsistencies, are characteristic of the new Israeli narrative, and are symptomatic of the evolution of historiography, the impossibility of continuing to spread the propagandistic account of the past, and the attempt to keep the writing of history anchored in the consensual self-justification previously mentioned. Yes, we are told, the "departure" of the Palestinians did indeed begin before the war with the Arab countries, and yes, the term *refugees* did indeed cover their situation, contrary to the view maintained in Israel for such a long time. But no, there was no wish to expel them. Yes, young Israelis are told in a few words about the central notion, the *Naqba*, constituting the perceived reality of the other, but the victim's behavior remains the basic cause of his wretched lot. The Arab leadership had no clear policy and contributed to the stampede. As for the Palestinian elite, they were the first to leave, abandoning their compatriots to their fate.

If a new exodus of the Palestinians were to occur tomorrow, desired and instigated by the Israeli authorities, something that can be imagined only under exceptional conditions of warfare, and if, the day after that, Israel forbade any possible return for these new refugees and seized their property and possessions, would Israeli history books later explain that, when the intifada broke, out many middle-class families in Ramallah and Gaza sent their children to study in Amman and Cairo though they themselves did not leave, giving the storm time to pass and thereby weakening the determination of those remaining behind? And that the deplorable policies of Yasser Arafat, of whom the least that can be said is that he, too, issued no clear orders to his people in the recent intifada, had contributed to their new misfortune? From the factual point of view, this would be correct. Yet, as in the explanation provided by Israeli textbooks for the Palestinian exodus of 1948, it would be deeply perverse if these correct facts were presented only to deny any Israeli initiative in this new expulsion and to establish a kind of shared responsibility in its advent.

In Israel today Avieli-Tabibian's textbook is considered the most progressive account of the Palestinian expulsion. We must also note that 58.6 percent of Israeli students do not complete high school, and that in any case fewer than 60 percent of young people attend public schools.[12] The other 40 percent attend various religious institutions, where they are subjected to a presentation of facts essentially based on the divine allocation of the Land of Israel to the Jews and revolving around the demonization of the Arab (see Chapter 13). Moreover, this textbook was not recommended in all public high schools and did not stand in good repute in the Ministry of Education, whose minister, Limor Livnat of the Likud Party, declared when she took office that, in contrast to her Labor predecessors, she accorded "the highest importance to Zionist, Jewish, and national education in the educational curriculum" and would not include "the post-Zionist works of the New Historians" among the textbooks accepted.[13] "I'd like students to study the Bible in every school, including the Book of Joshua," said Ariel Sharon at the same time.[14] The Book of Joshua, with its account of conquest, is the part of the Hebrew Bible that Israeli nationalists, religious or not, like best. "Students should not be taught the New Historians," the prime minister went on to say, "but Zionist Jewish values."

To tell the truth, Sharon's worry was misplaced. All Israeli students study the Hebrew Bible in public school for several hours a week, from the elementary grades through high school (knowledge of the Bible is tested in the high-school exit examination). As for Avi Schlaim, Ilan Pappe, and the like, none of their works has ever been reproduced in any Israeli textbook. But even Barnavi, Naveh, and Avieli-Tabibian, in their attempts to set forth a past free of the crudest mythological dross, are considered too risky by those who fear that any challenge to the image of the eternal victim of aggression, spotless in his purity, will inevitably lead to moral collapse. Such people reveal what is behind the risk that terrifies them, for anyone reading Barnavi and Naveh or Avieli-Tabibian closely might well note certain inconsistencies, ask questions, and, who knows, go on to read the New Historians, and from there go on to observe that their works are much more serious and logical that the sugar-coated and attenuated versions of official history, and that they therefore confirm much of what the Palestinians have kept on repeating for fifty-seven years.

THE IMPOSSIBILITY OF RETURNING
TO THE FORMER HISTORIC ORDER

In the end, this attempt to return to the former historic order, to the initial denial, is futile and even unrealistic. There is every chance that, with time, Israeli historiography will depart further and further from the accepted version — which is no longer taken seriously by anyone on the international academic level — and approach historical facts with less passion and more concern for the truth. Just as history textbooks in France can no longer discuss the former colonial empire in the same way as those written in the 1950s, which were marked by an effort to promote the benefits of colonialism for the native populations, so Israeli textbooks, if they are not to seem ridiculous, will be unable to return to the truncated history in effect until recently. In this way they will be part of the emancipation of a constantly growing minority of young Israeli scholars who, in the areas of Jewish and Israeli history; Middle Eastern, Islamic, and Arabic studies; sociology and anthropology, are throwing off the ideological shackles of the past, even though, at the same time, most of the Israeli university world has been caught up in the regression affecting the entire society after the beginning of the second intifada.

As for the divergence of views between Segev and Levy, it remains the case that the fundamental Israeli codex, the self-justifying historical narrative accompanied by the ethnicist view of the Palestinian other, centered on making the despoiler a victim, has deeply marked generations of Israelis and is still firmly in place despite the many flaws that have increasingly come to light. This global perception makes it harder to break free of fabrications, denials, and the fear of what introspection might entail. It also sets boundaries to debate in Israel and to the effort required for any deviation from the consensus. As we have seen in the case of the Tantura Affair, one of the major pressures put on Teddy Katz by those around him was the argument that, given the renewal of Arab attacks on Israel, this was not the right moment to reveal the facts he had discovered, even if those facts were proven. Finally, this perception limits the access to knowledge and the will to acquire it.

How many Israelis know exactly what became of the property and possessions of the "absent" Palestinians? How many know that, when Israel was established, the Jewish National Fund owned no more than 7 percent of the land of the Jewish state and 13 percent of the urban area, but, following the Palestinians' "departure," it owned 89 percent of the total? This concealment, intentional or not, conscious or half conscious, of the essential questions about the past continues to exert its effect on the way people behave today.

In the Palestinian territories, colonization has been going on, in successive and irregular waves, for thirty-nine years. According to the nongovernmental organization B'Tselem, the state of Israel has used various quasi-legal dodges to gain possession of 46 percent of the West Bank. Before the Israeli withdrawal, the IDF and the five thousand settlers in Gaza owned 30 percent of this thin strip of territory into which over a million souls are crowded.[15]

How did this territorial transfer occur? Who and what was on this land before? The settlers living in the occupied territories are given parcels of land (generally the best and best irrigated), and the so-called "municipal territories" of the settlements can be ten times larger than their actual physical boundaries. What happened to the previous occupants? Did they give up their land voluntarily? All these questions, which very few Israelis ask themselves, refer not to a remote past but to current daily life. Yet everyone knows that Gaza and the West Bank were not exactly deserts before the Israeli occupation.

The result was that when, at the onset of the intifada, Palestinian snipers lying in wait in the village of Beit Jalah opened fire on Gilo, a nearby district built in the 1980s in the annexed eastern part of Jerusalem, its inhabitants, and the vast majority of Israelis, were outraged. Because an inhabited area was being fired on, obviously, but even more because the Palestinians were attacking a district in Jerusalem, their capital, and the very existence of the country was felt to be at stake. Most of the people living in Gilo had never known a Jerusalem other than the city said to have been "reunified" in 1967. Like 99.5 percent of Israelis, they know nothing about the means undertaken by the Ministries of Infrastructure, Housing, and Defense to promote settlement and develop "Greater Jerusalem," basically by confiscation. The plans and means of implementation for these undertakings are often unspoken or wrapped in a thick fog. And that is fine, since most people prefer not to know about them.

Almost no one saw the connection between the name Gilo and the name of the village across the way from which they were being fired on. But Gilo in Hebrew has the same root as Jalah in Arabic. Gilo had been built on land belonging to inhabitants of Beit Jalah (and the neighboring town of Beit Hanina), land confiscated by force. It was not by chance that, at the beginning of the intifada, Palestinian snipers fired on the Israelis in Gilo, though few of the latter were able to understand why.

In all recent negotiations between the Palestinians and Israel, formal or informal, at Camp David, or Taba, or in the Geneva Pact of October 2003, the Palestinian representatives never asked for the return of Gilo, accepting the principle that Israel would keep the Jewish districts built in East Jerusalem since 1967. In six generations an Israeli society has been created, with its own constituents. No one imagines that it could give up overnight the attitude of *tzadkanut*, the permanent self-justification in which it is steeped. But this society will not enter into peaceful—and hence egalitarian and respectful—relations with its neighbors unless it begins a process of disengagement from its colonialist and ethnicist tropisms in which a new, common narrative is forged, one that takes into account not only the events of 1948 but also the way in which the inhabitants of Beit Jalah and so many other Palestinians since 1967 have been dispossessed.

This long and painful process can't get underway unless it is at least partially free of the delegitimization of Israel's existence systematically advocated by some Palestinians, and also, paradoxically, by some Israelis who promote the denial of the facts. Interviewed in 1998, Shabtai Teveth, a prolific Israeli historian who specializes in the modern period and has writ-ten biographies of David Ben Gurion and Moshe Dayan, expressed the opinion that the arguments of the New Historians, especially the notion that Israel was, as it were, born in sin, challenge the very legitimacy of the state and of Zionism itself. If Israel was born in sin and has perpetrated injustices against others, he concludes, then it has no right to exist.[16]

Teveth's inverted logic sums up what is involved in denial: since Israel is legitimate, it can only be pure; it can't have committed injustices and crimes. For if it had done so this would make it impure and hence ille-gitimate. According to this closed logic any state, any society, any human community can be deemed legitimate only if its birth and development have been spotless.

Here we are at the very heart of ethnicist thinking. Let us imagine for a moment that Teveth is facing a Palestinian who is making the same argument: "Since the Palestinian national movement is legitimate, all the acts and conditions of its emergence can only be immaculate, and any Palestinian who, for example, calls suicide attacks a crime thereby delegitimizes the right of the Palestinians to a state." Addressed to the face in the mirror, this logic leads to the conclusion that one is legitimately Palestinian only if one denies that terrorism is in any way criminal.

To escape these confining arguments that focus on the defects of the other and completely ignore one's own, self-justifying arguments that whitewash facts and demonize the opposite side, Ruth Firer, an educational psychologist and head of the Education for Peace Project at the Truman Institute of Hebrew University, has spent years delineating their underlying assumptions, often in collaboration with Professor Sami Adwan, a Palestinian who is an Israeli citizen.[17] For the need to repudiate denial with regard both to the other and to oneself is equally important on the Palestinian side.

SEVEN

AN "ARTIFICIAL STATE"
Internal Palestinian Obstacles to Understanding the Israelis

THE PALESTINIAN RELATIONSHIP
TO THE ISRAELIS

*A*rtificial: this term, even more than *colonial*, is often found in the political discourse of the Palestinians from the 1920s on. Israel is said to be an artificial state, and Israeli Jewish society is artificial as well. In a boomerang effect, just as Palestine and the Palestinians were ignored, made invisible, by the Jewish *yishuv* and then found themselves denied an identity in 1948, "erased, nameless, as though they didn't exist and had never existed," says the Palestinian historian Elias Sanbar,[1] Israel and the Israelis would also be deprived of their reality. "For a very long time we have used in our jargon terms like *the Zionist entity* and *the artificial state*," observes Eyad El-Sarraj, a psychiatrist in Gaza.[2] "Anything to avoid uttering the name *Israel*. This is because we couldn't accept that the Jews' right to return was carried out at our expense. But also because we didn't perceive the enemy's real nature."

The notion of Israeli artificiality goes back to the first settlements by Jewish pioneers. Coming from Central Europe, speaking Yiddish or beginning to express themselves in a totally new language, modern Hebrew, they seemed utterly foreign to the native inhabitants. And threatening as well, because the newcomers intended to appropriate their land. These strangers had no ties to Middle-Eastern Arab culture or to local customs, and they intentionally kept themselves apart. They were very different from the small Jewish communities that had lived among the Palestinians in Jerusalem, Safed, Tiberias, and Hebron for centuries, speaking and dealing with them in Arabic. With their growing numbers in Ottoman, then British, Palestine, these new Jews emerged as an organized force with their own institutions and national claims.

It was at this point that the notion of the artificiality of Zionism and Israel began to constitute a major handicap for the Palestinian national movement. For, as the decades passed and an intrinsically Israeli society took form, the theme of its artificiality proved increasingly invalid, and maintaining its central role in the Palestinian intellectual and cultural apparatus led its advocates from one failure to another.

The notion had a twofold basis: the general view of the Jew and Judaism according to religious parameters, and the characterization of Zionism as colonial. The issue of the importance of Zionism's colonial propensities had been raised earlier. But, for a great many Palestinians, if Zionism was nothing more than a form of colonial domination, this was precisely because the Jews were identified solely in terms of religion and could not constitute a nation. The problem lay in discerning the contradictory elements in Zionism and Israel: the Jews as both a religion and a nation; both the aspiration to national emancipation and the ethnicist tendency; both the construction of a nation-state and colonialism, but a colonialism that differed in its aspirations from other forms of that practice; both secularism and the mythological biblical foundations; and so forth. It was also a problem related to the Palestinians' own difficulty in constituting themselves as a national movement, one that, if not comparable to national movements in the modern West, was at least distinct from the Arab national movement as a whole.

The Palestinians' inability to perceive the complex identity of their adversary was clearly exacerbated by the setbacks they were dealt by that foe. During a long initial phase of Palestinian history, as the Palestinians went from one defeat to another, one illegitimate despoilment to another, they found it increasingly difficult to understand what lay behind these events. Any number of extremely incomplete, inept, and racist characterizations of Zionism can be found in Palestinian textbooks, as Israeli organizations, often highly ethnicist themselves, have pointed out.

As in the study of Israeli textbooks, in analyzing the serious defects of the Palestinian viewpoint it is most interesting to examine one of the most detailed and open recent attempts at a mutual understanding of the other, *Learning Each Other's Historical Narrative* (Bar-On and Adwan, 2003). This is a textbook conjointly written in 2003 by twelve teachers, six Palestinians and six Israelis, each group presenting its historiographic viewpoint to students on each side. It is the most advanced project in terms of taking the other camp's narrative and identity into account.

The Israeli group of teachers takes up the arguments set forth in Ketziah Avieli-Tabibian's book (discussed in Chapter 6), though it modifies them in the direction of greater honesty. Thus the authors acknowledge that in 1948 "there were a number of massacres, robberies and rapes by Jewish fighters" (p. 26), and that the Israeli forces carried out intentional expulsions of Palestinians ("During the course of Plan Daled, Hagana forces began to deport Arabs" [p. 25]), but without presenting this fact as a fundamental aspect of the war. As for the Palestinian authors, their presentation of the origins of Zionism includes the fact that "Eastern European Jews, particularly those living in Czarist Russia, whose living conditions were poor in any case, suffered cruel persecution" (p. 2). But, they immediately add, "Zionism appeared as a drastic international solution to the Jewish problem, transforming the Jewish religion into a nationalistic attachment to a special Jewish state" (p. 2). Here we have the idea that Jewish national identity is an artifice, a mutation, the illegitimate by-product of the only permissible Jewish identity, namely religion. According to these Palestinian historians, Zionism is the root of this artificiality, its architect, whereas it was in fact one of the manifestations of the progressive constitution of a national identity, emerging among the Jews at the same time as similar movements among other peoples of Eastern Europe.

The second major weakness of the Palestinian narrative lies in the account of the other side's colonialism. "British imperialism, it is claimed, found in Zionism a perfect tool for attaining its own interests in the Arab East. . . . Likewise, Zionism used British colonialist aspirations to gain international backing and economic resources for its project of establishing a Jewish national home in Palestine" (p. 2). This view is true in part, and the Israeli authors of this textbook also mention it.[3] But to the extent that it is the only view of Zionism that is presented, it fails to understand what was really at stake for the Jewish *yishuv* of Palestine. The reduction of the *yishuv* by the Palestinian teachers to a single role, that of an armed branch of British colonialism, reaches the point of absurdity when they write that "first and foremost, Britain bears responsibility for the defeat of the Palestinian people in 1948" (p. 21). After Britain," they add, "the Arabs and their leaders had the lion's share of responsibility for the defeat" (p. 22). It follows from these arguments that, if the *yishuv* was merely an extension of the British Empire, a colonial formation whose mother city was London, if it existed solely by virtue of what the authors call its constitutive union with Great Britain, if, in short, it had no autonomy, it cannot be considered the prime mover in the catastrophe!

The difficulty the Palestinians have had in dealing with the constitution of an Israeli Jewish society, the time lost by their leaders, generation after generation, in letting history roll over them instead of mastering it, stems from the difficulty they have in breaking with blind generalizations, namely that the Jews are only a religion, and that Zionism has no reality of its own outside the colonial context. These generalizations explain the evolving changes of position in the Palestinian national movement. First, the idea of a mass return to their countries of origin of the Jews who had moved to Palestine; then, beginning in the 1960s, the idea of the return of the Jews who had emigrated there, with the possibility that those who had been born there could remain and live in a future Arab Palestine; and then, in the 1970s, the idea of a secular, democratic Palestine in which Muslims, Christians, and Jews (that is, members of different *religions*) would live together—until 1988 and the de facto recognition of the state of Israel, forty years after the *Naqba*.

Neither the Zionist movement nor the state of Israel is a mere channel of imperialism, as Palestinian nationalism has held for so long. On the contrary, it is because they are not, because from the outset their ambitions were internal, demarcated from the direct interests of the dominant power in the Middle East, that they have known how to navigate politically in their relations with this power as circumstances dictated, generally in association with it, sometimes in conflict, but always with a view to preserving their own interest, a national interest. It is for this same reason that two divergent tendencies existed side by side within the Zionist movement for a long time. A majority was in favor of maintaining a privileged tie to the dominant British power in an ongoing relationship of both hostility and association, benefiting from British support as much as possible, pushing their luck if need be but systematically avoiding a rupture. Another group, with ultranationalist leanings, was willing to confront the imperialist godfather directly if necessary. It was not Arab nationalists but very young members of the Stern Group ("[Lehi] terrorists," writes Benny Morris [1999, p. 171]) who, on November 6, 1944, when the World War was still going on, murdered Lord Moyne, the British resident minister in Cairo, His Majesty's most eminent representative in the Middle East.

If the Zionist movement was nothing more than an offshoot of British colonial policy, what would explain the fact that its adherents were able to build a completely new society, different from the Jewish communities in their European cities of origin? Or the fact that they took a dead language used for religion, made it a contemporary[4] language, and brought it into everyday life with an astounding rapidity unique in modern times? What would explain the brilliant political intuition of its leader, David Ben Gurion, who understood that the British presence in the Middle East would be reduced to shreds by the Second World War and that the United States would emerge not only as the primary power on the international stage but also as the dominant power in his region? What would explain the fact that, from 1942 on, he bent all the efforts of his movement toward a closer relationship with Washington and easily managed to persuade a vast majority of his people to follow him, if this movement had no existence of its own beyond its alleged union with London?

Though they serve as the reference points of Palestinian historiography, the emergence of Israel is not in fact comparable to the classic colonial movement of transfering populations from a mother city. Such a transfer was in its past, but if we want to look for a closer resemblance the Israeli society arising from the war of 1948 is much more like what a Boer society in South Africa would have been like had it managed to free itself from its colonial patron, as it had attempted to do early in the twentieth century, and to create an apartheid society separate from its African environment. In the case of the Israelis, the powerful aspiration to national emancipation and the immediate memory of the Shoah brought them together in a solidarity of a very distinctively national character. But once the Jewish community in Palestine transferred its allegiance from the United Kingdom to the United States, Palestinian nationalism simply followed suit and transferred its former concept toward this new imperialism without making any changes in its view. It thus continued to be in error with regard to the nature of Israeli society.

"Right up to the present time, even in intellectual circles, many Palestinians see Israel as a colonial, artificial state," notes Nazmi El-Jubeh, professor of Byzantine History at Al-Quds University in East Jerusalem, former activist in the Democratic Front for the Liberation of Palestine, and codirector of the Riwaq Center for the architectural preservation of the Arab city in Jerusalem. Such a state, he says,

> runs counter to the direction of history and will be swept away by it. This approach ignores the actual existence of an Israeli society with its own logic of development, a society that has been rooted here for a long time now. Israel isn't an artificial state, an emanation of a distant metropolis. The vast majority of Israelis are the product of its history, not of immigration. Many of our intellectuals still prefer to believe that this is an artificial society. That's simpler; it enables them to avoid facing the Israeli reality. It also guarantees that a strategy based on this idea is doomed to certain failure.[5]

The national character of Israeli Jewish society is accepted by an Israeli Palestinian citizen like the philosopher and deputy Azmi Bishara, promoter of a binationality that would put Israel's Arab and Jewish citizens on an equal footing. But denial of this national character serves as an inverted mirror of the Israel Orientalist belief in the nonexistence of a Palestinian people and the illegitimacy of its nationalism. Like the other denial, it is accompanied by the certainty that there will be a long, insoluble conflict if the other is not eradicated. In Palestinians and Israelis alike it reinforces the ideological tendency to take a long-term view of history, on the one hand with the cult of origins and roots, and on the other the vision of a better, but very distant, tomorrow among the ultranationalists and the religious, and especially among those who are both: Israelis who worship the Land of Israel, and Palestinian Islamists.

What of the war? "It was and remains the role of my generation. And it will also be the role of generations to come. Time is not against us," said Ariel Sharon in 2001.[6] The conquest of the land to the detriment of the local usurpers is a divine mission, add the religious nationalists who share Sharon's warlike position and his long-term view. Ezzedine Khatib (a pseudonym), a student leader of Hamas in Gaza, echoes this sentiment: "Zionism is a component of an imperialist project. Like all forms of colonialism, it will ultimately disappear. Freeing Palestine through armed struggle will be very hard, but reaching a just peace through negotiation is sheer utopia. So we have to hold out, again and again. Time is on our side. Whatever they do, we're not going away."[7]

THE NAQBA: *A Catastrophe, but Not a Defeat?*

"I was taking part in a debate on the Al-Jazeera network," recalls Nazmi El-Jubeh. "We were discussing the war of June 1967, and I used the word *hazima*, which means "defeat" in Arabic. My interlocutors shot murderous glances at me. This word is taboo in the Arab world. Nineteen sixty-seven was not a defeat," he continued:

> It is said to be a *naksa*, which means "accident," or rather "minor accident." The battle was lost, but this wasn't serious. Why is it necessary to exclude the word *hazima*? Because it suggests capitulation. But as long as there is the least bit of ability to resist, we aren't defeated. This is a set formula, an evasion. When we refuse to call reality what it is, when we sugar-coat it, we can't confront it and hence overcome it, nor can we change our strategy. We remain within the fiction. This is, unfortunately, a very strong cultural tendency among us Palestinians.[8]

When Nasser resigned following the military debacle of 1967, El-Jubeh continued in the same interview, "the Egyptian and Arab masses refused to let him step down. Why? Because this was just an episode. Honor was safe: Nasser remained a hero who had made a glorious attempt to fight Israel. The war wasn't over. There was no need to draw up a balance sheet."

Yet Nasser had led his people, and the entire Arab world along with them, into their most serious defeat since the end of colonization. And he had done so because he had let language erase reality. The Palestinian writer Tawfik Abu Bakr recalls the boasting on Egyptian radios before the hostilities: the Israelis were "cowards who would take flight as soon as they came face to face with our heroic lions."[9] Carried away by the magic of language, Nasser offered Israel every pretext to launch an offensive and justify it in the eyes of the international community (with the exception of De Gaulle), especially thanks to the mad diatribes of his accomplice, the PLO leader Ahmed Shukeiry ("It will be us or Israel. There will be hardly any Jewish survivors in Palestine"[10]).

Submission to the magic of language continued during the war, as in this surrealistic dialogue between Nasser and King Hussein of Jordan on the first day of the conflict. When his air force was destroyed and his troops overwhelmed, Nasser was reassuring: "The battles are continuing. Do you think we could say that the United States is attacking with Israel?" Hussein suggested adding Great Britain to the list of alleged attackers. "Good," Nasser replied. "We had some problems at first but it's nothing. Allah is with us. I'm going to issue a communiqué, and you should too" (quoted in Hazan 1989, p. 31).

No sooner said than done. The next morning the following announcement was made on Radio Cairo: "We have evidence that several English and American aircraft carriers are conducting large-scale operations on the Israeli coast." Four days later the IDF, with no support whatsoever and like a knife cutting through butter, had tripled the territory under its control, achieving what had been beyond its reach in 1948: the occupation of the entire Land of Israel, all of Mandatory Palestine.

This tendency to manufacture appearances so as to ward off reality, to get drunk, to transform a terrible defeat into a temporary accident, has serious implications for Arab societies. "It is always dangerous to apply general concepts to groups unilaterally," says the Princeton anthropologist Abdallah Hammoudi. "But Arab societies are indeed often societies in denial. This is also a form of sociability, for defending honor. But certain forms of this denial are very powerful: to deny defeat is also to deny one's possible role in it. It is a form of over-negation, a way of saying "no, no no," a closure that fosters illusion and a contrived approach to the facts."[11]

This emphatic negation has had enormous repercussions when it comes to the Palestinians and their tragedy. They, and the entire Arab world after them, call the war of 1948 and the expulsion from their land the *Naqba*, the catastrophe, the disaster. And yet, notes Elias Sanbar, "the first Palestinian historians clearly used the term *hazima*, defeat."[12] But this term gradually disappeared. All that remained, in popular awareness and in the writings of commentators, was "disaster."

"A *naqba* isn't a defeat," El-Jubeh observes. "This word is used for the abrupt disappearance of a close friend or relative or for a natural disaster. It's an event you have no control over. We don't ask the inhabitants of Pompeii what role they played in the eruption of Vesuvius. Our expulsion in 1948 was certainly a catastrophe. But it was also a terrible defeat. In objecting to this word, excluding it from collective awareness, we too are falling into the terrible denial of reality that affects the Arab world."

"The exclusive reference to the *Naqba*," he goes on to say, "poses three problems. If all that happened is that we experienced a natural calamity, we don't have to assess our errors. If Israel is a kind of intangible natural element, we Palestinians can do nothing to make any changes. Finally, when we don't acknowledge a past defeat, we don't enable ourselves to build a victory in the present."[13] Behind the transformation of the word *naqba* into an exclusive icon, he concludes, lies the idea of a return to the past, a reconstruction of exactly what things were like before the cataclysm — an unreal perspective.

The reasons for the Palestinian defeat in 1948 are clear. The Palestinians had no chance whatsoever of avoiding a military debacle. They were confronted by a unique alliance between the Soviet Union and the United States, the two superpowers at the time that, when the cold war between them began, supported the partitioning of Palestine, and by an Israeli opponent who quickly became much better armed. They were abandoned by the Arab states, whose aid came in dribs and drabs. And they themselves had barely emerged from the terrible colonial crushing of their revolt in 1936–1939 and were highly disorganized. Their national leadership had been not only discredited but decapitated. Their society, unified along clearly nationalistic lines, was left drained and dislocated, and its powerful particularist, regionalist, and feudal tendencies were able to prevail. That national uprising had begun with a general strike in mid-April 1936, after a series of bloody clashes between communities. The feudal Palestinian leaders who were in contact with the British occupier, beginning with the grand mufti of Jerusalem, were overtaken by the event and tried, until June, to put an end to it in order to preserve their relationship with London, though they finally got on board so as not to be discredited. The uprising then turned into guerrilla warfare accompanied by internal civil wars and the renewal of old quarrels among the great families, in particular between the Husseini, who headed the Arab High Commission, and the Nashashibi, who continued to seek a compromise with London. After savage attacks by the British the revolt ended in chaos. The Palestinian fighters, often left to their own devices and no longer obeying orders, turned on the native villages, which they robbed and pillaged in order to survive, and on their adversaries, the British forces and the *yishuv*.

The details of the failure of their revolt, which ended in May 1939, do not explain in themselves why the Palestinians were militarily defeated in 1948. Anyway, between them and the *yishuv*, and later Israel, the forces, military and diplomatic, were too imbalanced. Yet these details are essential for the understanding of why and how the Palestinians were so easily expelled. In all wars, to be sure, civilians flee before the advancing armies. But the way in which the Israelis were able to empty out entire villages, sometimes in very organized fashion, piling the Palestinians into trucks and buses or accompanying the columns of refugees right to the border, the methodical manner of the expulsion, conquered zone after conquered zone, as well as the absence of organized opposition, are largely explained by the level of national awareness among the Palestinians. This in turn had much to do with the failure of the revolt.

Let us return to the fragmentation of Palestinian society in 1939. As Elias Sanbar observes, in contrast to Syria with Damascus or Iraq with Baghdad, Palestine originally "had no single center but a religious center, Jerusalem, and regional capitals, the coastal cities of Gaza, Jaffa, Haifa, and Acre, and those of the interior, Jerusalem, Nablus, Hebron, and the like." In the political and social domains the weight of the great families and a regionalist culture had a profound effect on the Palestinian national movement. "Throughout its entire history," Sanbar continues, "chiefdoms in Palestine operated at the junctions. To establish his power a national leader had to place himself at the intersection of these junctions in order to link them. The mufti of Jerusalem understood this. So did Arafat, in an entirely different context, after his return to Palestine. With the failure of 1939, the interconnections of Palestinian society were broken and the junction between regional powers was undone."[14]

This disjoining explains why, when the Israelis evacuated the Palestinians from Tiberias in 1948, those in Safed did not make a move, nor, when Safed was emptied, did those in Jaffa make a move, and the same happened with the people of Acre after the conquest and departure of the inhabitants of Haifa. On each of these occasions the local powers withdrew into themselves and watched their step, hoping to avoid their neighbors' fate until, with rare exceptions such as Nazareth, they too succumbed.

But although this regional withdrawal increased with the defeat suffered nine years earlier, it was a deeply ingrained feature of Palestinian society. Fifty-two years later it would characterize the second intifada as soon as that uprising became an armed struggle, as, for example, the heads of Fatah in Ramallah, Nablus, Jenin, and Gaza tried to establish autonomous fiefdoms. In this sense, the temptation to withdraw when the Israelis undertook to drive the Palestinians from their land reveals a temporary inability to constitute a distinct nation. There were also the complications stemming from the co-existence of multiple identities (Arab, Palestinian, religious, clan-based). Israel was able to carry out an ethnic cleansing because, in the conflict, one camp was motivated by national solidarity reinforced by the recent tragedy — the Shoah — while the solidarity of the other camp was crumbling. Thus the *Naqba* was the result of a conflict between a nation in the making and one that was in regression when it came to constituting itself.

This is how the Palestinian sociologist Anis Gandil sums up the war of 1948: "On one side there had been an established and efficiently functioning state machine long before the founding of the state, on the other a people without a state and without the ability to form one at that time."[15] The most important task the Palestinians have to face is understanding that what made the Israeli victory of 1948 so easy had less to do with colonial tendencies than with the collective adherence to a project of resurrection, of building a nation-state. Gandil's father was born in a village near Jaffa. "When I asked him why our family left," Gandil relates,

> he said, "Everything was happening so fast that people didn't know what was going on." An old man from the Bourrej camp told me: "We had been attacked, and there was no one to defend us. We had to protect the women and children." In the refugee camps, the older people often refuse to hand down their memories, because it was an incomprehensible defeat and there was a lot of shame involved. The truth is that almost all of those who were urged to leave thought they would soon return to their homes. As long as this incomprehension persists, it is very hard to form a positive outlook. Courage consists, first of all, in admitting that it was a defeat and in understanding why it happened.

Georges Giacaman, who heads Muwatin, the Palestinian Institute for the Study of Democracy in Ramallah, is even more outspoken: "In 1948 we not only lacked an autonomous political Palestinian leadership and state structures, we lacked the cohesion that binds a national society. For the most part we were a clan society."[16]

Ilan Pappe agrees that his Arab students at Haifa University don't like to hear that their ancestors didn't fight or fought only a little. But, he says, they have to face that reality.[17] Many victims of a misfortune suffered passively feel shame, but the cultivated memory of the Naqba alone is the source of the sense of victimization that, as we shall see, is so constraining to the Palestinian national movement. The concealment of the defeat acts as a strong inner brake on the understanding both of the opponent's real nature and of one's own faults. It is the natural accompaniment to the idea of the artificiality of Israeli society, the stubborn refusal to see that society in terms other than those of classical colonialism, the conviction or hope that it will inevitably disappear, and the illusion of a coming restoration of the old order. It has been an enduring influence on the Palestinian national movement and weighs even more heavily on it now that the Islamists have taken up the torch dropped by the national leadership.

The Palestinian Liberation Organization (PLO), representing a people deprived of rights, was, to be sure, the first to recognize the de facto existence of the people denying them these rights, doing so five years before the Oslo Accords. But in its concepts and modes of activity the PLO remains steeped in denial of the way in which it was created. "As early as 1973 the DFLP [Democratic Front for the Liberation of Palestine] suggested the formation of a Palestinian state alongside Israel," recalls Nazmi El-Jubeh, who belonged to that organization at the time:

> We didn't formally recognize the Jewish state, but that was implicit. What was Fatah doing in Lebanon then? Shooting at us! Fifteen years later it came around to this obvious conclusion. And it took twenty years to get to mutual recognition. Our difficulty in taking into account what the Israelis are still persists. It prevents us from carrying out a policy that would make them trust us more, freeing them from the fear they're imprisoned in. I told Arafat twenty times that the warm welcome he gave Neturei Karta [a small ultra-orthodox and fiercely anti-Zionist Jewish sect] was disgusting. That he was making a fool of himself and of the Palestinians. This same failure to take the Israeli national reality into account is what has historically led the PLO to favor armed struggle and led Arafat to allow the second intifada to turn in this same direction again without offering the people anything else, a path that has proved catastrophic.[18]

This failure, finally, is what leads certain Palestinian intellectuals to promote a Palestinian identity separate from the relation to the other. It is certainly easier to understand than the failure of the Israelis, for whom, as Georges Bensoussan (2002) has written, establishing the Jewish state presupposed ignoring the native population. This tendency in reverse, the erasure of the Israeli, is thus a reaction to the denial of identity of which the Palestinians were themselves the object. It is clearly set forth in a scholarly work on Palestinian identity by the historian Rashid Khalidi (1997), an example I choose by design because Khalidi is in fact among those who are most inclined to understand the Israeli adversary/partner.

Khalidi's book, which studies the period from the middle of the nineteenth century to 1923, does take into account the phenomenon of the multiple loyalties that affect the Palestinian population, but is chiefly aimed at demonstrating the emergence of a distinct Palestinian national identity, one separate from Arab nationalism, and beginning during the period of the decline of the Ottoman Empire. This intention is understandable. It seeks to dismantle the Israeli Orientalist argument according to which the Palestinians, other than as Arabs, have no independent existence. Yes, we did exist, and as Palestinians, even before the arrival of your first settlers, Khalidi objects. Thus, in his final chapter on present-day Palestinian identity, he speaks of a "reemergence" after the disappearance of 1948.

This view tends to downplay two major elements: first, the internal handicaps to the constitution of a Palestinian national movement, and second, the fact that present-day Palestinian identity is not the mere reemergence of a preexisting formation but has been profoundly shaped by the presence of the Israelis. The relation to the Jews is just as essential a factor in the gradual development of Palestinian identity as the relation to the Arabs is to Israeli Jewish identity. The absence of any reference to this relation, except in the area of diplomacy, in a work describing "the construction of modern national consciousness" reveals an internal contradiction: that one can have the idea of constructing oneself without the other, apart from him, and in turn erase him from his national narrative, despite the fact that one can't avoid seeing him every day. Thus one sees the mirror image of the phenomenon prevailing in Israel.

The absence, deracination, dispossession, and ongoing oppression, along with the denial of rights and the international endorsement of this denial, all constitutive of present-day Palestinian identity, are hardly conducive to introspection or an assessment of one's own faults, and even less so to openness vis-à-vis the people who are the source of this situation.

"In order to criticize one's own history and insert other narratives into it, the self-criticism must stop being perceived as a threat, a sign of weakness," says Georges Giacaman. "If it is to develop, we'll have to have our own state."[19] Meanwhile, the need to move toward a critical assessment can be seen as a condition of the ability of the Palestinian national movement, both in order to fulfill its ambitions, and to resist the new fragmentation and chaos that Israel is trying to impose on it. As Giacaman observes, the absence of such a critical assessment is a major handicap.

Israelis, Palestinians:

The Temptation to Do the Worst

MUTE ORACLES

The Transformation of Israel After the Six Days' War

THE EMERGENCE OF THE BLOC OF
THE FAITHFUL AND ITS IMPACT

In 1904, when he knew that he was dying, Theodor Herzl, the founder of Zionism, wrote a letter to his successors in which he told them not to "make any stupid mistakes" when he was gone (cited in Elon 2002). Many stupid things had been done during and after the establishment of the state, and there would be yet another one at the end of the Six Days' War.

Immediately after this war, between the sixth and eleventh of June 1967, in which Israel conquered the Egyptian Sinai, the Jordanian West Bank, and the Syrian Golan, Itzhak Raphael, a highly placed leader of Mizrahi, the religious Zionist party, expressed the opinion that Israel ought to give up the newly conquered territories. Otherwise, he predicted, the country would be headed toward disaster. Who remembers this nowadays?

Raphael's party, which became the National Religious Party (NRP), came to be dominated by Gush Emunim, the ultranationalist and mystical "Bloc of the Faithful" formally created in 1974. It is the guiding light for the settlement of the Palestinian territories. Cultivated and cunning, Raphael and his alter ego Yossef Burg, the other great leader of the religious

Zionists at the time, were traditional allies of the Labor Party, governing since 1948, and were in general more moderate in regard to the Arab environment. Thirty-eight years later, their place at the head of the NRP was held by a member of the Sharon government, Effi Eitam, a former secular kibbutznik who became religious and a former brigadier general as well, and whose advancement in the military had been checked by the staff on account of violent personal behavior deemed unworthy of his rank.

In an interview he granted me on the day he was appointed to the government in 2002, Eitam told me that "from the sea to the Jordan River: that is the vital space of the Jewish people" (2002a).[1] Smitten with Judaism (or rather with a particular kind of Judaism, that of the extreme religious right), but staggeringly uncultured in general, the general was no doubt unaware that the two last Europeans to claim a vital space for their people so as to enlarge their territory were named Hitler and Milosevic. The entire interview was similar in its content and even more in its tone. For example, Eitam castigated the "incredible psychopathic syndrome of the Europeans who are hurrying to save the murderer Arafat," adding that "among us [in Israel] as well, there are defenders of 'human rights' and 'peace' who are just as psychopathic."

Zionism, he said in conclusion,

> dreamed of a normal state. The Jews would become like other nations, living in security in their national homeland, and anti-Semitism would disappear, Well, Israel is the most dangerous place in the world for Jews. The secular concept of Zionism has failed. To be like others, Jews don't have to live in the Middle East. Israel's sole raison d'être is to be a really Jewish state. Now for many years the paradigm of peace, in its liberal sense, has prevailed there. Its central component, Judaism, has been marginalized. It has to be placed at the heart of our society. A truly Jewish state will have three pillars: One, land. Two, identity: our history, our culture, our language. Three, the specificity of the Jewish people. . . . This is our distinctiveness: we are the only ones in the world who maintain a dialogue with God as a nation.

Two weeks earlier, in an interminable interview in *Haaretz*, Eitam had said that these three pillars implied the expulsion of the Palestinians from the Land of Israel.[2]

How did religious Zionism go from the moderate political culture of a Burg[3] and a Raphael to the mystical coarseness of an Eitam, with his phobia of the peace paradigm? How did the values of Judaism as espoused by Gush Emunim, Eitam's group—the sanctification of the land, the distinctiveness of the Jewish people as "chosen"—spread far beyond the sect into a large part of the country's religious population and also, in a more diffuse way, among the nonobservant? The answer lies in one event: the war of 1967 and, following it, the ongoing occupation of another people. These have resulted in the denial not only of the consequences of this occupation for the population in question but also of the way in which this occupation affects Israel and the Israelis.

Effi Eitam's arguments had been made in Israel even before 1967, but in a highly theoretical manner and in a religious Zionist setting that was itself a minority position both in Zionism and in religious Judaism. Israeli society in general, historically dominated by the culture of the labor movement, was largely unmarked by deep religiosity. Yet I recall my first contact with an adherent of what would later become the Bloc of the Faithful.

It was 1964. I was in a seminar, a secular one, in which my professor of Judaism was a certain Yehoshua Zuckerman. He belonged to the *yeshiva* (rabbinical school) Merkaz Harav, founded by Avraham Yitzhak Hacohen Kook, the first Ashkenazic grand rabbi of Israel. In the minority within his party, the Mizrahi, but respected for his knowledge of Jewish exegesis, Kook was already developing a mystical view in which the Zionists and the state of Israel, unbelievers though they were, paradoxically constituted the first step toward redemption and the coming of the messiah. Just as Molière's Monsieur Jourdain was delighted to learn that what he was speaking was prose, Zionism was messianic without knowing it. Zionism, said its proponents, was the messiah's donkey, carrying him without knowing where it was being taken.

I was 17 years old, with little knowledge of or inclination for philosophy, and this Zuckerman, a disciple of Rabbi Kook, dominated the students with all his learning. Highly erudite, or at least so he appeared to us, he would quote from the Bible, the Talmud, Plato, Descartes, Kant, Hegel, and Marx one after the other. His view of Judaism, very different from the one I had been taught in the Zionist youth movement I belonged to, made me very uneasy, but I was hard put to contradict him.

One day I asked him this: "You claim that spirit and body are one, and that the Jewish soul is radically different from the non-Jewish soul. If that is the case, what of the Jew's body? Is it different as well?" He came right back with his reply: "I haven't the slightest doubt that genetics will one day prove that we, the Jews, are different from other people." Genetically different, then! For me, he could parade his learning as much as he wanted to, but I was through with that kind of Judaism. And I was not alone. A deeply religious man, and one who did not mince words, the famous Professor Yeshaayahu Leibowitz, a confirmed Zionist, would soon compare the followers of Gush Emunim to the Hitler Youth.

After 1967 the enraged diatribes of men like Leibowitz were swept away on the wind like the cries of a bird in the middle of the ocean. For although in 1964 arguments like Zuckerman's were still marginal in religious Zionism, three years later the Merkaz Harav yeshiva of Rabbi Kook and his emulators would become the spearhead of the settlement movement. The conquest of the remaining territories of Mandatory Palestinian, which they considered a dazzling stage of the journey toward redemption, would confer on them an increasing aura and intellectual influence. In ten years' time they would storm and gain control of the former NRP.

These are people who bring up their children (and many other children) in the belief that the Ten Commandments do not say "Thou shalt not kill," as non-Jews claim. The Hebrew words, they remind us, are "Thou shalt not commit murder." Now since killing an Arab under any circumstances can only be an act of self-defense, all Arabs being our enemies, it does not constitute murder. Some, like that other great sage Rabbi Ginsburg, add that the Arabs, as the reincarnations of Amalek, are not really human beings.[4]

Whereas, philosophically, the Jewish religion places life above all other considerations, people like Zuckerman and Ginsburg place a Jew's life above that of anyone else in any situation. "Protecting Jews' lives" is the slogan they deploy in their demands for increased repression of the Palestinians and the loosening of restrictions on what the armed forces may do, as they told me on various occasions during the second intifada, bringing to mind the famous grievance of extremist Algerian colonists against the metropolis. The phrase most often cited in the Bible (seventy times) is "Remember that you were a stranger in Egypt."[5] But, the members of Gush Emunim explain, this is not to be understood as urging respect for the stranger or foreigner, as the rabbinical tradition has it, for, they say, being a foreigner is always a despicable state (and besides, the Palestinians are foreigners who are unjustly occupying the Land of Israel). The biblical phrase, they say, means "You have no land other than this one, since everywhere else you are a foreigner and must never be one again."

It might be objected that this is still a marginal phenomenon, even if it has made a lot of progress. That is incorrect. In the strict sense, the disciples of Rabbi Kook are indeed confined to the NRP (7 percent of the votes) and other groups on the extreme right that some of them have managed to infiltrate (10 to 12 percent). Rabbi Benny Elon, the current head of the Moledet (Homeland) Party, also called the "transfer party," which has both religious and secular members, also comes from the ranks of Gush Emunim, as does Moshe Feiglin, who has had some success with a policy of entrism in Likud, this being a political strategy that consists in entering another party with the intention to influence it from within. Moreover, the general cultural influence of the Bloc of the Faithful is now on a different scale from where it was initially. In the years immediately following the Six Days' War, this colonialist and mystico-nationalist movement was not only legitimized but glorified, presented by a number of politicians—and not only on the right—as the cream of the younger generation, Israel's new pioneers. Yes, these young people were turbulent and sometimes a bit violent, but they were so idealistic! When they seized Palestinian land to found an extra-legal colony, weren't they rediscovering the pioneer spirit of the young labor movement of the 1930s, who did likewise with their famous operations known as *Khoma Umigdal* (Fence and Tower)?

As for their rabbis, their status as masters of Judaism is accepted. And the values they preach of the Jews as the chosen people are gaining ground. One of their best students, Effi Eitam, whom we have met as the head of the NRP, said in an interview that an "anomaly" allowed the Jewish people to "traverse all of human history." This, he explained, "is not just a historical and biological fact: it is a commitment. I believe we have a mission in the world." What mission? "To reveal God's image in the world" (2002b, p. 10). Genetics for Rabbi Zuckerman forty years ago, biology for the head of his party today: racism is an integral part of the Bloc of the Faithful.

Over the years this current has structured the informal "settlers' party," the political and social circle that, in Israel and in the territories, supports the settlements. Apart from the brief period following the Oslo Accords, when it really feared the worst, a withdrawal from the territories that it would not be able to stem, this group has constantly maneuvered, gained influence in government and the army, and stepped back so as to evade the few obstacles placed in its path—in short, it has imposed its will and held hostage all Israeli governments since the 1970s (until the withdrawal from Gaza in 2005). These governments were hostages forced or persuaded to make use of it to their benefit when the left was in charge of the country, eager hostages when the right was in power. Right and left alike, in varying degrees and for different motives, advocated the pursuit of the settlement policy. In this sense, the relationship of the settlers' party to their government has always been quite similar to that of its informal counterpart in French Algeria to the metropolis up to 1959. It functions as a lobby in Israel, relying on the government without ever foregoing an innate mistrust of it, and forming links with the military to ensure that what it considers its rights will prevail in all circumstances, namely to enlarge its prerogatives and to sabotage any political initiative that might endanger Greater Israel.

Why and how did this movement, the Bloc of the Faithful, come to structure the settlers' party? Basically because, once Israel found itself occupying another population after 1967, this bloc, with its emphasis on "the land," "the primacy of the Jew," and a scandalous anti-Arab racism, provided the most coherent intellectual, rational, and moral arguments for the necessity of this occupation. Forget about security imperatives and the need to reach an accord with an enemy who, in their view, always hated the Jews and would always hate them; Israel had to remain in the territories because this land belonged to Israel. Period. The rest is just a matter of tactical maneuvering, fine for the *goyim*, the non-Jews.

Most Israelis do not hold this view, but many of them share the values of Gush Emunim more or less enthusiastically. The longer Israel has remained in the occupied territories, the more they too have come to believe that giving back this land to its original residents would amount to an abandonment, a renunciation.

1967: *The Establishment of Omnipotence*

We may speculate about what Israel would have become, how its relations with neighboring countries would have evolved, and how the Palestinian national movement would have been rebuilt had the Jewish state restored—rapidly and unilaterally, or through the opportunities for negotiation that, as we now know, were available between 1969 and 1972—the conquered territories to the Arab countries, in particular Gaza to Egypt and the West Bank to Jordan. It would in any event have remained a Jewish state, much closer to what it was before 1967, even if demographic growth and the emergence of its Arab minority from the despondency following the defeat of 1948 would inevitably have posed new problems over time.

For, until 1967, Israel presented a great paradox. There was really no longer a Palestinian question. The Palestinians who remained there and became Israeli citizens (under a military governorship until 1963) numbered only 150,000 souls. In 1952, after new waves of Jewish immigration, they were only 10 percent of the population; today they are 20 percent. Above all, they were broken: politically, by the defeat, the disappearance of any national leadership, and the scattering into exile of their elite, but even more so socially, by the sudden vanishing of over 80 percent of their people. As we have seen, the Jewish state was quick to establish the notion of minorities on the basis of origin and religion, favoring some (Druses, certain Bedouin tribes) at the expense of others so as to fragment their unity and gain accomplices. "Since Israel could not impose cultural assimilation on them, the best way to manage the minorities is to divide and subdivide them," suggested an internal government report in 1949.[6]

And so for nineteen years Israel would be built on a foundation of nearly complete ethnic homogeneity. The Israeli nation was torn between attachment to the diaspora and rejection of it, between the general relationship to Judaism and the Israeliness of the "new Jew." Orientalism of an ethnicist type persisted in people's minds and in intellectual theory, but for all practical purposes the Palestinians no longer posed a concrete problem inside the country. Nor outside it, for that matter, where the Palestinian diaspora was politically downtrodden and under the control of those Arab regimes in place. The "Arab question" was only an external threat stemming from the ongoing hostility of the Arab states, and these, except for Iraq, which had no common border with Israel, had signed cease-fire agreements with it. In that arena security concerns continued to shape political thought; they were evident, for example, in the so-called retaliatory measures taken outside the country's borders in the early 1950s and in the Suez campaign in October 1956, where Israel joined Great Britain and France in a joint attempt at military invasion aimed at destabilizing the regime of Colonel Nasser in Egypt.

In Israel some Arab militants did try to establish a legal nationalist party (the pro-Nasser El-Ard, "The Earth") in 1958, but it was banned without further ado. To express political protest the Palestinians of Israel, even if they were religious or nationalists, had no choice other than the Communist party. This party had followed Stalin's orders in supporting the plan for partition in 1947 and its members had fought alongside Israeli forces in 1948,[7] but it alone took Palestinian oppression into account. Mapam, the Zionist party of the left, which liked to see itself as similarly compassionate toward the minorities, never managed to make inroads into this population because it was part of the various Labor administrations that imposed the military governorship with its growing list of prohibitions, and because it was in the vanguard of the kibbutz movement, one of the primary beneficiaries of the confiscation of the land of the "absent" Palestinians.

Before 1967 there was nothing colonialist, in the classical sense of the term, about Israel's relationship with the native population. With the exception of some cities, like Jaffa, Haifa, Lod, and Acre, where small Palestinian minorities remained,[8] generations of young Israelis grew up without

ever encountering the Arabs, who for the most part were confined to their
residential zones in Galilee or the Triangle. The situation was similar to
that in some parts of the southern United States during the era of racial
segregation.

This Israel gradually became transformed after 1967 under the influence of the occupation. This change frightened part of its Labor establishment, though in most others it released very old currents of thought,
tinged with the regret, rarely expressed but very vivid for some, for both
having accepted the partitioning of Palestine in 1947 for geopolitical reasons, and for not having conquered more land in 1948.

I had seen signs of this lively regret earlier on, though it did not make
any special impression on me. In 1962 or 1963, when I was about 15, my
parents invited to lunch an Israeli deputy named Itzhak Korn, who held
a high position in the international apparatus of the Labor Party that, at
the time, dominated the Zionist movement. Several leaders of the French
Zionist labor movement were also invited. The conversation was conducted in Yiddish. Korn said that, sooner or later, Israel would have to
grow larger, since the state was too small to accommodate all the Jews it
wanted to welcome. One of the guests pointed out that there were still
large empty tracts in the Negev in which people could live. After the deputy
left, I told my father that I was confused. "Yes," he replied, "there are Labor
Party members in Israel who think that way. It's a kind of dream. In Herut
[the nationalist right] this is still a very important idea. But there aren't
many Laborites who would agree."

There were more of them that he was willing to admit, especially among
those with roots in the movement known as Ahdut Haavodah (Labor
Union), which Ben Gurion had had a hard time persuading to accept the
partition of Palestine in 1947. The head of Ahdut Haavodah, Yigal Allon,
had written this in 1966: "In . . . a new war, we must avoid the historic
mistake of the War of Independence . . . and must not cease fighting until
we achieve total victory, the territorial fulfilment of the Land of Israel."[9]

The dream became real the following year. June 1967 saw the first of
the modern preventive wars, as they have been called since George W.
Bush made them a strategic doctrine.[10] No one will ever know whether
Colonel Nasser, then in power in Egypt, really intended to attack Israel at

that time, whether he had gotten himself into a trap or, as many historians believe, was trapped by his Soviet partners.[11] And even if he did not want war, no one can say that he wouldn't have been led to declare it by the inept political mechanism he had set in motion with his own rhetoric, namely his mobilization of the "Arab street," and the bragging about winning back Palestine in the deeply anti-Semitic diatribes of the head of the PLO in Cairo, Ahmed Shukeiry.

Let us briefly recall the facts. In mid-May 1967 Israel threatened to take military action against Syria, which had begun diverting the sources of the Jordan River in response to Israel, which had been pumping water from Lake Tiberias since June 1964. There had been continual border skirmishes. On April 7 Israel downed six Syrian MIG-21 airplanes. Cairo had diplomatic and military connections with Damascus at the time, and Nasser, who had conducted secret negotiations with Israel with a view toward a political accord, negotiations that Israel did not pursue, came to the defense of his ally. On May 16 he got the United Nations to agree to the withdrawal of the Blue Berets deployed on his border with Israel, and on the 22nd announced the closure of the Strait of Tiran, cutting off access to the Israeli port of Eilat through the Red Sea, which, for Jerusalem, constituted a casus belli. Finally, he massed troops in the Sinai.

Israel was gripped by the sense of a new existential threat. On June 1 a cabinet of national unity was formed; this was the first time the nationalist right gained a role in the government. Early in the morning of the 6th Israel attacked preemptively. The Egyptian air force was wiped out in eighty minutes. In three days the IDF reached the Suez Canal, in four the Jordan, whose west bank was inhabited by Palestinians. In the evening of the 8th Cairo and Damascus agreed to a cease-fire proposed by the U.N. But Israel pursued its offensive, and, the following day, its government decided to seize the Golan Heights of Syria when that country, whose air force had been destroyed on June 5, did not join battle.[12] Fighting ended on the sixth day. The battle of the seventh day, as the Israeli essayist Amos Elon (2002) called it,[13] began with the thought, What was to be done with this splendid triumph?

Two things are certain. The first is that the instigators of the allegedly preemptive attack—Defense Minister Moshe Dayan, who was their intellectual leader, and the generals around him—did not have a moment's fear for the survival of Israel. The second is that the Jewish population of the country, for its part, was intensely fearful of annihilation[14] and saw the victory as miraculous. The Israeli government reinforced this perception once the war was over. The day after the cease-fire Prime Minister Levy Eshkol told the Knesset that Israel's existence had been hanging by a thread.[15]

As is often the case in Israel, some time had to pass before certain truths came to light. In the spring of 1972, for example, on the fifth anniversary of the "miracle," some of its protagonists lifted a corner of the veil. Thus Chief of Staff Haim Bar-Lev stated that Israel had not been threatened with genocide on the eve of the Six Days' War, nor had that possibility been envisioned.[16] That same day General Haim Herzog, former head of military intelligence and future president of the nation, likewise stated that there was no actual or perceived danger of annihilation. The headquarters never believed in that, he added. Ezer Weizmann, former head of the army's air division and, like Herzog, a future president, confirmed that there had been no serious consideration of a major threat.[17] Mordehai Hod, whose planes had won the war in its first hour and a half, stated that these initial eighty minutes had been unceasingly and minutely planned down to the last detail for sixteen years.

And General Matti Peled, in charge of logistics for the general staff in 1967, had this to say:

> All these stories that were churned out about the enormous risk we were facing because our territory was so small, an argument put forth once the war was over, were never taken into consideration in our calculations before the hostilities. No sensible person has come forth who believed that all this power was absolutely necessary to "defend" ourselves against the Egyptian threat. This power was necessary for the definitive crushing of the Egyptians on the military level and their patrons, the Soviets, on the political level. To claim that the Egyptian

forces massed on the border were capable of threatening the existence of Israel is an insult not only to the intelligence of anyone who is able to analyze this type of situation but, above all, an insult to the IDF.[18]

Former minister Mordechai Ben-Tov was given the final word. He said that "this whole story about the danger of extermination was exaggerated after the fact to justify the annexation of new territory."[19]

Yet these statements by officials at the highest level did not change the Israelis' perception of what the Six Days' War was really about, any more than the later revelations about the reality of the expulsion of the Palestinians in 1948 would change their conviction about that reality. This is so because the idea of existential threat underlying the security relation to the other is always stronger than a rational look at relative military strength and thus validates all the cover-ups. And because this idea reflects a need that is existential in its own right, the need of the Israelis for a self-image in which they are never the instigators of violence but merely its victims. And, finally, because the state apparatus played a large role in cultivating the image of a little David attacked by a monstrous Goliath and beating him, as Firer (2002) has shown in her study of how the war of 1967 is represented in Israeli textbooks.

In a statement broadcast to the nation announcing the beginning of hostilities on the morning of June 6, Moshe Dayan had declared that Israel was not undertaking a war of conquest. Yet by the evening of the sixth day Israel had more than tripled its territory. A week earlier there had been 2.7 million Jews and 300,000 Arabs, a demographic ratio of one to nine. Afterward there were 1.3 million Palestinians under Israeli control, and the ratio was now one to two. What would become of this "non-conquest"? The question had been asked even before the end of the hostilities. As the war got underway, Meir Amit, head of Mossad, had asked the prime minister for clarification about Israel's objectives on the West Bank: Would the Israelis establish themselves there? Was there to be a union, or something else?[20] The raising of these issues *before* the offensive on the West Bank indicates that victory was considered a certainty and that the idea of a genocide facing Israel did not enter the minds of officials at this high level. What Prime Minister Eshkol replied was that, even if Israel won the Old City of Jerusalem and the West Bank, it would have to leave that area sooner or later.

One month later the framework of discourse underwent a change. There was no longer a question of leaving the conquered territories. As Levy Eshkol told the leaders of the Labor Party:

> In winning the victory we received a fine dowry in territories but also a bride we don't like. The entire government thinks that the Gaza Strip must remain in Israel and wants the Jordan River to be our border. It knows that there is a refugee problem to be dealt with. [He is referring explicitly to the population of Gaza.] . . . Without peace, we won't budge. If we consider the Jordan River to be the border with Jordan, our only choice is to create a zone in which a million Arabs [the number of Palestinians in Gaza and on the West Bank at the time] will have a special status.

In the same breath Eshkol discussed the problem his country would face in the future:

> What will happen in a generation, when they want to separate from us? I don't know. An important commission of experts is looking into the possibility of finding areas on the West Bank where, with additional water, refugees might possibly be settled [again he is referring to the Palestinians of Gaza]. . . . And so I see a semi-independent region in which defense and foreign affairs would be in Israeli hands. I don't care if, in the end, they demand representation in the U.N. I began with an autonomous region. If that is impossible, they will have independence. I fear the integration of a large number of Arabs into the [Jewish] state.[21]

Here we have it all. On the one hand, there is the powerful resurgence of the Orientalist relation to the Palestinians. Perhaps one day they will enjoy semi-independence, however it may be configured — autonomy or virtual independence — under Israeli control. Thirty-three years later Ehud Barak, with exactly this in mind at Camp David, would negotiate a rump state divided into four parts, minus East Jerusalem, surrounded and intersected by Israeli troops. And they were to call this "independence" and go to the U.N. if they wanted to. In 1967 practical measures were being considered to relocate the population of Gaza, too large for a such a small area, to the West Bank. The Arabs could simply be transferred at Israel's whim. In the meantime, there was no longer a question of retreating from the conquered territories.

On the other hand, we can also see the growing fears about this occupation and the integration of a large number of Arabs within the country's new borders. What would happen in a generation, the prime minister had wondered. A generation, exactly twenty years, later, the first intifada erupted. And now, on the historic territory of Mandatory Palestine, there are 5.2 million Israeli Jews and 4.3 million Palestinians. A demographic ratio of nine to one has become a ratio of near equality. In one and the same region half of the population imposes its will on the other half: this is what Levy Eshkol said he feared most of all. Many Labor leaders, beginning with Ben Gurion, then in retirement, shared these fears.

In 1969 my father, who was close to a number of senior Labor officials in Israel, told me this: "We'll have to give back all the territories, without exception. If not, there'll be another Algeria here." The memory of the war in Algeria was still fresh at that time, and my father was not the only one in the Labor Party to think in these terms. In 1977 Housing Minister Avraham Ofer, who had been suspected of corruption, committed suicide. "How sad," my father said. "He was one of ours." One of ours? Who was he talking about? "Well, the people in the party who think, as I do, that we have to leave the territories if there isn't to be a catastrophe." But why did they never speak out in public? "Impossible," he shot back. "The others can't hear that."

And so these mute oracles, greatly distressed about the course of events, would get together among themselves and lament, but in public they were silent. Their ostensible leader was Pinhas Sapir, the minister of finance, an old Labor apparatchik. And just as the religious leader Itzhak Raphael soon stopped mentioning the idea of a retreat from the territories in the face of pressure from his flock in Gush Emunim, Sapir and his friends fell silent in the face of the enormous euphoria that was pressuring the "other" Laborites, those who could hear nothing, the major leaders Golda Meir, Moshe Dayan, Shimon Peres, and Ygal Allon, to pursue an active policy of faits accomplis in the conquered territories.

The political leadership in Israel at that time was animated by a feeling of omnipotence on account of the ease with which they had won the war and the collapse of the surrounding Arab world. So what if the facts on the ground aroused the ire of the international community. In Israel, who cared about that? And who, in this bipolar world, and at a time when the war in Vietnam was in full swing, would prevent them? So went their thinking. So what if, during the Six Days' War itself, Israel had already expelled 250,000 Palestinians to Jordan and 100,000 Syrian Arabs from the Golan. In the outside world who reacted to this, and who was discussing it in Israel? The expulsions took place without any media coverage whatsoever. It would be ten years before the first revelations filtered in. And thirty years—that is, not until 1996—before an Israeli documentary filmmaker, Irit Gal, devoted a long television program to the expulsions in the Golan.

Given the general euphoria, a feeling of impunity set in. Nothing and no one was capable of thwarting the policy of facts on the ground, the foremost of which involved the settlements. As Amos Elon (2002) has pointed out, this policy was never put to a vote in the Israeli parliament.[22] Finance Minister Sapir and his minister of housing and infrastructure, who did not believe that new settlements had a future, signed checks for their construction. In private they thought that, at some future time they hoped would not be too far off, these settlements would inevitably have to be evacuated. But, they added with a certain degree of cynicism, when that day came the United States would fully compensate Israel for all the money it had spent in vain.[23] So go ahead with Allon's plan for establishing settlement blocs. Go ahead with the plan to build a city, Yamit, right in the middle of the Sinai, a major undertaking by Moshe Dayan. Both plans were adopted by the government.

In settling permanently in the Palestinian territories Israel was engaged in a process that would gradually change it profoundly from within. It would become "Algerianized," as Pierre Vidal-Naquet prophesied right after the Six Days' War.[24] What he meant was that little by little, almost mechanically, Israel would reinforce its most extreme colonialist tendencies, tendencies that were already in place but had been largely marginalized, after 1949, by a society that was focusing on its own construction. Ten years after the Six Days' War, the nationalist right under Menahem Begin, which had been a minority throughout the entire history of Zionism and, except for the brief period of national unity before and after the war, had been excluded from power since the creation of the state, swept the elections. For if the Israeli occupation and settlement of the Palestinian territories were justified, why vote for Labor, a party that was more hesitant when it came to establishing settlements? In 1977, with Gush Emunim now at the head of the National Religious Party, Begin was able to form the first nationalist right-wing government with his new group, the Gahal, ancestor of the Likud, conceived and built by Generals Ariel Sharon and Ezer Weizmann.

ESTABLISHING THE ROUTINE OF OCCUPATION

How did the occupation disrupt Israeli society? As Amos Elon (2002) notes, paraphrasing the famous historian Isaiah Berlin, Israel had always had "more history than geography." Now, it had both. And it also had two populations.

The IDF now had to add to its traditional military functions the daily management of a native civilian population. From the outset, through its so-called civilian government of the territories, a euphemism for the military control of people who *were* actually civilians, the army made all decisions about where they could work, study, and move. With time the IDF even drew up a list of books that could not be made available in Palestinian libraries and bookstores under penalty of imprisonment. When I consulted this list as a reporter in 1984, it contained some eight hundred items, including several works of Shakespeare, in which the Palestinians might have found some dire analogies to their own situation. An artist was arrested and tortured for having used the colors of the Palestinian flag in a painting.

And terrorist infrastructures had to be dismantled, though at that time they were very weak in the territories. The populace was for independence, but nationalist organizations had few representatives. Fatah was in limbo. The militant groups, which were few and small, had no weapons or explosives apart from some old guns. But Israel claimed that it had to ensure its security, which meant hunting down the nationalists. The IDF and Shin Bet, the domestic intelligence service, took charge of this task. The commander of the southern front, General Ariel Sharon, carried it out with unprecedented ferocity in Gaza in the years 1970–1971, while secretly promoting the development of mosques and the Muslim Brotherhood in the belief that any means were justified to block the primary foe, nationalism. Within a few years' time tens of thousands of Palestinians had passed through Israeli jails, and, in the course of their active military service or annual reserve duty, generations of young Israelis grew accustomed to these police functions. This was not yet a response to the intifada but simply routine procedure to make sure the Palestinians were kept in their place. Given the swiftness of Israeli repression and the weakness of their own forces, they remained in their place for twenty years. With few exceptions their political leaders were in prison or had been sent into exile.

At the same time the Palestinian, never named as such because he supposedly did not exist, reappeared in the visual field of the average Israeli, from which he had all but disappeared since the end of the War of Independence. Employers were turning more and more to this potential, and much less costly, labor force. Palestinians from Gaza and the West Bank came to find jobs in factories and fields, workshops and restaurants, and Israelis got used to being in contact with this mass of humanity that was there but transparent.

In Rishon Letzion, a large town south of Tel Aviv, was a place called the "slave market." The expression was familiar to all those who spent any time in that area in the 1970s. Every day at 6 a.m. panel trucks from Gaza unloaded their cargo, and Israelis—division heads at the Amcor refrigerator factory, which was owned by the Histadrut trade-union confederation; civil engineering contractors; and landowners—came to find workers, bricklayers, and field hands, all paid by the day. In the evening these laborers could be seen hurrying back to the trucks that took them back to their territories. The term *slave market* reveals the Israelis' growing familiarity with a new population that, deprived of all political and social rights and forbidden to organize or vote, could only work and keep silent. In the general passivity with which the Israelis accepted this situation, there developed a relationship of domination over people who were known to exist but remained essentially unseen.

And before long a vocabulary specific to the occupation emerged, one that reflected this invisibility. The best-known example is the very term *territories*. Should they be described as "occupied"? Absolutely not. This was the common international usage, found in the U.N. resolutions. In Israel, however, only the leftists used it; the nationalist right called them "the liberated territories." This was to be expected if one favors a Greater Israel, but what should a Laborite say? "Palestinian territories"? Unthinkable, for that adjective was taboo. "Arab territories," perhaps? Never that, for the Israelis' biblical roots are there, in Hebron and Jericho. Moshe Dayan, an unbeliever from way back, someone who would eat pork on Passover, is described by Amos Elon (2002) as "the adored victor in a glorious war and, for some years, the most famous Jew since Jesus Christ," and also as the first high-ranking secular politician to stuff his speeches with biblical images, saying, for example, "We've returned to Shilo [a house of worship in the Bronze Age] and Anatot [the prophet Isaiah's birthplace], never to part from them again," and so on. Shiloh and Anatot can't be Arab places.

And soon we found the expression *shtakhim mukhzakim*, "the territories held in possession" by Israel. This is a neutral and nonspecific term, and everyone knew what it referred to. On a famous TV show in the mid-1970s a comedian observed that the same term—held in possession—is used of prisoners. Soon all adjectives disappeared. In daily conversation as well as in the press, the only term used was "the territories." Simply "territories," with no identity, like the people who lived there.

Israel went on this way for twenty years, practicing a repression and a segregation that were not called by those names and that the international community barely noticed. The legitimacy of this situation evolved in such an imperceptible way that it easily became a feature of the Israeli mind-set. Even the term *territories* fell into disuse. In common parlance it was replaced by the geographic designations of the places in question, following biblical usage. At the beginning of the occupation only the ultranationalists called the West Bank "Judea and Samaria," but as the years passed these became the usual terms. The press, always following trends in public opinion, adopted them as well, speaking, for example, of "the opening of a new settlement yesterday in Samaria" or describing how "the farmers of Judea have succeeded in growing plums in winter." This happened wherever there were places with Hebrew names—in other words, in Israel.

During this time the government, left and then right, was at work. On an unofficial basis the settlement policy followed the Allon Plan, presented in 1968 by this former general who had been one of the most determined proponents of transfer in 1948 and later became the Labor Party's minister of agriculture. Except for the establishment of a "safety belt" surrounding Jerusalem, his plan called for large blocs of settlements on the West Bank, both along the former 1967 border (the Green Line) in the Jordan Valley, and transversely, with the aim of cutting this area into three separate regions. The motivation was said to be solely a matter of security, assuring of strategic depth by moving the eastern border of the country to the Jordan River and better control of the native population.

Once in power, the right then presented its own plan, adding more ideological motives to the security considerations that were the official basis of the Allon Plan. Drawn up in 1982 by Ariel Sharon, his so-called Master Plan called for major improvements in the infrastructure of the settlements in the territories, with special emphasis on the construction of as many settlements as possible so as to encircle the large cities of the Palestinians and divide the native inhabitants of the West Bank into a multitude of enclaves, ultimately leaving them only about 40 percent of their space.

These two plans served as marching orders for all subsequent governments, which, on the right and the left alike, followed them more or less energetically according to their political coloration and the situation at a given time. The least enthusiastic was Itzhak Rabin (1992–1995), the most zealous Menahem Begin (1977–1983) and Ehud Barak (1998–2000). But none of them questioned the logic of the settlement policy. In seven years, between 1993 and 2000, that is, during the period of peace negotiations with the PLO, almost as many settlers moved to the occupied territories as in the preceding sixteen years.

THE MECHANISMS OF COLONIZATION

But how to go about it? Imposing the "facts on the ground" called for a certain discretion. The settlements came about indirectly. Beginning in the late 1960s with the presentation of the Allon Plan, committees were formed very circumspectly in the ministries concerned: defense, supplies, housing, and agriculture. With time an entire bureaucracy was established to oversee Israel's gradual monopolization of the Palestinian territories, but nowhere was it readily apparent. The development of the settlements was written into the general budgets of these ministries without a specific line item, so that it is most often impossible to determine what its specific allocations were. The Knesset did not legislate on the matter—in thirty-nine years the principle underlying the settlements never came up for a parliamentary vote—and governments proceeded by way of directives. For the most part the Palestinians affected by these decisions, like the Israelis opposed to the settlements, learned of new settlement projects only when the bulldozers were already at work.

Once the financial means were made available, land for the settlements had to be found. Apart from a desert region in Judea, the West Bank and Gaza were heavily populated. In 2002 the nongovernmental organization B'Tselem published a detailed account of the multiple methods Israel used to gain control of land and give these appropriations the appearance of legality. Two of these can be mentioned here.

Article 49 of the Fourth Geneva Convention forbids an occupying power to seize land except when this is necessary for security purposes. Hence the Israeli army continually claimed this necessity as it carried out its confiscations. These areas were immediately dubbed "closed military zones." Shortly afterward, settlers began to move in in increasing numbers, while on paper these places remained military zones "closed" to

Palestinians but to no one else. Any Israeli, even a mere tourist, could go there without having to obtain any military authorization.

Elsewhere Israel made use of an old Ottoman law dating from 1858, according to which any land left fallow for ten years was to be considered abandoned and hence public property. This period was shortened by Israeli law to three years. All that had to be done was deny Palestinian landowners access to their property for three years for one reason or another, generally said to involve security, and then declare that property abandoned. Settlers soon moved in.[25]

According to B'Tselem's figures, which have never been contradicted, in thirty-seven years 46 percent of the West Bank came under Israeli control in this way, 20 percent of which was allocated to settlements and to the "Greater Jerusalem" annexed to Israel. This is not far from the 60 percent of land that, according to Ariel Sharon's Master Plan of 1982, Israel planned to appropriate by the year 2010.

Israel's juridical ingenuity is boundless. Specifically, it permits the arbitrary choice, according to what the state considers its best interests, from among three legal systems: (1) Egyptian or Jordanian law in accordance with the Geneva Convention's ruling on military occupation (since Gaza and the West Bank formerly belonged to these two countries, respectively); (2) decrees issued by the so-called "civilian government" of the IDF; or (3) Israeli law itself, in cases directly involving the settlers, who are residents of the territories but not subject to the laws prevailing there. This triple jurisdiction always makes it possible to find a statute that confers legality on the confiscations as well as on the systematic destruction of homes said to have been illegally built by the Palestinians on their own land, at the same time that Israeli authorities almost never issue building permits to the native inhabitants. For the most part there is no recourse against the rulings of military courts. If need be, the civilian courts of appeal in Israel will confirm them.

Why so much effort? Why is it considered absolutely necessary to confer the appearance of legality on the appropriations? Surely in order to preserve Israel's reputation as a democracy. And no doubt to avoid problems with its supreme court, for, when Palestinians appeal decisions, that court dismisses them 99 percent of the time, accepting the arguments of the authorities in the name of the public good, especially when security is invoked. In the thirty-nine years of the occupation, it has sided with Palestinians only very rarely, when it judges that, in a given situation, the public powers went too far or were unable to contrive an adequate legal case. The law must remain in effect.

Not always, however, for there are so-called "extra-legal" settlements, that is, those founded by private initiative as opposed to governmental decree. One third of the settlements in the Palestinian territories were once extra-legal, established by private (usually religious) groups. In such cases the government is not considered responsible. It can distance itself from them, especially if the international community shows concern. But by the time the United Nations has voted to condemn such a settlement, the roads, water supply, and electric and telephone lines duly provided by the state have lent it the appearance of legitimacy. The international agitation is forgotten, and, one after the other, these settlements are legalized.

Impunity is the rule, especially since wherever settlers, legal or illegal, establish themselves the army always follows or precedes them with a military encampment in their midst or nearby. After all, isn't it obliged to protect Israelis, and aren't the settlers, scattered in hostile areas, the most highly threatened? As we shall see, the IDF's development has been determined by the role it has taken on in maintaining order in the occupied territories, supporting the settlements, and gradually forging local ties with settlement leaders.

The slow but methodical despoliation that has taken place since the 1970s is, to be sure, less extensive than its counterpart during and after the war of 1948, but, paradoxically, its consequences are much more severe. For this time there is no concomitant expulsion of the owners, who, impotent in the face of faits accomplis and subject to the irrevocable decisions of the military authorities, brood on their rage. Their children swear never to be like their parents, powerless and passive. And this entire population is right there in the heart of Israel. The Israelis, however, swept up in the general euphoria after the 1967 victory and enjoying judicial impunity, were blind to what was happening, to the tragic consequences of the occupation and the settlement movement for their new neighbors.

And some people profited from it. With the construction of military bases and of housing for the settlers and private roads for them and the soldiers, plus the increase in opportunities for manufacturing, farming, and import-export businesses, an entire occupation economy arose. Some *kablanim*, entrepreneurs who had influence with the authorities, amassed fortunes, as did some Palestinian middlemen who had influence with the IDF's "civilian government" and furnished a labor force. A social economy of the occupation emerged as well. What with financial incentives, tax relief, subsidized loans, free school tuition, and the like, there was no end to the advantages offered by successive governments to those who wished to settle in Palestinian lands. Life was easier there, or at any rate cheaper.

It is no accident that the ultra-Orthodox and people living in the so-called "development towns" moved in large numbers to the settlements, writes Hannah Kim.[26] Many Orthodox Jews, not to be confused with the ideologues of Gush Emunim, are at the lowest income level, and they filled new cities like Betar Ilit and Emmanuel on the West Bank. Public investments were more generous there, nearly double what they are in the disadvantaged Israeli development towns.[27] Children were soon born in the settlements, and there was nothing, much less a road sign, to indicate that they were not in Israel. And then there was "Greater Jerusalem," which annexed dozens of square kilometers to the east. No one asked what miracle had caused these lands to be liberated, lands on which new suburbs were growing in the eastern part of the capital, new cities and small settlements elsewhere. For the new inhabitants, all this was Israel. As the years passed, their offspring could not even imagine a time when this was not the case, still less that it could stop being so.

Denial played its part as well. The settlers, and with them the majority of Israelis, persuaded themselves that before them there had been nothing. Before they moved in, there were no Palestinians living, working, and cultivating or even owning land. Israel did not confiscate, the settlers did nothing reprehensible. "At the outset there was no one on these hills except for some Bedouins. We developed it. It belongs to us," explained Gabi Bar Zakai, deputy mayor of the largest settlement on the West Bank, Maaleh Adumim, which was formed in 1982.[28]

The Palestinian occupied territories are among the most densely populated areas on the planet. But anyone taking a walk yesterday in Gaza, or today on the West Bank, and who talks to the settlers, will have heard them say, again and again, and as though it were obvious, that where they now live there was no one, nothing, before.

THE PARADOXES OF THE OCCUPATION

The occupation automatically reinforced the most ethnicist tendencies within Israel. The more instruments of domination were put in place, the more it became necessary to deny this: either to render invisible the bullying, arrests, collective punishments as a means of repression, and institutionalized torture in the territories, or to justify them with the excuse that "terrorists" could not be treated with kid gloves. The first intifada was still far off, and there was as yet no question of breaking kids' arms, as Itzhak Rabin would put it, not to mention the outbursts against an entire civilian population that characterized the second intifada. But Israelis were growing accustomed to dealing with the other through the imposition of force, with little regard for the means employed.

And the more accustomed they became, the more they refused to see what was going on, the more they withdrew into an insistence on what they regarded as their own rights and interests, forgetting that these were illegitimate. International law? What international law? The right of the Jewish people on the land was much more legitimate. And it didn't matter what the goyim, the non-Jews, thought. The country gradually changed its character: the movement advocating return to the faith, which generally brought with it the adoption of increasingly mystical arguments, got underway in the 1970s. More explicit forms of racism appeared and were not considered illegitimate. The opinions and governmental influence of people like Effi Eitam and Benny Elon were not on the horizon at that time, but the premises were there.

In ten years' time, not only had the right seized power and Gush Emunim gained control of the NRP, but openly annexationist groups had emerged on the right. "Gandhi," a retired general whose real name was Rehavaam

Zeevi, a man skilled in the strong-arm tactics he had long practiced in person and a good friend of certain figures in the Israeli underworld, founded a party called Moledet (Fatherland), which was the first to call for the transfer of the Palestinians out of Palestine. Later, when he was a minister in the Sharon government, "Gandhi" was assassinated by militants of the Popular Front for the Liberation of Palestinian (PFLP) in revenge for the targeted killing of their leader. Though he had been renowned for his unprecedented brutality toward "the Arabs," he was mourned as a great founder of the state and a visionary.

In these earlier years, though, Israel was still far from what Avraham Burg, the former Labor president of the Knesset, called the "insensitivity" and "loss of moral feeling" that would take hold of the country with the second intifada. Recently," he said in a 2003 interview, "I paid a visit to a high school. Many of the students were saying frightening things: 'When we're soldiers, we'll kill old people, women, and children.' And they were saying, 'We'll expel them. By the hundreds of thousands, by the millions.' And most of the students were applauding. I tried in vain to point out that this is what people were saying about us sixty years ago."[29] True, not many young people were expressing such destructive views in the 1970s. But ethnicism was strongly on the upswing. Hostility toward "the Arabs," as a category, was displayed more openly. It was less potential, more concrete: "the Arabs" were said to be not just an external threat but a very numerous presence right in the middle of Israel. The "pied-noirization"[30] of the Israeli mind-set was underway.

But why worry? On the whole, things were calm. The Palestinian street did not rise up against the settlement movement. On the contrary: thanks to some good middlemen, it was Palestinian workers who were building the houses intended for the settlers and the roads leading there. Well, they have to eat too, it was said. The employment of Palestinians, especially in small businesses, private agriculture, and the crafts industries often took paternalistic forms. Now and then armed terrorists tried to infiltrate by crossing the Jordan River or the Lebanese border or by entering from the seacoast, but without great success. They would sometimes mount attacks and take schoolchildren or other civilians hostage. These terrible acts had no effect whatsoever other than to confirm the Israelis in their belief that

Palestinian nationalists were simply barbarians. They constituted a threat but an external one. Because they were unable to confront Israel in their armed struggle, certain groups within the Palestinian Liberation Organization (PLO) soon began to attack Israeli or Jewish institutions abroad, hijacking airplanes all over the world. These people were, most assuredly, dangerous, anti-Semitic madmen. They were hunted down and executed in commando raids in Lebanon, Europe, and even Kenya.

By establishing a permanent presence on the West Bank and in Gaza the leaders of Israel as well as the vast majority of its civilians did not realize that the country was systematically altering the internal composition of the Palestinian national movement. At first the "internal Palestinians" did not count in the PLO, which was the national organization of a refugee people and represented the Palestinian diaspora. In the occupied territories its leaders were quickly imprisoned, as were those, for example the Communists, who did not belong to it. Thanks to repression, its influence was limited. Yet without understanding what it was doing, Israel would give it an unexpected gift by closing off all political options that included a withdrawal from the territories.

Thus Jerusalem negotiated with its old partner and adversary Jordan from 1969 to 1971. King Hussein even came, incognito, to spend an evening in East Jerusalem at the invitation of Moshe Dayan. In exchange for recognition of Israel he demanded the restoration of nearly all of the West Bank and the Old City of Jerusalem, agreeing to leave Israel access to the Wailing Wall (which was what Arafat would ask for, thirty years later, at Camp David). Dayan did not follow up on this. Similarly, David Kimche, who later became second in command of Mossad and secretary general of the Foreign Ministry, met with a great many civilian and religious leaders in 1968 and 1969. These people were prepared to establish in Gaza and on the West Bank a demilitarized state that would recognize Israel if that state withdrew its troops. Kimche's report was apparently not even examined by the government. Thus, by pursuing a policy of sheer denial of the Palestinian national movement and eradication of its activists, and by closing the door to any overtures by other forces, Israel did the PLO a major service.

It may well be that the PLO would have imposed itself on the Arab states under any circumstances. But it is Israel that turned away those that had the most to lose by the coming to power of that organization, namely Jordan and local Palestinian leaders, ultimately leaving them no choice other than to acknowledge the PLO as the sole representative of the Palestinian people. Which is just what they all did soon after being snubbed, Hussein going so far as to officially renounce all territorial claim to the West Bank. Thus Israel had broken the tacit agreement made with Jordan in 1947 to assure that no Palestinian state would ever see the light of day. The Palestinians did not exist, the PLO was merely a terrorist organization, but Israel had created a vacuum and, like it or not, had no other de facto interlocutor besides Arafat. Denial of the political nature of the Palestinian national movement had led to the opposite of what had been intended. But that was of little concern, for all that had to be done was to crush the PLO.

The war of 1973, known as the Yom Kippur War, launched by the Egyptian Anwar El-Sadat and the Syrian Hafez El-Assad, shattered the feeling of omnipotence in which the country had basked. Their military successes in the first three days aroused enormous fear. But Israel once again won a major victory, ultimately invading the opposite bank of the Suez Canal and entering Syria beyond the Golan, and so this war changed nothing in the relationship to the occupied territories. On the contrary, those areas had remained calm during the battles, a sign that they were quite submissive. And the war had demonstrated that, more than ever, Israel needed to reinforce its security measures.

The day after the war broke out I was speaking with my uncle on the telephone. The news from the front was very alarming: Israeli troops were being overwhelmed, and soldiers were dying by the hundreds. My uncle seemed to be panicked: "What do they want? The Sinai? The West Bank?" he cried. "They have to be given back the territories, and that's that!" Six weeks later, on my first leave (my reserve unit had been called up and sent to Syrian territory), I met him. "Let them all go to hell! Now it's clear that they'll never get the territories back." That's how the thinking goes with regard to security, always putting politics second to relative strength, or at least to its appearance. The result was that the settlement movement took on new vigor.

The right, which came to power in 1977, would soon show that its policy was paying off. Sadat, the very man who had made war against Israel, came to the Knesset. Negotiations were held under the aegis of President Carter and left the Israeli political class feeling that their country had been the winner by far. To be sure, Israel had to return every last centimeter of the Sinai to Egypt, after having claimed for ten years that the strategic depth offered by this desert was a vital necessity. But Sadat established diplomatic relations with Israel without having to commit himself to anything other than a vague project for Palestinian autonomy in five years. Almost the entire political class in Israel drew the conclusion that an Arab state, in fact, the most important such state, could be led to make peace without the need to surrender the Palestinian territories. An extraordinary success.

One more additional stage in the denial of what the "internal Palestinians" represented had been reached. They obviously didn't count. So what if they all, in their hearts, supported the PLO? They would be shown the vanity of their illusions. In 1982 Sharon persuaded Menahem Begin to undertake a wondrous adventure: conquering Lebanon and liquidating the PLO there once and for all, putting in power a "friendly" Christian regime. The offensive ended in a major political defeat. After the assassination, probably by the Syrians, of Beshir Gemayel, the president supposedly "elected" under the Israeli heel, his forces, the Israelis' allies, committed a massacre in the Palestinian refugee camps of Sabra and Shatila, killing between 800 and 1,500 civilians: men, women, children, and old people.[31]

At that point President Reagan, who up to then had let Israel conduct its operation, demanded its immediate withdrawal from Beirut. Ariel Sharon, minister of defense and instigator of this war, became the most discredited politician in the country. Israel had to retreat from Beirut, and it would soon see the triumph of Syria, whose presence in Lebanon was sanctioned by the Arab states in the Taef Accords seven years later. The PLO had been expelled from Lebanon, but it was far from eradicated, François Mitterand, with Reagan's tacit approval, having seen to the expatriation of its cadres to Tunis. The Israelis had a sense of bitter political failure but consoled themselves with the thought that, militarily, the PLO had been vanquished. Tunis, where the PLO's headquarters had moved, was a lot further away than Beirut. Security was what mattered most.

What of the Palestinians in the occupied territories during this time? Once again they did not make a move. The occupation was under control, the Israelis said, and there was no reason to think it might be otherwise in the future. The settlement movement proceeded unchecked. Confined as they were by the Orientalist certainties taught in most of the departments of Middle-Eastern studies they had been trained in, analysts in the security services, like academicians and media experts who specialized in the territories, saw nothing on the horizon. Like the settler Smilanski at the beginning of the century, they were convinced that an Arab would of course submit once he sensed that force would be applied, and so they pursued the hunt for nationalist activists. Apart from this routine, there was nothing to worry about.

"What would happen in a generation?" the Israeli prime minister had wondered in 1967. A generation later, in 1987, the question, and the vague unease it carried, were considered irrelevant. The occupation had become a way of life. Israeli families were picnicking by the Dead Sea, near Jericho. Household appliances manufactured in the territories and stamped "Made in Jordan" were exported to the Arab countries. The Laborite oracles who, twenty years earlier, had privately feared a catastrophe if the occupation continued no longer held meetings. Most of them had ended up persuading themselves that their anxieties were unfounded. In the political class only a few people protested the blindness, the establishment of colonialism in a new form: Communist leaders, whose group was seen as an Arab party and hence off the screen, Deputy Uri Avnery, and Reserve General Matti Peled. Theirs were voices in the wilderness.

The denial of reality had definitively won out in the minds of the Israelis and their political thinking. The Palestinians were a security question and nothing else.

NINE

"WE MISSED AN EXTRAORDINARY OPPORTUNITY"

The Great Waste of the Peace Talks

THE OSLO UPHEAVAL (AUGUST 1993)

By 1987 there had been twenty years of this calm apartheid in the occupied territories, years in which the daily life of a population deprived of elementary rights was managed by the "civil government" of the IDF and its regulations that changed in accordance with what it deemed necessary for security. Twenty years in which the intelligence service, Shin Bet, had been arresting people at will, setting no limits to the length of internment for alleged suspects; under Israeli emergency laws, months and years could pass without a trial or indictment. Twenty years in which it had a blank endorsement from the Supreme Court to torture suspects with full impunity,[1] and in which it expelled and exiled and wove its networks of collaborators among the occupied. Twenty years, too, in which politicians continued to seek desperately for local leaders willing to serve as intermediaries. Obsessed with security, the Israelis did not see the slow maturation of a new generation of Palestinians whose anger was equalled only by their determination. Anger at repression, humiliation, and a sense of impotence, and anger at the generation of their conquered and submissive parents.

To say that the first intifada, the "stone-throwing revolt" waged by Palestinian youth in 1987, stunned Israeli leaders is to put it mildly. They hadn't seen it coming. In conformity with the old Orientalist perception regarding security, they at first saw the uprising as an itch, an explosion of violence to be put down without delay. Once again, as the historian Zeev Sternhell recalled, it was thought that gangs were responsible. If need be, stated Yitzhak Rabin, defense minister in a coalition government comprising both left and right, the Israelis would break their bones.

This intifada would reveal the change that had come over Israel in its twenty-first year of occupation. It ended the phase of construction of a nation-state begun in 1948, a phase in which the Jewish state was, or could pretend it was, rid of the Palestinian question. From now on that problem would be unavoidable, once again an integral part of Israeli society's relationship to itself. And the results were paradoxical. In the interests of the national ethos, the construction of a national Jewish Israeli society had been marked by a consensus often based on institutionalized lies with regard to the Arabs. The media were subject to military censorship. The chief security agencies regularly briefed newspaper editors on sensitive subjects, pointing out the accepted version to be offered to the public. This was the case, for example, with the massacres of civilians committed by the army at Kybia in 1953 and at Kfar Kassem in 1956, which were presented as reprisals for attacks. Without balking, the press had taken on the job of transmitting rewritten facts. For journalists, then, the intifada marked the beginning of emancipation. In newspaper reporting and even on television, fault lines gradually appeared as journalists freed themselves from security constraints. What they were supposed to conceal now became so glaring that accepting censorship or self-censorship meant renouncing their primary duty, namely to inform.

With the first intifada signs of the general brutalization of the army began to come to light, signs that, with the second uprising, would be on an altogether different scale. Repression and torture were no longer confined to the special services in confined places; the rank and file were now directly implicated. The use of force became the soldiers' ordinary means of going about their duty:

> Blunders and excessive brutality toward the civilian populations multiplied. In the hospitals of Ramallah and Nablus young people, adults,

and the elderly were treated for injuries sustained in lengthy and
severe beatings: lips were split, teeth broken, arms and legs fractured.
An insane act of violence took place in early February 1988 in the
town of Salem: four teenagers were hit and then buried alive by a
bulldozer manned by soldiers. They were rescued on the brink of
death by inhabitants of the town. This episode led General Amran
Mitzna, the commandant on the West Bank [and future Labor candidate for the office of prime minister], to say this: "In my worst nightmare I could not have imagined that Israeli soldiers would commit
such an act." The daily newspaper *Haaretz* wrote that "heavy-handed
policy has become sadistic policy." [Baron 2003, p, 522]

One year after the onset of the first intifada — 400 dead, 10,000 wounded,
and 6,000 arrests later — Palestinian mobilization had not weakened. Israel soldiers were becoming exhausted by a repression that was often absurd, taking Palestinian flags down from walls and flagpoles only to see
them reappear the next day. The heads of Shin Bet finally understood that
their old thought patterns were no longer working, in particular the idea
that this was a new edition of the Arab revolt of 1936–1939. That event
had been a huge popular uprising, accompanied by guerrilla warfare,
against the British occupying power. What was taking place now was a
general youth movement. This isn't guerrilla warfare. The army has no
adversary; it's fighting against kids and stones, Shin Bet leaders told Defense Minister Itzhak Rabin.

The former head of the general staff, later a diplomat and former head
of government, Itzhak Rabin, affectionately dubbed *Hamoakh Haanaliti*
(The Analytic Brain) by his supporters, was really not a very brilliant politician. But he was a pragmatist, and he had no sympathy for the ultranationalists. He adopted the view that, if breaking the insurgents' bones did
not work, other means would have to be undertaken. Heading the Labor
slate in the 1992 elections, Rabin, a man who knew what firm control
meant, promised that he would be able to put an end to this intifada that
had lasted four years. Like de Gaulle in 1958, he did not go into detail
about how he would accomplish this. He was elected. The path to Oslo
was paved.

And, simultaneously, it had long been paved by Yasser Arafat. If truth be told, the leaders of the PLO, too, cut off in their Tunisian offices from events inside the territories, had not seen the intifada coming. But they quickly saw how to profit from it. The political movement of a diaspora, an essentially terrorist organization of armed struggle, the PLO now became the representative of a people fighting against its occupation and for its independence. It took quite some time for Arafat to realize that Israel would not be vanquished militarily. His emissaries had been conferring with Israelis of the progressive camp, and, with the help of King Hassan II of Morocco and the Romanian Nicolae Ceausescu, his adjutants had held secret meetings with highly placed Israeli politicians. His leading terrorists had sometimes negotiated with leaders of the Israeli special services. Since 1983 Arafat had been launching trial balloons toward effective recognition of Israel and gradually teaching Palestinian public opinion to accept the coming historic turn of events. On November 15, 1988, the Palestinian National Council adopted a declaration of independence acknowledging United Nations Resolution 242[2] and stipulating the establishment of a Palestinian state *alongside* Israel. In a press conference in Paris on May 9, 1989, Arafat announced that the PLO charter, which anticipated the disappearance of Israel, was null and void.

In 1991, immediately following the first Gulf War, the PLO rejoined the diplomatic game. Included in the Jordanian delegation, its representatives participated in the Madrid Conference, which brought together international and Arab partners to resolve the Israeli–Palestinian problem. The Letter of Assurances provided by Washington to Jerusalem on October 18, 1991, in which the United States undertook not to ask for the PLO's entry into the peace process,[3] did not fool anyone. Madrid offered the possibility of an enormous upheaval, opening the door for each of the two protagonists to end its nonrecognition of the other.

Announced at the end of August and signed on September 13, 1993, in front of the White House, the Oslo Accords of mutual recognition between Israel and the PLO were the culmination of this upheaval. My immediate reaction was one of heartfelt support. In August 1993 I felt the same emotion that had overcome me, four years earlier, when the Berlin Wall collapsed. In a sudden acceleration of history, the unthinkable had come

to pass. In 1989 there had been the announcement of the end of dictatorship in the Soviet Union and the achievement of freedom for so many
peoples who had been thwarted for decades; in 1993 the announcement
of the end of a hundred-year-old conflict and the possibility that Israelis
and Palestinians could live together in shared dignity. Three weeks before Oslo, the IDF had still been bombing the Palestinians in South Lebanon, and here were Rabin and Arafat, shaking hands. From what I knew
of them, I had little confidence in their political stature. No matter: the
mutual recognition was a historic breakthrough.

And yet, in comparing Oslo to Berlin my astonishment and emotion
did not entail similar assumptions about the future. While it was clear to
me that the collapse of the Wall created an irreversible situation—there
would be no recurrence of "true socialism," as it was called by the world
Communist movement—I had the immediate conviction that while the
Oslo Accords created a promise, there was nothing irreversible about it.
Most of my colleagues were of the opinion that Oslo would lead to a process with no return, that the recognition of Israel by the Arab world was
becoming inevitable, as was its corollary, the imminent formation of a
Palestinian state. I did not share these certainties. Oslo seemed to me to
represent a unique opening for mutual acceptance, the prelude to a possible reconciliation in the acknowledgment of the other and his identity.
But nothing, I felt, was spelled out in advance. When incremental negotiations got underway, I was convinced that they were heading in the wrong
direction. And as security needs in Israel soon overrode the political conditions for the implementation of Oslo—that is, the willingness to end
the occupation—the more those accords seemed to me to be a fleeting
moment of lucidity on Israel's part, a brief recognition of the validity of
the national Palestinian movement.

The Oslo Accords[4] were diplomatically shaky. Their preamble sums
up their ambiguities. It stipulates that Israel and the PLO "recognize their
mutual legitimate and political rights, and strive to live in peaceful coexistence and mutual dignity and security and achieve a just, lasting, and
comprehensive peace settlement and historic reconciliation." Each phrase
was negotiated down to the last comma. In each key term we can discern
what each of the signatories considered imperative.

Rights? For Israel, they had to be acknowledged as "legitimate," since the "historic rights" of the Jews are the basis of Zionism. For the Palestinians, they are "political": respect for the U.N. Resolutions, sovereignty, and independence.

Coexistence? For the Israelis, it implies security. For the Palestinians, it implies dignity, a status of equality, the absence of any act unilaterally founded on the notion that might makes right.

Peace? It must be "lasting and comprehensive" for the Israelis, assuring the Jewish state definitive recognition regardless of the final status of the Palestinians. Fine, the latter replied, but on condition that this peace is "just," that it take into account the origin of the conflict and its consequences.

Thus there was one document, but from the outset each party invested it with different content. For the Israelis, the future peace meant the legitimization of Zionism and perpetual security. For the Palestinians, it meant accession to statehood and acknowlegment of the fraud that had been perpetrated against them. And these were not the only ambiguities in the Oslo Accords. Nowhere is the creation of a future Palestinian state explicitly mentioned. Nor is there any formal stipulation of the abandonment of the settlements. The refugee question is evaded. But there was a sense of confidence in the document's basic philosophy, which was believed to imply all these ideas. On the one hand, land would be exchanged for peace; that is, Israel would withdraw from the occupied territories in return for a Palestinian state that would live in peace with it. On the other hand, since the signatories were coming from positions that had been very far apart, trust had to be established and time allowed for. But not too much time: a period not exceeding five years was given for completing incremental negotiations.

The accords are certainly multivocal, if not equivocal, but at the beginning their impact was enormous. On the Palestinian side they marked not only the end of the illusion that Israel was going to disappear, but also, on a deeper level, the recognition of the national identity of Israeli society. The Israelis were no longer Jews with an exclusively religious identity whose formation into a national group was said to be the artificial result of a distinctively colonial process.

And on the opposite side the accords marked the end of even greater illusions, illusions in which the Palestinians were reduced to an undifferentiated "Arab" identity and the PLO was denied the character of a national
movement. The handshake between Arafat and Rabin was a groundbreaking
event for the Palestinians, but for the former terrorist leader it was a victory signaling his legitimate entry into the international community. For
Rabin, the man who had carried out the expulsion of 70,000 Palestinians from Lydda and Ramleh in 1948, shaking Arafat's hand represented
a shock at the very deepest level: the collapse of the Orientalist vision
that for a century had structured the Israeli relationship to the native
inhabitants. In Israel, many saw this handshake as the historic defeat of
a vision that up to then had been consensual. But the advocates of the
old approach were stunned, unable to offer an alternative to the new
dispensation.

Someone unfamiliar with Israel and Palestine in the months immediately following the Oslo Accords can perhaps not imagine the enormous
sense of relief that came over a part of each group. For a number of Israelis it was as though they had been waiting for this for a long time without
daring to say so or even think so, as if the collapse of the mythologies that
had been erected to demonize the adversary was finally making it possible
for them to glimpse the end of imprisonment. On the other side, when
Arafat returned to Palestine in May 1994, the people of Gaza welcomed
him with wild enthusiasm, some of them even waving pennants with the
colors of the Israeli and American flags.

This was 1994. Yesterday the intifada, though in decline, was still going
on. From now on it would recede into the distance. Each side rushed
toward the other. Not everyone, of course, at most some of the elites, but
many more than just the militant left. For several months there was an
atmosphere of discovery of the other. Professors exchanged invitations;
colloquia were organized. These meetings with yesterday's opponent sometimes took unforeseen turns, with Mossad agents spending the evening
with former terrorist leaders and recalling together their past battles in an
ambience of macho brotherhood: "Remember how we screwed you that
time?" "Yeah, but that other time *we* left *you* in the dust." They would
clink glasses and reminisce about their heroic exploits: a surrealistic sce-

nario. The political figure, Abu Daud, who organized the massacre of Israeli athletes at the Munich Olympics in 1972 was permitted to come and live in Gaza.

On the Palestinian side—in Palestine proper, since in the diaspora matters were different—the change was obvious. The Islamists kept a very low profile. In the PLO, the Popular Front and the Democratic Front for the Liberation of Palestine, which had opposed the Oslo Accords, were at a loss. When the PFLP acted in a disciplined manner and followed the orders of their leaders in Damascus to boycott the first Palestinian elections, Ghazi Abu Jayyab, one of its highly respected figures in Gaza, broke with them and decided to present himself as an independent candidate. Arrested in 1969 at the age of 16½ and convicted of having fired on Israeli military vehicles, Abu Jayyab had been sentenced to life in prison. He remained in captivity for sixteen years, during which he went on long and terrible hunger strikes to bring about improvements in the treatment of political prisoners. He also learned Hebrew, "because to attain peace you have to begin by understanding the other,"[5] and became a translator. Freed in 1985 during an exchange of prisoners, he was arrested again in 1988. This time he was tortured, severely beaten, and deprived of sleep for days on end. Shin Bet believed that he was the author of the first tract distributed in Gaza that called for the uprising. This was false. A court admitted as much, but only after he had spent six more months in prison. Israeli human-rights lawyers were active on his behalf. When local PFLP leaders who had recently been released tried to tell him that the Oslo Accords were a capitulation, Ghazi replied, "Without Oslo you'd be issuing your calls for a boycott of the elections from jail, because you'd still be there." They could not deny this, and the general population, too, found the argument convincing. Not all prisoners had been freed, but it was believed they soon would be. Hope for a political solution overrode the problems of the moment.

On the Israeli side a new mood of introspection set in. The New Historians, who had been ignored before, provoked endless debates. Should the files from the War of Independence be opened? The official historians were alarmed: Zionism would be dead! But the press was suddenly very interested in all those former Israeli activists who, only yesterday, had been considered traitors and in some cases had even been imprisoned for meeting with PLO leaders. Today they were called precursors. And the once-vague notion of post-Zionism, put forth by essayists like Tom Segev, became fashionable. Underlying this notion was the simple idea that, with peace now within reach, Israel could achieve normality. With the threat of annihilation on the wane, it could look at itself in the mirror, subjecting its history and society to a critical evaluation untainted by evasion and whitewashing, without fearing that this would give aid and comfort to the enemy. Zionism had had its glories and its defects. It had won, since Israel existed, strong and, at long last, recognized by its historic enemy. But it was now time for it to yield to a new Israel, one that could do without its complexes and be more honest with itself, becoming even stronger in the process. The post-Zionists symbolized the retreat from ethnicism and the concomitant openness to the other.

Openness to the other certainly did seem to be taking root in Israeli democracy. For example, Ghazi Abu Jayyab, the former PFLP leader in Gaza, was invited to be on one of the most popular Israeli talk shows. Similarly, a Palestinian press freed from Israeli military censorship came into being and reprinted articles from Hebrew publications. These articles were, to be sure, favorable to the Palestinian point of view, but this was a start, a way of showing the Palestinians that the Israelis weren't monsters. Some people began to think that the two societies could never go back to where they had been: they were in motion. On the political and diplomatic level, however, the enthusiasm would soon collapse.

SEVEN YEARS TO NEGOTIATE A "JUST AND COMPREHENSIVE" PEACE

The explicit objective of the Oslo Accords was to achieve what was termed "a historic reconciliation." But how to go about reconciling with a hereditary enemy? Beyond the diplomatic vicissitudes of the negotiations, the errors committed on one side or the other, this is the question facing anyone who wants to understand why such great hope would slowly fall apart, ending in the Camp David fiasco seven years later. In the view of

Admiral Ami Ayalon, and contrary to the perceived idea, it was the Israeli Labor leaders, the signatories to the accords, who "missed an extraordinary opportunity" to attain reconciliation.[6]

The stakes were epoch-making: nothing less than a final agreement with the PLO to win acceptence of the Jewish state by the Arab world and a comprehensive peace with that world. At the time of the signing, the Palestinians, at least those within Israel, hoped for nothing but that. They were favorable to the accords by a much larger percentage than the Israelis, because they wanted a state but, even more, because the first phase of the agreement, Israeli withdrawal from the two tiny enclaves of Gaza and Jericho, enabled them to envision what really mattered, namely the imminent end of military occupation throughout their territories. The Palestinians of the diaspora were shaken, fearing that gains and losses would make them the forgotten people of history, yet the vast majority of them still considered Arafat their leader. Moreover, Israel knew that a number of Arab states, in the Gulf and in the Maghreb, were only waiting for the creation of an independent Palestine before signing a peace treaty with the Jewish state.

With Oslo signed, Israeli leaders faced a choice. They could understand that this was in fact a historic moment. Alternatively, once the ink had dried on the document and its codicil, the end of the "stone-throwing revolt" of the Palestinians, had been attained, they could revert to the former mode of relating to the Palestinians via domination.

Understanding what was at stake would not be a simple matter. It would mean understanding why, after Israel had claimed for so long that it would never recognize the PLO, it finally did so. Understanding that the country had gone astray, all those years, in its denial of the reality of the other, and therefore that in the future it would have to think and act differently. Understanding that, once the interim accord was signed, the Palestinians were in a position of total dependence and had nothing to offer the Israelis but a final peace as sole guarantee of their security. That the end of the occupation was therefore inevitable. And, finally, that Israel's vastly greater military and diplomatic strength (its own state had been recognized, and no Palestine existed) was also its weakness: that no final accord would be reached on the sole basis of relative strength. On the contrary, reconciliation could come about only through generosity—after all, it was the Palestinians who had been expelled, they who had been occupied—and acknowledgment of the fraud and suffering inflicted on them. Understanding also implied making a commitment to a pedagogical effort with regard to the Israeli population, explaining that only a withdrawal from the occupied territories would bring the security they hoped for. And it implied showing both sides, in tangible acts, that the general system of occupation would soon come to an end.

Failure to understand what was at stake meant pretending that Oslo had basically changed nothing, and a return to the traditional view of the need for relative superiority of forces and the security imperative that had been so deeply entrenched. Doing otherwise was surely too difficult for the Israelis, given how heavily ethnicist Orientalism counted for its leadership, despite efforts toward openness to the other in the intelligentsia. At the subsequent talks in Cairo, Israeli negotiators had only one issue in mind: security. And generals played a much larger role in committees than politicians. Delays began to accumulate. Arafat was not authorized to return to Palestine until May 1994, four months later than the Oslo Accords had envisioned.

I will not chronicle the negotiations and confrontations, or the accompanying sociopolitical developments, of the seven years that followed. The journalist Charles Enderlin (2002) has analyzed the diplomatic aspects in detail. Amira Hass, the correspondent in the occupied territories for *Haaretz*, has brilliantly described in two books (1999, 2003a) and innumerable articles the changes in the Israeli mind-set and the gap that slowly formed between the initial hopes of the Palestinian population and the actual implementation of the interim accords on the ground. Without minimizing the faults of Arafat and his Palestinian Authority, it is necessary to examine why the primary responsibility for the failure lies with the Labor leaders of Israel.

Yes, the heads of the PLO, most of them "Tunisians" (members of the movement expelled from Beirut to Tunis in 1982–1983), were obsessed with the regaining of the territories and proved unable to negotiate effectively and intelligently with the Israelis after years of armed struggle. But it was the Israelis who almost immediately and reflexively restored security interests to their primary position. Instead of attending to the fundamental issue, the search for a viable solution based on the equality of the two partners, they gradually brought the negotiations to an impasse, kindling in their fellow citizens a growing disaffection for the peace process and an increasingly angry exasperation with the Palestinians.

The first turning point was the murder, on February 25, 1994, of twenty-nine Palestinians praying in the Cave of the Patriarchs in Hebron by Baruch Goldstein, a doctor and religious settler belonging to a small ultra-nationalist sect called Kakh (an acronym of Kahane Khai).[7] This attack took place four months after the signing of the accords at the White House. Arafat had not yet returned to Palestine. Some of the most fanatic of the religious nationalist settlers had been living in this Arab city of 100,000 inhabitants since 1968. In 1994 they numbered only 300 people (there are 800 today). Strictly speaking, their settlement had always been considered illegal, yet all successive governments had accorded them the necessary facilities and protection. They are among the most "God-crazed" Israelis, profoundly racist in their hatred of Arabs and Muslims and (apart from the American Christian fundamentalists, whom they have recently discovered)[8] basically hostile to almost everything that is not Jewish. Under military protection, and hence with impunity, they have done untold damage to the property of many residents. In Israel even those in favor of the occupation admitted that these people were out of bounds. Everyone knew that, if there were a peace treaty, the settlers in Hebron, a fixed abscess of the occupation, would inevitably be evacuated.

What was to be done after this massacre? The heads of Shin Bet asked Itzhak Rabin for a clear signal that these very peculiar settlers should be thrown out of Hebron. After Goldstein's crime, they said in effect, no one would dare to oppose this. The prime minister hesitated. Removing these settlers would send a wrong signal to the PLO, showing that Israel was withdrawing from an area without getting anything in return. The overriding philosophy of Israel in the negotiations was not to let go of anything without compensation, and the interests of security and the relative strength of forces called for equal exchange. Rabin had nothing but scorn for what he regarded as fanatic settlers, but his negotiation strategy dictated that he maintain an Israeli presence in Hebron. In the future, he thought, this presence could be a bargaining chip.

Yet doing nothing would send another signal, this time to the settlers, who would see this as a form of impunity. So Rabin had an idea: the IDF would not evacuate all the settlers from Hebron but only those of Tel Rumeida, a minuscule trailer encampment of forty or fifty people (today they live in permanent structures). In other words, a symbolic gesture. His security adviser, Ehud Sprinzak, had been told that the settlers of Tel Rumeida were threatening to commit mass suicide; if there was a hue and cry, he told Rabin, the prime minister would be accused of fomenting war among Jews. Rabin was persuaded to do nothing. Or, rather, he did do something: the Arab population of Hebron was placed under a total curfew on the grounds that, after Goldstein's suicide attack, reprisals against settlers and soldiers, perhaps even attacks in Israel itself, had to be prevented.

When all was said and done, no one was evacuated from Hebron. The pro-settlement side won. If, in the period immediately after Oslo, Rabin had announced the evacuation in six months' time of half of the settlements, given the euphoria of the moment and the support of the Israeli Arab minority he would have had a comfortable majority of Israelis behind him. And he would have sent a powerful signal to the Palestinians regarding Israel's true intentions. According to Oslo, didn't trust have to be established? Apparently not; critical decisions would have to wait. And there was no question of telling people where, exactly, the government was heading. The result was that, in seven years of negotiations, no Israeli settlement was evacuated from the occupied territories. On the contrary, the pace of settlement increased.

Rabin had refused to evacuate the extremists from Hebron. His opponents, quick to use his argument—that Jews should not fight Jews—against those favoring an evacuation, had no such scruples. After Rabin stepped back the pro-settlement group, which had been numbed by Oslo, gained new courage. Everything wasn't lost, after all. Bibi Netanyahu and Ariel Sharon, leaders of the nationalist right, put in appearances at demonstrations in which Itzhak Rabin and Shimon Peres were caricatured as SS-men. Soon rabbis were launching what amounted to fatwas against Rabin and Peres: giving up even one square centimeter of the Land of Israel was a sacrilege, they claimed, an unpardonable offense against God, so any means could legitimately be used to prevent this. And more of the like.

Twenty months later, on November 4, 1995, five weeks after the signing of an interim accord that was known as Oslo II and envisioned a new, very minor, withdrawal from the territories, one of their disciples, Ygal Amir, would assassinate the prime minister.

For the Palestinians, the signal sent by the Goldstein incident was much more explicit. When one of their people commits an attack, a curfew is imposed; collective punishment is in the order of things. But when an Israeli is the perpetrator, it is again the Palestinians who are put under curfew! The logic of the occupation, according to which security prevails over politics, came down to this: whether a terrorist was a Palestinian or an Israeli, the Palestinians would be constrained. And this logic was not about to undergo a change.

This security-minded logic, curbing any political vision aimed at a future reconciliation, had another consequence: Israel demanded that the PLO demonstrate its willingness to be a partner in peace by maintaining order so as to ensure Israel's security. In practical terms, Israeli leaders were expecting the Palestinian Authority to turn itself into a conduit for Israeli security needs. The occupation continued, as did expropriations. The West Bank and Gaza were divided into some two hundred pieces of confetti, each with its own status, A, B, or C, granting the resident populations different rights and making travel between them much more difficult. The settlements were reinforced. The mission of the multiple police forces put in place by Arafat, as single units or in supposed cooperation with the Israeli services, was to make sure that this did not cause a stir among his people. And this happened with hardly anything being offered in return.

To be sure, Israel and the PLO were negotiating during this time. Negotiating what? Nothing essential, basically. Israel was still locked into the most restrictive interpretation of the accords. Contrary to the repeated assertion by the PLO that, according to Oslo, neither party would take any initiative in changing the status of the West Bank and Gaza pending negotiations on their permanent status, this clause does not appear in the text of the document. The conclusion drawn by Israel was that, since putting an end to the settlements was not explicitly stipulated, there was no question of Israel doing so. Did this go against what was called "the spirit of Oslo"? The Israeli negotiators were concerned not with interpretations but with ensuring the security of their fellow citizens in the face of terrorism, which had begun anew.

There are countless instances in which Israel cited security reasons for postponing the implementation of signed agreements or for applying them only in part. The Palestinians could do nothing other than be shocked and hope for better times. But such times were not likely to come, for restrictions in the name of security methodically undermined the possibility that the Palestinian Authority could become just that, a legitimate authority, in the eyes of its population.

The final point would be reached in the "prisoners' week" of mid-May 2000. Seven years after Oslo, some two thousand political prisoners were still in Israeli jails. From one negotiation to the next, Israel freed them only in dribs and drabs and delayed releases previously agreed on. Families and friends could no longer contain their exasperation, and the Palestinian street exploded. Their anger was directed not only at the occupation but also at Arafat and his inability to obtain what everyone wanted. There were three days of violent confrontations with the IDF before calm was restored. But for the first time since 1993 the militants of Fatah, Arafat's party, demonstrated side by side with those of the PFLP and the Islamists of Hamas, organizations that had rejected the Oslo Accords. For the political scientist Menahem Klein, at the time an adviser to Shlomo Ben Ami, minister for foreign affairs and internal security, the tragedy was "that Israel had not seen this coming, that no one in the cabinet had ever mentioned the issue of these developments in the territories."[9]

When Benyamin Netanyahu negotiated at Wye River in October 1998 under the aegis of President Clinton he proposed that the new phase of redeployment of the Israeli army envisioned by the accords be extended to an additional one percent of the territory of the Palestinians. Why not one-tenth of a percent? asked the caustic Palestinians. Then he signed an agreement for the release of three hundred prisoners, almost all of whom had been jailed for nonpolitical reasons, though the families of political prisoners detained for years had been hoping to see them free at last. The arrogance of the colonial occupier was fully evident in these attitudes. Israel was a thousand miles away from the Oslo Accords and recognition of the Palestinian national movement.

As time passed, the Palestinian population saw its conditions deteriorate more and more. It became harder to find work in Israel. Successive governments had deliberately brought in over 200,000 immigrants from the Philippines, Malaysia, Rumania, and elsewhere to replace the Palestinian labor force. Nor could they move about freely. In the seven-year period from 1994 to July 2000, the Palestinians were completely cordoned off for three hundred and thirty days, nearly a full year in total.[10] This happened after attacks, of course, but also on Jewish holidays, so that the settlers would not be disturbed. And, as time passed, Palestinian society came to have increasing doubts about Arafat and his Palestinian Authority, which was bringing them nothing beyond a degradation of their freedoms and their living standards, and Hamas grew in influence. If the Islamists are expanding, thought the Israelis, this was because security was vulnerable. And so further pressure had to be put on the Palestinians, allowing them as little leeway as possible until they had proved themselves. Security became the sole criterion for negotiation and debate in Israel, and there was increasing denial of the very reason for insecurity, namely the occupation of another people.

In a discussion with a noncomissioned officer in 1999 I pointed out that the Palestinians were desperate, with the repeated closures and restrictions on movement adding to their frustration. "It's distressing," he said. "Personally, I'm for giving them back the territories. In the meantime, we have to ensure security. But our actions have an educational effect. The worse life becomes for the Palestinians, the more inclined they'll be to accept our final offers, because they'll be all too happy to see us go." Even in the best-intentioned logic of security, people can persuade themselves that repression has a positive effect.

In July 2000 Arafat was obliged to participate in the Camp David summit by the Laborite Ehud Barak, who had succeeded Netanyahu as prime minister, and President Clinton. The talks were intended to settle all outstanding issues. The situation at the time was as follows: seven years after Oslo, two years after the date set for the end of the peace process, and after five new interim accords, the Palestinian Authority owned 70 percent of the territory of Gaza and 13.1 percent of the West Bank. Relative to what it had gotten in 1993–1994, it had regained 12.5 percent of additional territory, the so-called Zone A, including the large cities and towns (excluding 30 percent of Hebron and East Jerusalem), amounting to 70 percent of the population. In signing Oslo it had hoped to regain 100 percent of the occupied territory in five years so as to construct its state. Seven years later, it was in charge of 20 percent, and only under total Israeli control.

During the same period 30,000 Israelis had come to live in the eastern part of what was called "Greater Jerusalem," 78,000 in the rest of the territories. Nineteen new settlements had been created and half of the 122 already in existence "enlarged in response to the needs of their natural growth," as official Israeli policy put it. Eleven thousand one hundred ninety new housing units had been built there. Of the three Israeli prime ministers who held office in the years since Oslo, it was Barak, not the Likudnik Netanyahu, who constructed the most colonies.[11] In the thirteen years following the outbreak of the first intifada in 1987, the number of Israelis on the West Bank had gone from 65,000 to 220,000, in East Jerusalem from 80,000 to 200,000, in Gaza from 2,700 to 6,000.[12]

Thirty-five thousand additional hectares had been confiscated by Israel in occupied territory, 5.8 percent of their total area, the equivalent of the entire Gaza Strip. Eight hundred ninety-five houses had been destroyed by the Israeli army in East Jerusalem and the rest of the territories, on the grounds that they belonged to the families of terrorists or had been built illegally. Between 1988 and 2000, 13,000 Palestinians had been left homeless.

Because of the multiplication of zones dispersed throughout the territories (Zones A, B, and C), the need to control checkpoints and protect the bypass roads reserved for the use of the settlers, the massive closures, and similar measures, the IDF increased its forces on the West Bank by 30 percent, the largest military presence ever for that population.

In the period from September 1993 to July 2000, between Israeli retaliation and renewed Palestinian attacks, 385 Palestinian civilians and 23 members of their security services had been killed; on the Israeli side 171 civilians had fallen victim to Palestinian attacks, and 92 soldiers or police officers had died in confrontations or abductions.

It is hardly surprising that, on the eve of Camp David, very few Palestinians trusted the peace process. For most of them, Israel had shown no intention whatsoever of leaving the occupied territories. In addition, their standard of living had declined, unemployment was rife, the officials of their nascent state were incompetent and corrupt, and there was no democracy: no wonder the territories had become a seething cauldron.

In November 2000, six months after the Camp David summit, in the course of examining the reasons for its failure, I had a long meeting with Dennis Ross. For ten years this diplomat had been the United States go-between in the Middle East, serving in the Republican administration of the first George Bush and the Democratic one of Bill Clinton. Of all the American officials he was by far one of the most favorable toward Israel.[13] When I asked him whether, in hindsight, he thought he had made mistakes, he replied, "Yes. The diplomatic process didn't pay enough attention to the changes on the ground and their consequences." Which consequences, specifically? "First of all, the settlements," he explained.[14]

The situation had deteriorated considerably for Israel as well. The right kept on repeating that Oslo had brought neither peace nor security, since the attacks were continuing. The peace process had become bogged down in hundreds of security measures, the Palestinian Authority had been unable to offer any substantial political benefit, and the increasing intensity of the occupation had not put an end to terrorism: as a result, Israelis had become convinced that Oslo wasn't working. And if things weren't going well, according to what Gideon Levy has called the mental Pavlovian reflex, this could only be the other side's fault.

In civilian society the pacifists had all but disappeared from the landscape; they considered their mission accomplished. They were ardently in favor of the negotiations, and, like Dennis Ross, failed to take the situation on the ground into account and hence to question the way in which the overriding appeal to security had imposed a catastrophic logic. On January 5, 1996, the Israeli Special Services assassinated the Hamas "engineer" Yehia Ayash, who had fomented several attacks. The pacifist left, the group to which Prime Minister Shimon Peres belonged, was uneasy. They refused to distance themselves from the act, although there had been no Palestinian attacks in the country for six months and Arafat had imprisoned dozens of Hamas military leaders and, in the Cairo talks, had negotiated a commitment on the part of the Islamists to cease their attacks in Israel.

The liquidation of Ayash is a typical example of the way the security perspective lay down the law for policy. The Israel government knew that, in authorizing this act, it risked setting off a political firestorm, justifying the conviction of Arafat and the Islamists that Israel would never follow through on its commitments and considerably weakening its ostensible peace partner, the Palestinian Authority. As for the heads of the security services, they were technicians. They had received orders to kill Ayash, who was in hiding. For months they had been trying to target him. When they finally did so and asked for authorization to kill him, Peres hesitated, aware of the risks. At that point the security services gave him their usual pitch, saying in effect: "Today we have him; tomorrow who knows? If you say no, don't come blaming us for not bringing him down. It's up to you now." The security cabinet had given the green light. The consequences would be disastrous.

Six weeks after the liquidation of Ayash, the "engineer" was avenged in three terrifying suicide attacks by Hamas, killing dozens of Israelis. Peres had to react, to show under pressure from the right, which was denouncing his impotence in the face of terrorism, that he knew what security meant. And so Israel mounted heavy attacks against Hezbollah in South Lebanon, going as far as to fire missiles at the headquarters of the United Nations troops in Cana on April 18. In the carnage, dozens of Fijian Blue Berets lost their lives, as did 102 Lebanese civilian refugees, both Shiites and Christians. In the wake of international outrage, Peres agreed to a truce in Lebanon. The operation had been a fiasco, and Israel was condemned throughout the world, with the exception of the United States. Five weeks later, Shimon Peres lost the election to Benyamin Netanyahu; Israeli voters reasoned that, if security was the prime consideration and no one was talking about leaving the territories, they might as well trust a hardliner who promised to rule with an iron hand, not his pale Laborite clone.

The pacifist left condemned the way Likud, now back in power, sought to sabotage the principles of the Oslo Accords. Three years later Netanyahu, having failed on the level of internal affairs, returned the government to Labor. This time the pacifist left had nothing further to say when Ehud Barak, the new prime minister, taking precisely the same approach to negotiations as Netanyahu, demanded that the Palestinians give up the implementation of the third redeployment of Israel forces outside the territories, as specified by Oslo, and, under the conditions mentioned above, proceed directly to the discussion of the final status.

Israel had undergone major changes during this time. Shaul Mofaz, the chief of staff appointed by Netanyahu, was an avowed Likudnik. There were now more religious ultranationalists in the mid-level officer corps of the IDF, and the number of religious schools had increased by 15 percent as a result of the growth of Shas, a new Sephardic Orthodox party that was very active with regard to education. Its leaders, the former Sephardic grand rabbi of Israel Ovadiah Yossef and Rabbi Arieh Derhi, seemed to be moderates on the issue of the territories. But the base of Shas, influenced by rabbis for whom the hand of God explained the slightest event, was strongly ethnicist and superstitious, and they loathed the Arabs. In an alliance with the Laborites, its ministers resigned just before Barak left for Camp David.

Thus when he got on the plane for the United States the prime minister no longer had a cabinet. For seven years no Israeli leader had ever dared to confront the settlers' party head on. None had explicitly told the people what they must surely have known: that a "just and comprehensive peace" as stipulated by Oslo could never be signed if it did not conform to international law, ensure a viable Palestinian state with East Jerusalem as its capital, provide for a near-total Israeli withdrawal from the occupied territories, and deal with the refugee question in good faith. For, it will be recalled, Oslo had made it clear that peace must be just if it was to be comprehensive.

The Israeli leaders knew all this and didn't want to know it. For seven years the Palestinians had been repeating the same thing, and what had they gotten? A rump Authority, dependent on Israel for its every slightest action, presiding over a mere 20 percent of their territory. As he set out for Camp David, Barak felt confident that he could show them that their illusions were empty. They would finally have to take Israel's superior military strength into account, he thought. Hadn't reality proved him right up to that point?

THE CAMP DAVID FIASCO

No one knows what would have happened if Itzhak Rabin had not been assassinated in 1995. There is evidence that he underwent an important transformation in the months preceding his death, coming to understand that, if there was to be peace, a difficult confrontation inside Israel with proponents of an ongoing occupation was inevitable. In the revised edition of his memoirs (Rabin 1996)[15] he attempted to tell the truth about the expulsion, ordered by Ben Gurion, of the populations of Lydda and Ramleh in 1948, an event left unmentioned in the first edition (1979). This represented a new awareness of the Palestinian reality and a significant personal reassessment on Rabin's part.

At the same time, it was Rabin who had chosen Barak as his successor. Barak was considered an enigma, adored by some people close to him as "an Israeli Churchill, gifted with an uncommon capacity for synthesis,"[16] reviled by some former associates as a man having a "unilateral and simplistic" turn of mind who tended to think he could get everything he wanted "by virtue of his skill in manipulating the people he's talking to" and who was given to "shaping reality" to bring it into accord with his own view.[17] One of his Israeli biographers, Raviv Drucker (2002), describes a deeply disturbed, psychologically rigid man. From what I have been able to learn from my contacts, the expression *khakham tipesh* (intelligent idiot), which the Israelis used to describe the late Abba Eban, former minister of foreign affairs, fits Barak very well. On one point, however, there is agreement: the man was obsessed with security. It was for this reason that, on September 28, 1995, he abstained when Oslo II came to a vote in the Knesset.

Nor do we know whether Rabin would have chosen the negotiation strategy adopted by Barak when he came to power in May 1999, namely refusing to implement the accords previously signed and to negotiate the third phase of Israeli redeployment that they stipulated, the major military retreat that the Palestinians hoped for. His aim was to force Arafat to undertake the final round of negotiations after receiving the fewest possible concessions. This strategy was contrary not only to the spirit of Oslo (namely to build trust), but also to the letter of the accords (to proceed by

increments). In order to emphasize it, Barak excluded from the delegation he formed for the Camp David summit everyone who had taken part
in drawing up the Oslo Accords, including Shimon Peres and Yossi Beilin,
who were members of his government.

By July 2000 Oslo was far in the past. Negotiations had gotten bogged
down and mistrust was on the increase once again in the two populations:
among the Israelis, fear that the time would come when the taboo issues of
Jerusalem, the Palestinian refugees, and the settlements would have to be
addressed; among the Palestinians, exasperation with a peace process that
had led only to the reinforcement of the occupation and the collapse of their
living standards. On both sides there was a dangerous mounting of tension.
Arafat's image was now besmirched, and many Palestinians, including
members of Fatah, were prepared for the possible failure of the negotiated
process and the renewal of attacks. The Israeli army was conducting ex-
ercises in retaking Palestinian cities. Perhaps the time had come to resolve matters once and for all, to get down to brass tacks. Contrary to
the countless efforts by the Israeli media to inspire belief in an imminent accord, preliminary secret negotiations[18] on essential questions had
broken down, and as a result preparations for the summit talks were
clearly inadequate. But resolving matters once and for all implied being
politically and intellectually aware of the conditions for the "just, lasting, and comprehensive peace" and the "historic reconciliation" stipulated in the Oslo Accords.

I will not offer a chronicle of the summit here, since many investigations, eyewitness reports, and other studies have been published that are
in broad agreement about the facts, though they often disagree about how
those facts are to be interpreted.[19] But before I draw up the balance sheet,
I want to make one thing clear. At the end of Charles Enderlin's television documentary *Shattered Dreams* (cf. Enderlin 2002), Shlomo Ben
Ami, former minister of foreign affairs in Israel, comments on the failure
of the summit. Basically, he says, it was due to the fact that "each side
proved unable to take into account the other's myths." This way of putting it immediately struck me as sound and courageous.

Sound, because the fiasco seemed to revolve about a mythological issue
if there ever was one: Jerusalem is a holy place common to Jews and

Muslims, since Haram Al-Sharif, or the Esplanade of the Mosques, is built on the Temple Mount of the Jews. On this subject each side was in blatant denial of the other's reality. The Israeli delegates to Camp David proposed that a synagogue be built on the plaza so that Jews could pray there, scorning the emotional and political connections of this place to hundreds of millions of Muslims.[20] To which Arafat replied no evidence whatsoever of the existence of the First Temple had ever been found. It was as though the reality of the traces was what mattered, and not the emotional and political connections maintained by millions of Jews to that site. Ben Ami is right that ignorance and disdain for the other side's myths played a role in the failure of the summit. And his statement is courageous as well, since it showed a dawning awareness of Israel's role in that failure, even if, in his book (Ben Ami 2001), the former second in command in the government held the Palestinians solely responsible for the inability to take the other's myths into account.

But I soon saw that this attempt at Israeli self-criticism was basically a sophisticated way of evading key issues. For it was not the attitude toward the opponent's real or supposed myths that caused the failure of the summit but the attitude toward tangible realities. The difficulty a substantial majority of Israelis (and Palestinians) have, especially in the political class and the intelligentsia, is not primarily due to a stubborn refusal to consider the *other's* myths. It stems from an inability to give up their *own* presuppositions, their *own* preexisting perceptions of the Palestinians, views formed in response to what they thought was in Israel's national interest and necessary to preserve its self-image. From this perspective, contrary to the usual view of an evolved Israeli society facing a more archaic Palestinian one, the handicap is heavier on the Israeli side.

Beyond the diplomatic aspects—the degree of preparation for the summit, the quality of the negotiators, the personal stature and character of Ehud Barak and Yasser Arafat, the type of accord that each could accept given public opinion, and so forth—the failure of Camp David stems from Israel's incomprehension not of myths but of reality. The reality of the Palestinian people who, because of Israel, had become and still remain a nation of refugees, their core population subject, since 1967, to a military occupation. The Israelis did not regard the end of this occupation as the

crucial factor in the resolution of the conflict, a matter calling for immediate attention.

They did see that, in the long run, their country would have to give up
the major part of its presence in the occupied territories. But they did not
accept this except on their own conditions, which, as we shall see, were
many, all marked by the wish to perpetuate a form of domination. For
Barak, the need to put an immediate end to the occupation of another
people was not an imperative but a price to be paid, a renunciation of a
presence on other people's land that he and his negotiators did not view
as illegitimate in itself.

In 1962, when de Gaulle was holding secret negotiations with the Algerian National Liberation Front, he knew that he was heading for a very
short-term withdrawal of French troops. He also knew that Algeria's accession to independence in the whole of its territory was not only inevitable but also necessary for France, and that consigning French Algeria
to the past was the sole option if there was to be peace. His negotiators
were given the task of preserving French interests as best they could *within
this configuration*. Without going further into the similarities and differences between the two situations, it can be said that in strictly political
terms the negotiating position of Barak at Camp David was the opposite
of what de Gaulle's had been.

In Barak's view, the signing of a preliminary peace accord was the condition for the end of the occupation. And in that regard it mattered little
whether Israel's proposals were really generous, as its leaders subsequently
proclaimed, or incompatible with the creation of a viable state, as the
Palestinians held. What was most problematic about the Israelis at Camp
David was their negotiators' belief that, while the domination of another
people was a potential source of future danger, the political and military
presence of Israel in the occupied territories was legitimate.

The Israelis likewise sought, throughout the negotiations, to avoid the
refugee question, in the hope that an agreement on the other issues would
ultimately enable them to get around this huge obstacle. As they saw it,
the Palestinians were not likely to make the resolution of the tangled refugee question the condition for a comprehensive accord. Israeli negotiators clung to the view that Israel had had no initial responsibility for the

refugee problem, which should be resolved through an international fund to which Israel would be one of the contributors. Here one might agree with Shimon Peres that, from the outset, the refugee problem should not have been linked to the signing of an accord that aimed to be definitive. But since this question had been under discussion from the time of the Madrid Conference in 1991, and since Israel was demanding that Arafat sign an accord in which he would give up all further claims, how could the Israeli negotiators have imagined that the Palestinians would sign a peace agreement renouncing a situation that, for fifty-three years, had mentally and physically structured their identity?

If real generosity on Israel's part was to be expected, it would have been shown on precisely this issue, at least on the symbolic level, through acknowledgment of the responsibility of the Jewish state for the expulsion. Such an acknowledgment was essential if Arafat was to close this chapter and return to Palestine with an accord, making the V sign for victory to ease the acceptance of the fact that, in reality, there would be no *effective* return of the refugees. Then he could have announced, they finally acknowledged the injustice. In the same way that the Armenians cannot be reconciled with the Turks as long as Ankara persists in denying its responsibility for their mass murder in 1915, Israel's admission of responsibility was the condition for the Palestinians to come to terms with their grief and reconcile themselves to the present situation.

But it was on the refugee question that the Israeli negotiators were especially stubborn in their denial. Why? Because, for Shlomo Ben Ami, the expulsion in 1948 was something of a Palestinian myth, one that Israel should no doubt have taken into account, but a myth nonetheless, not a reality. It was in fact the Israelis who were steeped in a myth, repeated time again for decades, namely that the Palestinians had fled voluntarily. To call a spade a spade, it was the Israelis' refusal to admit, or political inability to come to terms with, what had really happened—namely an ethnic cleansing— that had led to the transformation of Palestinian reality into a nearly unquestioned myth.

After the failure of Camp David this same self-image led to the Israeli claims of generosity in the face of a Palestinian refusal that was held to be incomprehensible or manipulative. The Israeli proposals were said to have been the most generous that the Palestinians could ever get; they went beyond the most that could be imagined, exclaimed the returning Israeli negotiators in chorus. This conviction was undoubtedly rooted in the image that the Jewish leaders and inhabitants of Israel have of themselves and their state as a result, first, of the beliefs they have been taught concerning their history and their right to the land, and, second, of the way most of them spontaneously relate to the Palestinians.

What was the real nature of this supposedly maximal generosity? Let us compare the Israeli proposals at Camp David to those put forth at the new negotiations at Taba, in January 2001 (after the start of the new intifada) by a delegation led by Shlomo Ben Ami and including representatives absent from Camp David, especially the Laborite Yossi Beilin and, from the Zionist left party Meretz, Yossi Sarid.[21] Next, let us compare them with the Geneva Pact, the informal document signed in 2003 by Yossi Beilin and Yasser Abed Rabbo, former ministers of Barak and Arafat, respectively, and purporting to constitute the juridical infrastructure of what might one day become a definitive peace agreement.

TABA, GENEVA: *Camp David Laid Bare*

The outcome of the Taba negotiations,[22] which were concluded on January 21, 2002, makes explicit the inanity of the "line in the sand" Israel claimed at Camp David that it could not cross without endangering its existence. Taba was a major breakthrough, responding point by point to the demands the Palestinians had made at the summit.

THE REFUGEES

This issue had led to a standstill at Camp David. Points 1 and 2 of the Israeli proposal rejected all responsibility on Israel's part,[23] referring to the events preceding and following the War of 1948 only in terms of the suffering experienced on both sides. Israel proposed an international financial effort on behalf of the refugees, to which its own contribution was unspecified. On the opposite side, Articles 2 and 3 of the Palestinians'

proposal stipulated that Israel would acknowledge moral and legal responsibility for the expulsions and confiscations imposed on that population
in 1948 and admit that it had prevented the refugees from returning to
their homes. Resolution of the refugee problem, in their view, was incum-
bent on Israel. In other words, the two positions at Camp David were
completely incompatible.

Six months later, the proposals Yossi Beilin submitted to the Palestinians at Taba represented the most significant advance to date in Israel's
acknowledgment of its responsibilities.[24] After observing that "the problem of the Palestinian refugees is central to Israeli–Palestinian relations,"
and that the need for "its comprehensive and just solution is essential for
the creation of a durable and morally irreproachable peace," he acknowledges that "the nascent state of Israel was drawn into the War of 1948–
1949, which had its victims and led to suffering on both sides, including
the displacement and expropriation of the civilian Palestinian population,
who thereby became refugees. Since that time the refugees have for decades lived without dignity, citizenship, or property." He noted "the tragedy of the Palestinian refugees, their sufferings and losses," and added that
Israel "will be an active partner in closing this terrible chapter."

Never before had the state of Israel formally acknowledged its part in
"the displacement and expropriation" of the Palestinians and their territory. Nor had it ever agreed that, in the words of Beilin's text, "a just solution to the problem . . . must lead to the application of United Nations
Resolution 194." Here in Taba, and in black and white, an official representative of Israel was for the first time seeking a solution to the refugee
problem on the basis of the famous U.N. Resolution that had recognized
the refugees' right of return,[25] something Israel had programmatically
refused to include in its propoals at Camp David. Further proposals on
this question clearly led in the direction sought by the Palestinian negotiator Nabil Shaath six months earlier. They offered the refugees five options: return to Israel within limits to be agreed on, repatriation in a future
Palestinian state, relocation to their host countries or elsewhere, compensation, and additional international financing.

These proposals largely endorse what the Palestinians had asked for at
Camp David. The issue of determining the number of refugees autho-

rized to return to the Hebrew state was left unresolved, the Palestinians indicating that any number below 100,000 would be considered ridiculous, but the Taba negotiations formulated an agreement in principle based on international law, Israel's acknowledgment of its wrongdoings, and the Palestinians' acceptance of practical limitations to the right of return. Yossi Beilin tried to make his compatriots understand that "it is impossible to ask the Palestinians to give up the right of return. If we ask them [to do so], there will be no final accord."[26] For the first time, Israel was admitting the illegitimacy of its demand that the Palestinians forget their own history. This history was no myth.

It was not the fear of an alleged influx of millions of refugees returning to their country that had led the Israelis at Camp David to refuse to accept international law and acknowledge their wrongdoings. The Palestinians had made it clear that only an acknowledgment of fraud on Israel's part could lead to a solution that, in practical terms, would bar the implementation of the right of return. As Nabil Shaath explained,

> We asked Israel to subscribe to international law, as we had done. The Israeli acceptance of Resolution 194 did not call for a return of all the refugees, as Israel had claimed, anymore than our acceptance of Resolution 181 for the partitioning of Palestine, in 1947, which Israel demanded of us, led them to respond, to our demand that Israel return to the borders of that partition. They were well aware that we accept Israel in its 1967 borders. They also knew perfectly well that, once they accepted Resolution 194, we were not going to demand the return of four million refugees. What we had in mind was a solution for the refugees in Lebanon: 300,000 people to be divided half and half between Israel and the future Palestine.[27]

Israel's stubborn refusal at Camp David to acknowledge responsibility for the creation of the refugee problem, then, had to do not with the fear of an influx but with something that could not be mentioned: the consequences that acknowledging the past posed to the image the Israelis had of themselves. What would people have had to be told? That everything they had been taught for fifty-two years was false? This is why, after the failure of Camp David, a version had to be presented that demonized the other side. The Israeli media and their house intellectuals stated on every possible occasion that, in calling for recognition of Resolution 194, Arafat and the PLO had shown their true colors, their wish to destroy Israel from within by flooding it with refugees. In rejecting reality, they effectively created an additional myth.

The Geneva Pact spelled out the principles set forth in Taba on this point. The Palestinians were finally giving up the right of return, exclaimed these same intellectuals, though, three years earlier, they had denounced as scandalous the Palestinian call for recognition of Resolution 194. They were not concerned with what had really gone on at Camp David, nor did they read exactly what the Geneva Pact stipulated. For it expressly recognized that resolution, which endorsed the right of return.[28] Even better, though this pact avoids all explicit reference to Israeli responsibility in the refugee problem, it inscribes it beyond all doubt in reality. For it indicates the precise way to calculate the sum Israel has to pay by way of compensation to the heirs of the Palestinians it expelled.[29] For the first time Israel was undertaking to compensate the victims in its own name. Could there be a more explicit acknowledgment of responsibility?

Thus what the PLO had proposed at Camp David, and what Ehud Barak and his toadies presented as a threatening Palestinian refusal, was in fact the basis for a possible accord. This accord was accepted by Israeli political leaders as dangerous to the survival of the Jewish state as Yossi Beilin, Barak's former minister of justice, and General Amram Mitzna, who headed the Labor slate in the Israeli legislative elections. The talks at Taba and Geneva show what *real* generosity, what understanding of the issues confronting the two peoples and their shared dignity, could have led to at Camp David. Ehud Barak entirely lacked it.

BORDERS AND SETTLEMENTS

Of the territories conquered in 1967, the highest Israeli offer at Camp David involved returning to the Palestinians 91 percent of the West Bank and 100 percent of Gaza, maintaining the annexation of 9 percent of the occupied area. In reality this annexation would have amounted to about

From the "Generosity" of Camp David to the Informal Geneva Pact

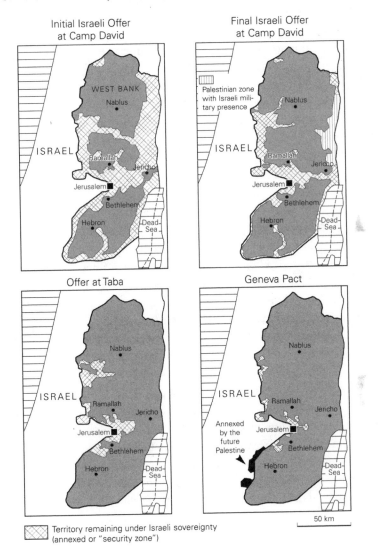

Initial Israeli Offer
at Camp David

Final Israeli Offer
at Camp David

Palestinian zone
with Israeli mili-
tary presence

Offer at Taba

Geneva Pact

Annexed
by the
future
Palestine

50 km

Territory remaining under Israeli sovereignty
(annexed or "security zone")

Sources: A. Keller, *L'Accord de Genève*, Paris: Labor et Fides, 2004. *Le Monde*. Clayton E.
Swisher, *The Truth about Camp David* (*La Vérité sur Camp David*), New York: Nation Books, 2004

15 percent, since the so-called "Zone of Jerusalem" (ZOJ), larger than the "Greater Jerusalem" that was already annexed to Israel, was excluded from negotiation. In exchange, the Israelis were restoring to the Palestinians 1 percent of their own land. In addition, the final card the Israeli negotiators laid on the table, their most progressive offer, cut the West Bank into two parts. Finally, Israel would retain control of the Dead Sea and two strips of land north and south of the Jordan River.

Here too, the Israeli delegation to Taba went in the direction of the Palestinians. It agreed to an "equitable" exchange of territories on each side of the 1967 border.

The principle of the real territorial contiguity of the Palestinian state on the West Bank was also accepted. Israeli negotiators proposed to annex not 15 percent but only 6 percent of the West Bank, which would be offset by 3 percent of Israeli territory, with the "protected passages" linking the West Bank to Gaza being considered equivalent to an additional 3 percent. In short, instead of the Camp David ratio of fifteen to one, the exchange would now be on a one-to-one basis.

At the point when the Taba talks were broken off by Ehud Barak, the Palestinians hoped to reduce the territory swaps to a basis of 2 percent to 3 percent. The Geneva Pact showed that here too, when Israel gave up a position of domination it inevitably drew closer to the Palestinian perspective. The definitive map finalized in Geneva endorsed the borders prior to June 5, 1967, as those separating the two states, modifying their lines only in joint exchanges amounting to 3.5 percent of the territory. In concrete terms, only the most important settlement area of East Jerusalem, the large settlement Maale Adumim and others contiguous to the Green Line, remained Israeli. All the other settlements were to be evacuated and ceded intact to the Palestinians. Once again, from the Israeli view, nothing remained of the "generosity" of Camp David.

JERUSALEM

At no time during the Camp David summit did Israel agree to the Palestinian offer of shared sovereignty of Jerusalem, according to which the areas primarily inhabited by Israelis would go to Israel, those primarily inhabited by Palestinians to Palestine. At no time did its negotiators accept Palestinian sovereignty over the Esplanade of the Mosques / Temple Mount. As for the Palestinian capital, they were willing to have the PLO establish it, not in East Jerusalem but in the suburb of Abu Dis, near the city, even if they called it Al-Qods (the Arab name for Jerusalem).

According to Yossi Sarid, one of the new Israeli negotiators at the Taba talks, the two parties were in complete agreement "on the principle of the partition of the city: the Jewish quarters would go to us, and the Arab quarters would go to the Palestinians."[30] The Israelis also agreed that the two states would establish their capitals there. This twofold advance was the only way to end the standstill arising from national and religious demands on both sides. There remained the thorny issues of the Old City of Jerusalem and the Haram al-Sharif / Temple Mount.[31] The deadlock had persisted in Taba, but it was resolved in the Geneva Pact. And, again, even though both sides made concessions it was resolved essentially in favor of the Palestinians. All of the Esplanade was to come under Palestinian sovereignty, as the PLO had been demanding since day one. They would exercise this sovereignty under the control of an international group. In addition to the Jewish quarter of the Old City and the Wailing Wall, Israel would retain access to the Mount Olive cemetery.

BARAK'S "GENEROUS OFFER"

Thus, point for point, Taba and Geneva showed what real generosity at Camp David would have entailed had Ehud Barak truly sought a reconciliation, and had he made ending the occupation an imperative for Israel. He had ordered his negotiators to halt the Taba talks, which did not prevent Israeli diplomats from promoting a new legend, namely that, after Camp David, the PLO had once more refused Israeli offers. In reality, Barak knew that he would lose the impending elections, and his military staff had warned him that, while the intifada was in progress there could be no question of signing an accord in Taba that would be more favorable to the Palestinians than the one offered at Camp David. To do so, the armed forces argued, would make Israel seem to be yielding to the Palestinian recourse to violence.

When the Geneva Pact was announced, Ariel Sharon minimized the scope of an accord with what he called "unofficial" Palestinian negotiators, signed by Israelis who "represented only themselves"[32] and were, he intimated, close to being traitors. As for Barak, he attacked Geneva with fierce aggressiveness, denouncing an accord "of capitulation," one that "included only Israeli concessions [that were] unacceptable" and was "an illusion that rewards terrorism."[33] Sharon's reaction was to assure his listeners that the pact was null and void, that there still was no Palestinian negotiating partner. Barak knew that there were indeed such partners: the primary Palestinian signatory to the Geneva Pact, Yasser Abed Rabbo, had been at Camp David, where he had been one of the strongest opponents of the agreement formulated there. It was not a question of the representatives involved in the pact that enraged Barak, but its contents, for his entire argument regarding his "generosity" at Camp David now seemed naked as a jaybird.

This conviction of Israel's alleged utmost generosity at Camp David on the part of Barak and his negotiators was not a sham. The Israeli offer at the summit had gone beyond what they had ever thought they could give up. But this generosity existed only in the head of a man who likened Israel to "a villa in the jungle," and whose entire training and belief system led him to favor domination over the Palestinians. He could not work his way out of this conviction at Camp David. However, escaping the hold of fundamental historical beliefs, accepting the other as an equal, was the course that all the Israelis pursuing the negotiations had to take, despite the intifada. For most of them, this was a major change. Nearly all of the negotiators of the Geneva Pact had had to make a long journey, personal and intellectual, to get to the point of accepting the compromises made on the refugees, the borders, and Jerusalem: the point of accepting the equality of the occupied and the occupier.

Let us listen to Shaul Arieli, the former paratrooper colonel who later became an adviser to Ehud Barak until the summer of 2000. It was he who, with Samir Al-Abed, the Palestinian deputy minister for planning, had negotiated the future borderlines at Geneva: "In 1994 I would never have imagined drawing maps like that. At that time I was convinced that Israel could make peace without, for example, having to give up land in exchange for annexed settlements. Barak thought essentially the same thing at Camp David." Yet he found the Geneva agreement "very just: we were giving up as much land as we were taking."[34] This relationship of parity was what had been lacking at Camp David.

Let us also listen to Avraham Burg, a Labor deputy and former president of the Jewish Agency and the Knesset, a man who wears the skullcap: "It took me three weeks before I agreed to sign the rough draft of the Geneva Pact. I had criticized Ehud Barak for his concessions on Jerusalem. The truth is that I changed. I'm devoting all my energy to a central aim: saving Israel from the occupation and saving Zionism from itself." He added that the greatly feared destruction of his country would come not from the Palestinian struggle but from its internal "decay": "We are neither a country of evil or a society of evil, but we have lost the sense of evil. We no longer feel, we no longer see. . . . I swear to you that there are nights when I can't close my eyes because I feel that I am an occupier."[35]

"The truth is that I changed." The change between the Avraham Burg of Camp David to the one in Geneva was the understanding that the occupation had to come to an end, and as soon as possible. But in July 2000 the Israeli position ultimately amounted to this: demanding a comprehensive and definitive accord without taking into account what was essential if this goal was to be reached, and demanding that the other party sign it and go back on their commitment to their historical roots—a "just solution" to the refugee question—so as to be able to accuse them, later, of having preferred war to peace and then make war on them. Changing meant freeing oneself of this attitude, from ethnicism and perpetual self-justification, from the feeling of superiority poisoning one's own society. This was the road that men like Beilin, Burg, Arieli, Ben Yair, and Menahem Klein were beginning to take, all of whom had departed from the historical Israeli consensus and were horrified at the role their country was playing in the intifada.

They remain a small minority in Israel. But they are not alone in accepting, today, things they would never have imagined before, for all of Israeli society has undergone a change in the past seven years. By placing the fundamental historical questions of the Israeli–Palestinian conflict right in the center of current events, says the sociologist Uri Ram, the intifada "has radicalized everyone's mind between two distant poles, leaving no more room at the soft center."[36] A majority of Israelis have headed into a much more aggressive ethnicism, a much more confirmed racism. The minority, frightened at this development, have totally or partially discarded the outmoded views of the past and are seeking ways to achieve coexistence, either alongside the Palestinians or together with them.

After a year of the intifada, when asked whether Israel had missed a rare opportunity to make peace at Camp David, the former head of Shin Bet, Admiral Ami Ayalon, replied: "Yes. The Palestinians and the international community have their share of responsibility. But we missed an extraordinary opportunity; the international situation was incredibly favorable after the fall of Communism, the Gulf War, and the emergence of globalization, all phenomena leading Israel to reexamine its own axioms. Now we are going backwards."[37]

Israel's ability to reexamine its own fundamental axioms is indeed what is at stake. Contrary to what the vast majority of Israelis believe, the Oslo Accords represented an exceptional opportunity for their country to become part of the Middle East. The country's leaders totally failed to understand the issues. They were unable or afraid to confront the ghosts of their history and the flaws of their identity, unable to free themselves of reliance on the spontaneous inclinations of a dominant power (which, as Albert Memmi brilliantly observes, give rise to their mirror image in the behavior of the dominated). Whatever the negligence on the Palestinian side, it was essentially these leaders who turned a historic possibility into an immense waste.

TEN

"SERIAL LIARS"
Creating a Useful Image of the Enemy

THE STEAMROLLER AFTER CAMP DAVID

Two years after Camp David, in an interview with Benny Morris, Ehud Barak called Arafat and the Palestinians "serial liars." "They are products of a culture in which to tell a lie . . . creates no dissonance," he said. "They don't suffer from the problem of telling lies that exists in Judeo-Christian culture. Truth is seen as an irrelevant category. . . . The deputy director of the US Federal Bureau of Investigation once told me that there are societies in which lie detector tests don't work, societies in which lies do not create cognitive dissonance [the response on which the tests are based]" (Morris 2002a).

Someone who wants to kill his dog claims that it is rabid. What shall we call this tendency to project one's own defect onto the object of one's rage? Because when it came to serial lies, half-truths, garbled assertions ascribed to the opponent, and vagueness on the precise details of the negotiations, in the immediate aftermath of Camp David Israeli leaders did not hold back. There was a veritable steamroller effect, profiting from Bill Clinton's accusation that Yasser Arafat bore the primary responsibility for the failure. This declaration had been obtained from Clinton by Ehud Barak, who was afraid of being ruined politically on his return to Israel, despite the prior understanding among Clinton, Barak, and Arafat, in the interest of pursuing the negotiations, that none of the parties would be assigned blame publicly.

Let us recall the major points of the Israeli version. At Camp David, the story went, an agreement was within reach[1] when Arafat showed his true face. The so-called Palestinian lie about the desire for peace was revealed. In an analogy that sums up his entire frame of mind, on September 6, 2000, Barak explained to his entourage that at Camp David he had "put Arafat up against the wall, the way he was in Beirut in 1982" (cited in Enderlin 2002, p. 276). Popular opinion expressed the simplistic view that Israel had offered everything but the Palestinians had refused. With regard to Jerusalem, it was said, Israel had proposed original solutions but had also, legitimately, rejected any Palestinian sovereignty over a part of the country's capital.

Arafat, it was repeated again and again, had shown that he was no statesman. The heads of the Labor Party harped on the claim that, like all the Arabs since the beginning of Israel's conflict with them, the Palestinians never missed an opportunity to miss an opportunity. Six months later, the second intifada was said to prove that Arafat had responded to Israeli generosity with terror. Then there was a new argument: the question of the refugees' right of return having been put back on the table, seen as proof that Arafat wanted to destroy Israel was that he was trying to get through force what he had been unable to get through diplomacy.

With time, the zealous opponents of the peace process got down to business, and the factory producing the demonization of Arafat and the Palestinians ran at full capacity. The fact is that the lies and half-truths (as Gideon Levy termed the Israeli version of the War of 1948) initially enjoyed widespread collective support among Israelis, including those in the peace camp. This was not solely due to their transmission by a battery of devoted or blind intermediaries and intellectuals, for these claims corresponded to what the Israelis wanted to believe. Once again, lies and half-truths reinforced the majority's ingrained need for self-justification. The blame must always lie with the other; it can't even be shared, let alone taken on as primarily one's own.

If these arguments had not had such dramatic consequences, one might be tempted to smile at them. Since the publication of Charles Enderlin's *Shattered Dreams* (2002), we now know the truth about the biased version presented to the public. Contrary to Israeli claims, the negotiators were at no point on the brink of an agreement. And we know what to think about the alleged generosity of the final Israeli offer. What about the refugee question? One would have to be obtuse to believe that it had arisen unexpectedly; it had been on the agenda since the Madrid Conference nine years earlier. As for the demand that Israel recognize the right of return, from the diplomatic point of view it was as integral to Palestinian identity as the Israeli demand that the Palestinians recognize Resolution 181 establishing a Jewish state in Palestine. We have seen how, in reality as opposed to fantasy, the Palestinian delegates envisioned the practical application of this right of return. In 2004 it was learned that Israeli military intelligence had informed Barak what the Palestinian position would be: accept Resolution 194 officially, and we'll be able to publicly renounce its application.

What of the claim that the Palestinian refusal at Camp David prefigured a vague intention to destroy Israel? After the summit Gilead Sher, Barak's major political adviser, revealed actual disgust with Arafat, who, he told me, was "as slippery as a cake of soap." "Abed Rabbo," he added, "is a tough negotiator, but he's honest. If you conclude an agreement with him, you can trust him."[2] How can we explain that Yasser Abed Rabbo, who at Camp David was firmly against accepting the Israeli proposals, pursued his contacts with some Israelis during the intifada, even heading the delegation that signed the Geneva Pact, if his previous refusal led to a wish to destroy Israel?

There remains Arafat. A year after Camp David Shlomo Ben Ami (2001) set forth his perception of Arafat, one he shared with Ehud Barak, minus the vulgarity. Arafat's personality is that of a Moses, not a Joshua, Ben Ami writes. In making a decision, he adds, Arafat is afraid of losing his status as the mythological expression of the general will of the Palestinian people. He would rather play the role of the mythic hero of Palestine than assume the role of a leader ready to go against the general consensus. Yet a great leader is precisely one who proves capable of making a decision when he is not satisfied. In Ben Ami's opinion, the underlying reason for this attitude on Arafat's part is that he does not acknowledge the legitimacy of the Jewish state despite the various accords that have been reached. Ben Ami's mother, he writes, taught him an Arab proverb that goes as follows: "To know the truth, you have to follow the liar right into his house." And, he continues, the Israelis have followed Arafat to the end in order to learn whether he was capable of arriving at an accord. But, according to Ben Ami, the Arafat myth cannot be reconciled with reality; the man is removed from real life and unable to reach a reasonable compromise with the state of Israel. He is to be blamed for transposing to the mythic level of the diaspora the problem of the refugees, the Palestinian cause, to the point where the Palestinians are no longer able to negotiate on the basis of reality. At the crucial moment Arafat always hedges. He tells stories. He is a clown, Ben Ami concludes, and can never be pinned down.

In each of these assertions one could replace Arafat's name with that of Barak, substitute Palestinians for Israelis, and so on. For some Palestinians have exactly the same view of Ehud Barak: he is a liar, a man who is evasive and unable to make decisions contrary to the Israeli consensus because he ultimately fails to recognize the legitimacy of the Palestinian state. He hedges at the crucial moment. He's a clown who can never be pinned down. We may recall how, in 1999, Barak was evasive at the very moment he had to sign an accord restoring the Golan to Syria (see Enderlin 2002, pp. 140–142). But what matters is the way in which Ben Ami emphasizes certain real traits of Arafat and invents others so as to create the image of the adversary that suits him.

What he needs is to depict an interlocutor cut off from reality, the opposite of Ben Gurion, the genuine leader Ben Ami has in mind, who had been realistic enough in 1947 to agree to a partitioning that he basically rejected. And this contrast between the statesman Ben Gurion and the ideologue Arafat steeped in his mythology became a constant among the Israeli Laborite left. Uri Avnery (2002), the former independent member of parliament, has observed that if Arafat were really the manipulative liar they described, he would, on the contrary, have acted like Ben Gurion by accepting Barak's conditions and signing a bargain-rate accord so as to obtain the advantage of an internationally recognized state, with the idea of challenging it all again at the first opportunity. Recall that in 1947, shortly before the partitioning of Palestine, Ben Gurion declared before the United Nations commission that he was prepared to accept the creation of a Jewish state on a significant part of

Palestine even as he claimed his right to all of that area (see Chapter 2). Just imagine how Barak and Ben Ami would have reacted to a so-called realistic Arafat, one who declared that he was signing an accord but did not renounce his right to all of Palestine.

Ben Ami's argument about Arafat's lack of realism says more about the man who is making it than about his target, for it masks the absence of reality on Israel's part. It is not Arafat who is transposing the refugee problem to the mythic level. He has to take its very tangible *reality* into account. The refugees, at least half of whom still live in camps, were not despoiled mythologically but in actuality. Arafat and the PLO can't make believe they are dealing with a myth. In demanding that the Palestinians negotiate on the basis of reality, Ben Ami is merely expressing a more prosaic idea: at Camp David they should have accepted Israel's superior military strength, agreeing to an unfair accord exonerating Israel of responsibility regarding the refugees.

In failing to understand that, despite the unfavorable balance of power, the Palestinians will not give up their claim to equality, if not in territory (the Israeli borders of 1967 include 73 percent of mandatory Palestine) then at least in dignity, it is Ben Ami (2001) who demonstrates a lack of realism. At Camp David and Taba, he says, his nation was pushed as far as they could go as Jews and as Israelis. In driving them still further back, the Geneva Pact, negotiated by certain Israelis very close to him, undertook to show that the man who was unable to reconcile himself to reality was Shlomo Ben Ami, not the Palestinian negotiators.

The denials of what really happened at Camp David at first drew the vast majority of Israelis together into a movement of deepest chauvinism that, for some, found its justification in the alleged proof of what they had always claimed (the baneful nature of Arafat in particular and the Palestinians in general), for others in a kind of lover's disappointment: they would have so much liked to love the Palestinians, and now look how the Palestinians were rejecting them. In all this, it is impossible to overestimate the responsibility of the Laborite Ehud Barak, whose version of the facts paved the way for the return of the far right. If the Palestinians were so deceitful, those who had opposed Oslo were right after all. Power fell into Sharon's hand like a ripe fruit.

Apart from people like Uri Avnery and the former Labor minister Shulamit Aloni, who clearly saw what was ultimately at stake in the peace process and what Barak was really like, the voices raised in Israel at that time to contest the official version of the facts could be counted on the fingers of one hand, or at any rate two hands. This challenge called for a great deal of perspicacity and independence of mind. In stressful times most Israelis are slow to discard the tendency to automatic self-justification. Since then the voices contesting the official truths about Camp David and the outbreak of the intifada have become much more numerous. In 2004, interviewing secondary-school students in Tel Aviv, I heard the following: "Barak gave the Palestinians everything they wanted, and they refused," asserted one student. "He told them, 'Take it or leave it.' It was an ultimatum." "Let's stop telling tall stories," was the reply of his friend.

These "tall stories" were unmasked as such by very few people at first. Working in great solitude, journalists like Akiva Eldar and Gideon Levy of the daily newspaper *Haaretz* took on this task. Eldar tirelessly revealed the extent to which the official version contained obvious contradictions and errors.[3] Ami Ayalon (2001), the former head of Shin Bet, condemned the erroneous perception of the peace process and the failure of Camp David. The writer David Grossman (2002) described how Barak conducted the talks, presenting Arafat with ultimatums.

And Colonel Shaul Arieli (2003), former director of the "peace administration" in Barak's cabinet, broke with his old mentor. The myth according to which Barak gave almost everything and Arafat responded with terror, he wrote in *Haaretz*, has become a major obstacle to the search for a peaceful solution. Fiercely critical of the way in which the army had imposed the logic of security during the Oslo process, leading to one delay after another, Colonel Arieli vouched for the fact that his services knew from the beginning that there was no chance that Arafat would agree to be the subcontractor of the security services in exchange for anything less than a state within the 1967 borders, including adjustments of borders and land swaps. Arieli would become the Israeli cartographer of the Geneva Pact.

As for Menahem Klein, he would successfully conduct the negotiations on Jerusalem in the context of that same pact. Wearing the skullcap, this former special adviser to Shlomo Ben Ami considered the latter's book "a disgrace, a travesty of the facts." "In November 1999," he said,

> when Barak excluded [Yossi] Beilin from the negotiations with the PLO, he told him, "I'm going to offer them 50 percent of the territories, and they'll have to accept that." All the politicians on the left knew that Barak intended to let go of as little as possible, that he functioned only to impose the balance of power. But they continued to let it be believed that Barak was a dove. They didn't prepare people for what was really at stake in the final negotiation, though they knew this. Then, after the failure, when Barak launched his big brainwashing operation in Israel, Ben Ami went along with him, and the others were trapped and kept silent.[4]

At Camp David, Klein believes

> Barak kept the Temple Mount up his sleeve. I can assure you that the issue of the Temple Mount was not raised in any form in the preliminary negotiations. Israelis were asking that a Jewish compound be built there! An idea never put forth in Israel, one that could not have been more pleasing to Gershom Salomon and Yehuda Etzion, those people who want to "reconstruct the Temple." Barak thought that in this way he could protect himself from the rage of the most extremist Israelis should there be an accord. But this was a far-fetched idea. There could be no better way to go about capsizing a negotiation.

And this is a religious Israeli speaking. In the statements of Menahem Klein, Barak appears as a master manipulator. But why did Klein and others like him remain unheard in Israel for so long? Because they were contradicting the "good conscience" that was so firmly entrenched? Yes, but also because the Israelis, unprepared by any government for what a real peace accord would imply, were very confused about what was actually at stake. At Camp David, for the first time since 1948 and 1967, fundamental questions had been put back on the table. What were the borders of Israel? What were the rights of the Palestinians, hence also of the refugees? Camp

David was about the future. Its repercussions in people's minds put the
big issues of the past back on the agenda.

THE PALESTINIAN UPRISING AND
ITS RETROACTIVE "CONCEPTION"

The peace process had failed, but during the two weeks of negotiations at
Camp David it became clear that achieving peace would mean leaving
the territories occupied for so long, abandoning once and for all a part of
the Land of Israel, and risking a difficult confrontation with the settlers
and their supporters. And it meant accepting the fact that the Palestinian
flag would fly in East Jerusalem. A paradoxical feeling came over most
Israelis, a mixture of relief (Barak hadn't given everything to the Arabs),
regret (even so, it took seven years to get to this fiasco), and vague fear for
the future (What would happen now that the negotiations had failed?).
Barak's explanation provided a simple, reassuring answer to the disarray:
the Palestinians were entirely to blame.

This explanation, moreover, "brought about a natural mental association with the past," explains the sociologist Daniel Dor of the University
of Tel Aviv:

> In 1948 we accepted the partition and they rejected it. This view has
> been the basis of the Israeli justification vis-à-vis the Palestinians for
> decades. So what did public opinion retain from this? Once again
> we were inclined toward a partitioning, and once again they rejected
> it. The conclusion was obvious: we'd had some doubts, but now we
> were sure that "they" didn't want peace. What was at stake in 1948,
> the existence of the Jewish state, was back on the agenda. The en-
> tire perception was falsified.[5]

When the intifada broke out three months later, fear immediately took
priority over all other feelings. The relative strength of the two sides did
not matter, nor did "who started it." The machinery of denying the facts
went into overdrive. Past and future came together: Israel was again in an

existential situation, a matter of survival, and this legitimized all forms of repression.

The Israelis were not completely wrong. Camp David had indeed posed questions of an existential order for them. Which Israel did they want? And what relationship with the Palestinians? But by activating a mass of binary reflexes—the good guys versus the bad guys, no alternative to ending up as either conqueror or conquered—fear blotted out all rationality. From the beginning of the Palestinian mobilization on the day following the death by Israeli bullets of six worshipers on the Plaza of Al-Aqsa, a place of faith and a national symbol for the Palestinians, public opinion turned irrational. "No one in Israel is explaining reality anymore," was the way the situation was summed up by Admiral Ami Ayalon (2001), one of the rare individuals within the political-military complex to retain independent thinking.

No one was explaining reality anymore because the reference points were topsy-turvy. The police had fired on an unarmed crowd? The contrary was hammered home: the Palestinians had initiated the violence. The rest followed from there. In the first weeks, when there had not yet been the slightest terrorist attack, the army opened heavy fire against stone throwers, most of them very young; later they were faced with armed Palestinian groups and police began to respond with submachine guns. There were new Palestinian victims almost every day, three-fourths of them civilians. Were there more than ten times as many of them as there were Israeli soldiers? No matter. Israel was fighting for survival. As David Grossman (2004) said, "it's a great temptation to be strong and perceive ourselves as weak. . . . We have dozens of atomic bombs, tanks, planes. We're confronting people stripped of all these arms. Yet mentally we remain victims. . . . This inability to see ourselves as we are in relation to the other constitutes our principal weakness."

The most inept, not to say revolting, arguments began to be heard. Distinguished humanists and former pacifists declared that they would never forgive the disgraceful Palestinian mothers for sending their own children to their deaths, unaware that they themselves were lapsing into an old colonialist state of mind. Charles Enderlin (2000) recalls how, when the British Army fired on young Jews demonstrating for independence in

November 1945, His Majesty's representatives in Palestine had been scandalized at the behavior of "these Zionists who stay home and send their children to attack our brave soldiers" and fall beneath their gunfire.

"It's him, the other, who puts us in a situation where we use force. Excuse me: where we are obliged to use force. Since after all he started it. All we did was react," in the caustic words of the Israeli professor Yaakov Raz (2002). This is the automatic belief of those who are convinced of the purity of their weapons. The famous Palestinian negotiator Hanan Ashrawi (2000) pulls even fewer punches: "Accusing the victim is a common recourse of the guilty to rationalize and mask the horror of his own crime."

The fact is that the repression of the Palestinian demonstrators instantly attained a level never reached in the first intifada (1987–1993). On day three the Israeli army in Gaza killed a ten-year-old child hiding behind his father in view of the cameras of the television channel France 2. On the day after that, two Israeli reservists who had lost their way in Ramallah were lynched and hung from windows by young people in a rage, here too under the eye of the cameras. All at once, on both sides, there was an additional emotional charge based on a symbolic issue: the imposition of the monstrous image of the enemy and the appropriation of the posture of the real and sole victim. At that time the first Palestinian attack of the intifada, on November 2, 2000, was still in the distance. The first suicide attack, on December 22, was even further away.[6]

The Israeli political and security authorities, who were the de facto initiators of the violence, set out to hammer home a point of view aimed at persuading the public, a public that did not wish to hear anything different: the slaughter on the Al-Aqsa Plaza had not, in itself, been provocative, since the Palestinians, having readied themselves for an insurrection, were only awaiting a pretext. Since they bore full responsibility for the violence, it was solely up to them to put an end to it.

In 1996, under the right-wing Netanyahu administration, violent clashes had already occurred after the opening of a tunnel along the Esplanade of the Mosques, and Shin Bet had had to take strong measures to stop them. Its second in command, Israel Hasson, had negotiated a return to calm with the heads of the Palestinian special services. In 2000 nothing of the sort took place. Not only did Barak not seek a negotiated stop to the confrontation, but he demanded that the Palestinians immediately cease all acts of violence prior to any discussion. On October 8 he gave the Palestinian Authority forty-eight hours to comply. During this interval elite Israeli marksmen and soldiers continued to fire on the demonstrators with real bullets, not rubberized ones. Nabil Shaath, the Palestinian minister of foreign affairs, replied, "Oh well. In forty-eight hours Barak will give us another forty-eight hours."[7] And indeed, on the evening of the ninth, he postponed the cessation of violence for another three or four days. With no collaboration between the two parties, how could there have been a decrease in tension?

Why did the Israeli leaders ignore the principle set forth by Itzhak Rabin—fight terrorism (in this case, the acts of violence) as though there were no negotiations, negotiate as though there were no acts of violence—and insist only on ultimatums? Had the Palestinian Authority and Fatah really decided to undertake a test of strength with Israel, including the transition to armed combat and the return to terrorism? What knowledge of the other, what mastery of events, what perspectives did the political and military leaders of the two camps have?

Beyond the propaganda and self-justifying arguments on each side, what did they think at the outset? Was this just the beginning of a new episode in a relationship that had had its ups and downs for years, or were they entering upon a confrontation of a different order? And in the latter case, what was at issue? On the Palestinian side, destroying Israel or gaining the independent Palestine in the occupied territories that Israel had refused at Camp David? On the Israeli side, rejecting any Palestinian state or imposing on the PLO the solution it had rejected as inadequate at Camp David? Depending on the answers to these questions, people's views on the outbreak of the intifada and the blame for its subsequent development will differ radically. A great deal of information necessary for a categorical response remains unavailable. But enough elements have come to light, along with enough first-hand testimony, to reveal the contradictions of the Israeli argument.

Fourteen months after leaving his position of leadership Barak said the Israelis knew, "from hard intelligence, that Arafat intended to unleash a violent confrontation, terrorism. [Sharon's visit and the riots that followed] fell into his hands like an excellent excuse, a pretext" (cited in Morris 2002a). Secretly planning the disappearance of Israel even as they sign temporary truces, Barak said, Arafat and the Palestinian Authority want a state in all of Palestine. This argument would be taken up by Ariel Sharon.

Did reliable intelligence sources, then, reveal *before* the intifada what Barak claims they did? Such sources have never been publicly presented, and their existence has been challenged in no uncertain terms by very highly placed intelligence officials. An article by Akiva Eldar (2004) in *Haaretz* could in the future be a sign of one of the biggest scandals ever known in Israel if this matter is revived. (Or, like the lies with regard to 1948, it could turn into a textbook case for historians.) This scandal would then be similar to that following the revelation of the intelligence reports that, according to George W. Bush and Tony Blair, asserted the existence of weapons of mass destruction in Iraq and justified the war they have conducted there.

Eldar reveals that the source mentioned by Barak is Amos Gilad, who confirms this. In 2002 this general, third in command in military intelligence (in Hebrew: Aman), headed the research department issuing situational analyses. Gilad has always believed that Oslo was a plot to destroy Israel and claims that he did indeed issue the reports Barak mentions. Later appointed coordinator of actions in the territories (2001–2003), today he occupies a very high position in the ministry of defense. On June 6, 2004, he was still arguing before the government that Oslo furthered Arafat's strategic objective, according to which Israel had no right to exist.

Now according to Eldar, the version of the facts given by another general, Amos Malka, head of military intelligence from 1998 to 2001 and thus Amos Gilad's direct superior, completely contradicts the argument of Gilad's alleged reports before Camp David, and even before the intifada, reports claiming Arafat's decision to launch a violent confrontation and terrorism. When questioned by Eldar, Ami Ayalon, head of Shin Bet until shortly before Camp David; Matti Steinberg, in charge of Palestinian affairs in Shin Bet; and Colonel Ephraim Lavie, a member of the Aman research department and specialist in the area of Palestinian politics directly under Amos Gilad at the time, all confirmed that no report of the kind mentioned by Ehud Barak was ever written before Camp David or before the intifada. According to Eldar, "Malka challenges Gilad's professional integrity: 'I say, with full responsibility, that during my entire period as head of military intelligence, there was not a single research department document that expressed the assessment that Gilad claims to have presented to the prime minister. . . . Therefore I argue that only after the Taba talks were broken off, on the eve of the 2001 elections, Gilad began retroactively rewriting'" the assessments of military intelligence.

In short, the head of military intelligence states that the "hard intelligence" sources on which Barak says he based his analysis and his attitude never existed. He challenges his subordinate, who is supposed to have written them, to produce them, and finally he accuses him in advance of predating them should he ever do so. General Gilad has never sued his superior, General Malka, for libel. Nor has he ever presented the slightest written document.

Let us put forth a hypothesis: like Bush and Blair later, Barak lied. His allegedly reliable intelligence sources never existed. But this is only half a lie. General Gilad, Chief of Staff Shaul Mofaz, and Mofaz's deputy Moshe "Bugi" Yaalon shared the convictions expressed in the nonexistent reports and presented them *orally* to Ehud Barak, since they were based only on opinions, not on the official reports that would have contradicted them. Barak tended to credit them precisely because they corresponded exactly to what he wanted to hear or to what he feared. This sort of thing has occurred very often in the history of intelligence: certain sources present their convictions as established facts at the political level, either because they firmly believe them ("there's no proof, but according to all indications . . ."), or because they sense that this is what the politician expects. At the same time they omit or marginalize contrary reports, sensing that the politician does not want to know about them.

The statement by Amos Malka, former head of Israeli military intelligence, is an essential key to what would happen both at Camp David and with the intifada. Shortly before Camp David, Eldar reports, Malka reviewed Arafat's positions for the cabinet:

> I said there was no chance that he would compromise on 90 percent of the territories or even on 93 percent. Barak said to me: 'You are telling me that if I offer him 90 percent, he isn't going to take it?'

I told [Barak and his minister, Haim Ramon] that the difference between me and them is that they are speaking from hope and I am trying to neutralize my hope and give a professional assessment. But Barak saw himself as able to make his assessments without assessments from MI [military intelligence], because he is his own intelligence, and he thought he was smarter. Afterward, it was convenient for him to explain his failure by a distorted description of the reality.

According to General Malka, the viewpoint presented to the government by Aman, which he headed, was this:

We assumed that it [was] possible to reach an agreement with Arafat under the following conditions: a Palestinian state with Jerusalem as its capital and sovereignty on the Temple Mount; 97 percent of the West Bank plus exchanges of territory in the ratio of 1:1 with respect to the remaining territory; some kind of formula that includes the acknowledgment of Israel's responsibility for the refugee problem, and a willingness to accept 20,000–30,000 refugees. All along the way . . . it was MI's assessment that he had to get some kind of statement that would not depict him as having relinquished this, but would be prepared for a very limited implementation.

In short, the assessment of military intelligence before the final summit of July 2000 was that an accord with Arafat was possible on the basis of the Geneva Pact.

On the refugee question, later transformed into a bugaboo by Barak, Sharon, and the Israeli information services, a document presented by Eldar finally does away with the argument that, in demanding the refugees' right of return at Camp David, Arafat showed his ambition to destroy Israel from within. Delivered before the summit, a memo from Gilad's own services, the research department of Aman, indicated that "Even those who hold an 'extreme' position on the issue, among them Arafat, have adopted the position that if Israel recognizes the right of return in principle, its implementation can be partial and limited."

Thus before Camp David Barak had, on the one hand, reports spelling out in black and white the conditions under which an agreement was possible, and, on the other, viewpoints according to which the only thing Arafat was aiming at was the destruction of Israel. Barak had no intention of giving in to the Palestinians' demands, but he was convinced that he could succeed in imposing his own on them despite the warnings of his intelligence services. And if the Palestinians refused, this would be because his "reliable sources"—not the official, written ones but the oral ones from a subordinate supported by the chief of staff—had gotten things right: Arafat did not want peace. Now we can better understand the anecdote related by Barak's spokesman Gadi Baltianski. Before leaving for Camp David, Barak had taken a pencil and stood it upright in the palm of his hand. Either Arafat will take it, he told Baltianski, or (accompanying his words with the gesture) "I'll let go and the pencil will fall." Peace would be down and Arafat would have "revealed his true face" (Enderlin 2003).

This is how self-persuasion comes about: one creates an image of the enemy corresponding to one's own needs—discard all opinions that contradict yours, then interpret the attitude of your interlocutor/adversary in accordance with your own presuppositions. In the fabrication of the Israeli line of argument after Camp David, the reaction to the intifada, and the successive stages in the development of this line of argument, each new event was interpreted according to the foundational assumptions. Once the intifada had broken out, the initial lie formed the basis of the underlying Israeli "conception." *Konceptzia*: this is the term used after 2000 by the military to characterize the view of a demonic Arafat who planned the Oslo trap so as to bring the refugees back and destroy Israel from within, an Arafat who, before his failure, would once again be the terrorist he had always been (see Eldar 2004).

This is why the Palestinian Authority had to be seen as having initiated the violence—they had planned it in advance. For Menahem Klein, the former adviser to Shlomo Ben Ami, minister of internal security at the time, the entire Israeli analysis of the outbreak of the intifada is a rewriting of events. In reality, he says, the Israeli establishment had no idea about plans being hatched in Fatah before the intifada, or about the development of an opposition that was highly critical of Arafat and was demanding the democritization of the Palestinian Authority and an end to its corruption. Nor did it have any idea of the exasperation of the Palestinian people over the ongoing occupation. There was a total blindness. All the intelligence memos, before the intifada, focused on the fact that Arafat was liable to make a unilateral announcement of the creation of the Palestinian state on September 13, 2000, and assessed how Israel might best react. Barak claims today that he had information about preparations by the Palestinian Authority for an uprising. This is absolutely false. There is not a single preexisting Israeli document to this effect. This entire theory was devised after the fact to justify the Israeli reaction.[8]

And indeed nothing in the first days of the intifada lends credence to the idea that Arafat planned the demonstrations with a view to beginning the final struggle. On the contrary, everything indicates that he was overwhelmed by their scope and by the brutality of the repression, and that politically he rode the surf of this mobilization, both because he could not risk losing his position of leadership in the movement and because he believed it could put him in a better position for a renewal of negotiations. He probably pictured himself saying to the Israelis: "If you don't go along with me, soon I won't guarantee anything anymore." There is also every indication that Barak, too, did not for a moment imagine that the final struggle was underway. Surprised by the magnitude of the revolt, he gave in to the wish of his general staff to strike very fast and very hard, in the belief that, if the IDF really bared its fangs this time, the Palestinian street would rapidly submit. He did not envision the continuation of the intifada.

In this initial phase, when the *konceptzia* was still far from being erected into a closed system, Barak probably judged that after the failure of Camp David Arafat ought to be given a lesson he would remember, one that would bring him around to a supposedly more realistic position. He had to be put under pressure to accept what he had previously refused. And the pressure of the military hierarchy on Barak was probably strong as well. The general staff at that time was led by Shaul Mofaz, a Netanyahu appointee who was fiercely opposed to the Oslo process. General Mofaz represented the group of high-echelon officers who had not coped well with the outcome of the first intifada. For Rabin had signed the Oslo Accords when the Palestinian uprising had lost a lot of impetus. This group felt betrayed by Israel's recognition of the PLO at the very moment when they felt that the IDF was winning, somewhat like the French generals in Algeria who didn't accept de Gaulle's undertaking of the process leading to Algerian independence at a time when military victory was in sight.

These officers, of whom General Gilad, author of the false intelligence report, was the archetype, then formulated the notion that Oslo was a major political defeat for Israel. If Israel had capitulated at Oslo, this notion went, it was because the Palestinians had won a war of attrition; seven years of the first intifada had worn down Israeli society and the political class. If they had pulled out all the stops, breaking the intifada very quickly instead of dragging the confrontation out on a small scale, if the Palestinians had had a taste of tanks and missiles, Israel would never have known this defeat.

With these ideas in mind, Mofaz intervened right at the outset of the new intifada, telling Barak that this time they had to strike without holding back, and with increasing strength if necessary, until the Palestinians got the message; if that did not happen, the Israelis would be beaten politically once again.[9] The prime minister, himself a former chief of staff, was not unreceptive to this argument even though he was annoyed by the pressure being applied by Mofaz and his generals. The military correspondent of an Israeli daily newspaper told me the following anecdote. At the beginning of the intifada, Barak required that he alone authorize the shooting of a missile into an inhabited area. What if a second missile is necessary, the liaison officer of the general staff mockingly asked; did authorization have to be requested again? Barak, fed up, replied that, yes, a second authorization would be necessary.

Despite the increasing number of Palestinian civilian deaths, the gradual rise in the level of repression did not attain its objective. Demonstrations became more intense. Armed groups appeared, and Palestinian police

officers joined the demonstrators. After the stones, Israeli soldiers began
to receive the first bullets. The Palestinians, in short, were not letting themselves be gunned down like rabbits, to use the expression of the former
head of Shin Bet. "On October 10, 2000 [the eleventh day of the upris-
ing]," Menahem Klein related,

> I drafted a memo for my minister, explicitly setting forth the risk of
> matters developing as in Algeria. I wrote to Ben Ami that we don't
> understand the depth of the crisis, that we have to go back to negotia-
> tion with a shock treatment. If you don't do this, I added, you'll soon
> have Ariel Sharon and Rehavaam Zeevi [leader of the transfer party]
> in your place. Put out the fire, I said, by political means, or you'll also
> have the return of terrorism inside Israel. But he paid no attention to
> this. Instead, Barak and his people chose the demonization of Arafat.
> They thought: if the Palestinians have deaths every day, there'll be a
> quick end to this. At the beginning of the intifada our leaders didn't
> think for a moment that a new stage, of a different nature, was being
> established right under their eyes. Or that by acting as they did they
> were contributing to it.[10]

It is less certain, on the other hand, that generals like Mofaz and Yaalon
hoped for a quick end to the hostilities. Like Sharon and the Likud, they
thought they finally had an opportunity to get out of the detested Oslo framework, redraw the map of the Israeli–Palestinian relationship and break the
enemy's back once and for all. It was Sharon, the leader of the opposition,
whose view of what was brewing was undoubtedly the most acute. He was
the first to understand that Israel was returning to a conflict that would be
long—long precisely because it was of existential importance for the opposite side—if the Oslo framework and the prospect of a Palestinian state in
all the territories won in 1967 were abandoned, and to understand that, as
Klein said, an Algeria-style struggle would develop.

Sharon, too, thought the situation called for a shock treatment, but not
the kind advocated by Ben Ami's former adviser, namely a rapid end to
the occupation. On the contrary, Sharon thought Israel had to win that
Algerian War. As a young officer in 1961 he had been very sympathetic to

the French officers involved in the putsch and their aim of preserving French Algeria. "It's like you [French] in Algeria, except that we are going to stay on," he declared in September 2001 to a French magazine, after a year of intifada.[11] Thus he himself made the comparison with the French occupation of Algeria and the war of independence of the National Liberation Front. His war involved maintaining the Israeli presence in the Palestinian territories, just as people spoke of maintaining France in Algeria. Once in power, he waged what those Israelis opposing his plans called a "war for the colonies"—that is, the settlements. And, in contrast to the French, he was confident that he could win it.

Soon, after thirty-four straight days of demonstrations, 160 Palestinian killed (along with 7 Israeli soldiers) and hundreds wounded, there came what Klein had predicted: the first attack of Hamas in Israel. As was reported in Le Monde on November 4, 2000, the bomb had been expected for weeks both on the Israeli side and among the Palestinians, whose political leaders, still hoping for a negotiated settlement, feared its consequences. And there it was, on Thursday, November 2, at 3 p.m., at the Mahane Yehuda market in a heavily populated district of Jewish Jerusalem where some of the bloodiest attacks of recent years had taken place, the last of them in November 1998. For the advocates of the konceptzia, this was proof that, as predicted, Arafat was proceeding to terrorism. And since he could stop everything instantly with a snap of his fingers, here too he must have been preparing in advance.

From "proof" to "proof" the konceptzia retrospectively reinterpreted the entire process in accordance with a failure to understand what was at issue in the present. It offered no rational explanation for what was happening, or rather it explained everything in terms of the enemy's irrationality. Why had the Palestinians risen up? Because of their irrational, destructive nature. As David Grossman noted, this was the official and popular truth current in Israel. The Palestinians' actual situation was irrelevant. This view, he concluded, was fraudulent and dangerous.[12] Dangerous indeed. Menahem Klein was right: established by Barak and expressed with more force and coherence by Sharon, it would soon enable Sharon to win the elections and his old accomplice, the transferist Rehavaam Zeevi, to enter the government.

THE FUNCTION OF *HASBARA*, OFFICIAL COMMUNICATION

Because the *konceptzia* had been fashioned on the basis of a political perspective that truncated the facts, with the coming to power of Ariel Sharon the machinery for producing justifications went into full operation. The longer the intifada went on, the more this machinery found daily confirmation in each movement of the enemy, as a well-oiled communication system increased its supportive output.

The army, in particular, was a driving force behind this heightened pace. Headed by Generals Mofaz and Yaalon, it interpreted everything in terms of the *konceptzia* that demonized Arafat. Communiqués from the IDF uniformly explained the killing of Palestinians as the response to attacks on Israeli soldiers. This was sometimes accurate, sometimes deceptive. It is almost never possible to verify these claims, any more than it is possible to verify the claims of the Palestinians, whose own tendencies to victimization and exaggeration are not the best guarantee of trustworthy information.

The Israeli military communiqués proceeded from the logic of troops in the field, especially the logic of armies of occupation faced with guerrilla warfare and a popular uprising. Yet they were effective. Provided ready-made by Dover Tsahal, the army's well-staffed mouthpiece service, they were accepted without question by military correspondents. Only a few journalists like Amira Hass and Gideon Levy of *Haaretz*, working in the territories though not accredited by the army, reasserted the truth of the matter and, if necessary, revealed the official lies. But they reported only one out of every hundred cases each day. International correspondents and news agencies paid attention. When the IDF was the sole source and the information was unverifiable, which occurred 95 percent of the time, they added the words "according to the Israeli army." This proviso was often deleted when newspapers repeated the accounts; the official communiqué became a piece of information. For several reasons—the blockades, their insufficient resources—the Palestinians were much less able to compete in the media arena, which only heightened their tendency to exaggerate.

All this was just routine military communication. When the house of a terrorist was razed and his family put out into the street, the army let this be known. It was widely believed that only the homes of actual or presumed terrorists were destroyed, but this was not so. Most of these homes belonged to people who lived where the IDF did not want them to. Their houses were said to interfere with the army's ability to maintain security or with the visibility needed by soldiers, or they were too close to a settlement that required protection, or terrorists could hide there, and so forth. It was the same with the fields and orchards that were laid waste. The result is that, in the minds of Israelis and even abroad, it is believed that only the houses of terrorists were being destroyed. The communication system functioned well.

As time passed and the ongoing intifada was no longer surprising, newspaper reports about the daily life of the Palestinians were generally relegated to six lines on an inside page: a woman held up for five hours at a checkpoint gave birth in the taxi and the infant died, a 3-year-old child was killed in a confrontation with terrorists, an 8-year-old was killed by a soldier mounting guard who felt threatened, and the like. In contrast, when events deemed important took place, the *konceptzia* strengthened its foundational arguments. When Yasser Arafat was declared irrelevant, or it was decided to disengage from signed accords in order to increase the military presence in Gaza and the supposedly autonomous Palestinian cities; when a one-ton bomb was dropped on a building to ensure the "targeted liquidation" of an Islamist political leader (leaving seventeen people dead, including ten children); when a "wall against terrorism" was built, leaving two million Palestinians in a cage and four hundred thousand wedged in between its path and the Israeli border, these were the moments when *hasbara* showed its true worth.

Hasbara—literally, "explanation," the term applied to official communications intended to be read abroad—is one of the keywords of Israeli political language. It refers to the line of argument, the version of facts, provided by the public powers. This notion has always been at the heart of media concern and public opinion. It is not seen for what it is: a self-interested plea on behalf of the government, to be taken as such with the requisite distance. It is everyone's common property in the face of the international community.

The Israelis have at all times maintained a paradoxical attitude toward their *hasbara*. In brief, though the powers that be have always paid special attention to *hasbara* and granted it impressive resources, at difficult moments when international criticism is directed at Israel its citizens blame it for being either ineffective (the justice of our cause is so obvious, but our services can't explain it),[13] or useless (no matter what we do, no one in the world will understand us). This is the ground in which the logic of the "conception" takes root: whatever the circumstances, it must be shown that Israel is struggling for survival against a terrorist monster bent on destroying it.

In covering news stories I have often seen the way the *konceptzia* influences *hasbara*. At the beginning of Operation Defensive Shield (March 28–April 17, 2002) I asked Olivier Rafowitz, the military spokesman in Jerusalem, to spend a day in a tank and share the daily life of soldiers in the field. This colonel was the laughingstock of correspondents, but he had always behaved perfectly with me. He agreed to my request on the telephone. When we met to establish the details of the news report, his cell phone rang. He suddenly turned pale, listened, hung up, and told me, "I have to go; we'll see about your report later." What had happened that was so serious? "Terrorists have entered the Church of the Nativity in Bethlehem and are holding priests hostage." During the day I called the archdiocese of Jerusalem and got the cell-phone number of one of these priests. He told me calmly, without seeming to be under threat from anyone, that no one had been taken hostage. "A church is always a place of refuge," he said. People were fleeing in panic, including some who were being sought by the Israeli army, which was combing the area house by house. The priests had opened the church doors, their only condition being that those who were armed had to lay down their weapons. It soon became apparent that all sorts of people had taken refuge: armed men and militants, ordinary people who were terrified, and very young people. But no sooner had the event emerged than Rafowitz had been briefed by the leaders of Dover Tsahal to the effect that hostages had been taken. This was to be the *hasbara*, the official explanation. Taking their own priests hostage: these people really are vile.

On another occasion Rafowitz had arranged for me to meet with General Kuperwasser, the second in command of military intelligence. When

I arrived at Tsahal headquarters in Tel Aviv, his team was in disarray. At that time the Bush administration, via its special envoy Anthony Zinni, was trying to reduce the tension. It had not yet officially committed itself to getting rid of Yasser Arafat, who was shut up in what remained of his so-called presidential palace in Ramallah. Washington had asked Arafat to make an unambiguous public denunciation of suicidal terrorism, and to do so in Arabic and on Palestinian television. This was the very moment he was about to deliver his speech. During our meeting Kuperwasser's associates kept trying to pass him several notes, the translation of Arafat's remarks.

After the speech the general's automatic assessment was a prime example of the *konceptzia*. Yes, he admitted, Arafat had indeed demanded an immediate stop to suicidal terrorism. And yes, to refer to those who perpetrated it he had not used the usual word, *shahid* (martyr), but a clearly opprobrious term. And he had spoken of two states side by side, Israel and Palestine, in the future. But, Kuperwasser added, "he didn't utter the words: 'recognition of Israel as a Jewish state.'" Which, he concluded, shows that "Arafat is still the liar, the clown." Regardless of what this "liar" had said publicly and in Arabic, his speech hadn't managed to conceal his "duplicity": "He still wants to destroy Israel by force."[14]

This was the first time I had heard this argument, which would soon become a classic *hasbara* line. Not only must the PLO "recognize Israel," which it had done in 1988, five years before Israel recognized it in turn, but it had to admit the country's "Jewish nature." No matter that this demand had never been inscribed in any prior negotiation with the PLO or presented to Egypt or Jordan at the signing of peace accords. No matter that in recognizing Resolution 181 Arafat recognized the Jewish state de facto, since the term is explicitly used there. This line of argument serves only to persuade people of the validity of their image of the other, to justify his demonization. Hoping to inspire trust in their interlocutors or do away with this wretched argument, the Palestinian negotiators of the Geneva Pact had stated in writing their recognition "of the right of the Jewish people to a state" (Keller 2004, p. 78). But this did not prevent the supporters of the *konceptzia* from regarding this pact as meaningless and condemning its Israeli signatories as traitors. If the PLO were to recognize the "Jewish nature" of Israel tomorrow, these supporters would no doubt stipulate as an additional condition that the PLO similarly recognize Jerusalem as the eternal and indivisible capital of the Jewish people. And if it went that far, it would ultimately have to adhere to Zionist principles and thank Israel for the expulsion of the Palestinians. Otherwise these "serial liars" would be unmasked anew each time.

It remains the case both that Israeli *hasbara* can be highly effective on some occasions and that on others its mission can prove to be impossible. The Jenin Affair is an instance of the remarkable success of *hasbara*, which was able to exploit the exceptional incompetence of Arafat and the partisans of the Palestinian cause. During Operation Defensive Shield an ambush led to thirteen deaths in an Israeli unit in the refugee camp of that city, which had been totally besieged. According to Amnesty International, its occupation by Tsahal resulted in at least fifty-four deaths among the Palestinians, including fewer than half of the armed militia,[15] and ten additional victims were Israeli soldiers. The army bulldozed all the dwellings inside the camp.[16] With his customary vainglory, Arafat immediately spoke of "Jeningrad," and his entourage hastened to denounce "a new Sabra and Shatila."[17]

Anxious about possible negative reactions on the international scene, Israel blocked access to the site to prevent any eyewitness testimony. Its major political columnist, Nahum Barnea, advised the authorities to evacuate the bodies from the streets and the ruins quickly, lest Israel become an international outcast.[18] Sharon rejected the possibility of an international commission of inquiry until the United Nations accepted his conditions, which placed broad limitations on the gathering of evidence. Yet Jenin rapidly took on symbolic import. Had a massacre taken place? If so, it would be seen as demonstrating "Israeli barbarity"; if not, "Palestinian mendacity" and the imperatives of the struggle against terrorism. The *hasbara* took every possible advantage of the situation.

Diverting attention from the facts and focusing only on their representation is one of the most prized methods of what specialists call crisis communication. The facts in themselves prove nothing, we are told. The best way to ignore them is to discuss only their interpretation. And so the communications services became preoccupied with *how* to describe the events at Jenin. No one was concerned about what had really happened—the terror inflicted on the population, the devastation, the ambulances forbidden to make their trips, the blockaded hospital, and the like — but only about whether there had been "a massacre" or simply "fighting." Nor did anyone care about the fact that, less than a hundred kilometers away, in the casbah of Nablus, another combat during this same operation had resulted in eighty Palestinian deaths and a single Israeli casualty, which gives a more realistic sense of the actual balance of forces in the armed confrontations. Finally, and this was the crucial point, the "battle" of Jenin and the "(non-)massacre" made it possible to hide the true nature of Operation Defensive Shield, which lasted three weeks; apart from these two cases, the fighting in this operation was made to seem nonexistent.

The journalist Uri Blau has stated, on the basis of military evidence, that this operation had been planned for over a year,[19] that is, ever since Ariel Sharon gained power and long before the dreadful terrorist attack on the eve of Easter, an attack that plunged Israel into mourning and served as the justification for launching Defensive Shield. On the political level this involved abolishing the accords previously signed so as to impose, and legitimize in the eyes of the world, Israel's military reoccupation of the A zones on the West Bank — basically the large cities formally under the leadership of the Palestinian Authority. Israel's second aim was to get the international community to validate the de facto exclusion of Yasser Arafat from the proceedings and to wipe out what remained of Palestinian political institutions.

Operation Defensive Shield was in essence one huge roundup. All Palestinian males between the ages of 14 and 50 were screened, with tens of thousands held for questioning and thousands cross-examined as an entire civilian population was subjected to terror by military force. Troops seized a vast number of private apartments and public places, moving into them and cordoning off the families into one room of their own dwelling, humiliating thousands of parents before their children's eyes and committing numerous acts of vandalism. The correspondent for *Le Monde* reported first-hand how the cultural center of Ramallah was pillaged and Israeli soldiers defecated everywhere.[20] An "authorized source" from the army acknowledged that an internal report of the IDF referred to "significant, massive, and futile acts of destruction," while a "very high-level source in the military courts" admitted that there had been "acts of vandalism on a much larger scale than one would have imagined."[21] These acts occurred in schools, mosques, offices, factories, nongovernmental organizations, workshops, and private dwellings. Soldiers seemed to be especially intent on the computers they found. Palestinians could only be fellahs, housewives, or garage mechanics; they could not be engineers, doctors, or literature professors and own a personal computer.

In addition to Jenin and Nablus, the Israeli army reoccupied all of the West Bank, encountering no, or only anecdotal, armed resistance. But, for their separate reasons, Arafat and the Israeli *hasbara* found themselves in agreement in focusing exclusively on the "Battle of Jenin," the former in order to glorify "armed resistance," a ridiculous palliative for the impotence and political incoherence of his Authority and the lack of prospects and tangible directives offered to his people, the latter to lend credence to the idea that the entire operation had consisted of fighting terrorists. Its political and social reality was largely concealed and rapidly forgotten. When, several months later, a United Nations commission of inquiry concluded that no massacre had been committed in Jenin, the Israeli authorities were exultant. In international opinion this was the only lasting impression left by Operation Defensive Shield.

And yet this victory of *hasbara* remains anecdotal in a war of communications that is lost in advance. In the long run *hasbara* comes up against an insoluble problem, one that spells trouble for those who are the most automatically sympathetic to Israel. For how can the occupation of another people be "sold" in any lasting way? Each time they appeared on television screens, the unbearable images of the results of the attacks in Israel evoked emotion and understanding in the international view of Israel and compassion for the victims. Each time, the international media made much of these attacks, whereas the almost constant slow trickle of Palestinian deaths earned only a few lines. But in relative terms the images of the attacks are rare in comparison to those seen abroad from day to day: lines of people at the checkpoints, Palestinian populations subjected to curfews, the small atrocities committed by soldiers against civilians—or more serious atrocities, as when the IDF razed a hundred houses in Rafah. In short, images of armed soldiers repressing ordinary people, of tanks and helicopters on one side, and on the other side images of kalashnikovs and makeshift mortars. As long as these images continue to be shown, the *hasbara* is chasing a chimera. It will win intermittent victories but lose the overall war. No *hasbara* will save Israel from the regular deterioration of its image.

The decision in July 2004 by the Court of International Justice in The Hague concerning the building by Israel of a wall of separation inside the West Bank, ostensibly to protect itself from terrorism, offers a striking example. The verdict declaring this wall illegal and calling for its demolition led to an uproar in Israel. The right, and also a large number of Laborites, competed in denouncing the unworthiness of a tribunal that had, it was claimed, condemned Israel without devoting a single word to terrorism. As in all such situations, the word *anti-Semitism* appeared. The communications and diplomatic services were mobilized to defend this argument, which was, however, incorrect; the court *had* recognized Israel's right to defend itself against terrorism, though to be sure it did not dwell on this point, considering it irrelevant to the tenor of the lawsuit.

It had based its verdict on the illegal and inhumane effects of the wall on the Palestinian populations, following a jurisprudence reflecting the rather simple principle of social coexistence in civilized societies. If you are afraid of a neighbor whom you know or suspect to be a thief, a person of violence, or a potential criminal, you have the right to padlock your doors, reinforcing them with steel and as many locks as you wish. But you may not imprison him in his own house, let alone his wife and children, his parents, and all the neighbors in the area, preventing them from moving about and working so as to ensure your own protection. To do so is to disrespect common law and set up your own law, in which might makes right.

The *hasbara* seemed not to understand this simple truth. Had Israel built its wall on its own border, one might have expounded on the fate of a movement of national emancipation that had had the historic aim of freeing its people from the ghetto yet wound up building the walls of a huge new ghetto,[22] but there would have been no lawsuit. And if there had been one, it would have been declared inadmissible. It is because Israel is immuring its neighbors in *their* own land that the wall has been condemned. Recognized within its 1967 borders, once it goes beyond them

Israel is an occupying power and must yield to the principles of international law governing an occupation. Confronted by this truth, *hasbara* may call the critics of the Jewish state serial liars and condemn international anti-Semitism and what it sees as the disinformation campaign against Israel, but in the long run that will prove both useless and ineffectual.

In situations in which their country is condemned for reprehensible acts, Israelis divide into two camps. The first, and larger, one sinks deeper into victimization, persuading itself that Israel is beset by inherent and historic misunderstanding, a position accompanied by accusations of anti-Semitism that are leveled against anyone who criticizes the nation. Here, the inevitable and unbearable deterioration of Israel's image, as long as its military occupation of another people continues, gives rise to the desperate and aggressive hysteria of its unconditional admirers. At the other pole, a minority works to break free of the usual ethnicist reflexes and shows itself ready, whether radically or gradually and with pain, to undertake what Admiral Ami Ayalon has called a reexamination of one's axioms.

ELEVEN

"SHARON IS SHARON IS SHARON"
The Creeping "Pied-Noirization"[1] of Israel

ARIEL SHARON AND THE PALESTINIANS

It would be wrong to accuse Ariel Sharon of being the origin of all the Palestinians' misfortunes. Everything, or almost everything, he undertook after coming to power in March 2001 had been tried previously, under his predecessor Ehud Barak, in the months following the Palestinian uprising. And it had all been previously suggested by the Laborites. Checkpoints; blockades; extended curfews; collective punishments; destruction of homes and industrial or agricultural property; deliberate shooting of civilian protesters; "administrative detentions" without a charge being brought, an inquiry opened, or a verdict rendered; not to mention "targeted liquidations"[2] and the "defensive" firing of missiles and tank guns[3] — the implementation of all these methods for crushing the intifada had been authorized by the army before Sharon arrived.

The plan to take Arafat out of play? Barak had practically announced it after the Taba negotiations were broken off. Besieging Palestinian cities again? Barak had asked the IDF to practice for this eventuality long before Camp David, so as to guard against any failure of the talks. The separation wall? It was originally an idea of the Laborites. Only one innovation can be attributed to Sharon—the use of fighter planes to drop bombs in urban areas.

But it would also be wrong to see Sharon as merely continuing what Barak had begun, though in a tougher fashion. Sharon came to the highest public office with a vision rooted in old convictions, convictions that had been strengthened by long military and political experience. According to Shimon Shiffer, a veteran political reporter for *Yediot Ahronot* who had accompanied him on all his governmental travels since 1977, "Sharon learned two lessons from the war in Lebanon in 1982: never divide the people, never break off with the Americans."[4]

For, after the massacre of Sabra and Shatila, Sharon, the defense minister at that time, had become the most discredited political figure in the country. He had seen one hundred thousand Israelis (equivalent to five million on a U.S. scale) march in protest, chanting "Sharon is a murderer." And President Reagan had abruptly withdrawn his support for the intervention of the IDF in Beirut. Sharon never forgot this. When he came to power nineteen years later, he made an effort to keep an eye on the national consensus and maintain better relations with the new American president, George W. Bush.

Sharon was able to analyze the nature of the conflict more coherently than Barak. And "Arik, king of Israel," as his supporters call him, had an ambition: to achieve the breakdown of Palestinian society and fragment its solidarity, beating the nationalists, whom he had always considered his only dangerous opponents, to the punch. If he had learned anything from his experience, it was to retain the reflexive assumptions of his fundamental vision of the conflict with the Palestinians. In his biography of Sharon, whose Hebrew title, *The Man Who Doesn't Stop at Red Lights*, says everything, Uzi Benziman (1985) sees as the basis of these assumptions Sharon's placing of force above all other considerations. After all, on November 1, 1980, Sharon, then a minister, had declared before the government that security prevailed over the law.[5]

Sharon had been a brilliant and unusually brave soldier. And a fighter too, as the Israelis say, a man who risked confrontation. Head of a criminal squadron in the 1950s, he had planned numerous killings of civilians,[6] and he had been a general of extraordinary intuition in the war of October 1973. He had always been exceptionally eager to annihilate the enemy, military or civilian, and had on occasion been criticized for blatant disregard for the lives of his own men.[7] This did not prevent him from winning the greatest adulation from his direct subordinates in the history of the Israeli military (Moshe Dayan was admired and feared, but not loved). Sharon was a man who never concealed his deepest opinions, and paid for this by being regularly marginalized in the IDF when he made his colleagues uneasy; he was also a confirmed liar who did not hesitate to resort to any type of demagogy that would promote his ambitions, and a tactician who would take any measures necessary to crush an opponent— or even a friend—in his path.[8]

Sharon grew up in the labor movement, specifically Ahdut Haavodah, the radical Zionist workers' group that was not content to stop at the cease-fire borders in 1948. But along with another general, Ezer Weizmann, he was also the founder of the present-day Israeli right, Likud. Finally, and this is not the least of his paradoxes, Sharon was impulsive, a man who rushed headlong into action, yet he was also, at heart, a planner. As a very young soldier, in the 1950s, he carefully planned the creation of a special battalion of paracommandos to carry out special operations beyond the borders against the advice of his superior, General Dayan, skillfully maneuvering to win the approval of Prime Minister Ben Gurion. He remained a planner upon entering politics. As defense minister he meticulously planned the 1982 invasion of Lebanon up to Beirut far in advance and waited for the right moment to go into action. He was a past master of "provocations," always well thought out.

Sharon had always envisioned a basically insoluble, permanent conflict in which Israel would have to impose its will on a hostile environment unable to accept it. In this he shared the historical perspective of the founder of Zionist revisionism, Vladimir Zeev Jabotinsky,[9] as well as Jabotinsky's argument for an "iron wall" to be erected by Israel as protection against aggression from without.

And he was also like his first mentor, Ben Gurion, in seeing the conflict continuing for another hundred years. It was this long-term concept that underlay Ben Gurion's relation to space; the "father of Israel" balked at speaking of his country as having borders. In his memoirs he relates a discussion held in 1948 in the Minhalat Haam (People's Council), the governing body before the creation of the state:

A comrade raised the issue of borders. A state could not be declared
without the fixing of its borders. I was against specifying them. I indicated that, in the Declaration of Independence of the United
States, there was no mention of borders. Why say nothing about our
boundaries? Because we don't know whether the U.N. will maintain its positions [the anticipated partition of Palestine]. And if the
U.N. does not exist in this matter, and war is waged against us, we'll
conquer them [the Arabs]. We'll seize Western Galilee and both sides
of the road to Jerusalem [granted to the future Palestine by the U.N.],
and all that will become part of our state if we're strong enough. So
why make a commitment [regarding boundaries]? [Tsahal Historical Service 1959, p. 58]

Ariel Sharon remained in this mental configuration, the notion of a
state with a territory evolving, according to circumstances, with inde-
terminate borders. What is more, in the 1950s, when "Arik" was a young
officer, the very term *boundaries* did not exist in the political jargon of
his country; what people spoke of was the "territorial extent" of the state.
But, even as he was careful never to burn his bridges with the tutelary
powers in the region (British, then American),[10] Ben Gurion was able
to play a game of carrot and stick and make compromises. As with the
historical position of the Israeli right, Sharon knew only binary situations in which the confrontation of two camps is obvious. He reduced
all reality to this antagonism, both in international relations and in the
Israeli–Arab conflict. The concept of the clash of civilizations fit him
like a glove.

Though he also shared other values with the historical hard-right wing
of Zionism, such as its intransigence regarding exclusive possession of the
Land of Israel, he was not imbued with this ideology. Uzi Landau, Likud
minister and member of a large family associated with the revisionist party
Herut, was scandalized when Israel contemplated a withdrawal from Gaza.
A pragmatist within the context of his convictions, Sharon was prepared
to dismantle all the settlements there, although, when he came to power,
he had made a public commitment to retaining them all at any price,[11] if
doing so would serve other ambitions aimed at destroying the Palestinian

nation and consolidating the territory of Israel in accordance with Ben Gurion's long-term perspective.

Sharon was much less of an ideologue, for example, than Benyamin Netanyahu; he was a determined and tactically skilled politician who knew only one rule, namely to gain time so as to advance his objectives. Any compromise or retreat was always temporary and did not alter his fundamental perception. He could let go of Gaza today, if necessary, in order to strengthen his position on the West Bank tomorrow, just as he could retake Gaza militarily should later events so dictate, or, on the contrary, proceed to a supplementary disengagement on the West Bank in the hope of ensuring the permanence of certain settlements. It all depended on circumstances. When they were favorable, he moved ahead as far as possible. When they were less so, he maneuvered, pointing to his willingness to accept "painful concessions" in order to play for time and await better days.

Two months after his landslide victory over Ehud Barak in the 2001 elections, "Arik" held his first major press interview as prime minister. *Haaretz* entitled it "Sharon is Sharon is Sharon" (Shavit 2004b). It tells all there is to know about his relation to time and space.

The Israeli–Palestinian conflict? "The War of Independence has not ended," Sharon said. "No. 1948 was just one chapter. . . . What was right then, before the state was established, is still right today. Basic things have not changed in any fundamental way. . . . [Fighting] was and remains the role of my generation. And it is also the role of the coming generations. . . . It is a very long road. We need forbearance and decisiveness and inner quiet. And will. The Jewish people need a great deal of will."

The Palestinians? He knew only two kinds: those "who want to bring home a piece of bread and raise their children," and these he could accept within Israel, and the others, who have larger ambitions, political ambitions, for example—all of whom are involved in the terrorism he was combating.

Israel? "Look, people today don't get so excited by the idea of 'another dunam and another dunam' [of land].[12] But I still get excited." What mattered was not to lose sight of the fact that the aim of Zionism is to keep moving forward.

The settlements? "I see no reason for evacuating any settlements. In any event, as long as there is no peace, we are there. And if in the future, with God's help, there is peace, there will certainly be no reason for not being there."

Ending the intifada? "I see two stages in this campaign. The first stage is to restore security and create the conditions for negotiations. The second stage is to formulate a realistic political plan." In the meantime, "we have to view things with our eyes wide open and be cautious. Very cautious. To give them the necessary minimum."

His "realistic political plan"? "[T]here are no quick solutions." "[W]hat I am proposing is to take a . . . less pretentious road. To go for a long-term, gradual solution . . . ," first an interim accord for ten or fifteen years, ending in a Palestinian state on 42 percent of the occupied territories, perhaps a bit more. But giving more than that would leave Israel without the fruits of its historical and strategic possessions and would not bring the conflict to an end." A cruel dilemma.

Sharon himself? "Personally, I am a sensitive man. I always like to see a tree in the wind with the corner of my eye, or to hear music in the background."

THE INTIFADA AND THE ISRAELI "MATRIX OF CONTROL"

What can be added to this profession of faith, except that it reveals all the colonialist Orientalism of Sharon's youth as depicted by Uzi Benziman in his biography, as well as the idea that the borders of Israel are never definitive—certainly not the internationally recognized borders—but remain in a state of development? In the course of this interview the old general also showed a warm nostalgia for the epic events of 1948 and the expansion of 1967. At those times the Israelis were conquerors, he said. Even at the hardest moments "our spirit did not falter." And he lamented the insufficient morale of present-day Israelis, to the point of envying the Palestinians' determination in their struggle.

Continuing the War of 1948 and moving ahead: this was the basis of everything Ariel Sharon wanted to undertake once he returned to political affairs. His priority was to crush the Palestinian national movement: there was no room for two nations. The rest was contingent. Given his belief that Israel had returned to its long-term conflict, this view and the lessons he learned from his political experience led him to plan what he would do once in power: take Arafat out of play, destroy the civil organs of the Palestinian Authority, gradually fragment Palestinian society in a process of cantonization, proceed in stages to increase the level of repression of the Palestinians so as to habituate international opinion to it and guarantee American support. At that time he could not imagine that the "Hanukkah miracle" of the September 11 attacks in the United States, as the head of Mossad called them, would lead the Bush administration to forge tighter ties with him and the president himself to describe Sharon as a man of peace.

General Meir Dagan, Sharon's political adviser during the electoral campaign of 2000–2001, confirmed the existence of this plan. It was December 14, 2001, two days after Sharon had declared Yasser Arafat "null and void." Earlier that day there had been a terrible attack on a bus carrying people who lived in the religious settlement Emmanuel. Dagan had conceived the plan, written "in black and white" before the elections, according to the journalist Alex Fishman.[13] Its two fundamental points were, first, that Arafat was a murderer, and hence no negotiation with him was possible; and, second, that the Oslo Accords were a major disaster for Israel and must be undone at any cost.

Sharon's initial aim was to gradually weaken Arafat, both internally and diplomatically. This implied the de facto political strengthening of his Islamist opponents, the aim being to push him into making a mistake that would end his role as head of the Palestinian Authority. How was this to be done? By slowly and relentlessly ratcheting up the level of repression to which the Palestinians were subject, and by maneuvering politically until the Americans were no longer in opposition.

Dagan gave several examples of how the plan would work. Thus, the first time the IDF used F-16 fighter planes to bomb the Palestinians in an urban area, there had been an international outcry but very little reaction in Israel. But, Fishman reports Dagan as saying, by now the world had grown accustomed to seeing F-16s in the skies over the West Bank and Gaza and no longer protested. A further example: on his recent visit, President Bush's special envoy had been eager to meet with Arafat, which made it impossible to declare Arafat out of play. But with the Emmanuel attack Hamas had done the work of bringing Arafat down in American and international opinion, and the decision about declaring the Palestinian leader null and void could be made.

The next stage, Dagan said, was already under way. This was to isolate Arafat within his own circle and among the Palestinians in general, and to that end Israel had begun to bomb their communications infrastructure (telephone, radio, television). At the same time the plan aimed at fragmenting the Palestinian Authority. The prime minister, the defense minister, and the general staff were meeting together to discuss when it would be possible to reoccupy Palestinian cities, beginning with Jenin, so as to put them in order. This was a tough challenge, since it would require national mobilization and the problematical issue of calling upon reservists. Fishman comments that, while no firm decision had yet been made, should there be a bloody attack coming from Jenin the balance might tip in favor of retaking the city. Four months later, a dreadful attack in Netanya, in the wake of the targeted liquidations of several Palestinian leaders and massive Israeli strikes, provided Sharon with the opportunity to go into action. Operation Defensive Shield, aimed at reoccupying Palestinian cities, had been planned for a long time and could now be launched.

Where was all this heading? Once Arafat was out for good, the Palestinian Authority dismantled, the intifada stamped out, the territories cantonized, and Palestinian society weakened, Dagan said, Israel would negotiate separately with those in power in each territorial unit. This dream was as old as the Israeli occupation, as old as the emphasis on *bitakhon*, security: with the disintegration of the Palestinian national movement, there would be many local notables willing to negotiate with the conqueror.

The author of such a plan was deserving of the highest distinctions. In 2003 Sharon named General Meir Dagan head of Mossad, the foreign intelligence service.

Plans have no more value than hopes. We know what became of the Sharon plan to eradicate the PLO in Lebanon and install a puppet government there. It failed, and the result was eighteen years of Israeli occupation in South Lebanon, thousands of dead on both sides combined, and a unilateral retreat by the IDF with no prior accord having been reached with either Syria or Lebanon.

The new Sharon plan, carried out to the letter, worked remarkably well until the death of Arafat on November 11, 2004. Washington is the only political power that counts in Israel's eyes, and the administration of George W. Bush has been a reliable ally despite the reservations of people like Colin Powell. When the IDF made its first incursion into Gaza (which was in A zone, forbidden, by agreement, to Israeli forces), Powell, the American secretary of state at that time, publicly demanded that the Israeli army evacuate the area in six hours. As Dagan predicted, the second time there was nothing more than an angry phone call. The third time, Powell had a subordinate place the call. The fourth time there was no phone call at all; Washington and the world had gotten used to such an event . . .

Since then incursions into the Palestinian A Zones have become an everyday occurrence. Three years after the first such incursion, the razing of a hundred residential buildings along Philadelphia Road in South Gaza caused no great stir on the international level.[14]

To be sure, Jenin, Hebron, and Nablus have not become Grozny. There has been no Sétif atrocity,[15] though there are those who can envision such a thing; at a government meeting Uzi Landau suggested that Israel do to the Palestinians what the Iraqis did to the Kurds.[16] Landau, who admires the gassings committed by Saddam Hussein at Halabja, was the Israeli minister of internal security at the time he made this remark. IDF soldiers were skilled at shooting at sight on the least pretext, the slightest suspicion. "The Aim: To Kill As Many of Them As Possible" was the banner headline of a 2002 article by Uri Blau in the weekly magazine *Kol Ha'Ir*[17] that cited orders given by officers.

One time out of a hundred the IDF offers excuses, as on July 7, 2002. Two weeks earlier, a tank had killed two brothers, 13 and 6, in Jenin. A regrettable error, said the army. Before that, it had claimed, as usual, that its soldiers had been threatened, but here the BBC had pictures clearly exposing the lie. Believing that the curfew had been lifted, the children had gone out to buy chocolate. A curfew is a curfew. If anyone infringes it, shoot first and verify later. This is the logic of all occupations. To date, over a thousand Palestinian minors have been killed by the Israeli army, half of whom were between a few days and 13 years old. At the onset of the intifada, an elite Israeli sharpshooter questioned by the journalist Amira Hass observed that, according to military rules, a minor was someone "under the age of 12."[18]

To be sure, Israel does not build huge detention camps as the colonial powers did. But the arrests and incarcerations involve tens of thousands of people. According to the World Organization Against Torture, a non-governmental organization, between October 2000 and March 2001 alone 300 children under the age of 18, some as young as 14, were sent to prison.[19] This United Nations agency also mentioned allegations of the widespread use of torture against children. Another NGO, B'Tselem, has stated that 850 Palestinians were tortured in 2001.[20] And, to be sure, this torture is not routine, as it was, for example, in colonial Algeria, nor is it of mindless and indiscriminate cruelty as today in Chechnya. Legally employed in Israel at all times by the special forces, it may even be on the decline according to the lawyer Leah Tsemel. "Shabak," she says, "infiltrates everything; it almost doesn't need torture nowadays because its methods are so effective."[21] The number of people imprisoned through "administrative detention," the legal Israel counterpart of the American prison at Guantánamo, rose from 34 on December 5, 2000 to 960 on December 8, 2001. There were 781 on September 2, 2004, after having reached a peak of 1,140 in April 2003.[22] Reports by various Israeli and Palestinian human-rights organizations would fill several library shelves.

But the repression has gradually passed through several stages. After months of being confined to their apartments, the Palestinians are now being walled in inside their own country. For example, between June 19 and August 30, 2002, the inhabitants of Ramallah, subjected to a total curfew, were permitted to leave their homes for only fifty-one hours, that is, a total of four hours each week for ten weeks.[23] There were hundreds of identical curfews.[24] Schools and universities are regularly closed. Contrary to what is generally believed, the homes that are razed are not only those of the families of suicide bombers; the vast majority are destroyed for "military reasons," to satisfy the needs of adjacent settlements, or simply by way of humiliation. At Ramallah, the army razed thirty-four dwelling units built by an association of Palestinian workers on the grounds that the apartment complex exceeded the municipal domain accorded to cities in Zone A.[25]

Internal transfers, the forced displacements in which people living in entire zones are made to live elsewhere, forbidden to move about freely or to gain access to their fields, are regular. In Gaza, the pumping stations for two wells that provided fresh water for nearly half of the households of Rafah were deliberately destroyed by military bulldozers.[26] A great many similar examples could be cited. Fanatic settlers who kill or injure Palestinians have never been called to account, even when complaints are filed against them. These settlers also go in for sacking fields and orchards. On September 22, 2002, the IDF declared that it was unable to protect Palestinian peasants and issued a temporary order forbidding them to harvest their olives.

In Hebron there were once 30,000 Arabs living in the so-called Jewish Quarter (inhabited by 500–800 settlers); subject to repeated curfews for four years, they now number only 15,000. In the historic Old City, under the army's control, fanatic settlers have painted on the walls and metal curtains of long-closed shops biblical phrases accompanied by slurs: "The Arabs are pigs," "Death to Arabs," and the like. The main thoroughfare between the Cave of the Patriarchs to the site of Tel Rumeida was full of such slogans when I traveled along it in December 2002. One of them was said to have been "Arabs to the gas chambers" before someone in Israel paid attention and made the soldiers erase it.

Entire towns have been deserted. Palestinian society is an advanced state of disintegration. Day in and day out there is an unbearable sense of being constantly subject to the unpredictable whims of Israeli soldiers, the indifference, arrogance, and, sometimes, the sadism of these kids in uniform, who, weapons in hand, keep the "savages" in their cages—not to mention the sense of being offered as prey to extremist settlers who do as they wish with impunity.

This is the "necessary minimum" planned by Sharon. It is the result of what the Israeli anthropologist Jeff Halper (2000) calls the "matrix of control"[27] imposed by the Hebrew state on the occupied population: the increase in settlements and the expropriation of land; the networking of these settlements; the allocation of one liter of water to each Palestinian peasant in contrast to seven to each settler; the multiplication of bypass roads reserved for Israelis and barred to the inhabitants of the West Bank; multiple statutes determining the right to work and move about, varying from one residential area to another and sometimes different within the same family; the dire impoverishment resulting from the closures; the tearing down of olive groves (some of them hundreds of years old) and orchards, or their pollarding so that they are no higher than ten centimeters; the filling in of wells—and as a grand finale, the wall.

Then there are the humiliations that leave a deeper impression than all the difficulties of daily life. After Operation Defensive Shield a Palestinian woman described to me the worst such experience her family had undergone. She, her husband, and their children had been confined to one room of their own apartment, the others being occupied by Israeli soldiers. Early one morning her 14-year-old daughter needed to go to the toilet. Knocking at the door to indicate that she wanted to leave the room, asking the soldiers for permission, and walking past these 18-year-old strangers in her nightgown under the eyes of her mortified father: both the girl and the father found this more unbearable than the imprisonment itself.

In daily life this sort of thing weighs more heavily by far on the Palestinian population as a whole than the deaths that, likewise, happen often but concern individual families. There are the deaths of people, who, if they were affiliated directly or indirectly with armed groups, are buried amid loud cries for revenge and bursts of gunfire. And then there are the deaths of people who almost never get media exposure: the "collateral victims." These victims are laid in their coffins secretly by the poor outside the range of television cameras and mourned within the family: a little girl on her way to school, an old man who thought the curfew had been lifted, men heading for the fields, all of whom were going about their business where the army had decided they should not be present. Such deaths occur more or less everywhere in the territories, perhaps one in a good week, ten in a bad week. These are the grand battalions of victims.

Among the bereaved sons, brothers, and cousins, how many young people swear that they will die the death of martyrs? Not "for nothing."

Yet, like all plans of its kind, Dagan's plan had to come to terms with reality, in order to deal, first of all, with the Palestinians' resolve to overcome their misfortunes. Anyone who has seen the women of Beit Hanun, in Gaza, women whose olive and orange trees had all been cut down by Tsahal's special bulldozers over an area of hundreds of meters, intent on placing new seedlings in the ground cannot fail to be impressed by such perseverance in rising up again from each blow. The Palestinians call this attitude *sumud*, "constancy." And the plan had to come to terms with the way the Palestinians ingeniously adapt from day to day and, without taking too many risks, contravene the new rules regularly imposed by the occupier's "matrix of control."

And it had to come to terms with the mild diplomatic pressures exerted on Israel. The decision, in June 2004, to proceed at long last with the dismantling of the settlements in Gaza was due to three factors. First there was the impossibility of making one million Arab inhabitants of the area, cooped up in their enclave as in a zoo, capitulate. Second, there was the need to take a political initiative in order to nullify the "road map" jointly drawn up by the United States, the European Union, Russia, and the United Nations, a document providing for the establishment of a Palestinian state in the occupied territories. And, finally, there was Israeli public opinion, which was largely convinced that continuing the occupation of the Gaza Strip was too complicated an undertaking for the future.[28]

Even if the withdrawal from Gaza was presented to the public as the way to strengthen Israel's hold on the West Bank, it is still a political defeat for the country after four years in which the Sharon government repeated its assurances that it would not dismantle the settlements.

THE "ALGERIANIZATION" OF THE ISRAELIS

Speaking in 2004, Moshe Negbi characterized the Sharon government as follows: "Sharon is the symbol of the way the Israeli mentality has evolved. The man who knew only the balance of power and who, before 1995, had appeared before demonstrators caricaturing Rabin as an SS man, became prime minister. And [the Labor Party leader] Peres entered his administration. Even better: so did Rabin's daughter! The cult of force is taking hold in general acceptance."[29] Negbi is an Israeli professor of public law and presenter of a law program broadcast on public radio. For eight years he wrote a column on law for the conservative newspaper *Maariv*; today he has become an advocate for a unilateral withdrawal from the occupied territories.

What are we to make of the societal transformation that saw a large majority of Israeli Jews run into the arms of Ariel Sharon, a man with his controversial past, his ideas, his brutality? What does it mean that this same man very quickly forged a centrist position for himself on the political chessboard, between a clueless Laborite left and a well-provisioned far right that was making horrendous plans? And how to explain all the paradoxical polls, which regularly show a majority of Israelis calling for the increased repression and the "transfer" of the Palestinians and, at the same time, coming out in favor of withdrawal from the territories?

The answer to this third question is the key to the first two answers. Basically, most Israelis would like to live without Arabs, but they also know that the Arabs are there and will not go away. And they are all more or less aware of the fact that what their politicians and generals tell them is often contradictory and hence not very trustworthy. The office of the general staff has assured them on a number of occasions that victory is near, but Sharon also told them that the struggle would be long and painful, that future generations would still know war. Israelis are told that, with the measures being taken, terrorism will soon be largely, if not entirely, stamped out. But the generals keep repeating that they need more resources because terrorism is growing. What to make of this?

When the intifada broke out, no Israeli, including those at the highest level, believed it would last so long. After six years and all the resources invested in its repression, most people in the country are overcome with distress and a sense of fatalism. And they have a vague sense that a radical solution for resolving the present situation, one way or another, is inevitable. This is why one of the comments most often heard in Israel nowadays is, "It would be best to get all the Arabs out of here if we could. But

that's not possible, so let's get out of the territories and be done with it."
This means that the same individual can perfectly well answer "Yes" to
the question, "Are you in favor of transfer?" and also "Yes" to "Are you in
favor of an Israeli withdrawal from the territories?"

Why, then, did the Israelis support Sharon so massively? Because, they
were following the very old logic, reactivated with unprecedented intensity by the intifada, the attacks, and the sense of being isolated on the international scene, that the Palestinians simply cannot be allowed to "win."
Give them something, sure. But let them get it themselves, and by force
at that—never! This is how the collective self-image works. And, though
most Israelis are unaware of the degree to which this is the case, such a
mind-set also gives rise to behavior that leads the opposite side to believe
that force is the only thing the Israelis understand.

When I was covering a story in 2002 I stayed at the Hotel Zion in Jerusalem, which is adjacent to a cinema complex for film archives and film
festivals. A series of recent suicide attacks had plunged the city into mourning. That evening almost no one was at the cinema complex or in its cafeteria. Financially comfortable Jerusalemites had chosen to eat out only
in restaurants that had security doors with peepholes through which those
who wished to enter could be screened. All the talk was of terrorism and
the Palestinians in general: What should be done? How to put an end to
the situation?

A few months later I returned to the same hotel. Under international
pressure, the PLO had announced a *hudna*, a truce, and there had been
no attacks for several weeks. The cinema complex was packed every
evening, and the mood in its cafeteria was happy and carefree. Most of
the people eating there, trendy young people and adults from intellectual
circles, began by saying how much they hoped the truce would last. Then
they quickly went on to other topics: their lives and loves, their friends,
their work. This is an entirely legitimate phenomenon and a sign of vital-
ity, a sigh of relief, the return to a normal existence. But the sigh of relief
was also full of meaning. No sooner did the Palestinians stop posing a threat
than they were forgotten: their lives and loves, their work. Forgotten were
the checkpoints, the expropriations, and the destruction of homes and
orchards. But those were continuing without interruption.

And yet most of the people who come to this kind of cinema complex are in favor of peace. The tendency to remain unaware of the other while behaving in a domineering way explains why, as soon as the first intifada ended, the pacifists stopped taking an interest in the daily lot of the Palestinians, whether it was the increasing restrictions being imposed in the occupied territories, or the heightened security requirements on the part of the Israeli authorities. Everything was fine since negotiations were being held.

This is why people felt betrayed when the Palestinians rejected Barak's offer at Camp David. And why most of them learn no lessons from the fact that it is the Israeli government that has in fact broken the truce after a long period with no attacks, something that has occurred several times during the intifada, for example by killing an important Palestinian leader, Islamist or secular. Each time this happened, Israeli editorialists wrote that, by committing a targeted liquidation, Israel was risking a resumption of terrorism. But as soon as a terrorist act was actually committed by way of reprisal, a huge majority of the population became frantic in urging that the most extreme measures be taken against the terrorists. As the most consistent proponent of this tendency, Sharon was a master at exploiting it.

For with the Palestinian uprising a large majority of Israelis have developed an attitude in which the ethnicism and the colonialist[30] features of the country's original national movement have taken over, relegating to the margins the other elements that, until then, had counterbalanced it. And so who else but the settlers and the military, that is, the two forces directly implicated in the occupation, could more coherently express these features, then about to spread with astonishing speed throughout almost the entire society?

"We aren't the *pieds-noirs* of Algeria at all, but in certain respects we're like them. The settlers have dragged all of Israel into a process in which the mechanisms of the occupation get the society accustomed to apartheid and racism," said the writer David Grossman in 2004.[31] He was telling the truth. Although, as we have seen in the preceding chapters, many of its members share the mentality of the "whites" in colonialist societies to varying degrees, Israel as such is not a *pied-noir* society. This is because (within the limits of a comparison) in relation to the settlers in the territories it is what metropolitan France was to the French in Algeria. On the one hand there is Israel, its society, its state, its recognized borders, its population, and on the other there are the conquered Palestinian territories with the Israeli settlers who have moved there; it is these settlers who can be compared to the colonial "whites" living among the native inhabitants.

Yet there are two obvious differences between the relationship of the metropolitan French to the French of Algeria in the decade 1950–1960 and that of the Israelis to their fellow citizens in the Palestinian territories. First of all, there is physical proximity. No sea, border, or distance separates the Israeli settlers from their "metropolis." Like the others, and in the eyes of the others, they live in what is considered to be Israel. With the total abrogation in daily life of the Green Line (the international border before the Six Days' War in June 1967), there are all kinds of natural, frequently used bridges between the country's two kinds of citizens. Settlers come to work every day in Tel Aviv and Jerusalem. Many hold jobs in Israel and return to their settlements in the evening. Without further knowledge, it is often impossible to tell whether a given person lives in Israel or the territories.

Hence the second difference: the metropolitan French of the colonial period had a special way of referring to those in Algeria and automatically differentiated themselves from them. People did not speak of "the French of Berry" or "of Brittany," but they would say "the French of Algeria." There was clearly a sense that these citizens were elsewhere, in the colony, apart from the daily life of the metropolis. In Israel, with its 250,000 settlers (not counting the 200,000 living in the annexed part of Jerusalem), there is hardly any extended family that does not include one or several of them. Almost every Israeli has a son, sister, mother-in-law, or cousin living in the territories, a friend or colleague who moved there. Many Israelis have a rather low opinion of the settlers and will readily say so: "They're spoiling our lives with their hard-line demands." The setters are perceived as "never being satisfied with what they're given." More vulgarly, "They're a pain in the ass." But they are never "Israelis from somewhere else."

With the logic of repression undertaken by Barak and intensified by Sharon once the intifada got underway, the mind-set of the informal settlers' party, its characteristic arguments, the violence its hard core had perpetrated on the occupied people for years, spread far and wide into the society through a thousand channels. Most of the political and mental mechanisms mentioned by David Grossman were set in place, and Israel became intoxicated with this ethnicist, obscurantist consensus. Ideas that had previously been expressed only in extremist circles or small parties of the far right, and that, while not seen as illegitimate, were nevertheless held by only a tiny minority, quickly became commonplace, reaching into normally moderate domains. The first of these ideas was the mad hope to transfer the Arabs somewhere else.

We may recall that a small transfer party, Moledet, had been formed at the time of the first intifada, sending two representatives to the Knesset. But at that time no institute would have thought to conduct a poll on a subject considered both unrealistic and immoral. In 1991, when Moledet was first invited to take part in the government during the administration of Itzhak Shamir, Benyamin Begin, son of Menahem Begin, the historic leader of the nationalist right, exclaimed, "The transfer party's joining the government is a profound political, moral, and social stain on Israel. Anyone who includes such a party in the coalition is in effect confirming UN resolutions that declare Zionism to be racism."[32] Under Sharon, not only would the transfer party join Likud and the Laborites in a cabinet of national union, but its favorite theme would appear repeatedly when opinion polls asked whether people were in favor of transferring Arabs out of Israel. Yes? No? Don't know?

Expel the Palestinians? Most Israelis no longer realized how scandalous it was merely to pose that question. An astonishing number of them answered "yes." As long as the Arabs were to be "crushed once and for all," in the phrase used by generals and political figures, why not think in terms of the most radical solution? They had in fact already been expelled once before, long ago. An entire national community denied this, frantically expunging the trace from their memory. But in the deepest recesses of collective awareness people knew very well that it had taken place and had brought nothing but advantages. In 2002, 73 percent of those living in poor Jewish towns and neighborhoods, 87 percent of whom were religious, 76 percent recent immigrants from the former Soviet Union, held that the emigration of Israeli Arabs should be encouraged (Hass 2003c).

Two years later, a national poll revealed that 63.7 percent of Israeli Jews favored "encouraging" their Arab fellow citizens to "leave the country,"

48.6 percent considered Ariel Sharon's government "too understanding" when it came to Arabs of Israeli nationality, and 45.3 percent were for denying them the franchise and access to political office. Dafna Kaneti-Nissim, who conducted the poll, explained that it typified a worldwide tendency: when people feel threatened, they develop hostility toward the minorities who live among them.[33] Kaneti-Nissim, a sociologist, admitted that this phenomenon wasn't too enlightened, but, as she saw it, the Israelis were ultimately no different from others. Really? In France, for example, xenophobia seems to be doing quite well. Aggressive manifestations of racism, primarily anti-Semitic and anti-Muslim, have increased significantly. The far-right politician Jean-Marie Le Pen won 17 percent of the votes in 2002. Yet it is hard to imagine that a polling institute would ask the French whether they are in favor of having the government take measures to "encourage" their fellow citizens who are Jewish, black, swarthy, yellow, or members of any other minority, to leave the country. What an uproar that would incite! It is even harder to imagine that 63.7 percent of the respondents would declare themselves in favor of such an idea.

This legitimized fantasy of getting rid of the Arabs, all of them, of living without them once and for all, reveals more than a breakdown of the democratic conscience of Jewish Israeli society. It is the crest of a groundswell that, before the intifada, brought preexisting ethnicist tendencies to unprecedented heights in a process of pied-noirization for a majority of Israelis. We may recall that Albert Memmi (1957) described the characteristics of this mind-set very well in advance. If it is not possible to live without the Arab, when he raises his head it must be lowered for him immediately. And hit—harder and harder if need be—until he once again agrees to be dominated. The Israelis have a well-known expression: "If it doesn't work with force, it'll work with more force."

THE LEXICON OF OCCUPATION

The reaction of the authorities in Israel to the Palestinian uprising in 2000 allowed the settlers' party to regain the upper hand and impose its vision. The great mass of Jewish citizens began to think like the colonizer, as described by Memmi, who seeks to legitimize domination, justifying the powers that be and the system, stubbornly pretending not to see the injustice and misery that are staring him in the face. And, again right on target, Memmi noted the ceaseless effort to absolve oneself, to proclaim one's own virtues and glory at the same time as the colonized are depicted in the darkest terms, devalued and even, should that prove necessary, annihilated.

At first stunned and, with few exceptions, mute, or marginalized and inaudible, the minority who resisted this tendency took awhile to get themselves together. During this time the majority grew accustomed to sanctioning the increasingly cruel measures imposed on the population of the territories, which greatly pleased the ultranationalist settlers pointing the way.

The question was, in such a case, how to maintain one's positive self-image? As Amira Hass (2003d) has written, an entire lexicon of occupation had been established to mitigate the true scope of the acts being committed by the army and make them easier to accept. This lexicon was created almost exclusively by the general staff and taken up by politicians and the media. Among other examples, Hass cites the expression "the closure was lifted." The listener or reader concludes that, in the town or village in question, freedom of movement has been restored. In reality, however, the closure on the Palestinians "is never lifted; it is only relaxed a little, sometimes," she writes. When the tanks or checkpoints are moved back 50 meters, the IDF immediately announces that "the closure was lifted." And everyone nods in agreement.

Hass's colleague Gideon Levy has delved even more intensively into this lexicon and the needs to which it responds. "Mythification is nothing new in our language," he says. "In 1948 it was said of an Arab village that it was 'abandoned' by its inhabitants. The people who had been expelled were always said to be 'absent.'"[34] Levy cites numerous examples of the way the meaning of words is twisted to alter the reality of the facts. Thus the military administration governing Palestinian civilians was officially called the "civil administration." He relates how different terms were used to designate one and the same thing, depending on whether one was a Jew or an Arab: "An 11-year-old boy killed by an Israeli soldier is a 'young

Palestinian.' When the victim is a 17-year-old Jewish girl, she's 'a Jewish child.' A Palestinian who dies at the hands of Israelis 'dies of his wounds.' We have no part in it."

"All the intifada did," he continues, "was enrich the terminology of the occupation." When an orchard is deliberately laid waste by its bulldozers, the army speaks of *khisuf*, literally "uncovering," "laying bare," or "revealing." An olive grove was "laid bare" for security reasons. When the IDF proceeds to what international news services call a "targeted liquidation," in Israel the term used is *sikul memukad*, "targeted thwarting." The person is "prevented" from continuing to live.

But, says Levy, "the most striking term in the language of occupation is *kitur*. The base word in Hebrew is *keter*, which means "crown." The nearest English equivalent of *kitur* would be "encirclement." In reality, it refers to the state of siege. But in military parlance the Palestinians are never subjected to a state of siege; they are merely "encircled."

"There does exist a Hebrew word for 'siege,'" Levy notes,

namely *matzor*. But it's never used for the Palestinians. Why not? Only the Israelis ever underwent a state of siege. In Jerusalem in 1948, for example. Like the word "massacre," immediately used when eleven IDF soldiers were slain by Palestinians at a checkpoint, but considered scandalous when our army kills seventeen people living in a house in one fell swoop. Only the Jews can be said to experience a state of siege; when the Arabs are besieged they're merely "encircled."

Why all these "apparently neutral terms," asks Gideon Levy, "that say things without saying them?" His explanation: "To conceal reality, sustain ambiguity." To convey what the situation is while enabling those who hear or read these words to preserve their sense of themselves, to prefer not to know exactly what is being hidden, and, for some, to remain truly ignorant. Yet "laying bare," "thwarting," and "encircling" are less brutal than "devastation," "assassination," and "state of siege." Such words permit tacit acquiescence in the worst: if that's all it is, it's not so serious. In France, the same mechanism led to the use of terms like "the events" and "the operations of maintaining order" during the war in Algeria, so as to avoid "war" and to hush up the raids, the torture, and the rest of what was being done.

Taken up wholesale by the political class in a feedback loop with the public media, the "uncoverings" and other "encirclings" are symptomatic of the way in which a society has completely withdrawn into its own axioms: "our rights," "the Arabs are monsters who have never wanted peace and never will,"[35] along with the cult of force. At the same time people are getting used to what is being done to the other, constantly hovering between concealment and support for the worst.

This "worst" has gradually set discussion within Israel on an unprecedented course. In 2002, anyone who compared the situation in the territories to South African apartheid, or the intifada to the Algerian War, would have been considered crazy; what was happening between Israelis and Palestinians had nothing to do with that. But little by little these parallels began to enter the debate spontaneously—and on both sides, not only by the opponents of the settlement policy. It was not long before the press interviewed Frederik De Klerk, the former South African president who had negotiated with the African National Congress. De Klerk immediately drew the parallel between the Israeli dilemma and apartheid.[36] And, after he retired from power, Barak spoke of the risk of ending up like Bosnia if the occupation of the Palestinian territories continued, likening the situation in Israel to Serbia under Milosevic in the 1990s.[37]

But it is the analogy to the war in Algeria that has emerged most strikingly. It had always been used by a small minority. Among the settlers of Gush Katif, in Gaza, for example, French speakers could be heard using florid and unambiguous language: "The Arabs fucked us over in Algeria. This time we'll fuck them over; we won't let ourselves be expelled." These settlers, who had come from France, were under the age of 50. They had not been born in Algeria or had left that country at a very early age. Theirs was the mind-set of getting even, avenging what had been done to their parents, who had been forced to leave when Algeria declared independence. For years only a tiny minority made this kind of comparison. But it soon began to slip into conversations and newspaper articles.

At first it appeared by way of negation. When I interviewed Dan Meridor in January 2002, the moderate right-wing minister in charge of special services at that time said, without my having made the slightest allusion, "Listen, this isn't Algeria here!" I then asked him why he had thought of Algeria in particular. "To tell you that it's completely different here," he insisted. Yes, but why Algeria? Why not say that the situation was completely different from Vietnam or other conflicts? "Well," he admitted, "because in some ways the Algerian War does come to mind."[38]

With the universal support in Israel for the neo-conservative view of the war on terrorism after September 11, this tendency to make the comparison to the Algerian War became widespread. In July 2002 I was in the cafeteria of Tel Aviv University and started a conversation with three students who seemed relatively unaffected by politics. The conversation quickly turned sour. I was French, a native of a country deemed hostile, and their enmity toward me mounted fast. "Anyway, you French bear the original responsibility for what's happening to us!" one of them lashed out. I asked him what he meant. "Well," he replied, "you were the first to capitulate to the terrorists. Because of you the Arabs in Algeria began to think that terrorism could pay off. And they were right, since you let go of Algeria."

The reference was fully accepted. Pied-noirization had become part and parcel of the Israeli mentality, and the country had passed smoothly into a process of "Algerianization," the very process that, as Pierre Vidal-Naquet wrote immediately after the Six Days' War, constituted the gravest danger for its future.[39] And a process that would lead a majority of Israelis to think that "conquering terrorism" would be enough to do away with a nation's aspiration to independence. In an almost mechanical way, such an end would justify all means.

Not everyone in Israel, of course, shared this student's rather hasty summary (any more than all *pieds-noirs* were blind supporters of the use of force). Yet, whether the comparison is accepted straight out, which is increasingly the case, or whether, in contrast, its terrible risks for the future of Israel are denounced, the analogy between the repression of the intifada and the French war against the *fellaghas*, like the analogy to apartheid, are made very often nowadays. Former Israeli ambassador Avi Primor has castigated "Sharon's South African strategy" in the Israeli press.[40] And

David Grossman himself manifested all the ambivalence these compari-sons evoke for him; they are complicated, he told me in an interview, "and not always applicable. I refuse any and all discussion of my country's right to exist that terms like *colonialism* or *apartheid* can imply." Then, in the same breath, he mentioned the fact that, in Israel, "society is growing accustomed to apartheid and racism,"[41] using the term he had judged inapplicable a moment before.

Consciously or unconsciously, the "colonial question" has entered the heart of the conflict. Once the first shock of the intifada had passed, not a week has gone by in Israel without an academician in a newspaper column, a journalist in an analysis, or a politician in a statement referring explicitly in one way or another to racial segregation or the war in Algeria.

TWELVE

"TERRORISM: TELL ARAFAT TO STOP THIS NONSENSE"
The Failure of the Palestinian Authority

EITHER ARMED STRUGGLE OR SECRET DIPLOMACY

In its war for independence, Algeria saw the triumph of armed struggle and its corollary, indiscriminate terrorism. Forty years later, the model would be replicated in Palestine. This time, however, the result was failure and chaos. Why?

Saleh Abdel Jawad, now 73 years old, is the former mayor of the village of El Bireh, near Ramallah. He was an advocate of recognition for Israel well before the PLO accepted that approach, and, an activist from day one, promoted nonviolent resistance to the occupation. After the Oslo Accords, he became a minister of agriculture in the Palestinian Authority, from which he resigned after a harsh critique of its incompetence. At the end of two years of intifada, he summed up his experience. During the first twenty years of Israeli occupation, he wrote,

> we organized nonviolent demonstrations and strikes, boycotted Israeli goods and banks. Israel reacted by dismantling elected municipal councils, undermining our judiciary apparatus, and exiling many mayors and representatives of groups advocating pacifism. Right from the beginning of the occupation a workers' movement was formed

under the aegis of elected municipal councils. This was a dynamic movement, creating jobs, building schools, founding youth clubs and libraries. Seven years later, the creation of the Palestinian National Front brought a central leadership into being. Its aim was to offer collective opposition to the Israeli occupation by nonviolent means. What good came of nonviolence? In the following ten years the authority of the Israeli occupation dissolved municipal councils, exiling the elected leaders and attempting to assassinate the others. On December 10, 1973, eight of the most moderate figures in the occupied territories were expelled; no charges were brought, and they were denied legal representation. Other expulsions and arrests followed. The local authorities found themselves subject to control. The effect of these acts was to weaken nonviolent resistance considerably. Then came months of closures of towns and villages, humiliations, ceaseless harassment, demolition of hundreds of dwellings, uprooting of vineyards and olive groves, filling in of wells, construction of tens of thousands of dwellings in the settlements, and confiscation of land.

Moving on to the current phase of the conflict, Abdel Jawad continued:

Above all, Ariel Sharon doesn't want a nonviolent resistant movement like Ghandi's, which won the sympathy of the international community. Israel wants the world to sympathize with it when it sends its army to destroy our houses. To weaken the Palestinians' nonviolent resistance, Israel has systematically dismantled and discredited the moderate political forces in the occupied territories. The argument that, if the Palestinians had acted differently, if we had mobilized in an effective pacifist manner, we would have a state today, is currently making its way into the Western media. But history will show that in the face of the occupation the Palestinians reacted by deploying a well organized nonviolent resistance movement that was crushed on all occasions.

Those who are asking us to organize peacefully are very lucky not to have experienced the problems that the people living on the West Bank and in Gaza come up against. Fortunately for them, these advocates of pacifism have never had to explain to their sons and daughters that family honor remains intact even after nearly forty years of oppression and humiliation. The second intifada arose from the quagmire of the occupation and its destructiveness. Israel's total contempt for and violation of all international rules, under a government of prolonged occupation, have brought about the collapse of the nonviolent resistance movement. It is becoming harder and harder to persuade young people that the outside world is aware of the pacifist strategy that will end in a just peace.[1]

During the "quiet occupation" of 1967–1987, Israel did indeed spare no effort in crushing any national pacifist organization of the occupied people. In order to thwart it, the Israeli government, hoping to contain the influence of the nationalists, favored Islamic religious leaders and sought in vain for docile public figures. After the Oslo Accords of 1993, security was placed above all else. Instead of an improvement in the conditions of daily life there followed an increasingly oppressive closure that, as the Palestinians saw it, undermined their leaders' negotiating strategy. Finally, the level of violence undertaken to repress their second uprising in 2000 quickly led even the best-intentioned Palestinians, especially among the young, to refuse "to stand there" without reacting and be shot down like ducks, as Israel Hasson, former deputy chief of Shin Bet, put it (Enderlin 2002, pp. 55–56). Since that time, anyone spending two days in a Palestinian town can't fail to note these young people's sense of impotence, the source of a boundless rage that makes them into recruits for indiscriminate terrorism.

But Saleh Abdel Jawad was too well-informed to rest content with this single explanation of the turn taken by the intifada. His paper was for external use, aimed at making Westerners understand the reality of daily life for the Palestinians and Israel's interest in having the conflict become one of weapons. Yes, the denial of the oppression imposed on the Palestinians is intolerable, but he also knows that Israel's policy is not the sole reason why the intifada became an armed struggle; still less is it the sole cause of suicidal terrorism. Abdel Jawad was a signatory to the Petition of Twenty drawn up in November 1999 by twenty prominent figures in the

occupied territories, a document critical of the corruption and antidemo-
cratic practices of the Palestinian Authority. It earned the old man a beating by Yasser Arafat's services, and he knows that all forms of violence are
not equivalent. He also knows that the illegitimacy and illegality of the
modes of Israeli repression can't justify all forms of counterviolence. Above
all, and he has said this from the outset, he knows that indiscriminate
terrorism directed against civilians can only lead the intifada to political
defeat, strengthen the Islamists, and bring about chaos.

He was not the only one to foresee this development. According to the
Palestinian professor Nazmi El-Jubeh,

> the first intifada had a huge influence on both societies, which began
> to think about the other differently. Accompanied by a larger politi-
> cal and social role for the Islamists, it was a movement of popular
> protest. Israel's recognition of the PLO instantly marginalized the
> Islamists once again. The failure of the peace negotiations and the
> outbreak of the second intifada had the opposite effect. Everyone
> stopped thinking. Most of the Israelis with whom I used to talk be-
> fore that time impulsively cast blame on the Palestinians.
>
> There was a similar drawing back on our side. The notion that
> Oslo had been merely a decoy, one that benefited the Israelis alone,
> became entrenched. If negotiation had led to an impasse, what else
> could be done? I was quick to tell Yasser Abed Rabbo [at the time
> minister of infrastructures and head of the splinter group to which
> El-Jubeh belonged], "We have to engage in a popular revolt, not in
> guerrilla warfare. Tell Arafat to stop this nonsense." The Israelis, of
> course, shooting right and left at our demonstrators, didn't leave us
> much choice. But the young leaders of Fatah were convinced that
> turning to armed struggle would lead us to independence, as the
> former intifada had led to the recognition of the PLO. And Arafat
> let it develop.[2]

The alternatives were secret diplomacy or armed struggle, which
amounted to terrorist action. Yasser Arafat seemed to know no other way,
just as he knew no form of government other than the autocracy and cor-

ruption he had established in his embryo state during the years of the Oslo process. This binary opposition, with its lack of balance, is deeply rooted in the old concepts of the PLO.

Created in 1964 under the aegis of the Arab League, and originally subordinate to the divergent interests of the nations forming that group, the PLO was heavily influenced by the defeat of 1948. When Yasser Arafat took over after the Arab debacle of 1967, he made it a front for several organizations. Its pillars were his own party, Fatah, which would always be in the majority, and the Palestinian movements stemming from Qaumiun el-Arab, the Arab Nationalist Movement (ANM), founded in 1951, one of whose leaders was George Habash, a Christian Palestinian doctor expelled to Lebanon in 1948. Alongside them a series of other organizations became active, most of which had ties to one or the other Arab regime.

It is no accident that the decade 1950–1960 was the gestational period of this nationalist revival. This was the high point of pan-Arabism in power and of the great anticolonialist struggles, most of which, in the context of the time, leaned toward Moscow or Peking, and were seen as the progressive camp. In addition, there was the feeling that the expulsion of 1948 had been possible only because the Palestinians were both politically defeated and militarily disarmed, and because the Arab monarchies had betrayed them. Under these circumstances the victory of the Algerian NLF by armed struggle came to serve as a fundamental reference point. As early as 1964 Fatah's journal, *Filistinuna* (*Our Palestine*), summed up its basic principles: "armed struggle is the sole path to winning Palestine back, and the movement has to be independent of control by the Arab countries" (Baron 2003, pp. 94–95).[3] When the first commando succeeded in carrying out an attack in Israel, Arafat broadcast his "military communiqué number 1."

All of Fatah's activity, not very extensive at the beginning, would now be geared toward armed struggle. For the Popular Front for the Liberation of Palestine (PFLP), this outgrowth of the ANM announced that "armed resistance is the only choice" (Baron 2003, p. 116). Like the Democratic Front (DFLP) that split off in 1968–1969, the PFLP adopted Marxism-Leninism. Their reference points were North Vietnam and Cuba, which were able to "fight imperialism" (p. 118), and they advocated popular war to bring about "a radical change in the Arab world" (p. 119). Fatah activists went to Boumediene's Algeria for training, those of the PFLP to Communist China. Moscow soon became the city Arafat visited most often outside the Middle East.

According to Abu Ayad, one of Arafat's first companions, the thinking in Fatah was that "the armed resistance of the Palestinian people would inevitably lead to a popular fight for liberation in the Arab world as a whole" (p. 99). Here we have the two historical principles of the PLO, armed struggle on the one hand, insertion in the Arab world on the other. But there was a subtle difference, for up to that time pan-Arab ideology had advocated unity first, the liberation of Palestine second. The PLO reversed the order: the liberation of Palestine was to become the road to Arab unity.

Although it reveals the PLO's wish for autonomy, this inversion does not alter the general stance regarding revolution in the Arab world. The nationalist regimes of the brother nations that had emerged from decolonization in Egypt, Syria, Iraq, Algeria, Libya, and elsewhere remained the reference points. And, despite their total failure, they remain so to this day.

In reality, apart from the ideological training of cadres and the strengthening of the PLO's presence among the refugees in Arab countries, the so-called Palestinian revolution consisted of inducing activists to commit attacks, terrorist acts aimed almost exclusively at civilians, the underlying assumption being that all Israelis represent the vanguard of imperialism. Before 1967 the number of such attacks was insignificant. Fatah's forces were still greatly reduced, and the borders of Israel were much less permeable than the Morice Line in Algeria. By bringing more than one million Palestinians under Israeli control, the war of June 1967 thereby propelled the PLO onto the political stage. From then on the central role of Palestine in Arab nationalism was taken for granted. Membership in Palestinian organizations grew rapidly. Finally, in 1974, when King Hussein became convinced that Israel had no intention of giving back the West Bank, which had belonged to his country from 1949 to 1967, and that a Palestinian state was an inevitability, Jordan became the last of the Arab states to recognize the PLO as the sole representative of the Palestinian people.

In contrast, the armed struggle pursued by the PLO was completely without results. In 1969–1970 Palestinian guerrillas made a huge effort to cross the Jordan River, only to be killed or quickly captured by the Israeli

Army. Fearing a destabilization of his state, where the Palestinian population exceeded 60 percent, King Hussein of Jordan put an end to the presence of the Palestinian militias on his soil during the Black September massacres of 1970.[4] The Palestinian organizations then emigrated to Lebanon, from which they once again tried to infiltrate terrorists into Israel without any greater success. A number of attacks were committed in hotels, schools, and public places, sometimes with the taking of hostages. The perpetrators generally sought the freeing of prisoners. They were systematically mown down, even at the cost of Israeli lives. The Jewish population was in agreement: these attacks just went to prove the demonic nature of the Palestinians.

There was no longer any armed struggle in the occupied territories. In Gaza a small surge of resistance to the occupying troops was harshly repressed in 1968–1971. After that, nothing. The PLO was a front preaching combat, but it had no popular base in the places where it intended to act.[5] Did it attempt to have such a base? Yes and no. Yes, because it cruelly lacked an occupied civilian population into which its *fedayeen* could melt. The people it tried to slip in were, with few exceptions, children of the 1948 exiles, who knew almost no one among the "internal Palestinians." They had no natural place in either Israel or the occupied territories comparable to the situation of those fighting on the liberation fronts in Algeria or Vietnam.

At the same time, the support of the internal Palestinians was not the PLO's primary concern, if it was even a concern at all. The Palestinians of Palestine were the great forgotten ones for the PLO. On the formal level, a place was reserved in its leadership organs for the "brothers" in the occupied territories, but in fact they played no role in these organs. In any case, people leaving Israel or the occupied territories to join a PLO organization knew they could never return unless they wanted to spend the rest of their lives in prison. The poet Mahmoud Darwish, who joined the PLO in 1969, did not see his native town in the Galilee again until after the Oslo Accords.

But the fundamental reason for the exclusion of the internal Palestinians from the political thinking of the PLO lay elsewhere, for that organization itself is a movement of exile. What structured it were the memory of the expulsion of 1948 and the resentment of the refugees, emotionally even more than politically. The PLO did not seek to build the framework of a future state; all its energy was aimed at expelling the despoiler, abolishing Israel. The lack of any success whatsoever in this direction by means of armed struggle had led it not to a questioning of its own axioms but to acts of indiscriminate terrorism against Israeli—and also Jewish—interests anyplace in the world it could perpetrate them.

And so there followed the attacks and taking of hostages that became its trademark: the murder of the Jewish athletes at the Munich Olympics (1972); the diversion toward Kenya of the Air France Tel Aviv–to–Paris flight (1976); the attack in rue des Rosiers (1982); the murder of an American Jew on a cruise ship, the *Achille Lauro* (1985); and more of the same. The list is long. Armed struggle amounted to nothing more than a confrontation on Lebanese territory, where Israel made constant incursions that left several thousand people dead, and bloody confrontations just about everywhere between Palestinian leaders and the Israeli services hunting them down. The writer Ghassan Kanafani, who headed the PFLP, was killed in Beirut (1972), as were three Fatah leaders (1973) and various PLO representatives in Europe between 1970 and 1980. The PLO headquarters in Tunis was bombed in 1985, and its second in command, Abu Jihad, was killed there in 1988.

In the case of the PLO, the model of armed struggle, including terrorism, as implemented by so many anticolonialist movements, came down to an indiscriminate terrorism, essentially outside Palestine, that was powerless either to formulate workable proposals for liberation or to set up bases in areas closely controlled by other Arab governments. After the PLO militias were expelled from Jordan in September 1970, their only truly active base was the one in Lebanon, but their arrogance gradually lost them the natural support of the Muslim populations, especially the Shiites, that they had long enjoyed. In 1982 Israel found allies among Christians of the far right in its attempt to eradicate the PLO. The Shiites of the Amal movement maintained neutrality during this time, which speaks volumes. Damascus, which had already strongly attacked the Palestinians in 1976, put the finishing touches on Arafat's expulsion from Lebanon in 1983. Twenty years after it was begun, armed struggle has proved to be a fiasco.

Politically, on the other hand, the PLO could claim success. The historical erasure of the Palestinians was no longer in effect, and the organization itself was taking on the role of interlocutor. The great Western capitals have authorized it to undertake representations. From 1973 on, Arafat denounced the recourse to terrorism on various occasions. In 1974 the PLO obtained an observer's seat at the United Nations. These successes went hand in hand with a slow political evolution within the organization that led it, in 1988, to recognize U.N. resolutions—and thus, de facto, Israel in the 1967 borders.[6] But they brought about no questioning of its fundamental assumptions about the major principles of its nationalism or its concept of armed struggle.

The PLO changed the fulcrum of its activity and, especially, its aim: the creation of a Palestinian state on the "liberated territories" of the West Bank and Gaza, replacing the ancient goal of establishing a secular, democratic Palestine on all of the territory it claimed. In this sense 1988 represented a fundamental political turning point. Nevertheless the PLO remained a conventional Arab anticolonial movement. It has never undertaken an assessment of the reasons for the failure of terrorism, nor of the nationalist Arab regimes in power and the reasons for their negligence. Not for a moment has the PLO analyzed the role played by the NLF's revolutionary violence in the later political failure of independent Algeria, though it quickly became obvious.

Nor has there been an assessment of Israeli reality. Like the Algerian NLF, whose original errors Mohammed Harbi (2004) has summed up so remarkably, the PLO continues to privilege an ethnicist vision of its relation to the Israelis, in which Israeli society remains characterized by its colonial artificiality. In the PLO, moreover, as Harbi writes of the NLF, an "ideologization of the precolonial past corresponds to a simplistic conception of the consequences of colonialization" (p. 44). On the internal level, this oversimplification, "by making colonization a homogeneous bloc, relegates to the dustbins of history the 'democratic invention'" (p. 44), a Western concept. The cult of the leader, the lack of internal democracy, the tradition of secret activity, the long-established corruption (which goes along with the tradition of prizing secrecy among diplomats and members of the special services, who would come to constitute the two pillars of the PLO): all these features, together with the absence of political stock-taking, would weigh heavily on the creation, in 1994, of the Palestinian Authority on the meager territory granted it by Israel.

THE PALESTINIAN AUTHORITY AT WORK

In 1994, as the head of the Palestinian Authority, Yasser Arafat found himself in a totally new position. From the chief of a liberation front representing exiles, he had become the leader of an embryo state on its own land. As for the PLO, in which only a small minority opposed the Oslo Accords, its internal equilibrium was upset, its center of gravity radically displaced. Whereas its mind-set and its view of the other had earlier been that of the refugees outside Palestine, now it spoke, above all, on behalf of the internal Palestinians. Between the "Tunisians" (the PLO officials who returned from Tunis, where they had retreated in 1982–1983) and the old leaders of the struggle against the occupation, people like Faisal Husseini, Saleh Abdel Jawad, and Hanan Ashrawi, along with the young people who had led the first intifada and those who often spent over ten years in Israeli jails, the shock of this change was sharp.

In the face of the occupation, which they dreamed would come to an end, the internal Palestinians had a different perspective in two crucial regards—the relation to Israel and to democracy. Whereas for the exiled Palestinians the revocation of the consequences of 1948 headed their list of aspirations, for those of Gaza, Ramallah, or Nablus what chiefly mattered was the abolition of the consequences of 1967, that is, getting the Israeli army to withdraw. But their day-to-day relation to the Israelis was not a figment of the imagination. Of all the Palestinians, when their first intifada was launched, those from "inside" were most eager to welcome the de facto recognition of Israel by the PLO in 1988 and the prospect of an independent state on the territories in which they were living. In the diaspora, especially in the refugee camps, minds were much less focused on political independence; the primary issue was how they could return and recover their lost land and property.

At the same time, as a result of contact with the enemy many Palestinians in the occupied territories gradually broke free of the abstract, generalizing view of Israel that they had held. The life the Israelis led, their economic and social successes, and the level of their internal discussions were like a permanent mirror reflecting an ongoing contrast to the Palestinians' own weaknesses. I don't wish to underestimate the retrograde tendencies that burden them, the weight of the great families, of clanism and ethnicism. But the point I am making is that, in all the Arab world, aspirations to democracy and access to knowledge are most highly developed among the internal Palestinians, and that these aspirations are not unrelated to contact, broadly speaking, with the occupier. Here we have one of the paradoxes of the occupation, similar to what the Algerian jurist Wassila Tamzali meant when, speaking retrospectively of her own people, she said, "It is *also* French colonization that made us progressive."[7] Contact, including conflictual contact, with Israel had made democrats of some Palestinians. The hope of putting an end to the occupation has given rise to hopes of emancipation from the social constraints of the past.

Ghazi Abu Jayyab learned Hebrew during his sixteen years in Israeli jails. "By the end of that time," related the former PFLP activist,

> I'd read in Hebrew the sixteen volumes of *The IDF and Its Beginnings*. There wasn't much else in the prison. When you look at what the hierarchy of the Hagana was like even before the creation of the state, its capacity for organization, the functioning of Jewish institutions, you can't help being an admirer. But it's mostly reading the Israeli press that made me change. I began to get to know its political class. I found Shulamit Aloni and Yossi Sarid interesting. But what this reading taught me was first of all the importance of democracy, debate, citizens' rights. When I say that to Israelis, they think it's an acknowledgment of their superiority on my part. Not at all; democracy isn't an Israeli value but a universal one. In Israel, it exists—at least for Jews. I want it to exist for us Palestinians, and in the Arab world. Of course we have to defend ourselves. But this doesn't conflict with the need for democracy. On the contrary, it's the only way

to let a political perspective emerge. We Palestinians have a serious
leadership problem. We don't need a *rais*, prophet, or emir but institutions that function properly and democratically. This is the condition of our liberation and our ability to avoid the chaos to which
the Israelis are driving us.[8]

A *rais* (head of state) who is half prophet, half emir. Institutions that
are not proper, democratic, or effective: Abu Jayyab's allusions are transparent. The way Yasser Arafat, like an Oriental despot, imposed his choices,
crushed all vague attempts to democratize his society, relied more on his
multiple security services than on his ministers; the way he systematically
favored secret channels of negotiation over real action by his semblance
of state apparatus and over the need to organize the defense of his people
against Israel's ongoing settlement policy; and the way he let corruption
proliferate, thereby leaving the field open for the *hamullas* (great families), and especially for the Islamists, in order to grow stronger in the face
of the negligence of those close to him — all this quickly became the hall-
mark of his power. The fact that during the entire Oslo period this manner of functioning was also encouraged by the Israeli leaders — before they
discovered, when the time came, how useful it was to denounce Arafat's
despotism — does not alter the despotic and impotent nature of the regime
he established, one that exactly replicates the worst defects of nationalist
Arab regimes, minus the real power and the means to implement change.
It was the result of the way the heads of the PLO historically operated and,
as previously mentioned, the complete absence of stocktaking.

The Palestinian historian Elias Sanbar rightly observes that the functions of what he calls the chieftain connect sociopolitics and geography
in a distinctive way among the Palestinians, namely, at their juncture. But
this special characteristic has its risks. When a leader locates himself at
the juncture of divergent or conflictual forces, and when his power depends first and foremost on maintaining the unstable equilibrium among
these forces, his policies are naturally inclined to preserve that equilibrium. Thus Arafat would promote the worst potentials of this balancing
act: the absence of initiative, the tendency never to make any decision that
might unlink these junctures — in short, inertia more often than not. He

would govern by hedging, instituting a patronage system, and giving the real power to those whose support was guaranteed, faithful accomplices who were dependent on him. As is often the case in Arab regimes, these would be the police services. Very soon after Oslo the way in which Arafat had conducted the negotiations was criticized in the ranks. Apart from the opponents of the accords (Islamists or secular members of the PFLP), the most critical figures among those in favor of the PLO's new line were often those people who knew the Israelis best. Their reservations concerned two issues: accepting the security logic imposed by Israel as the kingpin of the negotiations, and addressing the settlement policy, seen by the Palestinians as running counter to the formation of their future state. Arafat's entourage swept away the objections on these two points. The security logic? It served to strengthen the police organs on which Arafat relied, and he was not about to deprive them of their role. The settlements? The skeptics were told that they were basically unimportant; once a peace accord was signed, the towns and villages abandoned by the Israelis in the course of their withdrawal would be places where the needy could be moved in, beginning with the refugees who would come to live in Palestine. Though he acted shocked whenever Israel established or enlarged a settlement, between 1994 and 2000 Arafat systematically rejected any suggestion that he decline the framework of the negotiations with Israel as long as this enterprise, which was gradually suffocating the Palestinians, continued, and he blocked any mobilization in this direction.

To be sure, the balance of power was highly unfavorable to him in the security area and even more so in the political domain. Israel had much closer relations with Washington, which had played godfather to the peace process. But the crucial point was that the *rais*, a man who time and again had demonstrated his personal physical courage, was mortally afraid of the slightest movement that could destabilize his way of leading and negotiating. So above all he had to keep open the existing channel of negotiations, win the trust of the Israelis, and improve relations with the Clinton administration. Reassuring the Israelis meant giving *real* power to the security services, not to the cabinet or the elected parliament, and in failing to do so Arafat turned his back on democracy.

ARAFAT: *Muteness, Corruption, and Absence of Democracy*

When the Israeli leadership justified the marginalization of Arafat by pointing to the absence of democracy within the Palestinian Authority, his corruption, and the barbarity of terrorist suicide attacks, they were simply using their adversary's vices to deny his legitimacy. These were ad hoc accusations. The PLO was indeed corrupt, and had long been so. But during the Oslo process it was with the most corrupt of the Palestinians that the Israelis had had the closest relations. And this was no surprise, for it was the Israelis who could, at their leisure, block or unblock all the authorizations necessary to conduct business. At the outset, 80 percent of Palestinian corruption was an Israeli matter.

First there was the small-scale corruption on a daily basis. When a Palestinian contractor submitted to the so-called civil government of the IDF a request for authorization to transport workers to Israel, the reply would be long in coming. His counterpart, the Israeli contractor, would then tell him that he, the Israeli, could submit the request in order to expedite matters. But those seeking employment would have to pay a thousand shekels. Fifty-fifty, OK? There have been countless such cases since the occupation began.

And then there was corruption on a large scale. The Israelis have often favored the most corrupt partners, since they have a hold over them. Mohammed Rashid, the PLO financier, is one of the best known. He had been in business with Yossi Ginosar, a big shot in Shin Bet, from the time right after Oslo, though the scandal was revealed only at the end of 2002.[9] As Gilead Sher told me, Rashid was a man with whom one could get along; he had been in favor of signing an accord at Camp David.[10] The basics of the system of corruption in the occupied territories were laid down by Israel in order to gain accomplices. It is said that, just after his return to Palestine, Arafat named as one of his ministers the most corrupt man and the one most hated by the people, Jamal Tarifi, who had become a millionaire by providing Israel with the workforce to build the dwellings and roads reserved for the settlers, extracting his tithe from each Palestinian wage earner who got a job through him after his own palm had been generously greased by Israeli developers. In making this appointment Arafat thought he would win the trust of his interlocutors. Up to the time the intifada broke out, the only denunciations of the corruption came from Amira Hass, who covered the territories for *Haaretz*. But no sooner had the outbreak begun than Israel "discovered" the Palestinian Authority to be full of corrupt men.

The same is true of the accusation regarding the absence of democracy in the Palestinian Authority. During the entire time when there was cooperation on security matters during the peace process, Israel had demanded no reform whatsoever of that organization. On the contrary, the Palestinians who advocated democratic reform were considered a threat, and Israel's constant demands were for the increasing repression of the opponents of the PLO, without too much concern for the methods to be used. It was with the politicians who had the least respect for human rights, men like Mohammed Dahlan and Jibril Rajoub, that the Israeli powers on both the right and the left had the best relationships. Nowadays the absence of democracy among the Palestinians has become a leitmotiv of Israeli *hasbara*.

As for Hamas, after Oslo Itzhak Rabin authorized the return of its leaders, men he himself had previously expelled en masse, including Abdelaziz Rantisi. And, under joint pressure from King Hussein and Washington, Benyamin Netanyahu freed from prison its spiritual leader, the old, paralyzed Sheikh Ahmed Yassin. In the course of the intifada these two Palestinian equivalents of Bin Laden, as they were described, then became the victims of targeted assassinations. Whether the existence of a Palestinian national movement is recognized depends on circumstance. Stemming as they do from the occupier, these accusations seem shabby, a mask of virtue put on for the sole purpose of delegitimizing the other and his national struggle.

It remains the case that corruption, the absence of democracy, the incompetence of the leadership, and, of course, suicidal terrorism are very real flaws of the historical Palestinian nationalist movement. They are largely responsible for its inability to mount more effective resistance to Israeli oppression, avoid the chaos that threatens Palestinian society, and articulate a political vision leading to the satisfaction of its ambitions.

The corruption and absence of democracy that poisoned the Palestinian Authority had deep sources. These affected the way it functioned and its constitutive practice of buying votes and support. This was the cement at all the political and economic junctures. Nothing was permitted to escape the control of Arafat, who allocated subventions in accordance with the balance to be maintained.

At the time of the first intifada, for example, the psychiatrist Eyad El-Sarraj founded a children's health clinic in Gaza. After the Palestinian Authority came to power he was told that his establishment had to be absorbed by the Ministry of Health. El-Sarraj, who wanted to preserve his autonomy, explained that he was receiving private financing from Great Britain and Sweden. At that point he was arrested by the police services and beaten.

The Palestinian Authority under Arafat was not a one-party government. But, as in the Arab countries where similar governments prevail, everything had to be dependent on it. This was a structural given, since the Authority perceived whatever eluded it as a threat to its role as the guarantor of equilibrium. The two most concrete results of this demagoguery were the development of a bureaucracy that was all-powerful but overstaffed and lacking in initiative, and the return in force of the *hamullas*, the great extended families that traditionally held power in Palestine, favoring clan behavior as opposed to the establishment of democratic institutions.

According to Nazmi El-Jubeh, "The more ineffective the ministries proved to be, unable to respond to the most basic needs of the populace, and the more the *mukhtars* (heads of the great families) filled the vacuum of the Palestinian Authority, the more people turned to them to solve problems."[11] Interviewed in 2003, Georges Giacaman, director of Muwatin, the Palestinian Institute for the Study of Democracy, went further in characterizing the situation at that time: "The parliament is useless, laws are issued by the central power, the police are corrupt, the tribunals are not independent, and the courts are unable to enforce judicial decisions." And he continued: "How many accidents have there been in which the vehicle owner didn't have either a driver's license or insurance? In cases like that the police officer acts like a tribal judge, with a different attitude depending on whether the driver is the son of a good family or a nobody. That's how it is in all the branches of government."[12]

After seven years of this regime, together with the paradox by which both the physical presence of Israeli troops in Palestinian territories and the weight of daily restrictions had increased during the "peace process," not to mention the exponential growth of unemployment due to repeated closures, exasperation reached a peak on the eve of Camp David. The Islamists, who were sometimes the only ones to compensate for the deficiencies of the Palestinian Authority, felt a renewed sense of power. There was palpable tension among young people. Various forms of opposition to the Authority arose within the organization itself.

In the 1998 elections for local committees of Fatah, activists often chose to be led by popular figures not approved by Arafat. What united them was the wish to democratize the Authority. They denounced the corruption, wanted a role in the decision-making process, and called for transparency and greater attention to the needs of the people. They would become the non-Islamist leaders of the second intifada two years later, referred to as "terrorist leaders" by Israel.

What did Arafat do? He tried to divide this movement making democratic demands by playing one group against the other. He excluded from the cabinet anyone who expressed sympathy with his opponents and relied more and more on the services of the police and the great clanic families, all to the delight of his Israeli interlocutor (and the Americans). In early 2000, in refugee camps like Deheisheh, major confrontations took place between the populace and the Palestinian police. When, on May 15–18, riots brought the Palestinian street up against the IDF after Jerusalem refused to enforce an agreement freeing political prisoners, activists who for years had been asking for the democratization of institutions were in the forefront of the demonstrators. The more Arafat cut himself off from his own population, and the more ineffective his organization turned out to be, the more intent he became on authoritarianism and preservation of internal equilibrium—that is, on political inertia. He thus grew increasingly dependent on the future success of secret negotiations with Israel and increasingly unable to negotiate, given the risks of internal instability that he wanted above all to avoid.

This is why, when he was pushing for the Camp David summit meeting, Ehud Barak ignored the opinion of his chief of army intelligence, among others, and remained convinced that Arafat would have no choice but to accept his offer. What Barak did not want to see was that Arafat could not agree to Israel's "generous compromise," which he was aware of, without immediately seeming to be a capitulator. But Arafat, too, did not say what compromises he was willing to accept. He did nothing to prepare his people for the inevitable consequences of an accord, maintaining a vagueness around the positions he would defend at the talks so as not to arouse internal clashes.

Afterward, the Palestinian leadership constantly repeated that Arafat had not wanted to go to the tripartite summit, for which, he believed, there had been insufficient preparation. This is accurate. But if he felt trapped, what prevented him from trying to change the rules of play, declaring explicitly to his own people and the Israelis what his nonnegotiable demands were and what could be subject to negotiation? Yes, this would have infuriated the Israelis, and no doubt the Clinton administration as well, which would not have failed to reject the PLO's preliminary conditions. It might have imperiled the negotiation as it had been conducted up to that time. But this is not the main reason Arafat kept silent and agreed to negotiate under the worst conditions. He kept silent because of paralysis, because speaking out clearly would inevitably have led to violent internal debates and threatened his mode of functioning.

Arafat was often accused of double-talk by his adversaries. Like many politicians whose power depends on courting votes, he told each group what it wanted to hear. But his chief characteristic was not double-talk but political paralysis, and a mutism that left only the inability to speak out. All this in order not to offend anyone and to attempt to preserve a factitious national unity of which he was the keystone and proprietor.

This mutism and incapacity would be fully exploited by Israeli leaders as signs that Arafat did not rise to the level of statesmanship—statesmanship, for them, implying acceptance of their "generous" offer—but meanwhile they were very much on display at Camp David. Two participants in the talks, Dennis Ross from the United States Department of State, who was very close to the Israelis (to the point where he later became one of the directors of the Policy Planning Institute for the Jewish people), and Robert Malley from the National Security Council, who was much more critical of the Israeli attitude, spoke in identical terms of their mounting irritation in the face of Arafat's inability to take decisive steps, to present clear alternative proposals to Israel's demands.

The mutism and incapacity remained unchanged when the Israelis opened fire on the Esplanade of the Mosques on September 29, 2000, and when the intifada first began to be repressed. Apart from denunciations of Israeli "brutality," hymns to the glory of the "martyrs" cut down by the bullets and shellfire of the IDF, and hollow appeals for a return to the negotiations, addressed to an interlocutor who had no such intention, at least not under the previous conditions, Arafat and his entourage at no time provided clear leadership for the Palestinian uprising. Nor did they suggest modes of action that would enable the civilian population to mobilize, if only to organize its own protection. With the intifada, the Palestinian Authority, with its inchoate state apparatus, fell apart almost at once. All that remained was a directorate, incapable of political initiatives, around a mute leader.

Had the Authority planned the armed revolt, as Israel's leaders on both the left and the right insisted from day one? As we have seen (in Chapter 9), this argument was untenable, based as it was on supposed reports of military intelligence sent to Barak, reports that the general in charge at the time now says never existed. In reality, the situation was surely more prosaic: both interlocutors were preparing for a possible failure of the negotiations that *might* lead to a flare-up of violence. Barak and Arafat were at an impasse politically, not only because this is where the negotiation process had led, but because, after being welcomed as heroes by their adherents upon their return from Camp David, they were now in an extremely weak position within their respective governments. When the first shots were fired, each man acted in accordance with his objectives and his view of the other and the other's intentions. And, too, in accordance with his profound ignorance of the other.

It is well known how the situation stood on the Israeli side. Ehud Barak and his chief of staff, Shaul Mofaz, surely did not imagine for a moment that, after being hit with the power the Israeli army had demonstrated from the outset, the Palestinian resistance would continue for such a long time. Conversely, Arafat did not imagine for a moment that the repression would assume these proportions so quickly. With his mind locked into the bare alternatives of secret negotiations and armed struggle, he initially thought, just like Barak, that, since confrontation was underway, recourse to arms would enable him to return to the talks from a more favorable political position.

This is why he shilly-shallied, tightening the reins on those who advocated armed struggle as a way to get out of the blockage of the negotiations, just as the Lebanese Hezbollah had succeeded in getting the Israeli army to retreat. This is why the ministries of his Authority, for the most part inefficient and without directives, disintegrated in the face of the repression and were unable to meet the needs of the populace for protection. This was especially true for the ministry of health, which was in charge of hospitals, and the ministry of education, which did not reorganize its infrastructures in the face of the constant closing of schools and universities by Israel. And it is why, once the first terrorist act was committed after five weeks of almost daily Palestinian civilian casualties, Arafat kept going back and forth in his speeches, at some times praising the *shahids* (martyrs), that is, all the people dying in the confrontation, suicide bombers included, to meet the expectations of his people, embittered as they were at experiencing losses without inflicting any on the enemy, at other times denouncing the criminality of the attacks to satisfy international expectations. He never gave a clear reply to the question of what, exactly, was to be gained from armed struggle, and against whom was it directed.

The issue was not whether the Palestinian Authority was unable or unwilling to put an end to the terror, as the Israelis were demanding even as they systematically dismantled its institutions. After all, it was the Authority's dominated people who were being denied independence. To take an example that serves as an exact reflection: as long as Palestine was still colonized by the British, Ben Gurion hedged in his relationship with them on the matter of terrorism, sometimes denouncing misdeeds but consistently refusing to make a frontal attack on his own terrorists of Etzel. Five weeks after the creation of Israel, his forces sunk a gunboat intended for Etzel. In short, while national unity was appropriate in the face of the occupying power, there was no question of going along with its demands. Once independence was gained, it became politically possible for Ben

Gurion to bring his terrorists to heel. From the time of the first attack, Arafat was in the same scenario.

The issue is this: Why, right from the outset, did Arafat keep silent? Why did he give the impression that he was letting the course of events carry him along instead of seeking to control it? Why did he establish no political context for the insurrection, call for no kind of popular mobilization, apart from his magic formula of a return to the negotiations even when, with the accession of Ariel Sharon to power, the illusory nature of this incantation became obvious? And, if he was going to go back to armed struggle, why was he unable to say, once and for all, "Everything against the army and the settlers who are occupying our land, nothing against the Israelis as such"? Why didn't he understand that terrorism against civilians within Israel would only strengthen national unity as well as the sense of victimization on the part of the vast majority of Israelis? Why did he in fact think the reverse, that the Israelis would grow weary of the Palestinians? And finally, why was he unable to see that Sharon's accession to power had changed the game, since Sharon had a much more coherent plan than his predecessor?

The answer to all these questions lies in the foundational belief of the PLO that Israel was an artificial society with a congenital tendency to crumble, in the failure to assess the impact of terrorism, and in Arafat's own manner of functioning, where, as we have seen, he succumbed to inertia in situations of internal tension.

In the face of this paralysis, at a time when the increasing repression and matrix of control inflicted by the Israelis was dehumanizing the daily life of the Palestinians more and more, arousing the despair and rage of the young people in the face of the older generation's impotence, it was logical that Hamas, taking over the former political concepts of the PLO, gradually imposed its own mode of armed struggle and the unifying political principle underlying it, namely the eventual abolition of Israel. It was this that lent credence to the Israelis' conviction that they were indeed engaged in a fight for existence. "The most serious error of our leadership," said Professor Nazmi El-Jubeh in 2003, "is that it has been unable to speak to Israeli society over its army's machine guns and cannons and try to get them to trust us."[13]

INDISCRIMINATE SUICIDAL TERRORISM

The perpetrators of suicide attacks are the object of a double denial. Their supporters glorify them, denying the inhumanity of their acts, and in turn the vast majority of Israelis demonize the Palestinians as a group, denying the humanity of the attackers.

Why kill by choosing death instead of taking the risk of continuing with their lives? Every soldier, every fighter, knows in advance that he may die in combat. But the logic of the suicide terrorist is very different: he or she *decides* to die. Many political movements of national liberation have made use of terrorism, including indiscriminate terrorism against civilians. The Algerian NLF placed bombs in cafés, movie theaters, and buses. Some of its members heightened the terror by adding acts in which the victims were dehumanized: severing the sexual organs, evisceration. But suicidal terrorism as the principal modality of action is something new. In the Middle East it dates from the 1980s, and among the Palestinians from the 1990s. Why does it seem preferable from the perspective of the cause being promoted? Why blow oneself up with a bomb instead of setting it in the chosen place and moving away before the explosion, saving one's life so as to be able to go on with such acts? What are the meanings and implications of this choice for the perpetrators and for the society that produces or venerates them?

I've asked a number of Palestinians these questions, intellectuals and activists, Islamist or not, young and old, some of them confirmed supporters of terrorism, others "understanding" in regard to it, still others fierce opponents. Almost never have I gotten the same answer twice, nor, to tell the truth, a satisfactory one. Some respondents emphasized the despair of the suicide terrorists, the disgust aroused in them by a life of imposed humiliations. Others, in contrast, insisted on the difference between desperate people who put an end to their days and *istashahids* (voluntary martyrs), a term used by the suicide terrorists to distinguish themselves from the simple *shahids* who fell under the blows of the Israelis. The *istashahids* love life. Imbued with a powerful vital force, I was told, they act under an impulse contrary to the motive of the depressed person who has lost the will to live.

Some respondents gave me prosaic explanations of a logistic nature. Public places are so well protected in Israel that there would be no way to set down an explosive device and leave before it was found. That is why only terrorists wearing explosives on their bodies can hope to succeed. Others replied in the opposite way: logistics were irrelevant. The proof, they said, was that there had been "normal" attacks in Israel long before these acts took a suicidal turn.

Some assured me that only the overall development of the contemporary Arab–Muslim region could explain the trend toward suicidal terrorism through the dissemination of Shiite martyrology among the Sunnis, who were at first unfamiliar with it. The result is that the young Muslims who set out to die, and those who send them, deeply believe that they will join Allah at that very moment. If that were the case, other respondents wondered, why is it that the Islamist leaders don't send their own children to kill themselves? Still others reminded me that some Palestinian Christians have perpetrated suicidal terrorism, and that many such acts have been committed by the Al-Aqsa Brigades and the PFLP, secular organizations. Some Islamists assured me that the cumulative effect of terrorism would eventually cause a rift in Israeli society, which would not tolerate it indefinitely. Others told me they supported this form of armed struggle for the opposite reason: Jewish Israeli society seemed so powerful and cohesive that any hope of seeing it move toward acceptance of the Palestinian fact was futile; suicidal terrorism was intended not to undermine that society but to leave a trace, an indelible mark, on it.

Though these answers are contradictory, they do not necessarily exclude one another. They may be held by the same respondents at different moments, or even concomitantly. Thus Khaled Abu Ghanem (a pseudonym), a student of Hamas, told me this in one and the same breath: "The suicide attacks have no chance of putting an end to the occupation. They can't change anything about the Israelis. But as a potential threat this can be effective. It forces them to take us into account."[14] In other words, suicidal terrorism leads nowhere, but it serves some purpose.

As a form of political action terrorism has been a feature of very different movements since the nineteenth century: nationalism and anticolonialism, anarchism and communism, populism and the far right. Over the past fifty years, from Nelson Mandela to Itzhak Shamir, a long list can be made of former terrorists who became heads of states and governments, either of recognized, democratic states, or dictatorial ones. Quite a few "liberators" were once terrorists, but quite a few terrorists have had nothing of the liberator about them. In the past thirty years, however, suicidal terrorism has developed as a primary form of warfare only in certain specific areas, essentially in the Arab–Muslim region (even though the Tamil Tigers, who are not Muslims, originally promoted it in Sri Lanka). The Al Qaeda attacks in the United States on September 11, 2001, established it as the distinctive manifestation of the new world disorders.

Terrorism of this kind raises a set of questions. Why does it arise in some societies and not others, and what does it say about these societies? Its different political manifestations aside, is it essentially the same phenomenon in all cases, or are there very diverse forms of suicide terrorism, as there have been diverse form of terrorism over the past one hundred fifty years? Consider Bin Laden, Hamas as the offshoot of the Muslim Brotherhood, the Wahhabi Shamil Bassaev and his Chechen *boivikis*, the Shiite Lebanese Hezbollah, the Algerian Salafists, and the armed Iraqi groups: Are the shared support for jihad and the common mode of action more important than the differences among them, or are there fundamentally different stakes involved despite the apparent similarities? Even if Islamist Palestinian or Chechen terrorists are pursuing essentially nationalist aims initially separate from Al Qaeda's war of civilizations, what political, and possibly logistic, links do the use of identically barbaric modes of action establish between such groups in the new era begun on September 11, 2001? For those who have had recourse to a cult of death in the name of nationalism—the death of civilians, soldiers, men, women, old people, and babies as a wholly undifferentiated enemy, and their own death as well—what social and political regressions have emerged?

First of all, who are these new terrorists in Palestine? Ninety-five percent of them are between 15 and 25 years old. "The people who engage in suicide operations come from all backgrounds," says Professor Nazmi El-Jubeh, one of the Palestinian negotiators of the Geneva Accords:

Age, not social position, is the critical factor. Someone around the age of 20 has incredible energy, a boundless capacity for sacrifice. They have no wish to reject death, no fear, or, if they do, these are a function of individual needs and have nothing to do with responsibilities. The idea of a career, of building a life for oneself, is also absent or easily marginalized. It's no accident that all the armies in the world have imposed conscription at around age 18. In a situation in which the Islamists have made the suicide terrorist the archetype of the resister, they find their candidates among the 18-year-olds. The motive for acting out can be religious or simply nationalistic, but the age is always the key factor.[15]

El-Jubeh cites his own experience as an example. Arrested and tortured by the Israelis for his political activities in 1972, when he was 16, he refused to sign a confession and was sent to prison for the first time. "Today," he says, "I can't guarantee what I'd do under torture. I'm married; I have children. But at that age not confessing was a question of self-respect. Nothing would have broken me, not suffering or the fear of death."

Candidates for carrying out suicide attacks are generally Islamists, even if the involvement of non-Islamist currents rules out an absolute causal link between fundamentalism and suicidal terrorism. But among the Palestinians the initiative for this kind of armed struggle was at first exclusively Islamist. It reemerged in the intifada and then, as it were by fission, spread to Palestinian youth in the occupied territories. Why did the young people of the Al-Aqsa Brigade, who came out of Fatah, and those of the PFLP, an organization that formerly had Marxist leanings, all throw themselves into suicidal terrorism? Because once this form of action gained prestige they had to show that they too were ready to sacrifice themselves for the cause. And because religiosity imbues Palestinian society and organizations far beyond the fundamentalists. In the same way as secular Jews give the religious the right to represent essential "Jewish values," religion is a strong binding force in Palestinian nationalism. The secular members of Fatah named their terrorist group after the holy mosque in Jerusalem. And a number of the young people who blew their brains out in an Israeli café or bus were hardly observant up to the eve of their act, yet they presented on television the last will and testament they drew up in the name of Allah the merciful.

In the face of Israeli repression a young person's membership in a secular or Islamist cell very soon became the result not of ideology but of a confluence of circumstances. His boss, or the local hero, or some close friends belonged to one militant group or another; the would-be suicide bomber joined on the basis of this affinity. According to El-Jubeh, actual religious engagement was relegated to the sidelines in the context of "a sanctification of the *shahid* in which Palestinian culture and literature have been steeped for a long time, the term having little to do with gaining paradise."[16]

The Palestinian *shahid* was originally the warrior who fell in battle. His archetype is Abdel Qader Al-Husseini, killed in combat by the Haganah in 1948, or the preacher Ezzedin Al-Qassam, who was killed by the British in 1935 in a pitched battle. The term has gradually been extended to all those who die by Israel bullets and shellfire. The walls of Gaza are filled with paintings of *shahids* almost none of whom set out for suicide; they were killed in the course of Israeli repression. Thus the *shahid* became any victim who died unable to escape his fate. In this context the *istashahid*, or voluntary martyr, gradually became the most blessed of all, because he chose his end. The choice itself is religious only to a highly varying degree.

"They blow themselves up where we go to spend leisure time because their life is a torment, in our commercial centers because, unlike us, they don't even have the hope of being able to buy things. They shed blood in our restaurants to make us lose our appetites."[17] This is the explanation offered to the Israelis by Avraham Burg, former president of the Jewish Agency, in his despair at their indifference toward what he calls the "insane measures" taken against the Palestinians. Eyad El-Sarraj, a psychiatrist in Gaza who has a number of children and adolescents under his care in his health center, knows how strongly these measures influenced the psychology and behavior of his compatriots. During the first intifada he worked with a group of Israeli psychiatrists, psychologists, and social workers. The worst consequence of the conditions to which young Palestinians were subjected, he said in an interview in 2003, "even worse than the thousand difficulties of daily life, is the deterioration of the image of the father. A father who has been rendered impotent, passively accepting the life imposed on him by giving up any possibility of changing the course of things. The idea of dying by killing as many Jews as possible is where the rejection of this weakened image ends up, a compensation, the reestablishment of humiliated honor."[18]

Hussein Tawil, from El Bireh near Ramallah, has been a Communist union leader for a long time. In 2002 his son appeared on television, reading his last will and testament. This was how Tawil and his wife learned that he had just committed a suicide attack. A 21-year-old student, he had not been at all religious. His parents listened to him glorifying Hamas, saying that he was a "living shahid" as he set out for certain death. Nazmi El-Jubeh, a friend of the family, came to present his condolences. "The father," he relates, "was devastated, gnawed by a bottomless guilt. 'I brought up my children in the idea of progress, and I totally failed,' he kept on repeating. All evening I tried to console him, telling him he wasn't guilty. I said that parents aren't responsible for everything, that the external environment counts a lot. But Hussein was desperately trying to understand how his son, with the education he'd received, could have turned into what he regarded as madness."

"One month later," the professor continued,

I had the following experience. I live right opposite a permanent checkpoint. It was raining cats and dogs that day. Four women from Makhsom Watch [Israeli groups that keep watch on the roadblocks] were standing there shivering. Around seven p.m. I invited them in to get warm and have a cup of tea. They were glad to accept. I live on the fourth floor. My son Bashar, 15 years old, came downstairs when he saw me coming up with them. He turned aside and passed by stiffly, without saying hello.

I was in shock: an alarm went off in my head. What an idiot I am! I thought. You've just been consoling your friend whose son committed suicide, and maybe you're not seeing what's going on under your own roof. Bashar had always seen Israelis in my home. I thought he was able to differentiate between those who were oppressing us and those who were helping us. I was wrong. That very evening I got busy with him. He didn't speak a lot, but his look said everything. I read contempt for me in it: an idiot, dreamer, or coward who associates with Israelis while our people are oppressed.[19]

In his youth Nazmi El-Jubeh had spent five years in Israeli prisons. As an important activist in the PFLP he then experienced the Israeli invasion of Lebanon in 1982 and the bombing of Beirut. And now, because from the beginning he had considered terrorism in the intifada to be an error, because he continued to cultivate dialogue with progressive Israelis, because with all his being he rejected collective stigmatizations, he found himself a coward, or at best a dreamer, in the eyes of his son.

"Two months later," he continued,

> a second episode finally convinced me that a potential drama was underway in my home. One day I asked my son why he was spending so much time on the Internet instead of reading. In a word, I suspected him of surfing pornographic sites. That's the age he's at, I thought. "It doesn't matter," he answered. He suddenly stiffened, and I felt a doubt. I insisted that he turn on his computer. I stood there stunned. He had bookmarked dozens of sites explaining how to make a homemade bomb! I was in shock, terrified.

When I met with El-Jubeh in July 2003, he said that things were going better. This professor of Byzantine history is an intellectual, able to reflect on how best to keep his child from tipping over: "My wife and I spent hours talking with Bashar. We were torn between the fear of danger and the understanding that, in order to stop him, we had to give our son some room for freedom and personal development." But how many Palestinian parents, fearful of what the future may hold for their children, face this kind of situation without being aware of it or being able to confront it? How many remain paralyzed between understanding the rage that fills the young people because they have lived through the occupation for so long, and fear of seeing them turn toward suicidal action?

For years a cousin of mine in Jerusalem employed a Palestinian couple from the small town of Beit Jalah. The wife kept house, the husband took care of the garden. One day during the intifada my cousin got home from work earlier than usual and found the couple's three children, 14, 16, and 19 years old, in her house. She asked the mother not to let that happen again. Returning unexpectedly on another occasion, she again found these young people there and understood that the parents were bringing their children on a regular basis. She told the woman that she was ending her employment, and the Palestinian burst into tears. "Ma'am," she said, "my children are waiting till I've finished cleaning. They aren't bothering anyone. I take them in order to keep them close to me. While my husband and I are working, if we leave them alone, we don't know what they might do." By expressing her fear of what her children might become if left to themselves, the housekeeper could not have better convinced my cousin that they could really be dangerous.

It is this humanity that is masked by the Israeli discourse on the barbarity of the suicide terrorists and their environment. The underlying idea is that their actions are rooted in their nature, given the view of the Arab as an animal. Hence the great eagerness to repeat that the so-called despair and humiliation of the Palestinians are neither the cause nor the explanation of their morbid acts. This assertion, heard again and again, aims to reassure the Israelis, and to appease their consciences by negating the reality of this humiliation and despair, pretending that the terrorism is unconnected to the occupation.

To be sure, the conditions of life under the occupation are not *solely* responsible for the advent of the mass phenomenon of suicidal terrorism. But the idea that this phenomenon can be understood by concealing these conditions is an insult to the intelligence and, above all, constitutes a degrading ethnicist view of the opposite side. Hence the other phrases that are repeated by one and all: "The Arabs don't have the same sense of death as we do," or "How could Palestinian mothers glorify their sons' acts in front of the camera?" A given mother may well glorify her child in front of the camera. This is a question of dignity, of respect for the memory of the dead, a way of crying out to the world, "We're here, and, whatever our misfortunes, we aren't going to give up."

How can these Israelis be so deaf as not to hear what Avraham Burg is telling them? How can they believe or persuade themselves that the Palestinian mother is rejoicing at the death of her flesh and blood? How can they not know that, once away from the camera, like any mother she will burst into tears?

In July 2003 *Bamakhaneh*, the weekly magazine of the Israeli army, published the *Dokh Barko* (Barko Report), a long interview with a woman colonel, Anat Barko, who had taken a leave from the army between 1996 and 1998 to write a doctoral dissertation on the suicide terrorists. Passing as a student to hide her true identity, and accompanied by her husband, a highly placed official in Shin Bet, whom she introduced as her translator (though she herself spoke Arabic), she had spoken at length with Sheikh Yassin, the head of Hamas, and some forty imprisoned terrorists who had been captured before they were able to commit their dreadful crimes or who had been accused of leading terrorist cells. Her interview is exceptional in what it reveals about Barko's changing perception of her interlocutors in the course of her work, and what it reveals about the army journalist interviewing her.

When the journalist asks, "Wasn't there a risk for you in forming an emotional bond with these people and coming to forget that they're monstrous?" Colonel Barko replies that, although she "totally neutralized her affects," she was obviously interested in their former life and their environment in an attempt to understand how they had come to the point, mentally, where they "completely dehumanized the Jews, the Israelis, and maybe even all Westerners."

The journalist returns to the attack: "So they really are monsters?"

"They're monsters and human beings at the same time," Barko replies. She was surprised to find that in prison their attitudes are much more worthy than those of nonpolitical prisoners. After she gained their confidence, they "began to speak more humanely about the Jewish victims. We Israelis tend to see them as religious fanatics. They aren't." She describes people who were often educated, accorded the highest importance to moral values in their daily lives, and had no delinquent past. People who became deeply moved when, after speaking of their own children, she mentioned that she had children of the same age.

What conclusions did she draw from her study, asks the journalist. "That it's important to understand them. And that a whole part of what they're expressing can't be understood by a conventional interrogation by the security services. I think we have to find a way to stop this madness. If we value life, we have to find a way to live with the other without erasing him or canceling his right to life. Life, on the most basic level, must be permitted on both sides and for everyone."

Some will see in Colonel Barko's evolving view a new manifestation of Stockholm Syndrome, in which the victim manifests empathy for his executioner. This would be wrong. Those Israelis who see suicide terrorists only as monsters or animals are the same people who claim to "know the Arabs" although they have nothing to do with them. In trying to understand what transforms a human being into a candidate for suicidal terrorism, in bringing out the human being in him, Anat Barko, a colonel in the IDF, came to see that it is Israel's cancellation of his most basic right to life that explains his split personality, his morality on one side, the immorality of his act on the other. She recognized that the terrorist's own dehumanization led him to dehumanize the Jews and the Israelis in his mind. And that if the Israelis wanted to "find a way to live with the other" they had to stop erasing his reality. Before the intifada the three main leaders of the Al-Aqsa Brigades in Jenin were involved with an amateur theater company for young people. From Goldoni to suicidal terrorism: one wonders what process these "monsters" underwent.

In a sense it is reassuring to believe that the Palestinian suicide terrorists commit their acts because they think they are going to receive seventy virgins in paradise. Such a view seems to offer an explanatory key: the hysterical jihadist trend in Islam is sufficient to account for their behavior. But for the Palestinians in the occupied territories this is only rarely the case. Almost none of the people who set out to blow themselves up while killing Israelis were Salafists. From this perspective, and contrary to the views of those who hold the Orientalist view of an insane Islam, the development of the suicide phenomenon is even more serious and disturbing for the future of Palestinian youth.

The Palestinian form of denial is the exact opposite. If the terrorist's act leads so many Israelis to see him as nothing more than a monster, his original humanity leads a number of Palestinians to reject the inhumanity of his act. In an interview with me (conducted in Hebrew, which he knew much better than English after several years in Israeli jails), the militant Islamist Ezzedin Khatib (a pseudonym) was at first ill at ease, and began by saying that, "personally," he was "not in favor of attacks against civilians." He was not the first Palestinian I met who tried to escape responsibility. He added that he "preferred the activists to come back alive" after committing what he called "an attack." Then he set about justifying suicide attacks: "The *shahids* are not committing suicide; they're sacrificing themselves for the people. They aren't choosing death, as you put it. Even our psychologists don't understand this. These are talented people, sometimes with advanced degrees. There is simply no other way to commit an attack. If they got caught with an explosive charge in hand, they might break under torture later on, give up names. This way, if they're caught, they release the detonator."[20] He went on with a series of arguments all designed to downplay the savagery of the act for its Israeli victims, evading its self-destructiveness and its new specificity in Palestinian combat, and promoting the *istashahid* as the model fighter who falls not to advance a cause he knows is hopeless but to sanctify himself in a purifying gesture.

Palestinian denial, too, involves a global characterization of the enemy, who is seen as monolithic and vaguely demonic. Thus the death of Israelis in attacks is justified by the fact that "all of them, men and women, are serving or have served each year in the territories." What about the babies and children, I asked Khatib. "They'll all be soldiers themselves later," was the reply. "If they kill our children with impunity and without risk, protected in their airplanes and tanks, they have to expect to see their own children dying also."

Among Islamists, another typical response is that "Israel will never accept the Palestinians, and we shall never accept the presence of Jews as a state." Suicide attacks, which have been called war crimes by Human Rights Watch,[21] are the crudest manifestation of the conviction held by those Palestinians who, like their opposite numbers, take the unchangeable, long-term view of the conflict, certain that the more stubborn side will triumph at a time they themselves will not live to see. They are the counterpart, the reverse mirror image, of the long-term view deeply held by Sharon and his supporters in Israel.

But there is more to suicidal terrorism. As in Chechnya, where it eventually developed as well, it constitutes a profound regression even when it is part of a wish for national emancipation. Very generally speaking, terrorism is the weapon of the weak against the strong. The Basque ETA in Spain and the IRA in Northern Ireland are good examples of this kind of terrorism. As with the ETA, the movement may degenerate, driven solely by the need for organizational self-preservation, changing from an emancipatory movement under a dictatorship to an overtly reactionary force under a democratic government. By September 23, 2004, according to the nongovernmental Israeli organization B'Tselem, 635 Israeli civilians had been killed by Palestinians, including 110 minors, the vast majority of them in suicide attacks, in contrast with 284 members of various law-enforcement forces killed in attacks in the territories. Emerging as the primary vehicle of Palestinian armed struggle, suicidal terrorism, generally carried out inside Israel, has established itself in Israeli eyes as the substrate of the Palestinian wish to eradicate their presence. Moreover, by establishing itself in Palestinian eyes as the consummate form of resistance, it has in fact played a major role in forming their view that the conflict is immutable, its course not subject to change by anything they can do; hence it ultimately reinforces their passivity vis-à-vis an Israeli power perceived as beyond attack, unshakable by other means.

Finally, as Israel piles blow upon blow, suicidal terrorism has come more and more to be undertaken in a spirit of vendetta. And as blind violence has replaced the political void left by the Palestinian leadership, violence has come more and more to be a mode of social functioning within the society, which has undergone a brutalization — especially in the treatment of women — even more frightening than what it has experienced on account of Israeli occupation (see Chapter 13). "Our problem," says Ghazzi Abu Jayyab, who lives in Gaza, "is that with suicide terrorism our entire society has gotten used to the absence of respect for human life, the dignity of man. We're becoming the caricature of what Israel wants to make of us. It begins with the way the police officer treats passersby and extends into the violence of political and social relations."[22]

The failure of armed struggle, the chaos and desperation that have overwhelmed Palestinian society, and the internal violence that accompanies
them are also the result of the primacy of suicide terrorism over every other
form of resistance and the impunity it enjoys in the society. If this terrorism were to become entrenched as the chief mode of struggle, it could
lead to the worst-case scenario of chaos, of the kind imposed by the Iraqis
resisting American occupation in the Sunni zone, with its attendant
kidnappings, murders, and filmed throat-cutting, of foreigners to begin
with then very soon thereafter of Iraqis, a bloody and suicidal trend.

For Palestinian society has entirely concealed the questions posed by
the modalities of resistance. "Being subject to oppression and dehumanization doesn't favor making an assessment of the past or of present acts,"
says the sociologist Anis Gandil of Gaza.[23] By failing to formulate a political outcome that repudiates suicidal terrorist regression and making ambivalent statements about it in which all the *shahids* are glorified even as
the actions of suicide bombers are rejected, Palestinian political leaders
bear an even greater responsibility. Palestinian society today, walled in,
bled dry, shattered, largely reduced to the quest for daily bread and water,
and also politically adrift, has sunk into partial chaos. As early as January
2003 Amira Hass (2003e), the correspondent for *Haaretz* in the occupied
territories, drew up a balance sheet of responsibilities in an article entitled
"Rites of Death and Killing." "The failure of the official Palestinian leadership is clear," she wrote.

> But as opposed to what's presented in Israel, . . . [it's] disingenuous
> to claim that Yasser Arafat, imprisoned in the Muqata in Ramallah —
> and needing oxygen tanks to air out his room — could, even if he
> wanted to, order the security apparatus that he no longer has, the
> security officers who have been arrested [or] killed, or are at home,
> and the street spies who have been killed or wounded, to make their
> way through the checkpoints and trenches that surround the cities,
> to find potential suicide bombers.
>
> What he and his ministers and the aides around him do lack is
> the moral-ideological presence that could create the social-moral
> pressure and atmosphere against attacks on civilians, pressure that

could work on [organizations and individuals]. Nowadays there's not a single member of the Palestinian leadership who doesn't understand how Palestinian attacks on Israeli civilians sabotage the Palestinian cause. . . . Many are genuinely shocked by the scenes of bloodshed. But none . . . are left who have the charisma and authority that inspires respect—not even Arafat. . . .

This failure is also that of the more sympathetic . . . Fatah leaders on the ground. In the best case, some of them express their opposition to the bombings, but in vague terms qualified with buts. . . . But they don't dare come out in the open [against] the popular view, [namely that] the attacks inside Israel are an appropriate response to the killing and destruction perpetrated by [the Israeli army]. . . .

[These] Palestinian social and civil activists, including academics and others identified with the Palestinian intellectual elite, don't dare go to their publics and start an educational campaign against the rite of death and killing. Many of them say in private conversations that not only must the suicide attacks be condemned on pragmatic grounds, . . . but on moral grounds, the universal grounds of humanity.

Quite a few of them can be heard saying, "We must not deteriorate to the moral level of the Israeli occupiers," but they don't dare to do so openly. . . . Maybe they are afraid of being delegitimized or of physical harm.

The failure of the people who form these three layers of leadership also shows that they failed over the years to work together to form a joint strategy and working plan against the Israeli occupiers. Apparently they don't trust each other and each other's intentions.

There could be no better description of the intrinsic responsibility of Arafat and those around him for the growing power of the Islamists, for whom they have left the field open, and for the chaos, despair, and lack of prospects that now characterize Palestinian society. This society has disintegrated not only because Ariel Sharon, enjoying an impunity and an exceptionally favorable balance of power after September 11, 2001, managed to strike heavily at it, but also because the Palestinian leadership has permitted a regressive and politically impotent terrorism to fill the void it left. An Arab term often heard nowadays in the occupied territories sums up the condition of this society: *sumud*, which means holding on, clinging to what one has, in the absence of any ability to mount real resistance against the occupation, not to mention the absence of any tangible prospect for emancipation. Holding on: this is the despairing and desperate outcome of four years of armed struggle centered on suicidal terrorism.

DEMONIZATION OF THE ISRAELI AND ANTI-SEMITISM

In late October 2000 I met with six members of a youth club in the Wahdat refugee camp in Amman, Jordan, aged between 20 and 35. The second intifada had begun one month earlier, and every day the same images of Palestine appeared on television: assault helicopters and tanks on one side, stones and handguns on the other. What did they think of the situation? "The Jews are monsters," "cowards who fire on children." Did they hate these soldiers? "No, all the Jews without exception." One of them was overcome with emotion: "I can't describe how I feel. Look, if I had a Jew right here, I'd kill him before your eyes." What, exactly, did they know about the Jews? They had never met any.

My translator, who came from the camp, quickly skipped over what one of them had said. Looking uneasy, she told me that his remark was uninteresting. When I insisted, she translated: "He said that, among the Jews, there are people with big beards, called Ashkenazis. And that it's well known that they sleep with their daughters and sisters."[24]

After finishing the report I asked the translator where these wild fantasies came from. From reading *The Protocols of the Elders of Zion*? She had never heard of this scurrilous tract, which has been disseminated in certain Arab countries. I told her it was a famous anti-Semitic forgery written in the tsarist era in Russia, describing the Jews as monsters. "You don't have to look that far," she replied. "These people never read. No, they repeat what they hear every Friday in the mosque." And what about her; what did *she* think? She too had never met a Jew. She said that sleeping with one's daughter or sister seemed shocking, but ultimately she didn't know, "maybe it's true." She is an assistant lecturer in sociology at the University of Amman.

Palestinian leaders don't like people to talk about the widespread anti-Semitism in their society, because they are ashamed of it, and even more so because it is invoked by Israel in order to delegitimize their national movement. They often try to deny or minimize it, as though their people's predicament made anti-Semitism less serious, more comprehensible. Or they argue that this isn't precisely anti-Semitism but a form of popular hatred, despicable to be sure but explicable in view of the ordeals the Palestinians have undergone. Anna Jaber, for example, the scientific secretary of the Center for Middle East Studies and Research in Amman, did not excuse what the young people of Wahdat said. But, she added, "the refugees are dispossessed people who have been dehumanized. The Jew they speak of isn't the European anti-Semitic stereotype. He's the incarnation of the despoiler who drove them out of their land, the occupier. Their hate is like the hate Jews felt for the Germans after the war."[25]

These pseudo-rationalizations are wrong. Palestinian anti-Semitism was part of the Arab context and predates the expulsion. And the racism of the victims, the disinherited, the racism that August Bebel, in the nineteenth century, called the socialism of imbeciles,[26] is neither more excusable nor less dangerous than the racism of a superior group. The failure to take into account this real element in the racism of the oppressed involves all sorts of dangers for the Palestinians themselves. Its denial or minimization always works to the advantage of the most retrograde forces in their midst, nowadays essentially Islamist. If the condition set forth for colonized people before they could gain independence had been to renounce all ethnicism and shed all racism, the colonial empires would still be in fine form. But because, among others, most of the Arab regimes that emerged from decolonization remained entrenched in a narrow ethnicism, these forms of nationalism have failed, and their countries are now in a distressing state of regression, one in which anti-Semitism plays no small part.

The attempt to evade the question is clear in the discussions about Palestinian school textbooks. The debate about whether they are anti-Semitic generally takes misguided, manipulative forms. The books do indeed include passages that are crudely or implicitly anti-Semitic. But the Israeli or pro-Israeli organizations that carry on campaigns on this issue never have a word to say about the deliberate concealments and directly or indirectly racist passages that, now as in the past, are to be found in children's schoolbooks in Israel. And they deliberately merge in a single characterization passages that are straightforwardly anti-Semitic, where the Jews are called greedy, treacherous, lying, or corrupt, with others that are anti-Israeli in their political content. Thus, for example, the fact that Jerusalem, the capital of Israel, is called the capital of Palestine—that is, an ideological and political statement—is presented in some pro-Israeli publications as proof of anti-Semitism.[27] As for Israeli textbooks, they miss no opportunity to repeat that Jerusalem is the eternal and indivisible capital of the Jewish people. Would this have to be seen as a definitive sign of Arabo- or Islamophobia?

Similarly, it is claimed that the absence of Israel on maps of the region and its replacement with the word *Palestine* is clear evidence of anti-Semitism. By this measure one would have to see as racist the absolute omission of Palestine on maps in Israeli schoolbooks and the disappearance of the borders delimiting Israel not only in schoolbooks but on road maps, where the term *Israel* is used for the entire territory presently under that country's control. The undifferentiated accusation of anti-Semitism represents an ideological position in which the enemy is disparaged and one's own faults ignored. In such cases the outright or alleged anti-Semitism in Palestinian textbooks is pointed out solely to delegitimize the other or, more prosaically, to endorse expansionist aims.

Nevertheless, it remains the case that there is indeed anti-Semitism in these schoolbooks, and so the denial of this confirmed fact by those who defend the Palestinian cause often lacks conviction. Such people point to the efforts made by the Palestinian Authority to develop a new historiography for the use of schoolchildren, although they have few resources and are thwarted by the stranglehold Israel has maintained on Palestinian schools since 2000. The Israeli education specialist Ruth Firer acknowledges these efforts: "The new Palestinian textbooks contain many fewer negative stereotypes of the Jews and the Israelis than the Jordanian and Egyptian ones that were previously used," she wrote in a report for UNESCO and UNICEF in 2002.[28] It is true — and the Palestinians center their refutations on this fact — that the textbooks criticized as anti-Semitic were not Palestinian but had been sent over from Jordan and Egypt, two countries with which Israel had signed peace accords without the anti-Semitic nature of their textbooks ever posing an obstacle.

Yet, ultimately, what difference does the origin of these books make? They were certainly distributed in Palestinian schools, and their impact can only have been dire in the extreme. Instead of the usual waving away of criticism on the grounds that the guilt lies with others, isn't the point to confront the reality of the anti-Semitism in these books?

"It's absurd," says the Palestinian academician Georges Giacaman, "to deny the existence of anti-Semitism among us. It begins with the ongoing use of the term 'Jew' instead of 'Israeli.' This is a crucial problem, fueled by the fact that the Israelis tend to proceed in the same manner."[29] He is right. From the beginning up to the present time, the systematic trend of the Zionist movement and the Israeli leadership has been to liken all Palestinian hostility to anti-Semitism — "Arabs are killing Jews!" — and the tendency to present any victim in this light is stronger than ever today. Its aim is to lend credence to the claim that under all circumstances the Israelis, as Jews, are experiencing the same anti-Semitism as at the time of the ghetto. But the reverse tendency among the Palestinians to refer only to "the Jews" is equally well-rooted, as are the multiple forms of anti-Semitism that are on the increase in modern Islam and the Arabic space.

The history of the Jewish people under Islam, though it has known its share of pogroms, is far less tragic than under Christianity. The social inclusion of Jews was largely accepted. But Muslims tend to overvalue this fact, for example by idealizing the "golden age" in Andalusia, while concealing another fact, namely that this social acceptance, or lesser oppression, stemmed from the status of *dhimmis* — protected persons, but with fewer rights — conferred on Jews (and Christians) as monotheists, a status not enjoyed by other non-Muslims. Thus the protection of the Jews depended on their inferior condition. In the global reference to Israelis only as "Jews" we once again find the refusal to see Jewishness as anything other than a religion. From this follows the idea of its necessary submission to Islam.

When I was reporting from the Wahdat refugee camp Izdihar Saleh, an Islamist and revered figure who has dedicated her life to social programs, told me this: "I have nothing against the Jews as a religion. But those in Israel should go back to where they came from, all of them."[30] "I have no problem with the Jews as a religion. In the past we lived together. But the state of Israel is illegitimate," said Ezzedin Khatib, the Islamist from Gaza.[31] Those words—"I have nothing against the Jews as a religion"—recur as a leitmotiv among countless Palestinians, and not just Islamists. It is based on a partial reading of the role of the Jew in the Koran, a sacred text in which, as in the Old and New Testaments, the best exists alongside the worst. Today it is often used to convey the worst. Speaking of the *yahud*, "the Jew," as a generic category to refer to the Israelis serves as a screen for the rejection of the presence, in the midst of the Muslim world, of a different community *with a national character*. And, exactly as when the Israelis use the general category "the Arabs" to negate Palestinian national identity, it is found primarily among those who are in a permanent state of warfare with the other, and, even more often, among those who never have any contact with these demons they speak of.

In the Arab world today it is in fact the Palestinians who manifest the least degree of traditional Muslim anti-Semitism, precisely because their relations with Jews are the most concrete. The Palestinians can be divided into three geographical groups: those who live outside historical Palestine, in refugee camps in Arab countries; those who are occupied on their own territory; and those who are second-class citizens in Israel. The demonization of the Israelis is greater by far in the refugee camps of the neighboring countries than in the two other categories. There is very little chance of hearing the fantasy of the Ashkenaz with a long beard who sleeps with his daughters and sisters among the Palestinians of Palestine. On the contrary, among the latter "there is an extensive internalization of Israel and the Israelis," according to Georges Giacaman.[32] After English, Hebrew is studied more widely than French or Spanish at the University of Bir Zeit. The Society of Muslim Women has taken out advertisements in the West Bank newspapers to promote the learning of Hebrew.

Among the Palestinians of the occupied territories, two generations can be distinguished: those over the age of 30 or 35, and younger people. And there is a difference, as well, between men and women. Men who were 18 or older before 1987, during the so-called peaceful occupation, often worked in Israel or for Israelis. Many of them have learned to speak Hebrew. Others, political activists, spent long years in Israeli prisons, where almost all of them learned that language. For the vast majority of this group, the Israeli is not an abstract being, the embodiment of repression and nothing else. Even when they speak of the harshness of everyday life or express their rage at the constant tiny humiliations and their hate for the occupants, one of them will mention in the same breath "that terrific restaurant owner" in West Jerusalem for whom he washed dishes and who, during the first intifada, circumvented the military blockades to come get him at home and bring him back at night; another will mention the *moshavnik* whose land he worked and who always treated him with respect; a third, a teacher, will nostagically recall the Israeli professor with whom he corresponded.

For women and men from the younger generation the situation is very different. Since most Palestinian women do not work but remain at home, they tend not to know Hebrew. As for the youngsters, the policy of blockades and closures in the occupied territories set in with the first intifada, in 1987, which lasted for seven years. There followed another seven years of the Oslo negotiations, in which, after a very brief pause, this trend was not undone but, on the contrary, systematized and intensified. Since the end of 2000 the closing off has turned into a collective imprisonment. The Palestinians of the occupied territories who were under the age of 15 in 1987 know less Hebrew by far than the preceding generation. All they have seen is mounting unemployment and the inability of fathers to feed their families. Almost all of them have had no contact with Israelis other than soldiers or settlers, the two figures of the occupation. Like their mothers and sisters, most of them have always been confined to the closed circle of the family, the village. It is among this group that one finds people who say, "You don't know the Jews. All they understand is force," with as much conviction as their opposite numbers, who are equally certain that they "know the Arabs, who understand only force," though they have never meet any Arabs. This is the breeding ground of the ethnicist regression in which the Jews are hated generically; it is from this sediment that Islamism — and the anti-Semitism that accompanies it — emerges and proliferates.

"Regression": this is the term used by those Palestinians who can't stand it—when they are not depressed by it. From his splendid home in the fashionable district of Amman, Assad Abdel Rahman, who was then the Palestinian minister in charge of the refugees, said this to me in late October 2000:

> There's a terrible regression among the refugees. Most of them saw the Oslo Accords as a betrayal. Afterward some of them began to believe "We're going to have our state." No one is more dangerous than the radical who has turned moderate and sees that moderation doesn't pay. He then goes back to a worse radicalism. After our humiliation, and even more at Al-Aqsa, a pure madness, all distinction [between Jews and Israelis] disappeared. This return of the repressed horrifies me. I have secular intellectual friends. Since that time they've been saying, "Hezbollah and Hamas were right."[33]

"We don't know anything about Israeli society. We and they don't know one another anymore and don't want to meet. We're in regression." So says Anis Gandil, the sociologist from Gaza.[34] "In the 1980s in Beirut," relates Leila Shahid, the general delegate of Palestine to France, "people like me or Elias Sanbar kept on insisting that the Palestinians should not use the work *yahud* in speaking of the Israelis. And that the Israelis should no longer be seen as a monolithic bloc. Now the Palestinians are regressing to the old formulas."[35]

In this regression, this ethnicist demonization of the opponent, the methodical disintegration imposed on the Palestinians by Israeli policy plays a major role. But the inability of the Palestinian leadership to stem it, or at least to come out clearly against it, must be acknowledged. As is the case for both Israelis and Palestinians, not much can be expected from those who obsessively track manifestations of racism in the enemy without ever mentioning the racism that is rife in their own camp. On both sides those who seek coexistence in dignity feel tainted by the racism of their own people.

THIRTEEN

THE BRUTALIZATION OF ISRAELI SOCIETY AND THE RADICALIZATION OF NATIONALISM

THE NATIONALIST BLOC

The occupation of the Palestinians that began in 1967 would have an influence on what the Israeli legal analyst Moshe Negbi, borrowing a term from the German-American historian George L. Mosse, calls the progressive brutalization of social practices and discourse in Israel. We may recall that Chief of Staff "Bugi" Yaalon told his fellow citizens that they were David and the Palestinians Goliath. In the same interview, he compared the "existential threat" posed by the Palestinians to a cancer that he was treating with chemotherapy, reluctant to adopt the solution "recommended by some, [namely] to amputate organs." Like the "sensitive" Sharon, the general portrayed himself as "a humanist, a liberal, a democrat, someone who is seeking peace and security."[1]

The nationalist bloc in Israel, which is speeding up the brutalization of the entire society, is heterogeneous in nature. It includes tendencies that are radically inconsistent among themselves on other levels. Thus a number of clerics and members of Russian-speaking parties can come together on the same terrain of extreme racism regarding Arabs and Muslims while hating each other stubbornly (the great majority of Russian speakers are secular, and many are not even of Jewish origin). What links the nationalists in Israel—the huge national-religious camp, the "settlers' party," and almost the entire historical right along with a good part of the left, amounting to 70 to 80 percent of Israeli Jews—is the so-called war on terrorism. This is the conviction that what the Jewish state is dealing with is not a national movement, whatever its methods, but an enemy with no identity other than terror.

For this idea to take hold Yasser Arafat had to be put out of play, and the notion that the Palestinian Authority was a terrorist entity had to be gradually instilled. This is why, during the first thirty months of the intifada, Sharon and the leaders of the military reserved almost all their blame for the historical Palestinian nationalists, who were seen as the real threat; then, once the Palestinian Authority had been largely discredited internationally and internally, and chaos had overcome Palestinian society to the advantage of the Islamists, they organized the assassination of the political leaders of Hamas.

The attacks of September 11, 2001, in the United States would be of great help to Ariel Sharon and his governments in this enterprise. From that time on it could be stated that "Arafat is supporting terrorism the way Mullah Omar supported Bin Laden."[2] This is what I was told by Uzi Landau, minister of internal security, who compared the PLO to the Taliban. Like the Americans in Afghanistan, he said, Israel must "destroy the infrastructure of terror," namely the Palestinian Authority, "killing its soldiers, destroying its buildings, strangling it financially." What if that made Palestinian society tip over to the side of the Islamists? "I prefer a Hamas without a mask to a Palestinian Authority that moves forward masked," he replied. "That way things will at least be clear." Terrorism, Landau concluded, "is like organized crime": there is no point in looking for motives of any kind, still less for national order; it is never anything but a lethal will. Uzi Landau, a member of the Likud leadership, is the son of a very important leader of Herut, a party that, during the 1930s and 1940s, sent its activists to place bombs in Arab markets.

"Whoever thinks Arafat is equivalent to Bin Laden does not understand who Arafat is nor who Bin Laden is," replied Ami Ayalon, former head of internal secret services, amid general indifference. "Bin Laden is the guru of a very harmful sect that is bent on chaos and has no need for the international community. But Arafat dreams of being accepted. Since 1993 it has been Arafat who keeps on referring to the international community and demanding the application of the U.N. resolutions, and we Israelis who keep on refusing. If Arafat is killed, the Palestinian people will continue to want their independence."[3]

The reduction of the Palestinian Authority to a mere terrorist entity with no political character is a denial of reality. But reducing Hamas to this concept is equally so, whatever its methods of action and reactionary nature. Hamas is primarily a nationalist movement that inserts the national claim into a religious logic.[4] And so, under the heel of the occupier, it seems to be a resistance organization.

This is not the first time that resistance organizations have been both terrorist and reactionary. Yet what determines the political function of an organization is not its ideology but its position in the relationship of domination. The French resistance during the Second World War was overwhelmingly dominated by the communists, who justified all of Stalin's crimes and, in the East, hastened to copy them once their countries were liberated. As for the Gaullists at that time, they were in favor of maintaining the French colonial empire. The Serbian Chetniks who fought the Nazi occupier were already advocating the Greater Serbia that they would try to impose fifty years later. Yet all of these groups were resisters. From the outset the Algerian National Liberation Front had some profoundly reactionary tendencies. Its crimes against civilians vied in their horror with those of the Palestinian terrorists. Yet it still represented the aspirations of a people to independence.

All these subtleties are brushed aside by the Israeli nationalists. The mental universe that walls them in is a simple binary: it's us against them; we're civilized and virtuous, and they're backward and barbaric. Force, of whatever kind, is the only justifiable response to the total inhumanity of the enemy. This view is not without its consequences for the internal development of Israeli society. And it has produced its antidote, Israelis who reject its dangerous absurdity.

PLURALISM UP, DEMOCRACY DOWN

The evolution of nationalist discourse in terms of its tone and the terms used in public by the country's leaders is indicative that a breaching of mental dikes has taken place in Israel. When four thousand Palestinians held in detention undertook a hunger strike in August 2004 to improve their conditions, the Likud minister Tzakhi Hanegbi declared that, as far as he was concerned, they could starve themselves to death and it would make no difference.[5] Israeli authorities announced that the jailers would barbecue food in the courtyard in order to break the strike. Ghazi Abu Jayyab, who spent sixteen years in Israeli prisons and went on several hunger strikes in 1970–1980, one of which, a very long one, failed, told me how determined the prison authorities were not to give in. Even at that time they were using cooking aromas among other means (including force-feeding, with sometimes fatal consequences) designed to make the prisoners capitulate, knowing that for a hunger striker the smell of food cooking is like a torture.

Neither the wish to break the strike nor the method is new. What is new is that the method is affirmed without shame. Few Palestinians are imprisoned for blatant or premeditated acts of terrorism; the vast majority of them are political activists. But a minister can publicly declare that their starvation would mean nothing. The Palestinians are in effect "nothing."

The tone of this minister's public discourse is part of a general trend. Not only do the Israeli security forces operate with an unprecedented degree of impunity in the occupied territories, but inside Israel wheeling and dealing, political corruption, brutal budget cuts in social programs, and the incidence of spouse abuse and other crimes have never been so striking as they are today. Moshe Negbi, professor of civil law, gives this telling example of the way in which the brutalization of the Palestinians is reflected in Israeli society. Four youths were accused of repeatedly raping a girl of 14. They were subsequently drafted into the military. When they came to trial, the judge sentenced them only to fifty days of community service, justifying his clemency by saying he refused to compromise the future of these "good boys" who were serving in elite units.[6] In his mind the impunity of the uniform held good not just in the occupied territories but within Israel as well.

The shameful treatment of immigrant workers is the most striking example of this social brutalization. During the Oslo process, as the repeated blockades of the Palestinians created a certain disorganization of the rapidly growing Israeli economy, 300,000 immigrants were brought in from Thailand, the Philippines, Romania, and elsewhere (official eyes being deliberately closed to illegal entry) so as to offset the exclusion of Palestinians from the labor market. Severely exploited, often housed and paid in substandard conditions, fired at the whim of their employers, and holding a visa—unique in the annals of immigration—stipulating that legal foreign workers automatically became illegal upon the loss of employment, these immigrants became an issue when Israel entered a recession during the intifada.

Minister of the Interior Avraham Poraz explained at the time that the budget cuts in social programs were not only a necessity but "a very positive change: we are now going to send away the foreign workers living here—200,000 of whom are illegal, 100,000 legal—and put back to work Israelis who were living on welfare."[7] The cages of the Palestinians were opened and closed in accordance with alleged security reasons, so why not import and send back at will a foreign workforce in accordance with economic needs? To set an example, Ariel Sharon announced that he was letting go sixteen Thai workers employed on his ranch.[8] A religious action center, subsidized by public funds, began a campaign to rid Israel of these undesirables. Its chief slogan was the rejection of the *avoda zara*, playing on the double meaning of this Hebrew expression, which literally means "foreign work" and, in biblical usage, "idolatry." Out with these foreign idolators! So as to leave no doubt about the ethnicist basis of this campaign, the center accused the immigrants of threatening the Jewish character of the state "by marrying our women" (Cook 2002).

"It begins with indifference toward what is done to the Palestinians and is followed by indifference toward the corruption of democracy. We have imperceptibly gone from endorsing inadmissible acts of violence in the Palestinian territories to their acceptance in Israeli society," says Moshe Negbi. If Israel believes it is within its rights to ignore international law in the Palestinian territories, the result is a cult of force as a norm of behavior, including individual behavior. "The idea," Negbi continues, "is that the strongest or most cunning person wins out, and that this is how things are."[9] Another result is the disintegration of democratic awareness. One law, considered normal, now denies to a Palestinian from the territories who marries an Arab of Israeli nationality living in Israel, or the converse, the right to live with his or her spouse on Israeli territory. As the nongovernmental organization B'Tselem has written, an Israeli citizen who wants to marry someone living in the territories has to choose between two evils: not getting married or leaving the country.[10]

Judge Michael Ben Yair, former legal adviser to the Rabin government, says that he has been

> dreadfully disappointed by the way the society has developed. Before 1967 it was more closed in but more united, more patriotic but less nationalistic. There is more freedom of speech now, but also more intolerance. A few years ago only the extreme right called Itzhak Rabin a leftist.[11] Nowadays, if you say anything critical about the lot we impose on the Palestinians, you're called a leftist everywhere. The term is now a synonym for "bastard." We've become very aggressive, terribly intolerant. I'm considered a do-gooder, a moron who cares about such uninteresting things as human dignity. Something unhealthy has become deeply ingrained in the generation of sabras born after 1950. A willful ignorance and indifference in the face of cruelty. Frankly, today, I'd agree to let my children go abroad to live.[12]

Younger by fifteen years, the historian Shlomo Sand shares this view of the paradoxical way in which liberalization and intolerance have increased in tandem: "Israel is much more open and pluralistic than thirty or forty years ago, and much less democratic. Intellectually more diverse, socially more intolerant. Anything can be said aloud these days: the most racist arguments on one side, calling us colonialists on the other. But democratic awareness is collapsing, as we see in the legitimization of the idea of transfer, the relationship to the immigrants, and, more generally, in the way in which political life is conceived."[13]

With regard to pluralism, the range of ideas that can lawfully be expressed in Jewish Israeli society has become much broader. It extends from

Rabbi Ginzburg, who compares Arabs to animals, to Professor of Judaism Raz-Krakotzkin, who advocates binationality as the only solution for the future.

With regard to the decline in democratic spirit, the range extends from the general acceptance of discriminatory measures toward "the Arabs" as a general category, including those who are citizens of Israel, to the almost unfailing subordination of justice to the interests of politics, and not only because the Israeli Supreme Court has regularly declared legal blatant infractions of international law concerning human rights. The legal scholar Moshe Negbi has offered an example of the way in which the acceptance of the notion that might makes right has rubbed off on internal Israeli politics. In June 2004 Ariel Sharon expelled from his government two ministers from the far-right party Moledet in order to gain a majority for his plan for a future withdrawal from Gaza. This was an authoritarian measure with no legal foundation.[14] "I had no sympathy for the ousted ministers," Negbi told me. "But the legal adviser to the government should have told Sharon that his measure was illegal. Instead of which he defended his point of view before the Supreme Court, which endorsed it." A country "in which law exists formally but in which, when you're in power, you evade the common laws" will see its democracy fade, in Negbi's opinion. "In Israel," he added, "if you hold public, financial, religious, or military power you have incredible immunity nowadays."[15]

THE UNIVERSITY, THE MEDIA, AND THE "TRAITORS"

Examples of this paradox—an increase in the pluralism of opinions and a decrease in the spirit of democracy—are abundant. Corroborating what the sociologist Uri Ram has called the polarization of mentalities, they are found in intellectual, artistic, and academic spheres, which are now much more open. Never before have there been so many Israeli films and documentaries that harshly condemn the country. Never has academia produced so many critical texts in so many fields of research. Beer Sheva University has become a bastion of challenge to the historiographic and sociological consensus. After nearly fifty years of ignorance, one of the greatest Jewish intellectual figures, Hannah Arendt, who had been called a traitor, posthumously saw her book *Eichmann in Jerusalem*, written in 1963, translated into Hebrew in 2000.[16]

The 2002 study *Tohar Haneshek* (Purity of Arms) by the Laborite historian Dan Yahav lists the acts that, over the decades, have contradicted the Israelis' vision of their armed forces as being the world's most moral. In April 2002 a petition in support of Palestinian universities, entitled "Break the Conspiracy of Silence" and dealing with the ways higher education was being dismantled by the Israeli army in the occupied territories, was signed by 150 professors and researchers, a small minority of whom advocated an international boycott of the Israeli academy.[17]

The Bible Unearthed, the famous work by Israel Finkelstein, director of the Archeolocal Institute of Tel Aviv University, and his colleague, Professor Neil Asher Silberman (2001), is a typical example of the increasing liberalization of the intellectual domain in Israel. The book puts in question a long series of foundational claims in the Bible, the location of a number of places mentioned there, and the dating of the text. Above all, it categorically contests the reality of a temple in Jerusalem in the time of Solomon.[18] It could not have been published fifteen years earlier, says the historian Shlomo Sand, because it undermines the mythology serving as the basis for the "right of return" of the Jewish people to the land.[19]

Yet a number of researchers do not conceal their discontent. "Limor Livnat, the minister of education, and Benyamin Netanyahu have said that the role of the university is to educate the people in the right way," worries the astrophysicist Elia Leibowitz (who is much more measured in his opinions than his famous father, the philosopher Yeshaayahu Leibowitz). "I'm not claiming that the Israeli academy is a paradise, but its independence, which was taken for granted up to now, is being threatened."[20] In certain areas it had already been threatened by its own workings. Thus at Tel Aviv University there were no Arab instructors in the department of Near-Eastern Studies. Similarly, it is possible to specialize in Jewish history up to the doctoral level without ever studying general history, in accordance with the deeply entrenched view summed up by Itzhak Baer, one of the first instructors in Jewish history at Hebrew University: "There exists a force that raises the Jewish people above all the contingencies of causal history" (cited in Sand 2004).

The threat to which Elia Leibowitz is referring is more prosaic. In Israeli universities faculty members who do not adhere to accepted views often feel ostracized and subject to an inconspicuous but palpable surveillance on the part of nervous academic authorities. Their works are generally published abroad, not in Israel. Some, like Baruch Kimmerling (2003), draw conclusions that are plainly extreme. Kimmerling calls himself a patriot, someone who cares about the future of Israel, but, frightened by the trend sweeping the country, he says Israel is becoming fascistic. The fact remains that in the humanities and social sciences, a number of scholars who work outside the consensus feel a sense of suffocation. In the spring of 2002, at Beer Sheva, forty-three professors demanded the cancellation of a lecture that was to be held at the university by Yossi Beilin, the architect of Oslo. At the same time the minister of education, Limor Livnat, asked that charges be brought against two hundred academics who publicly supported soldiers refusing to serve in the Palestinian territories.

The misadventure befalling the historian Ilan Pappe says a great deal about this oppressive atmosphere. Professor of contemporary history at Haifa, Pappe, an Arabist, was one of the first to reveal in detail the ways official historiography had concealed the facts of what happened in 1948. On May 12, 2002, he was called before a disciplinary committee. Aryeh Ratner, dean of the humanities faculty, asked that he be expelled on the grounds that he had defamed the university in the Teddy Katz Affair (see Chapter 1). Already marginalized (his university had canceled his participation in three colloquia on his field of research), Pappe claimed that the real motive behind this attempted expulsion was to prevent him from giving, for the first time in the history of the Israeli university system, a course he had planned specifically on the Naqba, the Palestinian catastrophe. The controversy led to stirrings in Anglo-American academic circles, and the university chose not to pursue it. Pappe is still teaching there, but the episode revealed some of the strains in the atmosphere prevailing in the academy. Pappe received many letters from colleagues expressing their sympathy. When he wanted to make them public, nearly all of these colleagues refused.

When faculty members are hesitant to express their opinions publicly for fear of the consequences, it is no wonder that the intelligentsia is mobilized by the powers that be for ends that would horrify any democracy worthy of the name. In September 2002 the minister of labor and social affairs, Shlomo Benizri of the Orthodox Sephardic party Shas, convoked the first Israeli Council on Demography. Its thirty-seven members were selected from the cream of jurists, doctors, and scientists as well as from the heads of associations. The council had as its formal objective to increase the birthrate. Its real aim, presented unequivocally, was to encourage the birthrate among Jewish women and decrease that of Arab women.

As Gideon Levy wrote at the time, to define the Arab citizens of Israel

> as a "demographic problem" arouses painful memories and sends a highly aggressive message. What are they supposed to feel when their own government forms a committee whose avowed aim is to reduce their part of the population, as if they were a cancer whose propagation must be stopped? The Arabs of Israel would be neither a "problem" nor a "demographic demon" if the attitude toward them were fair and egalitarian.[21]

Levy was among the very few who were distressed. And among the most eminent representatives of Israeli science at this council were leaders willing to reflect on what they considered a national mission, pondering the most effective means to reduce the proportion of one category of citizens in relation to another on the basis of ethnic criteria.

The discussion of the so-called demographic risk posed by the Arab minority is as old as Israel. Ben Gurion had made the stemming of the Arab birthrate a matter of concern, but he kept quiet about it. The big difference today is not the project but its undisguised affirmation. The magnitude, bordering on hysteria, of the discussion of demographics in Israel is the most obvious sign of the decline of the spirit of democracy.

The results can sometimes be tragicomic. In 2003 Israeli universities stopped applying the affirmative-action measures they had begun to implement. This "positive discrimination" was intended to promote access to higher education for students from disadvantaged cities and districts. It turned out that the young Palestinians of Israel, generally the most disadvantaged, did better in competitive examinations, perhaps also because they were most determined to escape their situation. This was not what the game was about. Given that the number of available places in the universities had not increased, the universities explained, the admission of another population could occur at the expense of the original group.

As the journalist Aviad Kleinberg commented ironically, "One will appreciate the euphemism 'other population' used of the Israeli Arabs."[22] Even though they are citizens of the country, the "others," the Arabs, must not take places reserved for "us." "Don't we have the right to prevent any overrepresentation in the faculties of medicine?" replied the university officials, after noting the growing number of Arab students in this subject, although their proportion remained far below that of Arabs in the Israeli population. Kleinberg cuttingly recalled that between 1920 and 1930, when medical studies were especially prized by young Jews in Poland, the nationalists set about advocating a *numerus clausus*, a quota for this minority in order to avoid its "overrepresentation."

From hostility toward citizens who do not belong to the majority ethnicity it is but a short step to bringing pressure to bear on those who belong to it but do not share its ethnicism. Journalists, intellectuals, and artists, who have greater media exposure, are the first in the line of sight. The singer Yaffa Yarkoni, a national treasure and winner of the country's highest distinction, the Israel Prize, learned this to her cost. Called "the singer of all the wars," she did more than anyone to uphold the morale of the troops at the front in 1948, 1956, 1967, and 1973, up to the war in Lebanon in 1982. Thousands of photos have shown her at the side of the most celebrated generals, from Moshe Dayan to Ariel Sharon. Fifty-five years on the stage, a thousand songs recorded, some of which are taught in schools. Questioned by Galei Tsahal, the army radio station, on April 14, 2002, Yaffa

validated those who refuse to serve in the Palestinian territories. "I personally would give back all the territories," she said. She added that, if the collective repression of an entire people continued in this manner, she would advise her grandchildren to leave the country.

"Why is Sharon making war?" she demanded. "To kill peasants, bomb Gaza, and then discover that there are women and children among the victims? Our people experienced the Shoah. How are we able to commit these acts? The Palestinians are rising up, and I understand them."[23]

Stupefaction, uproar. Yaffa later explained that it occurred to her, in the heat of emotion, to mention the Shoah in connection with the numbers Israeli soldiers wrote on the arms of Palestinians arrested in round-ups, but that she never intended to compare the IDF to the SS. No matter. The publisher of the daily newspaper *Maariv* said she was one of the new European anti-Semites. She was called a Shoah denier and received hundreds of insults and threats. The Union of Israeli Artists canceled a large event planned in her honor. The muse of Israeli song had become the bearer of the plague. Like the academician Ilan Pappe, Yaffa received letters from colleagues outraged by what had befallen her. Only one, Gidi Gov, resigned from the Artists' Union.

What hurt the most, she remarked once the initial shock had passed, was hearing it said that she had insulted the memories of Israeli victims. This was a woman who had lost her first husband, a member of the Jewish Brigade of the British Army in Italy in 1944, a woman whose son-in-law, a pilot, had lost a leg on the Egyptian front in the 1970s. "What I say is said solely out of love for this country," she affirmed, adding: "The Palestinians have the right to have their state. Good God, that can't be helped. In the end, they'll have it. So why all this butchery, among us and among them?"[24]

Journalists, the people most aware of the realities on the ground, are equally subject to pressure. In the spring of 2002 Amnon Nadav, the new head of Kol Israel (the public radio and television channels), sent a note to journalists of Arabic-language networks indicating specific terms that were to be restricted or banned. Henceforth the word *victim* was to be used "only for Israelis who died in bloody attacks; with reference to Palestinian civilians, the notion that they are 'the dead' is to be used."[25] The list was long and detailed. A Palestinian leader was never "liquidated" but "killed." The phrase "according to the version" was banned with reference to "an official

Israeli spokesman, since it could raise a doubt about the veracity" of what he was saying. Official communiqués now had to be presented as confirmed truths. Some of the recommendations were symptomatic—to the point of absurdity—of the efforts being undertaken to codify language. Thus it was no longer permitted to speak on the air of "the Israeli–Arab conflict"; what had to be said was "the Arab–Israeli conflict."

Most journalists remained indifferent to these directives, in the belief either that they did not apply to them, since they did not broadcast in Arabic, or that current events would quickly prove the directives inapplicable. Others, however, were worried: if these measures were required of Israeli Arab journalists today, what would prevent their being required of Jews tomorrow, officially or subtly?

There had been a remarkable breakthough in freedom of the press during the first intifada, even though the media were still subject to military censorship. The initial phase of the second intifada brought an alignment on official truths roughly similar to the one found in the American press in the aftermath of September 11, 2001. Newspapers, radio networks, and especially television channels kept pace with or surpassed the general drawing inward of Israeli society. Very few journalists were able to keep an independent mind, to maintain a distance with regard to the official versions of events. For a long time military communiqués and bulletins delivered by the security organs were echoed by almost all the media as revealed truths. In 2003 Gideon Levy, the *Haaretz* columnist, mocked this trend:

> If you add up what our newspapers have published in the past three years, the army has liquidated 'the head' of the Ezzedin Al-Kassam Brigades in Jenin thirteen times, 'a high official' of Jihad in Nablus seventeen times, one hundred fifty 'terrorist leaders' in Gaza, etc. Either they don't give a crap about us, or the leaders were replaced each time and we should wonder what the point of these liquidations is. The reality is that no one has any idea what's going on, and when Tsahal [the IDF] kills these people it systematically announces that they were leaders. And our reporters stand at attention and echo these communiqués.[26]

On a number of occasions I was surprised at this automatic echoing by the media of statements that were clearly intended to sanction a future operation. One example among many: on May 7, 2002, an especially bloody suicide attack took place in a billiard room in the town of Rishon Letzion, leaving fifteen victims. The defense ministry immediately indicated that the suicide bomber came from Gaza. The very next day the entire press predicted, on the basis of "authorized sources," that there would be terrible reprisals in Gaza. At that time the Bush administration still maintained diplomatic contacts with the Palestinian Authority. Yasser Arafat announced that his police forces had imprisoned sixteen Islamists from Gaza, and President Bush was said to find this initiative very encouraging. The Israeli government got the message and gave up the plan to strike in Gaza. On the 11th, changing course, the army announced that the terrorist in question came not from Gaza but from the West Bank. Military correspondents immediately echoed this, with no comment on what they had written three days earlier.

But as time went by the credibility of military communications, too, began to erode. The evolution of the newspaper under discussion, Haaretz, is typical of this process. With the onset of the intifada, reporters like Amira Hass, Gideon Levy, and Akiva Eldar continued to write there, but they felt very isolated. Supposedly acting on the basis of a consensus, the editor in chief, Hanokh Marmari, a left-winger up to that time, made sweeping changes. Hass, who had reported from the occupied territories, was soon relieved of her regular duties and moved to the commentary section and the weekly supplement; another correspondent was named to her position. The refocusing lasted until Haaretz came to its senses. After three years the owner of the paper, Amos Schoken, who on principle never intervened in the editorial content, put an end to this change, stepping in when an editorial condemned the insubordinate pilots who refused to bomb the territories. Schoken (2003) wrote that the dishonor lay on the side of those who deliberately committed criminal acts, not on the side of those who refused to do so.

But the dramatic editorial shift imposed on Haaretz had not stemmed a tide of canceled subscriptions by those for whom the mere publication of articles by journalists like Levy or Hass had become unbearable despite the fact that they were a small minority of writers for the paper. These many readers felt that they had official power behind them. Thus Chief of Staff "Bugi" Yaalon, in the interview cited above in which he compared the Palestinians to a cancer, denounced "the pathological tendency of the Israeli media to criticize."[27] "Cancer," "pathology": the general is handy with medical analogies. Vice Minister of Internal Security Gideon Ezra, believing that "certain journalists are on the verge of supporting the fight against Israel," publicly suggested "placing people like Amira Hass and Gideon Levy under surveillance by Shabak, the internal secret service."[28] At this time, too, Israeli authorities denounced what they felt to be the partiality of the international media, calling in the BBC and even CNN and reprimanding them angrily and in no uncertain terms whenever they gave some space to the "Palestinian version" of events (only Fox News enjoyed the presumption of honesty). And measures would be taken to limit these networks' access to information, for example by not renewing the press cards of the Palestinian correspondents of the large Western news agencies and television channels.

These manifestations of exasperation, at the highest level, with freedom of the press, exclusively focused on accounts of the repression of the Palestinians, are regularly accompanied by direct threats against Israeli opponents of the occupation. Let us leave aside the bumper stickers sported by many vehicles, demanding "Bring the Oslo criminals to justice!" These are merely the signs of a vindictive and obdurate right wing seeking a scapegoat for all evils in what it calls the enemy within. But they reflect a mood, a general state of tension, in which newspapers are besieged with letters from readers denouncing "the saboteurs of national morale" and other Israeli "human-rights mongers." On April 14, 2002, Eliakim Rubinstein, the government's legal adviser, decried "the irresponsibility of the Association for the Defense of the Citizen and other human rights groups that—the shame of it!—confirm Palestinian allegations and broadcast them throughout the world."[29]

"Is there an attempt to silence people in Israel?" This was the theme of a televised discussion at the beginning of April 2002. The *Jerusalem Post* asked whether there was an Israeli version of McCarthyism and replied in the negative, with communications professor Gabi Weinmann explaining that, in adopting official information without distance, the media were simply reflecting the turn taken by public opinion: in the face of a national emergency, the people were rallying under the flag.[30] In the summer of 2002 Ariel Sharon stated before the cabinet that it was "inconceivable" that Gush Shalom (the Peace Bloc), which advocated IDF's unilateral withdrawal from the occupied territories, continue to pursue its activities.[31] Shortly before this Gush Shalom had called on pilots charged with bombing inhabited areas to refuse to obey clearly illegal orders, in accordance with the military code; in carrying out these orders they ran the risk of finding themselves before an international court one day. Sharon asked the government's legal counsel to verify the measures permitting him to ban the group. The attorney general's office established that, as matters stood, Israeli law did not allow his wish to be granted.

This must have disappointed Avigdor Lieberman, another Israeli minister who favored radical solutions such as revoking the citizenship of people like Uri Avnery, the head of Gush Shalom, and the lawyer Leah Tsemel, who defends activists from Palestinian organizations.[32] If one can calmly contemplate revoking the citizenship of an Israeli Arab who marries a Palestinian woman from the territories, why should Jewish "traitors" be exempt from this type of measure?

Traitors: this was the term used by General Dan Halutz, at the time commander in chief of the air force and today chief of staff, when he asked that the activists of Gush Shalom, the group led by the newspaper editor and former Knesset deputy Uri Avnery, be brought to justice. These activists, he said, are not even marginal but are outside the margins of the state.[33] Halutz used the word *traitors* to describe the twenty-seven pilots who, on September 26, 2003, announced their refusal to bomb the Palestinian territories.[34] Among these was the war hero Yftah Spector, the commanding officer of the IDF's school for pilots.

An Israeli psychologist told me that a patient of his, a 17-year-old high-school student, once asked him what his political views were. He hesitated, and then replied that he was far to the left. "Oh," exclaimed the young man, "but then you're for the Arabs! You think that all people have equal value!" This was uttered as a heartfelt cry; when you think that all people have equal value you must be for the Arabs.

The line of demarcation between the two major poles today in Israel is thus not so much political as moral. When all is said and done, this difference is what separates those for whom the members of their own ethnic group are worth more than others and those for whom all people are equally worthy. Between these two fundamental poles the gulf is growing deeper.

Those who, standing before the world and their own mirror, accept or justify everything, pretend they do not see glaring injustice, paint their opponents in the darkest colors, and are constantly busy absolving themselves of blame, to paraphrase Albert Memmi, are grouped around two axes: the army and the settlers' party.

THE NEW ROLE OF THE MILITARY

For the past decade or so the Israeli army has experienced an obvious change in its composition and attitude, a change that the intifada has made glaringly apparent. After a series of blatant speeches by Chief of Staff Shaul Mofaz, one of the leading columnists of *Haaretz*, Yoel Marcus (2002), a right-of-center moderate, asked bluntly, "Who's the boss around here? . . . Who makes the policy decisions, . . . the army or the government?" And he made the natural analogy: the IDF's role in the intifada recalls the days of the Fourth Republic in France, when "the army . . . was determining the rules of the game in Algeria."

These were not new criticisms. A year earlier, in 2001, Shimon Peres, minister of foreign affairs in the Sharon government, had complained to another well-known journalist, Nahum Barnea, that for every minor discussion the IDF was bringing in a battalion of officers from headquarters, all of whom had become experts on political matters such as how Israel should deal with the United States Congress or manage communications.[35]

The army has always played a large part in Israel's political life. But its interpretations of governmental directives, its interventionism, its taking charge of all sorts of issues in an increasingly broad view of what is involved in *bitakhon*, have never been more extensive. Other chiefs of staff have been "political," Moshe Dayan in the 1950s being the archetype. This protégé of Ben Gurion missed no opportunity to intervene in discussions. But neither Dayan nor those who followed him revealed their disagreements in public. Exceptions to this rule were few and far between. This was just the way things were done in Israel, where the IDF has always been more than simply an army; its leaders were consulted on a great many matters and provided a large number of the country's future politicians.

But Shaul Mofaz ushered in an entirely new practice; he increasingly encouraged overt public intervention by those in the army's highest ranks, and promoted an autonomous role for the IDF. In his book on the failure of Camp David, Gilead Sher (2001), Ehud Barak's chief adviser, noted that, ever since the appointment of Mofaz in 1998, the military had tended to appeal to public opinion directly, doing an end run around the government, and to take liberties in the ways it interpreted orders. These tendencies first appeared in the negotiations after Oslo, when, charged with increasingly political tasks, the army began to spread itself around. Sher observes that in the period prior to Camp David, government directives to reduce tension with the Palestinians all too often became dead letters. As opponents of the Oslo process, Mofaz and most of the officers around him developed a new viewpoint. As described by General Iri Kahn, head of IDF's operational research (cited in Schattner 2002), they came to believe that it was not enough to implement the government's vague and changing orders. What they had to do instead was interpret the government's wishes as an architect does with a client, reconceptualizing the struggle and introducing new ideas, keeping in mind international constraints and public opinion.

From that time on the IDF considered itself to be the architect, as it were, pondering the needs of its political client, the state. With the onset of the intifada, this approach took on an unprecedented scope. Convinced that it was necessary to strike harder than what Barak's "restraint" called for, though Barak's measures were much harsher than what had gone before, Mofaz began to air his views in public. Barak was still in power and intending to negotiate with Arafat when, in February 2001, the chief of staff announced before the press that the Palestinian Authority was "a terrorist entity." Again and again during the first Sharon administration he systematically countered each decision made by the Labor defense minister Benyamin "Fuad" Ben Eliezer, though, like him, Ben Eliezer was a general and a hawk. In the spring of 2002, for example, when the government imprisoned Arafat in Ramallah, Mofaz publicly called for his expulsion, and not a week went by when he did not make his opinion known. When there was no reaction at the political level, his generals were emboldened, one of the most extravagant in the public airing of his views being Dan Halutz, who demanded that anyone who supported the refusenik soldiers be considered a traitor.

The army's political weight soon became the key factor in political planning, basically because Ariel Sharon placed much more trust in generals than in politicians. Ministers, even those in the security department, began complaining that they were not informed of various decisions made by Sharon and the general staff. It was becoming more and more common for the military "architect" to develop his own ideas and apply them unilaterally. When the IDF bombed a Syrian radar station in Lebanon on April 16, 2001, attacking Damascus for the first time in twenty years, Zeev Schiff noted that the raid had taken place at the very moment when the government was discussing it: the army had not awaited the result of the discussion.[36]

This degree of initiative on the part of the general staff was accompanied by an expansion of the services in charge of the army's own communications and of influencing those of the government. "So who needs a government? The army has organized a forum for communications [hasbara] in charge of coordinating its messages to the country and the world," noted Uri Blau (2002), who covers defense issues for the weekly magazine Kol Ha'Ir. Under the authority of General Dan Harel, this forum was made up solely of high-ranking officers. At its first meeting, as recounted by Blau, Harel explained that there was a problem with the way the world viewed the legitimacy of the IDF's acts, so this legitimacy had to be found, strengthened, and preserved. The document prepared at the end of the meeting envisioned the regular issuing of "messages, including latent ones," on matters supposedly stemming from the political level. And indeed, with the intifada, the coordination of Israeli hasbara became increasingly determined by army organs, which were better staffed and clearly more aware of many facts and situations than the political services in charge of communications.

Not content with regular briefings of military reporters and other specialists in Arab affairs in the media, the vast majority of whom were in
contact with security organs, the IDF went beyond merely sending its so-
called experts to every little political meeting, as Shimon Peres had complained. Now its representatives invaded TV shows and radio talks. Uri
Avnery (2002b) made this daring comparison: "The chiefs of the Turkish
army, who are good friends of their Israeli colleagues, have a similar position in their country. Turkey is a democracy, there is a president, a parliament, an elected government. But the army considers itself as the supreme
guardian of the state and its values."

This tendency became so pronounced that Sharon, who had favored
the growing confidence of this Golem,[37] ultimately had to experience the
consequences himself. When he announced his plan for disengagement
from Gaza, Chief of Staff Moshe Yaalon immediately expressed reservations in public. The daily newspaper *Yediot Ahronot* reported that Sharon,
suddenly discovering that, in a democracy, the military is subordinate to
the elected government and does not normally criticize that government's
decisions publicly, had told his confidants that Yaalon was forcibly in-
truding into political affairs and attempting to influence government
ministers.[38]

But in Israel, as it had been evolving, there was no way Sharon could
silence his chief of staff once and for all. Informed of the prime minister's
wrath, Yaalon scornfully announced on the army's radio station that he
was unaware of any such crisis. And that is where matters remained.

Now that the debate was taking place in the town square, *Haaretz* described the general staff's reservations about Sharon's plan. The army believed that withdrawal from Gaza would give the Palestinians a sense of
victory that would only spur them on to further combat. A strategic error
was being put into effect, said several IDF leaders; the plan for separation
without political arrangements would end up as an Israeli retreat under fire.[39]

Here we see the position developed by the "planners" in the IDF since
the onset of the intifada, a position they tried to impose through an active
military lobby. There is no question of doing anything that might remotely
resemble a concession, in this view, because any backing down would
postpone the only acceptable outcome, namely victory and the crushing

of the terrorists. The majority of Israeli generals have constantly harped on this idea, which they set forth with much more consistency than the politicians in power, who have to take into account such unimportant factors as Washington and public opinion, even when, like Barak and then Sharon, they declare the end of violence to be a precondition to any talks with the Palestinians.

A champion of military victory and nothing less, since becoming the head of the IDF Moshe "Bugi" Yaalon has repeated this idea time and again. Here too we find an element of the current Algerianization of Israel. This is a mind-set oblivious of what is at stake politically, one privileging military necessity over reflection and automatically seeing any exit from the crisis short of total victory as a personal humiliation. It mechanically magnifies its successes whenever it can ("terrorism is on the wane") and demonizes a situation whenever it sees any advantage in doing so, when, for example, an exit strategy such as the "road map" appears on the horizon, or, more prosaically, when budget increases need to be justified; in such cases, the generals will note that "terrorism is on the increase." This has sometimes been asserted by the very people who, the day before, said it was on the wane.

This mentality will naturally seek to foil whatever runs counter to the promised victory, the final outpost of self-respect. The more this victory seems illusory, the more the army will mechanically entrench itself into the position of doing whatever it takes to achieve it, including measures that are increasingly illegitimate and brutal, transforming the enemy into a "terrorist nation," according to the term used by a number of Israeli political figures.

After laying siege to Balata with his troops in March 2002, the commander of a parachute brigade declared that the city had "capitulated." "A refugee camp was 'conquered' by elite troops, using the most sophisticated weapons: tanks and assault helicopters. If all this had not been so sad and grotesque, the terms would be amusing," wrote Professor Zeev Sternhell.[40] Israeli generals, Sternhell observed, are no longer ashamed to call colonialist police operations acts of war. Killing innocent people is becoming the norm, he said, carried out with a view to depriving another people of their freedom and human rights. Military actions undertaken by the Palestinians, such as attacks on checkpoints, are now brought under the heading of terrorism. It won't be long, Sternhell concluded, before Israelis will be told that soldiers who risked their lives in a tank along the Suez Canal and soldiers who destroy a car carrying a Palestinian mother and her three children are all taking part in the same war.

And in fact Zeev Sternhell did not have long to wait. Beginning with Operation Defensive Shield in the spring of 2002, all kinds of actions involving weapons—a suicide attack in a discotheque or the act of throwing a saucepan through a window at soldiers on guard by a Palestinian who had been imprisoned in his apartment for weeks—were considered similar acts of terrorism. If attacks on Israeli territory generally legitimize substantial operations planned in advance (and promote future attacks), the killing of soldiers carrying out the activities of occupation leads to bloody reprisals. As Sternhell told me,

> The way the Israelis are, the death of one soldier is enormously more serious for them than the death of civilians. With civilians, it's abominable, but that corresponds to how they see Arabs: cowards, bloodthirsty. So when hundreds of civilians are killed in attacks, it's awful but bearable. But when our soldiers fall, that's intolerable and gives rise to much more rage. No attack will induce as much emotion as when soldiers are killed.[41]

On January 9, 2002, four soldiers from a regular army unit made up of minorities (Druses, Bedouins, Tcherkassians) fell in an ambush in Gaza. The next day, the army let the same unit carry out reprisals, which is contrary to the norm. The unit went wild. Fifty buildings were destroyed, depriving five hundred civilians of all their possessions in an hour's time. "If that isn't pure vengeance, what is it?" asked Orit Shokhat in the weekly magazine Ha'Ir. "Vengeance has become the unifying element in Israel," she wrote, "and the army's permanent order of the day."[42]

As for impunity, it is almost always taken for granted. When the commander of the Hebron garrison, returning from leave, found that his vehicle had been stolen, soldiers raided the Arab city, leaving thirteen dead; an investigation went nowhere. When border guards beat a 14-year-old Palestinian to death in the street, the soldiers of their unit signed a letter claiming that they had not left the base. Everyone knew that this was collective false testimony. Case closed.

Questioned in July 2003 by a member of the Knesset about the failure to follow up on incidents identified as serious, General Menahem Finkelstein, attorney general for the military, said that in wartime "there are special considerations" before going ahead with the questioning. He indicated that not everything was up to him.[43] It was not until four years after the onset of the intifada that the army suddenly announced that "investigations of over six hundred instances of alleged abuse committed by Israeli soldiers against Palestinians" had been undertaken.[44] General Finkelstein explained that 217 files concerned instances of violence, 181 instances of damage to or theft of Palestinian property, and 88 instances of shooting without reason. There were 114 situations ranging from the use of civilians as human shields to unwarranted immobilization of Palestinian civilians by soldiers at transition points. Ninety charges had been brought, and fifty-six trials had taken place in military courts. Several soldiers, Finkelstein noted, had been sentenced to prison without possibility of parole, but he offered no details about exactly what they had been charged with, their rank, or the length of the prison terms.

Fifty-six trials, almost all of which surely involved subordinates, in four years: an average of one reprehensible act a month. During Operation Defensive Shield alone, in 2002, there must have been fifty-six a day. Under Sharon and Yaalon impunity reached unprecedented heights,[45] and military discourse confirmed this state of mind. On October 3, 2001, the Israeli government granted targeted assassinations the status of acts of preventive self-defense. When a one-ton bomb was dropped from a fighter plane on a residential building in Gaza, the journalist Vered Levy-Barzilai interviewed a pilot. "[That] is the uniqueness and the beauty of the world of the pilot," he explained. "You sit above, quietly, with your wide space. There are no noises, no booms, no shouts of people. You are totally focused on the target, you don't have the dirt and the horror of the battlefield. You do your thing and head home."[46] Dan Halutz, commander of the air force, had this to say: "If you really want to know what I feel when I release a bomb, I will tell you. I feel a slight bump to the plane as a result of the bomb's release. A second later it's gone and that's all. That's what I feel."

When an Israeli pacifist was wounded in a demonstration near the security wall, the officer in charge said that this was an unfortunate error; the shooter had believed his target was an Arab. In the summer of 2004 missiles were fired against a crowd in Rafah, and all observers on the scene agreed that the crowd was peaceful. But the army spokesman claimed that this was a misdirected shot; the intention had been to shoot in front of the demonstrators to prevent them from advancing, not into the middle of them.

So now the army shoots missiles at Palestinian demonstrators to show them that they must stop advancing. It is no wonder that such deviations from accepted security procedures take place without comment from the political class or, given the historical role of the IDF in Israeli society, that the press occasionally publishes articles reflecting their social impact. Thus *Yediot Ahronot*, the newspaper with the largest circulation in the country, presented on page one of its magazine, and continuing for a total of eight pages, a scoop on one of Israel's most secret units, the Sayeret Egoz (Hazelnut Squadron). This was an unprecedented report, written with sympathy, in which the members of this elite commando group, half of whom are religious ultranationalists, related in detail how they suddenly attack Palestinians and how, for each successful killing, they tattoo a little "x" on their arms. The article helps the reader share the fears and the pride of the squadron members: "Shimon is nervous. 'The cemetery guy, how'd we miss him?' he cries. 'I swear by my mother, that shit has seven lives!' Ronen displays with pride the tattoos on his left arm. 'I already have three x'es. Well, have to get back to my hideout,' he says."[47] I'll spare the reader the more macabre details.

The following week *Yediot Ahronot* published reactions from readers. Some of them thanked the newspaper for acquainting them with the life of "these true heroes of the Hazelnut Squadron." A parachute officer, however, indicated his "uneasiness" at the mentality that had developed in these commandos.[48]

And it is no wonder that the letters sent by elementary-school children to soldiers to sustain their morale tell us so much about the state of mind so many young people acquire in this atmosphere. "Dear soldier, I have a favor to ask you. Please kill a lot of Arabs." "I'm praying that you return home safe and sound. Do this for me: kill at least ten of them." "You don't give a damn about laws: a good Arab is a dead Arab." Here too the list will stop. *Yediot Ahronot* explained that a shocked reservist had brought these letters to the editorial office and that his unit had received dozens of them.[49]

Avraham Burg, former president of the Jewish Agency, was equally appalled when he listened to students in a high school he visited. They "were saying, 'When we're soldiers, we'll kill old people, women, and children.' They were saying, 'We'll drive them out, we'll put them on planes and send them to Iraq. Hundreds of thousands of them, millions.' And most of the students applauded."[50]

Not all Israeli young people, of course, have sunk to this level of madness. I met with a class of 15- and 16-year olds in Tel Aviv, in which the students said exactly the opposite. "If I were a Palestinian," said one girl, "maybe I'd be like them." A boy agreed: "In their place, maybe I'd fight against the occupation too."[51] Several of them challenged the argument that the Palestinians had refused to make peace at Camp David and advocated withdrawal from the occupied territories. Such people are called "beautiful souls" and "defeatists" in Israeli military and right-wing circles.

In such an atmosphere, and in exceptional cirumstances, are substantial portions of the largely "Algerianized" army capable of tipping over in the direction of a coup d'état? Nearly all military experts in Israel think not. They note the IDF's very deep entanglements with political and economic echelons, its legalist tradition, and its sustained, if weakened, popular roots. Uri Ben Eliezer, a sociologist at Haifa University specializing in military matters, is alone in believing that a coup is "implausible but, should there be a major internal crisis, possible." The IDF, he says,

has changed a lot in ten years, beginning with a reform, aimed at professionalizing it, that got underway in the 1990s. It's not so much "the people in arms" that it was for so long. The social composition of its higher levels has changed, and its intermediary hierarchy even more so. There has been a definite decline in the number of people from kibbutz or moshav backgrounds, who used to be overrepresented, and there are more settlers and even more students from military talmudic schools. These are the spearheads of a military society in training, who have as their mission reformulating the values of national identity.[52]

The parachute officer mentioned above, who was anxious about public approval of the crimes committed by the Hazelnut Squadron, went on to say this:

In my special parachute unit there are also a large proportion of religious people and settlers. They are found in all elite units. I am trying to articulate this carefully, because it is not pleasant to say, but a number of these religious people have no special sensitivity when they are shooting at Arabs and taking their lives. The ideology of the Jews as the chosen people, which is what they were brought up with, influences the way they behave in military operations.[53]

In other words, speaking less carefully, one might say that the ultrareligious, who are themselves often settlers as well, share the schoolchild's idea that "a good Arab is a dead Arab"—and apply it eagerly. Since they are led by generals like Moshe Yaalon and Dan Halutz (former and present chiefs of staff), and the defense ministry has most often been headed by General Amos Yaron, who commanded the Beirut garrison at the time of the 1982 massacre of Sabra and Shatila, it seems that their values are shared at the very highest level of the security hierarchy.

THE "SETTLERS' PARTY" AND THE DEVELOPMENT OF THE NATIONAL-RELIGIOUS MOVEMENT

The second intifada had been underway for only three weeks when an incident led the well-known Israeli military commentator Zeev Shiff to suspect that something was amiss.[54]

After the evacuation of the talmudic school at Joseph's Tomb (the army considered itself unable to preserve the safety of theology students in an isolated enclave in the middle of Nablus), the rabbi of a neighboring settlement of Gush Emunim led his flock on a walk to the nearby hill to steep themselves one last time in the sight of the holy gravesite. Under military escort, the settlers—men armed with light machine guns, as well as women, children, and infants—set out, happy, as they put it, to show that they were at home everywhere in the Land of Israel. They then continued on to the Palestinian refugee camp. Who opened fire? The rabbi was killed, as was a Palestinian. There were wounded people on both sides. The problem was that the IDF had formally proscribed all excursions into this zone, but the local commander had raised no objection and provided the escort. Who, the settlers or the military, was giving orders to whom? asked Shiff.

This was a legitimate question. For the spread of the settlers' mentality into the military hierarchy was due not only to the increasing number of officers trained in talmudic military schools, but also, more prosaically, to the constant and obligatory contact between the two groups. Where is the so-called war on terrorism basically taking place? In the occupied territories. The daily life of soldiers can be summed up as two activities: keeping the native population in line and protecting the Israelis who live there, that is, the settlers. As we have seen, the latter are very diverse in nature, but, as was the case in colonial Algeria, their informal "party" is controlled by the zealots among them, the most highly organized. So it is naturally with them that the military hierarchy has the most day-to-day contact.

Yzhar Beer, director of the nongovernmental organization Keshev (Listen), the Center for the Defense of Democracy in Israel, describes the role of the army in the territories as follows:

> [It] is always placed on the edge of, or within, a settlement whose location corresponds to strategic objectives. All the settlements have militias and armed residents, *kitot konenut* [warning groups], *merkazei bitakhon shotef* [permanent security centers], and the like. Their

leaders are remunerated by the army. *Hagana merkhavit* [Zone Defense] is a police force consisting entirely of settlers. They meet all the time with the local officers and agents of Shabak to share information. I was once in the home of Aharon Domb, head of the Hebron settlers. He showed me photos of slain Palestinian "collaborators." The photos came directly from Shabak. I was surprised that he was in possession of a copy. He told me proudly that he had a confidential hotline to the special services. The difference between the local officers and the settlers is that the former are there only temporarily and the latter remain there. Every officer appointed to a position in occupied territory knows that his advancement largely depends on the green light given or withheld by the settlers, that his interest therefore often lies in closing his eyes to their acts of violence.[55]

To show how far this cooperation can extend Beer cites the case of Rabbi Ginsburg, the settler who believes that Arabs have the souls of animals and who was invited by Shabak to give instruction in Judaism to recruits: "These determined settlers number only fifty thousand, and their direct supporters in Israel nearly two hundred thousand, but it would be mistaken to believe that their influence can be reduced to their numerical proportion. It is very widespread in the state apparatus, starting with the security organs," says Beer. Among Ariel Sharon's intimates was a certain Yaakov Katz, nicknamed Ketzeleh, the longtime liaison officer of Gush Emunim and founder of numerous settlements and the radio station Arutz 7, a deeply messianic man whom Sharon employed in all the administrative departments in which he served.

Uri Ben Eliezer, the sociologist whose specialty is the IDF, is in strong agreement with Beer. As he told me in 2003, when Israel still occupied the Gaza Strip, "with the possible exception of Gaza" it would be

very difficult to leave the territories without a serious internal crisis, because the arguments of the extremist settlers have permeated the social fabric and the military hierarchy to a great extent. In thirty-six years there hasn't been a single initiative in the territories that was not undertaken in consultation with them, if not at their instigation.

They usually know the little secrets of unpublicized activities on the part of the ministries of defense, public works, and housing that the general population and even certain ministers don't know about or discover only after action has been taken. For everything having to do with the occupation, a link of complicity between them and the army has been formed.[56]

Professor Ben Eliezer relates an incident that passed relatively unnoticed. In 1995, after the assassination of Itzhak Rabin, it was learned that the murderer, Ygal Amir, and his brother owned a veritable arsenal: light machine guns, grenades, explosives, and small rockets. An adjutant named Schwartz, who belonged to a prestigious squadron (Sayeret Golani), had stolen the weapons for them from his base. Schwartz was a student in a military talmudic school. When arrested he denied knowing anything about the deadly plans of the Amir brothers, claiming he believed the weapons were intended solely to kill Arabs. He was discharged from the army and sentenced to three years' imprisonment without possibility of parole. "The settlers are armed by the IDF for their defense," Ben Eliezer notes. "We know that weapons are disappearing from arsenals. But their number is one of the best-kept secrets."

Who are the people forming the backbone and activist base of the settlers' party today? According to Yzhar Beer, two-thirds of them are very religious, the rest traditionalist or even secular ultranationalists. All in all, he says, there are four groups. The most moderate faction

will not risk a major confrontation in the country to sustain their dream of a Greater Israel. Should there be a withdrawal from the West Bank, they'll kick up a fuss but submit to reasons of state. The pragmatists are more inclined to fight in order to preserve the maximum territory. These two groups are in the majority. Then there are the extremists, who find in *halakha* [religious law] the theological legitimation for all acts of violence and take an active part in hunting down Arabs on the grounds of lawful self-defense. Finally, the lunatic fringe doesn't differentiate among the Palestinians, all of whom are reduced to the status of Amalek [the biblical

archetype of the Hebrews' sworn enemy], who really has to be
exterminated.[57]

The two latter groups are the potential catalyst for an equivalent of the
OAS, the Secret Army Organization of settlers that rose up to defend
French Algeria against de Gaulle in 1961–1962. Ygal Amir, Rabin's assas-
sin, was active in their midst. They are relatively few in number in the
settlers' party today, but no one knows how much support they could
muster from unrest among the more moderate ultranationalists if wholesale withdrawal from the territories were the order of the day. For they all
share a strong sense of solidarity, based, according to Beer, "on two pillars, hatred of the Arabs and suspicion of the government, any government,
including Netanyahu and Sharon, even if they prefer them by far to Barak,
and hatred of the 'Oslo traitors.'"

Several books could be filled about this hatred. The report that the
nongovernmental organization Keshev covering Arutz 7, the FM station
of the extremist camp, provides sickening examples of the racism, including cases of implicit incitement to murder, that, along with denunciation
of the "crimes" of democracy, the station pours out every day.[58] Arutz 7 is
controlled by the most radical faction of the settlers' party. But every day
the Israeli mainstream media, too, report statements by representatives of
this movement that leave one flabbergasted. Outside of Israel it is hard to
imagine the extent of the blatant racism they express, racism that would
even make Jean-Marie Le Pen, who has to disguise his anti-Semitism and
hate of Arabs with wordplay or allusions in order not to run afoul of the
law, appear to be a model of brotherly love.

In March 2002 Haaretz published a long article on Ofra, a religious
settlement that has dozens of counterparts (Ushpiz 2002). The author
relates what people said to her. Two local rabbis, Yehuda Dinur and Avi
Gisser, were not among the most fanatic; on the other hand, they revealed
an extraordinary tendency to deny the Palestinians' reality. Dinur, for
example, said that they merely want "to be left to live quietly. . . . What
occupation are they talking about, what do they understand about occupation? What's an occupation? A word without meaning. . . . They don't
feel occupied. Only their leaders feel occupied" (p. B1). Gisser agreed: "I

don't know whether this sounds reliable or not, but a senior Israeli Defense Force officer told me that when they entered Jenin they encountered great support from the population. Masses of Palestinians cried out
to the soldiers: 'Go to the camps and bring order there'" (p. B1).

The local security company representative displayed less paternalism
but remained moderate in his views:

> "Look, there was Bibi [Benyamin Netanyahu], there was [Ehud]
> Barak, there was Sharon, and none of them has the balls to put an
> end to the situation, to clean them out and send them to Jordan. We
> have to go in for a total military campaign of two or three months, to
> clean them out. . . . Then if they want to give them a state, they
> should give them a state. I don't know. I don't have a firm opinion.
> I'm prepared to give something, but . . . they want to wipe us out."
> [p. B2]

"I don't agree," replied Yigal Sarbaro, another local settler:

> "This is our land. The solution is in the nation's ability not to leave
> even one of them here. Transfer or extermination; it's all the same
> to me. Anyone who wants to accept our rule and ownership, with-
> out civil rights and without ownership of land, can stay. Whoever
> doesn't will be eliminated. Even if we kill them all, the hostile popu-
> lation will give birth to new territorists. . . . [S]o we have to get rid of
> them, to wipe them out." [p. B2]

Sarbaro, who had immigrated from Ukraine nine years earlier, also said
that he feels "happiness, for the great days that are coming. . . . Now we
are seeing that the whole process is becoming faster. Every killing, every
death, brings us closer to redemption" (p. B2).

Everyone in Ofra shares a common fate. Everyone finds Sarbaro's ideas
legitimate, and many of the settlers subscribe to them to a greater or lesser
degree. This solidarity of interests is reflected in the values expressed by
those they respect the most, their rabbis and elected officials. Thus
Menahem Felix, a leader of Gush Emunim and founder of the famous

settlement Elon Moreh, said at a funeral, Psalm 149 of David in hand, that vengeance is a profoundly biblical concept.[59] Rabbi David Kavits, from the Ytzhar settlement, assures his followers that killing Arabs "is not a moral problem, in that by killing a Palestinian a Jew is not putting himself in danger."[60] Israel Rosen, member of the Forum of Rabbis of Judea-Samaria, suggests "razing the towns" from which Palestinian terrorists have come; this punishment would be "in accordance with Jewish ethics," which, he says, "unlike the ethics of Christianity or the Enlightenment, are based not on the principle of compassion" but on that of the preservation of life.[61] Well, it seems the lives of Jews living in the Land of Israel do have to be preserved.

Here too examples could be multiplied. Similar suggestions to be done with the enemy once and for all usually extend to those who, in Israel itself, do not share the same "values." Rabbi Shlomo Aviner, one of the settlers' spiritual leaders and head of Ateret Kohanim, an organization whose aim is the "Judaization" of East Jerusalem, issued the following public appeal on the fast day marking the fall of the First Temple: "The Israeli army has the right to execute those who weaken it by refusing to serve."

None of these suggestions has caused a major scandal. None has been punished. No wonder that a vice minister of defense, Zeev Boim, could declare in February 2004 that the Palestinians "have a genetic defect that leads them to commit acts of murder against Jews."[62] No wonder another vice minister, Gideon Ezra, was able to suggest that one way to fight terrorism is to kill family members of people who kill Israelis (Eldar 2001b). Or that, once the targeted liquidations of Palestinian leaders had begun and were arousing international disapproval (including, formally, Washington's), the Ashkenazic grand rabbi of Israel, a Shoah survivor though no friend to the settlers' party, was able to tour the country explaining that these murders had the full approval of Jewish religious law.[63]

The foundational principles of Gush Emunim, the primary ideological vector of the settlers' party, namely that the Jews are the chosen people and their land is sacred, have spread far beyond that sect into the religious movement in general. In contrast to the modernists of Gush Emunim, the Orthodox have traditionally not been nationalistic or have been so only slightly. Although the Land of Israel had great spiritual value for them, they did not care very much about territory (none of their leaders was a rabid annexationist) and still less about the state itself; their concern was to defend their own interests within its institutions, beginning with the public subventions they receive. Some, like the Neturei Karta and Satmar sects,[64] were even rabidly anti-Zionist and have remained that way, believing that the creation of the state of Israel is a major, even criminal, offense against God (see Rabkin 2004). But in one generation, with the growth of mysticism in the Jewish population, many more bridges have appeared between religious Zionism and the Orthodox. Each group had gradually blended into the other. Thus an increasing number of members of Gush Emunim are adopting the strict fervor and the customs of the Orthodox movement. And more and more "men in black," wearing frock coats and beards, subscribe to the belief in the sanctity of the Land of Israel.

This phenomenon has recently appeared in the vast, wealthy Lubavitch Hassidic sect known as Chabad.[65] Their rabbi, Menahem Mendel Schneerson, died in New York in 1994 (though many of his followers continue to believe that he is not really dead and will return as the messiah). Starting in the 1970s, Schneerson began to issue orders forbidding the restitution of even a square inch of the Land of Israel to non-Jews. But it was not until the 1990s that the mingling of the Orthodox and the national-religious movements became sufficiently widespread to be given concrete expression in the emergence of the Sephardic Orthodox party Shas (which in 1996, as the third party after Likud and Labor, had seventeen members of parliament). Ashkenazic Orthodox movements soon followed, so as not to see their influence decline. The result was the phenomenon that the Israelis call the *Khardelim*, an acronym formed from the first letters of *kharedim*, "the God-fearing," a name given to the "men in black," and *Datiim-Leumiim*," the national-religious. In other words, these are the ultranationalist Orthodox. Their nationalism is essentially a very new concept for them: the holiness of the Land of Israel. For them, Israel belongs solely to the Jews.

On June 6, 2000, Yzhar Beer, head of the Center for the Defense of Democracy, took me to a meeting at Yad Eliahu, in the country's largest covered stadium, organized by various movements. All eighteen thousand seats were filled. The featured speaker was Rabbi Ovadia Yossef, spiritual leader of Shas. This astonishing meeting went on for over four hours before the venerated rabbi put in an appearance and was introduced to the ecstatic flock as "the Moses and Prophet Elijah of our generation." Seven speakers had preceded him. I did not understand everything they said, since they mixed citations from the Talmud with their present-day Hebrew. But I understood enough to see the their fierce cultivation of a siege mentality, the invaders being the Arabs and secular Israelis, and their pride in representing what they held to be true Judaism. One of the speakers lambasted the secular Zionist left in insane terms ("evil toads," and the like). Another stated that, although some of the religious do not serve in the army, "when the secularists are done with their military service, they'll leave the country, but, come what may, we shall remain." Rabbi David Batzri ardently defended the settlers in Hebron, who, he said, "glorify the presence of God" there and are threatened by the *sonei Israel*, Israelis who hate their country, that is, nearly everyone who does not share his views on Jewish election.

Rabbi Eliezer Berland, who heads the talmudic school Shuvu Banim (Return, Sons [of Israel]) of the Breslau sect, spoke for an hour without stopping even for a drink of water. He ran on and on incredibly, swaying back and forth as though in prayer, interweaving current events; Abraham, Isaac, and Jacob; the pogroms of Khmelnitski in Ukraine; the scandal of the Israeli Supreme Court, which had ventured to decide a case concerning access to the Wailing Wall, which, the rabbi said, had been "granted by God to the Jewish people alone"; the pharaoh and Joseph; and the idolatrous threat of the corrupt West; Bill Clinton and Ehud Barak, those "faithless enemies of the Jews," who, he said, were leading the country toward "a Shoah even worse that the earlier one," but whose dangerous plans to give land back to the Arabs would be "halted by the hand of God, blessed be He" and punished.

And more of the same. He concluded, in a state of ecstasy, by speaking of "the chosen people, their purity and holiness." Berland is typical of this new movement. Originally from Gush Emunim, he went over to the ultra-Orthodox with their side curls. But he has retained the major teachings of his first spiritual master, Rabbi Kook of the Yeshiva Merkaz Harav, where he studied the "purity" of the Jew and the holiness of the Land of Israel.

Another rabbi, another profile: Amnon Itzhak. Moroccan in origin, a former secularist who returned to the faith, he is a speaker who, on August 15, 2000, was able to bring 22,000 disciples together in a Jerusalem stadium, and who has sold hundreds of thousands of tapes of his sermons. These sermons, tapes of which I happened to hear, take the form of repeated answers to questions he himself asks. For example, Itzhak will proclaim something like, "These Israeli secularists are not real Jews," and ask, "Do you know why?" "Why? Why? Why?" the audience cries. "I'll tell you why. Because . . ." Because the secularists are rotting Israel from within. Because they are terrified by the increasing numbers of their children who are returning to the faith. Because Zionism wanted a state for the Jews, but it was not really a Jewish movement. Because the Zionists are inclined to making compromises, to abandoning the Holy Land. Because the Eternal One hurls His wrath against His people when they turn their back on Him, sending Arab terrorists, those "poisonous snakes," those "cockroaches."

It would be wrong to consider Berland and Itzhak marginal figures. The former has preserved the fundamental tropisms of the religious Zionist school he comes from; the latter disparages Zionism but has adopted the belief in the holiness of the Land. Itzhak has been invited by the IDF to give talks to soldiers. Both exemplify the hideous side of religious Judaism, which, in Israel, has very largely become an ethnicist mystique of Jewish election and the divine allocation of the Land. In 2001, according to figures supplied by the Department of National Education, 41.4 percent of Israeli Jewish students were enrolled in religious schools.[66] Thirty years ago, fewer than 20 percent attended such schools.

FOURTEEN

"AN INSANE LOGIC,
A FORM OF SUICIDE"
The Israelis Confront Their Moral Failure

THE EMERGENCE OF THE "MORAL CAMP"

In a response to the ideology promoted by the army and the settlers' party, what has been called the moral camp has formed in Israel, consisting of those who make human dignity their touchstone. These people are Zionists, anti-Zionists, non- or post-Zionists. Often, especially among the young, they do not identify with any of these categories, judging them obsolete: they are simply Israelis. More or less active and determined, they can be found in all professional milieux—doctors, lawyers, senior officers in retirement, artists, scientists, and even some rabbis. Most of them are highly educated. They are also a small minority. But their voice, suppressed at the beginning of the intifada, carries beyond organized circles to a fringe of the population uneasy with certain acts and the image those acts convey of their nation.

The deterioration of Israel's image in world opinion is fundamentally due not to the alleged inefficiency of its official communications system, nor, as most Israelis would like to believe, to a supposedly intrinsic hostility of public opinion or the media, but to the ineluctable reality of the facts. As Israel entrenches itself ever deeper in the denial of these realities and this denial gives rise to its antidote, questions are being asked and the truth is being sought. The more the repression of the Palestinian people is denied or is held to verge on normality, the more an increasing number of Israelis are finding this denial or permanent self-justification intolerable. Never before have so many authors and artists in Israel taken an interest in the reality of the occupation today and, hence, in its historical origins, what really happened in 1948. The more they are maligned and accused of treason or self-hatred, the more numerous they become. In the early 1970s the annual June 5 demonstrations before the Knesset with the slogan "Down with the Occupation" drew about fifty people. Nowadays B'Tselem alone, the nongovernmental organization concerned with human rights in the occupied territories, has eight hundred members. Thousands of Israelis join together under the banner of an immediate end to the occupation.

The so-called refuseniks numbered fifty-two when, on January 25, 2002, they issued their call: "We, reserve combat officers and soldiers of the Israel Defense Forces, who were raised upon the principles of Zionism, sacrifice and giving to the people of Israel and to the State of Israel, [and] who have always served in the front lines . . . shall not continue to fight beyond the 1967 borders in order to dominate, expel, starve and humiliate an entire people" (*Combatants Letter* 2002). Some of the young men of this group spent over two years in prison after refusing for months on end to renounce their convictions. Since that time the number of signatories has exceeded five hundred, and the actual number of refuseniks is close to one thousand. This is a little, and it is a lot. In Israel, one thousand soldiers are the equivalent of ten thousand French soldiers refusing to serve in Algeria during that war (1954–1962).

What's the difference between a Jewish mother of the diaspora and an Israeli Jewish mother? asks a Hebrew joke. The former dreams of her son becoming a doctor and her daughter marrying a doctor. The latter dreams of her son becoming a pilot and her daughter marrying one. The army pilots have always been seen as the country's best sons. They enjoy an exceptional aura and are considered a true aristocracy. And so the entire country was stunned when, on September 25, 2003, twenty-seven pilots made public their letter to the head of the air force, announcing that from then on they would refuse to take part in actions in the occupied territories. The following day Major Yotam explained his decision, saying that pilots were, as he put it, being sent to carry out surgical strikes with an ax.

Not even the most experienced surgeon, he said, could operate using an ax as a scalpel. Their leader, General Halutz, indignantly exclaimed that no instructions or orders to attack innocent people had ever been given.[1] Of course not, replied the refuseniks, but who was talking about orders? With the measures being implemented, targeted missions were impossible to carry out without killing everyone in the vicinity of the target, and the air force was well aware of this. Denigrators accused the pilots of amorality, likening their refusal to bomb inhabited zones to an abandonment of their posts before the enemy and repeating over and over that the "purity of arms" remained the golden rule of the IDF, the most moral army in the world.

As we have seen, from the settler Tolkowsky, who stated in 1913 that the Jews, persecuted and mistreated for thousands of years, should be expected to show "a modicum of humanity" (see Chapter 3), to the writer Batya Gur ("It is not political stances we're talking about but about the image of man and his dignity" [2003]), it is the humanity and legitimacy of the opposite camp that are at issue in the personal crisis affecting a number of Israelis. This crisis is felt to be primarily moral in nature, the dehumanization of the other being experienced as one's own dehumanization. From this perspective the cumulative effect of members of the military elite joining the refuseniks, even after long hesitation, was symptomatic of the intensity of the moral crisis. Through fear of exclusion from the consensus, few people were able to step forward and say so openly. Yet as the writer David Grossman has noted, "There are many more people disturbed by the cult of force, a tragic error, than is thought outside Israel."[2]

Beyond their internal debates, what unites what I am calling this moral camp, in associations like Taayush, the Committee Against the Wall, Gush Shalom, Women in Black, the Makhsom Watch (groups monitoring the roadblocks), the refuseniks, Hamoked, Doctors for Human Rights, Rabbis for Human Rights, the Public Committee Against Torture, and others,[3] is not just hostility to the occupation and the conviction that, as Avraham Burg has said, quoting Memmi, the settlements are "rotting Israel from within."[4] It is a refusal to be associated with the ethnicist trend in their society, a feeling of shame regarding what that society has become, and fear of what the future might hold for it. Ruth Keidar, a 76-year-old retiree and longtime Laborite who spends entire days monitoring what happens to Palestinians at the checkpoints, sums up this feeling as follows: "When I return home, I'm devastated."[5]

Objections to the course being followed by the country focus on four themes.

THE CULT OF FORCE

First among these is the cult of force, that is, both the primacy accorded to security and the behavior of the army in what its opponents call the "dirty war."[6] Though the misdeeds have never sparked debates like those the discovery of torture in Iraqi prisons generated in the United States, they are so overt, so commonplace, that they are occasionally of concern at the highest level. The Israeli president himself, Moshe Katsav of Likud, has expressed regret that soldiers are now too trigger-happy. Minister Dan Meridor, of the center right, has spoken before parliament of the moral failure characterizing the behavior of soldiers at the checkpoints.[7] The IDF sometimes finds itself obliged to announce the opening of investigations, the precise outcomes of which are almost never known. One such investigation was held after two women in labor were detained at checkpoints and their newborns died; "I have the right to kill you, not to let you pass," one of them was told by a soldier on guard duty.

Sometimes the press, too, finds that too much is too much. After an air strike that was especially lethal for civilians in Gaza, an editorial in Haaretz held that Sharon had slipped Israel smoothly into an era of brutality.[8] After Operation Defensive Shield in the spring of 2002, a soldier who had taken part in it, a student in civilian life, told me this: "In order to dehumanize the Palestinians like this, we have to stop seeing them as men. In so doing we dehumanize ourselves."

What is being challenged at a deep level is the whole mythic relationship to the IDF. Many people have gotten used to frantically making light of the most terrible atrocities, even justifying them if need be. The majority cite what they see as the enemy's brutality as a reason for numbing themselves and, as Gideon Levy has said, looking the other way. But there are also many Israelis who no longer trust the official communiqués: "The army spokesman is lying" is a phrase heard more and more often, even from some who favor the repression. The list of obvious lies has become too long. When an Israeli unit destroyed fifty buildings in Gaza in an attack of pure revenge after the deaths of four of its soldiers, and the army justified this for "operational reasons," no independent media source took this announcement seriously. "We're digging ourselves deeper into the official lie. The behavior of units like the border guards is abominable. The IDF is now seen by everyone as a very violent army. Its influence on the education of the young is very negative. It has been corrupted by the occupation, no question about it," says Michael Ben Yair, former legal adviser to the Rabin government.[9]

REPRESSION AND THE ABSENCE OF POLITICAL VISIBILITY

This brings us to the second theme in the disapproval of the moral camp: the true nature of the repression and the absence of political visibility. We won't continue to wage "this war of the settlements," wrote the first refuseniks (*Combatants Letter* 2002). The idea that Israel is fighting a war for its existence, the watchword of the self-justification that spread through nearly all of the country at the outset of the intifada, clearly remains deeply rooted. It even serves as a leitmotiv in official discourse, playing a key role in the denial of the facts. But it is coming under increasing attack. More and more people are of the opinion that the IDF is conducting not a defensive war but an offensive one on behalf of the settlers. "This isn't a war of survival; it's a colonial war," writes Shulamit Aloni, the former leader of the secular left.[10] Now this view has been taken up again, its proponents including former generals like Dany Rothschild, Nehemia Dagan, and Dov Tamari.

In November 2003 former Shin Bet heads Ami Ayalon, Avraham Shalom, Carmi Gilon, and Yaakov Peri uttered a warning: "We're heading for a disaster."[11] They denounced the course of a war waged with the notion of achieving total victory, the absence of perspective characteristic of this notion, and the certainty of its failure in the long run. They called for a political accord that would evacuate the settlements, even at the price of an inevitable confrontation with some of the settlers, indicating above all that the intifada had made them question the basis of their traditional security vision. In so doing they were merely articulating a vague feeling shared by a growing number of Israelis: yes, this war would be won, or at any rate it couldn't be lost, but where would it lead them? As the former Shin Bet heads observed, the longer the conflict and the crushing of the Palestinians continues, the more cracks will appear in the dominance of *bitakhon* for those whose belief in hitting the Palestinians harder and harder until they give in is leading the country to an impasse. As early as the spring of 2002 a television journalist on the most widely viewed political program asked Ami Ayalon, the only one of the four to come forward since the onset of the intifada, "Don't you think we can win this war?" "Don't you understand that 'winning' it would be the worst thing that could happen to Israel?" the former master spy replied. And the journalist Aviad Kleinberg wrote as follows: "We're ignoring the danger inherent in too big a victory, one that would force us to live alongside a people from whom all honor and all hope have been snatched away. Israel's greater interest lies not in breaking the Palestinians but in living beside them in honor. War isn't the pursuit of politics by other means but the failure of politics."[12]

THE REFUGEE QUESTION

This challenge to the most firmly anchored element of Israel's historic relationship to its surroundings, namely the primacy of security, has had a ripple effect. A small but growing number of Israelis are challenging other foundational ideas as well. "Ten years ago I was saying, 'Let's forget 1948. There's no point in rewriting history; we have to think of the future.' I was one of those who imagined that we could achieve peace without mentioning the refugees," says Gideon Levy. "But the intifada brought the questions posed by 1948 back into our daily lives. Making peace by 'forgetting' the refugees is an illusion. This matter isn't only preventing the Palestinians from coming toward us; it's also preventing *us* from making peace with them and with ourselves."[13] The increasing awareness that this issue can't be gotten round, primarily because it has been the most strongly denied issue of all, is one of the most striking features in the development of the moral camp in Israel.

Merely mentioning the refugee question to the Israelis, who are easily persuaded on this score, is seen as an absolute horror, itself a demonstration of the Palestinian wish to do away with the nature of Israel as a Jewish state. Those who advocate a binational future for the two peoples are called anti-Semitic Jews. There is, of course, no magic solution that would enable the country to absorb all the suffering of the Palestinian refugees without infringing upon the integrity of Israeli society. Nor does it seem realistic, nowadays, to advocate an immediate binational future for Palestinians and Israelis. As Yasser Abed Rabbo told me, "The Israelis don't want that, they can't be forced, and, frankly, given what they're doing to us, very few of our people are willing to live with them."[14]

No one can know how many refugees would really wish to return and become Israeli citizens: 50,000? 100,000? 200,000? In 1951, when the Jewish state was demographically five times smaller than it is today, Ben Gurion planned to accept the return of 100,000 Palestinian refugees before abandoning this project. Yet it seems clear that no peaceful common future can be discerned without taking into account the origins and reality of the fate of the refugees, nor can it emerge without the acknowledgment of equality and dignity between the two parties.

Over and above the internal political differences in the moral camp, awareness of these two conditions is now increasingly recognized. Thus in June 2004 two hundred academics signed the so-called Olga Document (Bilitski and colleagues 2004), jointly drawn up by left-wing laborites from Yossi Beilin's Yahad party and members of Uri Avnery's Peace Bloc. Based on the idea of "truth and reconciliation," this document opened the debate on a binational future, not with the prospect of a unified state but as a state of mind based on a possible relationship between the two peoples. It advocates accepting the refugees' right of return, offering apologies for the expulsions and crimes committed in 1948, and ending the occupation as preliminaries to any real negotiation with the Palestinians.

A large majority of those favoring a definitive withdrawal from the occupied territories share the view expressed by Yossi Beilin (2001) at the time of the onset of the intifada: recognize their right of return but apply it in small doses. "It is impossible to demand of the Palestinians that they forgo the right of return. [We must arrive] at a solution that incorporates both narratives, ours and theirs. . . . If we demand that they forgo the right of return, there will be no settlement." Ami Ayalon was even more direct: "The refugee question is fundamental," he told me. "It structures the identity of the Palestinians. If we want to preserve Israel, we have to be aware of this. Especially if we want to make sure that, in practice, they don't come back, or very few of them. At that time we'll need a large-scale rehabilitation plan, and we Israelis will have to show special generosity on this point."[15]

On the other hand, some people do not believe in this solution. As the historian Shlomo Sand put it, "Saying yes to the principle of the refugees' right of return but not to its application is hypocritical. What would you say about a law that accepted divorce but in practice refused to let women apply it?" Sand opposed the refugees' right of return because this idea "creates terrible illusions among the Palestinians and terrible fears among the Israelis." The Palestinians, he adds, "have to do their mourning. But, if that is to happen, the Israelis have to stop denying their past and come to terms with it publicly. If the Palestinians are denied the right of return, Israel must also abolish its own law of return."[16] Michael Ben Yair, former legal adviser to the Rabin government, has come to the same conclusion: "It's impossible to have a law of return and deny them the same right. In a democratic state of equal citizens, Israel will no longer have room for discriminatory laws."[17]

What these two diametrically opposed views on the right of return have in common is the notion of equal treatment for the Palestinians. The proponents of return say that if they have this right the others should enjoy it as well. The opponents say that if it is denied to the Palestinians the Israelis should give it up for themselves. Both sides are in favor of equality of rights as stipulated in the Universal Declaration of Human Rights.

The same is true of the supporters of binationality and those who oppose it within the moral camp. The consensus in Israel is that the vindictive denouncers of the idea of binationality see in it an argument for the abolition of the Jewish state, a spearhead of anti-Zionism and hence of anti-Semitism. "People try to make it an absolute bogey," says Amnon Raz-Krakotzkin, professor of Judaism at Beer Sheva University and one of the most brilliant spokesmen for binationalism, a man who admires both Azmi

Bishara, the Arab nationalist representative in the Knesset, and Rabbi Arieh Deri, former leader of the Orthodox Sephardic party Shas. "Those who scorn us," he says,

> invoke Zionism, but they're forgetting their own history. The binational idea was advocated by a part of the Zionist movement from the 1920s to the 1950s, often including clergy and intellectuals like Scholem, Buber, and Magnes. It was formally claimed by the Mapam Party, even if they rejected it in practice. The Jewish state as agreed to by Ben Gurion in 1947 was supposed be over 40 percent Arab. Binationality was partially inscribed in the accepted plan for partition: Haifa and Jaffa were to be ports shared by both states, which were to have a common monetary system and the like. It is hard to predict how the conflict will evolve, but binationality can go hand in hand with two states, since, on both sides, it will be very hard today to accept a single country.

"For me," he concluded, "binationality is the acceptance of equality. The end of the occupation is its primary condition. Its two pillars are the recognition of U.N. Resolution 194 and the Palestinians' recognition of the rights of the Jews in Israel. On this basis we can build a common future, which history will define. But 'common' means that Israel will have to change its entire relationship to itself and its environment."[18]

This vision may be considered realistic or utopian, but, as voiced by Yossi Beilin and Ami Ayalon, for whom separation is key to preserving Israel's identity as a Jewish state, it is based on the notion that peace will come about through equality or not at all.

EQUALITY, ETHICS, AND MORALITY

Rejection of the present-day inequality and its consequences is by far the most common denominator in the moral camp. "Everything we're doing, everything, everything, is shameful; we're humiliating the Palestinians as individuals and as a collectivity. None of us could endure what we're making them go through," said Avraham Shalom,[19] former head of the internal security services. The shame is revealed every day in public speeches: "Under Moshe Yaalon, the IDF has lost all sense of ethics and morality," said Shmuel Toledano, once number two man in Mossad, in front of a thousand former superior officers and high-ranking agents of Shin Bet and Mossad.[20]

When General Yaalon succeeded Shaul Mofaz as chief of staff, Uri Avnery was reminded of a wonderful Jewish story. The rich guy in the shtetl has just died. Someone has to deliver the eulogy, but everyone refuses, since the man was despicable. The rabbi, in accordance with his role, is insistent: "My dear friends, all of you knew the deceased," he says. "You know as well as I do how greedy, stingy, cruel, disdainful, deceitful he was, and I could go on and on. But I'll tell you one good thing: compared to his son, who's here with us, he was an angel!"

According to the writer Sami Mikhael, "This conflict is corrupting us, destroying liberal, democratic values. Saying we're at war is just as stupid as saying there's a war between an elephant and a fly. We're a military power facing an occupied people."[21] And Professor Avishai Margalit of Hebrew University, author of a book called *The Decent Society*, said this: "We sometimes talk about Arab or Oriental honor and dignity. But the humiliations coming from the territories aren't about attacks on [people's] dignity as Arabs but as human beings." Margalit was reacting to cases in which soldiers shaved the heads of young people violating the curfew and a case in which a soldier had asked a Palestinian to choose the bone to be broken: "an arm, a leg, or a rib."[22]

Sometimes it is a minor incident that triggers this shame. "The three women soldiers who detained an old Palestinian on the main street of the German Colony in West Jerusalem didn't hit him; they didn't spit at him or kick him or shove him against a wall with the butt of a rifle, but there was something in the behavior of these three girls, border policewomen in uniform, detaining an old Palestinian on a narrow stretch of a main street in Jerusalem that made me pause," writes Batya Gur (2003).

> It was something undefined and awful, an evil, whose ripples forced me to return and take a second, more focused look at what was happening. The old man, a tall Arab of about 70, wearing a traditional

white keffiyeh, [had] an expression of disorientation and meek acceptance on his face. . . . One of [the soldiers] was holding the documents the Palestinian had handed them . . . and was talking on her mobile phone about personal matters, while the two others chatted and laughed . . .

This went on for a long while. I had seen them standing with him about half an hour earlier, on my way to the neighborhood grocery store. The soldiers were having a good time. And the old man stood there helpless, his face expressing the knowledge that he would have to wait until they finally decided to pay attention to him. . . . This was not one of the greater and more visible evils that take place around us daily, nor was it a disaster, only an insidious and consuming evil, one that is hard to pinpoint and define in words. . . . [It] was the glittering, sharp tip of a force of nature: the destructive power that has been penned up in the all-powerful authority of 18- and 19-year-old men and women. This power which we, the Jewish citizens of the state of Israel, have put in the hands of our children, the second and third generation of a very long occupation.

The author describes how she intervened, asking the soldiers to attend to the old gentleman. But they called the police, who arrested her

for disturbing a policewoman in the line of duty: "Move it lady, get in the car," yelled the pierced-tongued girl with victorious glee. That tiny stud, that shining metal bead, . . . in any other context would have been mischievous coquetry. . . . The glittering bead at the tip of her tongue, combined with the uniform, attest to the complete opposite: For her the uniform was a permit to do whatever she wanted. The glittering tip of her assaulting tongue is the tip of what we have become. . . . Time and again, every day and every hour, we see how we have turned our children into soldiers in hobnailed boots.

Sometimes it is the parents of young people killed in terrorist attacks who rebel:

My beloved son Arik, my own flesh and blood, was murdered by Palestinians. . . . Ethics have to be free of vengefulness and rashness. . . .
We lost sight of our ethics long before the suicide bombings. The
breaking point was when we started to control another nation. My
son Arik was born into a democracy, with a chance for a decent,
settled life. Arik's killer was born into an appalling occupation, into
an ethical chaos. Had my son had been born in his stead, he may
have ended up doing the same.

These words were spoken by Yitzhak Frankenthal, president of The Parents Circle, a group of families of victims of Palestinian attacks, in the
summer of 2002.[23]

Occasionally a very small minority of clergy express outrage: "The underlying question is the face of the other, the acceptance of the other. In
this case, does the Palestinian have a face? For me this is the key problem.
What insane logic is supposed to make us believe that we'll gain security by
multiplying the number of innocent victims? A politics of destruction and
manhunting is a form of suicide," exclaims Rabbi Daniel Epstein,[24] the
translator of the philosopher Emmanuel Levinas into Hebrew. This idea
of a suicidal course is becoming increasingly prominent in the moral camp.
No one within the historical consensus has expressed it with greater force
than Avraham Burg, the former Labor president of the Knesset: "We are
neither an evil state nor an evil society," said Burg in a 2003 interview, "but
we have lost the sense of evil. We no longer feel or see. I don't think we can
continue saying that beauty and morality are on our side because we were
persecuted for two thousand years. Today we are bad, frankly bad."[25]

Shortly before this, Burg, a former president of the Jewish Agency, the
son of one of the great families of religious Zionism, and himself a staunch
Zionist, had harshly condemned this perspective, which haunts him:
"Today the Israeli nation is nothing more than a shapeless heap of corruption, oppression, and injustice. Even if the Arabs bent their heads and
swallowed their humiliation, the moment will come when nothing will
work anymore. Any edifice built on another person's suffering is bound
to collapse."[26] In the interview referred to above, he continued this theme:

"We are at a crossroads. One path leads to destruction, the other to salvation and renewal. But the distance between these two paths is getting smaller. The threat of destruction is more concrete than ever."

Virtually all these Israelis believe themselves to be patriots. Their attachment to Israel cannot be contested. "The idea that this could end in a new expulsion of the Palestinians terrifies me," says Tom Segev. "As an Israeli, this would be my red line, the point in time when I'd stop identifying with this state."[27] As we can see, this is a distant prospect. Segev's country would have to reach the extreme limits before this famous historian-journalist would separate himself from it. Yet what his words show is that Israelis like him are finding it increasingly painful to identify with the acts committed in their name.

THE "SOFT UNDERBELLY" AND THE TEMPTATION TO LEAVE

Between the two poles of highly unequal power, the army and the settlers at one end, the moral camp at the other, the rank and file of Israelis—the "soft underbelly," as the sociologist Uri Ram calls it[28]—remains disoriented, hovering between a growing ethnicism and the hope for a normal, tranquil, and prosperous life. Most people, motivated by the urgent need to defend a state they perceive as aggressed against and misunderstood, are desperately eager to preserve a prestigious image of the country. Another Jewish joke:

— In one word, how are you?
— In one word? Fine.
— No, no, you can use two words to say it.
— In two words: Not fine.

How is Israel? Fine and not fine. Never before has the balance of power with its enemy been so strongly in its favor. The army has managed to fragment Palestinian society systematically to the point where it is at the brink of chaos. With regard to security, the imprisonment of the Palestin-

ians in Gaza and the construction of the wall on the West Bank are proving effective. Ariel Sharon and his successors could not dream of a more
compatible partnership than the one they enjoy with the Bush administration. Daily life under the occupation is certainly much less oppressive
than what Vladimir Putin has ordered for Chechnya, although it has more
media exposure by far. Yet even in the absence of silence the Israeli army
operates with the same impunity.

Moreover, the crisis undermining the country seems to be deeper
than ever. "Ask your children which of them is sure to be living here in
twenty-five years. The most perceptive answers may well shock you,
because the countdown has begun," wrote a desperate Avraham Burg.[29]
In 2002 a poll commissioned by the magazine *Kedma* showed that
25 percent of Israelis between the ages of 18 and 29 and 16 percent of
those between 30 and 39 "were thinking in pragmatic terms of the possibility of leaving Israel." Noting that there were more Palestinians under
the age of 10 than there were Israeli Jews on the shared territory of
Israel–Palestine, the sociologist Shalom Shittrit, commenting on the
study, wrote: "Disbanding the settlements and evacuating the settlers to
the area behind the 1967 borders is the solution Israel will beg to be
offered after another twenty years of occupation, or apartheid, when the
country will have become old, internally fragmented, and a great laun-
derer of dirty linen."[30]

Corruption, the failure of the rule of law, and societal violence: these
are recurrent themes in the Israeli media. The police worry periodically
about the porosity of the banking system, which pays little attention to the
origin of funds as long as they come with the label *new immigrant*, allowing the system to be enriched by mafia networks, particularly Russian ones.
The number of people seeking a thousand ways to escape the draft is increasing rapidly, a new phenomenon in a country in which military service has always been both a duty and a certificate of entry into active life.
Half of the draft evaders have social motives, the others ideological ones.
They disguise their refusal to enlist as chronic back trouble or major de-
pression. In 2002 General Gil Regev, head of personnel for the general
staff, noted a "great increase in the number of deserters" among draftees.[31]
Haaretz indicated that the rate of desertion grew by 7 percent in 1999,

and 31 percent in 2000, approaching 40 percent in 2001 and, according to military police, reaching 67 percent in 2002.[32]

Alongside intensive efforts to promote the *aliyah* ("ascent") of Jews from the diaspora to Israel, the most taboo issue in the land is the relative number of the *yordim*, those who are leaving the country, compared to the *olim*, those immigrating there. In the nearly sixty years of its existence, around 2.5 million Jews have come to live in Israel, and around one million have left. How many are leaving at present, and how many are moving in? Who are they? It is impossible to know the precise numbers, just as it is hard to distinguish those who are leaving for good from those who leave with the thought of returning someday because they are patriotic. The latter either return or they remain Israeli patriots — abroad.

"Departures from Israel are reaching gigantic proportions," announced *Yediot Ahronot* on July 20, 2003, a popular daily newspaper known for its spectacular headlines. All one has to do is walk in the East Village area of Manhattan to get a sense of how large this phenomenon is: around St. Mark's Place Hebrew is heard as often as English. These Israelis are almost always young, between 20 and 30. In comparison with the 5.2 million Jewish inhabitants in Israel, the number of Israelis listed as being in the United States has risen to 488,000. All in all, Israeli consular services put the number of *yordim* at 650,000, or about 12.5 percent of the Jewish population of the country. In reality the proportion is even higher, since the statistics count only those over 18 who have been away for at least four years without returning even for a vacation, while the number of those who are staying abroad without registering with their consulates is not known.

Who are the new *yordim*? Often they are sabras, born in the country, generally with a solid educational background (a high-school diploma or more), almost always secular, and strongly individualistic. In short, they are the most global in outlook, the least inclined to the sanctification of the Holy Land or the mystique of Jewish election. They often lived on the seacoast between Tel Aviv and Haifa. The historian Shlomo Sand has said of them that "if they constituted all of Israel, a peace accord would have been signed a long time ago."[33] They are not necessarily great progressives, and some are highly anti-Arab. They often live abroad feeling nostalgic for Israel.

But the lack of any prospect for a normal life in their country outweighs the physical or cultural attachment they feel for it. The phenomenon is not unique; globalization has everywhere led to a brain drain in the direction of rich countries. But this trend is very important in a country that is developed and at war, a country in which patriotism has always been a shared virtue.

In January 2002 Yossi Beilin spoke of the flight of the offspring of "beautiful Israel," the social stratum holding the reins of the country, families living there since the time of the *yishuv*. *Yediot Ahronot* decided to look into this more closely. To his dismay, under the title "The Parents are Running the Country; the Children are Overseas,"[34] the reporter determined that two sons of Minister Roni Milo (a right-wing moderate) were living in New York. Tali, daughter of Defense Minister Benyamin Ben Eliezer (a Labor hawk), was also in the United States. Yitzhak Rabin's son Yuval had settled in Washington. Orit, granddaughter of former prime minister Menahem Begin, had also left Israel. Ehud Barak had recently known the joy of becoming a grandfather; his daughter Michal had given birth in New York, where she lives with her husband. Ygal, the son of former defense minister Moshe Arens of Likud, lives in Los Angeles. The lawyer Yoel Herzog, son of former president Haim Herzog, had opted for Geneva. The list included a number of children of members of parliament and generals living in the West. Right and left wings were equally represented. The newspaper recalled that Alon Ben Gurion, grandson of David Ben Gurion, the father of the nation, was the director of the Waldorf Astoria hotel in New York.

As often happens in such cases, Beilin was accused of sapping the morale of the country by attacking its image. "Israel is a free country," he replied. "Whoever decides to emigrate doesn't become a failure, as I see it, and his parents don't have to apologize. The real debate is this: Isn't the government's policy, apart from reinforcing serious phenomena like the refusal of officers to serve in the territories or of young people to enlist in the army, giving rise to the most silent refusal of all, the refusal of those who are leaving?" And indeed, the departure of these young people does reveal something profound and complex. Many of them, in a vague way that is more social than political, can't see themselves living in a country where, as Ariel Sharon suggested, their "children and grandchildren will still know war." To Sharon's great displeasure, they have lost the determination of the generation of 1948, a determination recovered by the settlers of Greater Israel. "The danger," says David Grossman, "is not terrorism, which will never manage to bring us down. It's that our young people don't envision a normal life." [35] And it also lies in the fact that many parents of these young people do not look askance at their children's departure as long as this situation lasts.

Israel had already experienced two major phases of departure, in 1954–1956 and 1964–1966, due to economic recessions. This was the case in 2002–2004 as well. In the development town of Kiryat Malakhi, where the rate of unemployment was especially high, a young man of 18 told me in 2002, "If I don't make it as a career soldier, I'm out of here." [36] What the current departures reveal is a feeling that is seldom explicit yet runs very deep. How long will this Israel be able to exist in its environment? How long will it be able to keep the other population imprisoned behind walls and imprison itself within its own walls even as it arouses such great hatred? "Go to the Polish consulate," said David Grossman, "and you'll see people waiting in line to get Polish citizenship so as to have a European passport. What an absurd irony! We, who exist through a miracle of history, are wasting that miracle in a criminal fashion. As long as there is no prospect of normal life on the horizon, this phenomenon will increase." [37] "A race for passports is stimulating imaginations," wrote the correspondent for Le Monde. [38] Israelis born not only in Poland but also in the Czech Republic, Hungary, Lithuania, Romania, and Bulgaria, countries that have joined the European Union, are rushing en masse to their consulates to try to get dual nationality. According to an investigation by the Israeli institute Dahaf, more than 700,000 Israelis may be involved. Those who have already made such a request are said to number 140,000.

After filing his application, Mordekhai Gil, an Israeli who was born in Poland in 1940 and survived the Shoah, told Yediot Ahronot: "I love Israel and have no plans to leave, but, the situation being what it is, who knows what tomorrow will bring. Why not enjoy the advantages of the European Union? That can't hurt anyone." [39] Who knows what tomorrow will bring:

some people will no doubt see in these words proof that the Israeli is truly the modern figure of the Jewish outcast. Others, however, will see in them the failure of an ideology that had set out to provide these outcasts with a safe homeland but is now offering them the prospect of permanent war and the impossibility of a life, on the same territory, shared with a population of local outcasts who are just as numerous. More prosaically, the race for European passports reveals an inexpressible lack of confidence in the future of this state such as it is.

What of the others, the great mass of those who do not leave but still do not subscribe to the ideology of the settlers? They continue to live, love, and suffer in Israel, entrenching themselves in a fortress mentality. They protect themselves inwardly in the face of the most serious signs of brutalization, evading the reality of the occupation in voluntary or half-conscious ignorance of the facts and leaning more or less strongly toward one of the two fundamental poles, sometimes toward both in turn. Motivated by ethnicism, they protect themselves by focusing on the faults of the opposite side—the brutishness of terrorism, the corruption of the Palestinian Authority—and on the incomprehensible incomprehension that their plight arouses in the world. After all, aren't *they* the victims?

In April 2004, just after the Jenin Affair, I called Nahum Barnea, the most famous journalist for *Yediot*, who had just advised the authorities to hurry and remove the Palestinian corpses from that city: "If Israel doesn't find a way to give them an honorable burial, these corpses will bury us," he had written, making himself the spokesman of the military hierarchy that, after Jenin, was worried that "Israel was being seen all over the world as a war criminal on the scale of the Serbs in Bosnia."[40] He replied with irritation: "Are you calling me so that you can criticize us some more? I wrote what I had to say. But you French, what did you do in Algeria? Who are you to think you can stand in judgment?" I told him that I represented neither the history of France nor his own nation and imagined the same was true of him. I admitted that he was right on one point: the Israeli repression was not making mass torture an everyday matter, sending hundreds of thousands of people to detention camps, or bombing entire towns, as the French Army had done in Algeria. But, I added, his argument surprised me. What would be said of a man charged with a crime who proclaimed that his neighbor had committed crimes that were much more serious than his? Any court would consider this type of defense an admission of guilt.

"Right, right," said Barnea, calming down a bit. Then he once again became aggressive: "But you say that we're Nazis! The country is at war, for God's sake. Don't you understand?" I replied that I had never written any such thing, that my newspaper had never compared the IDF to the SS. I added that, here too, the argument struck me as bizarre, as though there were only two categories, Nazis and non-Nazis, the latter having no grounds for self-reproach. Between acting like a Nazi and being pure as the driven snow, I said, there was the whole range of human crime, from the minor to the very serious. One can be a criminal without automatically being a Nazi. "OK, OK, I know all that," he replied. "So what do you want to talk about?" Making himself available, often with a great deal of humor and excellent information, he then kept me on the phone for over an hour.

When Barnea's son was killed in a 1996 attack, this man, who tends to be on the political center-right, wrote a deeply moving public letter to him, thanking him for having convinced him of the benefits of the peace process. Among journalists he is known as a sponge, that is, he senses the situations, the states of mind, and the questionings of his compatriots. In his initial reaction to my phone call he showed the typically Israeli reflex in which, when someone is afraid of being reproached for unacceptable acts, he justifies himself in a way that seems very childish: "Other people do worse, and no one holds it against them."

You run into this kind of argument all the time in Israeli conversations: "What did the French do in Algeria? The Americans in Vietnam? The Russians in the countries they conquered? The English more or less everywhere, beginning with Palestine?" and so forth. This is a way of concealing one's own acts—"In comparative terms, what we're doing to the Palestinians is small potatoes, so stop criticizing us!"—and going right ahead with the agenda. Barnea also showed the second reflex, extremely widespread in Israel, a reflex that is related to the first and consists in turning Nazism into the sole reference point for criminal acts; since none of the crimes committed by the Israeli army reaches the level of Nazi barbarity, it follows that they are minor, not really crimes at all.

FIFTEEN

"THE HIDDEN PLOT OF OUR LIVES"
Competing for Victimhood

ISRAELIS, NAZISM, AND THE SHOAH

Five years ago, on January 28, 2002, I interviewed Gilead Sher, the former chief adviser to Ehud Barak. By now enough time has passed for me to feel free to relate this anecdote. As he was painting a very harsh portrait of the policies of Ariel Sharon, who had been in power for nearly a year, I pointed out: "But he was elected democratically to carry out such a policy," and I added, "and by a vast majority." "So what?" he replied. "Hitler, too, was democratically elected." Then, as he noticed that I was taking down what he had been saying, he interrupted himself: "Hey, no way. You're not going to publish that I compared Sharon and Hitler in your paper." I reassured him, saying that if he did not mean it I would certainly not publish his statement in *Le Monde*. But, I suggested, this seemed to be a comparison that had occurred rather spontaneously. "Well, sure," he replied. "That's how we Israelis are. The Nazis, the Shoah, that's our natural reference point for evil, for the negative. That's how it is. You personally should understand this."[1]

Yes, "that's how it is" in Israel. But it is a phenomenon that has always astonished me on account of its inconsistency: on the one hand, the Israelis hold Jewish suffering as sacrosanct and unique; on the other, they trivialize the Nazi universe by making it an everyday point of reference.

It's often thought that only someone like Yeshaayahu Leibowitz (1903–1994), a religious Zionist philosopher with an especially sharp tongue, would dare to call the rivals of the Bloc of the Faithful "Judeo-Nazis." But this is incorrect. From the decade 1940–1950 up to the early 1960s, during the time of Israeli negotiations with Germany on the indemnification of victims of the Shoah, with compensation paid to Israel as the sole collective legatee, both Menahem Begin, the opposition leader opposed to indemnification, and Prime Minister David Ben Gurion called one another "little Nazi," "Judenrat," "kapo," and the like, even in the Knesset.

This tendency to bring in Nazism on any occasion is by no means confined to politics. It is an amazingly everyday practice. The Shoah is a singular event, but the Nazi reference is made constantly, on the right and the left, and in all social classes. I have heard the infuriated owner of a car mutter *"khatikhat natzit,"* literally, "piece of Nazi" to the meter maid who had just written him up for parking illegally. For the Israelis "Nazi" has become an unremarkable synonym for "bastard," "stupid jerk," and the like. The Nazi is the bad guy, anyone who has it in for you.

At least this is the case among Jews. For there is a subject where any reference to Nazism instantly arouses rage: the domain of the repression of the Palestinians. When the writer Batya Gur (2003) intervened in favor of the old Arab that the two women soldiers were holding at their mercy (see Chapter 14, pp. 401–402), the spontaneous referent mentioned by Gilead Sher came up clearly: "The hidden plot of our lives, a plot that was engraved in us, was exposed suddenly in its full banality and in its truth," Gur wrote. "I found myself saying that I refuse to feel like a German walking past an abused Jew in Nazi Germany and turn away indifferently or fearfully. 'You're calling us Nazis!' shrieked the soldiers, and in moments this word became a precious possession upon their lips. They rejoiced in their justice, and I could already imagine all the self-righteous people gloating over the use of this word." This parallels my discussion with Nahum Barnea, because if the soldiers could *not* be compared to Nazis, they weren't doing anything reprehensible; in fact, they were within their rights.

After 1945, for an entire generation in Israel the Shoah was marginalized in favor of the heroic resisters against Nazi terror who came from the

Zionist youth movements. But beginning in the 1970s the memory of the extermination of the Jews gradually took over in the realm of education and became a concern for intellectuals in Israel. This is not a unique phenomenon. The Belgian scholar Jean-Michel Chaumont (2002) had analyzed how, throughout the West, the central focus on the prisoner interned in a concentration camp has gradually given way to that of the resistance fighter captured while still armed, and that in turn to the person without social standing who is sent to death solely on account of his identity, almost always Jewish. More generally, the interest in the great crimes against humanity—the Shoah, the Gulag, and the Chinese Laogai, along with the enslavement of Blacks and the massacre of the Indians—and the accompanying work of memory, are recent phenomena. But in Israel this shift has taken on much larger proportions and significance. As Tom Segev (2001) notes, "In the 1980s, the Shoah emerged as an essential element in Israeli identity, culture, and politics."

Segev, the author of an exhaustive study (1993) of the attitude of the *yishuv* toward the extermination of the Jews in Europe and that of Israeli society toward the survivors, sees the Eichmann trial of 1963 as the first turning point. "Before the trial, the Shoah was an almost complete taboo. . . . Horror, guilt, and shame shrouded [it] in a big silence" (Segev 2001). Many young Israelis, he writes, asked why the Jews had not defended themselves, letting themselves be led like lambs to the slaughter. In the initial phase of the construction of the Hebrew state, education focused on the emergence of the "new" Jew, strong, able to defend himself and impose his will, and generations of sabras came to view their parents with scorn, condemning their weakness as characteristic of the diaspora, in accordance with the attitude of the national movement toward the Jews of the *galut* (exile). "The survivors," Segev wrote, "often accused the Israelis of indifference."

This alleged indifference, arising directly in response to the ideology aimed at forging the "new Jew," inevitably had painful consequences. All the emancipatory movements within European Jewry in the nineteenth century—Haskala, nationalists, socialists—had the escape from the status of victim as their goal. If Zionism emerged as the sole survivor, this is chiefly because the others were devastated in the Nazi years (as well as the perpetuation of anti-Semitism in what was called by Communists during the Stalinist period as "true socialism"). But aside from its historical contingencies Zionist nationalism managed to form a state because it was the vehicle of a plan to get beyond victimhood. The construction of Israel and its preservation, that is, a plan directed toward the future and not toward the impotent cult of the past, played a major role in the ability of Judaism to overcome a tragedy of the magnitude of the Shoah, to regenerate and reconstruct itself instead of succumbing to collective neurasthenia.

Why, then, did David Ben Gurion successfully undertake the capture of Adolf Eichmann, the primary official in charge of the Nazi extermination program? According to Segev (2001), Ben Gurion had three objectives. The first was to "remind the nations of the world that the Shoah put them under an obligation to support the world's one Jewish state." The second was to integrate the new Jewish immigrants from Arab and Muslim countries into the Israeli ethos. "They lived in Asia or Africa," Ben Gurion said, "and they had no idea what was being done by Hitler, so we have to explain the thing to them from square one." His aim here, according to Segev, was "to unite Israeli society in a national catharsis, gripping, purifying, and patriotic." Finally, the Eichmann trial was intended to "counterbalance the historical charge that the Zionist movement under Ben Gurion had not done all it could to save the Jews of Europe, and to prove that the prime minister and his government were not indifferent to the Shoah, in spite of their efforts to establish close economic and military ties with Germany," an accusation that was then still frequently being made against Labor Party leaders by the nationalist right.

By bringing the Shoah into the heart of the country's concerns, the Israeli authorities generated a wide variety of consequences. On the highly positive side, the first message received was that the sabras had to stop being ashamed of their parents. After the Eichmann trial Moshe Dayan, the most famous soldier born in the land of Israel, made the rounds of Israeli high schools. Having enlisted in the British Army, he had taken part in the Italian campaign of 1944–1945, by the end of which, he told the students, his regiment had captured a thousand SS men. They were cooped up, surrounded by barbed wire, with only two soldiers, armed with simple rifles, to guard them. Their shoelaces and pants buttons had been taken away, that was all. With a thousand of them against two, it would have been easy for them to try to escape. Yet these *Übermenschen* made not the slightest attempt at rebellion, because, Dayan said, they were finished, mentally destroyed. The message to the Israeli youngsters was clear. The inmates of the concentration camps hadn't been sheep led to slaughter. They had previously been placed in conditions of dehumanization and terror so enormously greater than those in which the SS "supermen" prisoners found themselves that they were already more devastated even before being sent to the camps. The dead and the survivors must not be the objects of scorn. They had been absolute victims, with not the slightest responsibility for their fate.

Segev also mentions that the interest in the past sufferings, along with the appropriation of the status of being the absolute victims of history, inculcated in generations of Israelis, accompanied the rediscovery of diasporic Judaism and its roots, which Zionism had ignored. Today this phenomenon is astounding. Although few survivors had any wish to revisit the places of their martyrdom, or even the places they had lived before that, pilgrimages to Auschwitz, organized and actively encouraged by the authorities, as well as journeys made by individuals bringing their families to the cities and towns throughout Eastern Europe where their parents or grandparents used to live, are more important than ever before in Israel. The fall of the Berlin Wall has, to be sure, made this easier. But the sheer size of the phenomenon is remarkable. Segev also notes that, in Israel, this rediscovery of the diasporic Judaism of the past has gone hand in hand with the increase in religious fervor and mysticism, and, more generally, with a movement of return to tradition. But only to a certain degree. For in fact, among secularists, who have less attachment to traditional values, the Shoah plays an even more important identitarian role.

It is this identitarian function that explains both the tendency to transform the genocide of the Jews into an almost ahistorical and inexplicable event because it is seen as inconceivable, and the opposite tendency to trivialize references to Nazism in daily life to the utmost extent.

APPROPRIATION OF THE MEMORY
OF SUFFERING

The reemergence of deep traumas from the past and the wish to inscribe them in an identity, be it national, religious, or social, are a contemporary fact associated with the evaluation of the Second World War. The Geneva Convention of 1949 established the recognition of civilian victims in international law. Since that time the memory of suffering has become an intrinsic part of political, social, and cultural concerns on a global scale. The Jews, as well as the Armenians, the Gypsies, the descendants of Black slaves, colonized peoples, and many others who carry within them the memory of their sufferings, have risen up publicly.

In itself, the recognition of victims and their rights is a sign of democratic progress. The critical aspect at stake here, however, concerns the way in which this work of memory is carried out and the way this memory becomes part of the new identity. From this point of view, the issue for the Jewish survivors and their descendants — for this memory of suffering spreads through a thousand channels, including silence, far beyond the first generation — is not different from what others have had to deal with.

Generally speaking, the status of this memory is subject to an external threat and an internal risk. The threat is that of pure denial or less easily confirmed forms of negation — the concealment of facts or their minimization. The risk is that of exclusive appropriation placed in the service of unjustified ends. Both phenomena are, unfortunately, very common and very dangerous.

It is hard to imagine a real reconciliation of the Armenians with the Turks as long as the latter continue to deny or minimize the mass extermination they carried out against the former at the beginning of the twentieth century. We have also seen the way in which Japan, in its history textbooks and its official position, continues to evade responsibility for the crimes committed by its troops in China and Korea during their conquests. The absence of the work of memory on the significance of the Gulag is an obstacle to Russia's attainment of modernity and moreover acts as a support for the type of government established by Vladimir Putin and the war waged in Chechnya. With regard to concealment, Polish president

Lech Walesa delivered an astonishing speech at the site of Auschwitz on the fiftieth anniversary of its liberation. Before an audience of heads of state, government officials, and international delegates, he achieved the feat of speaking for an hour about the universal meaning of what had taken place there without once uttering the word *Jew*.

The tendency to appropriate the memory of suffering in the service of unworthy ends is likewise very common. What is President Mugabe of Zimbabwe saying when he undertakes a so-called agrarian reform that is a farce, the destruction of a nation's agriculture by the expropriation of white farmers in order to distribute their land to his clan, generals, and high officials? Whoever criticizes his decision is immediately termed a supporter of apartheid. Mugabe claims that he is waging a battle "in the name of the ancestors, the people oppressed by the whites for years."[2]

What did the Algerian generals say in the 1990s to cover up the massacres and disappearances? They attributed all of them to Islamists, during the "dirty war" with them in their country. Anyone who expressed the slightest doubt found himself pilloried, accused of furthering the interests of colonialism and forgetting the million dead of the Algerian War, those martyrs who shed their blood for the nation's independence.

What did Ariel Sharon say when he was threatened with being brought before a tribunal in Brussels for his responsibility in the massacre of Sabra and Shatila? That "it is the entire Jewish people"[3] who are being accused through him, with the implication that this is a clear indication of anti-Semitism. The Stalinists were longtime champions of this method. "The Great Patriotic War against Hitler and his 16 million dead" was the leitmotiv they used to counter any criticism, any mention of the Gulag or the German–Soviet Pact. In France, the French Communist Party called itself the party of the 75,000 people who were shot to death giving their blood for the Liberation. Past suffering served as a wall of protection for the party, silencing doubts within it and discrediting all criticism from without.

For its proponents this method has two advantages: it encloses its supporters in a fortress mentality, guaranteeing their adherence and intimidating them with the risk that would be incurred with a rupture (exclusion from the group and isolation). It also makes it possible to delegitimize criticism, either by avoiding discussion of the facts or by purely and simply denying them and directing a torrent of abuse concerning the pathology toward whoever reveals these facts and the evil intent of his actions. For years anyone who attacked the Communists was first called an enemy of the working class and then soon thereafter a fascist. So it goes with the recurrent tendency to view any critic of Israel, regardless of the facts on which his criticism is based, as an anti-Semite, avowed or disguised, and, when he is a Jew, as a non-Jewish Jew full of self-hatred.

Self-centered ethnicism is always fond of such speculation. The political appropriation of the memory of past suffering and its use as a means to perverse ends sometimes goes as far as the actual rewriting of history. Those who followed the course of the wars in the Balkans in the 1990s know the extent to which propaganda from Belgrade, contrary to the obvious historical facts, insisted that only the Serbs were oppressed by the Nazis in Yugoslavia during World War Two. The Milosevic regime and the Tchetniks of Seselj never missed an opportunity to recall the establishment of the fascist Ustash government in Croatia and the existence of a Bosnian SS division, in order to canonize the Serbs as the sole victims of Nazism and the only people to resist in Yugoslavia, forgetting about the nature of their government at the time and the deportation of the Jews of Serbia.

The linchpin of this mechanism is the claim of the uniqueness of one's own victim status, and it is the way in which those making the claim endow themselves with the legitimacy, prerogatives, and impunity they deny to others. In the case of Serbia, it was used in the service of ethnic cleansing. In the case of Israel, the truly singular magnitude of the crime committed against the Jews gives those who argue for the uniqueness of the Shoah an unequaled strength of conviction, one that plays a large role in setting up the mental walls behind which so many Israelis are imprisoned: the belief that they are the ones who are aggressed against, excusing the demonization of the Palestinian opponent, and offering a permanent self-justification.

The debate about whether the genocide of the Jews was unique is largely devoid of interest. The Shoah both was and was not unique. To be sure, it was singular and unprecedented, both in the way it unfolded and the way in which the putting to death of a specific population was planned and industrialized. At the same time, this genocide was an act perpetrated by human beings against other human beings, as was the enslavement of Blacks, the Spanish–Portuguese genocide of the Indians, the massacre and mutilation of Blacks in the Congo by hired killers at the behest of King Leopold of Belgium, and the Gulag, among many other examples. Its uniqueness does not place the Shoah outside of human history. Like all mass crimes, it may legitimately be compared to others, if only to understand what cannot be compared.

This debate about uniqueness is ultimately of interest only because of the issues it reveals. When Jean-Marie Le Pen announced that the extermination of the Jews was merely "a detail of World War Two" and created fewer victims than the Gulag, his aim was to reestablish the legitimacy of anti-Semitic feeling in France and to shift attention from the Nazis' crimes to those of the Communists. The opposite occurred in 1950–1960, when the Communist parties made it their mission to take over the organizations representing the victims of Nazism: by claiming that the Nazis' crimes were unique and incomparable, they hoped to turn attention away from the Gulag.

In Israel the claim of the uniqueness of the Shoah is associated with nationalism and, for a generation, has paralleled the increase in mysticism, as this brings with it the claim of impunity and lends it legitimacy. As a student in Jerusalem in 1969 I went to hear a lecture by the writer Amos Oz. The mind-set of the average Israeli, Oz said, was this: for two thousand years we have been the victims of pogroms, which culminated in genocide. So if by chance we happen to commit a pogrom, no one is going to pick a quarrel with us. And anyway, who would dare to reproach us?

That was thirty-six years ago. Since then the repression of the Palestinians has grown markedly, as has the role of the Shoah in the Israelis' collective identity, and the attitude Oz was condemning has become further entrenched. "I don't think we can continue to say that beauty and morality are on our side because we experienced a genocide sixty years ago," says Avraham Burg, the former president of the Jewish Agency, going against the tide.[4]

For a long time I have been shocked by the political appropriation of the memory of the Shoah. Among the victims of the genocide of the Jews some were Zionists, others anti-Zionists; some were Communists, others Bundists or on the far right; a great many were religious, others atheists; and many were assimilated or hoped to see their children become so, but none were exterminated by the *Einsatzgruppen* or sent to Belzec, Sobibor, or Treblinka for their opinions. All—women, men, babies, children, and old people—were dealt with this way on account of their identity alone: they were Jews or designated as such by the Nazis. Their only crime was their existence.

When I was a young Zionist activist during the 1960s I was vaguely disturbed when I saw the Zionist-Socialist movements, the ultranationalist Betar, the Jewish Communists, and the Bundists (Socialist supporters of Jewish cultural autonomy) separately commemorating each anniversary of the uprising in the Warsaw Ghetto. Later I came to understand the meaning of this division. No Israeli school child has ever heard of Marek Edelman, but all of them know the name of Mordekhai Anilewitz, who led the insurrection of the Jews remaining in the ghetto after the others had been deported. Yet Edelman, the only leader of the revolt to survive, was his assistant. Why was Edelman forgotten in Israel? Anilewitz had been active in Hashomer Hatzair, the most far-left of the Zionist youth movements, whereas Edelman had been a Bundist, which then meant an anti-Zionist.

Precisely because the Nazis did not differentiate among the Jews to be exterminated, the Jewish fighters had all grouped themselves together, right and left, Zionists and anti-Zionists. But when official Israeli historiography transformed the insurrection into a precursor of the advent of Israel, it excluded all reference to the Bundists and Communists among the fighters, keeping them out of textbooks. Edelman has remained largely unknown in Israel; his memoirs (Krall et al. 1986) were not translated into Hebrew until 2001, twenty-four years after their publication in Poland. His first book, *The Ghetto Fights*, which came out in Warsaw as early as 1945, was turned down by all Israeli publishers and, as the Israeli historian Idith Zertal (2004) has noted, appeared in Hebrew only in a private collection in 1981 "thanks to the stubborn perseverance of a handful of scholars resisting the exclusive imposition of the national-Israeli version of the insurrection" (p. 50). Edelman, she adds, "was not a suitable hero" (p. 51).

For a long time this exceptional insurrection was monopolized by the Zionist labor movement, with even the participation of Betar being set aside. Since then this kind of monopoly has extended to Israel's entire relation to the Shoah. The genocide of the Jews has gradually ceased being the extermination of all the Jews, the memory of which legitimately concerns all those who were affected by it directly or through familial transmission. It has become the property of the state of Israel and those who unconditionally support its politics. They alone are authorized to claim its memory. When I lived in Israel I knew survivors who were enraged beyond measure by this. Today I know children of former concentration-camp inmates who are still equally enraged.

TURNING THE SHOAH AND NAZISM INTO ABSTRACTIONS

The appropriation has several consequences. First, both Nazism and the Shoah are turned into abstractions. Nazism ceases to be a political movement with its ideological characteristics and concrete modes of action and becomes merely an indefinite, generic incarnation of the threat hanging over the Jews. As for the extermination of the Jews of Europe, it is no longer a specific human and historical tragedy but an immaterial armor, without tangible representation, of permanent victimhood. There is no other way to explain the ease with which any enemy—both the external foe and the policeman who gives you a ticket—is, absurdly, called *Nazi* in Israel, while at the same time Israelis act outraged and scandalized whenever anyone uses the same absurd analogy in describing their country.

This attitude could be said to be a further unfortunate but inevitable result of the Shoah. For likening Israel to Nazism is not just an absurdity. It is also a perversion, not invariably but often sustained by overt or latent anti-Semitism. The Israelis are right to feel outraged when the Nobel prizewinner José Saramago or the French anti-globalization activist José Bové compares the situation in Ramallah to Auschwitz. The problem is that they themselves are quite ready to use and abuse similar comparisons with regard to others. Thus many politicians and commentators do not hesitate to call Arafat the reincarnation of Hitler.

Turning the enemy into a "Nazi" is not a new practice. When Menahem Begin convened his government on June 5, 1982, to present his plan for the invasion of Lebanon as proposed by Ariel Sharon, he encountered opposition from several ministers led by the religious leader Yossef Burg. His reply was that the alternative to the invasion was Treblinka, and it had been decided that there was to be no second Treblinka.[5] When the head of Fatah in Ramallah, Marwan Barghouti, was captured, the Knesset member Tsvi Haendel applauded the arrest of the man he called the incarnation of Eichmann. The list of these comparisons to Nazism vaguely characterizing the Palestinians, the PLO, Hamas, and the like could go on and on. This invective is not just as ridiculous as Saramago's; it in fact "diminishes the scope of the atrocities committed by the Nazis, trivializing the exceptional agony of the victims and survivors," writes Idith Zertal (2004, p. 145). And it reduces Hitler, Eichmann, and Nazism to the level of a banal epiphenomenon.

The consequences within Israeli society of turning Nazism and the genocide of the Jews into abstractions can reach an appalling level. On January 25, 2002, Amir Oren, the chief expert on military matters for *Haaretz*, reported a discussion among high-ranking officers. The subject was the possible reoccupation of Palestinian cities. "In order to prepare properly for the next campaign," Oren wrote,

> one of the Israeli officers in the territories said not long ago [that if] the mission will be to seize a densely populated refugee camp, or take over the casbah in Nablus, and if the commander's obligation is to try to execute the mission without casualties on either side, then he must first analyze and internalize the lessons of earlier battles— even, however shocking it may sound, even how the German army fought in the Warsaw ghetto. . . . Many of his comrades agree that in order to save Israelis now, it is right to make use of knowledge that originated in that terrible war. . . . The Warsaw ghetto serves them only as an extreme.

Oren's article drew no comment from the IDF's spokesman. The jour-nalist later specified that Israeli generals were studying these situations from a pragmatic point of view and were not, obviously, identifying with the Nazi army. Nor with the Russian army, although Vyacheslav Ovchinnikov, former general of the special forces in Chechnya, had been invited to present his "experience" before the Israeli National Defense College.[6]

How could these high-ranking Israeli officers have "pragmatically" stud-ied the way the German army went about crushing the Warsaw Ghetto without putting their heads in their hands and asking themselves, at that moment, how such an unthinkable thought could have emerged from their brains and what it implied about the way they themselves regard the Pal-estinians? And how could officers attempting to "manage" a large num-ber of individuals held for questioning have ordered that a number be written on the arm of each Palestinian before his interrogation?[7] And yet this happened. The army spokesman justified the practice. The com-parison with the tattooing by the Nazis of a number on the arm of each concentration-camp inmate, he retorted, comes from people "who don't know history." To be sure, these arrests had nothing to do with the depor-tation of the Jews. Nevertheless, the comparison arose spontaneously in the mind of Knesset representative Tommy Lapid, who later became a minister. Lapid knows history; he is a survivor of the Shoah, and he was scandalized by the method the officers used.

Israeli generals and officers are neither dumber nor crazier than those of other armies of occupation. The assignment of numbers to civilian prisoners as they are examined is extremely common. Studying precedents before a military engagement is a conventional practice in all armies. The officers of the IDF could have found a hundred other ways to organize interrogations. Instead of Warsaw they could have studied the Battle of Algiers or a thousand other sieges in history before taking over Jenin and Nablus. What led these men, with their education and the constant refer-ence in Israel to Nazism and the Shoah, to contemplate *in addition* the methods employed by the Nazis? And to select one that, by its symbol-ism, instantly recalled them? And to do so without seeing anything wrong with it?

One major reason surely lies in the way Nazism and the Jewish extermination in Europe have been reduced to abstractions. Viewed as a symbol—the acme of universal and historical hatred of the Jews—this representation of Nazism tones down its concrete political reality, emptying it of precise content and separating it from its roots, its general ideology, the sociohistorical conditions of its accession to power, and their manifestations. Nazism becomes solely a matter of hatred of the Jews. Similarly, the Shoah ceases to be an elaborate process of subjugation and planned destruction, one that had a beginning and proceeded gradually to establish mechanisms of dehumanization, from the imprisonment in ghettos of starving and socially fragmented people to the final culmination of the gas chambers. It becomes "the wrong that was done to us," an ahistorical wrong and an incomparable one, but one that is not viewed in the context of many of its specific practices other than the gas chambers. Thus the vast majority of Israelis cannot imagine comparing it to anything else. Hence in contemplating the way in which the Wehrmacht seized the Warsaw Ghetto and wrote numbers on the arms of prisoners, the Israeli officers had no context and could not see the connection. How could their pragmatic reflection or this commonplace act be scandalous?

For the most part the experience of misfortune does not increase people's awareness of the misfortune of others. On the contrary, it leads them to fall back on themselves and their own kind, treating others with indifference and even with aggression. So it is with the Israelis. It isn't hard to find Israelis saying, "The Palestinians are suffering? What do they know about suffering? We're the ones who know what it is."

Among Israelis who resist this attitude, however, the reference to Nazism and the Shoah occurs just as often, but with exactly the opposite effect. They develop a heightened sensitivity to others' suffering, precisely because it evokes what they are carrying within themselves. Again, it is not only Israelis who react in this way. But such reactions are especially intense for them, because the Shoah was a crime outside all norms.

It is no longer possible to count the times politicians, writers, intellectuals, and artists refer to Nazism in order to stigmatize, not the Palestinians, but the brutality of their own oppression and the accompanying indifference. Writing in the literary supplement to *Haaretz*, Gideon Levy (2003) provoked outrage when he advised readers to think about what a book by the German historian Sebastian Haffner, recently translated into Hebrew, had to say about the way Weimar Germany had imperceptibly turned into the Third Reich. When the sociologist Baruch Kimmerling (2003) published a book on Ariel Sharon's policies with regard to the Palestinians, he called it *Politicide*. Professor Amnon Raz-Krakotzkin used the term *sociocide* to characterize the systematic destruction of Palestinian society.[8] In both cases the suffix -*cide* automatically brings genocide to mind.

When the writer B. Mikhael, the son of Shoah survivors, learned that numbers had been written on the arms of Palestinians held for questioning, he exclaimed that "in sixty years' time the Israelis had gone from being the ones marked and numbered to the ones doing the marking and numbering, from prisoners to jailers, from those being forced to march with their hands up to those making others do such marching. Nothing, he concluded, had been learned, nothing taken to heart in those sixty years; everything had been forgotten."[9] We may recall the way Batya Gur almost automatically compared the situation of an elderly Palestinian, humiliated in the street by two women soldiers, to that of a Jew called in for questioning at the beginning of the Hitler regime in Germany.

Shulamit Aloni (2003), former minister in the Rabin government, is haunted by the indifference of her people to the suffering of the Palestinians. "There is no one fixed method for genocide" she wrote on the day following especially savage atrocities.

> How is it possible to explain the expulsion of citizens from their homes at three o'clock in the morning on a rainy night, then depositing bombs in the house and then departing without warning? When those expelled returned to their home, the bombs were exploded and a brutal murder and destruction of property was thus committed. . . . [Israeli soldiers] enter a village, they kill, they destroy and they arrest, and then they retreat. Those who remain on the ashes and the ruins will take care of themselves. . . . [As] one of the smart generals told me, we do not have crematoria and gas chambers. Is anything less than that consistent with Jewish ethics? Did he ever hear how an entire people said that it did not know what was done in its name?

Attacked from all sides, Aloni explained herself in an interview.[10]

> These days you meet people around the country who say: "I don't
> want to know, I have given up reading the papers." Do you know
> how many people are unwilling to read Gideon Levy and Amira Hass
> [*Haaretz* reporters in the Occupied Territories] because they sim-
> ply don't want to know what is happening there? They do not deny
> the accuracy of these two journalists' articles, but they simply don't
> want to know. . . . We have always angrily and justly rejected the
> Germans' claim that they "did not know." They simply didn't want
> to know. . . .
>
> Our society is being undermined by gross insensitivity and by adu-
> lation of force. I am disturbed by our moral disintegration. I am dis-
> turbed by the arrogant and light-hearted way in which we kill and
> murder Palestinians. . . . I cannot find any peace of mind anymore,
> when I see this Wall that we are building. We are pillaging the land
> and destroying the way of life of people who have lived in the same
> place for centuries. . . . [W]e are busy destroying greenhouses, plan-
> tations, and the vital infrastructures of three million people, and then
> pretend that we are the victims. I cannot live with the way we con-
> tinually wail that we are the victim, and do not examine our own
> morality. What is happening to us? But people remain silent so as
> not to get into trouble.

In characterizing Israeli indifference to the fate of the Palestinians,
Aloni, the former leader of the Laborite left, turned to what Gilead Sher
called the natural referent of evil, of the negative, Nazi Germany, one
that automatically comes to mind for Israelis at both ends of the political spectrum. Amira Hass (2003b), the *Haaretz* reporter who has done
the most to bring to light the daily oppression of the Palestinians, rejects the use of this referent. "The Warsaw Ghetto is different from the
'Gaza Ghetto' not merely in 'extent,' but in essence," she wrote in an
article entitled "Making Stupid Comparisons" after Oona King, a Jewish member of the British parliament, had made this connection following a visit to Gaza.

Hass, like Aloni, is discouraged by the indifference of her people, and by the fact that the use of methods employed in the crushing of the insurrection in the Warsaw Ghetto is accepted as a matter of course as a topic for military study. But, as I do, she considers the tendency to reduce everything to the universe of Nazism to be "idiotic, inappropriate, and harmful."[11] "Descriptions of Israeli control over the Palestinians," she writes,

> naturally arouse certain associations in certain Jews. A child raising both hands in the air before a soldier pointing a rifle, . . . an enormous detention center buried somewhere in the Negev. . . , with more wire fences, more watchtowers and searchlights. . . . After all, one compares in order to warn, in order to stop the deterioration. But one cannot effect change if one misdiagnoses reality. . . . It is not necessary for the very worst to happen for opposition to what is happening to be justified.

Hass is, she says, "inhabited by the Shoah" as a result of her family history. Her father was a resister in a Romanian ghetto, and her mother was deported to Bergen-Belsen, where she conducted herself admirably.[12] "The Shoah," Hass told me, "explains me. I have this wound, a sensitivity to all dehumanization, that is the mark of certain children of survivors." Her parents, she adds, "handed down to me for all time the refusal of indifference and the sense of resistance. When forty thousand people are confined to their homes for a month like animals, it gives me gooseflesh."[13] Hass was speaking at the outset of the intifada, in connection with the case of Hebron, before these detentions had subsequently spread to the Palestinian inhabitants of all the cities of the West Bank.

Nazism and the Shoah thus leave their mark, on those Israelis who go along with, as well as those who look away from, all the ways in which the Intifada is repressed, and on those who are horrified by injustice and insensitivity. This is true of Jewry all over the world, not just in Israel. For example, over the past four years comparatively few rabbis of importance, American or French, have issued any public criticism of Israel regarding the fate of the Palestinians. In the United Kingdom, however, Chief Rabbi Jonathan Sacks has publicly stated that he regards "the current situation as nothing less than tragic, because it is forcing Israel into postures that are incompatible in the long run with our deepest ideals" (cited in Freedland 2002). Claude Lanzmann, the director of the most outstanding film on the subject, has made a lifetime's work of the memory of the Shoah; he sides with the diehards in Israel. In contrast, from 1967 on Primo Levi grew uneasy about the inevitable consequences of the occupation. On June 16, 1982, along with 150 well-known Italian Jews (including Natalia Ginsburg) he signed a petition in *La Repubblica* calling for opposition to the Begin government in what was called a "tragic moment for the Palestinian people."[14]

The author of *If This Is a Man* wrote that, in Israel, "nationalist authorities are prevailing in an aggressive direction, while the internationalist aspect of Judaism is relegated to the background." In connection with Operation Peace for Galilee, waged by Begin and Sharon in 1982, he expressed his "anguish and shame": "I mistrust successes won by the detrimental use of arms. I feel scorn for whoever likens Israeli generals to Nazi generals, and yet I must admit that Begin is bringing this judgment down on himself. I maintain a deep sentimental tie to Israel, but not with that Israel." It is true that, in contrast to those who find it necessary to defend Israel come what may, expressing their criticisms or their despair only within their community so as not to lend aid and comfort to the enemy, Primo Levi was convinced "that the Jews of the diaspora have the right to guide the Israelis along the paths of wisdom and tolerance." It is also true that, as he said, his Judaism was not "Israeli-centric": "I would say that the best of Jewish culture has to do with the fact that it is polycentric." And, finally, it is true that Levi strongly denounced the way in which Menahem Begin appealed to the victimization of the Jews by the Nazis as a justification for the victimization of the Palestinians.[15]

The difference is that those intent on justifying their actions refuse to tolerate any criticism of Israel or Zionism, readily labeling such criticism a modern form of anti-Semitism in order to continue their unbending attitude and their blindness, whereas those who oppose this, equally affected by the past sufferings of the Jews, use it to deepen their sensitivity to injustice, to all unwarranted human suffering. And it makes no difference whether the author of this injustice is a Jew, although, when that is the case, at a deep level this is felt as even worse.

Many other consequences accompany the Shoah, in itself and in the partisan monopolization of its memory. The most understandable of all is the curbing of criticism, not just of Israel but of Jewish institutions in general. It is motivated by the respect due the dead, for the extermination has sanctified the past. The tragedy has made people forget that the emancipation of the Jew came about by the collapse of ghetto walls, precisely because this collapse occurred through an annihilation. A modern version of the extraordinary novel *The Brothers Ashkenazi*, written in 1936 by Israel Joshua Singer, brother of the Nobel prizewinner, is an infinitely tender account of Jewish life in Central Europe, but it is also scathingly critical of the ghetto mentality, one described as a regressive milieu, a walled prison. Today this book would be seen as almost anti-Semitic, full of self-hatred. Jewish life in prewar Eastern Europe, that engulfed civilization with its exceptional vigor, its splendid political and cultural developments but also its flaws, is considered untouchable: compassion is the only permissible response. Israel and the Jewish institutions built in the heritage of its engulfment make use of this untouchability for their own personal ends, and in so doing once again activate the withdrawal into the self symptomatic of the ghetto mentality. People forget how strongly the ghetto, walled in by its environment but also by its own leaders, was rejected—in a manner that was full of contradictions but was nevertheless collective—by all those Jews who counted as modernists, reformers, revolutionaries, emancipators, or simply honorable men.

Finally, another common effect of this appropriation of the memory of suffering is the tendency to accept any reference to Nazism (even when it pertains to Israel), so long as it is expressed by a Jew, as though this were a legitimate internal matter, and to be scandalized as soon as a non-Jew expresses the same idea. Observations appearing in the international press are termed anti-Semitic where precisely similar comments in the Israeli press are held to be justifiable. Here too we might see the enduring and understandable aftereffects of the Shoah. Yet there is a striking difference between the treatment reserved for the imbeciles who, today, compare Sharon to Hitler and the absolute impunity of Sharon and Benyamin Netanyahu, who, in the 1990s, let their supporters carry portraits of Itzhak

Rabin and Shimon Peres on which had been drawn small mustaches, and who were shown with their hair combed diagonally, and swastikas.

THE VISION OF PRESENT-DAY ANTI-SEMITISM

From the exclusive monopoly on the right to Jewish martyrdom it is only a small step toward deciding according to one's own political interests whether an opponent is anti-Semitic. Thus, when Sadat succeeded Nasser, it was immediately recalled in Israel that, as a young officer, he had had dealings with Nazi Germany. In the years 1930–1940 Egypt was under the British Protectorate, and Sadat, like many nationalists in similar situations, had come to the conclusion that the enemy of his enemy could further his emancipatory ambitions. Hence in Israeli eyes Nasser, who had been likened by Israelis to Hitler in the 1950s, was followed by a former pro-Nazi. A few years later Sadat, now the first Arab head of state to visit Jerusalem, signed a peace treaty and shared a Nobel Prize with Menahem Begin. Any reference to his alleged Nazi past was immediately forgotten.

We may smile at this, but the tendency to decide who is, or is not, a Nazi or an anti-Semite according to circumstances and political interests can also lead to absurdity. Israel's strongest supporter in the United States nowadays is the Christian Coalition of America (CCA), a powerful organ of Protestant fundamentalism founded by the preacher Pat Robertson, with three million activists, eighteen million members, and its own television channels and radio stations. Its anti-Semitic leanings are at this time completely masked by the needs of the cause. Rabbi Benny Elon, the propagandist of the transfer of the Palestinians, is their chief ally. During a visit to Israel by the CCA leadership, Elon, who accompanied them half the time, explained the motives of this alliance to me: "Historical anti-Semitism was Christian. Now it comes from Islam, which sees in Israel the advanced bastion of civilization."[16] Christians and Jews, he said, must unite in the face of this threat.

I too accompanied this visit in December 2002. Roberta Combs, the president of the CCA, had come to support the settlers in Hebron and Shiloh, the most extreme of the extremists. But she had also been received by Likud deputies and the ministers Uzi Landau and Nathan Shcharansky, all of whom congratulated her on her staunch support for the Jewish state. To my astonishment I learned that the media director for the CCA was a seasoned Israeli-American activist from Betar, Ron Torossian, who made no secret of his organization's close ties to this American movement. Ehud Olmert, at the time the Likud mayor of Jerusalem, had been the guest of honor at the CCA convention in October of that year. "God is with us, you are with us," he told the delegates in Washington. One month earlier Ariel Sharon had won a standing ovation from four thousand evangelical Christians who came to his country at the behest of the International Christian Embassy of Jerusalem, a far-right mystical organization said to be working with the Jewish Agency. Sharon wrote to the leaders of Stand for Israel, a CCA affiliate created by its former vice president Ralph Reed, Jr. and the American rabbi Yechiel Eckstein: "The support of Christian Americans is a great encouragement for me, my government, and, above all, the people of Israel."[17]

Overtly hostile to Islam (its seminars on that religion are highly disconcerting), the Christian Coalition cannot be proven to be anti-Semitic. But these so-called best friends of Israel were the first to propagandize for Mel Gibson's scandalous film *The Passion of the Christ* without incurring the slightest charge of anti-Semitism on the part of Israeli leaders. The CCA is a group that includes a number of Southern conservatives with notorious historical ties to anti-Semitic organizations like the Ku Klux Klan and the John Birch Society. Its theological vision calls for the "reconstruction of the Kingdom of David" as a precondition for the apocalypse, in which the Jews will either recognize Jesus as the true messiah or disappear into the torments of Gehenna. In short, the CCA supports the Jews the way the rope supports the hanged man. But when the suspicion of anti-Semitism conflicts with their political interest, Olmert and men like Landau don't matter: the enemies of Israel's enemy Islam are their friends.

Anti-Semitism is viewed on two levels in Israel today. First of all it tends to function as a form of racial xenophobia in a class by itself, vastly more serious than other forms. Yet it is also seen as a constitutive by-product of Islam, such that any hostility to Israeli policy is said to represent an alliance between the left and the Islamists. From these two perspectives, the

Israeli right can give as reasons facts that are not without foundation. Vulgar anti-Semitism and anti-Americanism are the common lot of Islamism today (Turkey excepted). And as the oppression of the Palestinians increases and Iraq continues to be occupied, the Arab–Muslim world, sapped by reactionary regimes, digs itself ever deeper into a crisis mentality in which, carried along by the ethnicist hatred of Israel and America, anti-Semitism spreads all the more pervasively into Muslim populations.

Anti-Semitism is not more serious than any other form of racism. But since the Shoah is the most recent and the most "modern" of mass crimes committed on Western soil, its impact is rightfully incomparable. To erect it into a more serious kind of racism automatically leads to devaluing the other forms—especially colonial racism—and in doing so opens the door to their legitimization or minimization.

It remains the case that anti-Semitic motives are indeed to be found in critics of Israel, some of whom advocate its disappearance. But this does not make all critics avowed or potential anti-Semites, as the leaders of the Israeli right (and sometimes the left) would have one believe, nor does it make Sharon a man of honor. And neither does the support of outright Islamophobes for the policies of Ariel Sharon automatically make backers of Israel racists or Islamists paragons of virtue.

It also remains the case that, when it is reduced to the sole criterion of being for or against Israel, the charge of anti-Semitism is all the more effective because it depends on the person making it. Someone who is anti-Semitic can sometimes employ the same argument as someone who is not; its deeper meaning lies not in its content but in the way it is used. For example, when Jean-Marc Varraut, the lawyer for Maurice Papon, the prefect sentenced for having deported the Jews of Bordeaux during the Occupation, cited his client's relations with the grand rabbi of the city at that time, this was a disgraceful way of mitigating Papon's crime and placing the responsibility for the extermination of the Jews on the Jews themselves. When Hannah Arendt examined the behavior of the Judenrat in the ghettos, she was doing the work of a historian, and the accusations of anti-Semitism and self-hatred directed at her were a disgrace.

It is the system of instrumentalization of truths, their organization into a specific logic, that is racist, not the truths in themselves. In the recent past one could denounce the Gulag in the Soviet Union as a fascist or as a perfect democrat; it didn't change the fact that the Gulag indeed existed. The same goes for the relation to Israel. The fact that anti-Semites may turn to their advantage unworthy acts committed by the Israeli army cannot be used as an argument to deny, nullify, or mitigate the unworthiness of those acts, nor to lend credence to the idea that such criticism, regardless of its source, is a manifestation of anti-Semitism. When it is because it is a Jewish state that Israel's acts are criticized, that is a sign of anti-Semitic leanings. When these same acts are deemed criminal because they were committed by a state as such, as would be the case with any state bound by international conventions, the charge of anti-Semitism is simply a way to cover up these crimes. If this difference is not understood, the only conclusion can be that 25 or 30 percent of Israelis are themselves anti-Semitic.

When it is instrumentalized solely for the defense of Israeli policy, the charge of anti-Semitism is intended to carry a defamatory stigma or to put under suspicion anyone who utters a criticism of Israel. The very same people who, in Israel, cultivate the friendship of American fundamentalist Christians, just as, in the past, they entertained the warmest relationships with the apartheid regime of South Africa (which was tinged with anti-Semitism), are quick to make France the new hotbed of international anti-Semitism and, if possible, to connect that sentiment with the emergence of Islamism. They sometimes do so with arguments that are themselves racist, as when Sharon called on the Jews of France to emigrate to Israel in all haste on the grounds that the Muslim community in France is very large. At the end of one meeting, Sharon's friend, the deputy Avigdor Lieberman, asked me whether I am Jewish. When I said yes, he exclaimed, "You're crazy to remain in France. The country is infested with Muslims. They're like the plague. They're already beyond attack; soon they'll have taken over the whole country."[18]

The same kind of instrumentalization recurs in the endlessly repeated argument that today's anti-Zionism is just the hideous mask of anti-Semitism. That may well be so, but there is also nothing new there. In the Stalinist trials in the pivotal period between 1940 and 1950 in Eastern Europe the charge of Zionism was already being leveled against the

Jews, many of whom were in the dock. Its sole aim was to encourage the anti-Semitic tendencies of the local populations, who were often quick to believe that Communism had been imposed on them by the Jews and understood perfectly well that the word *Zionist* concealed a reference to that group. But there are countless anti-Zionists, non-Zionists, and even Zionists whose severe castigation of Israel's treatment of the Palestinians is motivated by anti-racism and support for human rights. Here too the equation anti-Zionist = anti-Semite is intended only to nullify or evade the content of the criticism by delegitimizing its author.

This equation does seem to have some partial basis in reality today. But in being raised to the status of a general theory it also seems to be a last-ditch, desperate argument intended to erect a wall of protection against criticism of Israel. There is no question that, with the repression of the intifada, a powerful anti-Semitic current, previously latent, has surfaced in the Arab–Muslim world. It is equally true that in certain European countries, France foremost among them, an initial effort undertaken by the far right has been supplemented by increasing ethnicism, a basic racism, in disadvantaged areas. Anti-Semitism in general has gotten a new lease on life in those countries, and an aggressive version of it, often under Islamist influence, has set in.

But the attempt to cite this anti-Semitism as a justification, to exaggerate its magnitude wildly, to seek to flush it out from behind any criticism so as to bind Jewish communities unfailingly around Israel and distract attention from what Jacques Julliard, an editorial writer for *Le Nouvel Observateur*, has called the Occupation with a capital O,[19] all this seems to be the final position of the Israeli *hasbara*, as futile as the others in stemming the impact on public opinion of the realities of the repression of the Palestinians. It can only foster, among those who promote it, a state of tension in which meanings are reversed so that the bearers of the new form of hate will no longer be the racists, or those who employ shameful means of oppression, but instead the anti-racists and defenders of human rights — in short, the "beautiful souls" who are overly concerned with the other, those who do not consider the war on terrorism grounds for depriving another nation of its freedom.

We can expect that such arguments will not be much more successful in the future than the efforts of Israeli communications system to condemn what it sees as the disinformation spread in the media. As long as the Palestinians of Gaza are pent up in a barbed-wire zoo with no prospects, as long as those on the West Bank are imprisoned behind a wall or in their own apartments—in short, as long as this occupation continues and worsens, the image of Israel will deteriorate and the charge of anti-Semitism leveled at all criticism can only lose credibility. At the same time, these realities can only promote any existing, vague tendencies toward anti-Semitism. Anti-Semites, of course, do not need them as fodder. But, as they see it, why not make happy use of the inhumane acts committed by some Jews?

As early as the Israeli invasion of Lebanon in 1982, carried out to eradicate the PLO, Primo Levi stated that this initiative had contaminated Israel's image, inflicting damage that would be hard to undo. The petition he signed noted that fighting against Begin's policies was also a way of combating the recrudescence of a new anti-Semitism to be added to the old anti-Semitic tendencies still lingering on (see Anassimov 1996). The acts committed for five years by the man who was the master strategist of the invasion of Lebanon, Ariel Sharon, and by those around him, have given rise to similar comments, even more enraged and upset than those of Primo Levi, from those Israelis who cannot bring themselves to endorse them.

For Shulamit Aloni, "modern anti-Semitism and the Shoah are at the origin of the creation of Israel. But by their acts our leaders are fueling this anti-Semitism the wrong way around, citing it as a justification of their acts and shutting the Israelis up in a mental prison, a permanent fear. If we don't say this, who will?"[20]

And what did Avraham Burg say in December 2003? "The hostility toward Israel that has emerged in the international community stems in part from the policies of the Israeli government. What I fear most of all is that, afraid of what the enemies of Israel will say, we won't wash our dirty linen in public, indeed that we'll get to the point of not washing it at all, and things will begin to stink."[21] Eight months later Burg announced his retirement from politics.

PALESTINIAN "VICTIMIZATION"

"How unlucky we are," says one Palestinian. "If we hadn't met up with the Jews, Israel would have been forced long ago by the international community to leave our territories, and we'd have our independence." "Idiot," the other replies. "It's the reverse: what a stroke of luck that we met up with the Jews. Who would be interested in us if we were Chechens, Tibetans, or Africans?" Behind this Palestinian joke is a comparison of misfortunes and the sympathy they arouse, characteristic of the competition for victimhood developing among their people.

Each of these Palestinians is right in his own way. For the cost of the impunity Israel enjoys has really been borne by them—an impunity that has for decades enabled Israel to violate international resolutions on the Palestinian question. Israel is not the only state to break these laws, but it is the one that, in so doing, has gotten around them by systematically and successfully adopting a victim position. It cannot be denied that, at least in the West, the Shoah weighs heavily against the ability to criticize Israel, not to mention impose sanctions on it.

The Palestinians, however, far from experiencing the worst horrors in today's world, enjoy much more diplomatic and media attention than other peoples who are victims of national oppression. This is due chiefly to the general importance of the Middle East in maintaining worldwide equilibrium (the risks posed by destabilization, Islamism, the oil supply, etc.), but also largely to the fact that it is Israel that the Palestinians are confronted by—by the Jews. In fifteen years of dirty war the Turkish Army has killed some 35,000 Kurds, including a great many civilians, razed hundreds of towns in Turkish Kurdistan, and displaced three million people, all without making a ripple on the international scene. And yet this took place in the Near East. The current war Moscow is waging in Chechnya, on the edge of the Middle East, is barbaric, with many more victims than in Palestine. Who, other than a few isolated Western intellectuals, cares about it?

If Shulamit Aloni can no longer endure the way her compatriots keep on presenting themselves as victims, what must be the feelings of those who directly experience Israeli domination? When the aggressor does not acknowledge his acts, or, worse, tries to make the victim bear responsibility for his own lot, adopting a position of self-righteousness and justifying his actions by the alleged behavior of the victim, he arouses rage or despondency in the victim, magnifying the latter's sense of injustice and impotence and often making it much harder for him to undertake the work of reconstruction. A number of studies support this view, for example in cases where a woman is raped and the attacker claims that she consented or was provocative. When the aggressor himself was abused as a child, his lawyer will seek to use this as a way to mitigate the scope of his client's act.

Just as the woman who has been raped is not responsible for whatever acts of violence the rapist may have been subjected to in his childhood, the Palestinians have no role in the extermination of European Jewry. And the Palestinians are right to find intolerable the constant tendency to cite this past extermination as an excuse for denying the present reality of their suffering. No one would compare a rape to mass crimes that are more loathsome by far. Yet, having "met up with the Jews," the Palestinians are often inclined to identify their own suffering with that of this group.

The publications of Palestinian nongovernmental organizations are crammed with this reference. The word *genocide*, totally inappropriate in this context, comes very easily to the lips of their spokesmen. Yasser Arafat used it several times, reflecting back to the Israelis the charge that he was the reincarnation of Hitler. Nabil Shaath, his minister of foreign affairs, told me that when the committees discussing the refugee issue at Camp David encountered the Israelis' refusal to admit any special responsibility for the expulsion of the Palestinians in 1948, he said to President Clinton, "Mr. President, you should lend us Stuart Eisenstadt so that we can negotiate better."[22]

Eisenstadt, undersecretary of commerce in the Clinton administration, was the man who had negotiated the restitution of, and compensation for, Jewish property that had been in escheat since the time of the Shoah. What Shaath was in effect saying was: "Lend him to us, and he'll know how to make the Israelis admit that they were wrong and that they have to give us back what was taken from us or compensate us for it." It was an attempt at humor, but his basic point was inappropriate: an ethnic cleansing like that of 1948 is in itself an act serious enough to call for reparation, but it is not the planned and industrialized extermination of a people.

After winning his case Eisenstadt had declared that the compensation of the victims of the Shoah, fifty years after the fact, showed that from now on there would be no statute of limitations on violations of human rights. A number of Palestinian organizations instantly seized on this statement, exclaiming, "Is that so? Well, what about us?" When it became known that Israeli soldiers were marking numbers on the arms of Palestinians being held for questioning, Yasser Arafat was quick to ask, "Isn't what's happening there a new Nazi racism?"[23]

Both the competition between victims and the recurring claim of a form of equivalence when it comes to misfortune are profoundly harmful to the Palestinian cause. First of all, they stem from a denial, for the equivalence in question does not exist. As Amira Hass has said, the Gaza ghetto is not the one in Warsaw, and the expulsion or disintegration of a society by means of violence is not the same thing as its physical extermination. The Palestinians will always lose this game—and their credibility along with it—in the same way the Israelis lose when they claim that they are the ones being attacked in the present conflict. Moreover, it is not necessary to have undergone what the Jews of Europe experienced in order to claim one's rights legitimately. By arguing for a nonexistent equivalence in suffering, the Palestinians ultimately validate the opposing view by a reductio ad absurdum: if rights are justified by the level of suffering, the Palestinians still have a long way to go.

This attempt to set up an equivalence is especially harmful because it is the culmination of a much stronger tendency to victimhood, one that severely curtails the possibility of assessment—of oneself, one's responsibility for one's lot, and the justice of the policy followed by one's leaders—and hence the ability to project oneself into a positive future. This victimhood is part of a still broader context, for most of the Arab–Muslim world cultivates it today in worship and in nostalgia for a glorious past. According to Hazem Saghieh, editorial writer for the daily newspaper Al Hayat, "In the collective psychology of the Arabs, the past is a faithful friend. The present is wholly negative."[24] And again: "We are victims; we have no responsibility for what happened,"[25] either back then or in the present situation. For a long time this has been the most common mind-set in the Arab world, Saghieh explains. It is a major obstacle to the as-sessment of fifty years of failure since the end of the colonial era.

For victimhood leads to systematic abdication of responsibility. No fail-ure can be imputed to oneself: American imperialism, the West, Israel, and the colonial past are always the cause. This attitude leads to the demonization of the real or imagined enemy and hence to his distor-tion. And it leads to conspiracy theories—imperialist plots, Jewish plots—flourishing today in the Arab–Muslim world. Many Egyptian newspapers, and not only Islamist ones, propagate ad nauseam the fantasy that all the evils besetting the country—corruption, prostitution, AIDS, drugs, ho-mosexuality, and the like—come from Israel. One could cite a hundred examples of this tendency to resort to Machiavellian explanations in or-der to excuse one's own flaws.

The most common of these insistent rumors in Muslim countries since September 11 is that Mossad was behind the attacks on the World Trade Center, or that the Jews predicted it, or that they stayed away from the two buildings on that day. It is useless to reply to those who hold such theories that a simple reading of the names inscribed on the wall set up in New York in memory of the victims would sweep away this absurd rumor: such ethnicist fantasies come from a split awareness. On one side, the fantasist inwardly rejoices at the misfortune of the American enemy ("In view of the grief they've caused us, they deserve what they got"). On the other, aware that this act is an abomination, he shrugs off all responsibil-ity, denying that the perpetrators came from his camp and placing the blame on the detested opponent Israel, "the Jews," those whom the Ameri-cans support or, worse, serve as valets.

Favoring the victim position to the exclusion of any other self-image and to the detriment of a constructive vision of the future promotes a fa-talism that can only be highly reactionary in nature. If all evil comes from the other, and this other (Israel, in the present case) appears invincible, mere human strength will never suffice. Only God can ward off this fate.

Victimhood and the avoidance of responsibility are now the powerful vehicles driving the political and social regression of the vast majority of Arab–Muslim societies. In this regression Palestine occupies the chief symbolic place of injustice and misfortune. "Arab nationalists and Islamists," writes the Egyptian psychiatrist Mohamed Mosaad (2002),

> like their Israeli right-wing counterparts, feel threatened. Their solidarity, their very existence, they think, is in danger. . . . For them, Israel is an essential element, or even the essential element, of their identity and their existence. Both the Muslim Brothers [Islamists] and the Leftists who persecuted and jailed them for decades believe fighting Israel must be the very heart of their programs. Islamists think this fighting will gather the Islamic world together. Nationalists think it will strongly unite the Arab world. The common essence of different Arab discourses, religious or secular, is resistance against Israel.
>
> What future could there be if Israel, the enemy, does not exist? The logical answer is that these discourses should change to encounter their national, political, economic, and social problems. However, these problems . . . are almost impossible to face, thanks to the autocratic regimes. Therefore it is naturally better to face Israel, though only with words. Although very impotent, this hypocritical position maintained by Arab "patriots" protects them from danger while granting them much popularity as heroes of this time! What a conspiracy they are making against their people and against themselves!

Placing the focus on Israel plays a central role, both in the way it demands submission of minds to authoritarian powers and in the conspiracy theories that are rife there. And just as an account of Israeli acts can be turned to the advantage of an anti-Semite without invalidating that account, the opposite is also true. That Islamophobes or fanatics in Israel keep harping on the argument that the instrumentalization of the Jewish state effectively distracts attention from the real problems of the Arab world nevertheless does not invalidate what they are saying.

The focus on Israel also confers on Palestine and the Palestinians their special status in Arab–Muslim martyrology. Why, from Morocco to

Bangladesh, have the Russian intervention in Afghanistan, the Serbian ethic cleansing in Bosnia and Kosovo, or the massacre of a nation in Chechnya, all of these being Muslim countries, never aroused as much turmoil and feeling of humiliation as the plight of the Palestinians? Why do young Muslims in France feel immensely more humiliated by that plight than by the fate that has been imposed on their own people back home? Why does the massacre of Palestinians in Sabra and Shatila in 1982, committed by Lebanese Phalangist Christians with logistical support from Israel, remain fresh in memory, when an identical massacre committed six years earlier in the refugee camp of Tel el-Zaatar by Syrian troops, called upon to help the Lebanese Phalangists and actively supported by pro-Syrian Palestinian factions, is all but forgotten? Just as the slaughter of Palestinians by King Hussein at Irbid and Wahdat in Jordan during the Black September of 1970 has been dispatched to the black holes of memory.

The explanation has to do with the despoliation and direct domination imposed on the Palestinians by Israel, and its refusal to acknowledge their national identity and right to self-determination. But it has even more to do with the fact that this dominator is Jewish. The Arab and Muslim forms of ethnicism, which are very striking, involve a sanctification of the land very similar to that found in Israel. The despoliation of Palestinian is felt to be all the more serious because Palestine is considered an Arab land, a Muslim land. And the domination is all the more intolerable because it is carried out not by Arabs or Muslims (as was the case for centuries under the Ottomans), but by Jews. "In the Israeli ethnocracy," notes the Moroccan anthropologist Abdallah Hammoudi, "the Arab is in a position of inferiority. Of *dhimmi* [protected person, in the Muslim tradition].[26] And the Jew is in the position of the dominator, the strong one. The Arab world has a great problem in facing this reality. The domination is unacceptable in itself, but it also activates ancient, deep-rooted tendencies that are likewise unacceptable." Yet Hammoudi says he is an optimist: "Misfortune has its good points. In the collective Arab psychology the idea of the inferiority of the Jew is no longer tenable. The problem now is the acknowledgment of equality."[27]

From a societal perspective, the tendency to claim victimhood and the failure to take responsibility constitute not only an obstacle to admitting the enemy's equal status and dignity, but also an obstacle to forming a positive self-construct. It leads to fatalism and to nostalgia for a happy time when one lived with honor and was treated with respect, a lost paradise that happens to correspond to a state in which one was the dominator oneself, where the land was Arab and nothing else, and the internal minorities—Jews, Berbers, Kurds, Copts, and others (even the Shiites)—could only knuckle under.

The part Palestine plays in the Arabs' feeling of humiliation, and in the resignation of entire segments of the Muslim world in the face of what is really at stake, works against the Palestinians. They see themselves as invested with the robe of martyrdom, borne aloft to the heights of general victimhood. This leads most of them to conform to this image. It is more than understandable that Palestinian nongovernmental organizations have the latest information on acts of violence committed by the IDF or the settlers. But their tendency to exaggerate the facts (though these are sufficient in themselves) is not a good sign, especially since in most cases it is accompanied by a marked absence of activity in all other areas. These are groups that were highly critical of the PLO's negligence under Arafat in responding to the needs of the population, including those having to do with daily resistance to the occupation, but they have seldom engaged in constructive projects to defend and organize that population.

Victimhood also imposes a strong constraint on self-assessment: when one is nothing but a victim one is irreproachable. And paralyzed as well: "We tend to see ourselves as a helpless people, caught up in world events too big and too powerful for us," says the Palestinian educator Sami Adwan. "And because we see ourselves as victims, there is very little reflection or self-criticism" (cited in Prince-Gibson 2002). Elias Sanbar, a history professor in France who, with his parents, was driven out of Haifa to Lebanon in 1948, expresses in radical terms his exasperation with the competition for victimhood:

> The status of victim doesn't interest me. It's first of all an ethical question: the memory of past misfortune doesn't confer any special right

on the victims' heirs, only duties. Then, when you see yourself solely as a victim, you don't see your own image in the mirror but that of your executioner. Finally, permanent victimhood is a powerful motivation for exemption from punishment. When you're a victim, you can't be guilty of anything. This is obviously true of the Israelis, but it's true of us as well.[28]

For the sociologist Anis Gandil, who as the head of the French nongovernmental organization Refugee Children of the World does important educational work in eighteen centers throughout the Gaza Strip, this fixation on the victim position is an "enormous handicap." "Our collective memory," he says,

remains stuck in 1948, our "catastrophe." But there's a problem. In reality, people know that they won't return and that we as a group won't go back to being what we were. In a refugee camp a man of 80 and a young person of 18 both define themselves as refugees. But the word has a different meaning for each of them. For the elderly man, Palestine is real; it's his village. For the teenager, it's an imaginary utopia. When he says, although he and his parents were born in Gaza, "I'm from Lydda," or "I come from Majdal" [Palestinian cities emptied of their populations by Israel in 1948 and 1950] he's living in a fantasy. What the Palestinians need is recognition of the wrong that was done them, justice, and reparation. Not going backwards. Victimhood leads to the idea of a utopian reparation, an annulment of the misfortune, a restoration of the prior state. This is why most of our historians are so concerned to safeguard the victimhood memory of the past but not to explain the defeat. To understand is to begin to distance oneself from the past.[29]

Gandil then assesses the magnitude of this task:

Most reflective Palestinian intellectuals, Elias Sanbar, Edward Said [who died in 2003], and Rashid Khalidi, are outside of Palestine. This

isn't by chance. Here we have neither the time nor the mental disposition to "understand." For us it's a matter of daily survival. No
reflection is possible under the occupier's boot. And yet this reflection is absolutely necessary. We even need Israeli historians to help
us understand ourselves. But in the present condition of Palestine
this is an almost impossible task that has to be carried out in terms of
managing not to seem complicit.

SIXTEEN

FORWARD
Israeli Society After the Evacuation of Gaza

THE WITHDRAWAL FROM GAZA:
A *"Prehistoric Event"*

On October 26, 2004, the Knesset approved a plan for the evacuation from Gaza that had been submitted by the prime minister. Ariel Sharon, the man who had symbolized the colonization of the occupied territories, put his plan into effect in August 2005. For the first time since the conquest of the territories in June 1967, Israel was dimantling its settlements there and repatriating their inhabitants to the interior of Israel.

Daniel Bensimon, a leading reporter for *Haaretz*, related two anecdotes. "Six weeks after the withdrawal from Gaza," he told me, "I suggested doing a major survey of the evacuated settlers. What had the withdrawal meant to them? How did they see the future? 'Drop it,' I was told. 'No one's interested in that anymore.' I couldn't believe my ears."[1] Several days later, shortly before the Jewish New Year and Yom Kippur (the Day of Atonement), a propitious time for Jews, Bensimon asked Defense Minister Shaul Mofaz of Likud for his assessment of the preceding year. Mofaz was forthcoming until the journalist mentioned the withdrawal from Gaza. "On to the next question," replied the former chief of staff, brushing the matter aside. "Six weeks after the event," Bensimon told me, "the evacuation of the settlers had been relegated to prehistory."

This is not the least of the paradoxes characteristic of Israeli society. In a country that has made the memory of the Jewish people's terrible sufferings into a symbol of identity, the concealment of the immediate past has become the rule. "Our society never looks back, either in war or in peace," states Bensimon. "If you don't step on the gas the second the traffic light turns green, you'll set horns blaring immediately. You have to keep going forward, get right down to business."

Daniel Dor, professor of communications at the University of Tel Aviv, tries to explain this tendency. "The Israelis," he says,

> have a culture of trauma. At the same time, they live in a very stressful environment: every day, or nearly, there's an event that is perceived as existential. When life is a whirlwind, with everything moving very fast, very hard, you just think about tomorrow, not about the day before, let alone the distant future. Collectively, we aren't inclined to draw lessons. Our chief mental means of defense lies in forgetting events and hiding problems. This is why there won't be a general assessment of what led us to leave Gaza or what that may mean for the future. The society doesn't want it. That's how it adapts to change.[2]

Yet many questions remain. Why, after thirty-eight years of refusing to dismantle settlements, did Israel do so for the first time? And why did it not demand anything in return, when before this the absence of a peace treaty had justified maintaining the settlements? Why, in a famous interview in 2001, did Prime Minister Ariel Sharon declare that he would never evacuate "the smallest settlement," not even the "most isolated one," and then decide to do so four years later? (see Chapter 11). Why did he order the evacuation at a time when the military power of the intifada was diminished and Palestinian society was bled dry? What did the repatriation of the settlers say about the legitimacy of the settlement policy established by all the earlier administrations, right and left alike, for thirty-eight years?

"The Israelis are incredibly slow to question themselves," says Adi Ofir, professor of philosophy at the University of Tel Aviv. The reason, he says, "is the refusal to take into account what we're inflicting on the Palestinians every day. We don't want to know what's going on. If, instead of evacuating Gaza, Israel had expelled 100,000 Palestinians, most people would have looked on with equal indifference. Nothing leads people to ask: Where are we headed now? No; whatever will happen, will happen."[3]

Professor Ofir's statement needs to be modified. The Israeli reluctance he speaks of is fading rapidly. Thus the year 2005 saw the appearance of a profusion of books radically challenging the policies of Israeli leaders and the army during the intifada, including the presuppositions underlying their decisions and the arguments put forth to justify them.

Raviv Drucker and Ofer Shela (2005) set out to show the blindness of the country's leadership, its stubborn refusal to understand either the premises of the intifada and what was at stake there, or the government's role in the outbreak and exacerbation of that uprising. They conclude is that there was a failure on the part of the prime minister himself. If, before he came to power, someone had told Ariel Sharon that he would preside over a unilateral disengagement from Gaza and Northern Samaria, order the construction of a wall leaving 94 percent of the West Bank on the other side, see the inevitable rise of Hamas as the leading force of Palestinian society, and call all this a victory, Sharon would have taken him for a madman, they write.

In the same vein Amos Harel and Avi Isasharoff (2005) write that their country won the war on terrorism militarily but lost it politically, gradually wearing itself out without managing to break the enemy's resolve or succeed in geting it to renounce the political convictions it held at the outbreak of the intifada.

Many other books candidly appraise the Israelis' tendency to delude themselves, to always blame the other side without ever acknowledging their own share of responsibility, to discover the limits of the politics of the iron hand only after repeated setbacks. Nor is it an accident that the most recent book by the historian Tom Segev (2005), whose title in English would be *How 1967 Shattered the Face of the Country*, appeared immediately after the withdrawal from Gaza. Segev radically questions one of Israel's fundamental assumptions, citing numerous documents to support his judgment that, far from being unavoidable, the war of that year was intended by part of the Israeli leadership, which chose to seize an extraordinary opportunity to fulfill the historic ambition of Zionism, namely the conquest of Mandatory Palestine (see Chapter 8). And, yes, he writes, that ambition plunged the country into a crisis in which it is still embroiled.

Thus, even though no extensive discussion of the lessons to be learned from the withdrawal from Gaza took place, much fruitful thinking was done on the sidelines. Not only has a rupture appeared in the collective mind-set, but the settlers' camp has clearly lost a great deal of influence and prestige as well. As can be seen from their publications, people with national-religious and Orthodox-religious leanings who worship the primacy of the Land of Israel are in a state of great distress. And there has been a rift in the bedrock of Israeli society as a whole.

REASONS FOR THE WITHDRAWAL

Why did Ariel Sharon, who championed the settlements for over thirty years, finally dismantle, in Gaza, establishments that he had personally promoted? Surprisingly, all the commentators, whether on the right or the left, secular or religious, were in agreement on three basic reasons: Israeli exhaustion in the face of the intifada; the international context; and, finally (a minor but frequently cited argument), the prime minister's need to distract public attention from matters of political corruption in which he might be implicated.

Akiva Eldar, the *Haaretz* political columnist, told me this:

> Seeing the United States sign the "road map" advocating the establishment of a viable Palestinian state in 2005, and seeing Yossi Beilin and Yasser Abed Rabbo, who promoted the Geneva Pact, being received in Washington by Colin Powell, set off an alarm signal in Sharon's mind. He was trying to regain the initiative. Who could possibly be against a withdrawal from Gaza? It allowed him to beat the international community to the draw, postpone Palestinian statehood indefinitely, and place Israel in a favorable position internationally. Moreover, it was consistent with what the polls were showing Israelis wanted after four years of intifada: a separation from the Pal-

estinians. Leaving Gaza meant giving back a very small piece of territory but one with a very large Arab population.[4]

According to Shlomo Sand, professor of contemporary history at the University of Tel Aviv,

> at a certain point in time, contrary to their previous statements, generals began to say that there would be no military solution to the intifada, that politicians would have to assume their responsibilities. And this was going on in a context in which society was dimly becoming aware that no military measures would make the Palestinians capitulate. Sharon is also very close to financial circles. Here too internal pressures played a role, so that investments would resume. Finally, the demographic question weighed heavily. Most Israelis would like to live without the Arabs. Since the Palestinians aren't giving up their national claims and their birth rate is much higher, how to remain on the same territory in which there will soon be more Arabs than Jews?[5]

And Uri Ram, a sociologist at the University of Beer Sheva, has this to say:

> At the beginning of the intifada ideological regression was triumphant: the Land of Israel became the supreme value and Palestinian nationalism was reduced to terrorism. With the passage of time and the growing wear and tear, the inclinations toward integrating Israel into the international community and achieving a better life got the upper hand. The withdrawal from Gaza is not a matter of chance. Of course Sharon and the general staff had ulterior motives: quitting Gaza went along with the wish to maintain as much control as possible over the West Bank. But the fact is that Israel unilaterally left Gaza in response to its intrinsic needs.[6]

All the commentators emphasize that the unilateralism on Israel's part is the salient feature of the withdrawal. It is a turning point in the relationship to the Palestinians, which up to then had been one of dominance. The decision to abandon the prospect of a victory that would lead the Palestinian Authority, or, better, a new, more comprehensive partner, to be more flexible in negotiation once calm was restored, gradually gained acceptance and force in the Israeli establishment during 2002–2003, well before taking the form of a political program.

The term *unilateral* was first uttered in 2003 by people close to Sharon and representatives from the general staff during the annual security forum at Herzliyah, which brings together the cream of Israel specialists on strategic matters. What lay behind it? The relinquishment of all illusions with regard to the Palestinians. From the time of the outbreak of the second intifada, the feeling that the Palestinians had triggered the violence to get what they had not been able to gain at Camp David, or, worse, that they had always aimed at the destruction of Israel, had taken hold in almost all of the political class and the Jewish population of the country. Israel had to conquer if it was not to disappear. Then, with the failure of the policy focused solely on security, the idea of separation emerged. "If we no longer trust the Palestinians at all and can no longer make them give up," says Dani Rabinowitch, an anthropologist at the University of Tel Aviv, summing up the process of collective reflection that brought about the shift in public opinion, "what remains is to live without them and preserve our interests as best we can."[7]

"Separation," adds Daniel Bensimon, "means establishing a certainty: there will be no peace, and so we have to divorce the Palestinians with or without their consent." This general change of attitude led Likud, the champion of a Greater Israel, to adopt the Laborite proposal to build a wall of protection that would include most of the settlements of the West Bank but interrupt the territorial continuity of Greater Israel, a project to which Likud had been initially opposed.

With the wall, construction of which began in 2003, Israel inaugurated its unilateral policy without saying so. Up to that time, with the exception of Jerusalem, called "the eternal and unified capital," all the territories — even those "unilaterally" inhabited by settlements for thirty-nine years – were supposedly up for discussion when it came time for negotiations. Now, despite the Palestinian Authority, which denounced the de facto

annexation of land, Israel drew "its" border—the border establishing the
separation most Israelis desired, and the most desirable one—without
concern for its interlocutor. As Yzhar Beer, head of the nongovernmental civil-rights organization Keshev, put it, repeating the words of Dov
Weisglass, one of Sharon's close advisers, "The Palestinians are not a
partner; they're a problem to be dealt with."[8]

The withdrawal from Gaza is part of this line of reasoning. "After thirty-
eight years of occupation," said Professor Daniel Dor in 2005, "the evacuation changes nothing in Israel's general view of the Palestinians. Nothing
has fundamentally altered in the relation between 'us and them.' But a
lot has changed in the relation between 'us and us.'" Like the wall, the
withdrawal from Gaza is primarily intended to set in motion the inevitable "divorce" on conditions imposed by Israel. But its further implications for the course of events are far from clear.

For a number of observers this separation is intended to shatter any
prospect for the establishment of a viable Palestinian state after an Israeli
withdrawal, that is if by this one means a state largely situated within the
1967 borders with a protected link between the West Bank and Gaza and
with East Jerusalem as its capital. Since the withdrawal from Gaza, Ariel
Sharon and his successors, beginning with the new prime minister, Ehud
Olmert, have sent various signals confirming this diagnosis. Not only is
the wall continuing to be built, but the idea of a "long-term interim accord" to replace the "final accord" with the Palestinians is being mentioned
much more often. And the de facto cantonization of the Palestinians is
taking shape.

On March 30, 2005, *Haaretz* published a map of the roadworks and
new roadblocks that would ultimately divide the West Bank into four distinct parts: (1) the east, encompassing Jerusalem and three large blocks of
settlements to be attached to Israel, (2) the north, around Jenin and Nablus,
(3) the center (Ramallah and Jericho), and (4) the south (Bethlehem and
Hebron). Similarly, in the Israeli political-military vocabulary, territorial
continuity on the West Bank, a key Palestinian demand, is increasingly
being replaced by the notion of "transportation continuity." The plan is
for Israelis and Palestinians to use entirely separate roads on the West Bank.
In crossing zones of demarcation in the hands of the IDF, communications

among Palestinian cantons would be assured by bridges and tunnels under Israeli sovereignty.

In a series of mid-October 2005 articles, Amira Hass showed how, despite the withdrawal, Israel domination was being perpetuated in Gaza through innumerable channels. The withdrawal did not do away with the Israeli Civil Administration. As on the West Bank, this IDF department must still be informed of every birth, death, marriage, and change of address. Every new identity card must be written in Arabic and Hebrew and must be obtained with the department's consent. The army reserves the right to refuse it, as well as to forbid a move on the part of anyone who has forgotten to inform it of a change of address or civil status. According to Hass, 54,000 Palestinians are forbidden to move for so-called administrative reasons, not to mention the nearly absolute prohibition on Gazaites to visit the West Bank, much less work or live there.

As Akiva Eldar, one of the most perceptive commentators on domestic policy for *Haaretz*, has observed, "Ariel Sharon didn't want any negotiation. He absolutely didn't want a final accord based on the Geneva Pact. What he most likely wanted is to withdraw from as many territories as possible on the other side of the wall on the West Bank, at the same time preserving an Israeli military presence around secured Palestinian 'cantons.' And," Eldar added, "he would also most likely have been forced by circumstances to abandon that plan."

For the strategy of unilateralism included an autistic component. How was one to manage the other side without taking it into account, without admitting the legitimacy of its aspirations, and hence without running the risk of a new self-deception? Judge Michael Ben Yair, former legal adviser to the Rabin government with the rank of minister from 1993 to 1995, is well aware of the limits of unilateralism. Yet he sees in its triumph more reason to hope than to fear:

> It can't be overemphasized what a fundamental precedent this unilateral withdrawal from Gaza constitutes for the Israelis. What finer demonstration that the occupation made no sense! Sharon didn't intend to withdraw from the West Bank also? No matter. Just as all of Gaza has been evacuated, all the occupied territories will be as

well, with the possible exception of the Jewish quarters of Jerusalem. At that time the precedent of Gaza will take on its full value.[9]

The sociologist Uri Ram agrees wholeheartedly: "This unilateral withdrawal has positive and negative aspects. On the negative side, unilateralism is a retreat into the self that reinforces Jewish ethnicism. On the positive side, this withdrawal traces an irreversible path: like it or not, the occupation will have to end. And this has happened with the support of the large majority of Israelis. Which is really terrific. The withdrawal is an alloy of the wall and the sea." What Ram means by this is that the wall is the physical manifestation of the Israelis' self-enclosure, their indifference toward their neighbors, while the sea implies looking outward toward the world, the other face of Israel, the industrious, dynamic, and secular society that massively supported the withdrawal from Gaza.

DRAWING UP THE BALANCE SHEET OF THE WITHDRAWAL

How to assess this event? "First of all," according to Uri Ram, "it demonstrated that the so-called settlement coalition has become a small minority. Second, the agenda of Greater Israel is now a dead letter. Apart from a mystico-nationalist fringe, no one refers to it anymore. Third, the ideological language that prevailed at the beginning of the intifada is bankrupt."

Finally, the initially powerful settlement coalition has lost momentum, to the point where it backfired once the evacuation was put into effect. Two elements were in play here. One was the opposition of the extremist settlers, which was presented as a resistance movement. Despite its dimmed luster, the Israeli army remains iconic in a country where, during the intifada, the political class has been largely discredited, corruption is rampant, and the social situation has deteriorated. In resisting their evacuation by the soldiers and sometimes even insulting them in front of the cameras, the settlers alienated many Israelis who cannot identify with open confrontation of the IDF, the most respected organ of the state. In addition, the behavior of the extremist fringe, who clothed themselves in the mantle of deportees and called the soldiers Nazis, discredited their camp. The analogy was appalling: the indemnification of each evacuated family to the tune of $150,000–$350,000 was not exactly a deportation to Auschwitz, a student told me with a grimace.

The settlement coalition "did not survive a major contradiction," concludes Dani Rabinowitch. "Prior to that time, the settlers claimed to be the true perpetuators of the deeply held ideal of Zionism: the conquest of the land. Suddenly they appeared as a subversive element with regard to the primary instrument to which Zionism aspired, namely the Jewish state. In scorning it they lost their status as Zionism's 'best servants.'"

Nowadays Greater Israel is indeed a dead letter. Although, in contrast to the West Bank, Gaza does not include the holy places of Judaism, this strip of land had always been included in Greater Israel by the promoters of that goal. What public opinion confirmed was that, by giving up Gaza and also (a phenomenon that occurred relatively unseen) a portion of the territory of the West Bank that was twice as important, the notion of the Land of Israel was unable to prevail over that of the state of Israel. This is a crucial sign for the future.

Speaking of what he calls the "knockout victory" of the Blues (supporters of the withdrawal) over the Oranges (the disciples of Greater Israel), the sociologist Uri Ram sees it as a profound disconnection that developed in Israel during the intifada: "The Blues want a democratic Jewish state. This is somewhat contradictory, since 20 percent of Israeli citizens are also Palestinians. But the idea of democracy is central here. In the withdrawal it became clear that Greater Israel, uniting mysticism and ultranationalism, runs counter to democracy." Dani Rabinowitch agrees: "The society has realized that, if the settlers prevailed, this would not be merely an ideological victory. It would lead to a change of government."

The defeat of ideological language is ultimately the most striking consequence of the withdrawal. The policy favoring security over all else has been crippled. For the withdrawal from Gaza is first and foremost the failure of the security *konceptzia*, which had been supported by the rage of certain opponents who kept on repeating that if, after five years of intifada, the Palestinians were given back territory that had been deemed necessary for security, this would lend definitive credence to those among them who believe that violence was finally paying off.

The weakening of the previously dominant "security concept"—that Palestinian capitulation had to precede any return to politics—can be summed up by an example. It will be recalled that Chief of Staff Shaul Mofaz intervened in December 2001 to block the Taba negotiations between Israel and the Palestinians, doing this so that Palestinian militants could not claim that their violence had gained them more concessions than Israel had been disposed to grant six months previously at Camp David. Four and a half years later, Mofaz, now the Likud defense minister, was in charge of the disengagement from Gaza. He fulfilled this task with no qualms. The precondition of the cessation of violence had proved ineffective operationally; to people's minds, even among the military, politics, not security measures, was now the way to go. As Akiva Eldar put it, Gaza marked the beginning of a "de-brainwashing." The return to reality brought the Israelis back to the obvious fact, often hateful in their eyes but unavoidable, that the Palestinians are there and nothing will make them either leave or accept the occupation. To be sure, this "exit from regression" has its limits, as can be seen in its political implementation. Separation and unilateralism offer other effective ways of averting one's gaze from the other. It can also be seen in the certitude, expressed by nearly everyone I spoke to, that if, during the intifada, a Labor government had proposed dismantling the Gaza settlements, it would have failed—Sharon would have led the demonstrators against such a plan. Only Sharon, with his past and his aura of security-mindedness, could lead this operation, just as only Rabin, chief of staff during the Six Days' War, could dare to announce the recognition of the PLO. The security policy, even after taking a beating in the second intifada, as in the first, remains deeply anchored in Israeli minds.

Following the withdrawal from Gaza, the Israeli general staff and security establishment have come to believe that although this evacuation was useful on the military level it also contained elements of political failure—if only because the Palestinians saw it as a sign that their intifada was successful. They immediately began to explain that Israel had lost some of its deterrence capacity and that the IDF absolutely had to reestablish it right away. There was to be no possibility, in these circles, of allowing the Palestinians to view the withdrawal as a political gain. Thus when Hamas won its electoral victory the general staff submitted to the Israeli government a plan for military intervention in Gaza, aimed at making the new, democratically elected Palestinian Authority experience the same fate as the former one. The politics of force, or rather force as a palliative measure in the absence of politics, continues to act on the Israeli elites as a deeply embedded reflex.

VICTORS AND VANQUISHED

The major losers in the post-Gaza period are thus the settlers and their supporters, who are undergoing an unprecedented crisis, a crisis of representation, image, and, above all, strategy even greater than the one they experienced after the Oslo Accords. This time the shakeup is immense, especially since the evacuation of the Gaza settlements changed with such disconcerting ease from a potential plan to an operational reality. Before then, says Yzhar Beer, most settlers had lived "with the sense that they had a right to veto" decisions made at the political level. No one had ever ventured to oppose them directly, and they had only seen their influence grow in the workings of the state and in everyday life. Right up to the time of the evacuation, Beer notes, such venerated masters as Rav Eliahu, the former Sephardic grand rabbi, had claimed that God would not allow it to happen.

God allowed it. Since then, two general views have emerged. "With them both, the conflict between the primacy of the Land of Israel and the support for the state of Israel has gone up a notch," observes Yagil Levy, a sociologist specializing in military matters:

> Some people belonging to the national-religious camp say, "We weren't able to conquer hearts." They add, "If we had constituted 35 percent of the troops instead of 20 percent, the general staff wouldn't have been able to marginalize us so easily and the withdrawal couldn't

have been accomplished." Such people conclude that "the people aren't yet ready for redemption," and that an extra effort has to be made to take over the machinery of state and prepare for the storms to come. But others urge the conclusion that Zionism has failed as an instrument of the awaited return of the Messiah, an idea that, up to then, had been part and parcel of national-religious activism.[10]

Those in the latter group are in favor of abandoning the strategy that collapsed at Gaza, and are focusing instead on forming an alternative society. In 2006, on the eve of Yom Haatzmaut (the Israeli Independence Day), a lively debate took place among ultranationalist Orthodox rabbis. Some of them advocated a modification of the prayers in the synagogue for that day: the people of Israel were to bless no longer the state of Israel, which had failed in its redemptive mission. Others were opposed to this change.

"More and more of the religious are saying that this isn't our army anymore," says Levy. As a result, the state has become "suspect," according to the philosopher Adi Ofir. As soon as it stops being an instrument of messianism, what comes to the fore is the tendency to ignore its institutions. This tendency is not new. Since the creation of Israel the leaders of the "God-fearing" have maintained a utilitarian relation to the state, extracting from it as many institutional and financial benefits as possible while maintaining a considerable ideological distance. The preferred battleground for the rejection of the secular state has long been the supreme court, although the Orthodox largely reject its authority. After the withdrawal from Gaza, especially among the Khardelim, ultrareligious worshipers of the Land of Israel (see Chapter 13), the tendency to disconnect from the state has regained a vigor it had lost.

And among the ultranationalist secular fringe of the settlement movement, which favors a new mass expulsion of the Palestinians and has taken part in various coalition governments, another crisis is brewing. This group has been represented in several terms of office in the Knesset (and several times in rightist governments) by Avigdor Lieberman. Much less prone to the sanctification of the land, it is ideologically animated by an avowed ethnicism. "For them," says Professor Shlomo Sand, "territory is of little importance. What matters is to preserve the Jewish purity of the state."

Immediately after the withdrawal from Gaza, Lieberman, who had been one of the first to define a plan for cantonizing the Palestinians in the 1990s, formulated a new version. This time what he proposed was to cantonize not just the Palestinians of Gaza and the West Bank but also the 1.2 million Israeli Palestinian citizens. The idea would be to carry separation to its logical end, doing so via an exchange of territories. To make it possible for Israel to constitute itself as an ethnically pure Jewish state, some areas inhabited by these Israeli Arabs would be attached to a Palestinian entity composed of multiple enclaves under Israeli authority, in the process revoking their citizenship and reclaiming the "useful areas" of the West Bank. What we have here is an avowed policy of apartheid, carried along by a very diffuse popular sentiment in favor of separate homelands.

In the optimistic view of Daniel Dor, "The settlement camp is in crisis because the umbilical link to 'Papa' Sharon has been cut. It is hard to predict what the messianists will do. But most of them are already thinking about their financial compensation should there be an evacuation of the West Bank." Yzhar Beer, who has published many studies of the national-religious and the "men in black," is more uneasy. He recalls that what he terms their "provocations" have always, up to now, turned into advantages for them. In 1994 the murder by the settler Baruch Goldstein of twenty-nine Muslim worshipers in the Cave of the Patriarchs put an end to all vague plans to evacuate Hebron. And in 1995 the assassination of Prime Minister Yitzhak Rabin ended in the return to power of Likud in the following year. After the evacuation of Gaza, Beer personally saw on the walls of Jerusalem graffiti proclaiming "Next step: an attack on Al-Aqsa." He is much less sure about the impact of the Gaza precedent. "The fanatics are in shock," he says, "but they're regrouping as they did on previous occasions. Withdrawing from the West Bank will be much harder than from Gaza, because it will affect the heart of biblical mysticism."

As for the army, it is the primary victor in the withdrawal. This may seem paradoxical, since it was the army that waged the war on terrorism and was behind the retaking of the entire Gaza Strip in 2002. After all, it was through the voice of Chief of Staff Moshe Yaalon that the army expressed public disapproval when Sharon's adviser Dov Weisglass first mentioned a withdrawal from Gaza. Moreover, in the intifada it was the army that increasingly freed itself from political constraints and set its own agenda.

The paradox is self-explanatory, however. The army has tended to become autonomous, yet it was also the first to reach the conclusion that maintaining Gaza under Israeli sovereignty was ultimately an illusion. As we recall, in the autumn of 2002 General Iri Kahn explained that "the command has understood that it must take into account international constraints and the weight of public opinion." Because the IDF perceived its role in this way it was the first to promote an evacuation of Gaza. The chief of staff did, to be sure, make his discontent apparent when the idea was broached by the people around Sharon, but this was because he had been excluded from the decision-making process. In reality the first report advocating the evacuation of Gaza had been written by General Eyal Giladi as early as 2003. "In contrast to the evacuation of South Lebanon," explains the military expert Yagil Levy, "the withdrawal from Gaza was not imposed on the army by society. It was a cool-headed, considered move of crisis management. The army was the source of the conceptual plan and prepared for it. This is why it carried it through without a major clash. It's also for this reason that the withdrawal is not a constitutive experience with a strong impact on Israeli minds."

A means of crisis management? "The organizational interest of every army is to win," admits Levy. This, he says, was also the IDF's initial reflex after the outbreak of the second intifada. But the impasse in which the army had become enmired by what Levy calls its "excessive aggression enjoying veritable impunity," the increasing disapproval, even within its own ranks, of its methods, and even more the reduction of its budget, the state having made sharp cuts in public expenditures, gradually led it to reformulate its objectives. The army, Levy says, then came to three conclusions: there was no one to talk with on the Palestinian side; the situation was ultimately unmanageable, and so the IDF had to take action in seeking a way out; and, finally, what was needed was a strong measure, logistically comfortable and internationally advantageous.

According to Levy, the unilateral withdrawal from Gaza, a tiny strip of land requiring the presence of 60,000 armed men to protect the 5,000 to 6,000 settlers actually living there, offered the best opportunity. The risk—setting the people's army over against a part of the people—was carefully assessed. IDF researchers came to the conclusion that the risk was small and even included some advantages. For part of the general staff was worried about the growing power of the national-religious in the army, in which four men wearing the *kippah* have now attained the rank of general. The appointment of two of them, General Yair Naveh, commander in chief of the central region, and General Eleazar Stern, head of the department of human resources, had given rise to hesitations. With both seen as highly ideological officers, the question was, how would they act in case of conflict with religious settlers?

The withdrawal from Gaza enabled the IDF to put their trustworthiness to the test in a crisis that was largely under control. They passed the test. General Naveh carried out the evacuation of four settlements in the West Bank. General Stern called for the closing of the *yeshivot hesder*, military talmudic schools in which young national-religious students combined extended active service with biblical studies. The IDF did not intervene in the operations of elite combat units, in which there are many national-religious, so as not to put them in what Levy calls a situation of symbolic dilemma. In exchange, very few rabbis summoned their flocks to disobedience. The army came out exceptionally well, Levy says; fidelity to the state won an easy victory, and religious officers proved obedient. The IDF once again became The Great Mute One. And in confirming its status as the country's most solid institution it amply made up for the deteriorating image it had begun to acquire.

According to polls taken after the withdrawal, 50 percent of the settlers on the West Bank would be willing to abandon their homes if circumstances so required and compensation were offered. Thousands of settlers have inquired of the authorities how much they would see in the way of indemnity if they decided spontaneously to return to the other side of the Green Line, the 1967 border. The request for information is generally concealed from neighbors, but it is discussed among friends.

This phenomenon is profoundly symptomatic of a premonition, not publicly admitted, that as in Gaza someday soon settlements on the West Bank might well be dismantled. And it shows that, among the 70 percent of Israelis who moved to the occupied territories for essentially social reasons, for the first time in thirty-nine years fault-lines are appearing in the certainty of an eternal Israeli presence. In the population at large the concept of the primacy of the Land of Israel is in the process of crumbling.

A NEW POLITICAL MAP FOR EACH SIDE

The larger context makes clear why the withdrawal from Gaza exploded the political map of Israel. The two large parties, right and left, experienced major upheavals in November 2005. Ariel Sharon quit Likud to form a new group positioning itself at the center, and Shimon Peres quit the Labor Party to join him. This is the most tangible consequence of the turning-point that occurred with the withdrawal from Gaza. In the legislative elections of March 28, 2006, three new currents became apparent, corresponding to fundamental movements in Israeli society.

THE SUCCESSORS OF ARIEL SHARON

The first is represented by the successors of Ariel Sharon. It is no accident that, before he was incapacitated by a stroke on January 4, 2006, Sharon changed the name he had originally chosen for his new party. He had initially called it the Party of National Responsibility, but the new name speaks volumes: Kadima, which means Forward. Sharon was going along with the Israeli tendency "to keep going forward without looking back," as Daniel Bensimon says. The Sharon–Peres coalition — which became an Olmert–Peretz government after the Israeli elections held on March 28, 2006 — was consistent with the views of the majority of the population. Lacking an overall assessment of the politics of the past forty years and its failures, as symbolized by the withdrawal from Gaza, this majority now favors unilateralism with regard to the Palestinians because, according to Bensimon, it is convinced "that Arafat didn't want peace and Abu Mazen can't bring it about." With the outbreak of the intifada the historic center of the Israeli political map, the Labor Party, literally collapsed. Although Sharon was the head of Likud, he seemed to be at the heart of a new political equilibrium that was now further to the right than in the 1990s. This new center constituted itself independently in Kadima.

Until his health removed him from the political stage, Ariel Sharon remained for many the country's only "strongman." Despite his age and the corruption that clung to his coattails, he was seen as the one best able to preserve Israel's security while navigating in troubled waters—the general situation in the Middle East, the sometimes tense relations with the United States—without giving up anything essential to the Palestinians. His party, Kadima, appears to be most closely attuned to the wishes of the majority of Israelis, namely a separation from the Palestinians on conditions imposed by Israel, along with the idea that the Hebrew state should go it alone without concern for others.

What does such a unilateral separation amount to? Politically, it is the implementation of wishful thinking, the wish on the part of so many Israelis to live without the Arabs and to do so to their own advantage with no consideration of what this might mean for the other, as though he did not exist and had no legitimate claims, and as though this wish, even if it were temporarily put into action by a very favorable balance of power, could be viable over the long run.

When a married couple divorce, either the two spouses agree on the division of assets and the judge endorses this, or they do not manage to come to an agreement and the judge decides the conditions. But the separation from the Palestinians, as it has been discussed by so many Israelis, entails the unilateral determination of the country's future boundaries through disengagement only from the zones densely inhabited by Palestinians, and retention of the territorial zones in which Israel has an interest (those in which many settlers are concentrated, those in which there is groundwater, etc.). Thus it is more like a repudiation than a divorce. In such a separation one of the two partners imagines that he or she can unilaterally decide to keep the apartment, the children, the car, and the appliances, suggesting that the other is free to declare independence under these conditions.

Despite the wall, whose construction continues without interruption; despite the increasing number of roads on their own territory forbidden to the Palestinians, and other measures in which the West Bank is parceled into a multitude of cantons and subcantons disconnected from one another, making life impossible; and despite the constant expropriations of land—or rather because of all this—such a unilateral separation, one aimed at putting an entire population in a cage, as Benny Morris suggested, will fail tomorrow as surely as the politics of force failed yesterday. Yet today a large number of Israeli Jews want to believe in it, even if, once one manages to chip away at their carapace of automatic certainties, many of them express skepticism regarding the ultimate success of this kind of separation.

On the right, the danger that threatened Likud was that it would fall back on a program identifying it with ultranationalism. This was a danger because it came up against competition from a coalition of ultranationalist parties around the NRP (National Religious Party), and because, on the social level, its figurehead, Benyamin Netanyahu, was associated with the extremist Thatcherite policy he had followed as minister of the economy, pauperizing large segments of the population. Likud seemed to be huddling around ideological positions that had been pounded to bits by Sharon's pragmatism and the majority's wish for a divorce from the Palestinians. And in fact its electoral collapse symbolized the collapse previously mentioned, that of the settlement coalition with its territorial mystique of the Land of Israel.

On the left, Amir Peretz won a surprise election as the head of the Laborites once the activists were consulted, beating out Shimon Peres, Labor's last historic figure, as well as General Benyamin Ben Eliezer, both of whom represented the governmental alliance with Ariel Sharon. This victory marked the possibility of a return to the fundamentals of the Israeli labor movement, and to its internal political fundamentals, with renewed importance accorded to the working and lower classes and to the fundamentals inherited from Oslo with respect to the relationship with the Palestinians.

Young (53 years old) and of modest background, the man born Armand
Pérez was brought to Israel from Morocco at the age of four, where he became Amir Peretz. Peretz is not just a Sephardic union leader anxious to
win the support of the underprivileged members of society who, like him,
mostly come from Arab–Muslim countries. Had he been merely this, he
would have spent his career in Likud, which has historically prevailed among
the Sephardim by flattering the racist inclinations of these down-and-out
Oriental Jews abandoned by the leading Ashkenazi classes. But Amir Peretz
opted for the labor movement very early on. After a career as an officer he
became a member of Peace Now. Elected to the Knesset in 1988, he joined
the Group of Eight—the eight Labor deputies led by Yossi Beilin—who
paved the way for the signing, five years later, of the Oslo Accords.

More than his past as a moderate pacifist, the program with which he
persuaded the activists over to his side indicates the potential developments
underway in the society. In the intifada the Laborites had agreed to serve
Ariel Sharon as a crutch in the hope of retaining a modicum of credit. In
contrast, Peretz got elected on the basis of a three-point program: ending
the coalition with the nationalist right, giving priority to solving urgent social problems, and returning to negotiations with the Palestinian Authority—
in other words, by rejecting unilateralism, by not pretending to negotiate
by moving Israel's pawns but negotiating seriously, and by taking the other
side into account. On several occasions he stated that, if he were to form a
government, "the money would go to the poor districts, not to the settlements." Before the election some of the people close to Peretz, concerned
about the repercussions of such views, urged him to smooth out his profile
as a dove, offer as few opinions as possible on the question of the occupied
territories, and to basically focus on social issues.

With this program Peretz managed to salvage enough of what he needed.
Despite the defection of some of his leaders to Kadima, followed by part
of the middle class that had previously voted Labor, he got enough of his
party's votes, winning the support of new sectors of the population. A Labor
victory in the general elections was more than unlikely, given their pacifist program, yet the party's turn toward Peretz is symptomatic of profound
shifts in the lower ranks of society, even though these represent a minority. For the absence of a balance sheet on the withdrawal from Gaza con-

ceals a deep questioning within the larger sectors with regard to the future of the Israeli presence on the West Bank. Without the evacuation of Gaza, Amir Peretz would never have assumed the leadership of the party with the program he initially presented.

In the current state of affairs there is no reason to predict a rapid movement of Israeli society toward a wholesale abandonment of the occupation and an actual recognition of the historic injustice committed against the Palestinians. A large majority of Israelis support the construction of the wall going up on the West Bank and the unilateralism of their leaders. From this point of view Peretz's Labor policy, which formally rejects unilateralism, seems out of touch with the majority view. Yet the direction he has taken may well be indicative of a possible evolution, still in limbo, of Israeli society in the future. For even if unilateralism is accompanied by new partial withdrawals from the territories, it will not put an end to the basic claims of the Palestinians. The primary error of unilateralism, as I have noted, lies in the wish to move forward without taking the other side into account. And so this policy is certain to fail in the long run.

For it is highly unlikely that Israeli leaders will find among the Palestinians negotiating partners willing to accept their cantonization, the wall, and a de facto submission to ongoing Israeli control of all movement within their territories, not to mention the blocking of access to East Jerusalem. Were any such interlocutors to be found, they would quickly be called collaborators by the population of the territories. And if no viable Palestinian state emerges, a new generation will arise, unacquainted with defeat. Like the current generation, or even more so, it will conclude that Israel will never yield except to violence, since this is how a great many Palestinians already explain the withdrawal from Gaza. As Amos Harel has predicted, if there is neither a viable Palestinian state nor a relinquishment of Israeli control, a new revolt will break out tomorrow or the day after (Harel and Isasharoff 2005).

THE VICTORY OF HAMAS

We are not yet at that point. Very soon after leaving Gaza, however, Israel found itself facing an unprecedented situation: the victory of Hamas in the Palestinian general elections on January 25, 2006, the most democratic elections ever to take place in an Arab country. As has happened each time the Israelis' biased viewpoint makes them bump up harshly against their inability to decipher the other side's reality, this failure to anticipate the Islamist landslide prompted a flood of criticism, aimed primarily at the secret services, the underlying point of which was this: Why were these people, capable of liquidating or arresting whomever they wished, whenever and wherever they chose, blind to the profound developments in Palestinian society?

And there were subsidiary questions as well. What accounts for the regular marginalization of the very few Shin Bet leaders who, far in advance, almost since the beginnings of the second intifada, had predicted the disastrous consequences for Israel of a policy aimed at discrediting the Palestinian Authority, systematically destroying its institutions, and refusing it any option to end the crisis through negotiation? Why were their reports shunted aside, unattended to by anyone highly placed in the special services or at the political level? Once the shock of the Hamas landslide had passed, these questions abounded in the Israeli press—before being quickly shunted aside in turn, as has happened on every similar occasion.

The reasons for the Hamas victory are well known. First of all, it was part of a general upsurge of political Islamism throughout the Arab–Muslim world. But this phenomenon must be modified by the specific conditions of the Palestinian election. Hamas is a nationalist political movement basing its actions on religion, not so much a classic fundamentalist party. Moreover, as is well demonstrated by a recent study of the Lebanese refugee camps (Rougier 2004), it is literally detested by the Palestinian jihadists. In the eyes of Bin Laden's disciples, Hamas is a traitor to the cause because it is primarily nationalist, continuing to emphasize the territorial nature of its struggle (Palestine), whereas for them the notion of territory is no longer meaningful. They do not distinguish among Palestine, Bosnia, Afghanistan, and Chechnya; all that matters in their view is the establishment of a new caliphate for the Muslim *umma* as a whole.

Its strong nationalist identity is the reason why the Palestinian Islamist party won the votes not just of the religious but also of a great many Palestinians who wanted to punish Fatah for its negligence in meeting the basic needs of the population, and, even more, for its negligence in the face of Israeli policy. Why vote for a party that calls for making peace through negotiating with a state that takes no account whatsoever of the wish for peace, and ignores the leaders making such an appeal if it does not hold them in utter contempt? Worse, a state that, as the Palestinians see it, never acts except in relation to force, never evacuates a territory or settlement except under constraint?

For this is precisely the essential political assessment the Palestinians made of the Israeli evacuation of Gaza. They themselves had been conquered militarily, but the IDF left only because it was worn out, the Israeli government having concluded that maintaining its forces in the Gaza Strip was more costly than an evacuation. And it was Hamas, the party that never put any faith in negotiations, not those favoring a return to the talks, to whom the Palestinians gave credit for this event, which they saw as a huge success—not the military withdrawal from Gaza (Israel had partially withdrawn in 1994), but, for the first time in thirty-eight years of occupation, the evacuation of settlements.

The day after the electoral victory of Hamas on January 25, 2006, Ehud Olmert, the new Israeli prime minister, declared that the Israeli government would not negotiate with a terrorist Palestinian power that did not recognize the Jewish state. We may wonder whether, this time, the Israeli refusal to negotiate came at just the right moment. Previously Olmert had had opposite him a man, Abu Mazen, who had been regularly elected, formally recognized Israel, and was eager to negotiate with him. But for an entire year, pursuing his unilateralist policy, Olmert had never undertaken the slightest negotiation with him. Now he had opposite him an interlocutor who had no more intention of negotiating than the Israeli government did.

For what is the credo of Hamas? It can be summed up as follows: (1) To end the conflict it is not necessary to recognize Israel; (2) It is not necessary to negotiate, because Israel has known for a long time, and very precisely, the conditions under which the conflict could end: what it would have to do is evacuate all the Palestinian territories conquered in June 1967; (3) If Israel carried out this evacuation, the Islamists would be prepared to offer a *hudna*, a long-term truce that would extend indefinitely.

Israeli leaders may not trust this offer, but they can't pretend it does not exist. At this point they have reached the end of the road. After nearly forty years of occupation it is clear beyond any shadow of a doubt that what is at stake for the two peoples is not just the occupation itself but the end of the domination, the matrix of control, of the one over the other. It is the admission of the equality between the two partners with regard to rights and dignity.

From 1967 to 1993 Israeli governments wanted to crush the PLO. They did not succeed. After trying in a thousand ways, political and military, to ignore and eradicate the Palestinian national movement, they finally had no choice but to recognize its existence. After the Oslo Accords, as we have seen, they never stopped trying to subjugate Palestinian nationalism to Israel's wishes, politically until Camp David, militarily in the intifada. Still they did not succeed. With the electoral victory of Hamas the Israelis will now have to confront the impasse to which their own policies have led.

Explaining his break with the ideology of Greater Israel that he had been brought up in and shared for a very long time, Dan Meridor, the former (right-wing) minister of the economy, told me this after the withdrawal from Gaza: "Zionism meant the Land of Israel for the Jews and only the Jews, plus democracy. But imagine that the Palestinians gave in, saying, 'You've won, and all this land is yours.' What would we do? Give them equal rights? That's democracy. On that day Israel would disappear as a Jewish state. We can't win a war we have no interest in winning."[11]

ISRAEL TODAY

This is where Israel is today. Its unilateralism, which aims at divorcing the Palestinians under Israeli conditions, retaining land and settlements in accordance with plans determined by Israel alone—once again, as if the Palestinians did not exist—will come up against the same rejection as their former policy of wholesale repression in the intifada. And the Israelis know this, because they have been told clearly. If they want a better life, one of calm and security, they must leave the territories, all the occupied territories, simply because pursuing the occupation there has no justification.

Worst of all, for them but also for the Palestinians, is that they are now confronted with this ineluctable reality after their conceptual and strategic blindness largely contributed to the accession to power of the very party that rejects their existence: Hamas. Just as, over thirty years ago, their refusal to restore to King Hussein of Jordan the territories they had taken from him largely contributed to establishing the PLO as an actor to be reckoned with in the conflict. And just as their refusal to resume negotiations with Yasser Arafat and the Palestinian Authority during the second intifada unless the Palestinian Authority first renounced acts of violence — and, beyond this, their systematic attempts to delegitimize the PA — worked to the sole advantage of the Islamists.

The repeated denial of reality has only made matters worse. As Mahmud Darwish, the greatest living Palestinian poet, observed in February 2006, "The sun, it is said, is more powerful than the wings of the crow that cover the horizon." In the end, Darwish went on to say,

> reality is always stronger than denial. When the intifada broke out, the Israelis declared that they had no partner. As it happens, only Yasser Arafat could get the people to accept concessions. But they kept on reducing him to nothing. When Mahmud Abbas succeeded him, they and the Americans were all lovey-dovey, but politically they didn't negotiate a thing. And so they discredited him, too, in the eyes of his population. They still think they can carry out a policy of unilateralism. But if they're trying to keep their settlement blocs and generously accord us some bantustans, this means they don't want peace. And that won't work. Until they have to bow to reality. The only way is to be done once and for all with the occupation.[12]

The Palestinian poet went on to add a further observation. For his society, he said, the accession to power of Hamas is a regressive phenomenon heavy with menace: "I can't hide my anxieties. The leaders of Hamas have said they want to refashion the society on an Islamic basis. Anyone in favor of a pluralist and secular Palestine can only fear for the rights of women, for young people and individual liberties, not to mention the Christian component."

Whatever the reasons for the victory of Hamas, escaping Islamist control is now an issue of crucial historic proportions for Palestinian society if they do not wish to see Hamas, in its turn, overcome in the future by the jihadists as has already happened in certain Lebanese refugee camps.

CONCLUSION
Salvation through Defeat

A victim and nothing but a victim confronts a perpetual enemy who can't accept the presence of the other except through violence. These two societies, having attempted a peace process that was badly handled, will not let go of this powerful, mutual tropism of their own accord but will have to be induced to do so by a political initiative or dramatic events coming from the outside. At the present time large majorities in each camp are locked into the vision of "us" against "them." Each concrete block added by the Israelis, each watchtower, each cubic meter of land dug to extend, broaden, and deepen the security wall and the barbed-wire ditch that are supposed to separate them from their enemy, increases their isolation, their alienation from their environment, and the hostility they arouse. Each additional panel of the wall brings them closer to a clash of civilizations.

In addition, such a clash between Israelis and Palestinians sets in opposition not only one camp against another but also, within each side, those who uphold the ethnicist way of thinking against those in favor of universalism and justice. But few are able to get far enough out from under the weight of ethnicism to recognize this perspective. Thus, in different ways, the two societies have been worn out. Neither society has been beaten, but inside each many people have been battered down. The Palestinians increasingly see resistance as their only option, even as they go from defeat to defeat, a conviction that is matched only by the growing sense of impasse in Israel and the idea that, even as it goes from victory to victory, the country is being morally destroyed.

Young Israelis with a global perspective are not the only ones to leave their country to see whether life is less crazy elsewhere. Young Palestinians also feel the need to study or work in Amman or Cairo in order to flee a future without prospects. Many of the Palestinians who returned to the territories from San Francisco or Detroit to help build a country after the Oslo Accords have gone back to the diaspora. On each side those who retain some hope in the possibility of a shared future are resisting the terrible pressure exerted by the armed confrontation. But they will not succeed in winning over their fellow citizens by intellectual means alone. Too much blood has been shed in this intifada, too much mutual hostility has piled up. And, on the Palestinian side, there have been too many impediments to a decent life, too much daily suffering.

The problem cannot be reduced to the claim that the birth of Israel was accompanied by a radical injustice toward a native population. Many states have arisen by committing acts of injustice or committed them after their establishment. In the case of Israel what makes this injustice fundamental is that it is constitutive of the state: Israel would not have been able to become what it is without the initial expulsion of the Palestinians, and its future primarily depends on settling the dispute with them. This is why the denial of this fact is such a serious handicap, and why the Israelis are so frightened of giving it up. Despite their overwhelming military superiority, their international recognition, and the support they enjoy from the United States, the Israelis' existential fear is rooted in reality. What would happen *for them* if their legitimacy began to seem less conclusive in their own eyes, or if they stopped seeing themselves as victims? After thirty-nine years of occupation, leaving all the occupied territories would constitute an unprecedented challenge to their basic assumptions. It would mean abandoning once and for all the mythic relation to the Land of Israel, fixing the necessary demarcation of definitive and inviolable borders along the 1967 boundaries, and abandoning the historical domination over the Palestinians. It would involve a profound questioning of the Israeli self-image and its key elements.

Right after the War of 1967 General de Gaulle said this: "Now Israel is organizing an occupation on the territories it seized, which can't go on without opposition, repression, and expulsions, and a resistance is becoming evident there that, in turn, it will call terrorism."[1] Since that time this occupation has become stronger and more systematic. It has been accompanied by settlements. But nothing has arisen to alter de Gaulle's prediction; today it is clearly more valid than ever. The situation he described has become ossified on the ground and in people's minds. By a wide majority the Israelis are now stuck in their view that the struggle against terrorism takes priority over everything, while the origins of that struggle have been concealed. Despite all the hopeful signs in the 1990s, as long as this relation to the Palestinians continues, it is impossible to envisage an Israeli society largely capable, on its own initiative, of seeing the other as he is, looking at itself in the mirror, and drawing up the balance sheet of its own acts and history. It is even harder to imagine that the Palestinians, now under Israel's heel, will undertake a task of this kind until they have attained true national independence.

GETTING OUT OF THE IMPASSE

Yasser Arafat is gone. George W. Bush has postponed the conditional establishment of a Palestinian state. Ariel Sharon's successors, too, are hedging, as a way of blocking for good and all the constitution of a viable Palestinian state, one able to cooperate peacefully with his neighbors—a requirement that, no matter how intrinsically difficult, is essential for its survival. But we must be cautious about making predictions. Much of what takes place between the Israelis and the Palestinians will depend on local developments, and even more so on regional developments. Anything can happen. The United States may become enmired in Iraq to an extent far beyond what it imagines, or it may achieve relative military control over the situation. With the Bush administration an extension of the war on terrorism beyond Iraq remains a possibility, as does the gradual withdrawal of his troops if they are threatened with collapse or, conversely, if stability should begin to emerge. Dependent as always on their security services but extraordinarily fragile socially, the regimes of the major Arab countries, chiefly Egypt and Saudi Arabia, may remain as they are or be blown away with the wind as suddenly as was the Shah of Iran twenty-seven years ago. The Middle East is a powder keg.

In Israel the nationalist right disintegrated in the face of the emergence of the so-called centrist Kadima party. Ariel Sharon's successors set a new course to lead an alliance between the nonideological, dyed-in-the-wool advocates of security and the labor movement, returning to the fold, as it were, in a society that had been profoundly altered in the meantime. If, after the Israeli military withdrawal, the population of Gaza remains imprisoned behind the barbed wire that has proved effective as a security measure, any Israeli government, like the present administration of Ehud Olmert, will pursue the building of the security wall restricting the population of the West Bank to its enclaves. If the war on terrorism continues, any government will have to tack among the vagaries of the international situation, benefiting from the alliance with the United States, perhaps occasionally straining but never breaking that tie.

As for Palestinian society, predictions are even more risky. Bled dry and fragmented, it may reconstitute itself, or, urged on by Ariel Sharon's successors, it may sink into even greater chaos. As he did with the Gaza withdrawal, Sharon undoubtedly had his services plan various options, and certain Palestinian groups can be counted on to provide a "justification" for pushing Palestinian society toward chaos. Six years after the outset of the second intifada, and after the success of the Islamist faction Hamas at the parliamentary elections, both the regionalist tendencies and the dissentions and temporary alliances between armed groups with partisan and concealed financing are stronger than ever among the Palestinians.[2] Gaza may fall into disarray, something that Sharon's successors are probably betting on to conclusively persuade their people and the international community that a Palestinian state must not be formed. But despite the blows they have received, the *sumud*, the determination to hang in there, has never been stronger in the collective Palestinian attitude.

While the direction the Israeli–Palestinian conflict will take is difficult to foresee, the conditions under which it might be diminished are crystal clear. When David Lloyd George decided to recognize the Irish Free State in 1921, he noted that one can't cross a gulf in two jumps; the British troops had to be withdrawn. There will be no solution in Palestine unless Israeli forces are withdrawn from the occupied territories. Not a partial withdrawal, one that occurs in stages, in two, three, or five jumps spread out over time, nor an inconsistent one in which Israel would maintain the core of its settlements at little expense, but an all-out, final withdrawal from all the occupied territories, including East Jerusalem. This is as essential as it was with the withdrawal from the whole of the occupied Sinai, and (apart from a still controversial few square kilometers) with South Lebanon, and it would have been the case with the Golan in 2000 had Ehud Barak not pulled back at the last minute from an accord with Syria.

Six years after the outset of the second intifada, Israeli society by and large accepts the principle of a withdrawal. And in addition to the polls, statements by pragmatically inclined leaders of the nationalist right show that, at heart, most Israelis basically know that there is no other way the conflict could possibly come to an end; the Palestinians are not going to disappear. Yet they can't resolve to undertake a full withdrawal to the 1967 borders.

For thirty-nine years, in fair weather or foul, whether holding negotiations or waging war, Israel has always had a thousand good reasons not to leave the occupied territories. If the settlement party, even if it is a small minority, continues to impose its mind-set on the entire society despite the difficulties anticipated in the withdrawal from Gaza, this is because the vast majority of Israelis can only imagine the opposite mind-set as a denial of their identity, of what they have thought, said, and done for nearly four decades.

It is now time to go. Not tomorrow, not conditionally, not after a hypothetical prior agreement in which each square kilometer would be haggled over as in the souk. Israel has to leave the territories, and the sooner the better. What other alternative is there? Will the waning intifada perhaps be broken? And then what? If terrorism were wiped out, if Israel achieved a return to calm and finally realized its old dream of negotiating with docile interlocutors who accepted its conditions—all highly unlikely—what would change? With the inhabitants of Gaza imprisoned in their barbed-wire cage and the charms of "peaceful occupation" restored on the West Bank, Israel would be transformed into a systematically segregationist country with a Palestinian populace equal to, and soon greater than, its own, deprived of rights and cantonized into Bantustans. The Jewish state would then no longer be Jewish on the ethno-demographic level but, by institutionalizing a new form of apartheid, would itself be cut off from any future and even from any moral right to its existence as such.

Most important, such an eventuality would be only a short respite. Palestinian national identity is now taken for granted. Even the ideological settlers can no longer avoid using the term *Palestinian*, banned for forty years, since it has become so ingrained. In three, five, or ten years the revolt would begin anew. What is worse, the Palestinians would no longer be asking for a state but simply for equal civil rights, and who could legitimately deny them this? By virtue of its own action, Israel would disappear the day ethnic segregation was abolished, and in the same way its leaders, denying the principle of the right of return, said they feared the PLO was attempting to do so, namely by invasion from within. For that goal to be reached, not a single refugee would have to return.

This would inevitably occur—unless the hopes or premonitions of Benny Elon and Benny Morris should come to pass. "Exceptional circumstances" might permit a new expulsion of the Palestinians—an unlikely and unrealistic prospect, but not a totally impossible one if the conflict went out of control and the region as a whole burst into flames. But even a new Palestinian exodus would not get to the core of the problem. Today's world is not the world of 1948. The international community would not be so quick to ratify the legitimacy of an expulsion. Not only would the newly expelled Palestinians not disappear, but, once deprived of any prospect of national existence on their own soil, their demand for the abolition of Israel in return would be all the stronger. Not only would Israel, for its part, have lost all moral direction, but the internal crisis of its society would worsen dramatically. Many Israeli Jews, like Tom Segev, would "stop identifying with this state."[3]

Even if most Israelis would rather banish these disturbing issues from their minds, they have premonitions about them. Time brings change. The vast majority will never evolve toward abandoning their founding tropisms except under the pressure of dramatic events. When the current intifada broke out, people like Avraham Burg, president of the Knesset, instinctively took Barak's side. The pacifist Amos Oz immediately blamed the Palestinians for every failure. Today both men have changed. Who would have imagined, four years ago, that intellectual Israelis from Meretz-Yahad, the party of Yossi Beilin, would even consider the idea of a binational future with the Palestinians? On the right, too, there is deep uneasiness. Ariel Sharon would never have decided to risk an explosion in Likud by evacuating the settlers from Gaza had he not known that this evacuation was supported by a majority of the population.

The Israeli left took thirty years to recognize the PLO. It took thirty-five years to consider sharing sovereignty over Jerusalem, forty for a minority of its members to acknowledge in a draft agreement the validity of the demand for the Palestinians' right of return as the basis for any solution to the refugee question that was honorable and as just as possible. Even if Israeli society today is walled into its denial of the other, deep down it senses that the present situation is not tenable in the long run. Apart from the ultranationalists and those who claim a mystical relationship to the land, though many of their fellow citizens share these values, a vague but deep sense of disquiet has come over people. "Where are we heading with this?" they ask. "We don't know where we're going," they say, in a tone that is as confused as it is fatalistic. In intellectual salons and cheap diners alike, this is what one most often hears when Israelis get together. And in a confused sort of way, too, they are well aware that any compromise solution—a bit of territory "given up" here, a moment of governmental initiative there—will be only a makeshift arrangement as long as the Palestinian national question lacks a political solution.

This being the case, why do men like Yossi Beilin and Ami Ayalon, both absolutely convinced of the inevitability of a total Israeli withdrawal from the occupied territories if Israel is to be saved, postpone the deadline until new negotiations have been undertaken? Why don't they unambiguously advocate a unilateral withdrawal of the Israeli army to the borders of June 1967? Why don't they proclaim: "We have to leave and let the Palestinians build their state. Then we'll make peace with it as we did with Egypt and Jordan. And if they don't want that and remain hostile, we'll have ample means of defending ourselves"? If they don't say this in public, it can only serve to perpetuate the illusions of a peace in which Israel would not have to "give up" everything.

They don't do so because their political calculations are based on the conviction that their society is not yet ready to hear these things said. And yet Ayalon is aware of the contradictory nature of this attitude. "We have to leave the territories because each additional day that passes makes this departure more difficult," he told me as early as the second year of the intifada.[4] The problem is that even those people for whom this is self-evident can't say so aloud. This being the case, for most Israelis leaving the territories without getting anything tangible in exchange would be a terrible defeat, and would be experienced as profoundly traumatic. Even those of their leaders who are most clear-minded in private find themselves caught in the trap that Ehud Barak and Ariel Sharon have made.

Departure after a bilateral agreement? That would have been preferable by far for Israel's image and even more so for the political and security guarantees such an agreement would have brought. But such an accord was not reached at Camp David. And, as we have seen, this was largely the fault not of the Palestinians but of the Israelis, who were unable to understand what was ultimately at stake. After nearly four decades of so-called peace initiatives, from the Rogers Plan of 1970 to the "road map" of 2003, including the first round of Camp David talks in 1977 (which envisaged Palestinian autonomy in five years' time, though this never came to pass) and the Madrid Conference in 1991, the fiasco of the Oslo process has by now condemned any new peace plan that is incremental or partial to failure in advance. And this for one simple reason: quite apart from the refugees living outside of Palestine, even the Palestinians most favorably inclined toward Israel no longer have any faith in such a plan. Eager to see Israel act first to end the occupation, and having lost all confidence in Israel's real willingness to do so, they would have nothing to do with it. If, tomorrow, a Palestinian leader were prepared to sign an accord that would not radically and rapidly put an end to the occupation, he would immediately be considered a capitulator and would lose the trust of his people.

The Mitchell Plan, the Tenet Plan, the Zinni Plan, the regional conference, the road map of the "quartet": all these initiatives have failed since the outbreak of the intifada. This is so not only because the heads of Likud, in Israel, have done everything to promote this failure, but also because the times have changed. Such a stepwise Israeli disengagement had once been foreseeable in the logic of the Oslo process, and might have been intelligently honored. Now it would seem to be only an obstacle to the end of the conflict. The Palestinians no longer trust this type of measure, even if, to maintain diplomatic appearances, their leaders call for a return to negotiations. The idea of a Peace of the Braves, an end to the conflict in which there would be no winner or loser, has had its day. If the Israelis are the only ones who can win a military victory, the Palestinians are the only ones who can win politically—or there will be no winner at all.

The first American opponents of the war in Vietnam had as their watchword "declare victory and get out." But the longer that war went on, the less possible it became for the Americans to plausibly declare victory. Similarly, even if it were implemented after an alleged eradication of all terrorists, a general withdrawal of Israel from the occupied territories would seem like a major political defeat. It would go against the one thing nearly all Israelis deeply believe, because they were brought up that way and their entire self-image depends on it, which is: not only must the enemy never win, but they themselves must never lose.

This is the trap in which Israel finds itself. The impossibility of withdrawing from the occupied territories without seeming to have been defeated politically is perfectly all right with those who take a long-term view, convinced as they are that the conflict will last for generations to come until the enemy gives up, and for whom there can be no other solution. It is all right with the Hamas militant in Gaza who told me, "They'll win all the battles until we win just one, and that'll be the end of them." It is also all right with all those in Israel who, imprisoned in the mentality of the "wall of steel," are convinced that the Arabs must never be given hope and that any withdrawal would be the beginning of the end. But this trap is incompatible with political reality. For at this point, and it makes no difference whether Israel does or does not evacuate "only Gaza," even as the Palestinians gain nothing by going from one defeat to the next by terrorism, the Israelis are destroying themselves by going from "victory" to "victory."

The alternatives are set in stone. The first is that the Jewish state will manage to crush the Palestinian insurrection temporarily, nullifying the accepted principle of Oslo—the de facto recognition of the Palestinian national movement—with the consequences previously mentioned: the establishment of an Israel institutionally segregationist in the view of the entire world. The other is that, to avoid this dire future, Israel will leave the occupied territories. At this point a negotiation and a peace treaty can no longer be preconditions of the withdrawal; that withdrawal is the precondition of a possible future peace. In short, Israel's "victory" will lead it to perdition. Salvation can come only through "defeat."

No such defeat is on the horizon today. There are political reasons for this. Israel is the most trustworthy regional ally of the United States in the war on terrorism, and its diplomatic, military, and socioeconomic superiority is too imposing for it to be made to give up domination over the occupied territories, nor can anyone imagine what might force it to do so. And, of paramount importance, Israeli society will not come to such a decision on its own, for it is convinced that such a "defeat" would be the end of everything. Fear is the prime mover of the Israelis' automatic political tendencies. It goes hand in hand with delusions of power, behind which lies an immense insecurity. As the writer David Grossman puts it, "It's an enormous temptation to be strong and feel weak."[5] Regardless of their actual strength vis-à-vis the enemy, this is a temptation to which most Israelis succumb, because, together with victimization, fear promotes a sense of legitimacy and impunity and justifies aggression.

What is the origin of this apparently irrational collective feeling that to give something up without compensation would be the beginning of the end? That losing a little, a little territory or a little domination of the other, would inevitably lead to the total disappearance of Israel, to the Jews' being thrown into the sea? This fear is not without roots and motives. As we have seen, the memory of the historical sufferings of the Jews, and the way that memory is echoed in education and all aspects of daily life, plays a major role here, structuring the cult of force of which Grossman speaks.

But the fear has other causes as well, ones that are more difficult to articulate because they are more deeply buried. Prominent among these is the perception of the Israeli presence in the region as alien. This perception is clearly very widespread in the Arab environment, where, to put it mildly, the uniqueness and oddity of the Israeli "fortress" are at best accepted unwillingly, at worst flatly rejected. But this perception of strangeness is also shared to the highest degree by the Israelis, who experience themselves as foreign to their surroundings. They know that their presence is not self-evident, that it is due solely to the imposition of force. The Israelis suffer from the foreigner syndrome, which, whatever the circumstances and however deeply rooted the population, always involves a deep fear of being driven out, especially if the surroundings are hostile. So as not to *imagine* the destruction of their own national existence, not to imagine themselves being thrown into the sea, they must drive out the other, subjugating him and denying him his own national existence *in reality*.

How to get out of the vicious circle? The only way to overcome this constitutive fear is to invalidate it in action, to ascertain and confirm, in practice, that Israel can give up the territories without incurring its disappearance. The Israelis will never be freed of their fears until the day they realize that when the occupied territories have been evacuated they and their state will still be there, alive, with their military and economic superiority and their anchoring in the Western tradition, the day they realize that evacuating the territories will have had no existential results.

For there is no risk whatsoever that, if it leaves the territories, Israel will immediately disappear. Militarily it enjoys an advantage of a thousand to one over the Palestinians, ten to one over the Arab countries. Moreover, just as thirty years ago a withdrawal from the Sinai was perceived as strategically impermissible but, once undertaken, turned out to be a huge political asset, there is every chance that a general withdrawal from the occupied Palestinian territories will strengthen an Israel applauded by the entire international community. Yet it is incontrovertible that such a withdrawal would then lead to very deep and painful questioning and a crisis of identity.

If Israel were to leave the territories and yet not disappear, on the day the last Israeli soldier departed the Palestinians would most certainly embrace, sing, and dance in the streets just the way the Israeli Jews did on May 15, 1948, when the last soldier of the British occupation set sail. A real, almost unbearable feeling of defeat would come over most Israelis. And countless questions would arise. Why did a decision that had been postponed for decades *not* lead to the end of everything, but instead the contrary? Why did we deceive ourselves so deeply and for so long? Why didn't we leave earlier? Why were there so many victims, such vast expenditures of resources, so much repression, so many manufactured myths and false ideas? Why such strong conviction that only the domination of the other would pay off, if this was where it got us?

Were there to be an announcement of a general withdrawal from the territories, especially from the West Bank, "the heart of the Land of Israel," as Kosovo was "the cradle of the Serbian people," the settlers would not be a threat on the practical level. As opposed to what a majority of Israelis imagine, a wholesale evacuation of the settlers would pose no major logistical difficulties. If, tomorrow, a government in Jerusalem announced that in less than six months, and no matter what, there would not be a single Israeli soldier left in the occupied territories, there would not be a single settler left there either. None of them, even the most fanatic, the ones most inclined to take risks like those of the OAS (the organization of French terrorists opposed to Algerian independence), would remain in Palestinian territory without the protection of the Israeli army. Their rabbis, who for so long cited biblical verses to justify the prohibition against abandoning a single square centimeter of the Land of Israel, would be quick to find in *halakha*, Jewish religious law, all the judgments requiring their flock to save their lives and beat a hasty retreat. No one would bewail the fate of the ultranationalist mystical settlers. But Israel would then have to go about appropriately relocating its "repatriated" citizens, who for decades had been sent to live in foreign territory under a policy of planned settlement.

On the other hand, the party in favor of the settlements and a Greater Israel would be plunged into despair and rage at its defeat, seeing Israel's withdrawal as a catastrophe, a *Naqba* in reverse. And they would not be alone. With the weight it has gathered over the years through its ideological networks and multiple institutional channels, including in the army, it would then potentially constitute an enormous political threat within Israel, perhaps a threat of civil war. "There will be no withdrawal from the territories without a terrible internal crisis in Israel," the sociologist Uri Ben Eliezer told me.[6] At the very least, strong centrifugal tendencies, long absorbed by the national consensus, would burst forth. In view of the fear that these discords will erupt, the greatest risk Israel faces today is that without the occupation of the Palestinian territories it will lose its primary social cement. Is the perpetuation of conflict its sole guarantee of cohesion?

THE PRICE OF RECONCILIATION

After the intifada and the dramas to which it gave rise, a prompt reconciliation between Israelis and Palestinians is hardly conceivable. An initial "cold peace," following upon an Israeli withdrawal, is easier to imagine. But even that seems highly unlikely in the near future, given the imprisonment of the Israelis within their own mental walls, the dispersion and chaos of Palestinian society within its own mental walls as well as the physical walls that have been imposed on it, the relative strength of the two opponents, and the reelection of George W. Bush. A peace of this kind is very unlikely to emerge through a sudden awareness on the part of the majority of Israelis of what is really at stake in their future, or by a thinning of the cement that ensures their cohesion. But at some unforeseeable time in the future the international community may well impose an evacuation of the occupied territories. That community could intervene only if the perpetuation of the Israeli–Palestinian conflict came to pose a threat to world peace, which is far from being the case. It could also, more prosaically, intervene if the regional disturbances aroused by this conflict came to threaten the interests of the United States, which, after the war in Iraq, is more than ever the "godfather" of the Middle East.

In the history of Israel each time the tutelary power has banged its fist on the table the Jewish state has given in. In 1948, when Israel's troops invaded the Sinai, President Truman demanded their immediate retreat. Ben Gurion immediately complied. And again in 1957, when Ben Gurion was forced by President Eisenhower to leave Gaza after the British/French/ Israeli war in the Sinai, he did so without hesitation. In 1973, after Tsahal had crossed the Suez Canal and encircled the Third Egyptian Army, Henry Kissinger, Nixon's secretary of state, threatened to cut off military supplies to Israel unless the blockade was lifted immediately and the Israelis returned at once to their own side of the canal. Golda Meir and Moshe

Dayan did not question this demand. In 1991, Prime Minister Itzhak Shamir wanted nothing to do with the Madrid Conference, at which the PLO was to be represented for the first time. Suit yourself, replied James Baker, secretary of state to the first George Bush, but don't expect to get the loan of ten billion dollars you're counting on for the integration of Russian immigrants. Israel took part in the Madrid Conference. In 1998, during the Clinton administration, Prime Minister Benyamin Netanyahu, the fierce opponent of the Oslo Accords and any restitution of land to the Palestinians, shook the hand of the man he had never called anything but "the terrorist Arafat" and signed the interim accord of Wye River, which provided for a new partial withdrawal of Israel from the West Bank.

Today more than ever, the state of Israel seems to be the most trustworthy and stable ally of the United States in the Middle East. It is also more than ever dependent on the U.S. for carrying out its own politics. Were circumstances to change, a turnaround in American policy would be disastrous for it, dependent as it is the most extremist fringe elements in Washington. Under the Bush administration such a reversal is highly unlikely, but in view of the widespread chaos in the region it is certainly conceivable at some future date. To prevent the Mashreq from sinking into Islamism, and to preserve its interests and the regimes that are its accomplices, another American administration might well consider it more useful to force Israel to withdraw from the occupied territories and form a viable Palestinian state. Like Ben Gurion, Golda Meir, and Itzhak Shamir in the past, no Israeli government would then risk breaking the tie to the godfather in Washington. Israel would, of course, seek to postpone that date and to obtain additional security and financial guarantees. But in the face of a determined American government, it would not be able to reverse the trend. And if Israel were confronted with a choice like the one Slobodan Milosevic faced in 1999 in Kosovo—withdrawing his troops from a territory or refusing at the risk of being a universal pariah—there is only an infinitesimal possibility that its government would opt for refusal. The country would have too much to lose.

History rarely occurs as one would imagine, and these speculations seem as improbable as they are distant. They leave little room for hope that the conflict can be resolved for the time being. We might just as well speculate on the widespread disorders in the Near East that would arise should the opposite set of circumstances occur, as for example if the war in Iraq led to an extension of the "clash of civilizations." Then the potential collapse of governments currently in power would strengthen Israel's role against the rise of jihadist Islamism, and the seizure of control over the Palestinian national movement by radical Islamism would convince even diehard Israelis of the futility of hoping for peace with it. Most important, if a cold peace were imposed on Israel from without, there would be no instantaneous solution to the problems of its insertion in the region and its acceptance there. Such a peace would simply be the necessary prelude. A true peace, binding for the future, would still have to be established in the context of reconciliation and acknowledgment of the true identity of the other.

As long as Israel does not own up to the constitutive facts of its own existence and those of its Palestinian partner, beginning with the foundational fact that Israel in effect created a nation of refugees, no real reconciliation will occur, either with that nation or with the Arab world in general. It goes without saying that, as soon as a "truth and reconciliation" process emerges, similar to the one in South Africa, both parties would be affected: the Palestinian national movement, too, would have to draw up a balance sheet of its past blunders and acts.

If a truly viable Palestinian state were established tomorrow, it would immediately have to deal with the basic issue of how to guarantee its democratic nature. Given the political tradition of the PLO and the growing influence within the Palestinian population of the Islamists, there is every reason to fear the worst here. The present marginalization of the intellectual elite, the sharp decline in the status of women, the spread of Islamism,[7] and the accompanying reemergence of anti-Semitism are indicators of the difficulties a Palestinian state would have to surmount. It would still have to build a modern, democratic country, break free of its attitude of systematic victimization, and, as the lawyer Wassila Tamzali has said with regard to the governmental failure of Algerian nationalism, "get out from under the yoke of liberation in order to get to liberty." "Liberation," she adds, "implies the assertion of one's difference from the other, with the hatred that goes along with that. In the context of liberation the individual is necessarily part of a whole, unique collective. But liberty makes it possible to recognize the other side in its own right."[8] A difficult path, but one that can be mapped out once independence is gained. The recognition of dignity depends on it.

Once Israel no longer has to face the risks stemming from its role as a perpetual occupying power, its challenge will be to build a truly modern state. This chiefly means getting beyond ethnicism, beginning with treating its own Palestinian national minority as full equals. It also means putting an end to the reactionary, ethnicist, and religious aspects of its legal system, abolishing the power of Orthodox rabbis over family law, honoring the identity of Oriental Jews, and raising children to respect others and know history. Ultimately this amounts to making a profound change in the political nature of the country, establishing a republic worthy of that name with a constitution guaranteeing the equality of all under the law. In an Israel rid of the burden of ethnicism, one in which religion and the state are truly separate, no one who claims to be a Jew will find his identity denied because it does not correspond to official canons, as is the case today, for example, with Jews who were converted by Reform rabbis and the progeny of these converts. In an Israel that has entered modernity, Jews will choose to be citizens because that seems best to them, that is, in a variety of individual ways, and not because the Jewish ethnicity of their country is imposed by law or the Orthodox rabbinate.

If the Palestinian state were formed, and the Israelis realized that its advent did not lead to their own disappearance, the way would lie open for each person to recognize the other as an equal. As has been the case elsewhere, this is the path to reconciliation, as is the admission—if not of the truth—at least of essential truths. As the linguist Daniel Dor of the University of Tel Aviv told me, "If a wholesale withdrawal from the Palestinian territories were to occur tomorrow and a true peace established, and if a Truth and Reconciliation Commission were set up, people—a lot of them—would spontaneously begin to tell the truth. Because these truths would once again become audible."[9] His prediction might be seen as overly optimistic today. Nevertheless, we do now know the conditions under which a shared historical narrative, leading to a shared future based on respect and equality, will be possible.

These prospects may seem distant. Yet the wear and tear, and the profound feeling of impasse experienced by both societies today, contain as many reasons to hope as to despair. Up to now, the century-long strategy of the *yishuv*, and later the state of Israel, namely to build a fortress and keep on enlarging it through a policy of faits accomplis, has paid off. But it is ineluctably approaching the threshold beyond which this logic will bring about the opposite results. For, so long as the Palestinians continue to exist, the future of Israel and its Jewish population lies in peaceful integration into the Middle East. If the decision to cross this threshold is not taken, Israel could survive as an excessively armed fortress owing its survival to the constant imposition of its power on the native inhabitants and on an environment that is much larger, and expanding. But it would then still owe its continuance to its status at the top of the geopolitical agenda of a larger world power, and face a future of ongoing war that would only conclude with its own brutal and definitive disappearance.

AFTERWORD
Haim Gouri

Haim Gouri is the last Israeli "national poet" still alive, a member of the "1948 generation." A bard who sings of the love of the Land of Israel, his heart steeped in the memory of Jewish sufferings, he is renowned for a number of literary and poetic works dealing with the War of Independence, in which he fought in the ranks of Palmakh, as well as for *Facing the Glass Booth*, his famous book on the Eichmann trial, which he covered for the newspaper *Davar*. Works like the poem "Bab El-Wad" and the film *The 81st Blow*, taught in every school, are classics of modern Hebrew literature. Several of his poems are known by every Israeli child.

In October 2004 Gouri, at the age of 81, published an anthology called *Ani, Milkhemet Ezrakhim* (I Am a Civil War). Its very title shows how torn apart Gouri feels today. Here, as he recalls the past, he includes some poems whose spirit radically contradicts that of his earlier works, tinged with the heroism and glorification of Israel. They sum up a life. An Israeli life.

Here are three passages from the anthology.

From "The Oriental Fair"

Don't worry.
Everything's preserved in the archives, in drawers of dust.
In attics, in hidden basement hiding places.
When it's permitted, by law,
after all the guilty ones have died,
the innocent ones will come
to open up the rare treasures.
It'll be a ball! Believe me!

"Nights of Dogs"

And I, who loved the Land of Israel with all his heart,
moved around inside it ceaselessly like a devious plot:
"Where is the home of the Mukhtar?" like a distant
prologue to T.N.T.

It was clear that the war would come sooner or later and we
called them "files on villages," "perspective outlines,"
"birds-eye outlines," "access routes" and "look-out points"
and "prepared-in-advance coordinates" for the day of wrath.

We walked. But often we forgot the purpose of the walk
and then it became a walk pure as the splendor of the
heavens and without a dagger in the heart.

Walking in the Land of Israel of relative peace and
neighborly relations. For we were mixed together with
them, field by field, house by house, and sometimes—
heart by heart.

I haven't mentioned the "mixed neighborhoods,"
"Romema" and "Shiekh Bader," "Menshaia" or "Wadi
Nisnas," and the streets of Tiberias and Safed. Not to
speak of Rehovot-Zarnuga and Zichron-Faradis, and the
other settlements of the Baron.[1]

That world was destroyed and is no longer. And my heart
cries in me, more than once, when I remember it. For it
was part of my life, my childhood, and it had beauty in it
and deep-reaching connections. Not only fear. Not only
death.

Many of us loved the villages we blew up, that world
destroyed that is no longer . . .

"That Get-Together"

What will we do with all our memories.
Better that they rest in peace.
For our good.

But the silent ones will rise and come,
and the ones expelled and the exile-arrangers will come.
And the chronic complainers will come
and the opportunity-missers will also come.
And every abandoned one will be counted and
    every rejected one will be remembered.
I am the witness, to my sorrow, I and no other.

And also those hidden, for whom the silence is appropriate,
will come out of their hiding places and darkened basements.
As ambassadors of once upon a time.
. . .
And these and those will see and be seen and man will
    recognize his brother,
and shake hands and fall all over each other, like at a class
    reunion,
and with great joy and great crying, will remember and
    remind.
. . .
And this is almost the last chance to get an impression, to
    be seen,
to recognize each other a bit,
to shed light on several enigmas, before the covering
    darkness.

[All translations from the original Hebrew by Linda Zisquit.]

Notes

INTRODUCTION

1. As of the tally made by Agence France Presse on November 21, 2004, the conflict had resulted in 4,582 deaths: 3,547 Palestinians and 961 Israelis.
2. On February 25, 1994, this ultranationalist religious settler machine-gunned twenty-nine Muslim worshipers in the Mosque of the Cave of the Patriarchs before killing himself. This was the first suicide attack committed after the Israeli–Palestinian accords at Oslo in 1993. In all likelihood it was Goldstein's way of protesting the accords.
3. The article, originally printed in *Yediot Ahronot*, was translated in *Le Monde* on September 11, 2003.
4. Interview of Avraham Burg with Avi Shavit in *Haaretz*, French translation in *Courrier international*, December 11–17, 2003.
5. *Le Monde*, June 19, 2004.
6. Interview of Ariel Sharon by Ari Shavit in the weekly supplement to *Haaretz*, April 13, 2001.
7. Interview, July 3, 2003.
8. Interview, October 31, 2000.
9. Translator's note: Here and throughout, where a source in a language other than English is cited in the Reference List, I am translating from the version given in Sylvain Cypel's French text.
10. This term, which means *extermination*, is preferred in Israel to *Holocaust*.
11. In a legal action taken against him in the early 1970s, when the Communist Polish government was quick to stir up anti-Semitism in order to overcome popular insurrection, Jacek Kuron, who would become the labor minister in the first post-Communist government, felt similarly. When the prosecutor accused him of the worst turpitude — antisocial and unpatriotic behavior, and so forth — Kuron replied, "You've forgotten to add that I'm Jewish." Taken aback, the prosecutor said, "But . . . you aren't!" "No," Kuron said, "not as a rule. But at this moment I am."
12. Interview with Ami Ayalon on December 18, 2000.
13. Interview with Nazmi El-Ju'beh on July 9, 2003.

CHAPTER 1 – TANTURA

1. Interview, July 6, 2003. The following citations concerning Katz's master's thesis and its legal consequences are taken from this interview, except in the case of citations from eyewitness testimony appearing in the thesis, which are indicated as such.
2. *Haaretz*, December 22, 2000.
3. Interview, July 14, 2003. The following statements by Feldman are from the same interview.
4. Interview, July 6, 2003.
5. Interview, July 3, 2003.
6. Interview, July 14, 2003.
7. *Haaretz*, June 29, 2001. The following quotations from Segev are translated from the same article.
8. Interview, July 14, 2003.
9. Margalit, who went from *Haaretz* to *Maariv*, did so in particular in July 2003, when an Israeli director was making a film that did not refer explicitly to Tantura but mentioned a massacre of Palestinian civilians in 1948 in a way that was highly reminiscent of Katz's thesis. Yoav Gelber (2004), an information specialist and professor of Israeli Studies at the University of Haifa who was never concerned to know what really happened, presents a summary of the ideological attacks on Katz's thesis (see *Critique du post-sionisme*, Paris 2004, pp. 135–206).
10. Interview, July 11, 2003. The following quotations from Pappe regarding Katz's master's thesis and its judicial consequences are taken from the same interview.
11. See Pappe 2004, pp. 70–71 and notes 82 and 84, based on the archives of the Israeli army, dossier 143 and the archives of Haganah, p. 121.
12. Interview, July 6, 2003.
13. *Haaretz*, June 29, 2001.
14. Interview, July 11, 2003.
15. Interview, July 10, 2003.
16. Interview, June 9, 2004.
17. This is the title of the best summary of the initial work of the New Historians, presented and discussed by Dominique Vidal and Joseph Algazy (1998). Since then work by Israeli historians and sociologists, for the most part in Hebrew and English has appeared: Benny Morris, Ilan Pappe, Yoram Nimrod, Gershon Shafir, Avi Shlaim, Baruch Kimmerling, and others.
18. Basing his work on official archives, Morris was the first to reveal the means by which the Palestinians had been uprooted in 1948, as well as the vague intentions for "transfer" made long before that by the leaders of the *yeshuv*.

19. After Camp David and the onset of the intifada, without ever going back on his earlier writings, Morris has favored the political interpretation and, often, even the political justification of the facts he described there, especially the "transfer" of the Palestinians. The results are sometimes harmful with regard to the writing of history. Thus, for example, in his last work, *Victims* (2003), he downplays the vague intentions for "transfer" that he himself had previously revealed. Morris's evolution is examined at the end of Chapter 5 and below.

20. Jabotinsky's followers "called themselves 'revisionists' because they intended to revise Zionist politics—not Zionism itself—by returning to the sources: the political Zionism of Herzl" (Schattner 1991, p. 77).

21. Interview, July 10, 2003.

22. Interview, July 4, 2003.

CHAPTER 2 – THE "PURITY OF ARMS"

1. The account of the Congress is given in Morris 2003, pp. 162–164.

2. Weizmann Archives, 2271, cited in Morris 2003, p. 189.

3. Ben Gurion Archives, CZA Z4-14632, October 15, 1941, cited in Morris 2003, p. 189.

4. Interview, July 10, 2003.

5. Simha Flapan (1987) is also persuasive on this point. I shall not comment on the debate about whether this initial alliance was broken by the entry of Jordan into the war, as David Ben Gurion and Golda Meir held, or whether, on the contrary, the events of this war confirmed a tacit alliance of interests between Israel and Jordan.

6. The term *Mandatory Palestine* refers to the territory allocated by the League of Nations mandate to Great Britain (1919–1948). Apart from the Golan, it corresponds almost exactly to the territory currently under Israeli control.

7. Various lists of the eradicated towns and villages have been circulated, their number varying from 383 to 418, the number given by the Palestinian historian Walid Khalidi (Khalidi and colleagues 1992).

8. The idea of a transfer out of Palestine of the native population or a part of it had been expressed ever since the earliest days of Zionism by its founder, Theodor Herzl, not as a central objective but as a necessary accompanying measure. See Benoussan 2002.

9. Morris (1987) cites Zaki Shalom as the source for this quotation from Ben Gurion.

10. Zeev Sternhell (1996), however, has brilliantly analyzed the way in which the "national socialism" of the founders of the Israeli labor movement subsumed

the internationalist and humanist values it formally claimed to the priority of national redemption.

11. As Raphael Eytan, the former chief of staff who became a politician on the far right (he died in 2004), once said, "I don't believe in peace, because if they had done to us what we did to them we'd never agree to make peace."

12. I shall not list the other historical reconstructions, concealments, or mythologies called into question in Israel in the 1990s, concerning the actual behavior of the British in 1948–1949, which had been portrayed as systematically pro-Arab (Avi Schlaim); the alleged wish for peace in the face of Arab refusal of any compromise (Simha Flapan, Charles Enderlin, and Motti Golani); the legends surrounding Israeli socialiam, the Histadrut, and the kibbutz (Zeev Sternhell); the way in which the writing of history presented the "eternity" of the Jewish people (Boaz Evron); or the alleged saving of the Oriental Jews by Israel (Yehuda Shenhav).

13. In an interview on January 30, 2002 in *Le Monde*, Elon declared as follows:

> Shimon Peres is right. The demographic problem is real, and there's no point in ignoring it. The Palestinians are more numerous than we are, and Jewish immigration will never be able to compete with their birthrate. And the current situation isn't viable because they have a right to national independence. But we can't give up ours. This is why I'm in favor of transfer. There is no room for two states between the sea and Jordan. The Palestinians should have their state, which is Jordan, where they are already a large majority.

14. Interview in *Le Figaro*, April 22, 2001. The Israeli negotiator at Taba, Yossi Beilin, had proposed a text in which, for the first time since the beginning of negotiations with the Palestinians, Israel admitted essential responsibility in the creation of the refugee problem.

15. See Morris 2000a.

16. "'The Jews, thanks to their large reserve of officers trained and experienced in warfare [many had apprenticed in the British Army or were trained by it during the "Palestinian revolt" of 1936–1939], have an incalculable advantage over the Arabs,' wrote a U.N. military reporter, Colonel Rosher Lund, before the attack of the Arab states" (Simha Flapan, in Vidal and Algazy 1998, p. 40).

17. According to Flapan (1987), before the conflict broke out the head of Haganah, Israel Galili, had declared his conviction that the Israeli forces could repel any attack by the Palestinian Arabs, even if the latter were supported by the Arab states.

18. Interview by Ari Shavit in *Haaretz*, August 31, 2001.

19. Interview, July 14, 2003. Ben Eliezer is the author of *Derekh Hakavenet Hivatsruto shel Hamilitarizm Haisraeli, 1936–1956*. Tel Aviv: Dvir, 1995.
20. See his paper on this subject in Dieckhoff and Leveau 2003.
21. *Haaretz*, January 4, 2004.
22. *Yediot Ahronot*, September 26, 2003.

CHAPTER 3 – "A VILLA IN THE JUNGLE"

1. The phrase has become famous (see Schiff and Yaari 1990, p. 150), although more recent studies in Israel reveal that Rabin may not have uttered these words. Still, several high-ranking noncommissioned officers have attributed them to him, in particular during court trials, without being contradicted.
2. Interview in *Haaretz*, April 13, 2001.
3. In the famous interview Barak gave to Benny Morris (Chapter 2, note 15 above), Uri Avnery expanded his critique of the line of argument in which Barak justified his attitude at Camp David, analyzing the vision of Israel as "a villa in the jungle."
4. Interview with Carmi Gilon, Ami Ayalon, Avraham Shalom, and Yaakov Peri in *Yediot Ahronot*, November 14, 2003. Three of these men were speaking out for the first time. The fourth, Admiral Ayalon, had already spoken publicly on several occasions to condemn the self-justifying security vision of the Israelis, in connection with the Camp David negotiations, the perception of the Palestinian national movement, and the means undertaken to put an end to the intifada. During the most important Saturday night political broadcast in Israel, in the spring of 2002, Ayalon was asked, "Don't you think we can win the war against the Palestinians?" Ayalon replied, "Don't you understand that 'winning' this war would be the worst thing that could happen to Israel?"
5. *Yediot Ahronot*, November 21, 2003.
6. Interview in *Le Monde*, June 19, 2004.
7. This commission, comprised of two High Court judges and an Orientalist, looked into the conditions under which thirteen Palestinian citizens of Israel were killed during demonstrations in Israel itself at the very beginning of the intifada. The Orr Commission extended its conclusions, which were harsh for the police, to a measured account of certain ways in which Israel Arab citizens are discriminated against.
8. *Haaretz*, March 10, 2000.
9. Interview, February 20, 2002.
10. Interview, April 2, 2002.

11. Halper, director of ICAHD, the Israeli Committee Against House Demolitions, has developed his view of what he calls the Israeli ethnocracy in a number of writings. See for example Halper 2002.

12. Interview, July 14, 2003.

13. Interview, February 20, 2002.

14. For a long time torture was almost systematic on the part of Shin Bet, the central service for internal security, with regard to Palestinian political activists, residents of the occupied territories and Israeli citizens alike. One of the arguments that persuaded the High Court to oppose it deserves mention. Leaders of Shin Bet claimed the crucial need to use torture as a preventive measure to obtain information in emergency situations, thereby avoiding acts of terrorism. Following a report by the nongovernmental Israeli organization B'Tselem, lawyers for the plaintiffs noted that physical atrocities were regularly interrupted at noon on Friday and resumed only on Sunday morning. Thus the agents of Shin Bet could spend the weekend with their families, the sabbath putting an immediate end to the allegedly urgent need to torture prisoners so as to prevent attacks.

15. The references to Memmi in the rest of this chapter are based on this work.

16. The idea of the impossibility of assimilation, at least for the disinherited Jews of Central and Eastern Europe, is at the heart of two theoretical founding texts of Zionism: Pinsker's *Auto-Emancipation*, published in 1882 in Odessa during the great wave of pogroms that descended on the Jews of the ghetto in the czarist empire, and Herzl's *The Jewish State* (1896), written after the author had followed the Dreyfus trial in France as a journalist. Before these events both Pinsker and Herzl had advocated the assimilation of the Jews into their environment (though they held different views of what this would mean).

17. The larger issue of "colonialism" and "colonization" as it is understood today in the Israeli context will be discussed further on, in Chapter 11.

18. This labor was provided by local intermediaries the most famous of whom, Jamal Tarifi, would become a minister in the Palestinian Authority after Oslo, a decision made by Yasser Arafat to "give confidence" to the Israelis!

19. *Haaretz*, October 8, 2000.

20. This statement was made on August 5, 2002, and reported in *Le Monde* on August 8 of that year. On this occasion Rabbi Yossef added that "God regretted creating the Arabs."

21. *Agence France Presse*, August 29, 2000. Two weeks after the failure of the Camp David summit, Barak made the following statement on Israeli radio: "In a few weeks we shall know whether the Palestinians want peace and are ready to

examine the compromise proposals on Jerusalem drawn up by the American President Clinton, or if, like crocodiles, the more you feed them, the hungrier they are."

22. *Maariv*, October 20, 2000.

23. But, Memmi adds, the colonialist realizes that the colony is meaningless without the colonized. In the case of Israel, however, this foundation, essentially economic, is without basis, for the deep historic aspiration is for the formation of an independent society devoid of a colonized population.

24. *Haaretz*, May 26, 1997.

CHAPTER 4 – "THESE SEMITES – THEY ARE ANTI-SEMITES"

1. Interview, November 10, 2003.

2. Translator's note: This and subsequent citations from works written in French have been translated by S. F.

3. Interview, December 1, 2000.

4. In 1911 the Jew Yakov Beilis of Kiev was arrested on a charge of ritual crime, accused of having used the blood of a murdered Christian baby to make matzoh. He was tried and acquitted in 1913. The charge of ritual crime was one of the forces behind the traditional anti-Semitism of the Roman Catholic and Orthodox churches in Eastern Europe.

5. A documentary film about Isaac Bashevis Singer made by Isy Morgenstern contains a scene that is very evocative of this blend of hatred and nostalgia for Yiddish. Just after the announcement that Singer has won the Nobel Prize, Menahem Begin, the Israeli prime minister, visits the writer in his home. Their conversation is conducted entirely in Yiddish. Though he had come to pay his respects, Begin soon turns very aggressive. "Why," he asks, "do you continue to write in a dead language?" Singer gradually stops arguing, until the point when Begin says, "Yiddish is a language of the weak, of the diaspora, of the dead and the vanquished. Besides, one can't say "Present arms!" in Yiddish." Whereupon Singer replies, "Oh, if it could be said in German, it could also have been said in Yiddish. But I grant you that it isn't a language invented for generals."

6. Morris does not hesitate to use the term *colonist* repeatedly. He emphasizes, however, that the Jews were not colonists in the ordinary sense of the term, that is, the sons or agents of an imperial metropolis extending its power overseas.

7. In reality, the demand that preference be accorded to Jewish labor met with resistance from the people living in the *moshavot* who wanted to employ salaried Arab workers, the latter being much more experienced than the young people, all of urban origins, who had recently arrived from Russia or Poland. In passing Morris also chips away at one of the great pioneer myths of the *yishuv*, the draining of swamps, showing that, although this effort began an a Jewish initiative, it was in practice accomplished by Arab workers.

8. Vidal and Algazy (1998), however, cite sources indicating that very few Mapam leaders denounced the soldiers' criminal acts and soon stopped doing so. They quote among others the poet Abba Kovner, an official of Hashomer Hatzair who had been a hero of the resistance to the Nazis in the Vilnius ghetto, saying the following to Israeli soldiers in 1948: "The bayonet is just and blood is free. For the appearance of punishment says: vengeance, vengeance, vengeance!" (p. 97).

9. Cited by Yossef Gorni, professor of Jewish history at the University of Tel Aviv, *Haaretz*, November 3, 2000 (translated from the French by S. F.).

10. Among the principal intellectual figures within Israel who were historically opposed to the ethnicist tendencies of Zionism, most (for example Buber, Sholem, Magnes, Arendt, and Leibowitz) were from Germany or had studied in German universities. This is probably not coincidental, since Germany, located at the juncture between the two Europes where the two nationalist callings, the universalist and the ethnicist, developed, was the country in which both the totalitarian ideologies of the twentieth century and the beginnings of antitotalitarian thinking came into being.

11. Interview, January 28, 2002.

12. Interview, February 10, 2001.

13. *Combatants Letter*, Petition of the first fifty-two refuseniks, January 25, 2002.

14. The following citations from the writings of members of the *yishuv* are taken from the same book.

15. *Haaretz*, October 1, 1997.

CHAPTER 5 – "SOMETHING LIKE A CAGE"

1. It was during this time that most of the future leaders of Palmakh, and later of the IDF, were trained by the British Captain Charles Orde Wingate, after whom various streets and institutions in Israel are named.

2. It is interesting to note that both in ordinary language and in Israeli textbooks the term used to describe the Palestinian revolt of 1936–1939 is *meoraot* ("the

events"). Sometimes the revolt is referred to as "the troubles." These are the very terms long used in France to avoid naming the Algerians' struggle for independence.

3. *Yediot Ahronot,* December 14, 2001. "To be sure," said Alex Fishman, the journalist who interviewed Dagan, "the attempts to achieve this have not been very successful up to now."

4. The same thing happened in the large Jewish communities of the West, especially in the United States and in France, where unconditional approval of Israel and its policies has been a constant for many years. Having largely supported the Israeli–Palestinian peace accords, almost all the leaders and intellectuals of these communities initially rallied to the unconditional defense of Israel, taking no distance as they went along with and justified Ariel Sharon's policy with regard to the Palestinians. But in so doing they gradually found themselves caught up in ethnicist ideas and positions contrary to their general philosophical positions. Eventually, a "moral" movement in Israel that, as we shall see in Chapter 14, extended to the highest levels of the security establishment, grew large enough to make a mockery of unconditional support.

5. Interview, May 20, 2002. The two following citations are from the same interview.

6. Cf. *Le Monde,* May 30, 2002.

7. Unless otherwise noted, all the following citations are from this interview. (Translator's note: the English-language texts were supplied by the author.)

8. Interview, May 2, 2002.

9. *Yediot Ahronot,* reprinted in *Le Monde* as "La révolution sioniste est morte," September 11, 2003.

10. From the letters to the editor section of the weekend supplement, January 16, 2004. (Translator's note: the English-language texts were supplied by the author.)

11. In the 2004 interview Morris says in connection with the "ethnic cleansing" of 1948: "If you expect me to burst into tears, I'm sorry to disappoint you. I will not do that." The interviewer asks: "So when the commanders of Operation Dani are standing there and observing the long and terrible column of the 50,000 people expelled from Lod walking eastward, you stand there with them? You justify them?" Morris replies: "I definitely understand them. I understand their motives. I don't think they felt any pangs of conscience, and in their place I wouldn't have felt any pangs of conscience. Without that act, they would not have won the war and the state would not have come into being." Interviewer: "You do not condemn them morally?" Morris: "No."

CHAPTER 6 – TOM SEGEV VS. GIDEON LEVY

1. "For from the least of them even unto the greatest of them every one is given to covetousness; and from the prophet even unto the priest every one dealeth falsely. They have healed also the hurt of the daughter of my people slightly, saying, Peace, peace; when there is no peace. Were they ashamed when they had committed abomination? Nay, they were not at all ashamed, neither could they blush" (*Jeremiah* 6:13–15).

2. *Haaretz*, April 4, 1969.

3. Interview, July 4, 2003. See also Raz-Krakotzkin 2001b. The quotation from Raz-Krakotzkin on the following page is taken from the same interview.

4. The Israeli writer-historian Boaz Evron (1988) has made a special effort to deconstruct this view, revealing that, historically, the Jewish religion was formed and evolved in opposition to the Hebraic collectivity preceding the time of the diaspora.

5. Dinour's views are cited in Podeh 2003.

6. The best metahistoriographic study of what the authors themselves call the myths of Israeli history is Naveh and Yogev 2002. Written with empathy for these myths and their usefulness in the construction of the Jewish state, the book shows how they are in the process of lapsing or may be hoped to do so in the future.

7. Ben Gurion indicated that the line to be followed was that the Arabs themselves bore the blame for their flight, that they must never be allowed to return, and that the Arabs remaining in Israel were to be treated as equal citizens. See Morris 1987, p. 27.

8. See also Peleg 1994, p. 261.

9. The Israeli educational system participates in the establishment or reinforcement of an ethnicist view of the Arab, with racist connotations. But it is not the only source of this view. Among the attackers carrying out the raids against Israeli Arabs at the onset of the intifada were an especially large number of young immigrants who had recently arrived from the former Soviet Union.

10. See also Naveh 1995.

11. Interview, July 10, 2003.

12. *Haaretz*, March 13, 2001. As for the Arab population, only 5 percent of students complete high school. All of them follow the obligatory Israeli curriculum until the legal age of 15 and are able to ascertain the extent to which the version of history presented in the Arabic textbooks sanctioned by the ministry contradicts familial memories handed down for three generations.

13. *Haaretz*, March 8, 2001.

14. *Haaretz*, March 13, 2001.

15. This chapter was written before the withdrawal from Gaza was decided on.
16. See Vidal and Algazy 1998, p. 199.
17. See Firer 2002, Firer and Adwan 1997.

CHAPTER 7 – AN "ARTIFICIAL STATE"

1. Interview, August 23, 2004
2. Interview, May 20, 2003.
3. They write as follows:

> At the heights of World War I, Britain tried to marshal support for its war efforts from Jewish organizations in the US and from Jews in Russia; the Balfour Declaration was aimed at gaining Jewish support. Government leaders believed that the Jewish community had a great influence on policy-makers in the world, especially upon those of two of the great powers—Russia and the United States. The British had information that Germany was about to make a similar commitment, and felt it was important to anticipate their enemy's move. [p. 6]

4. Though it is less innovative, one of the rare comparable cases of modernization and codification of a new spoken and literary language is the renewal of Czech by the so-called movement of national awakening in nineteenth-century Bohemia and Moravia.
5. Interview, July 9, 2003.
6. Interview, April 13, 2001.
7. Interview, July 7, 2003.
8. Interview, July 9, 2003.
9. Quoted in *Al Ayyam*, the daily newspaper of the Palestinian Authority, September 3, 2003.
10. Quoted in Hazan 1989, p. 31. The following quotations are from pp. 38 and 39, respectively.
11. Interview, November 15, 2003. Translated here from the French.
12. Interview, August 23, 2004.
13. Interview, July 9, 2003.
14. Interview, August 23, 2004.
15. Interview, July 6, 2003. The following quotation is from the same interview.
16. Interview, July 8, 2003.
17. Interview, July 11, 2003. See also Pappe 2004.
18. Interview, July 9, 2003.
19. Interview, July 8, 2003.

CHAPTER 8 – MUTE ORACLES

1. The quotations that follow are taken from this same interview.
2. *Haaretz*, Weekly Supplement, March 22, 2002.
3. Yossef Burg was the father of Avraham Burg. His son, also a religious man but a member of the Labor Party, became president of the Jewish Agency and later of the Knesset.
4. *Maariv*, October 20, 2000.
5. Translator's note: In French, the word for "stranger" also means "foreigner."
6. Cited in Louer 2003, p. 22.
7. Under Stalin, the Israeli Communist party strongly supported the Jewish state in the conduct of its war. When, in 1948, President Truman asked Ben Gurion to withdraw Israeli forces from Sinai, which they had begun to invade, because he feared that their advance toward the Suez Canal would cause the Egyptian monarchy to collapse, Ben Gurion complied at once. The Communist Arab representative in the first Knesset, Tewfik Tubi, thereupon accused the Israeli government of what it called shameful capitulation to the American imperialist. Two years later, Moscow completely changed its position toward Israel (apart from the issue of its legitimacy), as did the Israeli Communist party.
8. In Lod, formerly Lydda, the Jewish inhabitants spontaneously called the small Arab quarter "the ghetto."
9. Cited in Morris 1999, p. 321.
10. In 1959, long before the National Security Council of the United States put the finishing touches on the notion of a preemptive attack in 2001, General Allon had already codified it, making this oxymoron the official strategy of the state of Israel.
11. See Morris 1999 and Hazan 1989.
12. See Hazan 1989, p. 47, for an account of this episode.
13. This expression had been used earlier by Judge Michael Ben Yair.
14. This fear of the disappearance of the state was to play a cathartic role far beyond Israel, for the 1967 war would have a profound influence in two crucial areas. The first was the way in which other Jewish communities, above all in the United States but also in France, identified with Israel, and the second was the West's general attitude toward the Holocaust. There can be no doubt that 1967 was a turning point in historiographic interest in the Jewish genocide, which before then had been marginalized in favor of the political and military aspects of World War II and the resistance to the Nazis.
15. Reported in *Le Monde*, June 3, 1972.

16. Reported in *Maariv*, April 4, 1972. The following statement by Haim Herzog is from the same source.

17. Reported in *Haaretz*, March 29, 1972. The following statement by Mordechai Hod is from the same source.

18. Interview with Amnon Kapeliouk in *Le Monde*, June 3, 1972.

19. *Al Hamishmar*, April 14, 1972.

20. See Morris 1999 for an account of these discussions.

21. Quoted in Enderlin 1997, p. 258.

22. Two annexations, on the other hand, those of East Jerusalem and the Golan Heights, were approved by parliamentary vote.

23. As Elon points out, the currency at that time was the Israeli pound; since then a monetary reform has introduced the shekel.

24. *Le Monde*, June 13, 1967.

25. It should be noted that many settlements were allocated land far in excess of what they could make use of. It is not known whether this land, confiscated from Palestinians but not cultivated for three years, had ever been declared "abandoned" by the Israeli state.

26. *Haaretz*, July 2, 2002.

27. See the report by Dror Tsaban, former assistant director of the Finance Ministry, in *Haaretz*, January 23, 2003.

28. *Le Monde*, June 19, 2004.

29. *Haaretz*, November 28, 2003.

30. Translator's note: See Chapter 11. The *pieds-noirs* were people of French origin born in Algeria and living there during the years when that country was a French colony.

31. There has never been definitive proof of the IDF's direct participation in this massacre beyond the authorization given to the Christian militias to enter the camps and their illumination, at night, by Israeli airplanes. An Israeli commission of inquiry under Judge Kahane concluded that Ariel Sharon was indirectly responsible and suggested that he be permanently deprived of any political role in the domain of security. Yet throughout the war the Christian Phalangists had not carried out a single operation that was not previously coordinated with the Israeli general staff and Israeli intelligence. It is improbable that their undertaking at Sabra and Shatila was the only exception to this rule. Phalangist leaders had been seen by many witnesses at the IDF's Beirut headquarters throughout the day preceding their entry into the camps. According to a recent book of testimony, *Mibeyrut ad Jenin* (*From Beirut to Jenin*) (Hammerman and Gal 2003), it appears that General Raphael Eytan, chief of staff at the time, prearranged the testimony of his officers before the commission so as to deny

any planning or knowledge of what the Phalangists were going to perpetrate or what happened during the massacre itself.

CHAPTER 9 – "WE MISSED AN EXTRAORDINARY OPPORTUNITY"

1. "Moderate physical pressure," as the legal term has it, figured in Shin Bet's arsenal for a long time. For decades Israeli courts had systematically rejected the complaints of Palestinians (including Israeli citizens) who had been tortured in the course of their interrogations. In 1999 the Supreme Court finally ruled that "moderate physical pressure" constituted torture. Yet the special centers were not closed, for example, according to the nongovernmental organization Hamoked and the Israeli Commission Against Torture, Camp 1,391, a secret detention center created, it seems, at the time of the first intifada. It is still in use. No Israeli deputy had ever been granted access to it, nor has the Red Cross. Officially, this camp does not exist. Since the outbreak of the second intifada several thousand Palestinians are said to have passed through it, including minors.

2. Adopted by the Security Council on November 22, 1967, this resolution emphasized in its preamble the inadmissibility of acquiring land through war. It stipulated the withdrawal of Israeli forces from occupied territories (Article 1a); the recognition of the sovereignty, territorial integrity, and political independence of each state in the region and its right to live in peace within secure and recognized borders (1b); a just resolution of the refugee problem (2b); and the guarantee of the territorial inviolability and political independence of each state in the region (2c).

3. For the text of the letter, see Baron 2003, pp. 781–786.

4. Their official title is Declaration of Principles on the Interim Self-Government Arrangements.

5. Interview, July 6, 2003. The following quotation is from the same interview.

6. Interview, December 18, 2001.

7. Rabbi Meir Kahane, an American, founded the Jewish Defense League in the United States before becoming the head of an extreme right-wing party, banned in Israel for open racism.

8. *Le Monde*, December 17, 2002.

9. Speech given in Washington before the Foundation for Middle-East Peace and the Middle-East Institute, October 2, 2002.

10. Three hundred and twenty-four, according to the Israeli government; three hundred and thirty-one, according to the Palestinian Authority (official sources).

11. *Haaretz*, February 27, 2001.

12. The figures for 1987 are cited in Baron 2003, p. 513.

13. Before his decade as mediator in the Middle East, Ross had worked for AIPAC (American-Israeli Public Affairs Committee), the organized Israeli lobby in the United States, and with WINEP (Washington Institute for Near-East Policy), a think tank supporting Israeli policy with regard to the Palestinians. Today he is no longer in the State Department and is a "distinguished fellow" of WINEP and president of the Jewish People Policy Planning Institute, a group directly connected with the Jewish Agency. See Swisher 2004.

14. Interview, November 24, 2000. In his book of memoirs (Ross 2004), he holds Yasser Arafat primarily responsible for the failure of the negotiations. He has carried on a debate with Robert Malley, another member of the United States National Security Council, who also played a large role in the negotiations and was present at Camp David, who holds a different view on the apportionment of blame (Malley and Agha 2001; Ross et al. 2001).

15. This edition does not contain the passages withdrawn from the Hebrew version.

16. Interview with Gidi Grinstein, November 1, 2000.

17. Interview with Professor Menahem Klein, former adviser to Shlomo Ben Ami, July 13, 2003.

18. These had been held in Stockholm and at Bolling and Andrews Air Force Bases in the United States.

19. I met with eleven participants at the Camp David Summit—Americans, Israelis, and Palestinians—who provided me with extensive testimony and also with a number of maps and written documents at a time when they were still respecting President Clinton's wish that they maintain silence regarding the negotiations in the hope that they would resume. To my knowledge, I was the first to publish a large-scale study of the course of the summit (*Le Monde*, December 28 and 29, 2000). For diverging interpretations, see for example the polemic between two American negotiators, Robert Malley of the National Security Council and Dennis Ross of the State Department (Malley and Agha 2001; Ross et al. 2001).

20. In his memoirs, former defense minister Moshe Dayan explained why, in his view, Haram al-Sharif should be entirely under Arab sovereignty. The mosque is a holy place in the present, whereas, for the Jews, the Temple Mount is merely a historical vestige. See Shragai 2000.

21. The delegation comprised Shlomo Ben Ami; Yossi Beilin; Gilead Sher, Barak's confidant and leader of his cabinet; Yossi Sarid from Meretz; the general Amnon Lipkin-Shahak; and Israel Hasson from the security services. The

Palestinian delegation was led by Abu Alaa and included Saeb Erekat, Nabil
Shaath, Yasser Abed Rabbo, Hassan Asfur, and Mohamed Dahlan, all of whom
had been at Camp David.

22. The text was drawn up by the European special envoy to the Middle East, Angel
Moratinos, and agreed to by both parties.

23. For the principal points of the Israeli and Palestinian written official positions
on the refugee issue at Camp David, see *Le Monde*, December 29, 2000.

24. For the text of Beilin's proposals concerning the refugees, see *Le Monde diplomatique* 570, September 2001. Translator's note: This text is the basis for the
following translations of the proposals.

25. Article 11 of this resolution states that "the refugees wishing to return to their
homes and live in peace with their neighbors should be permitted to do so at
the earliest practicable date, and that compensation should be paid for the
property of those choosing not to return . . ."

26. *Haaretz*, June 15, 2001.

27. Interview, December 3, 2000.

28. Article 7.2.i reads as follows: "The parties [Israelis and Palestinians] recognize
that Resolution 194 of the United Nations General Assembly, Security Council Resolution 242, and the Arab peace intiative (Article 2.ii) concerning the
rights of Palestinian refugees represent the basis for the solution of the refugee problem" (cited in Keller 2004, p. 113).

29. Article 7.9.iii. See Keller 2004, pp. 116–117.

30. *Le Monde diplomatique* 570, September 2001.

31. The Haram al-Sharif (Noble Sanctuary) is the plaza on which stands the al-
Aqsa Mosque, the third holiest site in Islam after Mecca and Medina. It was
built, along with the Dome of the Rock, between 690 and 715 C.E. above the
ruins of the Temple venerated by the Jews, which had been destroyed by the
Romans in 70 C.E. Only the western wall of this temple remains; a portion of
this wall, standing above the surface, is the Wailing Wall.

32. On October 10, 2003, Sharon accused "leftist elements" of "collaborating with
the Palestinians in wartime behind the government's back" (*Yediot Ahronot*,
October 12, 2003). On the 18th, he spoke before the Knesset, declaring: "It's
too bad Israeli generals are helping the Palestinians escape the need to wage
war on terrorism" (*Yediot Ahronot*, October 19, 2003).

33. Statements made on Israeli television, November 4, November 14, and December 2, 2003.

34. *Le Monde*, December 1, 2003.

35. Interview in *Haaretz*, French translation in *Courrier international*, December
11–17, 2003.

36. Interview, June 11, 2004.

37. Interview, *Le Monde*, December 24, 2001.

CHAPTER 10 – "SERIAL LIARS"

1. Barak's adviser Gilead Sher (2001) published an account of the negotiations entitled *Bemerkhak Neguiah* (*Within Reach*). Cf. the title of an ironic article by Gideon Levy (2001), "Just when we were about to give them so much," which mocks all these presuppositions the Israelis wanted to believe in.

2. Interview, January 28, 2002.

3. See, for example, Eldar 2000 and 2001a.

4. Interview, July 17, 2003 (the following citation is from this same interview). Klein has published numerous articles and a book entitled *The Jerusalem Problem: The Struggle for Permanent Status*. Tallahassee: University Press of Florida, 2003.

5. Interview, July 10, 2003.

6. This first suicide attack thus took place nearly three months after the events at Al-Aqsa that triggered the intifada. The only victim was the perpetrator. The second attack, on January 1, 2001, wounded sixty people. The third, in Netanya on March 4, for the first time killed three Israelis along with the perpetrator.

7. Television news, TF1, October 9, 2000.

8. Interview, July 17, 2003.

9. Mofaz intervened during the Taba negotiations to warn Barak; there was no question, he said, of reaching an accord more favorable than at Camp David, since if the Palestinians got more after their uprising Israeli concessions would have justified the intifada.

10. Interview, July 13, 2000.

11. Reported in *L'Express*, December 27, 2001.

12. *International Herald Tribune*, October 2, 2002.

13. Certain devoted admirers of Israel abroad, who likewise regret the supposed inadequacy of Israeli communications, sometimes lose their minds. Thus Roger Cukierman, president of the Representative Council of Jewish Institutions in France, told *Haaretz* that when Sharon came to France "I told him he absolutely had to appoint a minister of propaganda like Goebbels" (September 26, 2001). Yet the man retained his official position in the Council.

14. Interview, December 16, 2002. See *Le Monde*, December 18, 2002.

15. According to Amnesty International (2002), most of the dead were not involved in combat, including seven women, four children, and six men over the age of 55; six of these people died in the ruins of their houses.

16. Under the title "I made them a stadium in the middle of the camp," *Yediot Ahronot* published on May 31, 2002, the terrifying statement of Moshe Nissim, whom the soldiers called Kurdi Bear. Nissim operated a D-9 bulldozer, a tank that can lift a truck as easily as a wisp of straw. He describes the joy he felt when he razed Palestinian houses, working for seventy hours without a break in a state of wild excitement in which he did not try to find out whether any of the inhabitants were still inside their homes. One of the sarcastic headings in the article is "The purity of our weapons" (Yeheskeli 2002).

17. See Chapter 8.

18. See *Yediot Ahronot*, April 10, 2002.

19. *Kol Ha'Ir*, March 8, 2002.

20. *Le Monde*, May 6, 2002.

21. *Haaretz*, April 30, 2002.

22. This is the theme of one of the first plays by the greatest contemporary Israeli dramatist, the late Hanokh Levine. Written in 1970, it is entitled *Malkat Haambatia*, which could be translated as *The Bathroom Queen*, or, more in keeping with the author's intention, *The Toilet Queen*. It is the story of a family that, unwilling to go on sharing their apartment with a dirty, rude, and detested cousin, finally lock themselves in their own bathroom.

CHAPTER 11 – "SHARON IS SHARON IS SHARON"

1. Translator's note: The *pieds-noirs* were French colonials who had lived in Algeria for generations during the French occupation of that country (1830–1962). See the author's ensuing discussion and note 29.

2. Contrary to what the official Israeli services would have one believe, the targeted liquidations are not directed solely against armed terrorists. One of the very first such attacks, on December 31, 2001 (hence committed under Barak), was aimed at the dentist Thabet Thabet, head of Fatah in Tulkarm, who was known for his many contacts over the years with Israeli pacifists, especially those of Peace Now. He was executed by a special unit.

3. In the first four months of the intifada Israeli bombing in urban areas led to the death of 25 civilians by explosions inside their homes; 730 Palestinians were wounded, and 3,000 buildings damaged, affecting 21,000 residents, almost half of whom were under the age of 14. Four thousand people were left homeless. Five hundred houses were razed. See *Haaretz*, January 31, 2001.

4. Interview, December 27, 2001.

5. See Benziman's article in *Haaretz*, January 21, 2001.

6. The most famous of these was the murder, on October 12, 1953, of sixty inhab-

itants of the Palestinian frontier town of Kibya, who were killed at night in their own homes by explosive charges set by Unit 1 under Sharon's command.

7. This was the case in Mitleh in the Sinai campaign of 1956. Having brought his men into a mountain passage in contravention of orders, they found themselves trapped; Sharon had to deal with an incipient revolt on the part of his own parachute officers.

8. Thus General Geva has never forgiven him for having schemed to delay the building of bridges over the Suez Canal in the war of October 1973 so that he could be the first to cross over and win all the glory.

9. See Chapter 1, note 5.

10. Ben Gurion's political genius was to understand very early on, during the Second World War, that in the Middle East, and in Palestine in particular, the British presence, on which he had always relied in a conflictual way even as he strengthened his own position of autonomy, was destined to be short-lived after the Allied victory. He knew that London would yield to Washington as the dominant power in the region. This conviction was clear as early as the 1942 Zionist Congress in the Biltmore Hotel in New York.

11. *Haaretz*, April 13, 2001.

12. This was the slogan of the labor movement in the *Yishuv* for the "conquest of the land" from 1930 to 1940.

13. *Yediot Ahronot*, December 14, 2001.

14. In compliance with the Israeli–Palestinian accords signed before the second intifada, the Palestinian occupied territories were divided in hundreds of separate little districts. There were three different levels. All the districts belonging to the A Zone (less than 20 percent of the territories) were placed under full Palestinian control in both internal security and civilian matters. The IDF and Shin Bet were not allowed to interfere in these A Zone districts, which compised two-thirds of Gaza and the cities of the West Bank. In the districts of the B Zone (around 35 percent of the territories), the Palestinian Authority had sole control over most of civilian matters, but security control was shared by its police forces and the Israeli security forces. The districts remaining in the C Zone (approximately 45 percent of the territories) were under full Israeli control.

15. On May 8, 1945, and the days that followed, the French Army in Algeria slaughtered some 15,000 demonstrators, chiefly in Sétif and Guelma.

16. *Haaretz*, February 20, 2002.

17. *Kol Ha'Ir*, March 22, 2002.

18. *Haaretz*, November 20, 2000.

19. Statement from the office of the organization's secretary general, Geneva, April 5, 2001.

20. Deposition before the court, March 26, 2002.

21. Interview, July 3, 2004. Shabak, which succeeded Shin Bet, included all the domestic intelligence and counterintelligence services, including those in the occupied territories. It is officially attached to the office of the prime minister.

22. Figures cited by B'Tselem on November 3, 2004.

23. *Agence France Presse*, August 30, 2002.

24. On April 12, 2001, two Israeli pacifists walked through the streets of Tel Aviv with a microphone at 7 in the evening. "A curfew has been declared," they announced. " You are asked to return home immediately. Anyone seen in the streets will run the risks involved by the application of this procedure." They were arrested, charged with attempting to terrorize the public, and given a light penalty.

25. *Haaretz*, October 2, 2002.

26. *Haaretz*, February 5, 2003.

27. This article has been widely reprinted. See also Weizman 2003.

28. Using more carefully chosen language, Sharon's adviser Dov Weisglas mentioned these three justifications for his boss's decision to evacuate the settlers from Gaza (*Haaretz*, October 8, 2004).

29. Interview, June 9, 2004. See also *Le Monde*, June 19, 2004.

30. Translator's note: In following the author's arguments, it should be kept in mind that where English-language media refer to "settlements" and "settlers" in Israel, the French use *colonies*, "colonies" and *colons*, "colonists." Similarly, "the settler movement" and "the settlers' party" are "the colonial movement" and "the colonists' party," and the like.

31. *Le Monde*, June 19, 2004.

32. Cited by Henry Siegman (2002), of the Council on Foreign Relations.

33. The poll, sponsored by the National Center for Security Studies at Haifa University, was reported in *Haaretz*, June 22, 2004.

34. Interview, July 10, 2003. The following quotations from Levy are from the same interview.

35. Hence, for example, the total indifference with which Israel greeted the Arab League's proposal for peace of March 28, 2002. The media critic Ariel Lavie, outraged, wrote an article entitled "So what if the Arabs want to make peace?" (2002). "If two years ago we were all echoing Barak that 'the real face of the Palestinians has been exposed,' what can be learned about Israel's real face if it is now the one to refuse the proposal?" he asked.

36. On May 16, 2003, he declared in *Haaretz* that the original aim of apartheid was what was now being proposed as the solution for Israel and the Palestinians, namely two nation states separated according to ethnicity, culture, and religion. But most blacks in South Africa, he continued, did not see this as the

way to gain their rights; the whites were claiming so much territory that the black state would not be viable, and partition could not be achieved. The result was a transition from an apartheid of separation to an apartheid of domination and exclusion.

37. At a seminar on security held in Herzlia on December 16–18, 2001, Barak mentioned the risk of "evolving in a South African or Bosnian direction" if Israel did not withdraw from the occupied territories. See *Le Monde*, December 24, 2001.

38. Interview of January 26, 2002.

39. *Le Monde*, June 12, 1967.

40. *Haaretz*, September 26, 2002.

41. *Le Monde*, June 19, 2004.

CHAPTER 12 – "TERRORISM": TELL ARAFAT TO STOP THIS NONSENSE

1. Privately published document of December 2002, translated into French by Annie Coussemant as "Le Mouvement palestinien de résistance par la non-violence." The English translation is based on this French text.

2. Interview, July 9, 2003.

3. The information in the following two paragraphs is likewise translated from Baron's study.

4. After the highjacking of three airplanes by the PFLP, Hussein had sent the Jordanian army to attack the camps on September 17. The battle continued until the 27th, leaving around 1,500 of the fedayeen dead. The Palestinian Red Cross claimed 3,440 civilian casualties and 10,840 wounded (Baron 2003, p. 235).

5. The only major armed event of Palestinian resistance in this period was the Battle of Karameh in Jordan, on March 21, 1968, in which three hundred fedayeen went up against four armored Israeli columns and parachute forces. The resistance put up by the Palestinians in this refugee camp surprised the Israelis, who ended with twenty-one dead and around sixty wounded. After fifteen hours of combat, the IDF managed to destroy much of the camp, kill two hundred fighters and civilians, and return with a hundred prisoners. In other words, the sole armed struggle worthy of the name took place outside of Palestine.

6. On November 15, 1988, "on the basis of Resolutions 242 and 338 of the Security Council," Yasser Arafat announced the "declaration of independence of Palestine . . . in the name of God and the Palestinian Arab people" (cited in Baron 2003, pp. 770–771).

7. Interview, July 7, 2004. See also the supplement on France and Algeria in *Le Monde*, October 28, 2004.

8.   Interview, July 6, 2004.

9.   *Maariv*, December 5, 2002.

10. Interview, December 5, 2000.

11. Interview, July 9, 2003.

12. Interview, July 8, 2003.

13. Interview, July 9, 2003.

14. Interview, July 12, 2003.

15. Interview, July 9, 2003. The following citation is from the same interview.

16. Interview, July 9, 2003.

17. Translation in *Le Monde*, November 9, 2003, from an article originally published in *Yediot Ahronot*.

18. Interview of May 20, 2003.

19. This and the following two citations are from the interview of July 9, 2003.

20. Interview, July 6, 2003.

21. *Le Monde*, November 3–4, 2002.

22. Interview, July 6, 2003.

23. Interview, July 6, 2003.

24. Interviews, October 29, 2000. See *Le Monde*, October 31, 2000.

25. *Le Monde*, October 31, 2000.

26. The expression referred to the fact that, in Bebel's view, some of the oppressed, instead of holding capitalism responsible, focused their hatred on a subset of the population, in this case the Jews.

27. See, for example, *Textbooks of the Palestinian Authority*, Center for Monitoring the Impact of Peace, Jerusalem, November 1999.

28. Report published by the Truman Institute of the Hebrew University. See also Morena 2001.

29. Interview, July 8, 2003.

30. Interview, October 29, 2000. See also *Le Monde*, October 31, 2000.

31. Interview, July 7, 2003.

32. Interview, July 8, 2003.

33. Interview, October 28. See also *Le Monde*, October 31, 2000.

34. Interview, July 6, 2003.

35. Interview, June 26, 2003.

CHAPTER 13 – THE BRUTALIZATION OF ISRAELI SOCIETY AND THE RADICALIZATION OF NATIONALISM

1.   *Haaretz*, August 31, 2002.

2.   *Le Monde*, December 14, 2001. The following quotation from Uzi Landau is from the same source.

3. *Le Monde*, December 24, 2001.
4. Hence the hostility with which it is regarded by Salafist Palestinians in Lebanese refugee camps. See Rougier 2004.
5. Reuters, August 15, 2004.
6. Interview, June 9, 1004. *Le Monde*, June 19, 2004.
7. Interview, *Le Monde*, September 28, 2003.
8. *Haaretz*, September 17, 2003.
9. *Le Monde*, June 19, 2004.
10. Communiqué, June 18, 2003. The law in question was adopted on this day.
11. In Israel the term *smolani*, "leftist," does not refer to the far left but is broadly applied to anyone firmly on the left and anyone who defends human rights. The negative connotation of the term recalls the way in which "liberal," in the United States, has become an insult in conservative political jargon.
12. Interview, July 3, 2003.
13. Interview, April 13, 2002.
14. The head of government cannot alter the composition of his coalition without a prior vote of confidence in the Knesset.
15. Interview, June 9, 2004. *Le Monde*, June 19, 2004.
16. The translation was published by Babel in Tel Aviv.
17. The petition was launched by Haydar Abdel Sharif, Hanan Ashrawi, Mustafa Barghouti, Rana Nashashibi, Eyad El-Saraj, Raji Surani, and others. The first Israeli signatories included, among others, Professors Aharon Eviatar, Amnon Raz, Avraham Oz, Baruch Kimmerling, Daphna Levit, Daniel Amit, Ilan Pappe, Lev Grinberg, and Ruchama Maton.
18. According to Finkelstein and Silverman 2001, at the time in which the Bible situates Solomon's construction of the temple in Jerusalem, the city was just a small, unfortified, and relatively poor town; when the text of the Bible was written later on, a mythic past was constructed in order to support the exclusive monotheistic tradition of the Jews.
19. Interview, July 10, 2003.
20. Iinterview, July 3, 2003.
21. *Haaretz*, September 9, 2002.
22. Article translated from *Haaretz*, appearing in French in *Courrier international*, December 24, 2003, pp. 686–687.
23. *Haaretz*, April 22, 2002, and weekly supplement of May 3, 2002.
24. *Yediot Ahronot*, May 3, 2002.
25. *Haaretz*, April 28, 2002. The memo from the head of Kol Israel was dated April 15, 2002.
26. Interview, July 10, 2003.

27. *Haaretz*, August 31, 2002.

28. *Haaretz*, April 8, 2002.

29. *Haaretz*, April 14, 2002.

30. *Jerusalem Post*, May 3, 2002.

31. *Haaretz*, August 5, 2002.

32. Statement of December 27, 2002. See also Avnery 2003.

33. *Haaretz*, August 21, 2002.

34. *Yediot Ahronot*, September 26, 2003.

35. *Yediot Ahronot*, October 1, 2001.

36. *Haaretz*, April 17, 2001.

37. The golem is a Jewish legend whose origin is attributed to the Maharal of Prague. A robot manufactured to protect the Jews, it turned against its creator, who had to destroy it.

38. March 9, 2004.

39. March 9, 2004.

40. *Haaretz*, March 8, 2002.

41. Interview, April 17, 2003.

42. *Ha'Ir*, January 11, 2002.

43. *Haaretz*, July 10, 2003.

44. *Agence France Presse*, August 18, 2004.

45. On November 24, 2004, B'Tselem announced that 1,369 unarmed Palestinians had been killed since the beginning of the intifada. Twenty-two soldiers had been suspected of firing their weapons illegally; only one was charged. On December 8, 2004, the same nongovernmental organization announced that two-thirds of the Palestinians killed on the West Bank had had no role in any fighting.

46. Cited in Avnery 2002c. The following quotation from General Halutz is taken from the same source.

47. December 14, 2001.

48. December 21, 2001.

49. May 7, 2002.

50. Interview in *Haaretz*, translated in *Courrier international*, December 11–17, 2003, p. 684.

51. *Le Monde*, July 19, 2004.

52. Interview, July 2003.

53. *Yediot Ahronot*, letter to the editor signed "Parachute Officer," December 21, 2001.

54. *Haaretz*, October 20, 2001.

55. Interview, July 12, 2003. The following quote from Mr. Beer is from the same interview.

56. Interview, July 14, 2003. The quotation from Professor Ben Eliezer in the following paragraph is from the same interview.
57. Interview, June 6, 2002. The following quotations from Mr. Beer are from the same interview.
58. See http://keshev.org.il/siteEn/FullNews.asp?NewsID=50&CategoryID=14.
59. *Haaretz*, June 20, 2001.
60. *Maarriv*, January 22, 2001.
61. *Haaretz*, January 28, 2002.
62. *Haaretz*, February 25, 2004.
63. Associated Press, July 26, 2001.
64. These sects are tiny in Israel, but the Satmar are important in the United States.
65. A mystical movement, the Hassidim ("charitable ones") arose in Ukraine in the eighteenth century in reaction to traditional Orthodoxy (whose members were called *mitnagdim*, "opponents"). In contrast to Jewish tradition, which places knowledge of the texts above all else, the Hassidim emphasize the love of God.
66. *Haaretz*, March 13, 2001. Some 18.9 percent of these children were studying in schools of the religious Zionist trend, while 22.5 percent came under the heading of the Orthodox.

CHAPTER 14 – "AN INSANE LOGIC, A FORM OF SUICIDE"

1. See *Yediot Ahronot*, September 26, 2003.
2. Interview, *Le Monde*, June 19, 2004.
3. I have intentionally omitted Peace Now from this list. Its activists sometimes find themselves side by side with those of other groups, but its leaders, with ties to the Labor Party, refuse to face head on the issue of ending the occupation, preferring to call for negotiation with the Palestinians. The official policy of Peace Now is in some respects reminiscent of the position of those people in France who, when the departure of French troops from Algeria and that country's independence were clearly at issue, called for peace in Algeria without demanding the end of the French presence there.
4. *Haaretz*, November 13, 2003.
5. *Le Monde*, June 19, 2004.
6. Letter to the minister of defense by the refusenik Sergio Yahni, March 19, 2002.
7. *Le Monde*, February 11, 2002. The following quotation is from the same source.
8. July 25, 2002.

9. Interview, July 3, 2003.
10. Interview on Ynet, the Web site of *Yediot Ahronot*, April 26, 2004.
11. *Yediot Ahronot*, November 14, 2003.
12. *Haaretz*, September 29, 2002.
13. Interview, July 10, 2003.
14. Interview, December 2, 2000.
15. Interview, December 18, 2001.
16. Interview, July 10, 2003. The Israeli law of return automatically confers citizenship on any Jew settling in that country.
17. Interview, July 3, 2003.
18. Interview, July 4, 2003.
19. *Yediot Ahronot*, November 14, 2003.
20. *Haaretz*, August 8, 2004.
21. *Haaretz*, reprinted in *Courrier international*, September 26, 2002.
22. Cited by Dany Rubinstein, *Haaretz*, January 5, 2003.
23. Frankenthal 2002, in a speech made at a meeting in Jerusalem on July 27.
24. Interview on Judaiques FM, March 20, 2003.
25. Interview by Ari Shavit in *Haaretz*, text taken from the translation in *Courrier international*, December 11–17, 2003, p. 684.
26. Article in *Yediot Ahronot*, text taken from the translation in *Le Monde*, September 11, 2003.
27. Interview, *Le Monde*, April 4, 2002.
28. *Le Monde*, June 19, 2004.
29. *Le Monde*, September 11, 2003.
30. *Kedma*, October 24, 2002.
31. *Haaretz*, November 12, 2002.
32. The statistics were reprinted in *The Guardian*, November 19, 2002. By that November there were 2,616 deserters, in contrast to 1,564 in the year 2001, in an army of 186,500 professional and conscripted soldiers.
33. Interview, February 20, 2002.
34. January 28, 2002. The quotation from Beilin in the following paragraph is from the same source.
35. *Le Monde*, June 19, 2004.
36. *Le Monde*, May 24, 2002.
37. *Le Monde*, May 24, 2002.
38. April 29, 2004. The statistics that follow are from the same source.
39. March 11, 2004.
40. *Yediot Ahronot*, April 10, 2002.

CHAPTER 15 – "THE HIDDEN PLOT OF OUR LIVES"

1. Interview, January 28, 2002.
2. *Le Monde*, September 10, 2002.
3. *Le Monde*, December 3, 2001.
4. *Haaretz*, based on the translation in *Courrier international*, December 11–17, 2003, p. 684.
5. See Morris 2003. The writer Amos Oz replied to Begin in an open letter, reminding him that Hitler had died thirty-seven years earlier and was not hiding in Nabatyieh, Saida, or Beirut.
6. *Haaretz*, February 1, 2002.
7. "Soldiers blindfold and handcuff the arrested men. In certain cases a prisoner number is written on the man's arm, a practice that led Palestinian President Yasser Arafat to compare these methods employed by the Israeli army to those of the Nazis" (*Agence France Presse*, March 12, 2002; the following citation is from the same source). Nor was Arafat last in line when it came to the semantic instrumentalization of the genocide.
8. Interview, July 4, 2003.
9. *Yediot Ahronot*, March 15, 2002.
10. See Aloni and Somfelvi 2004. The interview appeared on Ynet, the Web site associated with *Yediot Ahronot*, on April 26.
11. Interview, May 17, 2003.
12. Hannah Levy-Hass wrote a book, *Journal de Bergen-Belsen* (Paris: Seuil, 1989).
13. *Le Monde*, November 22, 2000.
14. This and the following passages are translated from the author's citations from Anissimov 1996.
15. On this last point see Thomson 2002, p. 428.
16. Interview, December 3, 2002.
17. *Le Monde*, December 17, 2002.
18. Interview, January 29, 2002.
19. May 27, 2004. "How can we describe this occupation," he wrote, "without thinking, even involuntarily, of the Occupation?"
20. Interview, April 2, 2002.
21. *Haaretz*, based on the translation in *Courrier international*, December 11–17, 2003.
22. Interview, December 3, 2000. See also *Le Monde*, December 20, 2000.
23. *Agence France Presse*, March 27, 2002.
24. This excerpt from *Al Hayat* is based on the translation in *Courrier international*, May 7–14, 2003.

25. Editorial in *Al Hayat*, translated from *Courrier international*, October 11–18, 2001.

26. See Chapter 7.

27. Interview, November 10, 2003.

28. Interview, August 23, 2004.

29. Interview, July 6, 2003. The following excerpt is from the same interview.

CHAPTER 16 – FORWARD

1. Interview, October 3, 2005. The following citations from Bensimon are from the same interview.

2. Interview, October 2, 2005. The following citations from Dor are from the same interview.

3. Interview, October 3, 2005. In fact, although every television screen in the country was full of touching pictures of settlers resisting evacuation during the withdrawal from Gaza, the Israeli population looked on with mounting indifference finally bordering on exasperation. After thirty-eight years of presence, the settlers were evacuated in one week without major opposition in Israel.

4. Interview, September 30, 2005. Subsequent citations from Eldar are from the same interview.

5. Interview, September 30, 2005. Subsequent citations from Sand are from the same interview.

6. Interview, September 30, 2005. Subsequent citations from Ram are from the same interview.

7. Interview, October 2, 2005. Subsequent citations from Rabinowitch are from the same interview.

8. Interview, October 2, 2005. Subsequent citations from Beer are from the same interview.

9. Interview, October 2, 2005. Subsequent citations from Ben Yair are from the same interview.

10. Interview, October 3, 2005. Subsequent citations from Levy are from the same interview.

11. Interview, January 12, 2006.

12. Interview published in *Le Monde*, February 13, 2006.

CONCLUSION

1. Press conference, November 27, 1967.

2. These alliances and dissentions cast a stark light on the emptiness and obtuseness

of the so-called war on terrorism, its failure to understand what is really at stake. The day after Arafat died, Mahmoud Abbas (Abu Mazen), the candidate favored by Bush and other Western leaders after him, formed an alliance with the boss of the major security service in Gaza, Mohamed Dahlan. The so-called terrorists of the Al-Aqsa Brigade then split into two groups, those who were faithful to Dahlan and had supported Abu Mazen, and those who opposed his designation as the new president of the PLO.

3. Interview with Segev, April 2, 2002. See *Le Monde*, April 4, 2002.
4. Interview, December 18, 2001.
5. *Le Monde*, June 19, 2004.
6. Interview, July 14, 2003.
7. Especially Salafist antinationalist Islamism among the refugees. See Rougier 2004.
8. *Le Monde*, Ocober 28, 2004.
9. Interview, July 10, 2003. See Chapter 1.

AFTERWORD

1. Romema and Sheikh Bader are districts in Jerusalem. Tel Aviv was built on the site of Manshyieh. Wadi Nisnass is located in Haifa. Zarnuga has become the Israeli town Gedera. The Palestinian village Faradis bordered the Jewish settlement Zikhron Yaakov. Baron Hirsch finanaced some of the first Jewish settlements in Ottoman Palestine.

BIBLIOGRAPHY

Aloni, S. (2003). Murder of a population under cover of righteousness. *Haaretz*, March 6. http://list.nowar-paix.ca/pipermail/nowar/2005-August/001003.html

Aloni, S., and Somfelvi, A. (2004). A remarkable Jewish woman speaks out. www.monabaker.com/pMachine/more.php?id=A2058_0_1_0_M

Amnesty International (2002). Israel/Occupied Territories: Israeli Defence Force war crimes must be investigated. Press release, November 4. http://web.amnesty.org/library/Index/engMDE151542002?OpenDocument&of=countries%5cisrael/occupied+territories.

Anissimov, M. (1996). *Primo Levi ou la tragédie d'un optimiste.* Paris: Lattès. (English version: *Primo Levi: Tragedy of an Optimist.* New York: Overlook, 2000.)

Arendt, H. (1963). *Eichmann in Jerusalem.* New York: Viking.

Ashrawi, H. (2000). *Anatomy of racism.* Speech delivered on October 18, Jerusalem.

Avieli-Tabibian, K., Michman, D., Vago, R., and Halamish, A. (2001). *Eidan Haeimah Vehatikvah.* Tel Aviv: Metah.

Avnery, U. (2002a). Barak: A villa in the jungle. www.gush-shalom.org/archives. html.

———(2002b). The army has a state. *Gush Shalom*, July 20, 2002. Http//:zmag.org/content/showarticle/cfm?SectionID=22&ItemID=2134.

———(2002c). Letter to a pilot. *Gush Shalom*, August 26, 2002. www.counterpunch.org/avnery0826.html.

———(2003). Liberman's supreme soviet. Www. gush-shalom.org/archives/ article 227.html.

Ayalon, A. (2001). L'urgence, c'est de se désengager inconditionnellement des territoires. Interview with Sylvain Cypel. *Le Monde*, December 24.

Barnavi, E., and Naveh, E. (1999). *Zmanim Modernim*, 2 vols. Tel Aviv: Sifrei Tel Aviv Ministry of Education

Bar-On, D., and Adwan, S. (2003). *Learning Each Other's Historical Narrative.* Beit Jalah: Peace Research Institute in the Middle East.

Baron, X. (2003). *Les Palestiniens: Genèse d'une nation.* Paris: Seuil.

Begin, M. (1972). *The Revolt.* New York: Nash.

Beilin, Y. (2001). "Sharon is a post-Zionist." http://memri.org/bin/articles.cgi?Page=countries&Area=israel&ID=SP23001.

Ben Ami, S. (2001). *Quel avenir pour Israël?* Paris: PUF.

Ben Eliezer, U. (1995). *Derekh Hakavenet: Hivatzruto Shel Hamilitarizm Haisraeli.* Tel Aviv: Dvir.

Benn, A. (2001). For Israel, September 11 was a Hanukkah miracle. *Haaretz* (English edition), December 18, pp.1–2.

Bensoussan, G. (2002). *Une histoire intellectuelle et politique du sionisme, 1860–1940.* Paris: Fayard.

Benziman, U. (1985). *Sharon: An Israeli Caesar.* New York: Adamas.

Bilitski, A., Drezdin, A., Harel, Y., Hanegbi, H., Medicks, O., and Warshawski, M. (2004). *Kol Kore Lemaan Emet Vepius, Lemaan Shivion Veakhdut.* www.kedma. co.il, June.

Blau, U. (2002). Tsava Hataamulah Leisrael. *Kol Ha'Ir.* April 26.

B'Tselem (2002). Land grab: Israel's settlement policy in the West Bank. www. btselem.org/English/Publications/Summaries/200205_Land_Grab.asp.

Carmi, D. (2002). *Samir et Jonathan.* Paris: Hachette.

Chaumont, J.-M. (2002). *La Concurrence des victimes. Génocide, identité, reconnaissance.* Paris: La Découverte.

Cohen, A. (1985). *Panim Mekhoarot Bamarah. Hishtakfut Hasiskhsukh Hayehudi-Aravi Basifrut Hayeladim Haivrit.* Tel Aviv: Reshafim.

Combatants Letter: Courage to Refuse. (Collective, 2002). www.seruv.org.il/ defauteng.asp.

Cook, J. (2002). Israel's politicians target minorities. *International Herald Tribune,* November 27.

Dieckhoff, A., and Leveau, R., eds. (2003). *Israéliens et Palestiniens, la guerre en partage.* Paris: Balland.

Drucker, R. (2002). *Hara Kiri. Ehud Barak Bemivkhan Hatotzaa.* Tel Aviv: Khemed & Yediot Ahronot.

Drucker, R., and Shelah, O. (2005). *Boomerang: Kishalon Hamanhigut Baintifada Hashniya.* Jerusalem: Keter.

Dumke, E. (1998). *Haolam Vehayehudim Badorot Haaharonim,* Tel Aviv: Ministry of Education.

Eitam, E. (2002a). J'entre au gouvernement pour qu'Ariel Sharon ne s'arrête pas au milieu du gué. Interview with Sylvain Cypel. *Le Monde,* April 8.

—— (2002b). Interview with Ari Shavit. *Haaretz* (English edition), March 22, pp. 9–11.

Eldar, A. (2000). What Barak is really offering Arafat. *Haaretz,* December 5.

—— (2001a). What went wrong at Camp David. *Haaretz,* July 24.

—— (2001b). Ask Clinton what he thinks about Camp David. *Haaretz,* August 21. www.abunimah.org/features/010821ezra.html.

———(2004). Popular misconceptions. *Haaretz*, June 11. www.aaiusa.org/news/must_read06_11_04.htm.

Elon, A. (2002). Israelis and Palestinians: What went wrong? *New York Review of Books* 49, December 19. www.nybooks.com/articles/15935.

Enderlin, C. (1997). *Paix ou guerres. Les secrets des négotiations israélo-arabes, 1917–1997*. Paris: Stock. Revised edition, 2004.

———(2000). *Le Nouvel Observateur*, November 9.

———(2002). *Shattered Dreams: The Failure of the Peace Process in the Middle East*, trans. S. Fairfield. New York: Other Press, 2003.

———(2003). *Shattered Dreams of Peace*. Documentary film.

Evron, B. (1988). *Jewish State or Israeli Nation?* Bloomington, IN: Indiana University Press, 1995. (First edited in Hebrew [1988]. *Hekheshbon Haleumi*. Or Yehuda: Dvir).

Fallaci, O. (2002). *The Rage and the Pride*. New York: Rizzoli.

Finkelstein, I., and Silberman, N. A. (2001). *The Bible Unearthed: Archeology's New Vision of Ancient Israel and the Origin of Its Sacred Text*. New York: Free Press.

Firer, R. (2002). *The Gordian Knot Between Peace Education and War Education*. Jerusalem: Harry S. Truman Institute for the Advancement of Peace.

Firer, R., and Adwan, S. (1997). Ani Gibor, Ani Korban. *Panim*, October 3.

Flapan, S. (1987). *The Birth of Israel: Myths and Realities*. New York: Pantheon.

Frankenthal. Y. (2002). The ethics of revenge. Cited in *Tikkun Communities*, July 31. http://wearemichigan.com/resources/jewish/news.htm.

Freedland, J. (2002). Prophet of hope. *The Guardian*, August 27. www.guardian.co.uk/g2/story/0,3604,781042,00.html.

Gerber, H. (2003). Zionism, Orientalism, and the Palestinians. *Journal of Palestine Studies* 33:23–41.

Golani, M. (2002). *Milkhamot lo Korot Meatzman. Al Zikaron, Koach Ubekhirah*. Modan: Moshav Ben Shemen.

Gouri, H. (2004). *Ani, Milkhemet Ezrahim*. Jerusalem: Mossad Bialik.

Gresh, A., and Vidal, D. (2003). *Les Cent clés du Proche-Orient*. Paris: Hachette.

Grossman, D. (2002). Israelis don't hear the whole story. *International Herald Tribune*, October 2.

———(2004). Le culte de la force, tragique erreur. Interview with Sylvain Cypel. *Le Monde*, June 19.

Gur, B. (2003). The glittering edge of the boot. *Haaretz*, September 12. www.thetruthseeker.co.uk/article.asp?ID=1080.

Haffner, S. (2000). *Defying Hitler*, trans. O. Pretzel. New York: Picador, 2003.

Halper, J. (2000). The key to peace: dismantling the matrix of control. *Middle East Report* 216, August 31. www.icahd.org/eng/articles.asp?menu=6&submenu=3.

———(2002). From ethnocracy to a democratic state. In *A Middle-East Confederation*. www.icahd.org, December 30.

Hammerman, I., and Gal, I. (2003). *Mibeyrut Ad Jenin*. Tel Aviv: Am Oved.

Harbi, M. (2004). L'Algérie en perspectives. In M. Harbi and B. Stora, eds., *La Guerre d'Algérie 1954–2004*, pp. 315–326. Paris: Robert Lafont.

Harel, A., and Isacharoff A. (2005). *Hamilkhama Hasheviit. Eikh Nitzakhnu Velama Hifsadnu Bamilkhama im Hapalestinaim*. Tel Aviv: Miskal.

Hass, A. (1999). *Drinking the Sea at Gaza*, trans. E. Wesley and M. Kaufman-Lacusta. New York: Metropolitan.

———(2003a). *Reporting from Ramallah*, trans. R. L. Jones. Cambridge, MA: MIT Press.

———(2003b). Making stupid comparisons. *Haaretz*, July 9. www.haaretz.com/hasen/pages/ShArt.jhtml?itemNo=315977&contrassID=2&subContrassID=4&sbSubContrassID=0&listSrc=Y.

———(2003c). Ces Israéliens qui rêvent du transfert. *Le Monde diplomatique*, February. www.monde-diplomatique.fr/2003/02/HASS/9752.

———(2003d). Clarifying the occupation lexicon. *Haaretz*, June 11. www.zmag.org/content/print_article.cfm?itemID=3757&sectionID=22.

———(2003e). Rites of death and killing. *Haaretz*, January 8.

Hazan, P. (1989). *La Guerre des Six-Jours. La victoire empoisonnée*. Brussels: Complexe.

Herzl, T. (1896). *The Jewish State*, trans. S. D'Avigdor. New York: American Zionist Emergency Council, 1946.

Histoire de l'autre, trans R. Pinhas-Delpuech and R. Akel (2004). [Collective author.] Paris: Liana Levi.

Honig-Parnass, T. (1998). Gaon Venadiv Veakhzar. *Mitsad Sheni* 11: Special issue on the partition of Palestine, February.

Israeli, A. (1961). *Shalom, Shalom Veein Shalom*. Jerusalem: Bochan. Revised edition, 1999.

Judt, T. (2003). Israel: the alternative. *New York Review of Books* 50:16, October 23.

Keller, A. (2004). *L'Accord de Genève. Un pari réaliste*. Paris: Seuil.

Khalidi, R. (1998). *Palestinian Identity: The Construction of Modern National Consciousness*. New York: Columbia University Press.

Khalidi, W., Elmusa, S. S., and Khalidi, M. A. (1992). *All That Remains: The Palestinian Villages Occupied and Depopulated by Israel in 1948*. Washington, DC: Institute for Palestinian Studies.

Kimmerling, B. (2001). *Kets Shilton Haakhuzalim-Ashkenazim, Khilonim, Vatikim, Sotsialistim Veleumiim*. Jerusalem: Keter.

———(2003). *Politicide: Ariel Sharon's War Against the Palestinians*. New York: Verso.

Krall, H., Stasinska, J., and Wechsler, L. (1986). *Shielding the Flame: An Intimate Conversation with Dr. Marek Edelman, the Last Surviving Leader of the Warsaw Ghetto Uprising*. New York: Henry Holt.

Lavie, A. (2002). So what if the Arabs want to make peace? *Haaretz*, April 5. www. occupationalhazard.org/article.php?IDD=520.

Lee, S., dir. (1991). *Jungle Fever*. Film.

Levy, G. (2000). Ytakhen Shelo Haita Efsharut Akheret, Aval Lama Leshaker Kol Hashanim? *Haaretz*, November 1.

——(2001). Just when we were about to give them so much. *Haaretz*, June 17.

——(2003). Nazis in Germany and the state of affairs in Israel. www.holyland trust.org/articles/essay03_05–15.html.

Louer, L. (2003). *Les Citoyens arabes d'Israël*. Paris: Balland.

Lozowick, Y. (2003). *The Right to Exist: A Moral Defense of Israel's Wars*. New York: Doubleday.

Malley, R., and Agha, H. (2001). Camp David: The tragedy of errors. *New York Review of Books*, August 9, pp. 59–65.

Marcus, I., et al. (2001). *The Palestinian Authority School Books and Teacher's Guide*. Jerusalem: Center for Monitoring the Impact of Peace. www.edume.org/reports/1/toc.htm.

Marcus, Y. (2002). Who's the boss? *Haaretz*, September 3, 2002. www.haaretzdaily. com/hasen/pages/ShArt.jhtml?itemNo=204303&contrassID=2&subContrass ID=4&sbSubContrassID=0&listSrc=Y&itemNo=204303.

Memmi, A. (1957). *The Colonizer and the Colonized*. New York: Beacon, 1991.

Morena, E. (2001). Les manuels scolaires palestiniens sont-ils antisémites? *Le Monde diplomatique*, April. www.monde-diplomatique.fr/2001/04/MORENA/15106.

Morris, B. (1987). *The Birth of the Palestinian Refugee Problem*. Cambridge, U.K.: Cambridge University Press.

——(1990). *1948 and After: Israel and the Palestinians*. New York and Oxford: Clarendon.

——(1999). *Righteous Victims. A History of the Zionist-Arab Conflict, 1881–2001*. New York: Vintage, 2001.

——(2000). *Tikkun Taut: Yehudim Vearavim Be-eretz Israel*. Tel Aviv: Am Oved.

——(2002a). Camp David and after: An exchange. *New York Review of Books* 49:10, June 13. www.nybooks.com/articles/15501.

——(2002b). A new exodus for the Middle East? www.guardian.co.uk/israel/ comment/0,10551,803417,00.html.

Mosaad, M. (2002). The one narrative crisis. *Viewpoints/Peace Watch*, September 5. www.mideastweb.org/onenarrative.htm.

Naveh, E. (1995). *Hameah Haesrim*. Tel Aviv: Sifrei Tel Aviv, Ministry of Education.

Naveh, E., and Yogev, E. (2002). *Historiot. Likrat Dialog im Haetmol.* Tel Aviv: Babel.

Navon, E. (2001). "Y a-t-il une vie après Oslo?" *Outre-Terre, revue française de géopolitique* 1: January–March.

Oren, A. (2002). At the gates of Yassergrad. www.haaretzdaily.com/hasen/pages/ShArt.jhtml?itemNo=121553&sw=warsaw.

Pappe, I. (2000). *La guerre de 1948 en Palestine.* Paris: La Fabrique.

——(2002). *Israel, a state in denial.* Lecture given at the School for Oriental and African Studies, London, September 16.

——(2004). *Les Démons de la Nakbah. Les libertés fondamentales dans l'université israélienne.* Paris: La Fabrique.

Peleg, Y. (1994). Otherness and Israel's Arab dilemma. In L. Silberstein and R. L. Cohen, eds., *The Other in Jewish Thought and History.* New York: New York University Press.

Pinsker, L. (1882). *Auto-Emancipation.* New York: Zionist Organization of America, 1944.

Podeh, E. (2003). *The Arab-Israeli Conflict in Israeli History Textbooks, 1948–2000.* Westport, CT: Bergin & Garvey.

Prince-Gibson, E. (2002). What do Israeli, Palestinian texts say about conflict? *Jerusalem Post Service,* February 1. www.jewishsf.com/bk020201/sup11.shtml.

Rabkin, Y. M. (2004). *Au nom de la Torah. Une histoire de l'opposition juive au sionisme.* Montreal: Presses de l'Université de Laval.

Ram, U. (1993). *Hakhevra Haisraelit. Hebetim Bikortiim.* Tel Aviv: Brerot.

Raviv, A., Oppenheimer, L., and D. Bar-Tal (1999). *How Children Understand War and Peace: A Call for International Peace Education.* San Francisco: Jossey-Bass.

Raz, Y. (2002). Introduction to M. Golani, *Milkhamot lo Korot Meatzman. Al Zikaron, Koach Ubekhirah.* Modan: Moshav Ben Shemen.

Raz-Krakotzkin, A. (2001a). Binationalism and Jewish identity: Hannah Arendt and the question of Palestine. In S. Asheim, ed., *Hannah Arendt in Jerusalem.* Berkeley: University of California Press.

——(2001b). History textbooks and the limits of Israeli consciousness. *Journal of Israeli History* 20.

Ross, D. (2004). *The Missing Peace: The Inside Story of the Fight for Middle-East Peace.* New York: Farrar, Straus and Giroux.

Ross, D., Grinstein, G., Malley, R., and H. Agha (2001). Camp David: An exchange. *New York Review of Books,* September 20, pp. 60–64.

Rougier, B. (2004). *Le Jihad au quotidien.* Paris: PUF.

Said, E. (1979). *Orientalism.* New York: Vintage. 2nd ed., 1991.

Sanbar, E. (1984). *Palestine 1948: l'expulsion*. Paris: Livres de la Rexue d'Etudes palestinienne.

Sand, S. (2004). Postsionisme, un bilan provisoire. À propos des historiens "agréés" et "non agréés" en Israël. *Annales-Histoire, sciences sociales* 1:143–160.

Schattner, M. (2002). Israel: the army in command. *Le Monde diplomatique*, October. Http://mondediplo.com/2002/10/07army.

Schiff, Z., and Yaari, E. (1990). *Intifada—the Palestinian Uprising: Israel's Third Front*. New York: Simon & Schuster.

Schlaim, A. (1988). *Collusion Across the Jordan: King Abdullah, the Zionist Movement and the Partition of Palestine*. Oxford, UK: Clarendon.

———(2000). *The Iron Wall*. New York: Norton.

Schoken, A. (2003). Refusal for the sake of democracy. www.seruv.org.il/english/article.asp?msgid=52.

Segev, T. (1984). *1949: The First Israelis*, trans. A. N. Weinstein. New York: Owl, 1998.

———(1993). *The Seventh Million. The Israelis and the Holocaust*, trans. H. Watzman. New York: Owl, 2000.

———(2001). Genocide, a modern sickness. *PREA Digest*, April 22. http://mondediplo .com/2001/04/13eichmann.

———(2002). *Elvis in Jerusalem: Post-Zionism and the Americanization of Israel*. New York: Henry Holt.

———(2005). *1967: Veharetz Shinta Et Paneiha*. Jerusalem: Keter.

Sela, I., dir. (1993). *Testimonies: Israeli Soldiers on the Intifada*. Film.

Shavit, A. (2004a). Survival of the fittest. *Haaretz*, January 9.

———(2004b). Sharon is Sharon is Sharon. *Haaretz*, April 12. www.cephasministry. com/israel_sharon_sharon.html.

Sher, G. (2001). *Bemerkhak Neguiah*. Tel Aviv: Khemed & Yediot Ahronot.

Shimoni, Y. (1947). *Arviyeh Etetz Israel*. Tel Aviv: Am Oved.

Shohat, E. (1991). *Israeli Cinema: History and Ideology*. Tel Aviv: Breirot.

Shragai, N. (2000). Temple Mount revisited. *Haaretz*, October 10.

Siegman, H. (2002). Sharon's real purpose is to create foreigners. *International Herald Tribune*, September 25. www.iht.com./articles/71634.html.

Singer, I. J. (1936). *The Brothers Ashkenazi*, trans. M. Samuel. New York: Grosset & Dunlap, 1967.

Sternhell, Z. (1996). *Aux origines d'Israël. Entre nationalisme et socialisme*. Paris: Fayard.

———(1997). On myths that refuse to die. *Haaretz* (English edition), October 1.

Swisher, C. E. (2004). *The Truth about Camp David: The Untold Story about the Collapse of the Middle-East Peace Process*. New York: Nation Books.

Thomson, I. (2002). *Primo Levi*. London: Hutchinson.

Tsahal Historical Service. (1959). *Toldot Milkhemet Hakomemiut*. Tel Aviv: Maarakhot.

Ushpiz, A. (2002). With a mighty hand. *Haaretz* (English edition), March 15, B1–B2.

Vidal, D., and Algazy, J. (1998). *Le Péché originel d'Israël*. Paris: L'Atelier.

Vischitz, Y. (1947). *Haaravim Beeretz Israel*. Tel Aviv: Sifriat Poalim.

Warschawski, M. (2000). *A tombeau ouvert. La crise de la société israélienne*. Paris: La Fabrique.

Weizman, A. (2003). *Ariel Sharon and the Geometry of Occupation*. Privately printed, September 9.

Yahav, D. (2002). *Tohar Hanesheq*. Tel Aviv: Tammuz.

Yeheskeli, T. (2002). I made them a stadium in the middle of the camp. *Yediot Aharonot*, May 31. http://electronicintifada.net/bytopic/200.shtml.

Zertal, I. (2004). *La Nation et la Mort. La Shoah dans le discours et la politique d'Israël*. Paris: La Découverte.

SELECTED READINGS

Giacaman, G., and Lonning, D. J. (1998). *After Oslo: New Realities, Old Problems*. London: Pluto.

Kimmerling, B. (2001). *The Invention and Decline of Israeliness: State, Society and the Military*. Berkeley: University of California Press.

Laor, I. (1995). *Anu Kotvim Otakh Moledet: Masot Al Sifrut Israelit*. Tel Aviv: Hakibbutz Hameukhad

Mardam Bey, F., and Sanbar, E. (2002). *Le droit au retour: le problème des réfugiés palestiniens*. Paris: Sinbad Actes Sud.

Mashalha, N. (2003). *The Politics of Denial: Israel and the Palestinian Refugee Problem*. London: Pluto.

Negbi, M. (2004). *KeSdom Hainu: Bamidron Mimedinat Khoq Lerpublikat bananot*. Jerusalem: Keter.

Pappe, I. (1988). *Britain and the Arab-Israeli Conflict, 1948–51*. Basingstoke, UK: Macmillan in association with St. Antony's College, Oxford.

—— (1995). *Aravim Veyehudim Betkufat Hamandat: Mabat Khadash Al Hamekhkar Haistori*. Givat Haviva: Hamakhon Lekheker Hashalom.

Sanbar, E. (2001). *Le bien des absents*. Arles, France: Actes Sud.

Slyomovics, S. (1998). *The Object of Memory: Arab and Jew Narrate the Palestinian Village*. Philadelphia: University of Pennsylvania Press.

Teveth, S. (1989). *The Evolution of Transfer in Zionist Thinking*. Tel Aviv: Shiloah Institute.

INDEX

xenophobia, in colonialism, 99

Yaalon, M., 357, 371, 382
    criticism of withdrawal from Gaza,
        376, 459
    IDF impunity under, 379, 401
    on intifada, 275, 280, 377
    on Palestinian threat, 65–66
Yaari, E., 109
Yaari, M., 127
Yadlin, A., 166
Yahad party, 398
Yahav, D., 364
Yahia, O., 27
Yamit, 213
Yarkoni, Y., 367–368
Yaron, A., 382
Yassin, Sheikh A., 328
Yiddish, Zionist rejection of, 121–122
yishuv, 96
    Arab Revolt and, 139, 152
    attitude toward Shoah, 413–414
    in civil war, 65
    ethnicism of, 59, 110–111, 123–124,
        132
    expulsions of Palestinians and, 58–
        59, 130–131, 146
    glorification of, 104, 165, 169–170,
        185
    leadership of, 41–42, 69–70
    level of danger to, 65, 150, 172
    minorities breaking with, 125
    negotiating with Hashemites, 171–
        172
    relations with British, 139–141
    UN partition plan and, 52–54
Yom Kippur War. *See* War of 1973
    (Yom Kippur War)

Yossef, O., 102–103, 247, 390
Yotam, 393–394
Yzhar, S. (Yzhar Smilanski), 61

Zangwill, I., 85
Zeevi, R. ("Ghandi"), 222–223, 281
Zertal, I., 420, 422
Zikhron Yaakov, 28, 174–175
Zinni, A., 285
Zinni Plan, failure of, 478
Zionism, 34, 95, 207, 233, 454. *See also*
        post-Zionism
    binationalism and, 54, 399–400
    British and, 184–186
    claiming purchase of land, 14–15
    colonialism and, 17–18, 94, 183–185,
        188
    expulsions planned by, 50–51, 167
    failure of, 86, 125, 457
    hard-right wing, 293–294
    Morris and, 147–148
    native residents ignored by, 163–
        164
    opposition to, 86, 93, 125, 308, 433–
        434, 468
    Orientalism and, 110
    rejecting Bund, 121–122
    religion and, 202, 388–391
    resistance to Shoah and, 412–413,
        420–421
    revisionist, 47, 59, 293
    textbooks on, 183–186
    vision of, 17, 127, 200–201, 413–414,
        447–448
Zisling, A., 127
Ziv, M., 166
Zone A, 244, 299
Zuckerman, Y., 201–202